the
canadian
connection

JEAN-PIERRE CHARBONNEAU

the canadian connection

Translated from the French by James Stewart

Preface by Judge Jean-L. Dutil

OPTIMUM PUBLISHING COMPANY LIMITED

To my wife Carole

Contents

Preface

It's hard enough to fight in the dark, but it's almost impossible to fight enemies you don't even know exist.

In America, in Canada, in Quebec, the phenomenon of organized crime is accepted by the public as a necessary evil. People resign themselves to it, as to a plague that cannot be contained. But we all suffer the ravages of these men who build fabulous fortunes for themselves through exploitation, not only of the wealthy, but of those of small means as well.

Special police teams have been formed to counter the activities of the underworld. In spite of this work, the hoped-for results have not always been achieved. The enemy sometimes seems untouchable as it spreads invisible but murderous tentacles over all its surroundings. The ingenuity and determination of certain police forces are often rewarded however, and drug traffickers put out of harm's way, as Jean-Pierre Charbonneau's book reveals.

But it has now become necessary for the ordinary citizen, the man in the street, to come to the aid of the police. For this fight he must understand what a gangster is and be able to recognize the world of crime. As the late Senator Robert F. Kennedy wrote :

The racketeer is not someone dressed in a black shirt, white tie, and diamond stick pin, whose activities affect only a remote underworld circle. He is more likely to be outfitted in a gray flannel suit and his influence is more likely to be as far-reaching as that of an important industrialist. The American public may not see him, but that makes the racketeer's power for evil in our society even greater. Lacking the direct confrontation with the racketeer, the American citizen fails to see the reason for alarm. The reason, decidedly, exists. The financial cost of organized crime is not limited to the vast illicit profits of gambling or narcotics. When the racketeers bore

IX

their way into legitimate business, the cost is borne by the public. When the infiltration is into labor relations, the racketeer's cut is paid by higher wages and higher prices—in other words, by the public. When the racketeer bribes local officials and secures immunity from police action, the price exacted by corrupt law enforcement — incalculable in dollars — is paid, again, by the public. In short, organized crime affects everyone. It cannot be the concern only of law enforcement officers. It must be the urgent and active concern of every citizen.

One of the underlying reasons for flourishing criminality, we must admit, is lack of knowledge and interest on the part of the general public. Thus the most honest citizen becomes the involuntary accomplice of the biggest criminals, even of drug traffickers. The efforts of police, of courts, of all the organizations dedicated to fighting crime, will come to nothing if the public is not aware of the dimensions of organized crime and its methods. Well-directed publicity and honest exposure of illegal activities are certainly the surest ways of drying up the revenue sources of crime magnates.

The U.S. Chamber of Commerce has described the difficulties encountered in efforts to control organized crime:

The fundamental problem facing our criminal courts at the national level is the apathy of citizens towards these questions. Why not, in fact, leave the problem of criminality to the professionals who are paid to combat it? Because professionals themselves fully realize and openly admit that without citizen cooperation they would be left without sufficient resources to accomplish the monumental task of fighting crime.

It is precisely this need for information which is met by a book like *The Canadian Connection*. The author, a skilled and experienced journalist, is one of those who have undertaken the mission of informing people on the world around them. In that respect, his book is a valuable instrument in the fight against the underworld of crime.

Specifically, Jean-Pierre Charbonneau has chosen to attack one of the most profitable of underworld operations: the traffic in narcotics.

In our time, drugs, which many describe as "living death," are at the root of an incredible number of major criminal acts. In the manner of Lucky Luciano and his like, traffickers use narcotics to enslave our innocent youth and their own henchmen as well. The

X

families and gangs of the underworld wage merciless wars for
control of the traffic and distribution of drugs. Persons who never
wished to be involved in organized crime may pay with their lives
for their allegiance to narcotics.

The trade in narcotics pours tens of millions of dollars into the
coffers of traffickers, financing their operations in other fields and
permitting them to spread their criminal activities over a much
larger surface.

If Charbonneau's book succeeds, even in a small way, in
unmasking these shameless exploiters, it will be a truly useful work.

Judge Jean-L. Dutil
*Chairman of the Quebec Police Commission Inquiry
into Organized Crime.*

This book is not intended to be a literary work of art; in fact, reviewers and literary critics may find stylistic short-comings when they review the contents. The great value of this book is its completeness, integrity and devotion to telling the entire story.

The Editors

Introduction

The big cities of the United States, with New York in the lead, have long been the world's major market for drugs of all description, including that costliest and most formidable narcotic—heroin. For almost as long a time, major Canadian cities like Vancouver, Toronto and especially Montreal have been choice staging points and operational bases for the international traffic in drugs. The closeness of the U.S. market and the affinities of Canadian gangsters for drug smugglers in other countries have made the Canadian Connection one of the most active and important links in this international commerce.

For the past 50 years, in fact, Montreal has been one of the North American continent's major ports of entry for illicit drugs. It is the Canadian centre for heroin imports and most other narcotics. This book, though it describes the activities of smuggling groups in Vancouver, Toronto and Winnipeg, concentrates on the Montreal traffickers, their enterprises, successes and failures. For the Canadian Connection is, above all else, the Montreal Connection.

This book is essentially a historical record. It reconstructs all the major investigations of the heroin traffic undertaken by the Montreal section of the Narcotics Squad of the Royal Canadian Mounted Police. It does not pretend to explain the sociological phenomenon of organized crime.

I have made no attempt to draw conclusions about the role of the underworld in society. I tried simply and honestly to present to the public, in a Canadian perspective, a comprehensive compilation of facts about the international traffic in drugs.

Certain people, and especially those prejudiced against the police, will no doubt complain that this account is incomplete and biased. It is! ... and it could not have been otherwise. Thanks to exceptional cooperation of RCMP authorities, I had almost unrestricted access to the archives of the Narcotics Squad. This historical reconstruction was made with the help of material from the archives, and with the testimony of police officers who conducted the investigations. Certainly, police files must be read with caution. They can shed only a partial light on what lives and stirs in the criminal world, even though they often contain the personal accounts of informers and key witnesses. Only those who inhabit the underworld can describe its real face, and for obvious reasons, such people rarely choose to speak openly and frankly about it. In any case, the reconstitution of history requires such copious testimony that any kind of account must be considered, at best, an incomplete picture.

But by approaching the subject from the outside, from the viewpoint of those who fought against the traffickers, one begins to see the continuity in this 50 year-old struggle. The story of the struggle by hundreds of investigators, secret agents and double agents to penetrate local and international underworlds and dismantle great networks of illicit trade in narcotics, is every bit as exciting as the story of the exploits of any crime lord. And probably a lot less fictional too. The history of the drug traffic, unfortunately not yet finished, has been written as much by the officers of the Narcotics Squad and their colleagues in other countries as by the "godfathers" and their soldiers.

This universe of the underworld is clothed in myth. Many people, because of the simplifications of sensation-seeking authors and journalists, think of it as a Super-organization, secret, highly-structured and controlled by criminals of Sicilian or Italian ancestry. For the uninitiated, the term "Mafia" is often synonymous with "underworld." This book tries to separate myth from reality however, and the reality is much more complex. The underworld is not an organization, but an environment, a "Milieu" of crooks, bandits, dealers, outlaws of all description. Within the Milieu a multitude of gangs, clans or organizations exist and co-exist. Some are powerful, well-organized and stable; others are loose, haphazard and even temporary coalitions of odd-job criminals and journeymen crooks. The Mafia as such is a collection of gangs or families and feudal chiefs of Italian origin united by cultural, family and ethnic links as well as by mutual interest. For various historical and cultural reasons the Italian clans of the Mafia have long been a dominating influence in the North American underworld. But they have no monopoly on criminality. And in drug trafficking, as this book tries to show, they are by no means the only interested parties.

Attempts to combat the plague of drugs date back many years.

The first Canadian legislation to control drugs and suppress illicit traffic goes back to 1908: the law passed that year prohibited the importation, manufacture and sale of opium for any purpose other than medical. The previous year, following riots in the Asian colony of Vancouver, it was discovered that opium had been in use there. Mackenzie King, then Minister of Labor, had been sent to Vancouver to study claims for riot compensation from the Chinese community. Two of the claimants who had suffered property damage during the riots turned out to be opium dealers. King, therefore, made an investigation of the opium trade at the same time as he inquired into the causes of labor agitation. In his report on "The Need to Suppress the Opium Traffic in Canada," he noted that the use of the drug was spreading "in the white race, not only among men and young people, but also among women and young girls." He recommended the adoption of rigorous legal countermeasures. (1)

Up until the 1920s, the Canadian public paid little attention to drugs, though the federal parliament had legislated several times in an attempt to increase control over the opium trade. The new law on opium and narcotic drugs prohibited not only opium but also its new derivatives, morphine and heroin, and cocaine, produced from coca leaves. In 1922 Mrs. Emily Murphy, a magistrate and judge of a juvenile court in Edmonton, published a series of articles in *Maclean's* magazine on the dangers of drugs. The articles, later collected in a book called *The Black Candle,* had such an impact that the law was amended again the following year, adding cannabis to the prohibited list.

In 1920 the federal government extended the jurisdiction of the Royal North-West Mounted Police to the entire territory of the Canadian federation, thereby creating a national police force. The Royal Canadian Mounted Police, given the mandate to enforce the drug laws, established the first section of its new Narcotics Squad in Vancouver in January 1921, and the second at Montreal in November of the same year. Toronto, Winnipeg and other cities soon had RCMP anti-drug squads also, and the battle against national and international traffickers was joined.

With severely limited manpower at the beginning, (but with steadily increasing personnel in the past ten years) the RCMP

---

1. See final report of the Le Dain Commission of Inquiry into the Non-Medical Use of Drugs in Canada, Ottawa, 1973.

Narcotics Squad relentlessly pursued drug financiers and smugglers, both Canadian and foreign. The work has produced impressive results, especially since the beginning of the 1930s, but the Canadian federal agents have rarely been given credit outside the country for their arduous and uninterrupted efforts. This book tries to allot them the fair share of their work and worth.

A book of this kind is obviously not possible without the cooperation of many people, not only in the research, but in matters of revision, proofreading, and transcribing of the manuscript.

I would like first to thank the members of the RCMP who instructed me in the subject with competence, impartiality and sympathy. Among them, Assistant Commissioner Jean-Paul Drapeau, Quebec division commander and a former member of the Narcotics Squad, was chiefly responsible for the aid given. He did everything in his power to ensure that the information provided was precise and complete. Without his intervention, the book in its present form could not have been written. Within the Narcotics Squad, commanded in Ottawa by Inspector Gordon Tomalty and in Montreal by Inspector Roger Perrier, two exceptional police officers greatly assisted my project. They are Staff Sergeant Gilles Poissant, chief investigator for the squad, and Staff Sergeant Paul Sauvé, who for more than a year devoted many hours guiding my research and acquainting me with the ways of the world of drugs. Their devotion, patience, competence and experience were essential factors in the realization of this book. Several other federal agents, active and former members of the Narcotics Squad, cooperated in notable ways. I am thinking particularly of Staff Sergeant Léonard Massé, Sergeants John Leduc, Ernest Bacqué, Réginald Beers, Gilbert Bishop, Renaud Lacroix, Guy David; Corporals Claude Savoie, Yvon Thibault, Walter Wafer, Richard Laperrière, Raymond Boisvert, John Philion and Conrad Plouffe. Two other former officers of the Narcotics Squad, who have since left the RCMP, also deserve my sincere thanks: Staff Sergeant Guy Houde, until recently in charge of the counterfeit squad, and Staff Sergeant Gérard Barbeau, now with the general directorate of public security of the Quebec department of Justice. To the latter I owe my first contacts with the Narcotics Squad. Thanks also to George Bessinger and Jack McCarthy of the Montreal bureau of the U.S. Drug Enforcement Administration.

I wish to state — surprising as this may seem to certain people — that the cooperation of the federal agents was at no time conditional. I did agree to keep certain information confidential or to modify — rarely — certain details in order to respect understandings, agreements or arrangements police officers had with their informants. As a journalist, I know the meaning of the word *confidential* and I know it is of prime importance in the pursuit of truth.

I wish also to thank Nicole Thomas for her care in typing the texts, journalists Michel Auger and Gilles Provost who gave me their valuable comments, and the management of *Le Devoir,* which granted me numerous unpaid leaves of absence during the preparation of the manuscript.

Two lawyers of renown, Réjean Paul, former prosecutor for the Narcotics Squad and chief prosecutor for the Quebec Commission of Inquiry into Organized Crime, and Jacques Dagenais, assistant chief prosecutor for the Crime Commission, studied the manuscript and suggested essential changes. My thanks to all of these and to other colleagues not here named.

JPC

Chapter 1

Charlie Talked Too Much

Montreal, August 21, 1934, 5:10 p.m. Charlie Feigenbaum drove up to his sister-in-law's home on Esplanade Street to take her to the family cottage at Val Morin. He entered the house, emerging a few minutes later with some packages which his 18-year-old son, Jackie, helped stow in the car. Neither noticed the three men in the Hudson parked across the street. In the cool of the late afternoon, half a dozen neighbors relaxed on their balconies. As Charlie handed the last package to his son, a man got out of the Hudson and casually crossed the street. Approaching Charlie, the stranger drew a revolver and nonchalantly, as though lighting a cigarette, fired six times. Charlie Feigenbaum fell, mortally wounded, before the horrified eyes of his son. The killer walked calmly back to the Hudson, stepping lightly on to the running board just as it sped away.

Charlie Feigenbaum — racketeer, smuggler and informer — was to have testified 20 days later at the trial of Pincus Brecher, a New York millionaire charged with trafficking in narcotics. His testimony had already led to a 14-year prison term for Harry Davis, one of the barons of the Montreal underworld.

The big, untidy, ambitious Feigenbaum had tried his hand at all the rackets. He started in the clothing industry, acquired an embossed-leather business called *Knit Shoe Company* and struck it rich in gambling and bookmaking operations. He turned to the slot machine racket and installed so many machines in Laurentian resort centres that he was nicknamed "King of the North." Then he got into smuggling, specializing in silk fabrics. At that time, in May 1930, business contacts introduced him to Pincus Brecher, a rich New Yorker who claimed he could help Feigenbaum make a lot of money.

First, Feigenbaum helped Brecher revenge himself on an associate who had pulled a double-cross in a fraudulent bankruptcy

19

affair. Later, he helped obtain false passports for some of Brecher's friends—Jack Pollakowitz, Louis Adelman and the brothers Sam and Joe Bernstein. In Montreal at the end of July 1930, Brecher introduced Feigenbaum to Charles Haims, a one-time bootlegger turned Swiss watch smuggler. The story was that Haims had been able to get his merchandise into the United States, but not into Montreal.

Brecher asked Feigenbaum if he could arrange things with Canadian Customs. Charlie said he knew an officer who would let in a few cases of goods on the quiet. Brecher then explained that another associate, Irving Stein, who was in Europe, would soon ship two trunks containing Swiss watches and French perfume. If Feigenbaum did his part, he'd get a percentage of all of Haims' future deals.

When the merchandise arrived in Montreal on August 15, 1930, Pincus Brecher was installed at the *LaSalle Hotel* with Mrs. Pollakowitz, whose husband was in Europe to supervise the shipment. That day Feigenbaum met three more of Brecher's New York associates—Hyman Holtz, Charlie Grah and Louis Buchalter, also known as Lepke. They had come to Montreal to pick up part of the merchandise.

Buchalter was the best known and most feared of the Jewish gangsters of New York. At the peak of his career he more or less controlled the leather, fancy-leather and footwear industries, the taxi and poultry businesses, laundries, bakeries and restaurants. By official estimates, the honest businessmen of New York were paying him $5 million to $10 million a year to be left in peace. Lepke Buchalter had links with some of the Italian crime lords who were beginning to impose their rule in the underworld. He was chief of the band of hired killers known as Murder Inc. (1), and a kingpin of the drug traffic in America. It was even said that he and other Jewish mobsters, including Meyer Lansky, Jacob Katzenberg and Jack (Gurrah) Shapiro, owned and operated a heroin manufacturing plant in Brooklyn. (2)

When he met Lepke in Montreal, Charlie Feigenbaum was still unaware that his main role in the arrangement would be to facilitate

---

1. "Murder Incorporated" was not the name of a specific organization, but a name invented by American journalists after a series of killings by gunmen of the Brooklyn mob leaders, the most formidable of the New York underworld.

2. This laboratory at 2919 Seymour Avenue in Brooklyn was destroyed by fire February 25, 1935.

the importation of large quantities of drugs. He knew, however, that Pincus Brecher was associated with Harry Davis, overlord of Montreal drug trafficking and an important figure in gambling and illegal betting. Feigenbaum knew Davis well as owner of a building in Lachine, a southwest suburb of Montreal. There, in the *White House Inn,* with Max Shapiro, Fred McBurney and Harry Baris, Davis ran the biggest gambling joint in the city. (3) He also owned a well-known night club, the *Frolics.* Brief spells in prison for possession of drugs had only increased his power and prestige in the underworld, where he was soon recognized as a big man, despite his diminutive physical stature.

After the meeting with Brecher and Buchalter, Feigenbaum made the necessary approaches to Customs, hoping to avoid inspection of the two trunks which had just arrived under the name of Irving Stein. The Customs officer on duty, however, refused to release the containers without opening them for inspection. On the advice of Brecher and Harry Davis, Feigenbaum then made an arrangement with Joe Lapalme, his pal in the Customs service. Pretending that the trunks had to be sent to New York, Lapalme managed to get them transferred to his custody, then had them delivered to the home of Max Feigenbaum, Charlie's brother.

Later Harry Davis picked up the two trunks, removed their contents and returned them to Max Feigenbaum's home, where Joe Lapalme's employees retrieved them to be forwarded to New York.

Satisfied with Feigenbaum's work, Brecher, Buchalter and Davis invited him to join them in their business of importing various merchandise from Europe. His next mission would be to join Pollakowitz in France to help prepare new shipments.

On the night of August 20, Feigenbaum and Brecher travelled to New York together. The following day Feigenbaum boarded the *S.S. Bremen* for Cherbourg. In Paris he linked up with Pollakowitz and advised him that cases destined for Montreal in future should be numbered so the Customs broker would know which ones to remove from regular inspection. After five days in France, Feigenbaum returned to New York where Pincus Brecher awaited him. The two returned to Montreal the following day. Harry Davis came to them immediately. There was a problem of how to get

---

3. In 1934 Montreal was an open city. Gambling dens, brothels, rackets — the supply exceeded the demand. Corruption and deceit infected the public administration, police and courts. Ten years earlier, at the end of the first public inquiry into the Montreal City Police, Judge Louis Coderre had written that "vice spread itself across the city with an ugliness and insolence that seemed assured of impunity."

$10,000 to Pollakowitz in a hurry. During Feigenbaum's visit to Paris, Brecher had already cabled $10,000 through Pollakowitz's son-in-law, a Montreal dentist. This time it was Harry Davis' wealthy associate, Max Shapiro, who took on the task of getting funds to Pollakowitz through a bank.

The first shipment from Pollakowitz arrived in Montreal on September 15 and was followed by four others, on September 22 and 29, October 13 and November 11. Each time, one of the two cases in the shipment was picked up by the broker, with the connivance of Customs officers, and delivered to the home of one of Charlie's brothers who was now in on the operation. The first shipment was a test. The case illegally brought in contained only valueless trinkets. But the four succeeding shipments held a rich cargo: nearly 300 kilos (660 pounds) of morphine, cocaine and heroin.

The operation might have continued for several years had it not been for Charlie's arrest a few days before the last shipment. Joe Lapalme, the customs officer, stricken with remorse, had told Customs investigators of Feigenbaum's shady activities. The investigators checked the records carefully and discovered that Feigenbaum and certain accomplices, including the former city councilor Julius Levine, had illegally imported more than $100,000 worth of silk fabrics. It was for this offense that Feigenbaum was convicted in the spring of 1931 and sentenced to five and a half years in penitentiary.

A few weeks after his conviction, Charlie Feigenbaum learned that friends who had promised to help him were instead taking advantage of his absence to cut him out of the rackets. He made a full confession. Between June 16 and June 20, 1931, he told his story in detail to three investigators from the Narcotics Squad of the RCMP and from the U.S. Customs service. The police immediately linked Feigenbaum's revelations to three earlier seizures of morphine in New York and Montreal.

On February 17 and March 4, 1930, U.S. Customs investigators had seized two suitcases filled with morphine shipped from France on the SS Majestic and SS Ile-de-France. They learned that just before each seizure, a certain Joe Bernstein, accompanied by two customs officers, had tried to take delivery of the suitcases by posing as the private secretary of Sir Duncan Orr Lewis, a British diplomat who had just arrived in New York. The baggagemaster, unconvinced, had refused to release the suitcases without written authorization from the diplomat. When the authorization didn't materialize, the cases were sent to the investigation office, where the secret of their contents was discovered.

Further investigation implicated a Jewish gangster, John Bloom, who had been arrested and sentenced to eight and a half years in prison. Joseph Bernstein, meanwhile, had disappeared from New York. Feigenbaum's statement revealed that Bernstein hid out in Montreal for a time, then disappeared after Feigenbaum got him a false passport.

Feigenbaum's story also confirmed the suspicions of U.S. investigators about the involvement of Jack Pollakowitz in the affair. Two days after the second seizure, a telegram sent to him in France from his wife had been intercepted. It read: HOT HERE — NOBODY SICK — DON'T STAY AT BROOKS — BE CAREFUL — DON'T ANSWER.

The "Brooks" in question was Nathan Brooks, an old comrade in arms of Pincus Brecher, whom Feigenbaum had already met in Montreal.

Charlie Feigenbaum also told the RCMP that Harry Davis had supplied the kilo (4) of morphine seized on the arrest of two Montreal peddlers, Sam Arcadi and Harry Tucker, on October 11, 1930. The dealers had been arrested as they delivered the drugs to two undercover agents of the Narcotics Squad of the U.S. Bureau of Narcotics. (5) After their arrest, Harry Davis confided to Feigenbaum that he had sold them the drugs.

Feigenbaum even recalled a heated discussion between Davis and Brecher, in his presence, when the New Yorker reproached his associate for endangering the security of the group.

Davis had replied that he had to sell that morphine in Montreal because the cubes were larger than the ones sold on the New York market.

On checking these disclosures, police discovered that the morphine cubes seized in New York were in fact smaller than those seized from Arcadi and Tucker.

Following Feigenbaum's confession, the Narcotics Squad, U.S. Customs, the U.S. Bureau of Narcotics and the French police, accelerated the search for evidence to corroborate and complete his statements.

---

4. One kilo equals 2.2 pounds.

5. The U.S. Federal Bureau of Narcotics of the Treasury department was founded in 1930 to combat the clandestine narcotics rings which had multiplied in the U.S. since 1924, when heroin was prohibited.

Newspapers report of the gang slaying of Feigenbaum and the Brecher suicide.

In June 1932, Jack Pollakowitz was arrested in Paris for illegal possession of drugs and sentenced to 18 months in prison. He was later extradited to the United States and convicted of drug trafficking.

On April 9, the RCMP arrested Harry Davis and charged him with traffic in 852 kilos (30,000 ounces) of opium, morphine and heroin, between January 1 and December 31, 1930. (6) He was also charged with corruption of public officials. The charge mentioned the names of Pollakowitz and Pincus Brecher, who were indicted in New York a few weeks later, along with Nathan Brooks, John Bell and several other members of the gang.

The trial of Harry Davis opened October 1, 1933 and lasted five days. The Crown summoned 56 witnesses, but called only 17 to the stand, including Charlie Feigenbaum and Sam Arcadi. The jury took less than an hour to declare the accused guilty. On October 19, Chief Justice R.A.E. Greenshields, of the Court of King's Bench, sentenced the Montreal mobster to 14 years in prison and 10 strokes of the lash. He also recommended the launching of extradition procedures against Pincus Brecher, who had just been freed in New York because the offenses charged against him had been committed in Montreal.

The conviction of Davis created shock-waves in the underworld. Never before had a crime boss of his importance been charged, convicted and sent to prison for such a long term.

Less than two months later, Charlie Feigenbaum was freed on parole. At the time of his assassination on August 21, 1934, not only was he preparing to testify again, this time against Brecher, but he had also resumed his underworld activities as though nothing had happened. He was even rumored to harbor the impudent ambition of dethroning Harry Davis.

On September 28, 1934, despite the elimination of Feigenbaum as a witness, the 57-year-old Pincus Brecher was found guilty of illicit trafficking in narcotics and corruption of public officials after a five-day trial and 45 minutes of deliberation by an Assizes jury. Taken to the common jail to await his sentence, he boasted to the assistant director there that he had nine out of ten chances to win on appeal. But ten minutes later he brushed aside his guards on a second-story balcony and threw himself head first into the prison courtyard. Death was instantaneous. For the RCMP, this unexpected and spectacular ending closed the file.

---

6. Nearly all the imported drugs came from the same company, *Hoffmann La Roche,* in Paris.

But in New York the investigation continued. Three years later, in November 1937, a New York grand jury indicted Louis "Lepke" Buchalter and his partner Jacob (Yasha) Katzenberg for trafficking in heroin. The U.S. Bureau of Narcotics produced evidence that Lepke had imported six cargos of heroin from Shanghai and Hong Kong, valued at $10 million. Once again, drugs had been brought to America through the complicity of New York Customs officers. But the two mob leaders, sensing the danger, had already fled. Katzenberg was captured later in Greece, and Lepke managed to arrange the elimination of seven embarrassing witnesses before giving himself up to police on August 4, 1939. He did this after his underworld friends, notably Albert Anastasia and Meyer Lansky had convinced him they had made a deal with the government. There was, in fact, no such deal. Police activity and pressure on the underworld had been intense since Lepke's disappearance. The underworld chieftains had simply decided that Lepke, as the most wanted criminal in the U.S., would be a serious hindrance to their normal operations if he remained at large.

Lepke was sentenced to 14 years in prison for drug trafficking and associating with criminals. Hardly had the sentence been pronounced when he was convicted and sentenced again, this time to 30 years for extortion of funds from New York bakers. Finally, on the testimony of one of his former strongmen, Abe Reles, he was sentenced to death on March 4, 1944, for the murder of a Brooklyn confectioner who had talked too freely. Lepke Buchalter died in the electric chair.

A few months later, the brothers George and Elias Eliopoulos, two Greeks nicknamed "The Drug Barons" in Europe, were charged with trafficking in heroin. In 1929, 1930 and 1931, they had virtually monopolized the European black market in narcotics. During his trip to Paris in August 1930, Charlie Feigenbaum had heard of them in a chance conversation between Jack Pollakowitz and another dealer of Russian origin. Unaware that Feigenbaum also spoke Russian, the two men discussed, in his presence, the monopoly of the market by a certain Greek supplier. These details may have helped the U.S. Bureau of Narcotics to trace the Eliopoulos brothers and bring charges against them after they had taken refuge in the U.S. at the beginning of the Second World War. Because of lack of evidence, unfortunately, they were freed on October 31, 1947.

The dismantling of the Davis-Brecher-Buchalter ring marks a stage in the history of international drug trafficking — the end of the reign of the Jewish crime bosses in North America. Lords and masters of many of the continent's big city underworlds since the beginning of the century, the Jewish gangsters were the first to seek profit from the wave of drug addiction that broke over America after the First World War. The smashing of several of their narcotics rings opened the door to their like-minded contemporaries of Italian origin, who had settled their rivalries and formed a secret society of family clans called, as in Sicily, the Mafia. The American mafiosi, first in partnership with Jewish traffickers and then alone, moved into narcotics traffic by progressively taking over distribution networks and then by taking over the importation of supplies. Their business was in full expansion when it was interrupted by the Second World War. The mobilization of maritime transport and the tightening of customs controls almost totally disrupted their supply routes and the international contraband in narcotics.

Harry Davis   *Meyer Lansky*

(Photos Playboy Press and Associated Press)

Lepke Bulchalter   *Albert Anastasia*

27

Chapter 2

A Priest and His Sins

The post-war years in North America brought rapid growth in drug addiction. The mass return of wounded soldiers and veterans who had developed a drug habit overseas gave vigorous stimulus to the illicit narcotic trade, particularly in heroin, which in the past 15 years had become the product most in demand.

For the RCMP, as for the U.S. Bureau of Narcotics, the flow of information about the trade resumed and steadily increased. By the beginning of 1949, the Narcotics Squad in Montreal had already identified some of the new moguls of the drug racket. One of them, Jean-Claude (Johnny) Laprès, 31, seemed particularly active. For months his name had been turning up constantly in reports from underworld informers. Johnny, a dealer in gold and a counterfeiter, was said to have access to large quantities of heroin. One of his agents, Roger Denizet, had been arrested in Vancouver the previous December as he tried to deliver 32 ounces (one kilo) of heroin with a market value of nearly one million dollars. Shortly before that another Laprès accomplice, Larry Petrov, had negotiated the sale of two kilos of heroin with Émile (Jack) Nadeau, one of the boss figures in the Montreal drug distribution network. (1)

Not much else, however, was known about Jean-Claude Laprès. Was he head of an important organization? Or just a front man for more important racketeers? Where did he get his merchandise? From whom? How was it delivered?

Most of these questions had still not been answered when, on the evening of March 31, 1949, a Gérard Gagnon telephoned the

---

1. In July 1957 Larry Petrov was assassinated for making certain wrong moves after a huge robbery of more than a million dollars at a branch of the Bank of Montreal. At the time of his death he was awaiting trial on a charge of possession of drugs.

Narcotics Squad claiming to have interesting things to say about Laprès. At Squad headquarters later, he gave the following account:

"I met Laprès some months ago through the parish priest of Sainte-Madeleine d'Outremont, Father Joseph-Arthur Taillefer, whom I knew from several years ago when we both served in anti-communist movements. He presented Laprès as a good guy, not too scrupulous, with whom it was possible to make all sorts of good deals. Before that, Father Taillefer had also introduced me to an American businessman, Louis Ponzini, proprietor of the *Mills Paper Company* of New York. As I was also interested in the paper business, we became good friends. One thing led to another, and he also met Laprès. A little while ago I realized that Laprès and Ponzini were involved in illegal matters. One day Laprès told me he had 600 ounces of heroin for sale, at prices ranging from $150 to $200 an ounce, depending on whether the customer bought brown or white heroin. (2) He asked me if I could find any serious buyers. Three weeks ago, when I visited Father Taillefer, he told me Laprès had entrusted him with some samples of heroin. He showed me two packets which he said contained 75 ounces of brown heroin and 125 ounces of white. Shortly afterwards, I met Laprès and the priest again and they told me they had a still in operation about 40 miles from Montreal and had 8,000 gallons of spirits ready for sale.

"Laprès told me he was getting protection in this business from two police officers of the RCMP.

"Furthermore, I know that Laprès is trying to sell a big lot of stolen bonds. He said he had $120,000 worth and was willing to sell them at 25 per cent of their value. He also showed me some samples at the priest's place. And he asked me to try and obtain some banknote paper. He asked Ponzini that too and said he knew people who would pay $12,000 for 50 pounds of the paper.

"Finally, I recently learned that Laprès and Ponzini were negotiating with a Vancouver businessman for the sale of a stock of gasoline from Texas. This man is supposed to be coming to Montreal soon and I think he's also interested in heroin. If you wish, I could introduce one of your agents to Ponzini."

Enthused by this windfall of information and the spontaneous offer of help, the Narcotics Squad quickly mobilized one of its

---

2. In drug trafficking circles "white" heroin, of French manufacture, is purer, more in demand and more expensive than the "brown" which is of Asian or, in this case, Mexican manufacture. The brown contains more impurities such as caffeine.

agents. Four days later, there was a first meeting with Louis Ponzini. The American partially confirmed the account given by Gérard Gagnon by mentioning that Jean-Claude Laprès had contacts with a priest which permitted him to operate almost without risk. The priest was said to be the middleman between Laprès and his customers for the exchange of merchandise and money. Ponzini said the Laprès heroin was of excellent quality, but professed to have no interest in it himself. (3)

A few days later, the secret agent met Ponzini again, but the New Yorker had become suspicious and wanted to return home. The federal investigators then decided that the best way to infiltrate the Laprès organization would be to introduce an undercover agent to Father Taillefer. But before risking that, a test was made. In the presence of police officers, the informer Gagnon telephoned the priest and asked:

"Do you still have the stolen bonds you talked to me about?"

"No," replied the priest, "Laprès came to get them, and the heroin too."

"Do you know anybody named Labonté?" asked Gagnon.

"Yes, he's a friend and partner of Laprès."

The last answer confirmed RCMP suspicions that Eddie Labonté, a rich underworld chieftain, was closely linked to Jean-Claude Laprès, perhaps as his boss, or at least as his financial backer.

The Narcotics Squad now tried to convince Gagnon to become a double agent with the first task of introducing an RCMP undercover agent to the priest. But the informer declined on the grounds that he was no longer on very good terms with Laprès. But Gagnon did not want to give the impression that he was backing out. He suggested that one of his assistants, a commercial traveller from Quebec City named Henri-Paul Papillon, who already knew the priest, might be ready to play the game. The proposition was quickly put to Papillon, and he agreed to cooperate.

Towards noon on April 12, 1949, Papillon turned up at the presbytery of Sainte-Madeleine d'Outremont to begin his mission. Father Taillefer, a middle-aged man, welcomed him warmly. In the

---

3. The RCMP later established that Ponzini had been brought in on this deal by the informer Gagnon who had also skilfully extracted $22,000 from him. The American made a full statement and was one of the first witnesses called by the RCMP.

course of conversation, the priest disclosed that Jean-Claude Laprès had been seeking a buyer for $80,000 worth of stolen bonds, as well as for 700-800 ounces of heroin.

As arranged, Papillon then replied that he knew someone who might be interested, a man named Frank Martin from western Canada. Papillon described Martin as well-off and not too scrupulous, his partner in a wartime racket producing counterfeit gasoline ration coupons. (In reality, Frank Martin would be Frank de Cheverry, an RCMP undercover agent and a new recruit to the Narcotics Squad.)

The priest showed immediate interest and tried to reach Laprès at once by telephone. Papillon noticed that one of the calls was made to the home of Eddie Labonté. After several attempts, the priest got Laprès on the line and he agreed to meet Martin that same night.

The encounter took place in the undercover agent's room in the *Mount Royal Hotel.* After some small talk, the dealer got to the point:

"I have 120 pounds of top-quality heroin. If you want, I'm ready to make a deal right away. All you've got to do is get $300 to the priest as a guarantee and I'll deliver an ounce to you tonight."

"O.K., agreed," said the agent quickly.

Perhaps too quickly! When Papillon took the money to Father Taillefer, Laprès told him the deal had been put off until the following day. The dealer was suspicious. He said this new customer Martin didn't look like a conventional crook, and wondered if he might be a federal agent. Laprès was obsessed with the fear of falling into the same trap as his friend Denizet. He telephoned de Cheverry and invited him on a tour of night clubs to meet some underworld friends. The undercover agent, wary of the invitation, politely declined.

Laprès would obviously have to be convinced that Frank Martin was a serious buyer, able to close a big deal. RCMP authorities agreed to make $35,000 available to be placed the following day in a safety deposit box at a bank. Papillon, resuming his role, contacted Father Taillefer to tell him of his friend's displeasure:

"Martin isn't too happy about what happened last night. He thinks Laprès is bluffing about the 120 pounds of stuff. That's a big lot, you know."

"Don't worry, I'll talk to him," said the priest.

"Anyway, you can tell him my friend is suspicious too, but he's ready to prove his good faith. Tell him to come and see him this afternoon. He won't regret it."

The priest transmitted the message. Early in the afternoon, Laprès came to meet de Cheverry at his hotel. The two men went together to the bank and the undercover agent displayed the bundle of money at his disposal.

"See," he told the dealer, "I can pay cash. You don't have to worry. But look, I don't flash money around like a lot of other guys. I don't want to attract attention. Don't forget this isn't my territory. Maybe for you there's no problem, but as for me, I don't want to be spotted. That's why I didn't want to go out with you last night."

But Laprès still wasn't convinced.

"I'd still like you to meet my friends," he insisted.

"Sorry, that's impossible. Besides, I have to leave town this evening."

The police officer had decided it would be best to make a show of independence and postpone the transaction. In this business, it was better to build respect and confidence gradually than to risk spoiling everything by moving too quickly. A little later that day, Papillon completed the strategy by telephoning Father Taillefer.

"Martin just left town," he said. "He didn't like Laprès' attitude at all... always so suspicious. My friend's not used to that, you know, he doesn't like it when his word is doubted."

The priest seemed disappointed. To prove his own good faith, he said he was willing to carry on negotiations. The federal investigators took him at his word: a few days later, Papillon wrote to the priest to say that his friend Martin would be returning to Montreal soon. In his letter of reply, Father Taillefer reported that Laprès would be willing to meet the buyer and talk business.

So far so good. On April 19 de Cheverry and Papillon were together at the *Mount Royal Hotel.* In the evening, Laprès joined them there. When the question of trustworthiness was raised again, the undercover agent suggested that he be introduced to the priest, make his explanations, and let the priest settle the matter. Laprès agreed and two days later de Cheverry met Father Taillefer for the first time. The meeting went off without a hitch. Satisfied with the agent's story, the priest reassured his partner, who then agreed to close the deal that same day. It was done in the afternoon, not far from Eddie Labonté's home. As agreed, Papillon acted as intermediary and Laprès exchanged one ounce of heroin for $300. After the deal, the priest contacted de Cheverry:

"Are you satisfied with the goods?"

"Yes, it's perfect," replied the police officer. "You can tell Jean-Claude that I'm ready to buy a stock of 50 ounces."

Negotiations resumed over the next few days, but despite the first sale, Laprès was still extremely suspicious. After much fruitless talk, de Cheverry concluded it was useless to force the issue. He preferred to let the whole thing drop for the time being. Papillon and Taillefer, however, agreed to keep in touch. This, at least, kept hopes alive for a deeper infiltration of the ring.

In May, an unforeseeable incident threatened the undercover operation. Gérard Gagnon, the original informer, had gone to the archbishop of Montreal and told Msgr. Joseph Charbonneau his whole story. He had denounced Father Taillefer to the RCMP, hoping to provoke the arrest of the American, Ponzini, who had been threatening to bring fraud charges against Gagnon. Ponzini had not been arrested. He had, however, made good on his threat about the fraud charges. Now Gagnon was hoping for support from the archbishop's palace to get him out of his jam in exchange for his help in nipping a parish scandal in the bud. The bishop rejected the proposition, choosing to let events follow their course.

When Narcotics Squad investigators heard about Gagnon's interview with the bishop, they brought him in for an explanation. Gagnon said he had gone to the bishop because Father Taillefer had refused to pay him $300 he had coming to him. He swore he had said nothing about the police undercover operation. As proof of good faith, he offered some additional information.

"The last time I saw the priest," he told the officers, "I learned that Eddie Labonté had just sold the last lot of stolen bonds to a certain Michel Sisco. According to what I heard, this guy is one of the bosses of the gang. He has two brothers, one in Rome and the other in Marseilles, and with them, he's involved in various international deals. To get in touch with him, you just have to call either of two numbers, Harbour 7-5044 or Lancaster 6-3174."

A quick check revealed that the number Harbour 7-5044 was listed under the name of Michel Sisco, commercial agent, 3515 University Street in Montreal. The number Lancaster 6-3174 was the listing for a business firm named *Contact,* with head office at 328 St. Catherine Street East in Montreal, whose registered owner was a certain John MacKay. At first glance, these facts bore no relationship to any information already in the possession of police. But before investigating any further, the police had to find out if Father Taillefer and his accomplices had been informed of what Gagnon had told the police, and if so, what had been their reaction.

Jean-Claude Laprès

Eddie Labonté

Vincenzo (Vic) Cotroni

At the beginning of June therefore, Papillon telephoned Father Taillefer. The priest said that Gagnon had been in to see him after his release on bail:

"Gagnon told me that you and Frank Martin are secret agents of the federal police ... He also told me that $1,000 could get the investigation called off. But Gagnon's just a liar. That's what Eddie Labonté and the boss Michel Sisco think too. They had a long talk with Laprès about this and they agreed that you and Martin are good guys. If Martin comes back to Montreal, we can surely make a deal."

This conversation encouraged the Narcotics Squad to hope for renewed approaches to the traffickers. But the investigators decided it would be better to negotiate through the priest whenever possible. From the beginning he had been much less suspicious than Laprès.

A few days after his telephone conversation with Papillon, the priest wrote to get Frank Martin's address. In the exchange of correspondence that followed, the priest confirmed Laprès' intention to meet Martin again.

The time had come for undercover agent de Cheverry to appear on stage again. On July 12, Henri-Paul Papillon met Father Taillefer to inform him that his friend was in town and ready to talk business. After Papillon's departure, the priest got in touch with the agent.

"I'm ready to organize a new heroin sale, and this time I'll be the only middleman. And you don't have to worry, Laprès won't meddle in this affair because I know someone who'll be easier to get along with."

"I think that will be better," replied de Cheverry. "Laprès made too much of a fuss about nothing."

The following day, during a meeting with Taillefer, the RCMP agent set his conditions.

"This time," he insisted, "the operation has to be done my way: the merchandise will be deposited in a locker at the station so its quality can be verified; then, before taking final delivery, we'll go to the bank to get the money. I'll hand over the money in exchange for the key to the locker. If these conditions are acceptable, I'm ready to buy about 30 ounces."

The priest was in agreement but had to consult his mysterious partner. This was quickly done, and an hour later, Taillefer was back.

"My partner is worried about handing over the key," he explained. "He doesn't want any personal contact at all."

"Well, in that case arrange to leave the key in some public place where it can easily be picked up."

The priest thought his partner would agree to that. He went off for another consultation and later in the afternoon returned to see the police officer. His partner had approved the deal, but for this time, preferred to sell only 10-12 ounces. The undercover agent accepted the counter-proposal and the deal was made. It was an agreement to buy six ounces at $250 an ounce and the exchange was to take place the following morning.

Towards 11 a.m. on July 14, Taillefer joined Martin at his hotel and told him the merchandise was in a locker at Central Station. The two men walked to the Cathedral, discreetly followed by agents of the Narcotics Squad who, from the beginning, had monitored every move of their undercover colleague. Taillefer retrieved the locker key from beneath a stone on the Cathedral grounds. At the station, in locker 504, de Cheverry found six small envelopes. He pocketed one of them and, with the excited priest, went to the head office of the Royal Bank of Canada on St. James Street. Taillefer waited while de Cheverry entered the safety deposit chamber where colleagues handed him $1,500 in cash and checked the nature of the white powder in the envelope. It was heroin. The two men then returned to Central Station where the agent took possession of the five other envelopes and paid the money to Taillefer.

Before leaving, de Cheverry suggested that the priest advise his partner of the outcome of the operation. Taillefer agreed and stepped into a telephone booth. Standing nearby, the agent saw the priest dial HA 7-5044 and heard him talk to a certain "Michel."

There was no longer any doubt that the priest's partner was the Michel Sisco whose name had come up in the past few weeks. The identification of Sisco, who was unknown to police, became a priority.

Back at his hotel, de Cheverry turned over the heroin to his colleagues installed in the next room, and telephoned the priest to express his satisfaction. Father Taillefer also seemed happy about the operation, even suggesting that it might now be possible to think of a regular collaboration. The agent took the opportunity to say how much he'd like to meet the silent partner: it had been such a pleasure to do business with him. Taillefer promised that a meeting could be arranged very soon.

To hasten this meeting, de Cheverry contacted Father Taillefer less than two weeks later. For two days he tried unsuccessfully to arrange an appointment with the mysterious Michel Sisco. But his contacts with Father Taillefer were not a waste of time. They built up a feeling of trust and when the agent said he would have to leave town shortly, the priest replied that they must get together soon for another business deal. But caution was the watchword. A month passed before any new contact was established with the traffickers.

The narcotics squad used the time to intensify its investigation of Michel Sisco. There were few leads, but one produced interesting results: one of the two telephone numbers where Sisco might be reached was a business firm, the *Contact Club*. Its address was the same as that of a night club, *Le Café de la Paix*. Familiar with underworld methods, the investigators suspected that the business firm was only a front for a gaming house or an illegal bookmaking operation. The suspicion was soon confirmed through a check with the electrical company: the firm was registered as a sporting club, in the name of Emile (Bébé) Caron, a well known keeper of gambling dens. In police files his name was linked with Armand Courville, another gambling house operator, known especially for his partnership with one of the new underworld chieftains, Vincenzo Cotroni, owner of the building which housed *Le Café de la Paix* and the *Contact Club*.

Vincenzo Cotroni, oldest son of a Calabrian family of immigrants who arrived in Montreal in 1924, was born in 1911. He started work as a carpenter-helper for his father before becoming a professional wrestler under the name of Vic Vincent. It was the well-known wrestler Armand Courville, who gave lessons at the *St. Paul Club* in Ville Emard, who initiated him to the game. Their enduring friendship dated from that time. During the '30s, Cotroni had faced various charges of theft and receipt of stolen goods, possession of counterfeit money, illegal sale of alcohol and assault and battery, but he got off without too much trouble and with minimum time in jail.

Cotroni, a thick-set, reserved and unemotional man, moved into the big time around 1942. With Courville, he bought *Le Café Royal*, a night club in the downtown red light district of bars, gambling dens and brothels. That year he rented an apartment on St. Catherine Street East, not far from the club, where Courville organized a prosperous gaming house with the help of Emile Caron, Hildège Gervais and Joe Tremblay. (4). With Tremblay, Courville

---

4. Tremblay was the right-hand man of one of the lieutenants of Harry Davis, Eddie (The Kid) Baker.

also opened a gambling house at the corner of St. Catherine and Amherst Streets.

Cotroni's influence, prestige and wealth grew steadily. In 1945 he acquired a building at 1410 de Bullion Street which quickly became one of the most prosperous gambling dens in the city. A year earlier, with Courville and the brothers Edmond and Marius Martin from Marseilles (who would later be exposed as brothel keepers and drug traffickers) he bought a night club, *Le Café Val d'Or.* At the time the Narcotics Squad was investigating Michel Sisco, the place had changed its style and had become one of the top cabarets in the country, under the name of *Faisan Doré.* People flocked in from all parts to hear what no other club had yet dared to present: French music and humor, in the Paris style. (5) Saint-Germain-des-Prés was alive and well on The Main. (6) Every night, at St. Lawrence and St. Catherine Streets, the well-to-do patiently queued up — doctors, businessmen, politicians, judges, lawyers — on the sidewalk outside the *Faison Doré,* among the prostitutes, rubbies and drifters of the red light district. Most of the spectators were unaware that this first French night club in America, the showmart of Quebec songs and rendezvous for the cream of Montreal society, was a headquarters for the upper levels of the local underworld.

Aside from these activities, Cotroni had a reputation as an excellent political organizer. So had Courville, who had even been chief of the Liberal party's special police force and was a good friend of the Provincial Police director. In 1936, Cotroni had benefited from the clemency of a court in Sorel when he was charged with inflicting serious bodily injury on a voter during the provincial election. In 1947 he was arrested for impersonation at a municipal election, but once again managed to get off scot-free.

With this information in hand, the detectives of the Narcotics Squad pondered the possible relationship between Michel Sisco and Vic Cotroni. They decided it would be worthwhile to check the telephone calls made from the *Contact Club.* They discovered that during the previous months of April and May, several calls had been

---

5. Among the big names who performed at the *Faisan Doré*: Jacques Normand, Charles Aznavour, Pierre Roche, Bourvil, Luis Mariano, Tino Rossi, Charles Trenet, Georges Guétary, Aglaé, Jean Rafa, Michèle Sandry, Monique Leyrac, Guylaine Guy, Murielle Millard, Denise Filiatrault, Gilles Pellerin, Roger Baulu, Fernand Gignac.

6. At that time St. Lawrence Street, which divides Montreal into east and west sectors, was the busiest street in the city. In the Red Light district, the street was called The Main, deriving from the English term main street.

made to New York to someone named Benny Blanka. A check with the U.S. Bureau of Narcotics revealed that this Mr. Blanka was really Sebastiano Bellanca, known as Benny the Sicilian, an important member of the New York Mafia and a notorious drug trafficker with a criminal record going back to 1939.

But there was more. In making their regular surveys of telephone calls, the federal agents noted that in the same months of April and May, Vic's younger brother Giuseppe, known as Pep, had also made several telephone calls to Benny Blanka. Pep Cotroni, not as brilliant or influential as his older brother, had made his name mainly as a specialist in robbery and receiving stolen goods. He'd been charged eight times since 1937 with offenses of that type and at the moment was appealing a prison sentence for receiving stolen bonds. The RCMP wondered if Michel Sisco and Giuseppe Cotroni were accomplices in the heroin traffic. The hypothesis was worth exploring, but at a time of reduced staff, the Narcotics Squad had other priorities. It was time for the undercover agent de Cheverry to renew contact with Father Taillefer and his movements had to be observed at all times so his testimony could later be corroborated in court.

On Tuesday, September 6, the agent took a room in the *Laurentian Hotel* and telephoned Father Taillefer. The priest seemed suspicious. The next night, at the presbytery, the police officer understood why: Jean-Claude Laprès had been arrested on July 19 on a charge of counterfeiting. Taken to RCMP headquarters he had recognized de Cheverry there and as soon as he had been released on bail, spread the word among his friends and allies. (7)

The police officer kept his composure.

"Hey, wait a minute. Laprès is nothing but a liar and I don't trust him at all. But to prove I've got nothing to hide, I'm ready to meet him, if necessary. Anyway, I didn't come to Montreal to waste my time and you know I want to meet your new partner because I want to be sure Laprès doesn't get in on the deal this time."

The firm and spontaneous reaction seemed to reassure the priest.

"I'll put the proposition to him right away. I'll let you know soon."

_____

7. On April 7, 1947, the RCMP raided the home of a repeat offender named Archie Black, and seized 358 counterfeit Canadian one-hundred dollar bills. This investigation, started in 1945, led to the arrest of Jean-Claude Laprès, Rosario Delisle and Maurice Leblanc for conspiring to manufacture false banknotes with a face value of $100,000.

The following afternoon the priest telephoned the agent to say that his friend had agreed to a meeting and did not think Laprès needed to be included. The meeting took place the following night at the presbytery. From the beginning, de Cheverry went on the offense.

"Are you involved with that good-for-nothing Laprès?" he asked Sisco.

"I know him," replied the dealer, "but I can tell you I don't trust him too much. Anyway, I don't do business with him any more ... I have nothing more to do with him ... But I'm the one who supplied the heroin for the first deal and as far as I know the amount was exact. I supplied the stuff for the second deal, too."

"O.K., I believe you but I'm warning you, if Laprès sticks his nose in, count me out. Aside from that, it strikes me that you have pretty interesting resources ... Do you think you could guarantee me regular supplies? For me, that's absolutely necessary. I've got to be able to count on the stuff regularly, otherwise I'll have to look elsewhere. I've got customers and I can't fool around."

"You don't have to worry about that," replied Sisco. "Unless there's another world war I can fill any order, no matter how big."

"If that's so, I think we'll be able to get along," said the agent, feeling increasingly relaxed in his role. "Within a couple of days I can probably give you an order, but first I have to get in touch with my customers. As soon as I have news, I'll let you know."

The meeting ended on that note. The next day, Saturday, September 10, the agent telephoned Father Taillefer.

"I talked to my customers," he said, "and I think I could make a deal on Monday for at least ten ounces. Get the message to Sisco and tell him I'll call back."

Monday evening de Cheverry called the priest and said he was prepared to buy 32 ounces of heroin at $225 an ounce. The priest contacted Sisco and the same night let the agent know there would be no problem. The transaction could take place two days later, using the baggage locker system.

On Wednesday, September 14, about 11 a.m., Taillefer joined de Cheverry at the hotel and the two men walked to the Cathedral. This time Sisco himself was there to hand over the key. But at Central Station, a surprise awaited the agent. Locker 505 contained only a newspaper and some sugar. Had the traffickers discovered the plot? No. Sisco arrived and hurriedly explained that he had been testing Martin's reactions. He wanted to be sure of his identity.

The group returned immediately to the Cathedral where, this time, Sisco handed the agent the key to locker 177 at Windsor Station. The 32 ounces were there. With the merchandise, and with Sisco and Taillefer, the agent went by taxi to the Royal Bank. Sisco waited outside while the priest accompanied the agent to the safety deposit chamber. Quickly, de Cheverry handed over $7,200 as agreed. Taillefer checked the amount, took leave of his customer and started towards the exit. That's when the curtain fell. Simultaneously, other agents of the Narcotics Squad, who had watched the entire transaction, arrested Taillefer and Sisco. A few hours later Laprès was also arrested, along with one of his underlings, Rosario Delisle, who had been an accessory in the first transaction with Henri-Paul Papillon and had also been charged in the counterfeit affair.

The preliminary hearing for the four accused began on October 5. Father Joseph-Arthur Taillefer, the first to appear, surprised everyone by pleading guilty to the five charges laid against him. Twelve years later, in a little book, he explained that he had pleaded guilty on orders from the Bishop of Montreal, who wished to avoid scandal. (8) The same day, he said, another message had reached him: "Plead guilty — not a word — $10,000 on your release — Sisco."

The narcotics dealer incidentally, had also got word to him that a hail of bullets awaited him if anything went wrong. On October 28, 1949, the curate of Sainte-Madeleine d'Outremont was sentenced to two years in penitentiary and a $3,000 fine. (9) The others — Michel Sisco, Jean-Claude Laprès and Rosario Delisle — on the testimony of Henri-Paul Papillon and the agent Frank de Cheverry — were sent to trial, fixed for February 1, 1950.

But these arrests did not end the investigation. Mystery still surrounded the identity of Michel Sisco and his role in the drug scene. It was still too early to close the files. When questioned by police officers, the dealer first claimed to have been born at Michel, British Columbia, of a family of Calabrian immigrants. After the death of his mother, shortly after his own birth, his father had taken him back to Italy where he lived until 1927. Then he claimed to

---

8. *Un prêtre et son péché,* , Alain Stanké, Editions de l'Homme, Montréal, 1961.

9. Father Taillefer was imprisoned in Montreal's Bordeaux Jail. On his release, profoundly marked by his misadventure, he was obliged to return to the laity. He had never abandoned religious practice however, and later was able to exercise certain priestly responsibilities. People who knew him well suggested that naiveté may have been partly responsible for his behaviour.

have lived in France for four years, returning to Italy after that. During the war he was imprisoned by the Germans but according to his story, escaped in December 1942, reached Casablanca, and from there managed to board a British ship which brought him to Halifax. He entered Canada as a refugee.

What to make of this fantastic story? The federal agents decided it was too vague, and at the same time too precise. There were also other indications that this biographical account might be a tissue of lies. Police searched Sisco's home and arrested his girlfriend, Suzanne Filleau, a Parisian. At first the young woman identified herself as Nicole Laplante but she quickly changed her story and admitted entering Canada illegally. Furthermore, just before his arrest, the dealer had applied for a restaurant licence in Montreal North. In the application he stated he had been born in Italy. Among his personal effects, police found a sheet of paper. On it, word for word, was written the story he had told about his family background.

With these facts in hand, the Narcotics Squad decided to make a full investigation, at home and abroad, of Sisco's identity. His fingerprints were transmitted to several countries through Interpol. (10) In Montreal, following certain tips, a search was launched for a Frank Sisco, said to be the brother of the accused man.

The RCMP had also obtained other information after the arrest of Michel Sisco. The search of his home revealed that he had been running a brothel there. Besides his girlfriend, two other women were on the premises at the time of the raid. One of them, another French woman named Gisèle Denizet, was the wife of Roger Denizet who had been arrested in Vancouver in December 1948 for possession of a kilo of heroin. Born in Saskatchewan, Denizet had spent a lot of time in France, where he was linked with some influential characters. In Montreal, they called him Roger the Frenchman.

Sisco had a key to the *Contact Club* on him when he was arrested, a club owned by one of Vic Cotroni's men. Another clue linked Sisco with the Cotroni brothers: his restaurant in Montreal North, *Le Chalet Blanc,* was co-owned by Pep Cotroni and it was

---

10. Contrary to popular belief, Interpol is not a Superforce of international police. It is an information bank, established in 1923, for the world's national police forces and plays no active role. Nor is it concerned only with drugs. Its formal name, since 1956, has been the International Criminal Police Organization.

Giuseppe (Pep) Cotroni

Antoine D'Agostino, alias Michel Sisco

François Spirito

Paul Bonaventure Carbone

Vic who had put up the money for it. In Sisco's personal papers, police found the name and address of Sebastiano Bellanca of New York, and the name of a Brooklyn company, *Carol Paper Products Corporation.* According to the U.S. Bureau of Narcotics, this firm belonged to the brothers Carlo and Paolo Gambino, chief lieutenants of the brothers Philip and Vincent Mangano and of Albert Anastasia, heads of one of the five families of the New York Mafia. (11)

All this information led police to believe that Michel Sisco was only a link in a very large chain.

As Sisco's Montreal friends went about collecting money for his cash bail, the RCMP continued its probe into his identity. The police managed to find his alleged brother, Frank Sisco, who also claimed to have been born in Michel, British Columbia of a family of Calabrian immigrants which included two other sons, Louis and Michel, and a daughter, Susy. Frank said the family had broken up early in his life, and he hardly knew his brothers and sister. He said he had returned to Canada in September 1948 after working for 18 years in a canning factory in California. He had met Michel by chance, in December of that year, in the *Faisan Doré* club in Montreal. During the conversation, he realized that this must be one of the brothers he had never known.

Shortly after this statement, the Narcotics Squad learned that it would be impossible to confirm the Sisco family history in Michel, B.C. because all records prior to 1910 had been destroyed. But long and patient investigation turned up a relative of the Sisco family in Manitoba. This person confirmed the origins of the Sisco family but declared that there had been only two children, Louis and Susy.

The original doubts, in effect, were confirmed. Michel Sisco was an alias. But the question remained: who was he?

The answer came on March 7. The French national police, with the help of photos and fingerprints provided by the RCMP, identified Michel Sisco as Antoine d'Agostino, one of the bosses of the French underworld. He was born of Neapolitan parents in Bône, Algeria, on December 18, 1918. On July 23, 1948, he had been condemned by a French tribunal, in his absence, to death and national disgrace for treason. His criminal record went back to

---

11. The Mangano brothers were eliminated in 1951 by their chief lieutenant Albert Anastasia (an associate of Lepke Buchalter) who was himself assassinated in June 1957 and replaced by Carlo Gambino. Gambino became the most powerful chief of the American Mafia, or Cosa Nostra.

March 1935 in Algeria when he was sentenced to two months in prison for robbery. In October 1938 he had been banned from Marseilles after being convicted of rape and procuring. Between 1941 and 1943 he lived among the Paris underworld in Montmartre, where he met Suzanne Filleau, a notorious prostitute who had been married to an international gangster.

During the German occupation, d'Agostino, like many another criminal, became a Gestapo agent and as such was able to commit many armed attacks with impunity. He disappeared after the Liberation, turning up in Paris again some months later, where he became owner of the cabaret *La Boule Blanche* and the restaurant *Le Chardon Bleu*. His brothers Joseph and Albert managed these establishments. In November 1947 a warrant was issued for d'Agostino's arrest for theft of ration coupons. On March 16, 1948, he was sentenced to five years in prison for this offense—in his absence. He had already skipped to Italy, where in San Remo he went into business counterfeiting French and U.S. banknotes. The counterfeit ring was smashed in August 15, 1948 and all his accomplices were arrested. But once again d'Agostino managed to escape using his brother Albert's passport.

This time he took refuge in Montreal where he renewed acquaintances with several colleagues from the French underworld including the brothers Edmond and Marius Martin, François Spirito and Joseph Orsini.

Before the war, the Naples-born Spirito and his friend Paul Bonaventure Carbone, grand master of the Corsican and Marseillaise underworld, had organized the first big international network for French heroin: the Orient Express. Spirito had been encouraged in his enterprise by some American Mafia clans who had seen a promising market opening up after the 1914-8 war and had observed the success of the Jewish gangs. With his excellent contacts in French Indochina, Turkey, Greece, and Yugoslavia, Spirito had been able to import tons of opium and morphine-base, converting them to heroin in secret laboratories in the Paris region (the first labs to be put into operation by drug traffickers). (12)

---

12. Scientists discovered the method of transforming morphine-base into heroin in 1874. Around 1900 the German firm Bayer marketed heroin as a cough depressant. But it was only towards the end of the thirties that addicts began to prefer heroin to opium, morphine and the very popular cocaine. Until the adoption of the International Convention on Narcotic Drugs in 1931, the manufacture of morphine, heroin and opium derivatives was virtually unrestricted in Europe, though that had not been so in the United States since the

During the war, again with Carbone, Spirito sided with the occupying forces and was one of the men in charge of the Gestapo's security services in Marseilles. After the death of Carbone in December 1943, Spirito had to take refuge in Spain with the French Resistance hot on his heels. From there he emigrated to America, spending some time in Montreal before settling permanently in the United States.

Before the war, Joseph Orsini had been one of the most loyal lieutenants of Carbone and Spirito. Like them, he joined forces with the Gestapo. This earned him a death sentence in absentia.

These three men — Spirito, Orsini and d'Agostino — were together in Montreal when the maritime seaways re-opened after the war. They decided to rebuild their fortunes by starting up their heroin network again with the help of old associates who were still in France and their new friends in America. Large and regular profits might be expected from the network, given the closeness of the U.S. market and Spirito's pre-war contacts there. In Marseilles, they linked up with Joseph Renucci, a Corsican crime lord of the time who with his band of young and ambitious brigands had plunged into black market and smuggling operations throughout the Mediterranean. Renucci had also established important contacts in the Middle East, mainly in Lebanon, the former French protectorate where traffic in morphine-base had made fortunes not only for dealers but for government officials who, like the dealers, had retained close links with France. With Marseilles, Tangiers (Morocco) and Ajaccio (Corsica) as operational bases for trafficking in drugs and American cigarettes, Renucci and his men had gone into partnership with the Mafia and particularly, it was said, with a powerful Italo-American who had been deported to Italy, Salvatore (Lucky) Luciano.

The Sicilian Luciano grew up in New York's poor and crowded "Little Italy." During the '20s he raised himself to the top level of the American underworld by leading the pacification of the warring

---

implementation of the Harrison Act in 1914. At first, French gangsters and others like Jack Pollakowitz of the Davis-Brecher-Buchalter band bought their drugs from various legitimate pharmaceutical firms and organized their shipment to the United States. After 1931 they used their contacts in these firms to recruit chemists and establish their own clandestine laboratories. Thus, before the Second World War, Dominique Albertini, who worked for Spirito and Carbone, was initiated into secrets of heroin manufacture by a depraved old scientist, habitué of Pigalle, lover of light films and easy ladies. Albertini's success established the "French school" of gangster chemists, renowned above all others in the world of international drug trafficking.

Lucky Luciano

slum gangs. At the same time he helped the various Italian-American crime families take control of the most lucrative rackets, in cooperation with Jewish mob leaders like Meyer Lansky and Lepke Buchalter. By the late '30s Luciano and his American Mafia, or l'Unione Siciliana as he called it, had control of various drug distribution networks across America and were importing heroin in collaboration with the Frenchmen Spirito and Carbone. In 1936

---

13. In his memoirs, written in 1961 and published in 1975, Luciano declared he had only once wished to involve himself in the drug traffic. That was in June 1925 when he agreed to finance a heroin shipment at the urging of one of his lieutenants, the Neapolitan Vito Genovese. It turned out badly, for he was arrested in possession of several packets of pure heroin. He got off by permitting the seizure of the entire cargo in exchange for his freedom. From then on, he claimed, he began to be described as one of the big shots of the drug traffic. Before that, in June 1916, he had been arrested at the door of a pool hall in possession of nearly two grams of heroin. That cost him six months in prison. He acknowledged many contacts with mafiosi drug dealers after the war, but claimed these contacts had nothing to do with drugs. He did admit introducing Joseph Biondo, one of the moguls of the drug trade, to Egidio Calascibetta, one of the owners of the *Saci* pharmaceutical laboratory in Milan. But as far as he was concerned the meeting had to do with the purchase of chemical products. Calascibetta and several other directors and scientists were arrested and imprisoned in 1953 for this heroin organization. Luciano was also charged, at the request of the U.S. Bureau of

however, his career was shattered at its peak by the exposure of a gigantic prostitution ring. He was found guilty on 62 charges of procuring and sentenced to 30 to 50 years in prison. Even in jail, Luciano retained great influence. In 1942 the secret services of the Navy called for his help in the interests of national security. Authorities feared an epidemic of sabotage in the port of New York by dockers and businessmen of Italian origin and doubtful loyalty to the United States. Luciano helped organize protection in the port by intervening with dockworkers' union leaders who were controlled by his men. This precious help won Luciano an early release from prison and in February 1946 he was deported to Italy. There he encountered several old friends who had also been shipped home from America. These deported mafiosi were the first to re-launch the heroin trade to the U.S. after the war. In Italy the manufacture of heroin was still legal. The mobsters made arrangements with certain Italian pharmaceutical companies for the diversion of a substantial part of the legal production towards the illegal market. (13) These corporate collaborators were of prime importance to Renucci and his partners.

In Marseilles, Spirito, Orsini and d'Agostino had also contacted Antoine Cordoliani, an important Corsican dealer. Cordoliani and his young partner Edouard Giribone had set up an important heroin connection with Sicilian dealers. He was also associated with the brothers Marius, Joseph, and Georges Aranci. These brothers had worked for Spirito and Carbone before the war but were now allied with the powerful clan of the Guérini brothers, the new chiefs of the Marseilles underworld. (14)

In Paris, Spirito and his friends made contacts with two prominent figures, Marius Ansaldi and Dominique Reissent who

---

Narcotics, but Italian authorities decided they had insufficient evidence to proceed against him. The affair, however, provoked strong reactions from the UN Commission on Narcotic Drugs and Italy later banned all production of heroin. When all was said and done, it was finally estimated that Luciano's friends, through falsification of official documents, had managed to export some 800 kilos of heroin to their New York associates, for a total value of nearly a billion dollars. (See *Lucky Luciano, his testament*, by Martin A. Gosch and Richard Hammer, Paris, Stock Editions, 1975.)

14. One-time strongmen on the Spirito-Carbone team, the Guérini brothers chose to ally themselves during the war with certain Resistance networks. This later brought them certain advantages. Closely linked to the Socialist Party, they helped control the power of the Communist Party in the Southeast of France after the war, in collaboration with the Central Intelligence Agency (CIA).

had put into operation the biggest clandestine laboratory of the post-war period. Without doubt, they had manufactured the heroin bought by the undercover agent de Cheverry.

Once the link with France had been well established, Spirito, Orsini and d'Agostino divided the responsibilities for the operation. The first two settled in New York with some of their accomplices to look after American customers. D'Agostino, who stayed in Montreal to receive the shipments from France, eased naturally into the Montreal underworld.

At first, reports from Interpol made no mention of d'Agostino's link with Spirito and Orsini. The RCMP, U.S. Bureau of Narcotics and the French police were not able to put together the story of this association until later. But the reports, which confirmed suspicions of the federal agents, arrived four weeks too late. Antoine d'Agostino (Michel Sisco), had been a fugitive since February 1, 1950, when he failed to appear in court for the opening of his trial.

He had been freed from custody on December 31, 1949, on bail of $10,000 put up by Armand Duhamel, a shady character with underworld backing, an underling of Pep Cotroni and other influential figures. (15) When d'Agostino was out on bail, he first tried to make a deal with the RCMP for special treatment by promising to provide information about two illegal laboratories in France. When these attempts failed, he fled the country.

The Montreal part of the affair ended on June 16, 1950, after a jury trial, when Judge Wilfrid Lazure sentenced Jean-Claude Laprès to three years in penitentiary. His underling, Rosario Delisle, got off with three months in jail.

---

15. Strange coincidence. When the court fixed bail at $10,000 for the French trafficker on September 28, 1949, Vic Cotroni and a close friend, Angelo Bizanti, operator of a chain of brothels, travelled to New York that same night. Questioned about the trip on his return, Cotroni said he had gone to buy clothing. As for Jean-Guy Laprès, as soon as he was released on bail he made the rounds of underworld clubs and gambling haunts looking for bail money for d'Agostino. One of his visits, observed by the Narcotic Squad, was to the *Palmina Lunch* on Riverside Street, a club run by Frank Puliafito and his wife Palmina Cotroni, sister of Vic and Pep.

Chapter 3

The Master-Chefs of
The Corso Pizzeria

In the struggle against drug traffickers, investigative leads bloom so thick and fast that the only possible tactic is to deal with the most urgent. As a result, trails that look promising must often be temporarily abandoned. That was the case in April 1949 when the RCMP launched its hot pursuit of Jean-Claude Laprès and Father Taillefer. At that time, Narcotics Squad investigators had also been attempting to corner Johnny Young, the most important drug pusher in the Montreal underworld. On March 1, 1949, federal agents arrested a Vancouver addict at Montreal International Airport in Dorval who had been on his way home with an ounce of pure heroin. Police learned that just before his arrest, the addict had met with Johnny Young.

Young's hang-out was the red light and low-life districts of the city, where he had a solid reputation. He had 19 convictions since 1935 for burglary, receiving stolen goods, and corruption. An election specialist, he had been popular some years before as a professional wrestler and then became bodyguard to Maurice Duplessis, who was premier of Quebec at the time. Later he acquired three gyms, the most popular being at 1110 Clark Street, and it was best known as a rendezvous for the whores and gangsters of the district. Young had also worked at the *Faisan Doré* for Vic Cotroni and at the *American Spaghetti House* for Angelo Bizanti, the biggest brothel operator in the city.

During the months of the Laprès-Taillefer operation, RCMP detectives could only make the occasional check on the movements of Johnny Young and his henchmen. But even that produced enough information to warrant police action once Laprès, Taillefer and d'Agostino had been arrested.

On September 15, 1940, the day after d'Agostino's arrest, officers of the Narcotics Squad and municipal police arrested two of

Young's friends—William Lamy and Frank Perreault. Several capsules of heroin, ready for sale, had been found in their homes. A few months earlier, Frank Perreault had been charged with complicity for having aided the escape of his brother Douglas and another friend, both of whom were wanted for the murder of two policeman during a bank holdup. (1) When police arrested him at that time, he had been in the company of Young and another notorious pusher, Robert (Bob) Tremblay. Tremblay, originally from British Columbia, was a former weight lifting champion whose long spell in the merchant marine had provided him with valuable contacts in the smuggling business.

The seizure of heroin from Lamy and Perreault convinced the RCMP it was time to pay a visit to Johnny Young. On Monday, September 26, 1949, a Narcotics Squad raiding party burst into his lair at 1061 St. Denis Street, apartment one. Young dashed for the stairway but Ross Andrews, just out of police training school, gave chase and brought him down with a masterful football block. The pusher got an injured knee out of it, a bit humiliating for such an athlete.

Inside the apartment, a tremendous surprise awaited the investigators. There they saw a veritable heroin-packaging factory. Lactose, gelatin capsules, rubberized envelopes and heroin, still littered the kitchen table, ready for mixing and packaging. (2) In all, 52 ounces of heroin were stored in the apartment, enough, given its degree of purity, to make 26,000 capsules each of which would sell

---

1. Towards 2 p.m. on September 23, 1948, three men with criminal records—Douglas Perreault, Donald Perreault (no relation to the first) and Noël Cloutier—raided the Banque Canadienne Nationale at Notre Dame and St. Just Streets in Montreal. While Cloutier waited in a car, the two Perreaults entered the bank and were still inside when a passerby alerted two Montreal police officers, Nelson Paquin and Paul Duranleau. As the policemen reached the door of the bank, the bandits opened fire. Paquin was hit in the thigh. Soon after, one of the bandits came out of the bank and finished Paquin off with four point-blank shots in the chest. Then he fled on foot, after realizing that Cloutier had driven off in the getaway car. The second bandit also emerged from the bank at that moment and shot and killed officer Duranleau. Reinforcements had been called and the car driven by Cloutier was pursued through city streets at speeds over 80 miles per hour. The chase ended in Cloutier's arrest. A huge manhunt was organized for the other two bandits and they were arrested about ten days later, in Alberta, for stealing gasoline. All three died on the scaffold.

2. Heroin which arrives pure in Montreal is never re-sold in that form. The dealer mixes it with lactose or quinine to increase its volume and multiply his profit. At the final sale on the street, the heroin may have been cut up to a dozen times and its purity may be as low as five per cent, especially in times of shortage.

Johnny Young during his appearance in court for trafficking in heroin.

for between $3 and $5 in Montreal, and $8 in Vancouver. In other words, a $200,000 jackpot! But that wasn't all . . . opening a drawer, detectives found a card-index of names and addresses. A quick examination revealed it to be Young's list of customers including the names of all the main heroin pushers in Quebec. Also on the list was Walter Sillanpaa, the Vancouver addict arrested on March 1 whose trail had led to Young. Finally, under the bed, police discovered a real arsenal of revolvers, ammunition, automatic rifle and a machine gun.

In criminal court, Johnny Young was first found guilty of being an accessory after the fact in the bank holdup and murder of two policemen. He was sentenced to four years in penitentiary. In February 1950 he was convicted of possession and trafficking in narcotics which brought him a five-year sentence and a $500 fine. Two months later he was judged a habitual criminal and, as a result, sentenced to prison for an indefinite period. It was the first such judgment in Canadian history. Young's cronies, Lamy and Perreault, were each sentenced to six months in prison.

These were significant police achievements, but they did not end the heroin traffic in Montreal. (Arrests rarely do end the traffic completely. They merely slow it down for a while until someone else takes on the business.) The new priority in the Narcotics Squad became the detailed analysis of Johnny Young's card-index. For weeks, Squad investigators checked the names and addresses that were so thoroughly and carefully compiled by the dealer. They decided on an undercover operation to try to infiltrate the underworld once again. But by now, the small staff of agents in the Montreal section of the Narcotics Squad had become somewhat over-exposed by their investigations of the past few months. They were too well known, so a call went out to the Toronto section for help with the operation. A Toronto agent named Hugh Walker was chosen to make contact with the Montreal traffickers.

On January 20, 1950, Walker went to the *Harmonie* restaurant on St. Catherine Street to meet Nick Shuba for the first time. Shuba was easily approached and came quickly to the point.

"I could get you 100 caps of heroin for $200," he told Walker.

Walker's first move was to try to meet Nick Shuba, a minor heroin pusher, hoping to be introduced to Shuba's supplier, Emile (Jack) Nadeau. A former pimp turned drug dealer, Nadeau was being mentioned as the man who had replaced Johnny Young as chief of the Montreal heroin suppliers.

"That's interesting," replied the agent. "But I'm interested in big deals. Could you introduce me to your supplier?"

"That could be arranged. He's in the restaurant right now, in fact, sitting at the back. It's a guy named Nadeau. Wait for me, I'll go have a talk with him."

Shuba went to the back of the restaurant and sat at Nadeau's table. A few minutes later he returned to Walker.

"The boss is willing to work with you, but first we need a little advance of $50."

"I don't trust that kind of deal," replied Walker, who knew his way around and thought it wise not to appear too hasty. "I'll think about it and let you know."

Over the next few weeks, Walker had further contacts with Shuba and with other Nadeau pushers like Cecil Chesson (an imposing, 200-pound addict known as Big Red), and Jack Dushin, an old dealer who had known hours of glory in the 1920s. Little by little, Walker convinced them that he was involved in drug distribution in Toronto. He built up his cover by returning frequently to the Queen City and from there, making long distance telephone calls to the Montreal traffickers. By mid-August, his efforts paid off with a meeting with Jack Nadeau in person.

On the agreed day, August 17, he arrived in Montreal and joined Cecil Chesson at the *Northeastern* restaurant, Nadeau's headquarters. Chesson told him to go to a nearby tavern where the boss was waiting. Nadeau was there with another gangster, Red Burke, who began questioning Walker on his relations with the underworld in Vancouver and Winnipeg. But the police agent was thoroughly versed in the history of Canadian narcotics traffickers; he answered all questions calmly and brilliantly. Satisfied on that score, Nadeau himself began discussing heroin prices and then asked Walker to meet him later at the *Northeastern*. It was Cecil Chesson who met the undercover agent there.

"Everything's fine," he said, "the deal will be made tonight."

At the appointed time, Walker met Chesson in a downtown pharmacy and the two went to a tavern near the Loew's theatre. There Chesson made a phone call. He returned to announce that the deal had been put off for a few days. The disappointed agent returned to his hotel.

At noon the next day Chesson telephoned Walker and asked him to meet him immediately. This time it was the real thing. As soon as the policeman arrived, Chesson told him everything was ready—the package was in the washroom of a nearby restaurant. Walker quickly handed over the agreed amount of $1,400 and then retrieved the four ounces of heroin. The first inning had been won. But the game wasn't over yet . . .

Several weeks went by before the agent Walker made any attempt to resume contact with the Montreal dealers. He returned to Montreal at the beginning of October and met Jack Nadeau and Cecil Chesson again. This time the meeting took place at the *Corso Pizzeria* on St. Catherine Street East. The establishment was owned by two henchmen of the Cotroni brothers: Diodato Mastracchio, known as Dulude, and Vincenzo (Jimmy) Soccio. Primarily known as operators of illicit gambling dens, they were associated with Giuseppe (Big Pep) Cocolicchio, co-founder of the *Corso Pizzeria* and manager of two gambling houses in buildings owned by Vic Cotroni and Angelo Bizanti.

Mastracchio and Soccio, according to rumors over the past few months, had become the new bosses of the heroin traffic in Montreal. The RCMP still had little information about them, but it did have some new leads.

Walker found both Nadeau and Chesson at the *Corso Pizzeria*. He began by complaining about the quality of the first delivery and

*Diodato Mastracchio (centre) and Jimmy Soccio (far right) with
Nicola Di Iorio.*

then raised the possibility of a second transaction. He said he was now in the market for a half-pound of heroin. This time, because of the size of the deal, the talks stretched over several days. During this period, the agent returned frequently to Toronto. To permit Nadeau to get in touch with him quickly, he had given him the name, address and telephone number of a garage where he could be reached. The garage belonged to Walker's brother, who had agreed to play the role. Everything had been foreseen to protect the identity of the undercover agent, except pure chance . . .

In October, Nadeau decided to spring a little surprise on his friend Walker. He travelled to Toronto and visited the garage in question. The garage owner was away and all the employees had been forewarned, but on that day the accountant who came in once or twice a month to do the books was there. The accountant knew the garage-owner's brother well, but he didn't know about his special mission. When Nadeau inquired about his friend Hugh Walker, the accountant replied without hesitation that Hugh was fine and still with the federal police!

Nadeau was stunned at the news and didn't know what to do. He had already sold heroin to the police officer and sooner or later would be arrested. There was only one solution. He telephoned RCMP offices and asked to speak to agent Walker. When Walker heard the voice of the dealer on the line he couldn't believe his ears. He saw all his efforts reduced to nothing. But the gangster quickly reassured him. He said he knew the agent's identity but had not told any of his associates or contacts in the underworld. Why not make a deal? In exchange for favorable treatment, he would present Walker to his suppliers, Dulude Mastracchio and Jimmy Soccio. Nadeau warned, however, that in case of his arrest, the two narcotics bosses would be immediately told the whole story. Nadeau said he had already instructed his wife to do that if he were arrested.

The police officer could not promise total immunity. That is not permitted in Canadian law. But considering the risks and the importance of the criminals involved, Walker thought it would be a fair and honest bargain if the prospect of a light sentence could be held out to Nadeau. Walker's superior officers came to the same conclusion when he put the proposition to them. The infiltration operation could therefore continue.

Back in Montreal, Nadeau brought together Mastracchio and the undercover agent. Walker, following the plan, mentioned to the owner of the *Corso Pizzeria* that he was trying to get in touch with a Frank Sisco. The Narcotics Squad knew that this man, who had passed himself off as the brother of Michel Sisco (real name—Antoine d'Agostino) (3), had close ties to the Cotroni organization and was perhaps a major link in the French connection.

Mastracchio, however, was cautious. For weeks, as Walker tried to gain his confidence, he remained discreet and noncommittal. So on December 9, when the agent decided to go for a grand slam, he had no idea what the reaction would be. From Toronto that day, he phoned Mastracchio:

"I'll be coming to Montreal next week."

"Perfect! You know, I know Frank Sisco well, but I haven't had any news of him for three or four weeks."

It was the first time Mastracchio admitted knowing Sisco. The following Tuesday, at the pre-arranged meeting, he went a little further.

"I think Sisco will be in Montreal very soon," he told Walker. "I'll be sure to give him your message."

"In that case, I'll come back in a few weeks."

On January 26, 1951, Walker returned to Montreal and went to the *Corso Pizzeria* to learn the latest developments. Jimmy Soccio was there to greet him and promised to get the information.

At noon the next day Soccio telephoned Walker at his hotel:

"I haven't seen Sisco yet, but I think I know why you're in Montreal. Maybe I could help you." (4)

"What I'm after," replied Walker, "are 'matchboxes.' " Understand? If the price is right I'd buy four or five."

"Come and meet me at the Corso. We can talk better there."

At the restaurant, the talks got down to business and soon an agreement was made. Soccio tore a cigarette pack in half, gave one half to Walker and told him to bring it with him to the place which would be indicated to him later. It would be his passport to the person who would complete the transaction.

---

3. See Chapter Two.

4. Frank Sisco never did take part in this transaction and the undercover agent was not able to make contact with him. A little later, Sisco was arrested in the United States for violation of immigration regulations. The arrest permitted the RCMP to obtain information which was useful in another investigation in 1955.

Back at his hotel, Walker printed his initials in invisible ink on his half of the cigarette pack, then slipped $1,900 into an envelope. This took place in the presence of colleagues from the Narcotics Squad who had never lost sight of him since he began the mission. He went to the Woolworth's store at St. Lawrence and St. Catherine Streets, where he handed the envelope to Soccio, then returned directly to his hotel room.

In late afternoon, his telephone rang. An unknown voice invited him to a meeting on Pine Avenue, in about 20 minutes, to compare cigarette pack halves. The contact was made without hitch. The stranger told Walker he would find his "matchboxes" under the stairs at 3655 St. Urbain Street. Walker and a colleague then went to the designated spot where they found the agreed quantity of heroin, wrapped in brown paper.

The Narcotics Squad was satisfied with the results so far but wanted to gather more direct evidence on the roles of Diodato Mastracchio and Jimmy Soccio in the heroin traffic. It wanted to be sure that the case against the traffickers, built up in months of efforts, would not be destroyed through lack of evidence.

On March 1, therefore, Walker again visited the *Corso Pizzeria.* After a brief chat with Mastracchio, he went on to Soccio's new establishment, the *Café Pionnier* where he discussed possible new deals and complained, as every good dealer should, about the last transaction. In the following weeks, the undercover agent met Mastracchio several times but not until May 30 did they have a conversation of any particular interest. On that day Walker asked Mastracchio if he could help him make a deal in which he, Walker, would not be cheated. The trafficker replied:

"I'll have some real good quality stuff for you next Friday. But I can't set a price until the merchandise arrives in Montreal. Things are going badly in New York just now and prices are going up after every arrest . . . ."

After several conversations during the following week, Mastracchio told Walker on June 6:

"I haven't been able to arrange anything in Montreal. Prices are too high. I'll try to get better conditions as soon as possible."

There was no further development however, until mid summer. On July 27, Mastracchio phoned Walker in Toronto to say that he and Soccio had spent the past week in New York and there should be some news in a few days. This time the wait was really over. Four days later the gangster called back:

Luigi Greco (centre) and Frank Petrula in a Paris cabaret, 1951.

François Spirito   *Gaetano (Thomas) Lucchese*

"O.K., everything's fine. You can come to Montreal. Only the price is a bit high, $650 an ounce. They've got problems in New York and the prices are going up fast . . ."

Walker came to Montreal on August 3. Discreetly followed by colleagues from the Narcotics Squad, who had been joined by an agent of the U.S. Bureau of Narcotics, he went to the *Corso Pizzeria* for a meeting with Mastracchio. The crime boss began by explaining that the market was getting tougher all the time and merchandise was hard to get, not only in Montreal but in the U.S. where prices were constantly rising. Mastracchio said he had been able to get only 15 ounces, and ten of them were reserved for an old customer in Vancouver who was ready to pay the high price. Walker could have the other five ounces and the deal could be made that night through Soccio. Walker didn't like that idea but the trafficker reassured him by offering himself as guarantor for the deal, the quality of the merchandise and the attitude of his partner.

At the 8:30 p.m. rendezvous, Walker met Soccio in the *Café Pionnier* and handed over the agreed sum of $3,250.

"Come and meet me on the street corner in a few minutes," said Soccio.

Walker, accompanied by a police colleague who had posed as his bodyguard, walked to the corner. Soccio was just getting out of a taxi. "The stuff is inside," he said. Walker grabbed the package quickly, while his companion drew a revolver and arrested the astonished Soccio.

Later that night Mastracchio was also arrested, along with John Sullivan, a waiter at the *Corso Pizzeria*. Charges were also laid against Jack Nadeau and his henchmen, Cecil Chesson, Jack Dushin and Nick Shuba, who was already in prison for robbery.

This local narcotics ring, an RCMP spokesman told journalists, was part of a vast chain which stretched across the ocean to one of its major links, Lucky Luciano in Naples. The Narcotics Squad, in fact, had recently learned of the visit to Italy of two men closely connected to the Cotroni brothers. Luigi Greco and Frank Petrula were said to have met Luciano during their visit. These two men had great prestige in the Montreal underworld. Greco and Petrula, sons of Italian and Ukrainian immigrants, respectively, had been bodyguards for Harry Davis when Davis was the king of narcotics in the city. Before that they had busied themselves at various tasks, ranging from auto theft to bank robbery. After the death of Davis in 1946, they took over some of his rackets and linked up with members of the Cotroni gang. (5)

But there was also another connection between the Lucky Luciano network and the arrest of Mastracchio and Soccio. The U.S. Bureau of Narcotics had just smashed the Spirito-Orsini ring which had collaborated with Cotroni's gang for several years. During July and August, about 15 French and American traffickers were indicted by a Grand Jury of the southern district of New York. (6) Most of them had links with the Gaetano Lucchese gang, the first American Mafia family to move into narcotics trafficking on a big scale towards the end of the 1930s. Lucchese was an old friend of Luciano and a former partner of the Jewish mobster Lepke Buchalter. (7)

The files of the Narcotics Squad revealed a direct link between the Mastracchio-Soccio investigation and the arrests by the U.S. Bureau of Narcotics in New York. The efforts of the RCMP undercover agent, Hugh Walker, to contact Frank Sisco were aimed at exposing the connection between Antoine d'Agostino (Michel Sisco) and the Spirito-Orsini Mafia group in New York.

Several convictions resulted from the New York arrests, François Spirito and Joseph Orsini among them. Spirito, after serving his two-

---

5. After serving his sentence for drug trafficking, Harry Davis was released from prison in 1945. On July 25, 1946, he was assassinated by a gangster from the fringes of the underworld to whom Davis had refused permission to open a gambling house. His murder, and the bomb attempt on his life 11 days earlier, raised a storm of civic protest which led to the dismissal of certain police officers and the appointment of a lawyer, Pacifique Plante, as head of the morality squad of the Montreal Police. For 18 months, Plante and his men carried out a merciless battle against the city's racketeers until they, in turn, were dismissed.

6. Heading the list were the Corsicans François Spirito, Joseph Orsini, Angel Abadalejo, Vincent Bernardini, as well as Antoine d'Agostino whose trail was picked up during the investigation but who could not be found when police drew in the net. During the next few months, the Frenchmen Lucien Ignaro, Jean David, alias Jean Laget, François Paoleschi and Paul Praticci were also charged. Mafia dealers involved were Carmelo Sansone, Vincent Randazzo, Salvatore Mezzesalma, Eugenio Giannini, Salvatore Shillitani, Anthony Martello and Rosario Tornello.

   On September 20, 1952, Eugenio Giannini was murdered in New York on orders from Lucky Luciano. In 1950 he had gone to Europe and met Luciano in Naples. Giannini was arrested by Italian police for smuggling penicillin and dealing in counterfeit money but was acquitted for lack of evidence. After he returned to New York, Luciano discovered his links with the U.S. Bureau of Narcotics and asked his partners to "take care of him."

7. Note that Carlo Gambino, whose name had been linked to d'Agostino's, had close ties with Lucchese. His oldest son, in fact, married Lucchese's daughter.

year sentence, returned secretly to Marseilles, was arrested and then released, despite the death sentence for treason which had been pronounced on him in his absence. He retired to Sausset-les-Pins where his name cropped up in public from time to time until his death in October 1967. Joseph Orsini was sentenced to a 10-year term in prison. When he was released in 1958 he was deported from the United States and resumed his underworld activities in Marseilles.

In Montreal in April 1952, Diodato Mastracchio and Jimmy Soccio both pleaded guilty. Each was sentenced to 23 months in prison. As they began serving their terms, the central office of narcotics in Paris exposed Marius Ansaldi's illicit laboratory, the main source of supplies for the Spirito-Orsini-d'Agostino organization. This lab, which had been in operation since the end of the war, was the biggest producer of its time supplying an estimated total of $50 million in heroin to the U.S. black market. When the police put this lab out of business, the production of heroin from morphine-base moved to Marseilles, a city which already specialized in the importation of raw materials from the Middle East. The French traffickers thought it logical to concentrate all production activities in a city like Marseilles which had been top-ranked for prostitution and smuggling for more than a century. Thus Marseilles became the world capital of heroin. The Marseilles underworld, mainly composed of gangsters of Corsican origin, is a closed society, much more so than the Paris underworld. Its members often consider themselves blood brothers, all of a family, in the image of the Mafia.

Chapter 4

On the Trail of
the Fugitives

After the arrest of the owners of the *Corso Pizzeria,* the work of the Narcotics Squad became much more difficult. Several of the post-war crime chiefs had been unmasked in the past three years and their successors were beginning to get the message. It became almost impossible to infiltrate a drug trafficking ring. The federal police agents had to be content with compiling bits and pieces of information picked up here and there from interested informers.

They also still had hopes of tracking down Antoine d'Agostino who had taken flight in January 1950. Since then, and since the arrests of François Spirito and Joseph Orsini in July 1951, d'Agostino had been seen in just about every part of the two Americas and even in Europe. But the information about him was never precise enough to permit a follow-up investigation.

On November 23, 1953, however, an anonymous telephone caller declared to the Narcotics Squad that he had met the famous fugitive ten days earlier in Mexico. The informer, who refused to give his name or agree to any meeting, said that d'Agostino frequented the French restaurant *Helena* in Mexico City and lived with a young woman in apartment 8 at 276 or 376 Plaza de la Reforma. He said the dealer had grown a moustache and wore dark glasses but had not changed much otherwise. Asked about the circumstances of his meeting with d'Agostino, the caller said he had nothing more to say and hung up.

This information, though far from ample, seemed detailed enough to warrant its transmittal to the Federal Bureau of Investigation (F.B.I.) and the Bureau of Narcotics in the United States. Both organizations had liaison officers in Mexico who could check the story. A short time later, however, it was New York that supplied the first interesting response: the local section of the Bureau of Narcotics there had linked the information to an important investigation it had going.

During the previous April, after an undercover operation, the New York Bureau had arrested one of the major partners of Spirito and Orsini. This was Jean David, alias John Laget, called the Silver Fox. David was born in 1898 at Arles, France, in the Bouches-du-Rhône. He fled France in 1939, after the murder of a bank messenger and took refuge in New York where he became a respectable businessman, well-regarded by the French colony. He was co-owner of the *Felice* restaurant on 46th Street and also one of the directors af a company called *Letourneur Sulky Wheels Inc.* After David's arrest, the investigating officer, Angelo Zurlo, discovered that he had been receiving a lot of correspondence through the intermediary of a de luxe Italian restaurant. Through his contacts, the officer even managed to obtain a letter from an Edwardo Gomez in Mexico, written in French and stating that the reply should be sent to the *Helena* restaurant, 9 Cella de Terma, Mexico. The letter, with the name "Paul" written in one of its corners, read as follows:

"Not having heard from you, I've taken the liberty of writing to you. Let me know the price of fabrics in New York. Why don't you take a vacation and come to Mexico. It's a beautiful city. Please give me an address where I can reach you and let me know the price of fabrics. If they're expensive, I can go to New York."

A few months later, another letter arrived at the Italian restaurant which David had frequented. This one was addressed to a "Mr. Dumont," a person who had previously come to the restaurant with David. The letter came from Marseilles and was signed "Charlot," a pseudonym for one of the trafficker's henchmen. The second letter was even shorter than the first:

"The people in Mexico want to know why you haven't written. I haven't had much luck in my business but I've become an expert in the manufacture of shirts. If you have friends with money, I'd be interested in coming to the U.S."

Although innocent in appearance, these letters were obviously coded messages related to international narcotics traffic. The police problem was: how to use them to best advantage.

It was finally the RCMP's information about the possible whereabouts of Antoine d'Agostino which gave the lead to the New York investigation. On December 7, 1953, the agent Zurlo addressed the following letter to Edwardo Gomez at the *Helena* restaurant:

"I'm terribly sorry, but I couldn't write to you. I've had a letter from Charlot asking me to write to you. The price of fabrics is very high here. Don't write to me at the bar. Use the following address and let me know."

The agent signed the letter and gave the address of the small apartment he shared with another agent in Brooklyn. No one at the Bureau of Narcotics really expected an answer; the chance of getting a reply was figured at about one in a million. On December 12, however, came a great surprise: a tall gentleman of aristocratic bearing presented himself at the Brooklyn apartment looking for Zurlo. Zurlo was not there, but fortunately his colleague was. The stranger, of French origin, said his name was Joe and he had just arrived from Mexico. He wished to see Mr. Zurlo on an urgent matter of great importance. The police officer easily managed to arrange a meeting with Zurlo for that night in a nearby restaurant.

During the meeting, Zurlo used his long experience of the world of criminals, skilfully making references to Mr. Dumont to gain the confidence of the visitor who was really Roger Coudert, 58, a big name in the Paris underworld. The dealer, who had not much use for idle chatter, came quickly to the point and asked the undercover agent if he wished to buy heroin. The agent expressed interest and the two men soon came to an agreement on a transaction involving eight kilos. The Parisian even provided a few grains of white powder as a sample and a token of good faith.

The next day a second meeting took place and as tests had shown the heroin to be of very good quality, Zurlo offered to pay $8,500 a kilo. The trafficker became angry, but not at Zurlo: he had just delivered six kilos to another member of his organization who had only paid him $6,500 a kilo. Finally Coudert, seeing that the undercover agent was interested in buying large amounts, agreed to organize a regular supply. But that would only be possible, he stipulated, if the New Yorker added to his list of customers the name of "a friend in Montreal"—Lucien Rivard.

This name was not unknown to the RCMP. For a little more than two years, Rivard's name had been making the list of the new chiefs of the Canadian drug trade. Not much was known about him except that he was an old friend of Johnny Young and that he was on excellent terms with several people in the Cotroni brothers circle, and particularly Angelo Bizanti, owner of the *American Spaghetti House* and Young's former boss. In 1951 and 1952, Rivard had been associated with a dealer named Rhéo Gauthier, who was later killed in an auto accident during a narcotics delivery to Windsor, Ontario. Since the jailing of Diodato Mastracchio and Jimmy Soccio, Rivard had acquired the reputation of being the number one man in the heroin traffic in Montreal and throughout Canada. He was accorded great respect in the underworld and was considered a peerless organizer. His chief lieutenants were Bob Tremblay, former sailor and comrade of Johnny Young, and Jean-Louis (Blackie) Bisson.

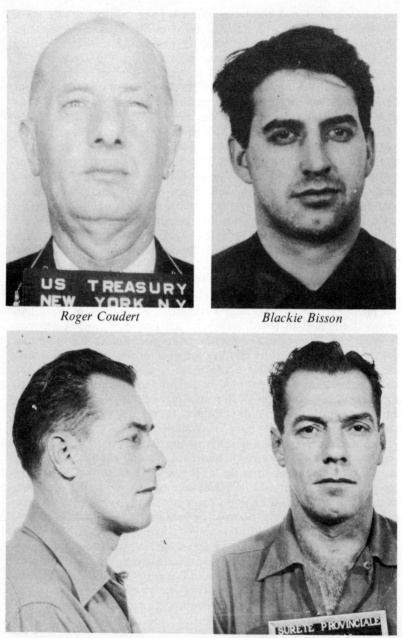

Roger Coudert

Blackie Bisson

Lucien Rivard, photo taken 1952.

In 1952 Tremblay was the major heroin wholesaler in Montreal. From his headquarters in *Dubé's Pool Room* on St. Lawrence Street, he supplied a team of street dealers through his trusted aide, Walter Ward. In the spring of 1952, a gambling loss forced him into greater involvement in drug traffic and to take a personal hand in sales to customers. Tremblay continued his activities until the end of 1952, when he went back to Vancouver, his home town. Supplied by Rivard, he took over heroin distribution on the west coast of Canada while Bisson replaced him in the Montreal market.

In January 1953, Narcotics Squad officers learned that a Frenchman named Jacques, in New York, was regularly supplying large quantities of heroin to Rivard. According to their information, the two traffickers met once a month in a Montreal tavern, *Le Sphinx*. A delivery of several kilos of heroin usually followed each meeting. Until Roger Coudert had mentioned the name Rivard to the agent Zurlo, it had been impossible to locate and identify the mysterious French supplier. Now the mystery was perhaps solved, thanks to the work of the Bureau of Narcotics undercover agent.

The Parisian, besides mentioning the name of Rivard, also asked Zurlo if he knew "my friend in Montreal" and "his partner, a big, fair-haired man." The agent had already been briefed on the RCMP information. He was able to reply smoothly that he had heard of Rivard and his partner, Rhéo Gauthier, The account the agent gave of the circumstances of Gauthier's death greatly interested Coudert and convinced him of the trustworthiness of his new customer. The Parisian dealer was encouraged to reveal even more confidences. He mentioned that Rivard was not only a very important figure in the international traffic, but also an active member of the ring that Coudert worked for. Once, he recalled, Rivard had even accompanied him on a trip to France when they brought back 15 kilos of heroin. The Montrealer had kept six for himself and the rest was distributed in the New York market.

The narcotics traffic situation in Canada seemed to hold no secrets for Roger Coudert. He could discourse with equal facility about the importance of the eastern market or about the profitability and risks of the western market. That brought him to inquire if Zurlo knew anyone in Vancouver. When the agent said he didn't, the trafficker offered another important revelation.

"Did you ever hear about those two brothers in Vancouver who skipped bail and disappeared. Well, they're with us now. They're members of the organization. One of them left Mexico, a year and a half ago, with five kilos. He only paid cash for three and we let him have the other two on credit. He never came back though and since he hadn't paid what he owed, his brother had to pay the bill. Lately I learned that the one in New York is now working with a guy from Brooklyn."

At the time of this conversation, Coudert did not know that on the eve of his first meeting with Zurlo, the Canadian fugitive he was talking about, George Mallock, had been captured in New York by the Bureau of Narcotics. Mallock and his brother, John, had been first arrested on September 28, 1950, after a joint undercover operation by the Bureau of Narcotics and the RCMP. They had sold an ounce of heroin to the agent Henry L. Giordano (who later became Commissioner-General of the Bureau of Narcotics). Out on $20,000 bail each, they failed to appear for their trial on January 21, 1951, and from that date became, with d'Agostino, the most wanted criminals in Canada.

The Mallock brothers, long active in the tough sections of Winnipeg, Manitoba, took control of the heroin traffic on the west coast of Canada in 1949. John was the first to get into the lucrative rackets, like drug trafficking and counterfeiting. He began selling heroin in 1947 while his brother, George, was serving a term for grievous assault. At first, he bought by the ounce and re-sold in capsules. The business prospered and he quickly established himself in force in Winnipeg, then in other Prairie cities where he eliminated competition by violence and terrorism. He had become a chief in the drug traffic by the time George, just out of prison, joined him in June 1949. He had also begun an invasion of the Vancouver market, thanks to the work of his two main representatives, Pete Jamaga, alias Joe Hall, and Peter Noveselski, alias Pete Novis.

Their organization was struck a first, hard blow on March 25, 1950, when John and Pete Novis, travelling in a car with a thousand caps of heroin, were arrested by the RCMP Narcotics Squad in Vancouver. Novis took all the blame, however, and John was freed. Backed up by a formidable scoundrel named William Carter and a small army of strong-arm troops, George came to Vancouver and succeeded in taking complete control of the market while John organized new deliveries through Lucien Rivard. Solidly established on their Canadian territory, the Mallocks soon turned towards the United States. In mid-July 1950, the Seattle section of the Bureau of Narcotics was advised of their presence in the region. The agent Giordano was then despatched to Vancouver where, through certain contacts in the underworld, he was able to approach William Carter first, then the Mallock brothers themselves.

Not until November 1951, 11 months after the disappearance of the Mallock brothers, did the RCMP learn that they had managed illegal entry to the United States with the help of Lucien Rivard, Rhéo Gauthier and Bob Tremblay. They had gone to Winnipeg where one of their men, Percy Greenwell, alias Melon, had driven them to Montreal by car. Supplied with false passports, they had finally made their way to Mexico. In return for these services the Mallocks introduced Percy Melon to the Montrealers who were able to use him for a time to supply the Vancouver market. Melon turned out to be a bit slow in paying his bills, however, and Rivard stopped dealing with him. Instead, distribution on the west coast was turned over to Bob Tremblay who was able to use the services of former members of the Mallock gang, like Pete Jamaga.

The RCMP and the U.S. Bureau of Narcotics learned almost simultaneously of the Mallock brothers' new activities in the drug traffic. Shortly after the mysterious telephone call about Antoine d'Agostino's place of refuge in Mexico, Montreal agents learned that George Mallock had visited Lucien Rivard in September 1953. He had taken advantage of his visit to Quebec to send a kilo of heroin to a former partner in Winnipeg, Peter Lahosky. [1] It was also reported that Mallock was accompanied in Montreal by Frank Sisco.

George Mallock's trail in New York had been picked up towards the end of November when a Bureau of Narcotics investigator met a gangster who claimed he could take him to the Canadian fugitive. On December 8, therefore, the day after the agent Zurlo had sent his letter to Mexico, another agent, Anthony Zirilli, had a first meeting with George Mallock. Zirilli was able to negotiate a deal for seven kilos of heroin from France. At the second meeting, on the afternoon of December 11, the dealer was arrested after an RCMP officer who had been sent to New York for that special purpose, had positively identified him. At that moment, of course, no one knew that Zurlo's letter would bear fruit the next day or that it would be an associate of Mallock who responded to it. If that could have been foreseen, police would no doubt have preferred to delay the arrest of the fugitive.

---

1. Peter Lahosky carried on his activities with impunity until January 26, 1972, when he was arrested in Winnipeg as he took delivery of a stock of heroin brought from Montreal by the wife of Emile Hogue, also known as Pit Lépine, a close friend of Lucien Rivard.

At midnight on December 17, Coudert, who was under special and constant police surveillance, received a telephone call from Mexico which caused him to leave his hotel in a hurry. Less than 15 minutes after the call, he left with his baggage even though his first transaction with Zurlo was set for the following day. The surveillance team tailed him to Grand Central Station where he checked two aluminum suitcases at the baggage office. The team, unfortunately, then lost sight of him in the traffic. During the night, however, the cab driver who had picked Coudert up was located. He had taken the trafficker to La Guardia airport. This incident was immediately related to privileged information to the effect that soon after George Mallock's arrest, a New York underworld lawyer had passed a warning to his brother John, who was at the *Maria Angelo* hotel in Mexico, right beside the *Helena* restaurant.

The Bureau of Narcotics agents thought they had seen the last of the French trafficker for a while but to their great surprise, he contacted Zurlo the following day at noon. When they met, Coudert explained that he had gone to Montreal to meet his courier but, because of misunderstanding, the courier, instead of waiting, had returned to Mexico with the merchandise. The Frenchman confided to Zurlo that the drugs were transported in secret compartments built into trunks or suitcases. Heroin from Marseilles was brought first to Montreal or Mexico by couriers using the airlines. Deliveries to New York were then made via Montreal because inspection on the direct Mexico-New York flights was too strict. All arrangements for supply shipments were made definitively in advance in order to keep overseas communications to a minimum. When Coudert was ready for a transaction, he had only to send a sum of money to be deposited in a certain Swiss bank account. When the account-holder was advised by the bank that a sum of money had been deposited, he knew from the amount involved how much heroin to ship.

After making these explanations, Coudert mentioned that he had two fake suitcases to be repaired. The secret compartments had been broken during the last transaction of six kilos. The police officer, alert to every opportunity, quickly seized this one; he said he had a trusted friend who could look after the repairs. The trafficker, happy to have his problem solved, suspected nothing. He took Zurlo to Grand Central and gave him the two aluminum suitcases he had placed in the baggage checkroom the night before. The undercover agent immediately took this loot to Bureau of Narcotics headquarters where meticulous examination revealed a thin layer of white powder on one of the partitions of a secret compartment. The quantity was small, but it was enough: chemical analysis comfirmed the substance to be pure heroin. It was now imperative that the trail of the trafficker not be lost a second time.

Left to himself, but followed constantly, Coudert went to the *St. George Hotel* in Brooklyn. During the night he received another telephone call from Mexico. The anonymous caller announced that Johnny the courier had left Mexico and should arrive in New York in three or four days. He would be carrying only three and a half kilos; the rest of the order would arrive later. After another meeting with the Parisian on December 20, Zurlo deduced that the Johnny in question could be John Mallock. The following night Coudert got another call from Mexico. This time he was told that Johnny had been injured in an auto accident and that he must come back at once because "something has gone wrong."

The investigators were convinced by this time that word of George Mallock's arrest had come to the ears of Coudert's associates and that nothing more could be hoped for from the undercover operation. The time had come to arrest the Frenchman; there was already enough evidence against him anyway. And while they were at it, they also arrested two notorious mafiosi who had often been seen in Coudert's company. One was Antonio Farina who used his small shirt factory in Mexico as a front for his work as an intermediary between the d'Agostino gang and New York buyers. His arrest came just in time—a day before he was scheduled to return to Mexico.

The other mafioso was Ugo Caneba, a key man in the ring which had been set up by Luciano's friends. With his older brother Salvatore, he had managed to intercept hundreds of cases of medical supplies destined for the U.S. military when the cases arrived in Sicily at the end of the war. Some of the supplies consisted of enormous quantities of drugs in raw form. The Caneba brothers were nephews of Pasquale Ania, who was called Don Pasquale, a grand master of the Sicilian Mafia. They were accomplices of the creators of the combine of pharmaceutical laboratories in Milan, had long been associated with the Corsican underworld, and were customers of François Spirito and Joseph Orsini. Salvatore Caneba, in fact, had known these last two men before the war, in France, where he had spent several years before being expelled in 1936. The arrest of Jean David, the Silver Fox, furthermore, followed the indictment of Salvatore which had come shortly after the indictment of Joseph Orsini in July 1951. After Ugo's arrest, both brothers were deported to Italy. There they immediately resumed their habitual activities until November 1966 when they were definitely put out of harm's way.

73

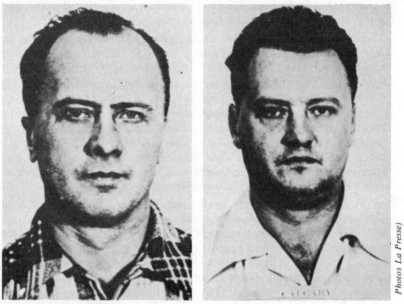

Photos La Presse

The Mallock brothers, George (left) and John (right).

Jean-Baptiste Croce

Paul Mondolini

On March 1, 1954, George Mallock was sentenced at Vancouver to 21 years in penitentiary and a $17,000 fine. In New York, a month later, Roger Coudert was given a ten-year prison term and fined $16,000. Antonio Farina got a five-year sentence and a $10,000 fine. These judgments, of course, were in addition to the conviction of Jean David and the deportations of his right-hand man Lucien Ignaro and of the Caneba brothers.

The Mexican police, meanwhile, had located the other Mallock brother, John, but once again the trafficker managed to escape. On the following April 9, however, John Mallock was identified as one of the victims in a serious road accident at Queretaro, about 200 miles north of Mexico City. He never regained consciousness in hospital and died from his injuries on April 22, 1954.

After this death and the round-ups in New York, police efforts in Canada, the U.S. and Mexico concentrated on Antoine d'Agostino and other members of his ring, some of whom were just beginning to make names for themselves. Two names in particular had surfaced shortly after the charges were brought against Roger Coudert: Jean-Baptiste Croce and Paul Mondolini, both Corsicans. In the spring of 1953, they had succeeded in delivering an important quantity of heroin to d'Agostino. They came to America hidden aboard the liner *SS Cavelier de la Salle* which had sailed from Bordeaux in France. The ship was destined for Mexico but en route received orders to make a stop in Florida. In a panic the two men left the ship in a lifeboat, landed on an isolated beach and finally managed to deliver their merchandise.

It was known that Croce and Mondolini were well-backed by the French underworld and that they had previously been arrested by U.S. Customs and the Mexican police. On August 14, 1953, Customs officers at Corpus Christi in Texas intercepted two Frenchmen, Paul-Marie Bégin and Jean Croce, who had attempted to enter the U.S. illegally. The two men were turned back to Mexico six days later, and later still, they were identified from their fingerprints as Paul Mondolini and Jean-Baptiste Croce.

On February 18, 1954, Mexico City police raided an apartment looking for John Mallock. The apartment was occupied by a Marseilles woman, Marcelle Senesi and a Mexican named Eduardo Dubian Chabolla, but had been rented by a Jean-Baptiste Croce who was living at the *Campastela Hotel.* Croce and his friends were questioned at length at the police station, but finally released. Only later, after further identity checks, did police learn that Chabolla was in reality Paul Mondolini and the Marseillaise with him was his girlfriend.

The two men were well known to French police. In February 1953 just before their secret departure for Mexico, they had been accosted by crime squad officers in a Parisian bar, *Le Laetitia,* and asked for their papers. Mondolini had false papers, but Croce's name had been taken and transmitted to Interpol.

Jean-Baptiste Croce, known as Bati, was born in Bastia, Corsica, in April 1920 and worked first as an ordinary sailor on the Far-East lines of *Messageries Maritimes.* He got into smuggling before the war by supplying morphine-base to the labs of François Spirito and Paul Carbone. Because of his extraordinary talent as a trafficker, he was taken under the wing of Ansan Albert Bistoni, the big boss of Marseilles, and the two became inseparable. Bistoni, who was called Mister Albert, was also a Corsican and had also started as a sailor on the Indochina routes. Before the war, Bistoni supplied the Carbone-Spirito ring with opium. Later, he joined Spirito in organizing a link with certain Mafia groups, especially with Francesco Pirico of Milan, a friend of Lucky Luciano and the Caneba brothers and one of the originators of the pharmaceutical laboratory combine. At the time Croce's moves in America were being investigated, in December 1953, the central office for narcotics of the French national police succeeded in charging him in connection with a seizure of four kilos of heroin in Paris. As a fugitive, he was convicted in his absence in 1956.

Paul Mondolini, also Corsican, was born in 1916 and had spent many years in Indochina. He had even been police chief of Saigon! In August 1949, he won notoriety for his part in an armed attack on The Begum, wife of the Ismailian prince Aga Khan, who had been holidaying on the French Riviera. He and his accomplices made off with royal jewelry valued at more than 200 million francs. This caper, one of the biggest crime stories of the post-war period, earned Mondolini the attention of almost every police force in the world. It also earned him, in December 1953 and in his absence, a life sentence at hard labor. The affair was forgotten, however, when the thieves turned the loot over to the police at the instigation of Mémé Guérini, a crime lord of the Marseilles underworld. Mondolini was also known for his close relations with another Corsican, Dominique Nicoli who was assassinated in Marseilles and replaced by Joseph Patrizzi, owner of the Marseille bar *L'Artistic,* and the Nice Cabaret *Maxim's.* (2)

---

2. Joseph Patrizzi was charged with trafficking in heroin in February 1975. He was arrested with Urbain Giaume, one of the participants in the robbery of The Begum's jewels.

Despite all this information, the search for the two Corsicans and for Antoine d'Agostino was difficult work. For weeks officers of the U.S. Bureau of Narcotics marked time. Finally, it was examination of Customs files which gave a firm lead. On January 14 and 18, 1954, a certain Albert Blain and his wife Madeleine, carrying Canadian passports, entered the United States at the Texas border point of Laredo. They claimed they were returning to Montreal. Putting various bits of information together, the Bureau of Narcotics concluded that the Blain couple were really Antoine d'Agostino and his wife, Suzanne Filleau. This conclusion was supported when the RCMP Narcotics Squad learned that the Blain passport numbers were false.

Shortly after this discovery, the Bureau of Narcotics gained more ground by turning up an important informer in the circle of French traffickers in Mexico. They learned that d'Agostino was also known as Alberto Dujardin or Carlos Alberto Ferrara and that he lived in an apartment in the Plaza de la Reforma (a confirmation of RCMP information).

In June, the Bureau of Narcotics learned that Paul Mondolini and Jean-Baptiste Croce had left Mexico the previous month. After delivering a supply of heroin in New York, they had gone on to Montreal to make contact with one of their partners. Mondolini had stayed in Montreal, according to the information obtained by the American agents, while Croce returned to France. RCMP efforts to find Mondolini in Montreal were not successful. The search was still going on when the U.S. Bureau of Narcotics and the Mexican federal police lost track of d'Agostino in Mexico. On the night of July 28, police had failed in an attempt to arrest Suzanne Filleau, as two Mexican members of the gang were going to meet her. The police action tipped off d'Agostino who disappeared from circulation with his henchmen. It also caused Bureau of Narcotics agents in New York to re-double their caution in another undercover operation which was about to come to a head. This time a secret agent had made direct contact with an important member of Luciano's organization, Sebastiano Bellanca, who was known as Benny the Sicilian and was believed to be one of the most active heroin importers on the American east coast. Bellanca had been known to the police since 1949, thanks to the checks the RCMP had made on the telephone calls of Michel Sisco (Antoine d'Agostino) and Giuseppe Cotroni. Bellanca was known to have made several trips to Montreal in that year accompanied by a certain Gaetano Martino from Brooklyn. Martino was identified as a personal courier for Luciano and for Vincent Mangano, one of the Dons of the New

York Mafia. The year before in Geneva, Bellanca's brother Antonio had been arrested in possession of 15 kilos (35 pounds) of heroin. Earlier, the two brothers had been involved in the traffic of immigrants. Since 1950 the name of Sebastiano Bellanca had figured in various investigations by the Bureau of Narcotics. (3)

On August 11, 1954, late in the afternoon, the approaches to the *Hemingway Trucking Company* in Paramour, New Jersey, were under heavy surveillance by agents of the U.S. Bureau of Narcotics. Earlier in the day, Benny Bellanca had contracted with the undercover agent to sell him a kilo of heroin that night. One deal had already taken place between the two men in April, and this time the police hoped to take the trafficker in. Early in the evening, therefore, when Bellanca left the offices of the *Hemingway* Company, an impressive team of agents was on his tail. He was followed right into New York to the intersection of 152nd Street and Morris Avenue. There he was joined by an accomplice, Pietro Beddia, who consulted with him for a few minutes. (4) The two men then got in their cars and drove, one behind the other, to 156th Street. About a hundred feet from the corner, the two cars drew up side by side and Beddia threw a package into Bellanca's car. At that moment the police moved in and surrounded the two cars. Bellanca offered no resistance. Beddia tried to crash the police barrier but a couple of shots through his windshield changed his mind about trying to escape.

---

3. The following mafiosi were on the files of the Bureau of Narcotics as associates of Sebastiano Bellanca: Jack Scarpulla, Frank Scalici, Settimo Accardo, Joe Pici, Peter Beddia and Albert Anastasia.

4. Five days earlier, U.S. agents had intercepted a telephone conversation between Pietro Beddia of White Plains, New Jersey, and an unknown man named Tony. It had to do with a trip Tony was to make to Montreal the following day to meet certain friends. Beddia was giving instructions on the route to be followed. Convinced that the trip involved the heroin traffic, agents put various border posts under surveillance and even travelled to Montreal to check certain addresses, including 1790 St. Timothy Street where Sebastiano Bellanca's other brother, Joseph, had lived for several years. On the morning of August 8, the agents watching the Champlain border post noted that a certain Mildred Renda had crossed into Canada the night before. They recalled that a man named Antonio Renda had often been seen with Pietro Beddia. In late afternoon Mildred Renda returned to the border point accompanied by her husband Antonio (Tony) and her son. They said they were returning home from a visit with a relative in Monteal. A search of their car produced nothing, and they were allowed to proceed into the U.S. A few months earlier, Benny Bellanca had confided to a Bureau of Narcotics undercover agent that he obtained his heroin supplies in Montreal.

The immediate search produced the kilo of heroin Beddia had just delivered, along with some revealing documents. A piece of paper found on Bellanca bore the name of Carlos Ferrara, one of the aliases of Antoine d'Agostino. On the other side of the paper a Montreal telephone number was written: Harbour 0459.

This telephone number, when it was checked, proved to be registered in the name of Joe Seminaro, 345 Emery Street, apartment 2, Montreal. At first sight, the name meant nothing to Narcotics Squad agents but after several weeks of research, they learned that Seminaro was the father-in-law of Giuseppe Cotroni. "Pep" Cotroni had been jailed in 1949 for receiving stolen bonds. Since his release from St. Vincent de Paul penitentiary in April 1953 he hadn't attracted much attention though it was known he had resumed his position at the side of his older brother, Vic. The role of the Cotronis in the heroin traffic had ceased to preoccupy the RCMP until this telephone number was found in Bellanca's pocket. For the federal police, Lucien Rivard had become the number one suspect in the international traffic.

But Rivard, too, it was noted with great interest, had close connections with Benny Bellanca. U.S. Bureau of Narcotics agents had seen him several times at the offices of *Hemingway Trucking* in Paramour and at the *Guy Restaurant* in New York, owned by Bellanca's nephew. Bellanca's arrest had added another element to the file: at his grilfriend's place police found a paper bearing Rivard's name, address and telephone number. Earlier investigations showed that in December 1953 and February 1954, the Montrealer had stayed at the *Taft Hotel* in New York and had made several telephone calls to the *Guy Restaurant.*

The discovery of the names of Rivard and Pep Cotroni in the company of an individual as important as Sebastiano Bellanca held a special significance for detectives of the Narcotics Squad. For some time it had been rumored that the Montreal Mafia had decided to regain its place in the international heroin traffic by joining up with Lucien Rivard. The most recent operations of the U.S. Bureau of Narcotics seemed to confirm that. Other significant indications soon came to light.

In the following October the Bureau of Narcotics raided the home of another New York mafioso, Tony Bianco, just out of Atlanta penitentiary where he had served several months with Roger Coudert. Among his personal effects was the following letter, addressed to Lucien Rivard, in care of the *Corso Pizzeria,* Montreal:

"Dear Lucien,
I just got out of Atlanta where I met one of our very good

friends, the big Frenchman, Roger. He says he got ten years because of certain people in Mexico. He needs money for an appeal and he asked me to help him get out. He told me to write to you at the Corso Pizzeria to ask you to meet me on your next trip to New York. If you have any good linen and the price is right, I have a good market which could make a little money to help Roger in his appeal. Let me know when I could see you. I'm sure we can do some business which would allow me to help Roger. Write to me.

Tony Bianco
c/o Frank's Restaurant
1140 — 2nd Avenue, N.Y."

This letter convinced the RCMP of Lucien Rivard's dealings with the d'Agostino organization as well as of his association with the Cotroni clan. The fact that the letter had been sent in care of the *Corso Pizzeria,* property of Diodato Mastracchio and Jimmy Soccio, was not a negligible clue.

Another element tended to confirm rumors of a new Rivard-Cotroni link in drug trafficking: the general situation of the Montreal underworld which for the past 18 months had been boiling with activity. A hundred or so U.S. gangsters, fleeing from the new ten per cent gambling tax voted by Congress after the Kefauver crime inquiry, had installed themselves in Montreal with the blessing of the top leaders of the underworld. Most of them were bookies who had been doing business with local contacts for decades. They came to Montreal with guarantees of immunity offered by the city's crime chiefs who exercised control over politicians and policemen in the city and the province.

RCMP agents were aware of the massive presence of strangers in town but could do little about it. Their authority in Quebec did not extend to enforcement of gambling laws. They had to be content with passive collection of information while waiting for a change in administration which would permit them to cooperate with municipal police forces.

Even so, the information coming in was far from useless. The Narcotics Squad, alert to major changes in the underworld, had noted the arrival in Montreal, at the end of 1953, of a New Yorker with the air of a conqueror. The newcomer, known as Mister Lillo, was in Montreal to supervise the activities of the American bookies and to collect a percentage of the profits for the Mafia chieftains.

Within a few weeks of his arrival, however, it became plain that this was no simple supervisor. According to police informers, Mister Lillo had taken control of the Montreal underworld on behalf

Frank Petrula   Joe Bonanno

Pep Cotroni   Pax Plante

of the American Mafia and with the agreement of local crime lords. In partnership with local leaders, he had already acquired a chic restaurant called the *Bonfire,* on Decarie Boulevard in the northwest part of the city. It quickly became the headquarters for the Organization. He also founded a finance company, *Alpha Investment Corporation,* with his official partners Luigi Greco, Frank Petrula, Max Shapiro, Harry Ship and Vic Cotroni (whose name did not appear on the books until 1966). Mister Lillo, with the backing of Vic Cotroni and Louis Greco, clamped his rule on night clubs, blind pigs, gambling dens, bookmakers, prostitutes and thieves: henceforth, all must pay tribute to The Syndicate.

But who was this Mister Lillo? The answer soon came from the F.B.I. and the U.S. Bureau of Narcotics. Carmine Galente, called Lillo, was a 44-year-old son of Sicilian immigrants, a tough, harsh, authoritarian chief of the Brooklyn underworld and an incomparable killer. More than 80 murders were ascribed to his hand; the most celebrated was that of Carlo Tresca, an anti-fascist journalist of an Italian weekly in New York, who had been assassinated in January 1943. The murder had been ordered by Vito Genovese, Luciano's assistant, who had taken refuge in Italy in 1934 following a killing and became one of the intimates of the fascist dictator Mussolini. Galente, a specialist in underworld diplomacy, was second-in-command to Giuseppe Bonanno (Joe Bananas) who was one of the five godfathers of the New York Mafia. In this role, he was in contact with all the big names of the American and Italian crime world including Lucky Luciano. Bureau of Narcotics files record a Galente-Luciano meeting in Italy in 1954.

In the autumn of 1954, when the RCMP learned that Giuseppe Cotroni and Lucien Rivard had apparently become partners in the heroin traffic, Narcotics Squad agents immediately suspected that Carmine Galente might also be involved perhaps even as the instigator of the affair. It was no secret that Galente always insisted on Mafia control of the rackets. He had, no doubt, obliged Rivard to join up with Cotroni by promising him greater opportunities in the U.S. market.

The theory about Galente's leadership in the Montreal heroin traffic was strengthened at the end of October 1954 by information passed to the RCMP from the U.S. Bureau of Narcotics. A few weeks earlier Frank Petrula, one of Galente's Montreal partners, had paid a visit to Luciano in Italy and had apparently returned with a stock of heroin. On October 29, in an attempt to verify this information, Sergeant Maurice Nadon and corporals Jean-Paul Drapeau and Frank de Cheverry of the Narcotics Squad carried out a thorough search of Petrula's luxurious home in Beaconsfield, a wealthy Montreal suburb. (5) The search lasted several hours but no trace of heroin was found. Nevertheless, the agents did not leave empty-handed.

Petrula's wife, worried about the way the federal agents were man-handling her paintings, decided it would be better to reveal the location of her husband's wall-safe. Hidden behind removable tiles in the upstairs bathroom the safe contained a hoard of $18,000 in ready cash and a few sheets of notes. When this discovery was made, Petrula tried to get the police to let him destroy the notes in exchange for the $18,000. But the police wanted to take a closer look at these slips of paper which seemed so precious. When they did, they were amazed: what they had in their hands was the list of journalists and politicians paid by the crime syndicate during the municipal election which had ended four days earlier. Petrula's notes indicated that the underworld had spent more than $100,000 in an attempt to defeat the Civic Action League and its star mayoralty candidate Jean Drapeau. Drapeau had been distinguishing himself for the past four years as assistant to Pacifique (Pax) Plante on the legal staff of the Commission of Inquiry into Gambling and Commercialized Vice in Montreal.

This inquiry, demanded since the early '40s by various groups of citizens, was finally established on May 31, 1950, five days after the start of the Kefauver Inquiry in the United States. It followed a long series of articles by Pax Plante in the daily newspaper *Le Devoir,* in which the former assistant police director of Montreal exposed in detail the well-oiled machine of the crime syndicate and its protection by politicians and policemen. With Judge François Caron of Superior Court presiding, Pax Plante and Jean Drapeau brought 373 of the city's most important police officers, politicians and gangsters to testify before the Commission. Convinced that the Plante accusations were well-founded, the judge craftily waited until October 8, 1954, 20 days before the municipal election, to make the Commission's report public. The report condemned the actions of 20 senior police officers, including the director Albert Langlois and his predecessor Fernand Dufresne. The politicians involved, though exonerated for lack of proof, were nevertheless badly shaken, and the underworld chieftains had been severely called to account. Vincent Cotroni, Luigi Greco, Max Shapiro, Harry Ship, Léo

---

5. In 1973, Sergeant Nadon and Corporal Drapeau were appointed, respectively, Commissioner and Assistant-Commissioner of the Royal Canadian Mounted Police.

Protection of the crime syndicate by politicians and policemen is exposed.

Bercovitch and Henry Manella, among others, had been exposed in clear and direct terms.

The report, published in full in all the major newspapers, so aroused the population that the mob leaders decided to make a massive attempt to counteract its possible adverse effects on the election results. On election day dozens of bully boys armed with sticks, clubs and revolvers roamed the city intimidating voters and sacking polling stations and committee rooms.

Petrula's notes were eloquent on this subject: they included the list of shock troops, with the budgets which had been granted them by underworld bosses (whose names were also listed in the notes). Among the names were: Carmine Galente and his jack-of-all-trades Mike Consolo; Luigi Greco; Vic Cotroni; the Organization's financial counselor Irving Ellis; Harry Ship, top man in illegal betting circles; Dominic de Francesco; Jimmy Orlando; Peter Adamo and Jimmy Soccio, key men in the Cotroni clan.

In spite of all its efforts, however, the underworld failed to prevent the victory of the Civic Action League and the election of Jean Drapeau as mayor. It was a failure the crime lords would bitterly regret over the next three years. (6)

Reinstated in his police functions, Pax Plante quickly resumed the battle against racketeers. His officers, with the help of the RCMP, soon rid the city of the American bookies and made life intolerable for local gangsters. One after another, the gambling dens, brothels, blind pigs and night clubs, were visited by police. Under the steady harassment, the Syndicate finally had to transfer some of its operations to adjacent suburbs. Even the federal income tax office got into the act, on the initiative of the RCMP, obliging Carmine Galente, in the spring of 1955, to give an account of his revenues. A short time later Galente was expelled from Canada along with his representative, Mike Consolo. He nevertheless retained a controlling hand on the Montreal rackets.

On the drug trafficking scene, the Narcotics Squad made life difficult for dealers and street sellers. In April 1955, after an investigation lasting several months, the Squad brought charges for

---

6. The war on crime which followed the victory of the Civic Action League ended abruptly in October 1957 when the Greater Montreal Rally (le Ralliement de Grand Montréal), led by Senator Sarto Fournier and supported by underworld financiers, defeated the Drapeau administration in the civic election and re-established on the municipal level the same shady politics which had never ceased to exist on the provincial level.

a second time against Jack Nadeau and his main henchmen. Unfortunately, the concentration of the Squad's limited manpower resources on the local traffic prevented it from giving adequate attention to the international traffic and especially to the Cotroni-Rivard organization. (7) The efforts that were made in that area produced slim results and police once again had to be content with painstaking gathering of clues.

The last positive result had been in November 1954 when U.S. Customs investigators in New York arrested a friend of Rivard, Emile Hogue, also known as Lépine. Returning from a trip to Europe, Hogue had brought back an automobile in which English customs officers had discovered a secret, though empty, compartment. Hogue claimed he knew nothing of the secret compartment in his car and, under lengthy questioning, denied any participation in drug trafficking. He did admit however — and this was no doubt the most important information — that he knew the traffickers Michel Sisco (d'Agostino), Lucien Rivard, Rhéo Gauthier and the brothers John and George Mallock. A further interesting fact: his passport indicated several visits to Mexico, including one in March 1953. Released for lack of evidence, Hogue became the object of the RCMP's special attention. So did William (Butch) Munroe, another Rivard henchman. The U.S. Bureau of Narcotics had asked for information about Munroe, a Scottish-origin croupier in a gambling establishment at 1408 St. Elizabeth Street, who had a criminal record for theft and receiving. During the summer of 1954 Munroe had spent several days at Lucien Rivard's chalet at Pointe Calumet, a small country resort much appreciated by Montreal racketeers, about 30 miles from the city. Before that, in January and February 1954, he had accompanied Rivard on a trip to Florida. This was known from a postcard addressed to Blackie Bisson which was found during a police search.

While the investigation in Montreal had to mark time, the trail of Antoine d'Agostino had been rediscovered in Mexico. Or, rather, the trail of his wife, Suzanne Filleau. On the evening of March 4, 1955, agents of the narcotics section of the Mexican police and of the U.S. Bureau of Narcotics followed the young woman to a clock shop on Bartaloache Street. Shortly after her arrival, a man came out of the building and got into a Chevrolet. The police arrested him thinking he was d'Agostino but he turned out to be merely the proprietor of the building. The surveillance continued and a little later two other men emerged from the shop. This time police had no

---

7. At that time, the Narcotics Squad had only about a dozen regular investigators.

difficulty recognizing the suspects: they were two notorious traffickers, Albert Carter Cantu, who had been marked the first time when Antonio Farina was arrested in New York, and Jorge Asaf y Bala, known as the Al Capone of the Mexican underworld. (8)

The two gangsters remained outside for a few minutes then went back into the shop. Their presence in the building with d'Agostino's wife was certainly no coincidence, and the police decided to strike. With no further delay, they burst into the shop and found themselves face to face with d'Agostino and another Corsican trafficker, Alfred Michiluci, who had arrived from France the night before and was about to return there. Taken by surprise, none of the five occupants offered any resistance. During the usual search which followed, agents discovered a basement workshop skilfully adapted for the manufacture of double-bottomed luggage and trick suitcases of the type Roger Coudert had mentioned two years earlier. Six of these suitcases, ready for use, were seized, including those which the Corsican Michiluci intended to take with him on his return to Marseilles the following day. There was only one flaw in the picture: no trace of heroin had been found.

Within the next few days, therefore, the Mexican police were obliged to release all the traffickers, except d'Agostino who was wanted by the police of three countries. He was deported without formality to San Antonio, Texas, where a court fixed bail at $100,000. Canadian authorities, informed of the arrest and deportation of this important French trafficker, took immediate steps to obtain his extradition. That was going to be a long drawn-out affair, however, since American authorities wished to charge d'Agostino first for his participation in the Spirito-Orsini ring. The trafficker, meanwhile, had launched legal proceedings to contest his hasty deportation to the United States. It was a full year later before d'Agostino reached trial in New York where he was convicted and sentenced to two years in penitentiary. Later, the Canadian government won its case for extradition and d'Agostino was deported to Montreal in June 1958. There he was sentenced to three more years in prison. Finally, in June 1960 he was deported to France where he was sought for several crimes and imprisoned at Le Havre on October 31, 1960. During his detention at St. Vincent de Paul penitentiary in Montreal, perhaps tormented by the jailing of

---

8. Jorge Asaf y Bala was arrested by Mexican police on November 11, 1959, along with an associate named Salvador Escabis. His arrest followed negotiation of a deal for three kilos of pure heroin with two undercover agents of the Bureau of Narcotics.

the unfortunate Father Taillefer, he was suddenly smitten with religious fervor and passed his time giving courses in Bible reading to his cellmates...

The arrest and deportation of d'Agostino forced his accomplices to flee Mexico and seek another refuge for the re-launching of their drug traffic. In April 1955 the Narcotics Squad was informed of Paul Mondolini's presence in Montreal. Further checks revealed that the Corsican was living in the Rosemont district under the name of Jacques Desmarais, in an apartment rented from Jimmy Curio, (9) a friend of the Cotroni family well known in sports and entertainment circles.

Mondolini could not be found, however, until July 8. On that day Corporal Jean-Paul Drapeau spotted him during his routine rounds as the trafficker entered the Emery Street residence of Joe Seminaro accompanied by Jimmy Curio and the youngest Cotroni brother, the 25-year-old Frank. (10) The RCMP had for several weeks been keeping a close watch on this house which was being used as a meeting place by Pep Cotroni, Seminaro's son-in-law. With increasing interest, agents had noted the comings and goings of Jimmy Curio, Frank Cotroni and Butch Munroe. It was learned, too, that Jimmy Curio and Frank Cotroni also had a chalet at Pointe-Calumet, near Rivard's. Police believed that Rivard's trip to Paris and Marseilles in the previous May had been for the purpose of reorganizing the network, which had been disrupted by d'Agostino's arrest.

The accumulation of these new clues encouraged the Narcotics Squad to redouble its efforts especially since the U.S. Bureau of Narcotics had passed on the information that Sebastiano Bellanca had skipped bail and disappeared. He was rumored to be in Montreal with Mondolini. Trying to trace the two mobsters, the RCMP accompanied Pax Plante's men, under Inspector William Fitzpatrick, in a raid on the *Auberge Durocher* in Piedmont in the Laurentians. The city police were looking for Frank Petrula for the smashing up of two night clubs two days earlier. (11) The *Auberge*

---

9. A pseudonym.

10. The Cotroni family had six children. The first four — Vincenzo (the oldest), Palmina, Marguerita and Giuseppe — were born in Calabria. The two youngest — Frank and Michel — were born in Montreal.

11. Since the departure of the American bookies with their millions and the victory of the new city administration, Frank Petrula's mood, never very calm, had changed for the worse and his star was declining dangerously. On the night of July 21, after attacking Harry Smith, a mob leader in the western sector, he

Durocher belonged to Pep Cotroni and was an ideal refuge for fugitives. Unfortunately, the raid produced no useful results; nor did subsequent raids on the homes of Rivard and Cotroni. Narcotics Squad agents were unable to break into the closed circle of the friends of Rivard and Cotroni. For weeks, their efforts produced nothing, or very little.

But the RCMP in Vancouver was having better luck. On August 9 federal agents and city police there carried out mass arrests of about 30 heroin distributors, dealers, and pushers, after a five-month undercover operation by two agents who had infiltrated the underworld. This round-up struck a hard blow at Lucien Rivard's new ambitions on the west coast. Among the traffickers who had been charged, in fact, was his old friend Bob Tremblay and several of his handymen, including Charles Talbot, Marcel Frenette, Lucien Mayer, James Malgren and Jean-Paul Chevrier.

Tremblay had gone back to Montreal in the spring of 1954 after Mallock had been convicted. But he returned to Vancouver in April 1955 with the firm intention of taking complete control of heroin traffic on the west coast. On his return, the pushers and wholesalers of the underworld had been required to link up with him, or to abandon their businesses. Those who resisted paid dearly. Jack Lenhardt Stone, a former distributor for the Mallock brothers, lost a leg when his car was dynamited; his partner, Silent Bill Semenick, and a pusher named Danny Brent, were killed. Harry Tranto, an independent wholesaler, was assaulted by a gang of hoods, while Thomas Kinna, an addict, was ambushed and beaten with iron bars. Underworld morals justified this attack on Kinna because the victim and his brother had stolen stocks of heroin from certain street-sellers. But it brought no luck to Bob Tremblay. A few hours after the attack, he and his men were arrested and charged with attempted murder. At the time of the round-up on August 9, sentences of 20 years in penitentiary had just been pronounced on Tremblay and the other accused.

---

sacked the *El Morocco* club and the *Down Beat Café* and had a run-in with a second-rate gangster who had been an informer for Pax Plante. He was said to have fallen from grace in the underworld because of his imprudent acts in the matter of documents concerning the participation of crime leaders in the last municipal election.

Chapter 5

A Seizure of Substance: The Saint-Malo

Police informers are generally held in low public esteem, their thankless role too easily forgotten. But without them the fight against drug traffickers would not be possible, as was seen in the first chapters of this book and will be even more evident by the final chapter.

On October 25, 1955, Raphaël Saïnas, an old friend of Paul Mondolini, was arrested in Milan in possession of a valise containing four kilos of pure heroin destined for the New York market. The source of the tip which led to the arrest was an informer who also told police that another cargo of 16 kilos was already on its way to Montreal. The drug was said to be on a French freighter, the SS Saint-Malo which had left Bordeaux on October 20 with a cargo of European automobiles and high quality champagne. The courier was a short, swarthy, moustached Corsican from Marseilles named Roberto, age about 30. During the stopover at Quebec, he was to deliver the heroin to the Peppe brothers, two Italian Calabrians well-known to Canadian police, and to a Corsican named Jean-Baptiste. They, in turn, would take charge of delivering the merchandise to an unidentified group in New York. On the Saint-Malo the precious powder was hidden in a trap fitted either in an air ventilator or in the cabin of a Negro sailor.

The Narcotics Squad of the RCMP received this information on October 31 and undertook immediate verification. The Saint-Malo, they learned, was to make a first stop at Pointe-au-Père, 400 miles down-river from Quebec City, to take on the Seaway pilots who would guide the ship up the St. Lawrence. RCMP investigators, along with two agents of the U.S. Bureau of Narcotics familiar with French and New York traffickers, decided to meet the ship there. But first they went to Quebec City on the chance that they might spot certain well-known faces.

(Photo La Presse)

Robert-Thomas Bianchi-Maliverno (left) escorted by a RCMP to the Palace of Justice.

The Saint-Malo *in the port of Montreal, November 10, 1955.*

When the *Saint-Malo* dropped anchor at Pointe-au-Père at 8:30 p.m. on November 8, the agents were already at the rendezvous. They boarded immediately and soon found their main suspect, Robert-Thomas Bianchi-Maliverno, 30, a sailor who answered the description of the courier provided by the Bureau of Narcotics informer. The black sailor, whose cabin was a suspected hiding place for the heroin, was also located. A preliminary search of the cabin of one of the two Negro crew members did, in fact, turn up 96 bottles of undeclared cognac and 200 contraband cigarettes. Near the engine room, a second hiding place was discovered containing another 188 bottles of alcohol. Questioned at length, the sailor finally admitted he had three accomplices and that one of them was Maliverno. Two of the accomplices, when they were questioned, agreed to talk but Maliverno absolutely refused to cooperate. When the *Saint-Malo* arrived at Quebec City the next day, Maliverno and two other sailors were charged in court with violations of the Customs law. They were convicted and fined a total of $450, while the ship was fined an additional $400. The federal agents were not really content with these results, nor with the ease with which they had been able to locate the contraband. They decided to stay with the ship until it reached Montreal where another thorough search could be made. When the *Saint-Malo* arrived at its destination in the early afternoon of November 10, a team of 44 police and Customs officers began a stem-to-stern search. Some hours later an RCMP agent noticed that the moulding on one of the panels in the ceiling of Maliverno's cabin seemed to have been recently removed. On closer examination, he saw that the panel had been freshly painted. The intrigued agent removed the panel and discovered 14 small sacks of white powder each weighing one kilo; in all, 31 pounds of pure heroin worth more than $14 million on the street. At that time, it was the biggest seizure of its kind ever made in America.

The captain of the *Saint-Malo* couldn't believe his eyes. This was the second "French Line" ship in the past couple of weeks to be involved in drug traffic! In the port of New York the previous month, U.S. Customs and the Bureau of Narcotics had seized 18 pounds of pure heroin hidden aboard the *Saint-Lo*. Like the *Saint-Malo,* it had sailed out of Bordeaux, but in the *Saint-Lo* case no one had been arrested. Bianchi-Maliverno, taken to Narcotics Squad offices, gave his version of the story. On a stopover at Hamburg, where the freighter had taken on its cargo, a man he met by chance in a bar had given him the sacks of white powder telling him it was perfume for a friend in America. Maliverno said the man gave him a few hundred dollars for his trouble. He did not know the

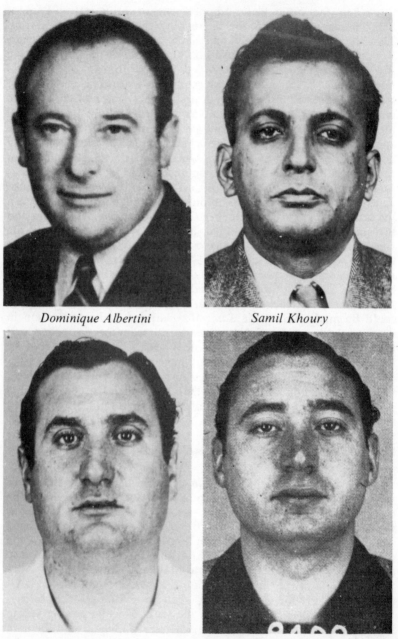

Dominique Albertini   Samil Khoury

The Venturi brothers, Jean (left) and Dominique (right).

was learned that he had close links with Antoine Galliano and that he had supplied the four kilos of heroin found in Raphaël Saïnas' valise in Milan. Albertini, recognized as the first great chemist of the French underworld, got his start as a pharmacist's assistant. Before the Second World War, he was initiated into the secret recipe for heroin by the degenerate old scientist mentioned earlier (see Chapter Two, Note 12). Associated with many celebrated traffickers like Dominique Nicoli, Paul Carbone, François Spirito and the Guérin brothers, he set up a great many illegal laboratories, mainly in the Marseilles area. In September 1952, Albertini tried to gain illegal entry to the United States by bribing a customs officer. The attempt failed and he was sentenced to a year in prison. Earlier he had been intercepted by immigration officers at Montreal as he attempted to pass through customs with a false passport. He was calling himself Antonio Trupino, a name that would surface later in an international gold trafficking affair. At that time Albertini was doing business in the United States with an influential Detroit Sicilian, Joseph Catalanotto, known as Cockeyed Joe, through the mediation of the Montreal Mafia and a gangster from Riverside, Ontario, Jimmy Renda.

The *Saint-Malo* affair took on considerable importance with Albertini's presence in the Maliverno circle. The shape of the gigantic international network, with him as a major link, was beginning to emerge. And early in the investigation further information came in which added appreciably to the dossier. On November 28, less than 20 days after the seizure of heroin in Montreal, an anonymous letter from Marseilles was received by the commander of the Narcotics Squad at Montreal:

"Sir,

I have the honor to inform you that the 14 kilos of heroin seized on board the Saint-Malo were shipped by Dominique Venturi and his brother Jean in Montreal. Use discretion. Thank you."

The RCMP had never heard of the Venturi brothers. The Narcotics Squad asked the French police to make inquiries about them and on December 10, 1955, and March 3, 1956, the central office for narcotics of the French police provided some valuable details about the two Venturi brothers.

Both had been born in Marseilles, one in 1921, the other in 1923, and their names figured prominently in the who's who of French gangsterism. They got their start, as did Croce and others mentioned above, as sailors for *Messageries Maritimes*. In the early fifties they were members of a gang led by Antoine Paoloni, known as Planche, who was a powerful leader of the Corsican underworld man's name. He had never heard of the Peppe brothers or of the Corsican, Jean-Baptiste. Naturally, this story convinced no one.

The police were particularly interested in the origins of the business card of a Montreal firm found in the sailor's baggage. The card bore the name of Ernie Ramaglia, *Riviera of Canada Co.,* 7076 St. Hubert Street. Maliverno explained that it had been given to him by a sailor who had come to Montreal before him. He wasn't much more talkative when asked for details of his relations with a certain Georgette Parcouet. According to the crew members of the *Saint-Malo,* this young woman, a prostitute from the *Trolley Bar* in Le Havre, came to meet Maliverno whenever the ship docked at any European port. Maliverno insisted she was just a girlfriend who had nothing to do at all with the narcotics affair.

Unable to obtain further explanations, the Narcotics Squad had no choice but to proceed with criminal charges against Maliverno and to try to follow up on the slim clues already available—such as the half-names and pseudonyms for whom the heroin had been destined; the *Trolley Bar* prostitute in Le Havre; the address of the Corsican courier; and the business card found in his possession. (1)

In the matter of the half-name "Jean-Baptiste," RCMP agents and their colleagues in the U.S. Bureau of Narcotics agreed that it probably referred to Jean-Baptiste Croce, the comrade-in-arms of d'Agostino and Mondolini. But opinions were divided on the identity of the Peppe brothers. During their stay in Quebec and Montreal, the U.S. agents had noticed two Italian restaurants called *Peppe's* and were convinced that the owners would be the suspects they were seeking. Narcotics Squad agents of the RCMP, on the other hand, believed that the Peppe brothers in question were really the Cotroni brothers, Calabrians whose names had already been linked to d'Agostino, Croce and Mondolini. Furthermore, the Monteal investigators noted that Giuseppe Cotroni was known in the under world as "Peppe" or "Pep." The RCMP officers were right

---

1. When his trial began on November 4, Robert-Thomas Bianchi-Maliverno pleaded guilty to the charges. Two days later he was sentenced to five years in prison. The government prosecutors appealed the sentence, however, and the Quebec Court of Appeal added another five years to Maliverno's sentence. Freed on parole on December 23, 1959, he was immediately deported to France where he became owner of a Marseilles bar called *Bar des Amis.* Maliverno was arrested again in June 1962 in connection with a holdup at the National Discount Bank. The year before, he had been implicated in a counterfeiting affair. A search of his home revealed that he had maintained contact with several former buddies in Quebec, including the trafficker Jack Dushin who was even offered the chance to transact heroin deals with Maliverno.

but it took several weeks of fruitless checking on the identity of the owners of *Peppe's* restaurants to convince their New York colleagues.

The French national police, meanwhile, at the request of Interpol, investigated the *Trolley Bar* in Le Havre. It was quickly learned that the place belonged to a notorious international trafficker named Guy Bégin. Jean-Baptiste Croce was a regular customer. The name of Bégin was not unknown. It had already appeared on police files. Paul Mondolini had identified himself as Paul Bégin when he was arrested with Croce at Corpus Christi, Texas, in April 1953. A coincidence, perhaps, but every detail has its importance. Furthermore, two sailors revealed during interrogation that in December 1954, they, like Maliverno, had transported 14 kilos of "perfume" powder to Canada. Sailing on the freighter *SS La Hague,* they had been acting on behalf of Guy Bégin and his associate, Antoine Galliano. (2) These two associates, according to Bureau of Narcotics information, recruited couriers for various teams of international traffickers, including the Croce-Mondolini team.

During his interrogation in Montreal, Maliverno gave his home address as 17 Quai de Saône, Le Havre. This proved to be the address of Joseph Campocasso, long suspected of trafficking in drugs, and the proprietor of another Le Havre night club, *L'étoile des Mariniers.* When Campocasso was questioned by the examining magistrate of a rogatory Commission, he said he barely knew Maliverno and his girlfriend. He said the sailor did not live at his home but sometimes used the address to receive letters from his mother. Campocasso did not deny that he had relationships with well-known traffickers such as Jean-Baptiste Croce and Albert Bistoni but he claimed they were simply relationships of the night club business. This claim was immediately contested. In New York, another French sailor who had been arrested in 1953 with five kilos of heroin, declared that he had previously been supplied with a load of drugs in the presence of Maliverno, Campocasso and a powerful Marseilles crime lord, Dominique Albertini. At that point, the Maliverno affair took on great importance. Albertini was considered one of the foremost leaders in international drug trafficking and had been the object of meticulous investigation for several months. It

---

2. It was learned during the investigation that Galliano was one of the main organizers, with Croce and Mondolini, of the *Saint-Malo* shipment. He was finally arrested in April 1961 after an undercover operation by the Bureau of Narcotics and French police.

in Marseilles and an accomplice of Joseph Renucci in the smuggling of American cigarettes between Tangiers and France. In October 1952, Dominique Venturi, with Paoloni and other well-known gangsters, intercepted and boarded the freighter *Combinatie* in mid-Mediterranean and made off with its cargo of 2,700 cases of American "blended" cigarettes which had been insured for $94,500. After a long investigation, Venturi was sentenced to four months in prison in February 1956. This affair became famous in France, especially for the series of underworld "settling of accounts" it inspired, ending with the assassination of Antoine Paoloni in November 1955. Everything began with a dispute between Paoloni and Jean Colonna, a veteran of the Corsican underworld in Paris. Colonna came out the winner thanks to the support of the Venturis and of the Francisci brothers, particularly the oldest Francisci, Marcel. French police believed that the anonymous letter to the RCMP, denouncing the Venturi brothers in the *Saint-Malo* affair, was related to this gang war.

After the pirating of the *Combinatie*, the Venturis and the Franciscis (Marcel, Jean and Xavier), formed a new gang with certain well-known criminals, notably Henri Codde, Jean Bozzo di Borgo and Jules Renucci. According to the information sent to the RCMP, the gang specialized in smuggling opium and morphine-base. Dominique (Nick) Venturi had even become proprietor of the *Bar Atlantique* in Marseilles and had bought a yacht called *Le Lion de Mer*. He used it for transporting narcotics. The yacht usually took on cargo off the Greek coast and unloaded it on the French coast between the Antibes and Marseilles. Marcel Francisci, whose travels around the Mediterranean had taken him often to Lebanon where he had founded several businesses, was believed to be in charge of obtaining supplies. He was also thought to have established close relations with Samil Khoury, considered by the U.S. Bureau of Narcotics to be the most important supplier of drugs between the Middle East and Europe. Khoury was one of Dominique Albertini's friends, to whom he supplied large quantities of opium and morphine-base. (3) An Arab married to a French singer, Khoury was involved in drugs, arms traffic and counterfeiting. He had influence and solid support among top-ranking policemen and politicians. One

---

3. On June 18, 1956, Lebanese Customs officers and the U.S. Bureau of Narcotics arrested one of Samil Khoury's partners, Ali Ahmad Halawi, a Beirut bar owner, the day after seizure of 100 kilos (220 pounds) of opium and 23 kilos (50 pounds) of morphine-base which the chief steward of the *SS Ronsard* was preparing to deliver to Marseilles. It was learned after the seizure that the drugs were destined for Dominique Albertini.

of his chief lieutenants, Mounir Alaouie, was a former officer of the narcotics section of the Lebanese police.

In the context of this new gang, the presence of Jean Venturi in Montreal took on particular significance. This oldest Venturi brother, according to the information supplied by the central office of narcotics in France, was the Montreal representative of the *Francavin-Ricard Company,* makers of the famous French liqueur, pastis. He had attracted the attention of French police in January 1955 on a tip from an informer. Venturi was said to be leaving France with a Ford car, with Quebec licence plates, in which a stock of heroin was hidden. The attempts by French police to find this car, however, were fruitless. (4)

As this information about the Venturi brothers was coming in, the RCMP Narcotics Squad was following up its latest clue—the business card found on Maliverno bearing the name of Ernie Ramaglia, proprietor of *Riviera of Canada Company.* This firm, manufacturing men's clothing, had declared bankruptcy just a few days before the seizure of heroin on the *Saint-Malo.* The federal investigators were sure they had heard the name Ramaglia before. They searched their files, and found their man in the reports on an investigation of Frank Sisco in 1952. Sisco had taken refuge at Ernest Ramaglia's home on Mount Royal Avenue and had claimed to be a partner of Ramaglia's brother who had a tailor shop on St. Roch Street. When Sisco was arrested in the United States for violation of immigration laws, the RCMP had interrogated the Ramaglia brothers as well as Sisco's girlfriend, Renée Galand. This woman had a small beauty products lab in her home which she ran in partnership with Jacques Mari, a brother-in-law of the Ramaglias. Mari's name, and that of another Ramaglia brother-in-law, Roland Mestre, had been found among the personal effects of Joseph Orsini when he was arrested in New York in July 1951.

At the end of March 1955, with all these leads in hand, the Narcotics Squad and the U.S. Bureau of Narcotics decided to search the homes of all the persons involved. The first visit was made at *Galand Products of Canada Ltd.,* Renée Galand's laboratory, where it was thought the powdered eggs the company claimed to use in the manufacture of its shampoo might also be used to conceal heroin powder. But confronted by police, the proprietress of the de Lanaudière Street firm confessed that the publicity was false, and that, in fact, no eggs were used in the manufacture of her products.

---

4. After the seizure on board the *Saint-Malo,* the vehicle was found in Montreal.

The next day, March 23, police visited the home of Jean Venturi on Pie IX Boulevard. Again, the search turned up no useful clues. But the questioning revealed that between the date of his first arrival in Montreal on June 4, 1950, and January 14, 1955, the Corsican had made four trips to France and several other trips to the United States. Venturi also admitted that he was a close acquaintance of Jacques Mari with whom he had served in the navy during the war.

Searches at the homes of the Ramaglia brothers proved equally unproductive. During the interrogation, however, Ernest revealed that Maliverno had come to Montreal for the first time in the summer of 1954 to see his brother-in-law Jacques Mari. Mari, who had settled in Montreal just after the war, was coming to be regarded by police agents as a key figure at the Montreal end of the French connection. He was the representative of a real estate firm, *Roma Gardens Real Estate Company,* as well as co-proprietor with his brother-in-law Roland Mestre of a beauty products company, *Marly of Paris.* No drugs were found at his home, but in an empty jewel case police found newspaper clippings about the *Saint-Malo* seizure and notes bearing the names of Jean and Dominique Venturi and Achille Cecchini, an important Marseilles mobster and member of the Venturi-Francisci gang. (5) This confirmed the involvement of this gang in the *Saint-Malo* affair.

While these inquiries were going on, other investigations by the U.S. Bureau of Narcotics gave some indication of the complexity of the French connection. Shortly after the seizure on the *Saint-Malo,* American agents learned that another well-known French trafficker, Jean Jehan, was the Montreal head of a narcotics ring linking Le Havre and New York. This Jehan was known as an old crony of Jean David, the Silver Fox, one of the New York members of the Spirito-Orsini-d'Agostino organization. Long before the war he had been involved in heroin traffic, behind the cover of his Le Havre bar, *Le Pilote,* which he managed under the pseudonym of Auguste. In March 1939, two French sailors who had been arrested in Le Havre with 16 kilos (35 pounds) of heroin admitted that they had previously smuggled 55 kilos (122 pounds) of the drug into New York. They had delivered it to two traffickers.

Sixteen years later, after the seizure on the *Saint-Malo,* it was learned that the two traffickers were Jean David and Jean Jehan. In

5. Achille Cecchini was arrested by French police in May 1966 for trafficking in heroin. This ring also involved other big names in the drug traffic, such as Paul Mondolini and Marcel Francisci.

1953, one of the two French sailors arrested in New York with five kilos of heroin which had been supplied to him by Dominique Albertini in the presence of Bianchi-Maliverno, also had in his possession the address of Jean David. This information, from the files of the Bureau of Narcotics, led to the belief that Jean Jehan, of Le Havre, could also be connected to the *Saint-Malo* affair.

The new priority of the Narcotics Squad in Montreal, therefore, became the search for Jean Jehan. There were not many clues beyond the fact that he was also known as Steve Martin. For months, he could not be found. Not until 1959 was he spotted in a St. Alexandre Street café *La Cave,* owned by the Marseillais Marius Martin, a former partner of Vic Cotroni in the *Faisan Doré.*

The *Saint-Malo* affair marked an important stage in the fight against international drug trafficking. It moved the RCMP towards closer surveillance of Lucien Rivard and Pep Cotroni with profitable results. A search of Rivard's home revealed that at the beginning of February 1956, Blackie Bisson, one of Rivard's senior henchmen, spent several days at the *Adriatic Hotel* in Paris. Rivard, a few months earlier, had made several trips to France.

On June 27, 1956, the Narcotics Squad heard that Jean-Baptiste Croce and Ansan Bistoni were in Montreal and preparing to leave the country. Federal agents who rushed to Dorval airport to check the records, however, learned that the two traffickers had left the city two days earlier on their way to Cuba. A week later the U.S. Bureau of Narcotics provided the information that the French freighter *SS Marquette,* which had docked at Montreal during the visit of Croce and Bistoni, was carrying a shipment of heroin. Agents in an RCMP yacht intercepted the ship in the Great Lakes and searched it thoroughly, but no trace of heroin was found. Nevertheless, the ship was escorted to Detroit where U.S. agents made a second search, also fruitless.

Additional information reached the RCMP a short time later. Croce and Bistoni were said to have returned to Montreal to make new arrangements with Lucien Rivard and Pep Cotroni for the international drug traffic. French and Corsican traffickers had been complaining for some time about the dishonest practices of many of their U.S. customers. When Roger Coudert had been arrested in New York, he grumbled about how the Mafia (particularly Sebastiano Bellanca and his suppliers Frank Saverino and Frank Pirico of Milan) had relieved Antoine d'Agostino of $40,000.

"The Italians always act in bad faith," said Coudert. "They're always ready to cheat the French. We'd prefer to have nothing to do with them, but they control the American market."

Jean-Baptiste (Bati) Croce

Paul Mondolini

Salvatore (Little Sal) Giglio

Charles Campo

Montrealers had a better reputation, observed their financial responsibilities well, and were therefore often used as intermediaries in transactions with the Americans. And to the French, the Montrealers were almost part of the family because they spoke the same language. In business, and particularly in the drug traffic, proper understanding between the parties is indispensable. Many deals were made easier by a Montrealer's bilingualism!

On the matter of the discussions in Montreal involving Croce, Bistoni, Rivard and Cotroni, some information was coming to the ears of the RCMP and the Bureau of Narcotics. This indicated that in future the French would make most of their transactions through Cotroni who, along with Carmine Galente, would then take responsibility for supplying the American market. Rivard, for his part, would join Croce, Bistoni and Mondolini in Cuba to assure the franco-american liaison and to see to the proper running of the payments system for heroin shipments. Rivard's departure from the Montreal scene might also relieve the strong tensions which had developed recently between him and Pep Cotroni. The previous autumn, several informers had commented on the growing animosity between Rivard and the Italians, who had become more and more demanding. There was even talk of a split between the two chieftains.

Lucien Rivard did in fact leave Montreal and install himself in Cuba, thereby confirming reports about his agreement with the Corsicans. Since the early '30s, Cuba had been a favorite haunt of underworld leaders from the east coast of the U.S. Through the influence of Meyer Lansky, financial counselor to the big bosses of the American underworld and great friend of Lucky Luciano, Cuba had become a paradise of forbidden pleasures, to the great benefit of its dictator, Fulgencio Batista. In Havana, where they settled, Jean-Baptiste Croce and Ansan Bistoni opened three night clubs: the *Eve,* the *Cupidon* and the *Pigalle.* Mondolini was associated with Santos Trafficante Jr. who ran a rich Havana casino called the *Sansoucy Club* for his father Santos Sr., boss of the Florida Mafia, and for Meyer Lansky.

At first Rivard worked with Croce and Bistoni but an unexpected incident soon moved him into a primary role. At the beginning of October 1956, the French government, under pressure from the United States, threatened Cuban authorities with a major international scandal if the Corsican drug traffickers were not forced to leave Cuba. Croce and Bistoni were therefore obliged to return to France where they were arrested on arrival, October 9. Croce was released after questioning, but Bistoni, who had been convicted at a trial in his absence the preceding February, was jailed. He had been sentenced to three years in prison, a fine of 200,000 francs and had been banned from Paris for five years. Mondolini, for his part, was arrested in Havana on December 14. On February 1, 1957, he was deported to France for the Aga Khan robbery. There he was sentenced by the appeal court in Aix-en-Provence on May 10 to two years in prison for armed robbery. Mondolini only served a few months of his sentence however. He was released from the Paris prison on July 3. (6)

Not affected by these expulsion orders, Rivard took over the interests of the Corsicans and become sole proprietor of their cabarets. These night clubs served him as a front not only for drug and gambling activities but also for the arms trafficking which he carried out on a large scale. Information coming to the RCMP led agents to believe Rivard had become Canada's biggest gun-runner. At one point, he was said to be buying guns on such a scale that the market ran dry and it became almost impossible to buy a rifle in Montreal.

In Cuba, Rivard was much in demand. Underworld leaders from many places came to see him and to talk business. Among them was Salvatore Giglio, known as Little Sal, a high-ranking New York mafioso whose name had often come up in investigations by the Bureau of Narcotics and the RCMP. Giglio, confidant of Carmine Galente, came to Montreal at the beginning of October, 1956 and according to Narcotics Squad investigators, contacted Vincent Cotroni, Jimmy Soccio, Blackie Bisson and Lucien Rivard. Since then it was rumored that Giglio had taken charge of Galente's interests and was trying to plan the heroin traffic in conjunction with both the Cotroni organization and with Lucien Rivard with whom he had developed close ties. On March 22, 1957, Giglio was married in Cuba to Florence Anderson, a waitress at *El Morocco,* the Montreal night club managed by Peter Adamo, one of Vic Cotroni's lieutenants. At the wedding, Rivard served as Giglio's

---

6. Some years later it was learned that Mondolini had received aid from Lucien Rivard during his detention in Cuba. Rivard had even gone to Paris to seek some financial support from an important leader in the Corsican underworld, Jean-Joseph Andréani, called le Vieux Joseph. Andréani was also known as Pio, and was a leading figure in the circle of Antoine d'Agostino, Albert Bistoni, Jean-Baptiste Croce, Roger Coudert and Paul Mondolini. Before the Second World War he acted as intermediary between French and American traffickers.

best man. (7) About a week earlier, Pep Cotroni had left Montreal on a trip to Paris. His arrival at Orly airport on March 14 was discreetly observed by agents of the French central office for narcotics who had been alerted by the RCMP. The following day, Cotroni's intentions were revealed. Agents who had been assigned to tail him noticed Jean-Baptiste Croce in *Le Français* bar, next to the *Claridge Hotel* where Cotroni was staying. The Corsican trafficker was seated at a table with a glass and a newspaper and seemed to be waiting for someone. Suddenly, his expression changed. He had seen a familiar face belonging to one of the police agents. That was enough to cause his hasty exit from the bar. A few minutes later, Pep entered the bar. He looked around carefully, then sat down at a table to wait. Several minutes passed and no one approached him. Finally, no doubt convinced that something unusual had happened, he returned to his hotel where he asked at the desk if there were any messages for him. Told there were none, he went back to his room.

In view of this, the agents of the French central office decided it would be better to proceed with immediate interrogation of the two traffickers. They put off the questioning, however, when they learned that Croce had a rendezvous at Orly airport at 11 o'clock the following night with an unknown traveller from Marseilles.

The man Croce met at the appointed time was another Corsican, Joseph Mari, known as le Frisé (Curly) and well-known to police. He owned several bars in the Old Port and had a solid reputation in the Marseilles and Bastia underworld. In 1949, Mari had been convicted of murder, sentenced to seven years in prison and banned from Corsica. Now he had come to Paris to turn over three million francs (about $10,000) to Croce. That was the amount found in his suitcase when he and Croce were arrested soon after his arrival. Taken to a central police station, the two Corsicans were questioned all night but without success. Croce categorically denied knowing Pep Cotroni even when confronted by photos seized at his girlfriend's place, showing him and the mafioso together in a Montreal night club.

In the morning, police agents went to the *Claridge Hotel* and arrested Cotroni as he was preparing to take a plane for Italy. The Montrealer was unable to give precise reasons for his presence in France. He admitted knowing Croce, but only by the first name,

---

7. During a later search of Rivard's home, RCMP agents found photos of the ceremony along with a newspaper reporting the Giglio couple's honeymoon trip to Summerside, Prince Edward Island, where Florence Anderson was born.

Jean, claiming they had met several years earlier in a Montreal restaurant. Cotroni could give no logical explanation for the half-section of a Canadian banknote found in his possession. (8) It appeared that he was to have given this half to Croce so that his men would later be able to check the identity of the couriers sent by the Corsican dealer. That was a classic trick, always effective.

Cotroni was also questioned about the notation in his passport showing his visit to Cuba on the preceding August 26. He explained that he had been in Miami at the time and could not resist the desire to go to Cuba and play at the casinos. This reply was hardly convincing to French, U.S. and Canadian police agents. They knew that on that day two important international traffickers, Jérôme Leca, a Corsican from Paris, and Antoine Araman from Beirut, right hand man of Samil Khoury, had arrived in Havana to meet Croce and Bistoni. To the police, Cotroni's presence in Havana at the same time was no coincidence. They had good evidence that the whole affair had been carefully planned.

First of all, Croce and Bistoni had paid a visit to Montreal two months earlier. Then there were the two telegrams sent to Leca in that same month. The first had been sent from Montreal on June 11, the second from St. Jerome four days later. Thanks to this information provided to French police by the cable delivery services, the RCMP Narcotics Squad learned that Leca had made two trips to Monteal in 1956. The first visit was at the end of January. He returned to Montreal on June 8 and left again on the 14th, the day before the second telegram was sent.

A check with Western Union in Paris had also led to the discovery of a telegram in transit, addressed to "Antoine Araman, Post Office Box 1017, Beirut" sent from Ottawa on August 22, 1956 and signed "Richard." The cable seized by French police read: "WITH PLEASURE – CABLE MEETING DATE – WILL SPEND VACATION TOGETHER – REGARDS." In view of the fact that Pep Cotroni and Tony Araman had been in Cuba together five days earlier, there was every reason to believe that the cable had to do with their drug trafficking activities.

---

8. On May 2, 1958, the RCMP received a letter from the director of the French judiciary police stating that a passbook for the City and District Savings Bank of Montreal had been found behind a filing cabinet when the central office for drugs had been moving out of its old quarters. The director speculated that the passbook, which bore no name, might have been slipped behind the cabinet by a suspect who wanted to get rid of it before police found it on him. He suggested it might belong to Pep Cotroni, a suggestion easily confirmed when the Narcotics Squad received a photocopy of the book.

These telegrams and others like them sent from Havana by Croce, Bistoni and Leca to Joseph Boldrini in Marseilles, one of Samil Khoury's Corsican representatives, induced the French central office for narcotics to charge Pep Cotroni with conspiracy in the traffic of heroin. The Montrealer was held in jail for a month before he was released on bail of 500,000 old francs (about $1,120). His passport was confiscated pending trial. While Cotroni was in jail, the RCMP sent to the French police a summary of his alleged activities since his release from prison in 1953. The latest material on his file had to do with the results of certain research in the records of the travel agency, Universe Travel Service, and of the Montreal office of Air France.

On December 26, 1956, for example, Cotroni had made a first trip to Paris. Two reservations had been made: one for Joseph (Pep) Cotroni and the other for Frank Cotroni. At the last moment Frank's reservation had been cancelled and another made in the name of Lucien Ignaro, the former right-hand man to Jean David, the Silver Fox (who has been mentioned earlier in this book). In February 1957, the RCMP Narcotics Squad, at the request of the U.S. Bureau of Narcotics, made inquiries about Ignaro's passage through Montreal. The report indicated that a Barclay Street couple in the Cote des Neiges district rented a room to Ignaro in July 1956. A popular French wrestler living in Montreal acted as intermediary for the rental. The Corsican trafficker stayed there till the end of December. The main thing noted about his five months stay there was the large number of telephone calls he received from a Mr. Philibert whose number, Pontiac 6-8263 was the listing for *Dominion Buffing Reg'd.*, 3056 La Salle Boulevard, Verdun. For some months RCMP investigators had known that this small chrome-plating firm was managed by none other than Jean Venturi.

Furthermore, Ignaro had been frequently visited at his Barclay Street residence by a local mafioso, Charles Campo, a relative of the Cotroni family. Campo, of Sicilian origin, had been arrested in New York on February 10, 1952. Arrested with him were: Matthew Cuomo, member of the Bronx organization of Frank Scalici and a friend of the Montrealer Diodato Mastracchio; Napoléon Colonna, a formidable Corsican gangster; Giovanni Maugeri, a Milanese hood considered an associate of Dominique Albertini and Antoine Galliano. Before the arrests, Bureau of Narcotics agents had made prolonged observations of Campo and his partners in the company of a sailor from the *SS Excambrion*. The search of this French freighter and interrogation of the sailor produced no results, but on April 10, when the ship made port again in Marseilles, the captain discovered a package of 17 kilos (37 pounds) of pure heroin in the hold. Agents concluded that the police action in New York had caused the suspect sailor to take the drugs back to France for re-shipment in other ships. In New York, Campo was sentenced to two years in penitentiary for violation of immigration laws. Colonna and Maugeri got six months each. The sentences were suspended, however, when the traffickers accepted immediate deportation. Meanwhile, the RCMP noted that on the same March day that Pep Cotroni had taken a flight to Paris, the Bureau of Narcotics passed on the information that Antonio Silvano, a Campo friend, had left Rome for Paris. Quite a coincidence!

All these details were of intense interest to the French central office for narcotics and its collaborators. They confirmed Giuseppe's importance in the international heroin traffic. But the information was of little use to the police in the prosecution of the specific charge of conspiracy laid against Cotroni. At first the French agents thought they had enough evidence to put Cotroni away for at least two years, but soon they had to recognize that they had acted precipitately and had collected insufficient proof against the Montrealer. They were therefore obliged to release him conditionally, and his Corsican accomplices as well. (9)

Pep Cotroni returned to Montreal on July 14, 1957, in time to celebrate the release of an old friend, Peter (The Russian) Stepanoff, a hardened criminal who had just finished a ten-year sentence for bank robbery. Pep organized a sumptuous party in his honor, attended by the cream of the underworld. Stepanoff's release had come at a good time for Cotroni, who for months had been looking for a specialist to supervise his new team of safecrackers and bank robbers. This team had already attracted attention early in 1957 with a spectacular robbery of an Outremont branch of the Bank of Montreal. On this job, 37 safety deposits boxes, marked with lipstick by an inside accomplice, had been systematically emptied. Total loot of more than a million dollars in cash, bonds and jewelry surpassed the previous record of the Brinks truck robbery in Boston in 1950.

The day after Stepanoff got out of prison, he became the new chief lieutenant for Pep Cotroni who, besides making him a partner in his restaurant, the *Ontario Spaghetti House,* installed him in a

---

9. Samil Khoury, also charged in this affair, got off as lightly as the others. He continued operating his rings with impunity until 1965 when he and his friend Mounir Alaouie were assassinated for having double-crossed a Jordanian hashish dealer.

luxurious apartment on Ridgewood Avenue. This apartment, not far from those of Peter Adamo and Salvatore Giglio on the same street, served for a long time to come as a meeting place for Cotroni and foreign traffickers.

There was another addition to Narcotics Squad files besides the arrest of Cotroni in Paris and the return of Peter Stepanoff: this was the voyage to France in 1957 of a Cotroni henchman, Michel Di Paolo, called The Penguin, who worked at the *Club Metropole,* the Montreal Mafia's main gambling joint. (10) Another addition, at the international level, was the summit conferences in Italy and the United States bringing together some of the most powerful overlords of the drug traffic.

Thus, on October 12, 1957, a security officer on patrol around Palermo, in Sicily, noticed an unusual procession at the *Delle Palme Inn.* Intrigued, he hid behind a bush to see what was happening. From there he recognized, as they arrived one after another, Santo Sorge, Carmine Galente, Joseph Bonanno, John Di Bella and Vito Vitale, all known for their membership in the American Mafia and for their participation in narcotics trafficking. Important Sicilian mafiosi arrived in turn. The last was Genco Russo, grand master of the old Sicilian Mafia, friend of Lucky Luciano. The meeting lasted four days. Then the participants dispersed, without having been unduly bothered by the police.

A month later, on November 14, 1957, a New York State police detective happened to notice an unusual number of black limousines parked around the one and only motel in the backwoods hamlet of Apalachin. Sergeant Edgar D. Crosswell made some inquiries at the reception desk of the motel and learned that the cars belonged to guests of Joe Barbara, owner of a rich estate in the area. Intrigued by the fact that these guests' names did not appear on the register, Crosswell made a tour of other hotels and motels in the region. He found that Barbara had made reservations for guests at several of these places, but no names, other than Barbara's, appeared on the registers.

---

10. Cotroni had sent his first envoy to France in 1956 in the person of Jack Croce, another employee of the *Club Metropole* which was managed by Giuseppe (Big Pep) Cocolicchoi, an associate of Jimmy Soccio and Diodato Mastracchio. Croce had been unable to accomplish his Paris mission very well, however, having blown all the money he had been given on drink. In September 1954, Croce had been arrested with Pep Cotroni at the Canadian-U.S. border. Agents of the Bureau of Narcotics thought Cotroni's companion was the Corsican dealer, Jean-Baptiste Croce. Checks by the RCMP later established Jack Croce's separate identity.

Crosswell, with increasing curiosity, then checked the Birghamton airport and learned that the Mohawk and TWA airlines had transported in the past few days an unusually large number of tourists from as far away as California, Colorado, Texas, Florida, Illinois, New York and even Cuba. Most of these "visitors" had been met by members of the Barbara family and taken to the various hotels. When Crosswell studied the passenger lists, he noted that the visitors — about 50 in all — had given false names.

The detective then had checks made on the ownership of the luxurious automobiles being seen in the region. The results soon came in, and the names of some of the limousine owners were not exactly unknown: Vito Genovese, Tony Anastasia, Joe Profaci, Big John Ormento, Johnny Dio.

That was enough to prompt Sergeant Crosswell into action. With only three men to help him at first, he set up two road blocks around Barbara's domain. The reaction wasn't long in coming. Tipped off by a fish market delivery man who had spotted Crosswell and his men on the road, Barbara's guests panicked. Some, including Vito Genovese, tried to escape by car. They were quickly intercepted and arrested. Others took to the woods but with the arrival of police reinforcements, several of them were also captured. In all, 60 underworld chiefs were caught in the net. Many others, however, managed to escape, at least 50, according to an estimate by the U.S. department of Justice. Among those who got away were all the members of the Montreal delegation which, according to the Bureau of Narcotics and the RCMP, had been led at the meeting by Luigi Greco and Pep Cotroni. (11) Like other representatives of "Cosa Nostra" families, the American Mafia, they had come to Apalachin to discuss methods of countering the action of the U.S. Bureau of Narcotics. The Bureau, by itself, had already imprisoned more members of the Organization than all other police forces on the continent combined.

Narcotics traffic, however, was not the only item on the agenda at the Apalachin summit conference. The meeting, called by Vito Genovese, also aimed at settling certain problems of succession and providing a solid base of authority for Luciano's powerful successor in the United States. But the unexpected turn of events was a

---

11. Pep Cotroni's presence at the Apalachin conference was publicly revealed for the first time in 1965 in *The Deadly Silence,* a book by Renée Buse, published by Doubleday and Company Inc., New York.

national disaster for the "Cosa Nostra." This incident revealed, as never before, how vast and well-organized was the empire of crime in America. Apalachin was a shock to the public and to many political leaders. Even police forces could hardly believe it. Only the U.S. Bureau of Narcotics in fact, first to be advised of Sergeant Crosswell's coup, was satisfied. For years its agents had been infiltrating the underworld and its informers had been describing the close links which united crime bosses all across the continent. But until Apalachin, most individuals and organizations, including the F.B.I., refused to believe it.

In Montreal, the weeks following the Apalachin fiasco were marked by another visit Lucien Rivard made to his sidekick, Blackie Bisson, a visit which led to the arrest of both men for illegal possession of arms. There was also another robbery of $1,800,000 from the Caisse nationale d'économie (National Credit Union), which seemed to carry the signature of the Cotroni-Stepanoff organization. Rivard's arrest, on January 8, 1958, followed a search by the Narcotics Squad at the home of Blackie Bisson, 3282 Place de Léry. Under a pillow in the room occupied by Rivard, investigators found a .38 calibre Smith & Wesson revolver and a .25 calibre automatic pistol. At first Rivard admitted owning these guns, but then changed his story and said the automatic pistol belonged to Bisson. Bisson in turn, informed of Rivard's version, hesitated for a few seconds and then admitted that the pistol did in fact belong to him. The two pals were taken to police headquarters and jailed. The next morning they appeared in criminal court on charges of possessing unregistered arms. Bisson immediately pleaded guilty and was fined $50. Rivard, however, managed to produce a registration certificate for his revolver and as a result, the charge against him was withdrawn.

On January 30, 1958, Rivard returned to Cuba via Miami where Vic Cotroni and his financial counselor Irving Ellis had been staying for the past week. Meanwhile, in Halifax on January 21, the RCMP and Canadian immigration authorities had arrested and later sent back to France another Marseilles trafficker, René Bruchon, listed as an associate of Lucien Ignaro. In the spring of 1947 he had been sentenced in New York to two years in prison after the seizure of 14 kilos (30 pounds) of heroin from the SS Saint-Tropez on which he was a crew member. In February 1953, this time in Algiers, Bruchon was given another year in jail for possession of 270 grams (.6 pounds) of cocaine. At the time of his arrest in Halifax, he was travelling incognito on the SS Arosa Sun which had left Le Havre five days earlier and was destined for Montreal (12). Bruchon refused to answer any questions and he was carrying enough money for a Montreal to Paris airline ticket. Perhaps his arrival in Canada did have something to do with Rivard's visit to Montreal. In any case, on January 26 he was deported to France.

The next chapter in the story opened on March 5, 1958, when the U.S. Bureau of Narcotics advised the RCMP that Jean-Baptiste Croce and Dominique Nicoli, an important Marseilles crime chief associated with Paul Mondolini, had been in Cuba since February 24. It was thought they were attempting to reorganize the drug traffic which had been in some disarray since the jailing of Albert Bistoni. It was also possible that they were negotiating some new deals. The Bureau of Narcotics was also aware that at this time the chemist Dominique Albertini, one of the traffickers' accomplices, was in Beirut negotiating the purchase of morphine-base with the Samil Khoury group. U.S. Treasury agents wanted to let the Corsican agents move freely until it could be seen who they would contact. But the Havana police chief did not see it that way and on March 13, Croce and Nicoli were arrested and deported to France.

After this incident, an unexpected event on April 8 set RCMP investigators on to another trail. On that day Walter Zymowec, manager of the Ridgewood Avenue building where Peter Stepanoff lived, was preparing apartment 303 for a new tenant. When Zymowec went to the basement to check the storage room for No. 303, he noticed that the door had been solidly padlocked. He assumed that one of the other tenants had either mistakenly made use of this storage room or had appropriated it deliberately, since it had been vacant for several months. He asked several tenants about the matter, but no one knew anything about the storage room or its contents. Zymowec concluded that the previous tenant of 303 must have forgotten to remove the padlock and that the room probably contained nothing of value. He decided to break the lock and clean the storage area for the incoming tenant.

As soon as he opened the door he saw three revolvers. Frightened, he looked no further, and hastened away to call the

---

12. The *Arosa Sun* was also the ship on which Giovanni Maugeri, partner of Charley Campo, illegally arrived in America in May 1956. His entry was aided by a sailor named Herbert Blaschevitsch, alias Herbert Suares, who was in reality a courier for Antoine Galliano of Le Havre. Galliano was also one of the organizers of the *Saint-Malo* shipment. Blaschevitsch took advantage of his voyage with Maugeri to bring two kilos (4.5 pounds) of heroin to Montreal which he delivered to the kitchen of the *Riverside Restaurant* owned by Palmina Cotroni.

René Bruchon   *Gabriel Graziani*

Antranik Paroutian   *Agop Kevorkian*

police. A few minutes later two officers of the city police arrived in a patrol car. Their quick search of the storage room turned up an astonishing hoard: stolen bonds to a total value of $75,000; four small sacks each containing a half-kilo of heroin; and the three revolvers.

The holdup squad of the Montreal police in charge of the investigation immediately alerted the RCMP Narcotics Squad. At RCMP headquarters, Zymowec was shown a series of photos of top-ranking bank robbers among whom he quickly identified Paul Mann (real name Peter Stepanoff), the tenant in apartment 104 of his building. Knowing the links between Stepanoff and Pep Cotroni, the police officers decided a small visit to apartment 104 might prove interesting. Stepanoff, naturally, did not share that opinion, especially when police arrived without notice just as he was entertaining a young lady. But after a meticulous search, the police had to leave empty-handed. Nothing could be found that would establish, in any legal way, that Cotroni's right-hand man knew about the contents of the storage room of apartment 303. The federal agents, however, were personally convinced that the loot really belonged to Stepanoff. A few days earlier they had learned about Stepanoff's efforts, since the beginning of the year, to take control of the Vancouver market on behalf of Cotroni and Rivard. This market had been free since the arrest of Bob Tremblay in 1955.

After the search of Stepanoff's premises, the federal agents paid a visit to Pep Cotroni's home, but here again, no useful evidence was obtained. The month of April, however, held more surprises . . . .

Just before the end of the month, the Narcotics Squad learned from Interpol of the arrest by Swiss police of two Marseilles traffickers, Gabriel Graziani and Marius Cau. At the time of their arrest they had been trying to negotiate, through a Geneva bank, certain bonds which had been stolen in Montreal from the Caisse nationale d'économie (National Credit Union). In response to this information, RCMP agents travelled to Europe where they learned that Gabriel Graziani was a member of the Corsican underworld with close links to Jean-Baptiste Croce and Dominique Nicoli. Additional information linked him to another Marseillais, of franco-american origin, Antranik Paroutian. The two men shared not only a grocery business in Marseilles but also an apartment in New York. This was the apartment where Graziani, before his return to Europe, was believed to have sold six kilos (15 pounds) of heroin to Peter Stepanoff in the presence of Paroutian. It was also learned that Graziani and Paroutian received their money from North-American traffickers through an exchange bank, later depositing it in Swiss banks.

When the U.S. Bureau of Narcotics was alerted, its agents visited the Graziani-Paroutian apartment in New York and discovered a concealed compartment which still contained a little heroin. Graziani had installed this hiding place after certain customers, including Peter Stepanoff, had tried to steal his drug supplies. (13) After this discovery, the U.S. agents decided to bring charges against Graziani and Paroutian, but first they approached Swiss authorities in an attempt to gain access to the secret accounts of the two traffickers. After many efforts, they succeeded. The documents established that over an 18-month period from the end of 1956, the two Marseillais had deposited at least half a million dollars in various accounts.

According to the French central office for narcotics, Paroutian made deposits into an account belonging to the Lebanese trafficker Antoine Araman, whom Pep Cotroni had met in Havana in August 1956. After splitting with his boss Samil Khoury, Araman had gone on his own. He was arrested in Beirut, January 27, 1959, along with his new partner Antoine Harrouk, Khoury's former bodyguard, and a Parisian trafficker of Armenian origin, Agop Kevorkian. These arrests followed the shipment of a large cargo of morphine-base to France in April 1958.

Subsequent inquiries into Kevorkian's movements established that he had made prolonged visits to Montreal at the end of 1956 and in the summer of 1958, and on each occasion had obtained visas to visit the United States. These trips, presumably, were for the purpose of collecting payments for heroin deliveries, since it was also learned that he had made visits to Switzerland to deposit funds for the benefit of Antoine Araman. The investigation of Kevorkian's transactions also led to the exposure of another important gang of French heroin traffickers using Montreal as a base. (14)

---

13. It was after this theft that Larry Petrov was assassinated. The former partner of J.C. Laprès disappeared from circulation on July 2, 1957, and two days later one of his legs was found in a Laurentian lake.

14. A notebook found on Kevorkian contained this notation: "Société de Banque Suisse CR 91 972" Swiss police reported that this corresponded to account number 91 972 opened at the Société de Banque Suisse on February 17, 1959, by Antoine Araman of Beirut. Bank records revealed that the account had received deposits to the amount of $140,000, most of the funds being transferred from another account at the Banque Privée de Genève, opened by an importer-exporter from the lower Pyrenees who used the pseudonym of Pachy Edward.

The traces of heroin found in the New York apartment of Graziani and Paroutian, along with the documentation from their secret Swiss bank accounts, led to their indictment by a grand jury for the district of New York. But by that time the two men had returned to France and their extradition was not possible. Graziani had been freed by the Swiss police because Canadian authorities had decided not to press for his extradition, considering that it would be difficult to convict him on any charge in Montreal. Graziani returned to Marseilles and joined up with Dominique Venturi as one of Venturi's chief lieutenants.

As for Paroutian, he continued his activities with impunity. He was not arrested until March 28, 1960, in Beirut, in connection with the seizure of two shipments of morphine-base which he had bought. The shippers who had been taken into custody declared that the drugs were to have been loaded onto a freighter destined for Marseilles. Later research by the U.S. Bureau of Narcotics revealed that Paroutian had gone to Turkey himself to negotiate the purchase of a large quantity of opium. But it wasn't in Lebanon that he was eventually convicted. It was in the United States. In Beirut he was acquitted when key witnesses changed their testimony. Deported to

---

Questioned by police, this individual declared that with the bank's approval, he had authorized a business acquaintance, Emile Michel, to use the account under the name of Pachy 2.

Michel was co-proprietor of an important pastry-catering firm but spent most of his time on under-the-table stock transactions and keeping company with gangsters. He, in turn, declared that he had authorized his friend Agop Kevorkian to use the account to receive deposits and make withdrawals. In this way, said Michel, he had frequently transferred to Antoine Araman's account, on behalf of Kevorkian, sums corresponding to amounts already deposited by Kevorkian in Michel's account, either through cash deposits at the wicket or bank transfers from America.

On this matter, the investigation revealed that between July 31, 1958, and April 3, 1959, Emile Michel had received $127,092, almost all of it coming through five transfers from bank accounts opened at the Royal Bank of Canada in Montreal and the Merchants Bank of Boston. These accounts were opened by an important Corsican trafficker named Gilbert Coscia. RCMP inquiries showed that Coscia had spent more than a year in Montreal. From April 20, 1959, to May 15, 1960, he lived at 3255 St. Zotique Street and had been in frequent contact with Jean Venturi. During this period he had made more than a dozen trips to the United States representing two Corsican crime chiefs from Paris; Antoine Marignani, called Lolo or Uncle, and Jean-Baptiste Jiacobetti, called Jeannot. These two were associated with the powerful Guérini family of Marseilles. With types like René Bruchon (arrested in Halifax, January 2, 1958) and Agop Kevorkian, Coscia's role was to ensure the connections for large quantities of heroin sent to Montreal and New York through diplomats.

the U.S. in June 1960, Paroutian was sentenced, after two trials, to 20 years in penitentiary and a $40,000 fine.

It is important to note that Paroutian's arrest in Beirut cast light on certain aspects of the Cotroni-Rivard file. His passport indicated two visits to Montreal in 1957 and 1958. He came to Canada the first time from the United States on December 23, 1957, and stayed in Montreal until February 27, 1958, when he took a flight to Cuba. He returned to Montreal from Havana on March 9 and left again for Cuba 13 days later. He returned to France soon after that via the United States.

Examined closely, this itinerary indicates that when Lucien Rivard was in Montreal at the beginning of 1958, Paroutian was there too. He went to Cuba exactly three days after the arrival of Jean-Baptiste Croce and Dominique Nicoli in Havana, where Rivard, in the meantime, had resumed his residence. Paroutian then returned to Montreal just before the two Corsicans were arrested and deported to France. There was not much doubt that Paroutian was an intermediary between the Corsicans and their Montreal clients, especially in view of the fact that soon after his travels his partner Graziani was arrested in Geneva in possession of bonds stolen by Pep Cotroni's gang.

At the end of April 1958, the Graziani-Paroutian investigation was just getting started when the Narcotics Squad learned that Salvatore Giglio had recently been in contact with Lucien Rivard. Giglio had been managing the Montreal interests of Carmine Galente and the Bonanno family for several months. Information on this New York mafioso was limited so federal agents thought it would be useful to search his Ridgewood Avenue home, as well as the premises of *Adams Theatrical Enterprises* on Bishop Street, an entertainment agency and a meeting place for Mafia bosses run by Giglio's friend and neighbor, Peter Adamo.

The searches, carried out May 7, uncovered nothing remarkable at the Adamo residence but turned up some interesting material at Giglio's apartment. Police found, for example, a detailed sketch of the route leading to Lucien Rivard's summer cottage. Giglio was confronted with the document, but said he had no idea what it was. In one of the bedrooms a coat was found which bore the name "R. Mancuso" in the lining. Giglio explained that he did not know anyone named Mancuso, but that a friend named Paul de Cocco came to visit him from time to time. This was true, but incomplete. Later it was learned that de Cocco, a restaurant owner from Schenectady, New York, had made a visit to Montreal. But he had also been accompanied by Rosario Mancuso, known as a man of influence in the Utica Mafia. The files of the U.S. Bureau of Narcotics listed Mancuso as one of the owners of the *Italian Village* restaurant at Plattsburg, a favoured haunt of Montreal and New York Mafia chiefs. He was also known as a union representative involved in the construction of the Strategic Air Command base at Plattsburg.

Finally, the federal agents found 240 Cuban cigars and 880 U.S. cigarettes which had not been declared to Customs. This may have been a minor sort of violation but it was enough to bring the mafioso into criminal court that same day. Giglio, not wanting to attract undue attention, quickly pleaded guilty and was fined $50. He was then taken to immigration officers who declared him to be an undesirable and ineligible to remain in Canada. As a result, he was given 48 hours to leave the country.

The following noon Giglio boarded a plane for New York. On his arrival at Idlewild he was searched by U.S. Customs agents who found two lists of names on him. The first list concerned the 21 Montreal bookies who were paying tribute to the Mafia. The second listed the names of eight others who refused to pay the weekly contribution.

A week after the forced departure of the New Yorker, Vincent Cotroni and Luigi Greco travelled to New York, no doubt to discuss Giglio's hasty exit and the matter of his successor as Galente's representative. On December 2, Cotroni attempted another visit to New York with his counselor Irving Ellis but U.S. authorities refused him entry.

The year 1958 ended with the explusion of Salvatore Giglio and the continuation of the investigation into the affairs of Gabriel Graziani and Antranik Paroutian, but there was not yet much hope for the early dismemberment of the Montreal Connection. For the past few years, however, the agents of the Narcotics Squad had been working steadily and by now they had good knowledge of the composition and operation of the complex international ring in which Lucien Rivard and his Mafia partners were involved. In fact, only one problem remained ... but what a problem! The closed circle of traffickers must be penetrated—either by getting hold of an insider ready to talk and testify, or by sending in an undercover agent who could set the decisive trap. Neither solution was easy, but the time had come for action.

Chapter 6

Pep in the Trap

In the early hours of Saturday, December 6, 1958, Giuseppe Cotroni arrived as usual at his Ste. Adèle cottage to spend the weekend. With him were his partner Luigi Greco and a few employees from the *Bonfire* restaurant. (1) Cotroni noticed that a side window of the cottage had been forced, but since nothing had been stolen, gave the matter no further thought. While his friends made coffee and cleared snow from the driveway, Pep went to the village grocery store. There he met a hotel owner from Lac Millette, Gaston Savard, proprietor of the *Manoir du Lac* and of a construction firm which had supplied building materials to Cotroni during the summer. Cotroni, an affable man who liked company, invited Savard for a drink at the cottage and Savard, perhaps thinking of the money Cotroni still owed him for materials, accepted.

The noon hour approached and the two men were still chatting. Two others had joined them: Savard's partner, Herbert Husson and Ernest Costello, manager of *Gatineau Power Company* at Ste. Adèle where Cotroni also had an outstanding account.

Cotroni, a man of the world, received his visitors amiably and offered them a drink before talking business. Costello, an Irishman, could stay only a short time because he had to meet his wife. He left after half an hour but promised to come back later that afternoon. Cotroni, Savard and Husson continued to drink and talk, until

---

1. Pep Cotroni acquired interests in the *Bonfire* after the mysterious disappearance of Frank Petrula, at the end of 1957, at a time when the federal Revenue department was claiming $400,000 in back income taxes from Petrula. Underworld rumors suggested that Petrula had been executed by his former partners to prevent him from confessing everything to authorities. Furthermore, he had never been forgiven for the discovery of his notebook on the 1954 Montreal municipal elections.

Costello returned at about 5 p.m. Still in a hurry, he didn't even sit down. Naturally, Cotroni offered him a drink, but Costello refused, saying he had just eaten. He accepted an after-dinner liqueur however, and Cotroni produced a bottle of anisette, filling all the glasses except Husson's, who had not finished his rye. Pressed for time, Costello downed the liqueur at a gulp and finding it bitter, asked for a glass of water before leaving.

As he drove home, Costello suddenly felt convulsions in his legs and stopped at the first garage. The pain in his legs increased. He asked the garage operator to drive him to a doctor who immediately began treatment for food poisoning.

Back at the cottage at about the same time, Cotroni and Savard also began feeling pains in their legs. Husson, who was not suffering the effects he observed in his companions, decided to go for a doctor since the telephone in the cottage was not in service at that time of year. He reached the doctor's office to find Costello under an oxygen tent and the doctor on the telephone calling for an ambulance. Husson immediately asked for another ambulance for his friends at the cottage who seemed to be suffering from the same illness. Their condition had worsened by the time Husson got back to the cottage. Savard and Cotroni were sick to their stomachs, their arms and legs were paralyzed, their mouths rigid and their eyes heavy-lidded. Husson decided there was no time to lose. Instead of waiting for the ambulance he drove them himself to the hospital at St. Jerome. He arrived at almost the same time as Costello, who died a few minutes later, even before the arrival of a doctor. Cotroni and Savard, given prompt treatment, survived.

Luigi Greco arrived at the hospital a short time later after getting the message from Husson. He returned to the cottage about 8:30 p.m. to tell the others of Costello's death. The party was over. Everyone went back to Montreal.

According to analyses, the anisette drunk by Cotroni and his two guests contained strychnine, a fatal poison. Costello died because he had absorbed more of the poison. He had swallowed the entire contents of his glass, while Cotroni and Savard had taken only a sip each. That was lucky for them, because there was enough poison in a half-ounce of the anisette to kill several men.

News of the affair quickly spread, naturally, and Provincial Police detectives started an investigation. Questioned in his hospital bed, Cotroni declared that he had no enemies and no one to suspect. Luigi Greco said the same thing. The coroner had no choice but to attribute the blame to a person or persons unknown.

(Photos Allô Police)

The bottle of poisoned anisette.

Cottage window indicating forced entry.

(Photo Allô Police)

Pep Cotroni

Luigi Greco

121

Agents of the Narcotics Squad, however, were asking themselves who had really been the intended victim. Rumors were flying in the underworld. Some believed that the attempt had been aimed at Greco, considered to have grown too powerful; others thought it the result of an old quarrel between Pep Cotroni and Lucien Rivard. The second hypothesis was strengthened on April 23, 1959, when René Robert, an ex-waiter who had become Cotroni's all-round man, was wounded with two revolver shots by Gérard Turcot, a friend of Rivard's who had just returned from Cuba. Robert and Turcot, however, had quarrelled in a bar a short time before the shooting which seemed to rule out the idea of a settling of accounts prepared long in advance.

Another theory was that the strychnine attempt was the work of New York Mafia bosses who some months earlier had ordered their men to get out of narcotics trafficking on pain of death. In 1958, the U.S. Bureau of Narcotics had struck hard. In January, following the seizure of 17 kilos (37 pounds) of heroin and 25 kilos (55 pounds) of opium, about fifteen traffickers had been arrested in New York and Philadelphia. (2)

During the summer, the Bureau had struck again, this time bringing charges against some 40 traffickers including some of the biggest underworld names on the continent, such as: Vito Genovese, Luciano's successor; Carmine Galente, Joe Bonanno's second-in-command and top boss in Montreal; John Ormento, one of the chief lieutenants of Thomas Lucchese; Rocco Mazzie, of Carlo Gambino's headquarters staff; Natale Evola, a protégé of Genovese and an Apalachin delegate who would later succeed Bonanno; Benjamin Levine, a former comrade of Lepke Buchalter, the narcotics financier of the 1930s. Accused of trafficking in more than 160 kilos (350) pounds) of heroin all across the U.S. since 1954, all were indicted following the testimony of a small Puerto Rican dealer, Nelson Silva Cantellops, who seemed to prefer to tell all rather than face a long prison sentence. (3) Patiently, for an entire year, Bureau

---

2. Among the most important were Vincent Todaro, a New York chieftain; George Nobile, one of Vito Genovese's men; James Santora and Peter Casella, lieutenants of Marco Reginelli in Philadelphia; Joseph Lo Piccolo, a friend of Santos Trafficante of Florida (Lucien Rivard's partner) and Charles Jérôme Leca, a Corsican from Croce's organization whom Pep Cotroni had met in Cuba in August 1956.

3. Nevertheless, he was kept in custody for his own protection for a considerable length of time. He was released at his own request and in 1965 was mysteriously assassinated in a bar brawl. Lucky Luciano, in his memoirs written in

of Narcotics agents verified his statement in all its detail before presenting their case to a New York grand jury. The result led to the arrest of the majority of the accused men, except for Carmine Galente and Big John Ormento, who had suddenly disappeared from circulation. They were still being sought at the time of the strychnine attempt against Pep Cotroni.

The day before this attack, an interesting report had come to the RCMP from the Bureau of Narcotics in New York. The report recalled that the six-month delay given to Mafia traffickers to get rid of all their stocks had now passed. It was also noted that Carmine Galente was one of the bosses who had forbidden his men to traffic in drugs. The report also indicated that the Montrealer, Cotroni, was one of the sources of supply for Vincent Todaro and his gang and that Cotroni also supplied several New York and New Jersey groups associated with Galente, Ormento and Genovese. This information, coming from underworld informers, was important because it helped to confirm that the new police operation recently mounted against the Montreal–New York ring was well-founded.

In early autumn, 1958, agents of the U.S. Bureau of Narcotics got in touch with a small-time dealer, Angelo Sonessa of Nutley, New Jersey, who had given them valuable information in the past. A few months earlier Sonessa had been working as a courier, visiting Montreal twice a week and bringing back supplies of heroin to New York. This time Sonessa hoped to avoid questioning. He suggested to the agents that another dealer named Joseph Vecchio had a better knowledge of the Montreal operation than he did. Vecchio was a soldier in the Genovese family and a former partner of Peter Stepanoff in a company importing American neckties. He was best known, however, as the partner of Settimo Accardo, called Big Sam, who had fled to Italy in 1955 after he had been released on $75,000 bail pending trial on heroin traffic charges. (4) Accardo was also a

---

collaboration with the producer Martin A. Gosch and the writer Richard Hammer, gave another version. He claimed that he had been responsible for Cantellops' testimony. Obsessed by the failure of the Apalachin summit, which had made the organization he built appear ridiculous, Luciano had conceived a plan to revenge himself on Vito Genovese, though without committing any spectacular murder. He said he prepared the plan with Frank Costello, Meyer Lansky and Carlo Gambino. An anonymous letter sent to the Bureau of Narcotics warning that the Puerto Rican was ready to close the deal had launched the investigation. In exchange, Cantellops was to receive $100,000 on his release from Sing Sing.

4. In 1963, Accardo was extradited to the United States where he was tried and convicted for the 1955 affair.

Big John Ormento   *Carmine Galente*

Frank Cotroni (left), Joseph Vecchio (centre), Michel Cotroni (right).

member of the Genovese clan closely linked to Lucky Luciano and one of his representatives, Cristoforo Rubino, a soldier in the Joseph Profaci family. (5) He had been an important customer of Pep Cotroni.

At the end of October, a Bureau of Narcotics agent named Stephen Giorgio sought out Vecchio, claiming he had just arrived from Sicily and had been sent by Accardo. From the very first meeting, the agent won the gangster's confidence, along with an invitiation to come along on the next trip to Montreal to buy a supply of "Christmas trees." The agent, who had not been authorized to go any further for the moment, deftly declined the invitation on the grounds that he had other business to look after. The investigation had reached this stage on the afternoon of December 6, the day Pep Cotroni swallowed the poisoned anisette.

On that same morning, New York State Police and Bureau of Narcotics agents had stopped two Cotroni men: Nicholas Elacqua and Joseph De Paolo. No trace of heroin was found in their car although police discovered an intriguing secret compartment under the back seat. The two men were likely on their way to join René Robert who had been staying at the *Edison Hotel* in New York for the past several days. (6) On the preceding July 10, Elacqua and Robert had accompanied Pep Cotroni to the *Lexington Hotel* in New York. Their visit may have had something to do with the visit to Montreal a week before, of Rocco Sancinella, an associate of Angelo Loiacano, an important Brooklyn heroin dealer and a collaborator of Vincent Todaro. In any case, RCMP agents believed that the premature interception of De Paolo and Elacqua had caused the ringleaders to change plans.

But the agents at the U.S. Bureau of Narcotics were not worried. They decided the time had come to re-establish contact with Joseph Vecchio. The undercover agent Giorgio, therefore got in touch with Vecchio just a few days after the strychnine attempt in Ste. Adele. Giorgio brought up the subject of drugs for the first time, and said he was looking for a supplier. Vecchio reacted violently, warning the agent of the dangers of drug trafficking.

"If the federal agents don't get you, the Syndicate will," he said.

The agent let the matter drop for the time being, but a few days

---

5. Cristoforo Rubino was assassinated in New York on July 18, 1958.

6. In October, Frank Cotroni and several of his men, including Yvon Duquette, Michel Delisle, Michel Di Paolo, Jack Croce and Robert Rocheleau, spent several days at the *Edison Hotel.*

later, he raised the question again. Finally, two days before Christmas, though still refusing to get involved personally, Vecchio said he knew someone who might help:

"This guy does a Montreal-New York run twice a week," he said. "He might take you along to Montreal if you ask him."

Vecchio added that this person always crossed the border at the same place, the Tappan Zee Bridge post. He drove a black Lincoln with a white roof and black and pink upholstery and had Quebec licence plates. His name was Eddie Smith. Giorgio thanked Vecchio. (7) His undercover mission was finished; other colleagues would move in on Smith.

The next phase of the operation began in February 1959 shortly after the surprise arrest of Peter Stepanoff by Montreal police. At the beginning of the month, a spectacular burglary had been carried out in the vaults of the *Premier Trust Company* of St. Catharines, Ontario. The loot amounted to $900,000 in cash and securities. Five days later, on February 7, two Montreal detectives happened to spot Peter Stepanoff and another mobster, Henri Samson, entering an Ontario Street clothing store. (8)

They decided to take a closer look at what Pep Cotroni's right-hand man was up to. They picked him up a few minutes later when he came out of the building and began looking nervously around. The city detectives, accompanied by RCMP agents, then searched the Yacknin store. They found 35 stock certificates valued at $9,600 which had been stolen during the robbery of the *Premier Trust Company*. (9)

Pep Cotroni still hadn't had time to get over the arrest of his chief lieutenant when Bureau of Narcotics agents John Dolce and Patrick Biase intercepted the suspected Lincoln of Eddie Smith at the Tappan Zee border point. The driver of the vehicle, however, didn't match the description given by Joseph Vecchio. Claiming to be a jeweler, he said the car belonged to his son-in-law to be, named Smith, who at that very moment was visiting his daughter in New York. The agents, trying not to arouse suspicion, told the driver they had a report that the car had been used in a robbery which they were investigating.

---

7. Joseph Vecchio did not outlive this error for long. A few weeks later he was assassinated in a simulated auto accident on the George Washington bridge.

8. The store belonged to the bookie Moe Yacknin, the new partner of Jimmy Soccio and Roméo Bucci in a St. Catherine Street East night club, the *Café Roméo*.

9. Found guilty on May 26, 1959, of receiving stolen bonds, Stepanoff was sentenced to eight years in penitentiary.

A search of the vehicle yielded nothing. The agents decided to go with the jeweler to his daughter's home, saying they wished to question the owner of the car. Detectives from the New York City police armed robbery squad joined them en route in order to make the ruse of a robbery investigation seem genuine. Smith was not home when they reached the daughter's residence but he was said to be expected soon. The agents waited. Smith didn't show up until nearly 2 a.m. The agent Biase, not wanting to scare Smith off, went to meet him and explained the presence of the police officers. He admitted to Smith that the searches of his car and apartment had produced nothing incriminating, and then asked him to identify himself and empty his pockets. His papers identified him as Edward Lawton Smith, 39, born in New Brunswick. He had lived in New York for some time and had applied for U.S. citizenship. At first sight, his address book seemed to contain nothing of special interest, but as a precaution, the police made a copy of it.

The agents then decided it would be better not to take the investigation any further at the moment. They left the apartment, offering apologies for their suspicions.

Over the next few days, police checked the contents of Smith's address book which revealed him to be a peerless Don Juan. Among the names of his numerous conquests, Bureau of Narcotics agents noted, in particular, that of a well-known model. Two weeks later, when they decided it was time to meet Smith again, they went to the home of the model. This time they hadn't long to wait. Smith arrived soon after they did. The agent Biase gave Smith no time to talk. He took him aside and told him that his goose was cooked, that police already had sufficient evidence on his activities in New York and Montreal. It was a bluff. All police had was what Vecchio had told them. But Smith was visibly shaken. The agent decided to go for broke:

"Why don't you be reasonable and try to help yourself?" he asked. "We know everything about you and Cotroni. So?"

Smith was cornered and it didn't take him long to react. Taken to Bureau of Narcotics headquarters, he agreed to discuss a way out for himself. In exchange for total immunity and full protection, he was asked to become a double agent and to introduce an undercover agent to Cotroni and his partners. The risks were great, but all in all, Smith figured they were preferable to a third long term in prison. He accepted the proposition on the spot on condition that he be allowed to choose his companion in the adventure. He wanted the agent Patrick Biase. Smith had been impressed by this police officer, barely 30 years of age, and was willing to take the risks with him.

Infiltrating the underworld is not a role that can be taken lightly. It must be learned and learned well. For the next few weeks the two men initiated each other into the secrets of their trade. Smith learned to become an undercover agent and to take account of the requirements for evidence that would stand up in court. Biase gradually familiarized himself with the composition and operations of the Cotroni ring. Smith was an excellent teacher on that subject. He had started in the organization around April 1957. At that time, a friend from New York, Frank (Chow) Mancino, who was a Brooklyn trafficker and member of the Bonanno family, had taken him to an apartment on Ridgewood Avenue in Montreal. (10) There, for the first time, Smith had met Pep Cotroni, his brothers Vincent and Frank, Peter Stepanoff and Carmine Galente. Mancino had taken possession of a stock of heroin for delivery and Galente had advised Smith to exercise the utmost caution on the trip back.

At first, Smith's job was to watch over the courier and the merchandise on trips between Montreal and New York. For that he was paid $300 a trip, later increased to $500. On arrival in New York, Smith drove Mancino to the various places where deliveries were to be made. He had followed the route dozens of times and was therefore able to provide a complete list of Cotroni organization customers.

Usually, the first stop on the route had been at a Manhattan snack-bar at Orchard and Houston Streets. Then came *Jay's Bar* on Houston Street and *Marconi's Restaurant* on Mulberry. Two Greenwich Village clubs were next: the *Squeeze-Inn Bar* on 4th Street, operated by Carmine Polizzano, a lieutenant of Genovese and Salvatore Sciremammano; and the *1717 Club* on 86th Street managed by the brothers Carmine and Salvatore Panico. Next was the *Vivere Bar* on Second Avenue, headquarters of Carlie (Charley) Di Pietro and Frank Mari of the Bonanno-Galente family, then *Chickie Jame's Stable* on 56th Street, Tony Mirra's hangout. Then drops were made at an apartment on 53rd Street, *Johnny's Keyboard Cafe* on 56th Street, *Marino's Restaurant* on Lexington Avenue, as well as the Brooklyn sanctuary of Rocco Sancinella and Angelo Loiacano and a Coney Island hotel. When the top bosses like Ormento, Galente or Genovese were personally involved in a transaction, deliveries were made in public places such as the *Edison, Park Sheraton, Forest* or *Lombardy* hotels.

---

10. On February 11, 1956, Frank Mancino had been arrested by RCMP in Montreal in connection with the indictments in New York of Settimo Accardo and Cristoforo Rubino. He had on him the telephone numbers of Lucien Rivard and Pep Cotroni.

At first Smith merely drove Mancino to a delivery point and waited outside for his return. But later he was admitted to the inner circle and came to know, personally, the big New York traffickers and their main clients. Smith had an excellent memory, and was able to provide Biase and the Bureau of Narcotics with a mass of detail which, without constituting legal proof, became valuable background material for numerous investigations. Among other things, this information clearly established the chain of command in the Cotroni organization and its volume of business. Each month, for example, Cotroni supplied about 50 kilos of pure heroin to Ormento, Galente and Genovese, at prices ranging from $6,000 to $10,000 a kilo. Cotroni bought from the Corsicans at $3,000 a kilo. The New York bosses, each with well-organized delivery and collection teams, supplied a number of regular customers who could usually count on getting three to five kilos a week. These intermediary customers were mafiosi like the brothers Marcantonio and Philip Orlandino, Angelo Loiacano and the Panico brothers who, in turn, supplied independent distributors like (The Jew) Sam Monastersky and his Irish partner Richard McGovern. (11) The independents in turn sold the merchandise to various dealers specializing in retail sales to pushers and addicts.

During his period of apprenticeship, Biase was able to meet some of the major heroin traffickers in New York which helped him to perfect his role as Dave Costa, Eddie Smith's new partner. By mid-April 1959 the Smith-Biase team, after testing the waters in the New York underworld and finding them about right, was ready to attempt the big strike at Cotroni. The U.S. Bureau of Narcotics informed the RCMP of the operation and the two forces jointly drew up a meticulous plan of action in order to protect the safety of the two special agents and the success of the project. Staff Sergeant Gérard Houle of the Narcotics Squad headed the operation.

Late in the afternoon of April 28, 1959, Patrick Biase and Eddie Smith, as planned, took a flight to Montreal. They arrived at the International Airport at Dorval about 6:45 p.m., checked into a

---

11. During January 1959 undercover agents of the U.S. Bureau of Narcotics managed to buy two and a half kilos (five and a half pounds) of pure heroin from the Monastersky-McGovern team. The investigation later revealed that they had procured the drugs from the Orlandino brothers. On February 14, Bureau of Narcotics agents and New York police arrested Monastersky, McGovern, the Orlandino brothers and two of their men, William Struzzieri and William Bentvena. Documents found at Marcantonio's place indicated that the 11 kilos (24 pounds) of heroin seized that night had been supplied by the Cotroni organization.

suburban motel and immediately began a tour of the city's night clubs looking for Cotroni. About 3 a.m. they met Giuseppe (Big Pep) Cocolicchio in the *Café Roméo.* (12) Smith, who knew him, explained that his friend was in Montreal on business and wanted to get in touch with Pep Cotroni personally. Cocolicchio, an agreeable fellow, promised to deliver the message, and the satisfied agents returned to their motel to sleep. Early the next afternoon they were awakened by a telephone call from Cocolicchio who announced that Cotroni would be arriving any moment. Fifteen minutes later the chief himself appeared, accompanied by one of his handymen, Arthur David. Smith introduced his friend and, over a well-laden table, the conversation quickly turned to the agent's background. Cotroni wanted to know whom he was dealing with, and demanded in a severe tone:

"Who are you? What's your name? Where do you come from? Who do you know down there? Who are your friends?"

"My name is Dave Costa," replied the agent. "Like Smitty said, my friends call me Pat. I'm Italian like you. As for my partners, I've got nothing to say about them for the moment. I don't want to know your business and I don't appreciate questions about mine. I'm from Harlem. That's all I've got to say for now."

The young man pleased Cotroni. He was Italian, which was a point in his favor, and his answers were frank. He asked Biase what it was he wanted, exactly.

"I've been distributing on the street, but I want to change things a bit and get into the wholesale business," replied the agent. "I need a supplier, somebody I can count on. I haven't got much capital but I've got somebody who's ready to finance me and I have some good customers. Smitty told me you were big in the business and the best man to see."

The trafficker replied that he could supply any amount of first quality merchandise—heroin or raw opium. He said he got it from overseas and its purity varied from 227 to 234 degrees Centigrade. Usually he received 227 but sometimes he got some 234. Everything was checked and that's why the packages from him were pierced. He said he'd been in business a long time and had learned a few things. He offered some advice to the agent as a young man just beginning: always do business in cash; that way, when you have a good customer who pays well, you don't have to worry. He gave the

---

12. Big Pep was the manager of the *Métropole Club,* the most prosperous gambling club in the city.

example of Orlandino who had been arrested a short time before in Hicksville and still owed Cotroni money. But Cotroni said he knew he would be paid eventually. Then he asked how much Biase was ready to buy.

The agent said he wanted two kilos to start with. Cotroni replied that that was a small sale, he usually sold in five-kilo lots only, but would make an exception for this time. But he said the price would be $7,000 a kilo instead of $6,500 or even $6,000, because the market was good and supplies were coming in regularly.

Cotroni then explained to the two agents how the delivery and preliminary contacts would be made. He said he would be ready for the deal about mid-May. On the 15th he would telephone Smitty and they would give him the number of a public telephone, using a code in which each digit, except for the zeroes and ones, would be increased by one. (13) He would call the right number ten minutes later and give the final instructions. The transaction would take place in Montreal and the agents were to use a Chevrolet convertible. This model was used because the arm-rests could be easily removed and the stuff hidden there without raising suspicions. The agents should then telephone Cotroni who would advise them on the best route to the border and the best time to cross it.

Cotroni said that if his instructions were followed to the letter there would be no problems for them or for him. Police had never been able to arrest any of his men, though he couldn't say the same for operations in New York. Bootsie and Angie, (14) two of his best customers, had narrowly escaped when their man in Hicksville had been arrested with a shipment.

The meeting ended and Cotroni left his new customers reminding them that he would be calling around May 15. With this promise in hand, Biase and Smith returned to New York the same night, after making a report to Sergeant Houle. Two Montreal police detectives, incidentally, had been at the same motel during the meeting and had noted the presence of two strangers at the table with Pep Cotroni and Arthur David. They would testify to this later.

On May 15, as promised, Cotroni telephoned Smith who gave him the required coded number. A few minutes later Cotroni called back on the number and asked if the buyer would be ready the following week. When the double agent said he would be ready,

---

13. For example, the number 4-5368 would in reality be 3-4257

14. Anthony Di Pasqua and Angelo Tuminaro, two members of the Lucchese family, for whom the Orlandino brothers worked.

Cotroni told him to arrive on Thursday morning and telephone him at the agreed number.

Biase and Smith left New York on May 21 in a Chevrolet convertible of that year and reached Montreal about 1:30 p.m. At Cotroni's suggestion, they registered at the *Cadillac* motel, on Sherbrooke Street East. A surveillance team from the Narcotics Squad was already in place at that motel. The agents then called the number Victor 9-0260, the *Métropole* gambling club, and asked Big Pep Cocolicchio to advise Cotroni of their arrival.

Cotroni arrived at the *Cadillac* motel about 4 p.m. He was accompanied by his all-round man, René Robert, who stayed in the car while his boss joined the two undercover agents. During the meeting Pep told Biase he could have received $7,500 a kilo for the merchandise, but in spite of that he was letting him have it for $7,000 cash, which was the price agreed upon. After verifying that his customers had the Chevrolet convertible he had recommended, Cotroni advised that someone would come to get the car and would hide the stuff in it. The delivery would be made at about nine o'clock the following night. He advised them not to leave for the border before 2 a.m. At that hour Customs surveillance was more relaxed and the officers less zealous and they shouldn't have any trouble.

Before he left, Pep invited Biase and Smith to move to the *Jacques Cartier* motel, further east on Sherbrooke Street, which belonged to one of his friends. (15) He said the *Cadillac* motel was too "hot." Morality squad officers were always checking it because of the prostitutes who hung around there.

The following morning Biase and Smith moved to the *Jacques Cartier*. Cotroni and Robert arrived there at 6 p.m. and the four had dinner together, afterwards going to the room to talk business. Cotroni then revealed to the two agents that he no longer wished to do business with them. He'd had a phone call from New York about the negotiations and he didn't like that. There could not be any deal if certain people in New York objected. Those people didn't like anyone trespassing on their territory. Cotroni wondered if the agents had told anyone they were coming to Montreal.

Biase, disappointed, showed anger. He said he had already lost

---

15. The proprietor of the *Jacques Cartier* motel was then Fernand Pierre Lefebvre, an old friend and associate of the Cotroni family. Later he became one of the owners of the *Casa Loma,* a popular night club belonging to members of the Cotroni clan, including Jos Di Maulo.

two days, this was his second trip, and now things were bogging down.

"The only guy I know is Chow Mancino," he added. "Smitty just told him we had a contact here and were coming to get some merchandise. He probably guessed you were our source because he knows Smitty knows you."

Cotroni thought it over and finally agreed that the explanation was probably true and that it had been Mancino who had told Angie Tuminaro that the Montrealer was negotiating with a new client. But he asked Biase to wait till the following Monday, May 25. By then he should have obtained more information and a decision could be taken. In the meantime he suggested that the two New Yorkers go out on the town a bit and enjoy themselves. Biase, not really having any choice, agreed to the delay.

For the next three days Biase and Smith made the rounds of the city's gambling joints. Everywhere they were received with grand welcomes and a show of respect. Biase had trouble holding back his buoyant companion who could not resist the advances of the numerous girls put at his disposal. Nevertheless, those three days gave the undercover agent the opportunity to get to know certain influential figures in the Montreal underworld. Among those who attracted his particular attention was Jack Lutherman, partner of Solomon Schnapps (also known as Solly Silvers), operator of the cabaret *Chez Paree*. Lutherman had offered to put Biase in contact with an important trafficker in Hamilton, but at that time, of course, the agent was unable to pursue this new lead.

On Saturday, René Robert phoned Biase to reassure him and tell him that everything would work out. The following day at 2 p.m., Robert phoned again. This time he announced that Cotroni would arrive in an hour to take Biase and Smith for a little outing. Worried, Biase alerted the Narcotics Squad which quickly organized teams to follow the agents. Plainclothes detectives from the RCMP were already in place when Cotroni and Robert arrived at the motel in their Oldsmobile and when they left a few minutes later, with Biase and Smith, heading for the Laurentians.

On the way, Biase quickly realized that Cotroni was trying to test him again. The conversation between the two men, though generally banal, was spiced from time to time with trick questions, so that the undercover agent had to be continually on his guard. With René Robert at the wheel, the group arrived at Cotroni's cottage at Ste. Adèle. Cotroni then explained that he had arranged a party that evening to which he had invited some important people from the United States whom he wished to introduce to Biase.

Always on guard, Biase sensed a danger and politely declined the invitation, pretending he had a date for the evening with a pretty girl in Montreal. The agent, a woman-chaser by nature, couldn't think of a better excuse. But Cotroni accepted it, despite its lack of originality, and the group returned to Montreal. Back at the motel, however, the mafioso insisted that Smith at least attend his party. This would be the first time since the beginning of the operation that the former trafficker was left on his own.

Before accompanying Cotroni and Robert back to Ste-Adèle, Smith went with them to the *Bonfire* where he met Carmine Galente, who had been wanted by police for more than a year. He was no doubt one of the eminent visiting Americans Cotroni wished to introduce to Biase. Other gangsters attended the party and Smith mingled with them in a friendly way.

Shortly before noon the next day, as planned, Smith returned to Montreal. Cotroni then told Biase that he had received no news from New York and that must mean that everything was in order. He said it would take a couple of hours to hide the stuff properly in the agents' car. In the meantime he offered them the use of his own car, warning them not to use it in Montreal. It was known to police and if they were found driving it they might get in trouble, perhaps even be accused of stealing it. It would be better to avoid any such trouble.

Robert then explained why a 1959 Chevrolet was absolutely essential for the transport of the drugs. This model of car was better than others because the arm-rests in the back seat had only to be unscrewed to reveal a convenient cavity in which the stuff could be hidden. It was simple, but efficient.

Before leaving with the Chevrolet, Cotroni told his new customers that the delivery would be made that night around eight o'clock. He also promised to supply them with a detailed road map to enable them to cross the border without difficulty.

As soon as Cotroni and Robert left, the two agents went to a locksmith where they had duplicates made of the keys to the Oldsmobile. Then they returned to the *Jacques-Cartier* motel where their precious cargo was to be delivered.

Cotroni and his companion arrived punctually. Pep quickly explained to Biase that he could not continue the transaction because his regular clients were reminding him that they had exclusive contracts with him. When Smith joined the group, Cotroni asked Biase to follow him outside on the balcony.

There Cotroni explained that while Smitty was a good guy who had done him some great favors and never betrayed him, it was better not to talk in the presence of a third person. He had confidence in Robert too, but between two people, one's word was as good as the other's and a third person was a useless risk for both. Cotroni went on to say that five men in the United States controlled the market and the price of the stuff. One of them had telephoned to tell him he should not accept any new customers because that would cut into the business and it would be impossible to control prices. Cotroni said that if he sold stuff to Biase, Biase would make between $150,000 and $200,000 in the first year. The guys in the U.S. were not ready to take that kind of loss. He thought the source of the problem was Chow Mancino who had told friends that Smith and Biase were in Montreal to buy stuff. Mancino was useful because he knew a lot of people, but because of him, Cotroni said he had been done out of $100,000. Cotroni suggested that Biase go back to New York and tell Mancino as many dirty and derogatory things about Cotroni as he wished. If Mancino could be made to believe that Biase considered Cotroni a low-down swindler and cheat, not fit to do business with, then it would be safe for Biase to come back to Montreal and for Cotroni to make a deal with him. Cotroni said that he would know whether or not Biase had talked with Mancino and whether or not he had convinced him of his disgust with Cotroni.

Cotroni then asked if Biase knew his friends Bootsie and Angie on the Lower East Side. Biase said he didn't and, unhappy at the turn of events, wanted to know why Robert had told him on Saturday that everything could be arranged, and why he had been made to waste five days for nothing.

Pep apologized, but said he had to consider the opinion of his customers. "They're powerful. They could make me or break me."

The two men walked back into the motel room then and Biase resorted to the classic ploy: money. He raised the mattress of his bed and showed the $14,000 (which Bureau of Narcotics authorities had provided). Robert then felt the need to intervene to reassure the New Yorkers and showed them a small sack of tools to demonstrate good faith. He said they had been ready to do business before the telephone call came, and even had the tools to remove the Chevrolet's arm-rests. Robert did not want the visitors to think that there was any trickery involved.

Again Cotroni advised the return to New York and the meeting with Mancino. He told Biase to call him Friday morning, at Victor 2-0067. He also suggested that if Biase came back to make a deal, he should bring some tarpaper to cover the hole behind the arm-rests.

This would throw off Customs officers who might raise the ashtrays and aim flashlights inside to see if anything had been hidden under the arm-rests.

Finally, to show his good faith, Cotroni told the two customers that on their next trip, if all went well, they would have an apartment and a garage at their disposal. That would be safer and more practical.

Deeply disappointed, Biase and Smith returned to New York that same night. The next day they went to see Mancino in his Brooklyn apartment, and found him feeding his pigeons on the roof. They followed Cotroni's instructions faithfully, painting him in colors as black as they could think of. They said they now intended to go to Florida to try to find another contact. Mancino promised to introduce them to someone useful when they returned.

On Friday, May 29, Biase telephoned Cotroni in Montreal from a public pay phone in New York. The mafioso asked him to call back the following day, saying he was very busy.

The next day, Saturday, Biase called again, from his home. He spoke first with a stranger, then with Robert, but could not get through to Cotroni. On Sunday Biase called again. This time Pep's father-in-law, Joe Seminaro, answered and explained that Pep was very busy at that time with municipal elections in St. Laurent, a northwest suburb of Montreal.

Finally on Monday morning Eddie Smith got a call from Cotroni announcing that everything had been worked out and the deal could be made that very day. Biase and his companion left Bureau of Narcotics headquarters about 1 p.m. and arrived at the *Jacques Cartier* motel at about 10:15 that night. They had just arrived in their room when the telephone rang. It was Cotroni saying that he was on his way. Less than an hour later, the group was re-united.

Biase began with an account of his meeting with Mancino which gave Cotroni great enjoyment. Then the Montrealer asked the agent if he had practised unscrewing the Chev arm-rests. He said Biase could do the operation right in the motel yard when he got the stuff. The proprietor of the motel was a Cotroni friend. .

Cotroni then told Robert to get the merchandise and a few minutes later Robert returned with two packages wrapped in brown paper. Pep assured his customers that he, himself, had verified the quality of the product which was 227 degrees of purity. There were two kilos and the price, as determined previously, was $14,000. Biase took out his money (the serial numbers of the bills had been recorded by the Bureau of Narcotics) and handed it to Cotroni who then handed it to Robert. Robert counted it and passed it back to Pep who also counted it. In a lordly gesture of apology, Cotroni then asked how much the trips to Montreal had cost the New Yorkers. Biase said $400 and Cotroni handed him $200, saying that he would share the expenses. Cotroni added that whenever Biase wanted to reach him, he should telephone Victor 2-0067 at 9 p.m. If Cotroni was not there, he should leave the message that Pat wanted him to call back. Cotroni said it might take as long as three days before he was able to return the call, but he would call, and Biase should wait.

By 11:30 p.m. on June 2 the first transaction was concluded, and discussion about the next one began immediately. Cotroni remarked that he usually received his merchandise between the 14th and 16th of each month and that, for the next time, he would again make an exception by selling a two-kilo lot, while holding the other three kilos in reserve. The undercover agent acknowledged the offer and the two traffickers left, after asking the New Yorkers to call in two or three days to say how things had worked out. Soon after their departure, Biase and Smith got in touch with the Narcotics Squad to arrange transfer of the heroin. At half-past midnight on June 3, in a quiet street of the east-end suburb of Repentigny, the agents handed over the two kilos of heroin to Sergeant Houle and agent Charles Ward of the Narcotics Squad. They returned then to New York where they learned that Carmine Galente had been found and arrested in New Jersey. (16) Two days later they advised Cotroni that their return trip had been made with no difficulty whatever.

The next development came on Saturday, June 13, when Cotroni telephoned Smith to find out why he had heard nothing from his new customers. The double agent replied that they had intended to call him on the 15th. Apparently satisfied, Cotroni said he would call again at the beginning of the week to find out when they would be coming back to Montreal. When he called about 11 a.m. on Wednesday, June 17, Biase and Smith were ready to go. They had already been supplied with the necessary $14,000. They told Cotroni they would be at the *Jacques Cartier* motel late that night.

In fact, the two agents arrived in Montreal much earlier than that. But as planned, they went first to the *Lucerne* motel, room 67, where they joined Sergeant Houle and the agent Ward. These two officers searched Biase and Smith carefully so as to be able to testify

---

16. Galente was released a short time later, after posting a cash bond.

later on how much money they were carrying. They made note of the serial numbers of the 13 one-thousand dollar bills and 10 hundred-dollar bills which had been provided by the Treasury department of the U.S., and they explained to the two agents the surveillance system which had been put into effect by RCMP detectives.

At 9:40 p.m. Biase and Smith were ready to resume their roles. They checked in again at the *Jacques-Cartier* motel, and were given the same room as they had the first time, No. 72. That was a stroke of luck, because a Narcotics Squad agent had already reserved No. 71. Cotroni and Robert arrived about an hour later and the new negotiations began. Once again, Biase pretended that he could only buy two kilos. He explained that a customer in Detroit had ordered another kilo from him but had refused to pay in advance. As a result, he only had $14,000 with him. Cotroni was prepared to supply an extra kilo on condition that he be paid for it without delay. Biase hesitated, but finally handed over the money. The trafficker then left, promising to return shortly.

The mafioso and his henchman, Robert, returned before 1 a.m. They explained to Biase that the deal could not be made before 6 a.m. because it had to be obtained from the cache and the man in charge of it was not someone who could be hurried. To prove their good faith, they waited with the agents.

In the next few hours, while Smith and Robert went out to get something to eat, Cotroni and Biase chatted. Cotroni found the undercover agent so likeable — perhaps because he was Italian — that he offered to sell him two more kilos on credit provided he paid within ten days and agreed to place another order. Naturally, Biase accepted the offer and added that in mid-July he might be able to buy a dozen and perhaps even 15 kilos. Cotroni, content with this, confided that he would be going to New York in a week and while there would like Biase to meet some of his best customers such as Rocky (Rocco Sancinella), Bootsie (Anthony Di Pasqua) and Angie (Angelo Tuminaro).

Cotroni said these were useful men to known. If Biase some day had an urgent need for stuff and couldn't come to Montreal, these men could help him out. On the other hand, if they needed stuff in a hurry, he might be able to help them. It was a question of good neighborliness.

In the middle of the night, Robert, who had returned from a restaurant with Smith, got the order to go and pick up the stuff. He returned about 6:15 a.m. and the deal was quickly concluded. At 7 a.m., June 18, 1959, Biase and Smith were back at the *Lucerne* motel handing over to the Narcotics Squad commander four kilos of 10 per cent pure heroin. They returned to New York the same day.

A week later Cotroni came to New York. With him were René Robert and another friend, Conrad Bouchard, an ex-singer who was wanted in connection with one of the bank robberies set up by Peter Stepanoff. Pep got in touch with Smith as soon as he arrived, but Smith told him that Biase was in Detroit on business. Biase, in fact, did not want to run the risk of meeting Pep's customers. Cotroni was annoyed and showed it by demanding an advance of $1,000 on the $14,000 owed. He said he was short of money because of his latest investments and a dirty trick by one of his customers. Smith immediately called the Bureau of Narcotics which sent an investigator to pose as Biase's partner. The investigator went with Smith to meet Cotroni and handed over the $1,000. That was on the afternoon of June 23.

Before he returned to Montreal, Pep, who had the impression that Smith was not on very good terms with his new partner, asked Smith to become his courier for certain of his New York customers, particularly Sancinella, Di Pasqua, Tuminaro, Mancino and Tony Bender (Anthony Strollo) who was Vito Genovese's right-hand man. (17) Cotroni even asked the double agent to come back with him to take charge of delivery of about a dozen kilos. Smith promised to think about it.

On June 29, as Cotroni had requested, Biase and Smith returned to Montreal. All day they tried to reach Cotroni, with no success. Biase then decided to go back to New York, leaving Smith to contact Cotroni in the hope that the trafficker might eventually lead him to where the heroin was stored.

At noon the next day Biase left and Smith found Cotroni, Robert and Bouchard. Together the four men went to the *Bonfire* where Luigi Greco awaited them. It was the first time Smith had met this associate of Carmine Galente and of Pep's older brother, Vincent, who at that time was in New York. (18) As usual at such meetings, Greco questioned Smith about his past and his contacts. It

---

17. Anthony Strollo, alias Tony Bender, was executed shortly afterwards, on orders of Genovese.

18. Vincent Cotroni entered the United States on June 27, 1959, with John Rao, a barber shop owner and with his bodyguard Michel Listorti, who claimed to be employed at a tailor shop belonging to Jimmy Curio (pseudonym), but who was also manager of the *Café Roméo*. On the preceding May 5, Vic Cotroni, his young brother Frank, and Jos De Francesco had gone to New York and stayed at the *Edison Hotel*.

soon became apparent to the double agent that Greco was one of Pep Cotroni's major financial backers and his superior in the hierarchy. Greco was a natural leader, very authoritarian, who let no one impose upon him. His decisions had the force of law in the underworld. When the meeting was over Smith accompanied Cotroni and his friends to Ste. Adèle. He noted that his companions still mistrusted Biase, asked themselves questions about his underworld relationships, and hoped that he would pay off his debt without delay. After this visit, Smith returned to New York to report to Biase and the U.S. Bureau of Narcotics.

Pat Biase was at his Long Island home when Cotroni telephoned him around 10:30 p.m. on July 5. The trafficker wanted to know when his new customers would be coming back to Montreal. The undercover agent replied that he and Smitty had planned to leave two days later. That satisfied Pep who fixed a meeting at the usual place, the *Jacques Cartier* motel.

The two agents arrived in Montreal early in the evening of July 7, stopping first at the *Lucerne* motel where they met, as before, colleagues from the RCMP and the Bureau of Narcotics and planned the details of the operation. It was a little after 9 p.m. when they got to the dining room of the *Jacques Cartier* motel. Cotroni and Robert, who had been waiting there for some time, welcomed them politely, but immediately after the usual exchange of greetings, Cotroni said that he wanted to talk to Biase alone. After dinner the undercover agent and his host left the two others and, at Cotroni's suggestion, sat in his car parked in front of the motel.

Cotroni said he did not want to talk in the room because it might be bugged. Before turning to business, he wanted to talk about Smitty. He hadn't liked Smith's attitude at the party at the cottage in Ste. Adèle. He had a big mouth and talked too much. Furthermore, Cotroni said that the last time he was in New York (when Biase was supposed to be in Detroit) he had told Smith he was sure they were being followed. But Smith had brushed this off, told him he was imagining things. Cotroni said he did not trust Smith, and advised Biase to drop him.

Biase realized that Cotroni had chosen Smith, a non-Italian, as a scapegoat and had transferred his suspicions to him.

"Don't worry about him, Pep," he said. "He's my partner and I'll keep him away from things. He gets paid regularly, but he doesn't want to get involved in the deals."

Cotroni then said he wished to do business only with Biase. He said he could help make Biase another $30,000 to $40,000 a month if he wanted. But he needed some names, references, people who could recommend Biase. He was ready to deliver the stuff but he had to have guarantees. Cotroni said he had 15 kilos on loan to Angie and Bootsie because he knew he could trust them. He had to be sure of all his customers.

Biase said he understood, but thought the last two deals should have convinced Cotroni that he was straight. However, if Cotroni wanted reassurance, he could call Smashy, Tony Bianca, and Ralph Fagilone. Biase said these men were well-known and respected in Philadelphia. They knew him well and were the best references he could give.

The agent then gave Cotroni the telephone number of a used car firm where these men could be reached. Naturally, he did not mention that Smashy was a "convert" like Smith, that Tony Bianca was the pseudonym of a Bureau of Narcotics agent who had infiltrated the underworld, and that Fagilone was a mobster whom the first two had brought into their control.

Cotroni seemed reassured. He said he knew Pat was a good guy. If everything turned out all right he would have an interesting offer for Biase. He could offer him eight kilos on credit, with not even a penny in advance, if he took charge of delivery of 15 kilos for Cotroni. He asked Biase to think it over and said he would call him the next day.

The meeting over, Robert rejoined his boss and the two left. The next day at noon the four men met again in the dining room of the *Jacques Cartier* motel. More relaxed than the night before, Cotroni renewed his proposition for delivery of a stock of heroin to New York, indicating this time that he could supply six kilos (13 pounds) that night. After the meal Cotroni suggested a drive in the city so they could talk a little.

Once inside the car, Cotroni asked Biase if he had the money he owed him and also if he could make a small advance on the six kilos.

"Didn't we agree that I'd pay back the $13,000 around July 15 and that the six kilos would be on credit?" asked Biase.

Yes, yes, said Cotroni, that was the agreement, but couldn't Biase pay something right away, even a small amount?

"You expect a lot, don't you?" replied the agent. "Anyway I've got $40,000 at home. Stop at a telephone booth and I'll call New York and see what I can do."

Robert stopped the car at a public pay phone and the

undercover agent called his wife who had been briefed in advance on what to do in such a case. She was to alert "Frank," the Bureau of Narcotics colleague who had already played a role as Biase's partner. On his return to the car, Biase said:

"My man will arrive tonight about 10 o'clock with the money. Is that O.K. with you?"

Cotroni said that was fine, but reminded Biase that he would do business only with him. He did not want to see anyone else, and Biase was not to bring his man to the motel.

On the way back, the trafficker assured Biase that if he could verify the references, everything would be ready for 10 p.m.: the six kilos along with the 15 other kilos destined for Tuminaro and Di Pasqua. At 2 p.m. they were all back at the *Jacques Cartier* motel. The Montrealers then took leave of their customers. Biase and Smith waited half an hour and then drove to the *Lucerne* motel to make a report on the latest developments. Nobody was happy with the situation. The question of the money was uppermost in the agents' minds because neither the U.S. Treasury nor the RCMP had any intention of investing large sums unless they were certain of recovering both the money and the drugs. They did not trust Cotroni. True, he had not asked for payment in advance, but there was no guarantee he would not do so at the last moment, especially since reports from Philadelphia indicated that he had not yet been in touch with Biase's friends there. After much discussion, it was decided to proceed immediately with arrests the moment Cotroni showed himself to be too demanding. In addition, as an added safeguard, an agent was sent to Dorval airport to mingle with passengers arriving from New York. In that way, if Cotroni had chanced to send someone out to watch for the arrival of Biase's partner, he wouldn't be disappointed.

Biase and Smith returned to their motel towards the end of the afternoon. As agreed, Smith took a taxi to Dorval at 8:20 p.m. to meet the fake partner. He had been gone some time when Biase realized that Smith had been carrying the keys to their automobile. And Cotroni was supposed to be coming to get the car in order to conceal the heroin in it. Furious, Biase went into the bathroom and pounded on the wall to signal his colleague from the Narcotics Squad, in the next room, to lean against his window. At his own window, Biase explained what had happened and asked the agent to arrange for someone to get to Dorval urgently and pick up the keys from Smith. The message was delivered and an agent was despatched on the mission. Unfortunately, Cotroni arrived a little earlier than expected, entering Biase's room at 10 p.m.

Cotroni greeted Biase, told him his stuff was ready, but that he had not yet received word about the other shipment. The clients in New York were not yet ready with their money. Then he asked for the keys to Biase's car so it could be prepared for the trip.

Biase, embarrassed and ill at ease, pretended to search everywhere for the keys, before bursting into angry tones:

"Smitty, that stupid bastard, he's so excited he left with the keys. Damn it to hell! How stupid can he be!"

Visibly annoyed, Cotroni decided to rejoin Robert and wait for Smith in his car. Biase had no choice but to go along with him. There Cotroni said again that Smitty was definitely not suited for this kind of business, that he talked too much, was too crude and too much of a braggart. He reminded Biase again of the incident in New York when Smith had brushed aside Cotroni's suspicions that they were being followed. Cotroni said that the manager of the *Edison Hotel* himself had told him that federal agents were watching them. That was why he left two days earlier than expected.

René Robert remarked at this point that it was a good thing they had left early, because they learned later that police wanted to take them to Chicago over a matter of some stolen bonds. (19)

Cotroni added that in this business you had to remain calm and not let anyone know what you were doing.

"And here I was thinking you didn't like me just because I wouldn't talk about myself," put in Biase.

---

19. The previous June 30, after an FBI investigation, a federal grand jury in Chicago formally indicted Cotroni, Robert, and three Americans in connection with receiving bonds stolen from the *Brockville Trust and Savings Company* in May 1958. The three Americans who were arrested on July 2 by the FBI were: Salvatore (Sam) Mannarino, a Pittsburgh Mafia boss with his brother Gabriel, a delegate to the Apalachin summit and a partner of Santos Trafficante in Havana's *Sansoucy Club;* William W. Rabin, a Chicago financial consultant and a former business partner of Mannarino; Norman Rothman, an arms and drug trafficker and gambling financier in Cuba where he had been closely linked to the dictator Batista and to the Corsican and Montreal traffickers.

The investigation of this affair showed that in October 1958, William Rabin, of *Central Trust Corporation,* had obtained a substantial loan from the *Central Bank* by using as collateral some $98,000 in bonds which had been stolen from the Brockville company by the Cotroni organization. With George E. Rosden, an international lawyer from Washington, Rabin had set up his *Central Trust Corporation* just four days before he applied for the loan. In January 1959, Rabin went to Switzerland with Rosden, who introduced him to a banker. The banker in turn introduced the two business crooks to *Crédit Suisse* which then lent Rabin $87,500 on the strength of Brockville bonds valued at $140,000. In these operations, Mannarino and Rothman were the brokers who introduced Rabin to Cotroni, who in turn supplied the stolen bonds.

"No," replied Cotroni, "That's why I decided to do business with you."

"I've been thinking, Pep," said Biase, "that my partner who's coming from New York probably won't want to hand over the money to Smith. He doesn't know him too well, and will probably need some word from me."

At that moment a motel employee approached the car and told Biase there was a telephone call for him. "It's probably Smitty wanting to know what to do," said Biase, as he left the car.

It was Smith on the line. Biase asked him to come back to the hotel for instructions and reminded him not to forget the car keys. Then he rejoined Cotroni and Robert in the car and told them of the conversation.

"What do you intend to do, Pep?" asked the agent.

Cotroni said that as soon as they got the car keys, he and Robert would take the car and stow the stuff in it. Then they would park the car somewhere and come back to get Biase and Smith to take them there. Cotroni thought that everything would be ready by Friday for the delivery of the 15 kilos to New York and added that the people Biase would be meeting there were the best. When Biase asked who these people were, Cotroni replied that he had already mentioned them. They were Angie and Bootsie.

Cotroni then handed a slip of paper to Robert, asking him to make a telephone call to see if all was going well. Robert went to the phone booth in the motel and a few moments later returned to ask Pep to come to the phone. Cotroni then returned to the automobile and told Biase that everything was in order. He said his friends from New York would be coming on Friday with $90,000. He would call Biase to come and get the stuff for delivery to them. But he said Biase should do this alone. He didn't want Smitty involved in it.

At that point, Smith arrived in a taxi. Biase rushed to meet him and to get the car keys which he handed to Cotroni. Then Biase got some paper at the reception desk and wrote the message: "Give everything to Eddy. Patty." As Smith departed in the taxi with the note, Biase rejoined the two traffickers.

"Listen, Pat," said Cotroni, "you should give me a phone number where I could reach you quickly in New York."

"There's nothing to write with here," replied Biase. "Come to my room where there's some paper."

In the room Biase wrote down his number and Cotroni transcribed it, using his personal code. The undercover agent then asked Cotroni to go over his method of delivery again to assure that everything would be ready on Smith's return. Cotroni reviewed the routine for a few minutes and the two men walked outside where Cotroni got into his car with Robert.

"We'll be back in an hour," said Robert.

Biase stood near the car as it moved off slowly. It had gone only a few feet when it stopped suddenly. Biase approached to find out what was happening.

"I think it will be safer if we wait till Smitty comes back with the money," said Cotroni, as Robert leaned over and said something to him.

"What did he say?" asked Biase.

Cotroni replied that Robert had just reminded him that the garage where they were going was being repaired and they wouldn't be able to get in. He asked if Biase would mind if they just put the stuff in the car instead of hiding it in the arm-rests.

"Fine," said Biase, "I'll look after that part myself, but hurry up. Smitty will soon be here."

But Cotroni insisted. He said it would be better to wait until Smith arrived with the money.

Biase didn't know what to do. If he refused the trafficker's demands, Cotroni would just drop the whole deal and leave. On the other hand, his own instructions were clear—no advance payment. He had no choice. Quickly Biase drew a white handkerchief from his pocket and waved it over his head. It was the signal. Within seconds dozens of agents from the RCMP and the Bureau of Narcotics (who had been working in the background from the beginning) surrounded the car and cut off any possibility of flight. Even so, René Robert made a dash for it, only to be grabbed and held by a Narcotics Squad detective before he had taken more than a few steps. Cotroni understood immediately what was happening.

"So that's it," he said. "Shit!"

A few minutes later, finding himself face to face with Biase in whom he had placed all his trust, he added angrily:

"We know how to treat guys like you."

"You're wrong, Pep," replied Biase, who realized that Cotroni was taking him for an informer and a traitor. "I'm not a stoolie, as you think. I am an agent of the U.S. Bureau of Narcotics."

The surprised Cotroni had nothing more to say. Taken to RCMP headquarters, he maintained his silence until his trial.

During the night, Narcotics Squad agents had plenty to do. They made dozens of raids. The cottage at Ste. Adèle was searched, the Ridgewood Street apartment, Pep's house and those of his brothers. Police visited every place that might produce some evidence and many gangsters and friends of Cotroni were brought in and questioned. Among them were Peter Stepanoff, who had already been convicted of receiving stolen bonds, and Conrad Bouchard. Bouchard was turned over to Quebec Provincial Police who had been looking for him for some time.

The representatives of the Bureau of Narcotics were also busy. Responsible for the two major witnesses, they quickly set up an impregnable system to protect them. Smith, who had the most reason to fear underworld reprisals, was taken under heavy guard to an isolated cottage in the United States. For months he was under day and night protection there to ensure his safety. Canadian court officials even travelled to New York to obtain his testimony.

Cotroni and his sidekick made their first appearance in criminal court the day after their arrest on charges of conspiracy in the sale of $8 million worth of heroin. They were both denied bail and Judge Marc-André Blain set their preliminary hearing for July 16. On that date, another charge was brought against Cotroni for receiving bonds stolen from the *Brockville Trust and Savings Company.*

The main witness in this affair was an Italian immigrant, Luigi Mariani, an engineering graduate of Zurich University. On his arrival in Canada, as he was unable yet to exercise his profession in this country, he was hired as manager of Cotroni's tavern on Ontario Street East. When Cotroni later decided to renovate the place, he put Mariani in charge of the work. Cotroni provided the manager with $9,700 in various stocks and bonds to buy material and pay the workers. Mariani deposited these in the Canadian National Bank which credited them to his account before discovering that some of the securities were stolen bonds.

The judge presiding over the heroin trafficking charges was Judge Wilfrid Lazure, of Court of Queen's Bench, who had also handled the d'Agostino case in 1949. Cotroni's trial began on October 19. The first witness was Patrick Biase. Questioned by the Crown prosecutor Jean-Paul Sainte-Marie (who would later become the personal lawyer of the big boss, Vincent Cotroni) (20), the

---

20. Sainte-Marie has since explained why Vincent Cotroni called on his services: he said that in Cotroni's view, he was without doubt the only lawyer who knew that Cotroni was not the underworld chieftain he was rumored to be.

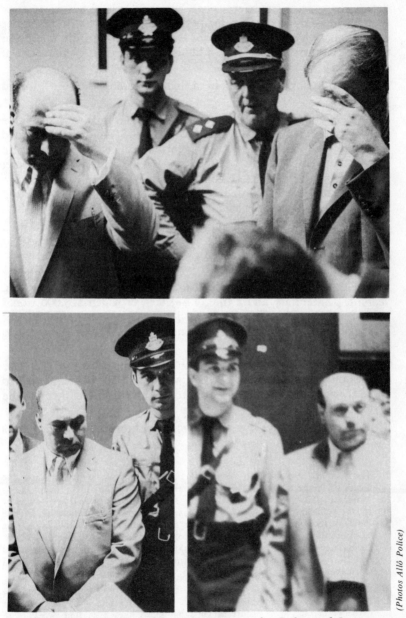

(Photos Allô Police)

Pep Cotroni and René Robert appearing at the Palace of Justice on charges of trafficking in heroin. Both pleaded guilty.

Bureau of Narcotics agent described his mission at length and in detail. His precise statements were corroborated from time to time by Narcotics Squad investigators who had kept the traffickers under discreet surveillance thoughout the operation. (21) In the middle of the third day, Biase was still continuing his testimony when Cotroni asked permission to speak.

"Your honor," he said, in a barely audible voice, "I plead quilty."

A few minutes earlier, his last hopes had vanished when Biase had shown his trump card. This was a small Schmidt transistorized transmitter which the undercover agent had carried on his person in all his meetings with Cotroni. All the supposedly secret conversations, all the negotiations between Biase, Smith and the two traffickers had been recorded, noted and dated to the day, hour and minute by RCMP technicians.

After his boss's surprise quilty plea, René Robert, who had been hospitalized after mysteriously absorbing some barbiturates, had little choice. He, in turn, pleaded guilty.

Sentences were pronounced in November 1959. On the 9th, for trafficking in heroin, Giuseppe Cotroni, 39, was sentenced to ten years in penitentiary and a fine of $88,000, of which $28,000 would go to reimburse the U.S. Treasury department and the RCMP for their expenses. (22) On the 20th, René Robert, 31, was sentenced to eight years in penitentiary.

In the matter of the stolen Brockville bonds, Cotroni was also found quilty in another trial and on May 18, 1960, was sentenced to an additional seven years in prison, to be served consecutively to the first sentence.

This second conviction, by coincidence, came only a few days

21. The trial and the copious incriminating testimony considerably damaged the facade of respectability the Cotroni family had always tried to maintain. In Montreal's Italian community, where the Mafia is always present and feared by all, the publishers of the newspaper *Cittadino Canadese,* Nick Ciamara and Emile Putalivo, received threats warning them not to publish information about the Cotroni affair. Alfred Gagliardi, owner of *Corriere Italiano,* the second largest Italian-language newspaper in Montreal, was not bothered. A municipal councilor and a good friend of the Cotroni family, Gagliardi published not a word about the case.

22. Just before sentence was pronounced, friends of Pep Cotroni contacted the Narcotics Squad hoping to obtain a light sentence for him in exchange for his cache of heroin. As a gesture of good intentions, they even sent two kilos of heroin (a little more than four pounds) to the federal agents.

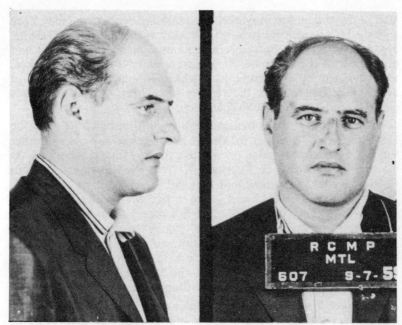

René Robert

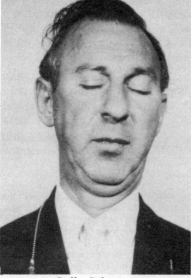

Solly Schnapps

Irving Ellis

after a federal grand jury for the southern district of New York brought indictments for heroin trafficking against Carmine Galente, Big John Ormento, Salvatore Giglio and many others who had dealings with them. In all, 29 Montreal and New York traffickers were indicted by the grand jury which estimated the amount of heroin they had put on the market since May 1957 at 600 kilos (1,320 pounds), valued at $633,660,000. (23)

Pep Cotroni's last conviction also came three months after the U.S. Bureau of Narcotics in Miami had arrested his older brother Vincent, suspected of being one of his principal financial backers. At the time of his arrest on February 7, 1960, Vic was returning from Cuba with a woman friend and Fernand Pierre Lefebvre, proprietor of the *Jacques Cartier* motel. Two other Montrealers were also arrested in Miami. Irving Ellis and Solomon Schnapps, two Jewish chieftains, had come to bring the money required for Cotroni's release on bail. Cited in the New York grand jury indictments, Solly Schnapps, like Vic Cotroni, had been held for a time for conspiracy to violate federal narcotics laws in the United States. For lack of evidence, however, the charges were dropped some months later.

In New York, the trials of Galente and the other American traffickers were much longer and more troublesome than those of Pep Cotroni and René Robert. Galente even had two trials, the first one being cancelled because of the withdrawal of several jury members, including the foreman who had been seriously injured in a mysterious accident. One of the most notable incidents of the 19 months of judicial debate was the public defection of a main witness, Suzanne Cadieux, René Robert's girlfriend.

Miss Cadieux, believing that her boyfriend's accomplices had done little to help him, went to the Narcotics Squad and the Bureau of Narcotics with an offer to testify against Carmine Galente and other traffickers she knew personally. She did in fact give such testimony at the first trial. But for the second trial, she went into reverse. Confidential information gathered by the RCMP indicated

---

23. Among the traffickers accused or denounced by the grand jury were: the Montrealers Guiseppe Cotroni, Luigi Greco, Peter Stepanoff, René Robert, Conrad Bouchard, Jack Lutherman and Solomon Schnapps; the Corsican Gabriel Graziani; the Americans Carmine Galente, John Ormento, Salvatore Giglio, Angelo Tuminaro, Anthony Di Pasqua, Carlie Di Pietro, Frank Mari, Frank Mancino, Joseph Vecchio, Rocco Sancinella, Carmine Polizzano, Salvatore and Carmine Panico, Philip and Marcantonio Orlandino, David Petillo, Salvatore Sciremammano, Angelo Loiacano, William Bentvena, William Struzzieri, Charles Gagliadatto, Benjamin Indiviglio, Anthony Mirra, Joseph Fernandez, Richard McGovern, Jack Gellman and Samuel Monastersky.

that Luigi Greco had arranged the about-face. He had sent one of his men, Conrad Bouchard, accompanied by a well-known criminologist, to visit René Robert in the penitentiary. The visit soon brought results. On January 17, 1962, Suzanne Cadieux called a press conference in the *Mount Royal Hotel.* Assisted by two lawyers, Léo-René Maranda and Jean Salois, who had defended members of the Cotroni clan, Miss Cadieux declared that she had given false testimony under the pressure of promises of moral and pecuniary gain and in particular, the promise of a quick parole for her lover. (24) In spite of her change in attitude, she was still required to testify in Montreal before a regatory commission from the United States. Though most of her answers were considered unsatisfactory, she did admit to helping the RCMP in several narcotics cases.

The second trial of the U.S. suspects ended in July 1962, 20 days after it began. Thirteen of those charged were found guilty and given heavy sentences. Carmine Galente was sentenced to 20 years in prison and a fine of $20,000, while Big John Ormento was given the same fine and 40 years in penitentiary. The 13 sentences added up to 266 years in prisons terms. Five other suspects were spared: one of them, Frank Mari, was acquitted while the four others — Savaltore Giglio, Angelo Tuminaro, Anthony Di Pasqua and Benjamin Indiviglio — took advantage of their release on bail to disappear from circulation. (25)

Two months later, in September 1962, the Marseillais Antranik Paroutian was also convicted in New York and sentenced to 20 years. He had been one of Pep Cotroni's principal suppliers and a partner of the Corsican Gabriel Graziani, one of the co-conspirators indicted by the grand jury. (26)

---

24. The lawyer who accompanied Conrad Bouchard on the visit to René Robert was not one of the two legal counselors of Miss Cadieux.

25. Salvatore Giglio, thought by many to be dead, turned up again in Los Angeles in 1972. He was arrested on charges which had been laid against him in 1960 and sentenced to prison.

26. After his release in the 1970s, Antranik Paroutian returned to Marseilles where, in the spring of 1975, he was kidnapped by unknown persons. Nothing has been heard of him since.

Chapter 7

Rivard and
the French Connection

Lucien Rivard returned to Montreal shortly before the arrest and conviction of Pep Cotroni. It was no longer possible to operate in Cuba where he had been installed since the summer of 1956. In early January 1959 Fidel Castro and Che Guevara became leaders of the Cuban government. With their guerillas they had overthrown the corrupt and dictatorial regime of Fulgencio Batista and had undertaken a vast clean-up. From the first days, already enjoying the diplomatic recognition of the great powers, including the United States, they created a ministry of purification and organized the pursuit of informers and collaborators of the Batista regime.

At first they attacked the native elite and their political adversaries, leaving foreigners, especially the gangsters, to go about their business, re-opening casinos, gambling dens and night clubs. This was a kind of compensation for the financial and material aid (especially arms) which underworld leaders had supplied to the guerillas, but the conciliatory attitude toward the mobsters did not last forever. Less than six months after taking power, Castro launched a grand offensive against gangsterism and foreign control of Cuban gambling establishments. In mid-May, most of the foreign gangsters who were still in Cuba were put in prison. Among them were several of Meyer Lansky's men, including his brother Jack, and some Canadians, including Lucien Rivard and his friends Gerry Turenne and Bill Lamy. Lamy, it will be recalled, had been sentenced to six months in prison in March 1950 for trafficking in heroin. Since then his name had often been linked to Rivard's. Turenne was a former Montreal wrestler well known in cabaret circles. He was Rivard's bodyguard.

Several of these men spent only a short time in Havana jails; just long enough for their deportations to be arranged. Bill Lamy, for example, was arrested May 6, and released five days later when he was able to show that he had nothing to do with the management of the gambling houses. Expelled to the United States, he was arrested again on his arrival in Miami where Customs officers questioned him on his role in the international heroin traffic. For lack of evidence he was released the next day.

Rivard's case was treated quite differently. He had become a personage on the island, as owner of night clubs transformed into slot machine heavens, as a trafficker in arms and drugs, as an associate of the Mafia. Like all the foreign mob leaders, he had given financial support to Batista who received a cut from all the rackets. The Narcotics Squad in Montreal had even heard that Rivard paid weekly fees of $20,000 to the dictator's regime. In any case, to the Castro revolutionaries, Rivard was an exploiter and a collaborator who deserved execution, despite his deliveries of arms. The authorities, therefore, were thinking about putting Rivard in front of a firing squad when, in the middle of June, Montreal lawyer Raymond Daoust appeared on the scene. After writing to the minister of External Affairs in Ottawa asking the minister to intercede with Cuban authorities on Rivard's behalf, Mr. Daoust travelled to Havana to plead his cause in person. The arguments he used are not known. But on June 19, 1959, ministerial decree No. 1514 ordered the expulsion of Rivard from Cuba for complicity in the trafficking of cocaine. Five days later, the trafficker was back in Montreal. Some time later, he confided to an RCMP agent that if he had been able to stay in Cuba for two more years he would have become a multimillionaire.

With the arrest of Pep Cotroni, Rivard was in a position to take over, in his own right, leadership of the importation of heroin into Canada. Unless his former partner had managed to introduce someone else to his suppliers, Rivard was now the only one who could count on supplies from the French traffickers. The Narcotics Squad was aware of this, and had placed Rivard under discreet surveillance since his return. But Rivard was cautious. He knew federal agents were interested in him. He sometimes even spotted the agents who were following him. Instead of taking evasive action to lose them, he would stop and, without losing his sardonic smile, ask them what they wanted.

In September 1959 Rivard took a vacation, spending a few months in the Oka region northwest of Montreal. He stayed at Bill Lamy's summer cottage (a man who would do anything for him) and frequented the *Saint-Placide Hotel* in the municipality of that name. The hotel belonged to one of his old friends, Lou Grégoire, who had been known to the Narcotics Squad since the beginning of the 1950s. In 1957, Rivard had asked him to manage one of his Cuban night clubs, *Las Vegas,* in Havana, which he did until the spring of 1958. Then he returned to Quebec and bought the hotel. During this tranquil period, Rivard was also in constant touch with some of his most faithful friends, such as Blackie Bisson, Butch Munroe, Larry Buckszar, Thomas Pythel and Joseph-Raymond Perreault. As we shall see, some of these men would later attract considerable attention.

It almost seemed that Rivard had abandoned his activities in heroin smuggling, but new facts soon indicated that this was not so. In the beginning of April 1960 RCMP detectives were informed that Rivard had gone to Acapulco some weeks earlier at the same time as four well-known international traffickers were visiting Mexico. According to the U.S. Treasury department the four were: Paul Mondolini (long-time associate of Rivard, mentioned before); Marius Cau (the Marseillais who had been with Gabriel Graziani when Graziani was arrested in Switzerland in April 1958 in possession of bonds stolen by the Cotroni-Stepanoff gang); and two mafiosi from Palermo, Pietro Davi and Rosario Mancino (noted for their association with Lucky Luciano, the brothers Ugo and Salvatore Caneba and Corsican smugglers). (1)

On April 8, alerted by U.S. Customs investigators, the Mexican federal police arrested Paul Mondolini at the Mexico City airport as he was about to board an airplane for Europe, via Cuba. The Corsican trafficker claimed he had come to Mexico on vacation. With no precise accusation against him — except perhaps for the illegal possession of ten gold pesos, worth $50 each — the Mexican authorities had no choice but to deport him to France.

On April 14, it was the RCMP's turn to go into action, intercepting Pietro Davi and Rosario Mancino on their arrival at the international airport at Dorval. The night before, the two mafiosi had been questioned for several hours by New York Customs officers when they arrived from Mexico. At Montreal, the police formalities lasted eight hours, at the end of which the two travellers decided it would be better to return to Italy without delay. That was fortunate for them, for the federal agents had decided to let them stay in Canada for a few days to see if they would make contact with certain members of the Ontario Mafia. The agents had some indications that the two men might have links with the

---

1. Rosario Mancino should not be confused with Frank Mancino, known as Chow, who was one of Pep Cotroni's customers mentioned in the previous chapter.

brothers Alberto and Vito Agueci, of Toronto, and Johnny Papalia, of Hamilton, who had started up an important heroin ring. (2)

On April 19, the RCMP intervened again. This time, Marius Cau was arrested as he got off a plane at Dorval. Like Davi and Mancino, he had come from Mexico with a stopover in New York where he had been questioned. He told the police officers that he had left France for Mexico in July 1959 and that his arrival in Montreal was only a stopover on his return to Europe. Cau, former boss of the *Bar des Routiers* in Marseilles, had become owner of a fish store in Varanges, a small town about 40 miles from Marseilles. Questioned about his previous voyages, he admitted having come to Montreal from New York in December 1957 at the time Antranik Paroutian was making the same journey. But Cau, confronted with photos of Paroutian, Graziani and Mondolini, refused to identify them and declared he had no contacts with known criminals. Judged an undesirable in Canada, Marius Cau was deported to Europe the same day.

In the next few months, the RCMP and the U.S. Bureau of Narcotics were unable to gather much information about Rivard's

---

2. In the spring of 1961 the brothers Agueci, Papalia (who had already worked in Montreal for Luigi Greco and Carmine Galente) and one of their couriers, Rocco Scopelletti, were arrested and charged in New York with international trafficking in heroin. With the agreement of Stefano Magaddino of Buffalo, whose authority extended to Ontario, they associated themselves with a New York group of the Genovese family, led by Anthony Strollo, alias Tony Bender, one of Pep Cotroni's clients. Originally from the village of Salemi, in Sicily's Trapani province, the Agueci brothers had been in business since the early 1950s with the local Mafia leaders—Salvatore Zizzo, Francesco Paolo Feliccia, Salvatore Valenti, Vincenzo Ditrapani, Cologaro Robino, Giuseppe Palmeri, Leonardo Crimi and the brothers Giuseppe and Serafino Mancuso. Supplied with heroin by the Corsicans Antoine Cordoliani (a former collaborator of François Spirito) and Joseph Césari, half-brother of Dominique Albertini, the Salemi Mafia shipped the drugs to a Toronto organization in double-bottomed suitcases transported by Italian immigrants, often without their knowledge.

Freed on bail in the summer of 1961, Alberto Agueci was assassinated in November of that year for threatening Magaddino, who had neglected to help him after his arrest. His horribly mutilated and charred body was found November 23, 1961, beside a highway near Rochester, N.Y. His brother and Papalia were sentenced to 15 years and ten years in penitentiary, respectively, in March 1963. On his release from prison, Papalia took over leadership of the Ontario Mafia with his associates in the Cotroni organization in Montreal.

Note, finally, that when Alberto Agueci immigrated to Canada in 1950, after having been rejected by the United States, he had a letter of recommendation to a Windsor travel agent signed by none other than Rosario Mancino. A short time later, he became co-owner of the *Queen* bakery in Toronto, in partnership with Benedetto Zizzo, brother of the Salemi Mafia boss whose name would surface in the 1970s.

Alberto Agueci   *Jean Jehan*

Johnny Papalia

activities. Rivard had become even more prudent and discreet. At the end of the summer and during autumn, 1960, it was learned, among other things, that he was supplying one of Pep Cotroni's former couriers who had gone into heroin distribution in the Vancouver market. Rivard was also suspected of supplying certain Toronto traffickers through accomplices in Montreal. At the end of January 1961 he went to Florida where he was joined by three friends, Gilles Brochu, Richard Foley and Georges Griffith, who were interested in auto racing. On their return to Quebec a month later, these three men were stopped by Customs officers at Blackpool, but a search of their car revealed nothing and they categorically denied any part in the heroin traffic. Rivard came back to Montreal at the end of March.

In October the RCMP learned that he had gone into legitimate business. With Gerry Turenne, he had bought a large summer resort centre at Auteuil, a small town about 15 miles northeast of Montreal. Registered under the name of Domaine Ideal, the centre included a marina, dance hall, swimming pool, restaurant, bar, cottages and a beach, and was valued at more than $200,000. Rivard managed the place, and supervised restorations. An able and tireless handyman, he spent hours repairing and improving the property. Agents charged with keeping an eye on him reported that he was spending most of his time on his new business and had apparently abandoned the drug trade. Information coming from the underworld confirmed these observations. Rivard was said to have retired and withdrawn from the heroin traffic.

But Narcotics Squad agents remained skeptical. And with reason, for at the very moment Rivard seemed to be losing interest in narcotics, two broad investigations were beginning in Montreal and New York. In both of them, Rivard would be among the suspects.

First, New York: late on the night of October 7, 1961, two police detectives from the city's narcotics section noted a tablefull of gangsters in an elegant Manhattan cabaret seated around a man of about 30 who had all the appearances of a mob leader of the prohibition era. Intrigued by the lordly airs of this individual who was receiving salutations from a series of persons of hang-dog countenance, the detectives decided to follow him when he left the club. In the next two hours the man's automobile stopped successively on Mott Street in the heart of Little Italy, fiefdom of the Mafia, then on Hester Street, Canal Street and Delancey Street. At each stop the detectives noted the same procedure: when the man got out of his car, another person came out of the shadows of a doorway to talk with him for a few minutes, then the man returned to his car and went on his unhurried way. The woman who was with him, a pretty blonde, remained in the car at each stop.

Towards 5 a.m. the mysterious stranger stopped on Meker Avenue in Brooklyn where the couple changed cars and left again. A few minutes later the car stopped and the couple went into *Barbara's Snack Bar*, just in front of St. Catherine's Hospital. The two detectives watched patiently until mid-afternoon when their man, apparently the operator of the snack bar, came out with the blonde. The couple were followed to 67th Street and Second Avenue where they entered building No. 1124.

The next morning, after a few hours of rest, the two detectives were back on the job. A check with the Bureau of Narcotics had quickly given them the information they were looking for. The mysterious snack bar operator with his pockets full of money was indeed an underworld figure. He was Pasquale Fuca, called Patsy, suspected of participating in the armed robbery at *Tiffany's* on Fifth Avenue. He was known to have carried out the assassination for the Mafia, in December 1958, of Joseph De Marco, a drug trafficker and member of the Lucchese family. More important still, Fuca's file noted that he was a nephew of the powerful Angelo (Little Angie) Tuminaro, one of Pep Cotroni's best customers and a leading narcotics chief in America. Tuminaro, who had been indicted with Cotroni, Carmine Galente, Big John Ormento and the others, was still being sought in connection with those cases. The two New York detectives were fired with enthusiasm. They were sure that by keeping a close watch on Fuca they might find the trail which would lead them to the fugitive.

With the help of the federal Bureau of Narcotics agents, the city detectives began constant surveillance of the movements of Patsy Fuca and his wife Barbara, the pretty blonde. They soon had information about the Fuca family. Barbara's father was an old gangster who had made his name in prohibition days by attacking convoys of bootleg liquor. He had since retired and worked occasionally at his son-in-law's snack bar. It was his old Dodge that Patsy used from time to time. Tony, Patsy's brother, who also worked at the snack bar, was a former sailor who had knocked about in the merchant marine. He had useful contacts all over the place. Their father, Giuseppe, had been known to police since his youth, when he took part in an impressive series of holdups. The only regular friends of Patsy and Barbara were a docker named Nick Travato and his wife. Police followed Travato several times after he had picked up Patsy for a little tour of Brooklyn, dropping in to several bars on quick visits.

At this period, Bureau of Narcotics informers were saying that a panic situation was arising again in the drug world. Heroin stocks were decreasing alarmingly and an important consignment of stuff was anxiously awaited from moment to moment. The police doubled their vigilance, sure that if the merchandise arrived safely, Patsy Fuca would most certainly be in on the deal.

In their attempt to get closer to Fuca, the investigators began to frequent *Barbara's* snack bar and soon became regular customers. On a Sunday in early November, as they were having coffee there, they saw two heroin distributors from Harlem meet Patsy in the back room to hand over an unknown amount of money. This was the first visit which linked Patsy to the heroin traffic; he was a wholesaler for drug distributors. Hopes of using him to get to Tuminaro increased.

On November 18, late in the evening, the agents were at their posts when a blue Buick stopped in front of *Barbara's* and sounded its horn. Patsy came out shortly afterwards and joined the two unknown men inside the car. The Buick drove off, eventually arriving at 245 - 7th Street, the home of Fuca's parents. The trio went into the apartment, emerging 20 minutes later. This time the agents recognized Patsy's companions—Barbara wearing a new wig and a red-haired girlfriend who had often been seen with her. The blue Buick took off again, heading on to East Broadway where it suddenly stopped. Fuca got out and quickly walked away. Without hesitation, one of the agents also got out to follow the trafficker. But Fuca walked only a short distance before he got into a big, beige Buick Invicta with foreign licence plates, which was parked at the sidewalk. In no time Patsy took off, made a U-turn and headed full speed along East Broadway Avenue, followed closely by his wife and the red-head in the blue Buick. An infernal chase began. At a certain point, as had to be expected, the pursuing agents lost the beige Buick. Sure that the mafioso had abandoned the vehicle somewhere along the route, two detectives began a search for the big car and found it a few minutes later. As predicted, Fuca had deserted the car and re-joined the two women. The agents noted the licence number: 45-477; the plates were from the province of Quebec.

The New York and Bureau of Narcotics agents decided to mount a discreet watch in the area to see if any mafiosi-type gangsters would come to get the mysterious vehicle which was perhaps loaded with heroin. In the middle of the night, a car came out of the shadows and stopped near the Buick. Four men got out, surrounded the de luxe vehicle and tried to open its doors. The police immediately rushed from their hiding places and arrested them. But the suspects were not the expected traffickers; merely hoodlums hoping to steal the expensive car. In view of this, the agents decided it would be useless to continue the surveillance. Instead they began to search the Buick. But the car contained nothing of interest. Discouraged and worn out with fatigue they decided to get some sleep and send some other colleagues to watch the car. They quickly regretted that decision. They had hardly reached home when their relief agents called to announce that the beige Buick had disappeared.

When the agents returned to their offices a few hours later, however, some good news renewed their hope. The RCMP Narcotics Squad in Montreal had been contacted and had checked the registration of the car. It belonged to the Marseillais Marius Martin, a former associate of Vic Cotroni in the *Faisan Doré*. Martin owned a small café, *La Cave*, on Saint-Alexander Street in the western part of Montreal. Two years earlier, the name of this club was mentioned shortly after Pep Cotroni's arrest when the RCMP received information that one of its regular customers, a certain "François," had been the heroin supplier to the Montreal mafioso. In their investigation of the bar, the RCMP learned that Marius Martin was not alone in the enterprise: he had two partners. The first was a former European champion of catch-wrestling, Roger (The Wrestler) Mollet, who was married to the French singer Michèle Sandry, a former star at the *Faisan Doré*. The files of the French national police showed that he had accidentally killed a man in 1943 in a street fight. The second partner had long been known by the name of Auguste Calmes, but lately he had been identified as the famous Jean Jehan, alias Auguste, alias Steve Martin. It was recalled that in late 1955 the RCMP had been warned that this person, a former partner of Jean David in the François Spirito-Antoine d'Agostino gang, was in Montreal directing a heroin trafficking group working out of Le Havre, France. Intensive police searches, however, had failed to locate Jehan.

All these details convinced the U.S. police officers that the presence of Marius Martin's automobile in the streets of New York had something to do with the drug traffic. This was confirmed by underworld informers only a few hours later who reported that an important shipment of heroin had arrived on the market within the past 24 hours. The next day the informers added that the panic caused by shortage had subsided and drugs were beginning to flow abundantly. The Buick had done its work well.

Even a large shipment of heroin, however, is quickly exhausted, especially in New York. At the beginning of December new information was coming in. The wholesalers were short of stock and were having trouble renewing their supplies. There were rumors that a new shipment, even larger than the one in November, was about to arrive. On December 16, two agents sitting in *Barbara's* overheard part of a conversation between Patsy Fuca and a stranger:

"Uncle Harry wants you to make a new order for cigarettes."

"When do they arrive?" asked Patsy.

" . . . next week."

"O.K., tell him I'll be ready."

This new clue was extremely significant for experienced investigators. Added to it, a week later, were further reports of shortages with drastic effects on New York addicts. The Bureau of Narcotics even wondered if the shortages were being deliberately provoked by the Mafia to bring about price increases.

Nothing much happened until the beginning of January when informers began talking of the imminent arrival of 50 kilos (110 pounds) of good quality heroin. Already detectives had noted unusual activity at *Barbara's;* notorious dealers had been coming in to give Fuca bundles of money. On the afternoon of January 9, another scrap of conversation was overheard. This time Patsy told someone on the telephone:

"O.K., I'll see you then."

Patsy hung up the phone and said to his father-in-law:

"Come in early tomorrow, papa, I'll be away all day."

Convinced that the big move would be made soon, the Bureau of Narcotics and New York police decided to stake everything. Two hundred municipal investigators and 100 federal agents were mobilized for the operation. Fifty unmarked radio cars were put at the disposal of this small army which was prepared for every eventuality.

On Wednesday, January 10, the team watching Fuca followed him to the *Roosevelt Hotel* where he met an elegant and aristocratic individual of about 60 years of age. After the usual greetings, Patsy and the stranger went out onto the sidewalk and had an animated conversation. Then they got into Fuca's blue Buick and drove four blocks to the *Edison Hotel.* The stranger got out and entered the hotel and Fuca drove away. The distinguished-looking man, followed by a detective, did not remain in the *Edison*. He walked through the lobby, out the door on another street, and then to the *Victoria Hotel* where he met another stranger, smaller and younger than himself. The two men exchanged a few words, left the hotel and went to a small restaurant nearby. They stayed there for the rest of the afternoon and then each returned to his hotel, the older to the *Edison*, the other to the *Victoria*.

As soon as the two men reached their rooms, the police agents quickly checked the hotel registries. The occupant of room 909 at the *Edison Hotel* was none other than Jean Jehan. He had registered under his real name and given his address in Montreal as 6085–21st Avenue, apartment 7, Rosemont. His companion who was in room 1128 of the *Victoria Hotel* had registered as François Barbier from Paris. This was an assumed name. His real identity was learned later: François Scaglia, 34, of Corsican origin, owner of a hang-out for traffickers, *Les Trois Canards* bar on La Rochefoucauld Street in Paris, and kidnapper of several wealthy persons since 1956. One of his kidnap victims had been Eugène Messina, of London, no doubt the most famous procurer on the European continent. In the French underworld, Scaglia was also renowned for the numerous gangland killings he had been assigned and for his vigor in carrying out various tasks in the white-slave trade.

Jean Jehan's presence in New York and his meetings with Fuca and Scaglia were of great significance. They indicated without a doubt that a large heroin transaction was about to be made. Officers in charge of the police operation were convinced of this and urged their men to even greater vigilance, for Fuca and the Frenchmen must not be lost from sight. In downtown New York, however, that is easier said than done. In the nights and days to come, the agents quickly realized this as they followed the many movements of the three traffickers and of a fourth who had joined them on the second day, another foreigner believed to be French. This one had registered at the *Hotel de l'Abbaye* under the name of J. Mouren, giving a Montreal address of 3585 Saint-Zotique Street.

For the first two days the agents managed quite well in the task of keeping the four suspects in sight and observing their meetings. Things turned sour on the third day Saturday, January 13, when they lost track of Scaglia and Mouren early in the morning. Then, late that afternoon, Jean Jehan also succeeded in losing his pursuers after he had spotted one of them in the subway. The police agents attempted to pick up the trail again but without success. The suspects did not return to their hotel rooms. The following day all three sent postal orders to pay their hotel bills, along with messages that they would not be coming back and requests that their baggage be held in storage for them.

The discouraged police could not know what was happening. They wondered if the transaction had already taken place, in whole or in part; if it had been cancelled, or merely postponed to a later date. All these possibilities were real. The only remaining hope of learning more was Patsy Fuca. He must be watched constantly. The Frenchmen might renew contact with him, especially if they hadn't been paid, or he might lead them to other New York traffickers, perhaps even his uncle Tuminaro.

Patsy spent most of Sunday at his snack bar. The agents covering him noted nothing of interest. That evening, however, the operator of the listening device which had been installed in the restaurant overheard a startling call. A man who could be Jehan telephoned Patsy and told him of his anxiety about the police actions. Skilfully, Fuca managed to calm his caller's fears and the two agreed that negotiations would continue. No more was needed to revive the ardor of the investigators.

Monday brought nothing new, except that Nick Travato came to get Patsy in the evening and took him for a car ride. It was the first time Fuca had left Brooklyn in three days. The following morning, Patsy went to an East End Avenue garage belonging to Sol Feinberg who was suspected of being involved in narcotics traffic. Agents set up an observation post across the street and watched the garage all day. They had been there 12 hours when, to their astonishment, Patsy arrived at the garage and then left for home after a few minutes. The agents only then realized that their quarry had spent the entire day somewhere else, free from the probing eyes of the police.

On Wednesday, Patsy came out of his home about 8:30 a.m., did a little shopping, and went to his snack bar where he worked until early afternoon. About 2 p.m. he came out and drove to another garage, this one on East Broadway in the Bronx. Suddenly the detectives remembered: it was here, in front of *Anthony's Garage,* that Fuca had picked up Marius Martin's Buick in November. This garage obviously played a role in the trafficker's activities. But Fuca did not give them much time to think about it. He came out of the garage after 20 minutes and returned to *Barbara's.* His brother Tony was waiting for him and the two drove off together. A few minutes later the police pursuit ended abruptly as the Fuca car was lost in traffic.

Over the next few hours, the police tailing teams cruised around the areas usually frequented by Patsy hoping to recover his trail. A little before 9 p.m., on a hunch, detectives decided to pay a visit to *Anthony's Garage*. It was a good hunch: Nick Travato's Cadillac was parked in front of the place. As the agents parked their own car nearby, they saw another car coming past them carrying Patsy and two other men. They tried to hide, but too late. The gangsters had seen them. The subsequent chase didn't last long. Once again Fuca managed to get away.

This was a serious development. Now that Fuca knew he was being followed he would probably increase his precautions. He might even decide to cut back his activities and stay out of sight for a while. At operations headquarters the agents were imagining the worst but at the end of the evening a telephone call renewed their confidence. An informer had chanced upon a friend of Patsy's in a bar who was joking about how unlucky the police were. More important, the friend had mentioned that Patsy and the others were going to make the deal the next morning at 9 o'clock.

At 8:30 a.m., Thursday, January 18, all the policemen were at their posts. Fifteen minutes later Patsy left home and headed for the East End Avenue garage. As police agents approached the garage they could hardly believe their eyes: two of the Frenchmen, Scaglia and Mouren were already there, pacing back and forth in front of the building. When they saw Fuca, Mouren went into the garage and came out almost immediately with a blue suitcase, identical to the one Jean Jehan had been carrying a few days earlier when he met Fuca. The two Frenchmen wasted no time getting into Patsy's automobile and the group drove quickly away. A few streets further on, the trafficker's car stopped again and a fourth person got in: it was Jehan!

The next few minutes were dramatic. Because of technical difficulties in radio communications, one police surveillance team, comprising two officers, found itself all alone to follow the traffickers' car. And Fuca's passengers were getting out one by one and going their separate ways. Jehan was the last to leave Fuca. He carried a black satchel, no doubt containing money from the Mafia, similar to one seen under Patsy's arm two days earlier. With Jehan's departure, there was only one thing the police team could do: follow Fuca, for the blue suitcase, probably full of heroin, was still in his possession.

Although cut off from other teams, the two agents managed to keep their man in sight. They were considering moving in to arrest him when suddenly the radio system miraculously began to function again, calling for help for two colleagues who said they had arrested two of the suspects. Reluctantly abandoning Fuca, the two officers joined their colleagues who were holding Scaglia and a stranger who was quickly identified as Jacques Angelvin, a popular performer in French television. A few moments earlier, the two men had left the East End Avenue garage in a black Buick with French licence plates, identical to Marius Martin's car. They were on their way to Montreal when police stopped them.

The search of the vehicle produced nothing, but the two men were nevertheless taken to a police station. In the meantime, the search for Fuca was resumed, but without much hope. Luck was with the police this time. A few minutes later the mafioso was spotted in front of one his favorite bars as he was leaving the place to go, first to his home, and then with his wife to his parents' home. By shortly after noon, police agents had been posted around Giuseppe Fuca's home. Twenty minutes later they saw Patsy come out of the house and take the blue suitcase from the car. This was it, the time to move. The agents burst into the house just as Patsy and his father finished hiding the heroin in a hole in the basement ceiling. There were 11 kilos, (24 pounds) of heroin, along with an arsenal of arms and ammunition.

At the end of the day, police officers summed up: Patsy Fuca, his wife, his brother Tony, his father and Nick Travato were under lock and key; Jean Jehan and Mouren had escaped with the money; no substantial accusations could yet be made against Scaglia; even fewer against Angelvin; Tuminaro still could not be found. As for

Principle figures in the "French Connection" from left to right: Pasquale Fuca, Jacques Angelvin, Anthony Fuca, François Scaglia.

the drug, it was an important amount, but far from the 50 kilos informers had talked about. Furthermore, it was still not known how it had been brought into the country. Another search of Angelvin's Buick produced no results.

On Monday, January 22, after a weekend's rest, one of the investigators immersed himself in a study of the papers found in Angelvin's hotel room. Among the documents he noticed some correspondence with the *United State Lines* company concerning the transport of the black Buick. On arrival in New York, the car and baggage weighed 2,343 kilos. But for the return trip, the television star had sent a note to the company advising that he had made an error in calculating the total weight of the car and his personal baggage. In fact, the total should be only 2,287 kilos, in other words 56 kilos less than he had calculated in the beginning. Why the difference?

The police officer could see only one explanation. Did not those 56 kilos represent approximately the amount of heroin the informers had talked about? There was only one way to check: the Buick would have to be taken apart. With the help of mechanics from General Motors, the dismantling operation gave the expected results: a series of cavities had been constructed under the chassis of the de luxe vehicle large enough to contain 56 kilos of heroin in one-pound packages. Laboratory examination of the dust found in the cavities confirmed the discovery. Shortly afterwards, the owner of *Anthony's Garage,* Tony Feola, admitted that Patsy Fuca had used his garage several times to recover stocks of heroin hidden in cars. He also confirmed that Marius Martin's beige Buick had been used to transport about 20 kilos (44 pounds) of pure heroin hidden in secret compartments built into the chassis. In each case, Feola had been responsible for restoring the cars to good condition.

The discovery of how the drugs had been transported did not end the affair. Only 11 kilos had been seized. More than 40 kilos, likely to turn up at any moment in the hands of street sellers, were still not accounted for. How could this stock be recovered, if it were not already too late to do so? Investigators recalled a telephone conversation between Patsy and his Uncle Harry. The night before the arrests, the uncle (suspected of being Tuminaro himself) advised his nephew to "wear only one suit at a time and leave the others in the closet." Perhaps these other "suits" were really the missing heroin. The first suit would be a designation for the heroin already seized at the Fuca home. It was now a question of finding the closet . . .

Convinced that the theory was worth testing, detectives from the

Bureau of Narcotics and the New York police decided to make a thorough search of the building in which Tony Fuca lived, the only one which had not yet been searched. On January 29, after an hour-long, intensive search, they finally found what they were looking for: in the basement, an old sea chest contained two suitcases; each suitcase contained 22 kilos of pure heroin, worth in total close to $50 million on the black market. (3)

With the 11 kilos already seized, this became the largest seizure of heroin ever made in America. It was more than double the catch on the *Saint-Malo*.

The drugs were not removed immediately however. They were left in place to facilitate the arrest of those who might come to get it. On the evening of February 24, Tony Fuca, recently released on bail, made the attempt . . . and was caught red-handed.

In Montreal, ever since the first seizure of the 11 kilos, the RCMP had been trying to collar Jean Jehan and J. Mouren. At 3585 Saint-Zotique Street there was no trace of Mouren. Furthermore, no one of that name had lived there, which was no great surprise to police. No trafficker of that name, in fact, appeared in any of the huge dossiers kept by the RCMP, the U.S. Bureau of Narcotics, the French central office for narcotics, or Interpol. For weeks Montreal detectives tried without success to track the suspect. They finally concluded that J. Mouren was an alias used by one of the partners in the café *La Cave*. This mystery, however, would never be definitely solved.

In the case of J an Jehan, the investigation showed that he had moved in at 6805—21st Avenue in Rosemont in April 1960. On January 28, 1962, ten days after the arrest of his accomplices, he notified his landlord that he would not be renewing his lease in May as he was going back to France. Witnesses saw him leaving his lodgings that day with a small satchel. He never came back. In the following week, RCMP agents saw Marius Martin several times, driving Jehan's car, a 1960 Monarch. Then the automobile disappeared from circulation. A month later Martin made a

---

3.   Ironically, Salvatore (Lucky) Luciano died in Naples that same day. Aged 65, he suffered a heart attack at Capodichino airport as he welcomed a Hollywood producer who intended to make a movie of his life. When the news came over the teletype machine in the Bureau of Narcotics hardly 30 minutes after Luciano's death, Commissioner Henry L. Giordano revealed that his men, in cooperation with Italian authorities, had been on the point of arresting the powerful mafioso for having introduced $150 million worth of heroin to American territory over the previous ten years.

complaint to police that his beige Buick had been stolen. He claimed to have left it in the parking lot of a Sherbrooke Street shopping centre. The vehicle was never found, which prevented the RCMP from establishing whether or not it was equipped with secret compartments like Angelvin's Buick.

On February 15, Martin went to Jehan's apartment twice to get some of his friend's personal belongings. Subsequent research showed that while Jehan was in Montreal he directed a fish importing business with the head office in Nimes, France, under the trade name *La Brandade de morue authentique.* In June 1961 he had received 20 cases of "fish," each one weighing 45 pounds. Was this one of his methods of importing heroin? The Narcotics Squad thought so.

At the end of August 1962 a new element was added to the dossier. Checks by the Quebec Vehicles Bureau confirmed certain information that Jehan's Monarch had become the property of Lucien Rivard. This was an important discovery for the RCMP. While it established that a new link had been made between the Montrealer and the French traffickers, it also indicated that rumors of Rivard's retirement from the narcotics racket were not necessarily true. Three years later, further information confirmed the Rivard-Jehan association. It was then learned that Rivard had met Jehan in Montreal in 1955 when Jehan and Jean Venturi were the permanent representatives for the d'Agostino ring. Pep Cotroni was believed to have introduced Rivard to Jehan, who in turn introduced Rivard to Jean-Baptiste Croce and Paul Mondolini. After the arrest of Patsy Fuca and his accomplices, Marius Martin is said to have contacted Rivard for help in getting Jehan and Venturi out of America. The story was that for $500 Rivard obtained false passports through Armand Duhamel who, it will be recalled, was among those who helped Antoine d'Agostino flee the United States in January 1950. After the departure of Jehan and Venturi, Marius introduced Rivard to their successor, former owner of the French restaurant *Le 400* and of a brothel at 312 Ontario Street East. This man had been involved in international drug traffic for 20 years, yet his name would not come out until 1965 when it was learned that, like Rivard, he had links with Salvatore Giglio on behalf of the Jehan-Venturi gang.

In New York, the Fuca affair ended with the conviction of all the suspects and heavy prison terms. In early summer, 1962, Angelo Tuminaro gave himself up to police. Some sources suggested that his failures had particularly displeased his associates in the Lucchese family who had large investments in the heroin trade. In any case, that did not prevent his younger brother Frank from succeeding him, though with no greater success. In February 1965 Frank, in turn, was arrested by Bureau of Narcotics agents along with 17 other traffickers.

As for Jean Jehan, he was finally located and arrested in Paris in May 1967. But because of his advanced age, French authorities rejected the extradition request made by the U.S. Bureau of Narcotics.

A year later, in April 1968, the whole affair was recreated by the pen of an American writer, Robin Moore, in a book called *The French Connection*. (4) The book was so successful it was made into a heavily fictionalized film which won an Academy Award for best film of the year in 1971.

A few years later, however, this great police victory was unfortunately compromised. In December 1972 all the heroin seized ten years earlier disappeared from the vaults of the New York police.

Following long and embarrassing inquiries, former agents of the narcotics section were held responsible for this crime, which put 300 pounds of heroin and cocaine back into circulation. Some of the drugs stolen from police property lockers had been replaced by packages of flour to delay detection of the theft.

4. *The French Connection,* Robin Moore, New York, Little, Brown & Company, 1969.

Chapter 8

The Return of Agent Biase

The second widespread investigation bringing Lucien Rivard's name to the surface began in Montreal in mid-summer of 1961. At that time informers advised the Narcotics Squad that Vincent Pacelli and Michel (Biff) Rinucci, two Lucchese family traffickers associated with Big John Ormento, had been doing business for some time with a Montreal gang led by a certain "Paul." This man, according to the information, was on good terms with Bill Lamy and Blackie Bisson, two of Rivard's principle acolytes, as we have already seen.

That was all Narcotics Squad detectives needed to identify the man in question. It was Jean-Paul Tremblay, 47, a notorious trafficker at the national level, who had recently been seen with Bisson and Lamy at the *Café Rialto* (1) on St. Lawrence Street. For the past ten years Tremblay, a good friend of Rivard, had been in Toronto looking after various rackets, including distribution of heroin. (2) In 1949 he had been arrested for drug possession and sentenced to nine months in prison. He had often provided bail for persons charged with trafficking or possession of narcotics. In early 1959 he had been questioned in connection with the murder of the one-time lover of his girlfriend Della Burns, alias Della Stonehouse, also known as a dealer in drugs. The victim, Lorne Gibson, an addict who had just got out of prison, accused the young woman of having denounced him to police. To avenge this insult, apparently, Gibson was lured into an alley and shot three times in the back.

For lack of evidence, Tremblay was released after being questioned about the murder. He left Toronto and settled in

---

1. A downtown cabaret of low repute.
2. Jean-Paul Tremblay should not be confused with Bob Tremblay, another Rivard friend who, as mentioned in an earlier chapter, was arrested in Vancouver in 1955.

Montreal where he bought a night club, the *Zanzibar,* on Christophe-Colomb Street near St. Catherine Street. In July 1960 he returned to Toronto to establish contacts for his new operation, the interprovincial traffic in heroin, and from then on was a frequent visitor to the Ontario capital. He had also launched a move to supply the west coast, but his emissary, Clovis Chapdelaine, was arrested in Vancouver the day he made his first delivery. (3)

On July 3, 1961, soon after they had received the information about Tremblay, RCMP officers were advised by the U.S. Bureau of Narcotics that members of the Pacelli-Rinucci gang planned a visit to Montreal that very day. They would be using an old Chevrolet with New York licence plates and would probably stay at the *LaSalle Hotel.* The U.S. agents added that the New York traffickers had made a telephone call to a Montreal number, UN 6-2137.

A quick check revealed that this number was listed to R. Laurier, 1274 Saint-Dominique Street, an employee of the *Café Rialto.* Observations at the Saint-Dominique Street apartment enabled police to establish, from the licence plates on the station-wagon parked outside, that R. Laurier was really Roger Laviolette, 44, Jean-Paul Tremblay's trusted aide. That confirmed the information received by the Narcotics Squad, two days before the call from the Bureau of Narcotics, that some Americans would soon be coming to Montreal to meet Jean-Paul Tremblay.

The following morning, July 4, as four Bureau of Narcotics agents arrived at Dorval airport to help Montreal officers with the investigation, a Narcotics Squad surveillance team spotted a blue, 1953 Chevrolet with New York plates, in the *LaSalle Hotel* parking lot. The automobile was registered in the name of Rocco Sparage, 441 East 117th Street in New York. It appeared to be the car the U.S. agents had described. The officers kept it under observation all day.

Late in the evening, they watched as an Italo-American of about 30 got into the car. He headed north, followed by police. His movements through city streets seemed strange until the agents noticed that he was following a Ford Thunderbird with Ontario licence plates, driven by none other than Jean-Paul Tremblay. The Thunderbird belonged to Della Burns. The two suspects drove around in Indian file until they reached the corner of Second Avenue and Laurier Street. There the American parked his car and

---

3. Chapdelaine served a couple of years in prison for this offense. In September 1969 he was arrested again for trafficking in heroin at Terrace, B.C., and this time was sentenced to ten years in penitentiary.

got in with Tremblay who then headed back towards the centre of town. Intrigued, the police officers divided the assignment. One team followed the trail of the two men in the car, which led them back to the *LaSalle Hotel,* where the stranger got out, and then to Tremblay's home where the Montrealer stayed for the rest of the night.

Another team of agents, meanwhile, was lying in wait not far from the Chevrolet. About 1:30 a.m. Roger Laviolette's station-wagon arrived carrying two men who were impossible to identify in the darkness. The station-wagon stopped beside the Chevrolet. One of the two men got into the Chev and drove off with a roar, followed at breakneck speed by the station-wagon. The federal agents tried to follow in their car but had to give up the chase when the two vehicles separated and went in opposite directions. They found Laviolette's station-wagon around 6 a.m., near Tremblay's home on Basile-Patenaude Street. But they could not locate the old Chev, or the Italo-American who had driven it and who had registered at the *LaSalle Hotel* under the name of T. Controne.

After this busy night, during which Tremblay and his pals had probably succeeded in making a new delivery of drugs, police had to wait a month for any further development. On the afternoon of August 1, the Bureau of Narcotics advised the Narcotics Squad of informers' reports that Tremblay would be delivering a supply of heroin to the Pacelli organization somewhere in the state of New York within the next 12 hours. That was enough reason to mobilize 30 or so federal agents to watch border points, bridges and places likely to be visited by Tremblay and his men. Patrols searched the city for any trace of the Tremblay gang, but without success. No one had seen him or his men all day.

About 3:30 a.m. the following day, after a watch of more than 12 hours, agents at the Blackpool border point noticed Tremblay entering Canada from the U.S. at the wheel of his Thunderbird. He seemed to be following another car, a red and white Pontiac driven by an unknown man. The agents discreetly followed both cars to Monteal. Once in the city, the tailing became more complicated. The agents had to use all their skill to avoid being seen and to avoid losing their quarry. The traffickers appeared to be suspicious. Several times they ran red lights and made U-turns at wild speeds. But in spite of these efforts, the police agents never lost sight of them.

After a half-hour's frantic chase through city streets, they arrived on Basile-Patenaude Street, near Tremblay's home. Tremblay got out of his car and went towards his house. The unknown man remained in his automobile and began stuffing something into a large paper bag. The police decided it was time to move in.

They accosted the two men and discovered that the driver of the Pontiac was Maurice Laviolette, brother of Roger. His paper bag contained $30,000 in U.S. currency, about enough to buy four kilos of pure heroin at $7,000 each.

The search of the cars turned up nothing, as might have been expected. The merchandise had already been delivered. The search of Tremblay's home, however, produced some worthwhile clues. Agents found his passport, issued the previous May 17 in the name of Georges Arnauld Tremblay. Examination of the passport, and checks with airline companies, showed that Tremblay had been to France three times since May: the first time he left on May 21, returning a week later; at the beginning of June he went to France again, coming back on June 12; on that day he stayed in Montreal only a few hours returning almost immediately to Paris where he remained until July 1.

These discoveries naturally led the investigators to wonder if the Laviolette brothers had not also treated themselves to a bit of European touring during the same period. The agents soon learned that Maurice had left Montreal on June 20 on an Air France flight and eight days later boarded the *R.M.S. Ivernia* at Le Havre which arrived at Quebec City on July 4. As for Roger, he had flown to Paris on July 7 and had returned to Quebec on the 25th of that month on board the *R.M.S. Ivernia,* just as his brother had earlier, which left Le Havre on July 19. It was later learned that he had been accompanied on his trip by the sister of another Montreal gangster, Gérard Généreux, who lived on Second Avenue in the Rosemont district. Généreux was not unknown to federal agents: it was almost in front of his home where, on July 4, Controne the New Yorker had abandoned the old Chev which had been picked up later by the men who arrived in Roger Laviolette's station-wagon.

All these visits to France by Tremblay and the Laviolettes were, by all indications, shopping trips for heroin. But who were the sellers? To find out, the RCMP sent a summary of the investigation to the French national police and asked the force to be on the watch. One member or other of the gang, no doubt, would soon be making another trip to France for further supplies. In a letter of September 1 to the director of the French judiciary police and the secretary general of Interpol, the RCMP emphasized the friendship between Lucien Rivard and Jean-Paul Tremblay and suggested that Rivard had probably been instrumental in Tremblay's success in obtaining a heroin supplier in France.

Meanwhile the investigation continued. On August 29, the U.S. Bureau of Narcotics learned that Tremblay was to come to New York two days later to work out terms of certain agreements with the Pacelli group. On September 1 the RCMP in turn learned that Tremblay had arrived in New York the night before and had promised to deliver a new shipment of heroin on Wednesday, September 6. Basing themselves on the method used so far by the Tremblay organization for bringing in drugs, Narcotics Squad detectives checked the schedule for ship arrivals in the near future. They noticed that the *R.M.S. Ivernia* was due to dock at Quebec City on September 5. Arrangements were immediately made for the search of all disembarking passengers and for the observation of members of the Tremblay gang who might be meeting a courier from the ship.

At 2 p.m. on September 5 the ship arrived at Quebec City and 50 of the 950 passengers disembarked. No drugs were found on any of them and no trafficker was seen in the vicinity. At 6 p.m. the *Ivernia* sailed for Montreal arriving at 7 o'clock the following morning. Again, police and Customs officers carried out careful inspections but with no better results. Neither Tremblay nor any of his henchmen came to meet anyone. Less than two hours after the ship's arrival, however, the U.S. Bureau of Narcotics advised the RCMP that Tremblay had notified his customers that the delivery would be made that day, at 5 p.m., at Lake George, N.Y. Believing that the drugs had been brought in by another route, the police authorities quickly established check points at bridges and border stations and at likely spots in Montreal.

By late afternoon, no trafficker had yet crossed the border. The police were worried. Had Tremblay once again managed to slip through the net? Reports from Lake George, however, indicated that no suspects had been spotted there. At 8 p.m. the RCMP received another message from the Bureau of Narcotics: Tremblay had just notified the Pacelli group that he would not be able to conclude the transaction that day because his cargo had not yet arrived. He expected to be able to deliver the merchandise about two weeks later.

Within a few minutes, another message was received at Narcotics Squad headquarters: Tremblay had been sighted in Montreal by a team of agents. That confirmed the information from the Bureau of Narcotics and for the time being there was no point in maintaining the bridge and border surveillance.

For the next three days there was nothing significant in the observed movements of Tremblay and his partners. But on Sunday,

September 10, the Bureau of Narcotics intercepted another call. Roger Laviolette telephoned a Pacelli friend to say that the delivery could be made on the following Friday. He or Tremblay would call to confirm the meeting place. The Narcotics Squad, informed of the traffickers' intentions, again checked shipping schedules and noted that another French liner, the *M.V. Saxonia,* had left Le Havre en route for Quebec.

When it arrived in the early afternoon of September 12, a "reception committee" awaited the 25 passengers who disembarked at Quebec City. No one was carrying any heroin, but on board, two agents spotted a French traveller who, in their opinion, could be the expected courier. Questioned by immigration officers, the 39-year-old man said he had made several trips to Montreal since July 1960 in order to deal with certain family problems. This time he had to go to Montreal again to meet a friend. The police officers were decidedly interested in this person and resolved to stay on his heels. The *Saxonia* arrived at Montreal about noon the following day and the suspect went directly to the *Taft Hotel.*

After renting a room, the man went out for a meal in the red light district then returned to his hotel and prepared for bed. The Narcotics Squad had taken the precaution of renting an adjacent room in order to observe his movements. At 11:30 p.m. the suspect left his room and went to the lobby, where he asked the manager to keep his money, an amount of $1,000, in the hotel safe. He then returned to his room and went to bed. The next morning, at 7:30, he left for the office of Air France where he reserved a seat on a flight to Paris that same night. He spent the rest of the day at the international airport.

Intrigued by the manner of this person and by the fact that he had met no one since his arrival, the investigators sent a colleague in to sit beside him. Almost immediately, the suspect began a conversation about his life and family problems. The monologue was convincing and after a few minutes, the police officer concluded that the man was suffering from nervous depression. But it could have been just a skilful pose. The surveillance was therefore maintained until his departure; then a request for information about him was made to the central office for narcotics in Paris.

Less than a week later the French police sent a reply to the Narcotics Squad. The solitary traveller was a farmer from Jura who had no connection with the underworld. His strange behaviour could be explained by serious family conflicts and his trips to Montreal had to do with offers to direct a large farming operation in Canada.

The RCMP investigators, in fact, had spent two days following a false trail. It was not a disastrous error though: the story from New York informers was that Tremblay had once again postponed delivery because he had not yet received his merchandise.

On September 22 this last information was confirmed by a discovery by Paris investigators. In their research into the previous voyages of the Montreal traffickers, the Paris detectives learned that Jean-Paul Tremblay and another Canadian named Anatole Ethier had stayed at the *Hotel Gare du Nord*. (4) The two men had arrived in Paris on September 16 and told the hotel manager they expected to be leaving on the 21st. In fact, they returned to Montreal on the 20th, and unfortunately the RCMP had not been alerted in time to give them a proper welcome. The two men had probably used the same tactic they had already used in Montreal — arriving at the airport just before flight time and counting on a usual number of cancellations in order to be able to buy tickets.

After this trip to France, Tremblay made another trip to New York on October 5. Alerted in time by the Narcotics Squad, agents of the U.S. Bureau of Narcotics covered several of his meetings with members of the Pacelli gang. In these discussions, Tremblay had appeared reluctant to continue doing business, mainly because of the RCMP intervention during the last transaction. He suspected that the police were on the trail of his clients. The talks lasted three days and at the end the Montrealer had agreed to resume the dealings as soon as his supply problems had been resolved.

Over the next few days, Tremblay's movements around Montreal convinced detectives who were following him that he was still active in the distribution of heroin to Canadian wholesalers. The investigators believed, however, that the quantities involved were not nearly as large as the sales to New York. In the agents' opinion, Tremblay's meetings with Canadian traffickers confirmed that he was in temporarily short supply of heroin.

During the week of October 16, the Narcotics Squad learned that a Frenchman had arrived in Montreal to meet Tremblay. The visitor's identity was unknown, but a brief description of him was available: he was said to be a man of about 50, perhaps more, over six feet tall, weighing at least 190 pounds, with greying hair, an elegant dresser who always wore dark glasses.

For several days the federal agents tried to establish the real

---

4. Anatole (Tony) Ethier had previously been seen by the RCMP during Tremblay's long stay in Toronto.

identity of this Frenchmen who was believed to be one of Tremblay's suppliers. Unfortunately, precautions taken by the traffickers made prolonged surveillance impossible. The gang usually met at the *Café Rialto* where an outsider would be quickly spotted. Movements by automobile placed an impossible burden on the agents. Often they had to abandon pursuit to avoid being spotted themselves. If the traffickers discovered they were being watched, months of investigative work would be wiped out.

Even so, additional information was coming to the investigators. It was learned, for example, that Tremblay and a woman named Hélène would soon be going to France at the invitation of the visitor. The date of the trip had not yet been set but it would probably be in November or during the Christmas period. In anticipation, the RCMP again called on the cooperation of the airlines. But the detectives, aware of Tremblay's habit of boarding at the last minute while employees were busy, assigned their own men the task of checking passenger lists for all overseas departures and arrivals.

Thus they learned that on November 13 a certain J. Tremblay, no address listed, had taken a flight for Paris three days earlier. There was no proof that this was indeed the Montreal trafficker, but two days later Jean-Paul Tremblay was identified among the passengers arriving from Paris. The search of his luggage produced nothing; nor did the police tail who followed him from the airport. Tremblay went directly home. But police were mindful of the trafficker's modus operandi in the past. The Narcotics Squad again checked sailing schedules from Le Havre: the *Ivernia,* which had been used by the Laviolette brothers before, was to dock in Quebec on November 26 on its last visit before winter.

In advance of the ship's arrival, a message was sent to the French central office for narcotics requesting a check on whether Jean-Paul Tremblay had been accompanied on his trip to Paris by an accomplice or an unknown person who might still be in France, ready to act as a courier on return to Canada. Paris authorities, however, were unable to produce any definite information on that score. Later, the search of passengers disembarking from the *Ivernia* was equally fruitless.

But the disappointment infecting Montreal investigators as a result of these setbacks was quickly dissipated. A few days later, confidential information established that the mysterious Frenchman who had come to visit Tremblay in October was none other than Roger Coudert, one of Lucien Rivard's old associates. Coudert had been arrested in New York in 1954 and sentenced to ten years in prison. He had been released from Atlanta penitentiary on September 21, 1960, and was immediately deported to France. His new association with Tremblay reinforced the theory that Lucien Rivard was no stranger to this international ring, especially in view of other information that Paul Mondolini, an associate of Coudert and Rivard, had also paid a visit to Montreal.

Over the next two months, the arduous surveillance of Tremblay's movements produced nothing of much importance. At the beginning of December, the trafficker was a victim of a burglary at his home in which he lost $13,000 in money and jewelry. Shortly after that he moved to a building on Fleury Street West, again locating in the north of the city. He met regularly with an old friend from Toronto, Bernard Vallée. He also hung out with Anatole Ethier, who had close links with another Toronto trafficker, Dominique (Nick the Greek) Baccari, who in turn had close links with Anatole's brother, Victor Ethier. The Narcotics Squad had learned through confidential sources that Tremblay was looking for two trustworthy men to take over daily delivery of 150 capsules of heroin to his friends in Toronto.

On the night of February 13, 1962, the officers in charge of the Tremblay investigation were awakened by members of the Montreal Police homicide squad. A call from Tremblay's new girlfriend had taken city detectives to the trafficker's home, where they found his lifeless and horribly mutilated body lying on the living room rug, under an overturned sofa. Blood stains throughout the place testified to a terrible struggle. All the drawers had been pulled out and searched.

The investigation established robbery as the motive for the murder. A gangster without class, Tremblay had the stupid habit of boasting about his financial success and flashing his money in the seedy clubs of The Main. He had been murdered by two pals he had been drinking with a few hours earlier. The two hoods killed him with a hammer, a club and a knife, and had then turned his rooms upside down looking for the loot from his last operation. They never did find the money. The police did, however, when they examined the basement ceiling of the two-story cottage. Officially, Tremblay had hidden $7,000 cash and two cheques for $1,000 each which he had endorsed. But according to certain reports, the hiding place had really contained several tens of thousands of additional dollars which were said to have been pocketed by unscrupulous detectives.

After Tremblay's death, Narcotics Squad agents concentrated on finding out as quickly as possible who would take over his

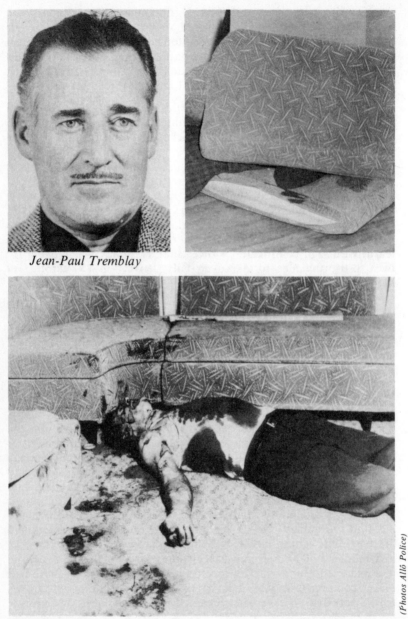

Jean-Paul Tremblay

(Photos Allô Police)

The mutilated body of the trafficker as he was found by police on the night of February 13, 1962.

operations — the Laviolette brothers, Anatole Ethier or Bernard Vallée. The answer came from New York on May 25. On that day informers had tipped the Bureau of Narcotics that George Farraco, the intermediary between Tremblay and the Pacelli gang, had telephoned Roger Laviolette who told him to be ready for a delivery in two weeks. Farraco was a talented crook who had been arrested for a great variety of offenses since 1939. In October 1953 he had been sentenced to ten years in prison for transporting supplies of heroin between New York and Detroit. In the federal penitentiary at Atlanta he had made friends with Roger Coudert who referred Farraco to his Montreal friends for heroin supplies when he got out of prison.

In the evening, six days after his phone call to Laviolette, Farraco left his home to go out and buy a newspaper. No one has seen him since. Underworld circles had come to suspect him of being in the pay of federal agents. He was blamed, among other things, for a number of raids that had been made on the homes of several Bronx traffickers.

In the week of June 11, for five evenings in a row, a white, French-speaking stranger of about 45, probably unaware of Farraco's disappearance, went to his door and asked to speak to him. These visits soon came to the ears of agents of the Bureau of Narcotics, who quickly confirmed that the stranger was Roger Laviolette. The police reasoned that if the Montrealer had come personally to New York to see Farraco he must be ready to make another deal. Why not give him a chance to do so?

On June 22, Patrick Biase, an undercover agent of the Bureau of Narcotics already very familiar with Montreal, telephoned Roger Laviolette and claimed to be Jack Farraco, the brother of George. (5) The trafficker reacted favorably to the call and invited Biase to come to see him a few days later.

On June 27, the Bureau of Narcotics agent arrived in Montreal and checked into the *Mount-Royal Hotel,* where George Farraco usually stayed. After a meeting with Narcotics Squad officers to plan details of the operation, he called Laviolette's hang-out, a garage on Papineau Avenue. The dealer wasn't there. His partner, Roger Lapierre, who was not then known to police, took the call and asked Biase to call back, which he did several times, without succeeding in reaching Laviolette.

---

5. Patrick Biase, it will be remembered, played an important undercover role in the Pep Cotroni affair. See Chapter Six.

The next day, after several more fruitless calls, Biase got angry:

"I'm fed up with the way Laviolette's acting," he told Lapierre on the phone. "How come he's not there yet? If he doesn't want to do business with me, let him say so."

"Listen Jack, I'm sorry, but you should be patient and wait for Roger."

"I've waited long enough. I'm going back to New York."

"Wait, I'm going to do something. Go to the airport bar at a quarter to nine tonight and I'll be there. We can have a little talk."

"Okay then, till tonight. So long."

At the agreed hour Biase met Lapierre in the *Caribou Lounge* at Dorval airport.

"My brother George had $75,000 on him when he disappeared," the undercover agent confided. "I'm convinced he was killed for the money. Anyway, I know he was doing business with Laviolette and I thought maybe he'd be interested in continuing with me. He never knew it, but I was always with my brother. He was out in front, but I was always right there behind him. The proof—I know that his "tires" are good and I also know that my brother knew an old Frenchman with the same first name as you. (6) If Laviolette wants to discuss with me, we could easily make a deal. He'll see that I'm O.K."

"Are you ready to do business right away?"

"Of course, what do you think I'm here for?"

"In that case I think everything will be okay with Laviolette. Anyway, call again in four days, at noon, he'll be there to answer."

That ended the conversation, and Lapierre escorted the American to his flight under the watchful eyes of Narcotics Squad agents.

The following week Biase called Laviolette as agreed. Laviolette told him that things were not too good in France and he'd have to wait a few weeks. Biase waited until August 20 to make the next contact and Biase then asked him to come to Montreal for a face-to-face talk. The following afternoon, after checking in with RCMP investigators, the undercover agent went to the Papineau Avenue garage for a first meeting with Jean-Paul Tremblay's successor. The

---

6. Biase's reference to the quality of the "tires" was really a reference to the quality of the heroin which the Tremblay-Laviolette gang often hid in the spare tires of their automobiles.

talk soon turned to Laviolette's ability to supply heroin in sufficient quantities.

"For the time being I have no stock," explained the trafficker. "My man in France has some problems and nobody in Montreal has any reserves. I can't supply anything at the moment but as soon as I get a new shipment, I guarantee that you'll be notified. In the meantime, would you be interested in buying some codeine? There was a robbery recently and less than two hours after I was asked if I wanted some." (7)

"Personally I'm not interested, but maybe one of my friends in New York would be. I'll talk to him and let you know."

"I could also get you some cocaine. A pal in Toronto has a connection. (8) He says the stuff comes from Argentina. I could call him, if you want."

---

7. On August 3, 1962, four masked bandits made off with 100 pounds of codeine from the *F.E. Cornell Co. Ltd.*, 370 Place Royale, in Montreal. The robbery was organized by a gangster named Maurice Cloutier (an associate of Lucien Rivard) who had gone into the drug traffic in early 1961. Cloutier first worked as a distributor in the Montreal market, and then attempted to supply certain Toronto wholesalers. But Tremblay's death and the arrest of several traffickers in the U.S. and Canada caused a considerable decline in business because of the difficulty of getting supplies. These difficulties were what caused Cloutier to organize a holdup at the *Cornell* pharmaceutical company, and Laviolette to postpone his transactions with the agent Biase.
    After the Cornell robbery, Cloutier and his henchmen distributed part of the codeine in capsules to Montreal addicts. But the effects of the drug were adverse: everyone who took it developed leg pains. Cloutier, hoping to correct this, tried to find another substance to mix with the codeine to make it acceptable to the addicts. Unfortunately, he never got the opportunity to test a new product. He was shot down on the street on October 28, 1962. The investigation revealed that his death was the result of a quarrel with another underworld figure, Pierre Ménard, manager of the *Hotel Moderne*. Ménard had stolen Cloutier's girlfriend along with the rooming house he had bought in her name. Cloutier had twice tried, unsuccessfully, to blow Ménard up with dynamite; he was the one who finally lost the contest.
    Ménard and a helper, Louis Côté, one of Conrad Bouchard's friends, were arrested for the murder but were released by the coroner for lack of evidence. On November 28, 1962, in a series of raids in Montreal, the RCMP counterfeit squad recovered most of the stolen codeine in a warehouse.

8. The Narcotics Squad investigation at the time of the murder of Jean-Paul Tremblay revealed that Roger "Le Français" (The Frenchman) Denizet, mentioned several times earlier in this book, had left Montreal to settle in Toronto. Denizet, who had been arrested in Vancouver in 1949, was known as an old friend of Antoine d'Agostino and Roger Coudert. After Pep Cotroni's arrest, he was seen at the café *La Cave,* the operations base for Lucien Rivard's friends, the traffickers Marius Martin and Jean Jehan. In August 1963 his name was found in Anatole Ethier's papers.

"Like I said, what I'm interested in is heroin. For the other stuff, I can always see what I can do in New York. But what I want is heroin and if necessary, I'll go and see Old Roger in France."

"Listen, you don't have to go to Paris. (9) I told you, as soon as I have the stuff, you'll be the first one to be notified. Roger has been having trouble with the police these days. Things aren't going too well there. But if you really want to go, what I could do is give you a letter of reference."

"Thanks but I haven't made up my mind yet. If I do go, though, I'll come and get your letter."

"You know, if Tremblay hadn't been killed, we would have had a stock of 100 kilos. Everything was ready. Roger was ready, but after that, he changed his mind. We've been waiting since then. Anyway, when I get the stuff, we can meet at my summer cottage. It's on Lake Saint-Francis, near the Ontario border. In front, just across the river, is the state of New York. If it ever becomes necessary, we can even use my outboard to transport the stuff. We could go by Lake Ontario."

The conversation continued on those lines, bearing on various future projects. Then Laviolette drove Biase back to his hotel, asking him again to be patient.

Patience was certainly required, because Biase's next meeting with the trafficker did not take place for another seven months. In the meantime the agent communicated several times with Laviolette but each time the promised transaction was put off. Laviolette justified the long delay by claiming difficulties in connecting with Tremblay's supplier, as well as his own problems with municipal police. He said Montreal police had accosted him one September night as he came out of the *Café Rialto*. They had found a stolen revolver in his car and he was charged with receiving stolen goods and illegal possession of arms. On February 26, 1963, during one of Biase's telephone calls, Laviolette said the charges against him should be settled by March 20 and after that he should be able to conclude a first transaction.

The police operation, in fact, resumed seriously on April 5, 1963. In a telephone conversation that day, Laviolette said he was ready to talk business and invited Biase to come to see him. Five days later, the undercover agent met the trafficker in Montreal at the *Palermo*

---

9. Like all gangsters, Laviolette was anxious to keep his precious overseas contacts to himself.

Café on Iberville Street. Laviolette considered this place discreet and secluded, safe from the prying eyes of federal agents!

"Here we can talk in peace! Like I told you on the phone, I'm ready to make a deal. My court cases are finished and I've already started to make arrangements with Old Roger. I have to see him in Paris on May 1 to buy ten kilos. My courier is already there awaiting my instructions. If you want, I could sell you eight. I have to keep two for other clients. I should have the stock in Montreal about May 15 and then we can organize the delivery. Aside from that, it could be Lapierre who'll be in charge of delivering the merchandise to you. We're partners in everything and the good thing is that he's not known by police. He's never been arrested."

"That's good, but how much are you asking?"

"Between $7,000 and $7,500 a kilo. It's not expensive, but there's another thing by the way. I need $3,000 in advance to pay the expenses of my trip and my courier. All my money is invested in the garage. I haven't got a penny to go over there."

"Yeah, in principle, that might be okay. I know my brother George worked that way with Tremblay. But all the same I'd like to think it over for awhile. I'll give you an answer in a few days."

"O.K., as you wish, but the sooner the better. You'll have to come back with the money by the 29th at the absolute latest. Anyway, you don't need to worry, it will be deducted from the final payment. Another thing, if we go ahead, you should arrange to stay at another hotel. You could go to the *Queen Elizabeth* or the *LaSalle.*"

"No problem. But I'm telling you right now, I don't like these meetings in public too much. You come to my room and we'll be able to talk in peace."

"When you arrive, give me a call and give me your room number. I'll come to see you."

The meeting over, Biase returned to New York and arrangements were made with authorities of the Bureau of Narcotics and the RCMP to supply the money required by the trafficker.

On April 29, the undercover agent returned to Montreal and checked in immediately at the *Queen Elizabeth.* His room had been reserved by agents of the Narcotics Squad who had rented an adjacent room and installed their electronic listening equipment there. Laviolette joined Biase in late afternoon and they talked for nearly an hour.

"Did you bring the money?" the trafficker began.

"Yes, there it is. But tell me one thing. Why do you always ask for money in advance? I didn't understand your explanation too well the other day."

"It's simple. For the last couple of years there's been a lot of fake money in circulation. We want to have time to make sure we're not being passed counterfeit bills. When we were dealing with your brother and the others it was always done like that. You don't need to worry. Just to show our good faith, we're even ready to sell you another two kilos."

"Ah? You don't have to keep them for yourself?"

"Yeah, but I want to prove we're glad to be doing business with you. You know, if you hadn't got in touch with me after Tremblay's death, we would have had to contact another one of Pacelli's guys to get the business going again ... Anyway, I'll tell you a good one. Two years ago in August we'd been to Lake George to deliver ten kilos. When they came back to Montreal, Tremblay and my brother were stopped by the federals who found the $30,000 they were bringing back. Me and Lapierre just got away. We were bringing back six kilos we hadn't sold because the guys didn't have enough money. Lucky we came back a bit later than the others or we'd have been caught like rats. You know, working with Lapierre is a real pleasure. He's an intelligent guy and you can trust him. He never says much and what's more important, he never puts pleasure ahead of business. He's not like Tremblay who drank too much and could never concentrate on the job."

"That's all very interesting, but what about your trip to Paris? Are you ready to leave?"

"Yes, yes, but I haven't decided whether I should go myself. Anyway, the way things are going, maybe I won't need to go."

During the meeting, Laviolette made several phone calls to his brother Maurice and to his partner Lapierre. He also tried to reach a certain Frank the Greek whom he apparently had to talk to before fixing a date for the delivery. Unable to reach him, Laviolette left, saying he would call Biase at 6 p.m. to give him the date for returning to Montreal to make the deal.

Laviolette did call Biase at the agreed time:

"Listen, I'll be ready between the 22nd and 25th of May. Anyway, call me on the 22nd and I'll give you the exact date."

"What about the money I gave you, is it O.K.?"

"Yes, no problem, everything's fine. The money is good."

On May 22, Biase telephoned Laviolette, who asked him to call back on June 10 because he had to go to Paris three days later. The conversation was brief, but Biase had time to ask the trafficker if his price was still the same.

"That depends on how things go over there," replied Laviolette.

By then, authorities of the Bureau of Narcotics and the RCMP had already agreed to share equally in providing a fund of $70,000 which Biase could use to impress the traffickers in the final negotiations. The plan of action, worked out with officers of the Narcotics Squad, called for the transaction to be made at the *Queen Elizabeth,* and for an armed police agent to act as the New York courier carrying and guarding the money for Jack Farraco. This second undercover agent would not occupy the same room as Biase, and like Biase, he would be surrounded by strict security measures, both electronic and human. In fact, the Narcotics Squad rented six rooms, four of which were occupied by agents responsible for covering and protecting the two undercover agents. Finally, Biase would not show the money to Laviolete until he was assured that the trafficker had the drug in his possession and was ready to make the exchange.

When this plan had been worked out, the Narcotics Squad concentrated on finding out as quickly as possible when Laviolette would leave for France and who and where were the couriers waiting in Paris. Agents were posted round-the-clock at Dorval airport while others checked the lists of maritime arrivals from Le Havre and Marseilles.

In spite of what he had told Biase, Laviolette did not leave Montreal on May 25, but on May 29, on an Air France flight. He returned on June 3. His stay in Paris had not been put under any police observation to avoid raising suspicions or provoking premature actions. On June 10, as planned, Biase telephoned Montreal from New York. Laviolette was not available. His partner Lapierre answered the phone and explained that Laviolette was spending the weekend at his summer cottage on the shores of Lake Saint-Francis. Biase called back the following day at noon. This time Laviolette answered and asked him to come to Montreal immediately. The trafficker did not confirm that he had the merchandise in his possession, and Biase suspected that Laviolette wished to renegotiate the price.

Biase arrived in Montreal that night, and after registering at the *Laurentien Hotel,* immediately got in touch with Laviolette. Laviolette, apparently under the influence of alcohol, refused to discuss anything on the telephone and asked his client to call him back at noon the next day.

The next meeting between the undercover agent and Laviolette took place first in the trafficker's automobile outside his service station, and then in the station itself with Lapierre and Maurice Laviolette present. According to agent Biase's later report, and that of Staff Sergeant Maurice Poitras who was in charge of the Narcotics Squad at the time of the investigation, the dialogue between Roger Laviolette and the undercover agent went like this:

"I saw Old Roger in Paris," said Laviolette, "but I had trouble. I had to go to Nice and Marseilles first. It was no party. When I finally met him he said he was glad to see me but he didn't want to do business with me the way he did with Tremblay. He said he gave Tremblay credit of $16,000 the last time he was in France and Tremblay never paid it back. Because of that Roger is demanding cash now and he won't sell less than five kilos. He showed me a cache he had built into a wall. It's amazing. He had at least 100 kilos of heroin in there. Anyway, since I didn't know what you'd think, I told him I'd wait a while and talk to my client. What about it? Are you ready to put up the money for ten kilos? It would take another $27,000."

"I don't know. That changes things a lot. I don't think the guys financing me will accept that. They'll say for sure that we'd be better off dealing directly with Old Roger."

"Listen," replied the trafficker who was anxious not to lose his first important client, "I have another proposition for you. Roger gave me two dates when I could meet him again, either between the 12th and 15th of June or the 29th and 30th of June. What do you say we both meet in Paris, at the *Gare du Nord Hotel,* on the 30th. I could introduce you to Old Roger. There's one condition though: you're not to talk price with him or to try to by-pass me in the deal. I want to remain the contact. Don't forget that."

"Don't get excited. You don't have to worry about that."

"O.K., but you'll have to have the money with you or be able to guarantee that it's in France. The payment won't be made until the merchandise arrives in Montreal and you've been able to verify it. As for me, I'm convinced Roger would agree to that kind of arrangement."

"It's an interesting idea, but me, I'll have to talk to my partners. For sure I can't give you an answer right off, just like that. I'll need a little time."

"I understand. What do you say we meet on the 19th, at 2 o'clock in the afternoon at the *Montcalm Hotel* at Lake George?"

"That might be O.K. I'll have time to meet my guys."

Then Laviolette got up and took Biase into another room where he showed him a small trunk.

"See that trunk? It's made many trips to Paris and every time it comes back it's full of stuff. When it's less than five kilos, we use the air route, but for bigger loads we send it by ship."

The trafficker then gave the undercover agent a slip of cardboard on which he had written the name and address of the hotel where they would meet in Paris on June 30. At the beginning of the meeting, he had given Biase $1,600, what was left of the $3,000 Biase had supplied for the trip to France.

About 5:10 p.m., Narcotics Squad agents who had been installed for some weeks in a permanent observation post in a building facing the Papineau Avenue service station, noticed Biase emerging from the station with Roger Laviolette. The trafficker drove the agent to the *Laurentian Hotel* and Biase then left to go back to New York.

On June 19, as agreed, Biase and Laviolette met in the parking lot of the *Montcalm Hotel* at Lake George, N.Y. The trafficker was accompanied by his partner Lapierre and another man who turned out to be Alain Phaneuf, 30, a sales representative and friend of Roger Lapierre.

The presence of this newcomer intrigued Biase and he asked Laviolette:

"Who's the guy in the car with Lapierre?"

"He's my courier. I wanted him to get a good look at you so he'll be able to recognize you easily later on. You know, he was there the last time you came to the garage but you didn't notice him because he was dressed as a mechanic."

The two men entered the hotel's *Garden Café* and sat at a table, carrying on the conversation under discreet observation of an RCMP agent who had sat down nearby.

"What have your guys decided to do?" asked Laviolette.

"They refuse to put up any money at all unless they can see the stuff first."

"Yeah, that's not too good. I've already made all the arrangements with Old Roger and I'm supposed to leave for Paris on the 29th to pick up five kilos for myself."

"Why don't you give me your five packages if Old Roger won't give you ten kilos without the rest of the money? If you do that, you could buy the rest with the money you get from me."

"That's not a bad idea. But I have the impression you and your friends have no confidence in me."

"It's not that, but with all the money we're putting up, me and my friends, we just want to be sure."

"O.K., let's say we meet in Paris on June 30 and that you'll have a guarantee that you have the necessary $70,000. O.K.?"

"That's O.K. I'll also have somebody to take delivery of the first five kilos and after that we'll arrange something together for delivery of the rest."

"Perfect. If your partners agree, come and meet me here in two days. If I don't hear from you by tomorrow afternoon, it'll mean that you'll be here. O.K.?"'

"Right."

Laviolette rejoined his companions and returned to Montreal. Since Biase didn't call the next day to change the appointment, the two men met at the same place, as agreed, at 4 p.m. on June 21. This time Laviolete was with his brother Maurice. The meeting was brief. The two men went over their plan once again. The New Yorker told the Montrealer his partners were agreed and that he would have $70,000 available when they met in Paris. The trafficker informed Biase that the trip to Paris would be at the beginning of July instead of on June 30.

Over the next few days, authorities of the U.S. Bureau of Narcotics made the necessary arrangements to provide Biase with a bank document showing him to have $100,000 at his disposal. On Saturday, June 29, Laviolette telephoned Biase and asked him for a $1,500 advance for travel expenses. The agent replied that he had to speak to his partners first and said he would give the answer the next day. On the next Sunday, Biase called the trafficker at his summer cottage and Laviolette asked him to come to see him as soon as possible.

So the Bureau of Narcotics undercover agent travelled once more to Montreal, on July 2. His room in the *Laurentian Hotel* was the site for the next meeting with Laviolette, at noon on the Wednesday. As usual, the adjacent room was occupied by agents of the Narcotics Squad who heard every word exchanged through their listening devices.

"I thought we could go to Paris together next Monday," said Laviolette.

"I thought we would go before that. I'd made all my plans to go right away."

"That could be arranged, but we have to settle the question of the money. For Old Roger, everything's O.K. on condition that I can be sure you've got the money for the ten kilos or that you could give me half to buy the first five kilos."

"I already told you, no money in advance until we've seen the stuff."

The conversation dragged on for about 20 minutes until Biase decided to show the trafficker the letter of credit he had for the Paris branch of the *First National City Bank.*

"That should be enough," he told Laviolette, "to prove that we're serious and ready to make a big deal."

Laviolette examined the document with undisguised satisfaction. Then he made several telephone calls to airlines to check on flight departures for Paris.

"Listen," he told Biase afterwards, "since you have the money, there's no need for you to come to Paris. I'll arrange things with Old Roger and all you'll have to do is come and get the stuff in Montreal."

"Thanks, but all my arrangements are already made. My courier is already in Paris waiting for me."

"Good, O.K. But you know, we'd never have had all these problems if I'd had all the money in cash at the beginning. I would have looked after everything and it would have been a lot simpler."

"I know, but enough of that. Now we have to figure out when we leave and how we're going to handle the expenses."

My courier will leave tonight and I'll look after his expenses. We'll leave tomorrow night and you'll look after buying the tickets for the flight to Paris. You stay at the *Ambassadeur Hotel* there and I'll check in at the *Gare du Nord Hotel.* Is that O.K. with you?"

"Yes, that's fine."

"Perfect. I'll go and get started now and I'll call you in an hour."

Laviolette returned to his garage. Two hours later, about 3:30 p.m., when Laviolette still had not called, Biase decided to call him.

"I just managed to get the money for my man's travel expenses," explained Laviolette on the telephone. "I'm going to make his plane reservations now. I'll call you back later."

At 5:20 p.m., the trafficker called the undercover agent:

"I've got a problem. I'm $400 short. Could you let me have that much in advance. I'll send someone to get it."

"O.K., O.K.," agreed the exasperated Biase, who knew he had no choice in the matter.

Half an hour later Alain Phaneuf arrived at the agent's room. Biase gave him $300, then went with him to the hotel lobby where, after calling Laviolette again, he gave Phaneuf another $100. All these actions were observed by a number of Narcotics Squad agents discreetly on duty in the lobby. At 6:10 p.m., Laviolette telephoned Biase again:

"Everything's O.K. My man has come back. I'll see you tomorrow between three and four o'clock."

That night, RCMP detectives watched the departure of Phaneuf for Paris. He was carrying a small white valise identical to the one carried by Laviolette on his last trip to France. Laviolette was also at the airport, waiting with his courier for the flight. As soon as he arrived in Paris, Phaneuf was put under continual surveillance by the central office for narcotics and by liaison agents of the U.S. Bureau of Narcotics in the French capital.

In Montreal, in the late afternoon of the following day, Laviolette was driven to the airport by Lapierre, after making a number of telephone calls. Biase met him there at 7:10 p.m. and handed him his airplane ticket. The agent left Montreal first, taking an Air France flight at 7:30 p.m. Laviolette, who also carried a white valise, left for Paris ten minutes later on an Air Canada flight.

At 8:30 a.m. on July 5, 1963, Biase and Laviolette met in Paris, at the Invalides terminus. The trafficker then advised Biase to go to his hotel and wait for a call the next day. Biase did so, but did not hear from Laviolette until two days later. Then Laviolette arranged a meeting with the agent in front of the Bristol Hotel, in the Saint-Honoré district.

Patrick Biase met Roger Laviolette and Alain Phaneuf at the appointed place in late afternoon Sunday, July 7. The trio then went to the *Le Roulis* café.

"I spoke to Old Roger," explained Laviolette, "but we can't do anything before Wednesday because we didn't come at the expected time. Tomorrow morning at 11 o'clock, I'll meet Jack (the agent) in front of the *First National City Bank*, on Champs-Elysées. We'll check to see if the money is O.K."

"There's no need to go in," said the trafficker, "I'm satisfied you've got the money. Come on, we'll go for a drink across the street at *Longchamps*. Alain is waiting for us there."

As agreed, Biase met Laviolette next day in front of the branch of the New York bank.

Roger Laviolette

Roger Lapierre

Roger Coudert

Alain Phaneuf

Salvador Pardo-Bolland

Juan Aritzi

At the table, Laviolette began talking about his former deals with Roger Coudert. Biase made careful mental notes.

"Old Roger has a big supply in reserve in Marseilles," said Laviolette. "The way I understand it, he gets his stuff from behind the Iron Curtain. He has a courier who travels between Marseilles and Paris to pick it up . . ."

After this session, Laviolette asked Biase to meet him again at the same place the next day, early in the afternoon.

On July 9, about 1 p.m., the trio met briefly again at *Longchamps.* Laviolette asked Biase for another $100 which, naturally, would be deducted from the price of the first kilo of heroin. The undercover agent didn't have that much money with him and proposed to meet the trafficker later in the afternoon. Laviolette then explained how the delivery would be made.

"Old Roger's courier will bring me a small trunk. The one they usually use measures three feet by four feet and has a false bottom practically impossible to detect. When I've got the trunk I'll give it to my man to take to you. As for you, you'll go and get your money from the bank. I'm supposed to meet Old Roger tomorrow morning at 10 o'clock."

"Perfect, I'll wait for your call."

At noon the next day Biase met Laviolette at the *Colisée,* a café on the Champs-Elysées.

"I met Old Roger and everything's fine. The delivery will be made in three days. If you want you could have the stuff sooner, even tomorrow, but it wouldn't be hidden in the trunk."

"That's O.K. Anyway, I'd have to break open the false bottom to check the merchandise. So there's no use wasting time hiding it in the first place.

"I'll be seeing Old Roger tomorrow. I'll tell him to deliver the stuff as it is."

On July 11, Biase did not meet Laviolette, but talked to him three times on the telephone. The first call was short: the trafficker was checking to see if his buyer was available. The second conversation took place while Laviolette was meeting with Coudert:

"Old Roger doesn't want to let the stuff go until you've got your money out," said Laviolette. "He wants to be paid as soon as he hands over the merchandise. And you'll have to take it in the trunk three days from now."

"That's no good," said the agent. "How come the plans are suddenly being changed?"

"What can I say? That's the way he wants it."

"I'd like to meet him myself. Try to arrange it. I could try to convince him."

"I'll see what I can do. I'll call you back."

A short time later, Biase got the third call.

"Old Roger doesn't want to see you. Everything's fallen through. I'll see you when you get back to the States."

The Bureau of Narcotics agent could hardly believe his ears: the whole deal cancelled so close to its conclusion! Why? He couldn't figure it out. Had the traffickers guessed his real identity? Determined to get to the bottom of this, he started out in search of Old Roger. He went to Lafayette Street, to the *Café de Paris,* which formerly belonged to the Parisian trafficker. The new owner had bought the place in February of that year and had no idea how to get in touch with the former proprietors. Biase had no better luck elsewhere. Disappointed, he returned to New York the following day. Laviolette and Phaneuf, without making any further contact with Biase, also returned empty-handed to Montreal.

For the next while, Narcotics Squad detectives increased their surveillance of the traffickers in Montreal, while Biase tried without success to reach Laviolette. On August 1, the Bureau of Narcotics advised the RCMP that their liaison agents in Paris had spotted Roger Laviolette. Narcotics Squad investigators quickly checked flight lists at Dorval airport and learned that the trafficker had left Montreal at 8 p.m. the night before. Half an hour earlier, his courier Alain Phaneuf had also taken a flight for Paris. The RCMP, after informing the Bureau of Narcotics, set up round-the-clock surveillance at Dorval airport and at the ports of Montreal and Quebec City.

To try to get a bit more information about what was happening, agent Biase telephoned the Papineau Avenue Garage. Roger Lapierre answered.

"Hello, Roger! Is Laviolette there? I want to talk to him. I've been trying to reach him for a long time."

"I'm sorry, but he's not here. He's gone on a trip, out of the country. He should be back next week, around the 9th or the 10th. But don't worry, I think he's going to have some good news for you."

"Oh yeah? How's that, out of the country?"

"He's gone with Alain to the place you visited recently."

"I see, I understand. In that case I'll wait."

On August 3, at 10:15 p.m., agents posted at Dorval noticed the arrival of a well-known individual, Anatole Ethier, former associate of Jean-Paul Tremblay, and proprietor now of a small hotel at Rockland, near Ottawa. The man was alone. He went to the parking lot where he got into an Oldsmobile with Ontario licence plates and drove directly home. The search of his luggage by Customs officers had produced nothing, but another check of airline passenger lists showed that he had taken the same plane as Laviolette two days earlier. That caused the detectives to speculate that Laviolette had obtained financing from Ethier for his first transaction with Coudert.

On August 7, the RCMP was notified that Laviolette and Phaneuf had made reservations to return to Montreal the following day. Laviolette was to arrive at 1:05 p.m., Phaneuf at 4:10 p.m.

At 1:15 p.m. on August 8, the Narcotics Squad received a call from the Bureau of Narcotics in New York. The Bureau had just learned that French police had arrested the two Montreal traffickers as they were about to board their flights. Alain Phaneuf had been carrying four kilos of pure heroin in a false-bottomed suitcase.

Interrogated separately, both men quickly came clean. Laviolette declared that Anatole Ethier had financed his latest trip and the purchase of the drugs. He said Ethier had himself given the money, $20,000, to Coudert during a meeting of the three men in a restaurant at the terminal building. Profits from the transaction were to be shared equally between Laviolette and Ethier. Phaneuf, for his part, was no hardened criminal and proved very cooperative. He told his whole story, explaining that he had been brought into the group by Roger Lapierre. Following these confessions, the French central office for narcotics arrested Roger Coudert. A search of his luxurious villa at Lamorlaye, in the suburbs of Paris, turned up the small trunk Phaneuf had brought, as well as a document showing that he had just converted $20,000 into French currency. Confronted with this evidence, the old trafficker admitted defeat and made his confession.

In Montreal, the Narcotics Squad made a series of raids on August 9 and 10, arresting Roger Lapierre and Anatole Ethier on charges of conspiracy to import heroin into Canada and trafficking in narcotics. A rogatory commission was later established which travelled to Paris to hear testimony from witnesses. Unfortunately, the procedures were not as successful as hoped. On November 29, 1963, after the preliminary inquiry, the RCMP was obliged to withdraw the charges against Ethier. Lapierre, however, thanks to the spectacular testimony of the agent, Patrick Biase, was sent to trial. Acquitted of the charge of conspiracy, he pleaded guilty to trafficking in heroin on October 26, 1964, and was sentenced to a year in prison and a $1,000 fine.

During the Paris hearings, it was established that Coudert, when he met Jean-Paul Tremblay and Roger Laviolette in Montreal on October 14, 1961, had also been on a mission for the Corsicans Antoine Marignani and Jean-Baptiste Jiacobetti and for their right-hand man Gilbert Coscia. After his meeting with Tremblay and Laviolette, Coudert went to Nice, where Gilbert Coscia introduced him to Mrs. Salvador Pardo-Bolland, wife of a Mexican diplomat who had been posted in Ottawa from 1954 to 1960, and who had acted as courier for Pep Cotroni's suppliers. After his trip to Nice, Coudert returned to Montreal where Mrs. Pardo-Bolland turned over to him two suitcases filled with heroin. (10)

---

10. The Marignani-Jiacobetti-Coscia organization specialized in the use of diplomatic couriers and was distinct from the Croce-Bistoni-Mondolini organization. At the beginning of October 1960, the Bureau of Narcotics in New York seized 52 kilos of heroin which was being transported by Mauricio Rosal, Guatemala's ambassador to Belgium and Holland. The diplomat had turned over the merchandise to Etienne Tarditi, a Corsican acting for two Parisians, Robert Le Coat and Félix Barnier who, like Gilbert Coscia, represented Marignani and Jiacobetti. The drug was to have been delivered, as usual, to Charles Bourbonnais, a controller for *Trans World Airlines,* who in turn was to deliver it to two New York traffickers, Joe Cahill and Nick Calamaras. These last two were associates of Joseph Biondo and the brothers Steve and Joseph Armore, all trusted aids of Carlo Gambino, one of the five bosses of the New York Mafia.

In February 1964, the Bureau of Narcotics in New York arrested Pardo-Bolland and a colleague, Juan Aritzi as they were turning over four suitcases of heroin to another well-known trafficker, René Bruchon whose previous arrest in Halifax has been mentioned. (See Note 14, Chapter Five.) Bruchon was acting for Gilbert Coscia who had supplied the drugs to the two diplomats. Aritzi, who had been transporting the merchandise on this trip, had stopped over in Montreal for three days on his way to New York. That permitted the Narcotics Squad to spirit away nearly all of the 60 kilos (132 pounds) of heroin contained in the diplomatic luggage. It was Pardo-Bolland's testimony in France which led to the conviction, in July 1966, of Roger Coudert, Gilbert Coscia, Antoine Marignani and a number of others, including Agop Kevorkian. (See Note 14, Chapter Five.)

Chapter 9

The Rivard Affair

It was nearly 8 o'clock in the morning of October 10, 1963, as Michel Caron, 33, and his 30-year-old wife Marie-Ida — both Montrealers — arrived at the Texas border post of Laredo. They told the three Customs officers there that they had come from Monterey, in Mexico, and had nothing to declare but their personal effects and a few souvenirs. Everything seemed in order, but the Customs officers were in a suspicious mood. The previous week, Customs investigators at Laredo had spotted Antonio Farina, an important international drug trafficker and liaison agent for New York and Sicilian mafiosi. He had been arrested in New York in December 1953, it may be recalled, with Roger Coudert and the brothers Salvatore and Ugo Caneba. (1) Farina, associated with Antoine d'Agostino, Jean-Baptiste Croce, Paul Mondolini and the others, had been sentenced to five years in prison and a $10,000 fine in April 1954. He disappeared when he was released in 1959, and there were good reasons to believe he had settled in Canada, South America or Mexico. Reports received in 1961 linked him once again to Roger Coudert, during Coudert's association with Jean-Paul Tremblay and Roger Laviolette. (2)

Because of Farina's presence in the area, Customs officers had been instructed to double-check everything. When the Carons drove up to the barrier in their Chevrolet Impala with Quebec licence plates, they were therefore asked to pull up beside an inspection table and unload their luggage. The search was meticulous: two officers checked the luggage on the table while the third examined the car. The car search was made by agent James E. Pagsdale of the department of Agriculture, who first checked the contents of some

---

1. See Chapter Four.
2. See preceding chapter.

pottery which had been placed on the back seat. There was nothing unusual about these souvenirs, but the officer sensed something not quite right. He leaned his knee on the back seat and noticed that it seemed remarkably rigid. Thinking some alcoholic beverages might be hidden under the seat, he asked Caron if he had declared all the alcohol he had bought. The Montrealer replied that he had no alcohol in his possession. The officer, after asking Caron to free the seat, raised it at one corner. He noticed that the seat seemed much heavier than it should be. Furthermore, as he groped beneath the seat, he felt an unusual kind of covering. The officer called his colleagues and together they removed the back seat and placed it on the inspection table.

A black plastic sheet covering the bottom of the seat, was quickly removed to reveal 27 transparent plastic bags hidden in the springs. The white powder contained in the bags was pure heroin. The Carons, utterly crushed, said not a word. They let themselves be taken into the station without the slightest resistance while the search of their car continued. A few minutes later, Pagsdale rejoined them. He and the other officers had found 39 more heroin-filled plastic bags inside the doors of the vehicle. In all, 34.5 kilos of the drug (76 pounds), valued at $35 million on the black market, had been discovered.

The appropriate authorities were immediately notified. By the end of the afternoon, Sergeant Walter Kelly, in charge of the RCMP Narcotics Squad in Montreal, had been informed of the Laredo Customs officers' catch, the second biggest of the kind ever made in the United States. The Carons were unknown to Kelly and his men. The husband, Michel, however, had had a few brushes with Montreal municipal police. At the time of his arrest in Laredo in fact, he was free on bail awaiting trial in a robbery and receiving case dating from the previous March. At that time he had been cooperative with detectives. But this time he refused to say a word, except that his wife knew nothing whatever of the matter and that the lives of his wife and four children, as well as his own, would be at risk if he talked.

His attitude didn't surprise the head of the Narcotics Squad, who could easily understand the state of mind the Montrealer must have been in, caught in a net so far from home. The same afternoon, therefore, arrangements were made for two RCMP investigators to go to Texas to question the prisoners. Sergeant Ronald Crevier and Constable Gilles Poissant were given the assignment. (3) They

---

3. Constable Poissant later became staff sergeant in charge of the operations of the Narcotics Squad in Montreal.

(Photo Allô Police)

The Customs officers of Laredo proudly exhibiting their seizure.

arrived in Texas two days later and on October 14 had their first interview with Michel Caron. They talked for four hours, but Caron refused to say anything about his relationships with traffickers, about his boss, the origin of the drugs he was transporting, or their destination. He would only say that his Texas lawyer had been sent to him following a telephone call he made to a Montreal tavern the day after his arrest, and that a celebrated Italian family of Montreal was behind the affair.

The next day Sergeant Crevier and Constable Poissant met with Caron again. The prisoner was a bit more cooperative but still refused to give names, identify photographs or offer precise details.

On October 16, a third interview took place in the Webb County prison. At the beginning, Caron absolutely refused to say any more, believing that he had already said enough to endanger his life. He had just received a telephone call from Montreal lawyer Claude Danis, advising him to say nothing and promising to provide the money required for bail for his wife which had been fixed, like his, at $250,000. The investigators, anxious not to panic their man, began talking of ordinary things. Then gradually, skilfully, they brought Caron to think about the drastic effects of heroin, the brutality of the world of traffickers and the enormous efforts deployed in the battle against these exploiters of human misery. The atmosphere was tense but the arguments of the police officers were reaching the target. Finally Caron broke down in tears and agreed to tell all he knew. For six days he told his story to the officers from the Narcotics Squad and then to U.S. authorities. Here is a summary of his statement:

"Everything I've told you so far is false. But now I'm going to tell the truth. The guy behind all this is Lucien Rivard."

"Two years ago I met somebody named Julien Gagnon on St. Helen's Island. He also called himself Jerry Massey. We met several times and talked about a lot of things. Last winter, in March, he introduced me to François Groleau, Rivard's right-hand man in the drug traffic. This was a guy who wasn't supposed to have any criminal record but had good contacts in Montreal and Chicago. His job was to recruit couriers and look after relations with them. For example, he was the one who would buy airplane or boat tickets, make reservations, give the couriers their instructions, arrange the place and date of deliveries, pay the boys their expenses and services. Sometimes he would be in charge of surveillance for certain transactions.

"When I met him, Groleau told me I was the guy he needed to go to France to get the stuff. He had confidence in me because I was a thief and because Gagnon knew me. He said I'd have to change my car because the one I had was too old and I'd need a newer one to make deliveries to the United States. He said Rivard could advance me the money and I could repay him from the money I'd make working as a courier. At first I didn't want to change my car; it was running well and besides, I told him what interested me was making money. If Rivard needed me, I was ready to help. I knew that he was the top man in the drug business in Montreal then and that I couldn't approach him myself to offer my services.

"Finally I accepted their offer and started working for Rivard. The first time I met him was in June. I was with Gagnon and we went to Saint-Eustache, to a hotel parking lot. After that Rivard sent Gagnon to France with his car to get some stuff. I was with him when he left. It was June 28 or 29, if I remember rightly. Anyway, a Saturday morning. He took a Greek boat called... ah, I remember that, the *Arkadia*. He had his Pontiac Grand Prix put on board. I think he stayed in Europe for about six weeks.

"A week after he left, I learned that Rivard had sent another courier to France. This guy was called Raymond Jones. Some called him Johnny and others le Grand Jaune. I knew him pretty well because he was often there when I met Groleau and Gagnon.

Besides, I'm the one who introduced him to Gagnon. Jones was just the same as Groleau, he didn't have any criminal record. His girlfriend worked in an east-end club.

"When Gagnon came back at the end of July, Groleau and I went to the port to meet him. Groleau had told me his car was supposed to contain 35 to 40 kilos (4) of heroin. We checked around to make sure everything was safe, then we told Gagnon to follow us in his car. We drove up to a hotel parking lot near Saint-Eustache. I think it was the *Chez Maurice* hotel in Laval West. There Groleau told us to leave Gagnon's car and to come back about six o'clock that night. Gagnon and I left and went to eat at a beach nearby. At 6 o'clock we returned to the hotel. We checked the car and noticed that the stuff was still in it. We left it there and came back at 9 p.m. By then the car had been emptied. After that we met Rivard at the hotel. I didn't talk to him but Gagnon got $1,500 for the job and $2,000 for expenses. Afterwards he told me had been to Belgium and Paris, Nice and Marseilles. It was at Nice where he was supposed to have met Rivard's partners, apparently Corsicans, but it was at Marseilles where he got the stuff. For the two days it took to load up the car, he stayed with the Marseillais.

"I got my first mission not long after Gagnon came back. In the first week of August, Rivard telephoned me and told me to come and see him in Jones' apartment on Sagard Street. There he explained that I was to deliver the stuff to the United States. There was about 35 kilos. He gave me $1,000 and told me to park my car at the corner of Belanger and Saint-André Streets, leaving one door open and the keys inside. I did what he said. About six hours later Groleau phoned me and told me my car was ready and was parked on my street, not far from my home.

"I left a couple of hours later. I think it was August 20. I brought my wife and two of my kids and we went to Plattsburg on Highway 9. At Customs I got out for a few minutes to put my jacket in the trunk of the car and I had a good look at a car which seemed to have been following me. At Plattsburg, as planned, I telephoned Rivard at NA 5-9080 and mentioned this to him. He said he had been told that I was driving too fast. He advised me to take my time and not take any chances of getting stopped by police highway patrol.

"Next I went to Bridgeport, Connecticut. We stopped at the *Bridgeport Motor Inn* and I registered under the name of Roberts as Rivard had suggested. After that, following the instructions I'd been

---

4. Between 77 and 88 pounds.

given, I wrote my room number on a piece of cigarette paper and put the paper on the dashboard of my car so it could be seen through the windshield. I waited two hours and then I got a phone call from a stranger. Now I know it was an Italian. Rivard told me his name was Frank or Frankie and that he was a hairdresser. I had made the comment that Frankie had very nice hair.

"Anyway, the guy on the phone said he'd meet me in the parking lot in 20 minutes. I met him and gave him the keys and registration for my car. He left and I waited in the motel. That evening he came back and knocked at the door of my room to give me back the keys and my papers. Naturally, the stuff had been removed from the car. I returned to Montreal that night with, believe it or not, two bedsheets from the motel. I couldn't resist stealing them. It had become a habit with me.

"I got $780 for that first trip. A few days later, probably September 6, Jones came back to Montreal with his wife. I learned that they had met Gagnon in Paris. Like Gagnon, Jones had taken his car with him. It was a Ford Galaxie 500 lent to him by a guy named Jerry Bourget and it came back stuffed with about 40 kilos of heroin. Gagnon and I met Jones at the dock. Before, we had gone to Saint-Eustache to make sure we weren't being followed by police. Rivard and Groleau had told us to make the first trip a test. But this time when Jones' car was unloaded at the dock, we escorted it into the city.

"But we had a few problems. I can tell you things got pretty damned hot. At the corner of St. Catherine and Pie IX, Jones' car broke down and caught fire. We had to call the fire department to put it out. I also called Groleau at his home to tell him what happened and ask him what we should do. Apparently he called Rivard because the both of them arrived on the scene soon after. Rivard saw that the stuff was intact and he had the car towed to a garage he knew. I can't tell you which one it was, I don't know. I learned later that Jones got $1,000 for the job and $2,000 for expenses. I can tell you he was furious. His damn car had broken down in France too and it had cost him between $740 and $780 for repairs. He told me the Frenchmen who did the job really screwed him.

"A week after Jones came back, Rivard called me to make another delivery to Bridgeport. I met him at the *Laval Curb Service* restaurant in Vimont, not far from his *Plage Idéale*. He told me to do the same as the first time and to leave my car near my place. About 4 o'clock in the afternoon Rivard called me to tell me to meet him at the corner of Sherbrooke and des Erables. When I got there

Rivard was waiting in my car. We talked a bit and he gave me $1,000 for the job and expenses. Before leaving, Rivard told me that Groleau had seen him in my car, near the intersection of Bélanger and de Lorimier. When he left, another gang member came to meet him.

"I drove to the *Brideport Motor Inn* again on September 21. My wife rented the room, under the name of Mrs. Welliston. That was her maiden name. I didn't want to check in myself in case they recognized me for the bedsheets I had stolen. The delivery was made as before. But this time Frankie was with another guy I didn't know. When he brought back my keys and papers he told me to tell Rivard that two trips to Bridgeport was enough. The next time it would have to be another city. He suggested Flint, Michigan, or some other place near the Canadian border.

"Back in Montreal, I met Rivard at the *Laval Curb Service*. He was very satisfied, and promised me a $100 bonus. Two or three days later I met him again at the *Plage Idéale*. When I arrived he was with some people I didn't know. As soon as he saw me he came to join me and gave me the $100 he had promised. Then he asked me if I was ready to go to Europe or Mexico to pick up a supply of about 35 kilos. I said I was, but that I would prefer to go to Mexico because I'd always promised my wife that I'd take her there some day. At that time I learned that Rivard was going to send another courier to France between September 15 and 30, and that on his return, Gagnon or Jones would take charge of making the delivery to the U.S.

"I've got to tell you this too, that in July, Groleau gave me $50 to get passports for me and my wife. Like he told me, I went to Bergeron, a justice of the peace in Montreal on Ontario Street. When I saw him the guy looked pretty drunk. I gave him $10 and he signed my application form swearing that he had known me for six years. With that, I never had any trouble getting my passports. I know Jones and Gagnon got theirs the same way.

"Another time Rivard gave $300 to one of his men, Gérard Turcot, who was called La Ploune, to have my car put in good condition. Turcot gave me $150 and kept the rest.

"On September 26, Rivard got in touch with me and I met him at *Laval Curb Service* at noon. First he gave me the tools I'd need to take out the front seat of my car where I was supposed to hide the stuff I got in Mexico. Then he gave me a piece of paper on which he'd written the name "George" and a telephone number in Mexico City. And he gave me $1,200 in U.S. fifty-dollar bills. He told me the money was for my expenses and when I got back to Montreal

(Photo Le Devoir)

(Photo Allô Police)

Lucien Rivard

François Groleau

(Photo Allô Police)

Julien Gagnon

Joseph Raymond Jones

with the 80 pounds of stuff I was to pick up, he'd give me $1,750. Before he left, he told me I had to be in Mexico at the beginning of October and that I'd receive further instructions there. He also told me that Gagnon and Jones would be making trips to Mexico to bring back loads just as big as the one I'd have. Gagnon would probably leave in the first week of January. From what I could understand, Rivard himself might be going to Mexico in December.

"After the meeting I went home and started packing my bags. I left with my wife the next day. She wasn't too anxious to come, but Gagnon had told her something might happen to her or the kids if she didn't go along. Rivard, for his part, had promised me a bonus of $200 if I brought my wife with me. We went via Cornwall and Prescott in Ontario and crossed into the States at Ogdensburg. Then we went to Buffalo and Columbus, Ohio, and stopped for the night at Shepherdsville in Kentucky. We slept at the *Blue Grass Lodge.* We arrived in San Antonio, Texas, on September 30 and stayed at the *Robert Lee.* The next day we reached Laredo and there I bought an auto insurance policy for the trip to Mexico. Rivard had suggested that. It was the *Carazos Insurance Agency.* In the afternoon we crossed the border at Falcon Dam Port. We arrived in Mexico City on October 2 and checked into the *El Diplomatico Hotel* under our real names.

"As soon as we got to our room I telephoned the number Rivard had given me to talk to George. I called twice. The second time a woman answered and told me George was in Acapulco. When I asked the hotel telephone operator to ring the number, she asked me how come I knew George. I said he was a friend. She then said that George was also one of her good friends.

"The next day I telephoned again and finally managed to talk to George. He arranged to meet me in a park near the hotel. When we met, he advised me to change hotels and to register at the *Beverly* under a false name. I did that the next day under the name of Bob Wesson. In the evening, about 10 o'clock, I called George again and we met in the park nearby. We talked a bit, then he took me by car to a house not far from the hotel where he introduced me to another guy, a Frenchman, probably from Marseilles, judging by his accent. George was a Mexican. He talked to me in English, but he talked to the Frenchman in Spanish.

"When we arrived at the house, the Frenchman was on the telephone to Rivard. He gave me the phone and I talked to Rivard too until he was satisfied that it was me. Then the Frenchman got on the phone again and Rivard assured him that I was his courier. After hanging up, the Frenchman told me I'd have to wait a few

207

days because the heroin was not yet available. The meeting didn't last much longer. George drove me back to the hotel.

"Nothing happened for the next two days. Mornings and afternoons my wife and I visited the city and each night I called George and met him near the hotel. On the evening of the third day, October 7, about 10:30, the Frenchman picked me up in front of my hotel and took me to his place. He had a grey Chevrolet, a 1962 Biscayne. At the house he showed me a piece of paper with the name "Adolfo" written on it. He told me Adolfo was the gang's driver. He tore the paper in two and gave me one of the pieces. He said a guy would come to see me in the evening, and if he had the other piece of paper, I should give him my car keys, driver's licence and automobile registration. The Frenchman drove me back to the hotel, and soon afterwards, a guy came with the piece of paper. He drove away in my car.

"The next morning I got a phone call to tell me my car was parked three streets from the hotel. I went down to the lobby where Adolfo had left my keys and papers. Soon after, the Frenchman phoned me to tell me not to leave Mexico right away because two guys wanted to see me. In the afternoon George came to get me and take me to the Frenchman's place. There were two strangers there. I got the impression they had just come from Montreal, because one of them, named Antonio, gave the Frenchman a bottle of liquor saying, "It's a gift from Montreal." The two men spoke French and Spanish.

"I asked the Frenchman where the stuff was hidden in my car. He told me some was in the doors, between the panels, and some in the springs under the back seat. I wasn't too happy about that, and told him the stuff wasn't supposed to be hidden there. Rivard had given me instructions to hide it under the front seat. Furthermore, I told them that I had been told in the beginning that I'd dealing with only one person and there were already five people involved.

"They all got together and talked for a few minutes in Spanish. Then the Frenchman came to me and said I was a good guy and gave me $500 in U.S. fifties and twenties. He told me to tell Rivard not to deduct that from my pay. I was pretty happy and calmed down. Then the Frenchman offered me a revolver and ammunition. It was a German Luger. I told him I didn't need it. Then he told me that they had worked for seven hours hiding the stuff and it was well and safely hidden.

"Before leaving, the one named Antonio gave a slip of green paper with a message in code that Rivard had written himself. The instructions were for me to be in Stratford, Connecticut on October

14 and to telephone Rivard from there at 9 p.m. at NA 5-9080. The Frenchman also gave me written instructions to call a certain Pancho in Mexico City as soon as I had crossed the U.S. border. When I was arrested, the Customs officers seized those papers. At the end of his talk, the Frenchman told me I could cross the border anywhere I liked. There were five different places, but he advised me not to try Falcon Dam because the highway traffic wasn't heavy enough and the officers had more time to search foreigners. He suggested I cross the frontier between 7 p.m. and 9 p.m., which was the busiest time.

"We left Mexico on October 9 about 11 a.m. We intended to cross into the States on the 12th, Christopher Columbus Day, taking advantage of the tourist rush to get through unnoticed. But we arrived at the border Thursday morning and I didn't want to wait. I should have. Maybe we wouldn't have got caught.

"The day after my arrest, I was able to telephone the *Grenier* tavern in Montreal, on St. Catherine Street East. I spoke to Marcel Choquette and told him to advise Gagnon or Gérard Turcot (La Ploune) so that they could contact Rivard to get me a lawyer. Not too much later a Laredo lawyer named Horace Hall came to the jail to tell me that Montreal lawyer Claude Danis had engaged his services for me. His fee was $7,000 plus costs. On October 19, in the afternoon, Danis himself came to see me. He told me everything would be all right as long as I kept my mouth shut and didn't talk to anyone. He said that if I talked, hoping to get a light sentence, the gang would get me wherever I was and my wife and children might be killed. I told him I hadn't said anything and had turned suspicions toward the Italians. He said that was good and I should continue to keep quiet. My trial would probably be in February and they'd work to get me a light sentence. In the meantime, he said my wife's bail would be reduced in a few days and the organization would put up the money.

"I've told you everything. Now, if you can protect my wife and kids, I'm willing to testify in court against Rivard and the others."

Michel Caron ended his confession by identifying photographs of most of his accomplices, including Rivard's partners in Mexico. It was then learned that the Frenchman was none other than the Corsican, Paul Mondolini, and that George was really Jorge Edouardo Moreno Chauvet, the most important Mexican trafficker of the moment. Antonio was identified as Tony Farina, and his companion was Frank Giovani Scalici, a member of the Gambino organization in New York. Remaining unidentified were Frankie the hairdresser, to whom Caron had made two deliveries of heroin at

Bridgeport; and Adolfo the driver, who had picked up Caron's car in Mexico for the heroin-loading operation. Thanks to the phone number Mondolini had given Caron, even Pancho was unmasked: he was Fulgentio Cruz Bonet, a Cuban refugee in Mexico involved in various rackets, including drugs.

As Caron signed his confession and offered his cooperation to U.S. authorities, analysis of the 76 pounds of seized heroin revealed it to be identical in quality to the 22 pounds seized at Houston, Texas, on November 7, 1962. In that affair, Customs investigators had brought charges against four men: Milton Abramson, Vincent Ferrara, Joe Stassi and Anthony Granza. The last two were known to police as active and influential members of the Gambino clan. Stassi in particular was considered as important a figure as Salvatore Giglio in the North American heroin traffic. He had close relationships with Mondolini and Chauvet who were suspected of having supplied the 22 pounds of heroin seized at Houston. Analysis of the heroin destined for Lucien Rivard and similar packaging methods used in both cases strengthened the suspicions. Furthermore, the quality and origin of the heroin supplied by Mondolini was identical to that of drugs in three important earlier seizures: on the *Saint-Malo* in November 1955; from Giuseppe

Paul Mondolini   Jorge Edouardo Moreno Chauvet

Cotroni in July 1959; from Roger Laviolette in Paris, in August 1963, hardly two months before Caron's arrest in Texas.

The French Connection had obviously not been broken — far from it. Caron's testimony therefore was essential. Every effort was made to ensure his protection, and that of his wife and their four children. On October 30, U.S. Attorney General Robert Kennedy telephoned his Canadian counterpart to say that Arnold Stone, a lawyer from the rackets division of his department, would go to Montreal to escort the Caron children to a safe place in the U.S. Ever since the Montreal lawyer Danis had communicated the threats to Caron, the RCMP had been providing constant protection of the children. On November 1, Mr. Stone arrived in Montreal and the following morning the children were taken to a secret place under the protection of U.S. Treasury agents.

Meanwhile, Narcotics Squad investigators had begun the task of confirming and corroborating Michel Caron's statements. Everything was being done to collect evidence as quickly as possible. Teams were established to find Rivard and his men and observe all their activities. There were indications from Laredo that Mondolini, Farina and Scalici might soon be arriving in Montreal to discuss the effects of the seizure with Rivard. Round-the-clock surveillance was mounted at the international airport. Other teams were assigned to assist Customs officers at the ports of Quebec City and Montreal on arrival of ships from France.

Informers also made a contribution. A month before Caron's arrest, some of them had advised the Narcotics Squad that Rivard had resumed his drug trafficking activities and had recently received a 40-kilo cargo (nearly 90 pounds), most of it destined for the U.S. market. A week earlier, heroin in capsules had reappeared on the local market after four months of extreme scarcity. The last signs of capsules dated back to the end of April, when a local distributor, Paul Lambert, was being supplied by the ounce by Roger Laviolette.

The latest information from the underworld, corroborated by the observations of federal agents, linked Lambert closely to Emile Hogue, also known as Pit Lépine, one of Rivard's most faithful companions. Hogue's name had come up the day after the arrest of the Caron couple when Narcotics Squad agents were checking on their passport numbers as transmitted from U.S. agents. It was at that moment, too, that the name of the justice of the peace, Jean-Paul Bergeron, appeared in the dossier for the first time. Police were about to interview Bergeron immediately, until they noticed he lived across the street from Emile Hogue. They decided it would be better to postpone the interview.

At the end of October, word was coming in that Caron was being blamed for disobeying Rivard's instructions, hiding the heroin under the back seat of the car instead of under the front seat as he should have. Nevertheless, his arrest had spread panic in the Rivard gang where there was talk of obtaining his release on bail so he could be eliminated. It was also being said that Rivard had connections with four other persons in Montreal, including one of the leaders of the local Mafia. (5) This group of four was said to have invested $50,000 as the down payment for the 76 pounds of heroin in Mexico. The rest was to be paid after delivery to Montreal. Another shipment was expected soon in Montreal, again via Mexico City, where another courier would take delivery.

Agents also noted with interest that Rivard and his wife had spent two months in Mexico during the previous winter. It was true that Rivard detested cold weather. But the visit may also have served to renew his links with Paul Mondolini and partners. In any case, all his movements were now being constantly observed. On November 11, for example, he met Julien Gagnon, alias Massey, at the *Champ de Lys* cabaret. Two days later the two men met again, this time at *Laval Curb Service* (mentioned by Michel Caron). This place belonged to one of Rivard's great friends, Gilles Brochu, who had been involved in the search by Customs officers at Blackpool in March 1961. (6)

On November 15, federal agents assigned to tail Gagnon and Raymond Jones, followed them through east-end Montreal in the early afternoon. At one point a third gangster, Fernand Lacoste, joined the two others. Soon afterwards, unfortunately, the police agents' car found itself in a traffic jam between two huge tractor-trailers. By the time the agents got clear, the suspects' vehicle had disappeared. A little later in the afternoon they learned that the two men answering the descriptions of Jones and Lacoste had held up the administrative offices of the *Saucisse Dionne* company on Sicard Street near the port at about 2:50 p.m. The bandits' car was the same one the RCMP agents had been following. It belonged to a city policeman who had just reported it stolen.

That evening, federal police surveillance teams patrolled around the east-end taverns and bars where Lucien Rivard's cronies often met. About 9 p.m. Jones, Lacoste and Gagnon were spotted in a St.

---

5. In 1965 the Narcotics Squad learned that during this period Rivard had been doing business with the Frenchman who had succeeded Jean Jehan and Jean Venturi.

6. See Chapter Seven.

Catherine Street East tavern. The information was immediately transmitted to city detectives who arrested the three suspects. RCMP detectives took no part in this operation so as not to awaken any suspicions among Rivard's couriers, who were still unaware of the Narcotics Squad's renewed interest in them. Searches at the homes of Jones and Gagnon produced new evidence about their trips to France on Rivard's behalf.

With Gagnon and Jones under arrest, the Narcotics Squad concentrated its surveillance on Rivard and on François Groleau, whose real first name was Charles-Emile. In the last two months of 1963 and in early January 1964, the two men were seen together several times, often in a Mount Royal Avenue furniture store, *Les Immeubles le Plateau.* The store belonged to Eddy Lechasseur, who had a record of criminal convictions. He and Rivard went on a visit to Japan together for a few days in mid-January. (7) Rivard was also observed in the company of his old friends Emile Hogue, Bill Lamy and Wilfrid Leclerc.

On January 11, the RCMP learned that another Rivard henchman, Paul Delaney, was preparing to leave for Mexico at the end of the month. The U.S. Bureau of Narcotics and U.S. Customs were immediately notified. Delaney was primarily known to police as proprietor of the *Key Bar,* a bootleg liquor joint on Dezery Street haunted mainly by habitual criminals. On January 24, the Narcotics Squad got further details: eleven days earlier, Delaney had gone to the *East-End Auto Body* garage on Aird Street, owned by Gaston Ethier, and had a secret compartment installed in his car. (8) Bill Lamy had been seen at the garage on the same day. Two days later Rivard was followed to Dorval airport. After asking at the Sabena Airlines counter if a certain Dusseault had been on the last flight from Mexico, he made a long distance telephone call to Mexico. One of the agents shadowing him managed to occupy the adjacent phone booth without being noticed. He heard the trafficker say in French:

---

7. On March 4, 1963, Lechasseur opened *Les Immeubles le Plateau* with the intention of arranging a fraudulent bankruptcy, which he did in the following December. A few months later he was charged not only for that bankruptcy, but also for his participation in a $300,000 bankruptcy fraud in which Judge Adrien Meunier, former Liberal Member of Parliament for Montreal-Papineau, was implicated.

8. There was no family relationship between Gaston Ethier and the brothers Anatole and Victor Ethier, who were cronies of Jean-Paul Tremblay and Roger Laviolette.

A few of Rivard's friends.

Paul Lambert

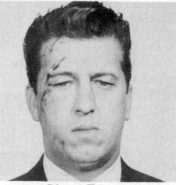

Gérard Turcot

Gaston Clermont

Paul Delaney

Gerry Turenne

Eddy Lechasseur

"The guy wasn't on the plane. I just checked. Reserve the same apartment we've been using for the past month. I think the boys will be there next Sunday."

On January 27, Rivard returned to Dorval airport to meet one of his friends who was coming back from Mexico. This was Gaston Clermont, a businessman from Ile-Jésus and a well-known political organizer for the Liberal party. When Rivard and his wife had returned from Mexico the previous year, they had been met at the airport by Clermont, who had also spent a few days with them in Acapulco. When Clermont arrived this time, he stayed at the airport for about an hour and 45 minutes and made new reservations for Mexico. On that same day, the 27th, Delaney and three friends left by car for Mexico.

Early the next morning Gaston Clermont took a flight to Mexico. Was he carrying a message from Rivard? No one knew. That evening Charles-Emile Groleau, who had not been seen for several days, arrived at Rivard's home and stayed for a few hours. Delaney and his friends, meanwhile, arrived in Mexico three days later. It was thought they would go to Acapulco the following Sunday, February 2. On February 4, U.S. Bureau of Narcotics agents observed a meeting of Delaney and one of his friends with unknown men. On the 7th, the Narcotics Squad in Montreal noted a meeting at the *Queen Elizabeth Hotel* of Rivard, Frank Cotroni and three strangers. All the detectives managed to find out was that part of the meeting took place in the Turkish bath and that at a certain moment there had been talk of a sum of $200,000. Late in the afternoon, Gaston Ethier and his girlfriend boarded a flight for Mexico. That night Clermont and two friends left Acapulco and went to Las Vegas.

About mid-February, the Bureau of Narcotics learned that the Mexican Jorge Moreno Chauvet was in France with an amount of $160,000. He was believed to be arranging with Mondolini for a shipment of heroin for Rivard. After the arrest of the Caron couple, Chauvet had gone to Paris, where the central office of narcotics established that he stayed at the *Georges Hotel* from October 28 to 31, with a 23-year-old Mexican, Alfonso Bonilla. As for Mondolini, he had occupied a room in the *25 Hotel* in Paris, from October 29 to November 4.

On February 23, Gaston Ethier, his girlfriend, two of Delaney's companions and another couple returned by air to Montreal. The search of their baggage turned up nothing of interest. A few days later it was learned that Delaney would come back to Montreal about the middle of March.

All these incidents and comings and goings seemed strange and disorganized to the Narcotics Squad. Were these trips actually related to Rivard's activities in narcotics trafficking? Were all these trips to Mexico in recent days somehow related to each other?

On March 7, Quebec Provincial Police detectives notified the RCMP that they had just taken into custody Lucien Rivard and two other men, Gilles Brochu and Roger Beauchemin! The three men had been arrested the night before by municipal police in Chomedey on a complaint from a local electrical contractor, Gaétan Raymond, who claimed he had been robbed and beaten by Rivard and his two accomplices. His wife had also been molested. An amount of $7,200 in cash and jewelry had been stolen, but police believed the robbery was only a pretext for beating up Raymond in revenge for his openly critical remarks about Rivard. Rivard and his friends had first been taken to the jail in Sainte-Dorothée, a municipality on Ile-Jésus. Then Chomedey police had delivered them to the Provincial Police, though not without some difficulty. As the police led out their prisoners, five hoodlums, led by a small-time gangster named Réjean Lavoie, rushed Rivard and gave him a pretty good beating, apparently on Raymond's behalf. (9) The police had been unable to prevent the incident, and had it not been for Rivard's own strength, the affair might have ended very badly.

Rivard, Brochu and Beauchemin appeared in Criminal Court on March 7 and were denied bail. Their preliminary inquiry was set for March 13. On the evening of March 9, Roger Beauchemin made a request to talk to officers of the RCMP. He said he had interesting things to say about Lucien Rivard. The Narcotics Squad was notified and the two officers in charge of the investigation, Sergeant Ronald Crevier and Constable Gilles Poissant went to meet Beauchemin that night in prison. He gave them this account:

"In 1962, I lived in Trois-Rivières and was working as a personnel officer for *Wabasso Cotton Ltd.* At the time, I was living with a woman, Jeannette Bergeron, whose brother Gérard was Gaston Clermont's partner in *B.C. Asphalt Ltd.* At the beginning of 1963, Jeannette and I went by car to Mexico with a friend, a Chinese, who was co-owner of a restaurant in Trois-Rivières. We went to Acapulco where we met Jeannette's brother and Gaston Clermont. At that time I met Lucien Rivard for the first time. He was in Acapulco too and Clermont introduced me to him.

---

9. A month later Lavoie was also arrested for theft and rape. He was attacked and beaten one night by an unknown assailant in Bordeaux Jail. On February 24, 1965, he was freed on parole but four days later in Chomedey he was shot in the head and killed...

"In June, two months after I got back to Trois-Rivières, I decided to move to Montreal. In fact I got a place in Chomedey, just across the street from Clermont's house on Saint-Antonio Street. Before I could get into my own apartment, I even stayed in Clermont's basement for a few weeks. As soon as I arrived I began doing pick and shovel work for Clermont and Bergeron. A little while later they hired me as a clerk at *B.C. Asphalt,* at $75 a week.

"Lucien Rivard often came to the office. I knew he was owner of *Plage Idéale* with Gerry Turenne. Since I had a lot of debts at that time, one day I asked Clermont if he could get me a weekend job as waiter at the Domaine Idéal. He said he'd fix it up with Rivard pretty soon. A week later he told me to get dressed as a waiter, with a bow tie, white shirt and dark suit and go to the Domaine Idéal. I worked there a couple of weekends.

"Naturally I saw Rivard often. At a certain point I made up my mind and asked him if he could help me pay off my debts quickly. I had already noticed that some funny things happened around there and I decided to try my luck. Rivard said he'd think it over and would talk to me again later because he had something going then. A couple of weeks later, at the beginning of August, he took me aside and asked me if I'd be interested in going to Mexico. I told him yes. Then he asked me if I had a passport. I did have one. Then he said: 'We'll pay all your expenses, $1,000, and when you get back, I'll give you $1,750.' I asked him what the gimmick was. He told me to think it over and not to ask any questions. If I was interested I should let him know.

"I talked it over with Jeannette, telling her it would help us pay our debts. At the time I thought it might involve bringing back a little gold. Anyway, I made up my mind. I went back to see Rivard and told him I accepted the offer. He said that was fine and when the time came he would notify me. A few days later he came to see me in the office of *B.C. Asphalt,* on Boulevard des Terrasses in Auteuil, and asked me if my car was in good condition. I told him the tires weren't much good. He asked me to let him have the car because he knew a garage which would fix everything up. I gave him my keys and he left with the car. It was a 1960 Pontiac Laurentian, a four-door. A week later, a black with a big cigar brought the car to my place. My girlfriend saw him and told me he left with Rivard after. The auto had been put into shape and four new tires had been installed. Around that time I asked Clermont if I could be away for three weeks or a month, on a job for Rivard. The next day he told me that would be O.K. I told him I'd be going to Mexico, all expenses paid by Rivard.

"Around August 8, Rivard asked me if I was ready to leave. I said yes. Then he gave me gave me half of a U.S. banknote. It was a ten dollar bill or a hundred dollar bill. He told me to go to *El Diplomatico Hotel* in Mexico City and register under a false name. Someone would come to see me there but before talking to him, I'd have to make sure he gave me the other half of the banknote. I was supposed to be at the hotel six days later, at exactly 9 p.m. I left with Jeannette, on August 10, at four in the afternoon. Just before we left Rivard came and gave me $900 in Canadian and U.S. bills. He advised me not to call him before I was ready to come back and not to send postcards to anyone for any reason.

"We went to Mexico by way of Toronto, Windsor, Detroit, Dallas and various cities. Even before we got to the U.S. border I had to have my brakes fixed in a garage. That cost me $20. We got to Mexico City about 8 p.m. on the 15th, 16th or 17th, I can't remember the exact date. I registered under the name Rivard had given me and 20 minutes later someone knocked at the door of our room. I opened it and the guy who was there greeted me by my assumed name. He spoke bad English and said he was sorry I hadn't been there at 7 p.m. Then he gave me half of a banknote. I took it into the bathroom to make sure the serial number corresponded with the half I had. It did. The guy introduced himself to me as George. Looking at the pictures you show me, I can see that he was Jorge Edouardo Moreno Chauvet.

"George left after the verification of the bill. He came back the same night about 10 o'clock. We went down to the lobby together and he asked if we could use my car. He said we wouldn't have to go far. In fact, we went a few streets and were joined by another car with two guys in it, Frenchmen I think. They'd been waiting for us and the one sitting in the right front seat was Paul Mondolini, judging by the photos you showed me. He seemed to be the leader of the group. George and I went and sat in their car with them and we talked about my trip, about Rivard, his operations, Plage Idéale. At the end, Mondolini told me he'd meet me at 2 o'clock the next afternoon. Jeannette could come with me and he'd show us Mexico City.

"The next day, at the agreed time, I went with my girlfriend to the same place I'd met the guys the night before. It was near a park, and their car, a Chrysler, was there. George was at the wheel and Mondolini was seated beside him. They showed us around the city. We didn't talk any business. At the end of the afternoon they drove us back to our hotel and before leaving, told us they'd take us to dine in a chic restaurant at noon the next day.

"The following noon a third man, a Frenchman from the south, came to meet us and take us out to lunch. He told me he was replacing George and that his name was Pierre. We did some sightseeing again and then came back to our hotel.

"About 11 o'clock the next morning, George telephoned me and told me to leave my keys in the car. Naturally, I did, and early in the afternoon I noticed that my car had gone. It was brought back to me late that night. Inside it were 78 plastic sacks containing white powder. Later George or Mondolini warned me not to use the car except for my trip home.

"The next day they let me know that everything was in order for my return to Montreal. Pierre came to see me in our hotel room and helped us pack our bags. Then he came with us and helped us find a quick way out of the city. When he left us after about 20 minutes, he gave me a slip of paper with a telephone number on it. He told me to call once we got into the United States. It took us three days to get to San Antonio, Texas. I called Pierre in Mexico from there to tell him everything was fine and that we had crossed the border.

"We came back to Montreal by the same route we had taken when we left. We arrived on August 30. Back in Montreal, I telephoned Rivard and he told me to come and meet him at *Laval Curb Service*. I went there right away and gave my car keys to Rivard. He told me to wait. A half-hour later he came back with my keys, and before leaving, gave me $1,100 or $1,200.

"About two weeks later, I met Rivard again. He gave me another $200. He had deducted the amount it had cost for the repairs to my car. After that, he never asked me to make any more trips for him. But once, Rivard asked me to go to the airport at Dorval to meet Pierre, the Frenchman I had met in Mexico City."

This was the first statement made by Roger Beauchemin. A little later, he completed the statement by declaring that before his return to Canada he had gone to Flint, Michigan, on Rivard's instructions where in a motel he delivered, to a certain Frank, 69 of the 78 sacks of white powder supplied by Chauvet and Mondolini. He had brought the nine remaining sacks to Rivard, who took delivery during the meeting at *Laval Curb Service*. Beauchemin identified Frank as the same man to whom Michel Caron had delivered two shipments of heroin at Bridgeport, and who had since been identified as Frank Jones Coppola, alias James Miller, of Milford, Connecticut. According to the Bureau of Narcotics, he was a partner of the mafioso David Iacovetti in several commercial enterprises. He was also operator of *Princess Beauty Salons* in Milford and Orange

Domaine Idéal

Laval Curb Service

(Photos La

and of the *Midas Realty Corp., Dolphie Realty Corp.,* and *Princess Academy of Hairdressing.*

On March 13, three days after his first statement, Beauchemin appeared with Rivard and Brochu before Judge A. Cloutier at their preliminary hearing on charges of robbery and assault. Beauchemin admitted having provided the others with the key to Raymond's residence. But Raymond, oddly enough, found himself unable to make a positive identification in court of Lucien Rivard as the man who had attacked him. Later the RCMP learned that the contractor and his wife had been threatened with death. Rivard was freed at the preliminary hearing, therefore, for lack of evidence. Only Brochu and Beauchemin were sent to trial.

The verdict did not unduly disappoint Narcotics Squad agents who knew that Rivard's days of glory were numbered. Though he was still unaware of it, he had been formally indicted on January 17 for international trafficking in heroin by a federal grand jury for the South Texas district, following testimony by Michel Caron. With the confession of Roger Beauchemin, who was also prepared to testify under oath before the grand jury, it was now possible to envisage the early arrest of Canada's number one narcotics trafficker.

Meanwhile, in Mexico, the Bureau of Narcotics was not idle. In cooperation with the Mexican federal police, the American agents broke up the Chauvet organization and seized at least 23 kilos (40 pounds) of heroin ready to be delivered. On March 9, 10 and 12, ten Mexican traffickers were arrested and ten others were being sought. Jorge Edouardo Moreno Chauvet was locked up and so was the young Alfonso Bonilla who had accompanied him to Paris at the end of October. Three other couriers were also charged. In all, they admitted transporting from France 100 kilos of pure heroin, of which only 23 had been seized (220 pounds and 40 pounds respectively).

On March 14, Mexican police made other arrests. This time the suspects were Rivard's friends: Paul Delaney and his girlfriend; Roger Roy, another employee at Domaine Idéal; and Lou Grégoire, owner of the *Saint-Placide Hotel,* who has been mentioned earlier. They were arrested at Acapulco and taken incommunicado to Mexico City. (10) Delaney was questioned on his contacts with

10. Thanks to Roger Beauchemin's statement, the RCMP were able to establish that Lucien Rivard's telephone call at Dorval airport on January 26 had been made to Roger Roy. Rivard asked Roy, who was visiting Mexico with Maurice Lévesque, another Domaine Idéal employee, to reserve rooms for Delaney and his group. Rivard had been accompanied by an unknown person when he made the call. Beauchemin revealed himself to be that person.

Gaston Clermont, Lucien Rivard and several other persons. Nothing of much interest was found in his luggage, except for half of a Canadian two-dollar bill. He claimed this was part of a bet he had made with a girl, but police knew it to be a method much-used by international traffickers to verify identities. In any case, on March 19, Delaney and his girlfriend were deported to Laredo, Texas, while the two others were freed. In Dallas, Delaney was arrested again and interrogated by the special services of the local police. Throughout his stay in the United States, he was under constant surveillance by the Bureau of Narcotics.

In Montreal, the Narcotics Squad was accelerating its efforts to collect all possible evidence supporting the new information that was coming in. In mid-May, everything was ready and on May 20, Roger Beauchemin testified before the grand jury in Houston. His testimony confirmed that given five months earlier by Michel Caron who, in the meantime, had been sentenced to ten years in prison. A few days later, U.S. Attorney General Robert Kennedy gave orders to seek the extradition from Canada of Lucien Rivard, Raymond Jones, Julien Gagnon and Charles-Emile Groleau.

On June 17, 1964, Pierre Lamontagne, a young prosecutor for the Canadian department of Justice, instituted the extradition procedures in Montreal on behalf of the U.S. government. The next day the U.S. consul-general in Montreal, Jérôme T. Gaspard, appeared in Superior Court before Judge Roger Ouimet and signed the charges issued by the grand jury in Texas. Rivard and his accomplices were then arrested by the Narcotics Squad on June 19, just as the U.S. Bureau of Narcotics was arresting Frank Coppola in Milford, Connecticut. Defended by a battery of well-known lawyers, the prisoners appeared in Superior Court that same day before Judge Claude Prévost who was acting as extradition commissioner. The judge made note of the prisoners' determination to present all possible resistance to the extradition request, and to force the U.S. government to prove, at least in summary form, that its accusations were well-founded. In the meantime, they were denied bail. The legal arguments continued until September 25, on which date Judge Prévost ordered the extradition of the four men. Petitions for habeas corpus, however, prevented the immediate execution of the judgment.

On November 23, these petitions were still under deliberation by the Court of Queen's Bench, when a national scandal, with Lucien Rivard at the heart of it, broke in the House of Commons in Ottawa. On that day the leader of the New Democratic Party, T.C. Douglas, and the member of Parliament for the Yukon, Eric

Nielsen, accused two federal government officials — Raymond Denis, former executive assistant to the Immigration minister and former assistant to the Justice minister, and Guy Lord, former special assistant to the Justice minister — of having attempted to bribe Pierre Lamontagne, who was the lawyer acting for the U.S. government in the extradition proceedings, in order to obtain bail for Lucien Rivard. Well-documented, Mr. Nielsen told the House of Commons that a criminal act had been committed, beyond all doubt, but that the Justice department, and the Commissioner of the RCMP had concluded that there was insufficient evidence to justify charges. Questioning the real motives behind the political authorities' refusal to press charges after the RCMP investigation, the NPD leader demanded a judicial inquiry to clarify the whole affair.

These charges exploded like a bomb in Parliament and throughout the country. The shock was so great that the acting prime minister, Paul Martin, tabled an order in council barely two days later creating a public commission of inquiry under the chief judge of the Quebec Superior Court, Frédéric Dorion. The judge's mandate required him to inquire into: "the truth of certain allegations concerning (a) the offer of a bribe to a lawyer whom the American government had retained to take action before the courts for the extradition of a certain Lucien Rivard, (b) pressures brought

Judge Frédéric Dorion

to bear on him; and the behavior of the Royal Canadian Mounted Police and the minister of Justice when the said allegations were brought to their attention."

Judge Dorion held public hearings through the winter of 1964-65 and into spring. He submitted his report to the government in June 1965. According to his report, Lucien Rivard enjoyed considerable support from within the Liberal party and his contacts had made strong efforts to obtain his release on bail and to prevent his extradition to the United States.

In brief, the inquiry showed that Mrs. Rivard and two of her husband's friends, Eddy Lechasseur, mentioned earlier in this book, and Robert-Emilien Gignac, a general contractor with few scruples, had conspired to obtain Rivard's release by bribery and political influence peddling. The group first sought to use the services of Guy Masson, a salesman who was also an important Liberal party organizer in federal, municipal and school board elections and former president of the Chambly Liberal Association on the south shore of Montreal. He was also associated with Gignac who was the first to think of using political influence on Rivard's behalf, the day after the trafficker's arrest.

On June 22, Gignac had met his friend Masson and introduced him to Mrs. Rivard and Eddy Lechasseur. Masson was given $1,000 and went that same night to Ottawa to meet one of his friends, Raymond Denis, a lawyer who had recently become executive assistant to the federal Immigration minister after having been special assistant to the Justice minister. He had known Masson since 1959 when they worked together in political organizations. With the knowledge that $50,000—$60,000 could be contributed to the Liberal party campaign fund, Denis agreed to intervene to help Rivard. On July 14, 1964, he asked his close friend, Pierre Lamontagne (the lawyer who was acting for the U.S. government) to come to Ottawa that same day to discuss an urgent matter. During the meeting Denis offered Lamontagne a sum of $20,000 if he agreed not to oppose Rivard's application for bail. Denis said that Rivard was a good friend of the party, that there were rumors of an imminent federal election, that his help would be needed in the future and it would be an advantage for the party if Rivard obtained bail. Lamontagne categorically refused the offer, but because of his friendship with Denis, kept the bribery attempt to himself.

Six days later, however, on June 20, while he was on vacation at his parents' home, Lamontagne received a telephone call from Raymond Daoust, one of Rivard's lawyers. Daoust asked him on what date the bail application for Rivard should be made, as he understood everything had been arranged in Ottawa. The same evening Lamontagne received a second call from Daoust, as well as two threatening calls from Gignac. In the days following, the 29-year-old prosecutor told Denis to tell his friends to leave him alone. Lamontagne also notified Sergeant Ronald Crevier of the Narcotics Squad, who was on vacation and advised him to call Inspector J.-Raoul Carrières if he was worried about something. He also met Daoust a few times.

During one of these meetings, Rivard's lawyer mentioned certain reports that Lamontagne had agreed not to oppose bail for Rivard in exchange for a payment of $20,000 of which half had already been paid to him. The rumor that Lamontagne had accepted money for his help in obtaining Rivard's release was current at that time in police and court circles as well as among politicians. Obviously, it was false. Following his meetings with Lamontagne, Daoust let it be known that he would not apply for bail. But on August 4 a request for bail signed by Daoust and his colleague Joe Cohen was made and notice of it received by Lamontagne. The same day another high official entered the scene: Guy Lord, special assistant to the Justice minister, telephoned Lamontagne to inquire about the possibilities of bail for Rivard.

A week later, on August 11, André Letendre, executive assistant to the Justice minister, also telephoned Lamontagne to encourage him to consent to bail. Letendre told Lamontagne that if he agreed, he could expect to be engaged for more cases by the federal government and would benefit greatly. That same day, Guy Rouleau, Liberal MP for Dollard and parliamentary secretary to the Prime Minister of Canada, Lester B. Pearson, also called Lamontagne for the same reason.

According to Judge Dorion's report, it was at Rouleau's instigation that Lord and Letendre intervened with the U.S. government's prosecutor. Rouleau himself had been approached by his own brother Raymond, who had been a friend of Rivard for about ten years and had received a request for help from Mrs. Rivard and Eddy Lechasseur. Another Rivard friend, Gaston Clermont, had been Guy Rouleau's chief organizer in the last federal election. In 1961 the Rouleau brothers had helped Rivard obtain a licence to sell beer at *Plage Idéale*. Furthermore, on June 17, 1964, just a few days before his arrest, Rivard had gone to Ottawa with Raymond Rouleau to see the MP Guy Rouleau about the possibility of getting bail or a transfer to Saint Vincent de Paul penitentiary for Robert (Bob) Tremblay, Rivard's friend who had been in jail in

Vancouver since 1955. The MP Rouleau had already made representations on Tremblay's behalf the previous year, producing a letter from Gaston Clermont offering Tremblay a job.

All these pressures finally impelled Lamontagne to seek the aid of RCMP authorities. On August 11, he made a first statement to Inspector Carrières, who submitted an immediate report to his superior officer, Superintendent J.-Adrien Thivierge, in charge of criminal investigations. On August 14, RCMP Commissioner George B. McClellan and his assistant J.-Rodolphe Lemieux met Justice minister Guy Favreau who ordered an investigation. Inspector Jean-Paul Drapeau, a former member of the Narcotics Squad, was put in charge of the investigation which lasted until September 18. In his report, Judge Dorion declared that this investigation could have been carried out with more speed and sureness had Inspector Drapeau not been obliged to make reports at each stage of the investigation and to wait for further instructions before continuing. The inspector was a competent investigator, but he had not been given the necessary latitude to conduct it to an effective end.

After the investigation, Commissioner McClellan and Assistant Commissioner Lemieux met the Justice minister and his colleague, Immigration minister René Tremblay, who had already suspended his employee, Raymond Denis. At this meeting on September 18, according to Judge Dorion, the RCMP authorities did not give judicious advice to the Justice minister, who therefore erroneously concluded that there was insufficient evidence to support the laying of any criminal charges. The Judge's report concluded: "There is no doubt that Mrs. Rivard, Eddy Lechasseur, Robert Gignac and Guy Masson conspired to obstruct the course of justice. There cannot be any doubt either that Lawyer Denis did offer to Lawyer Lamontagne a sum of $20,000 to obstruct the course of justice." Following the Dorion report, Denis was charged, convicted and sentenced to two years in prison, on December 15, 1967.

The Dorion inquiry also led to perjury charges against Lechasseur and Gignac but both were acquitted. Gignac was also later acquitted of the murder of Rocky Brunette, a small-time gangster who was said to have been given responsibility for delivering the $20,000 bribe Denis had offered to Lamontagne. Instead of handing the money over to another intermediary, Brunette was thought to have kept it for himself or shared it with an accomplice, and for this he was shot down on September 17, 1964. Two other friends of Rivard, Maurice Poirier and Robert Collins were also charged with Brunette's murder, but like Gignac, were acquitted for lack of evidence.

At the political level, the Dorion inquiry led to the resignations of the Justice minister Guy Favreau, the Member of Parliament Guy Rouleau and the ministerial official André Letendre. These were the darkest days of Lester B. Pearson's Liberal government.

For Lucien Rivard, the scandal broke at a bad moment and diminished his chances of preventing his extradition. On the following January 25, moreover, Judge François Caron of Superior Court rejected his request for a writ of habeas corpus. On February 19, Raymond Daoust carried the decision to Court of Appeal but Rivard knew he no longer had anything to gain by legal procedures. The best he could hope for would be to delay his extradition by a couple of weeks. Under the circumstances, there was only one solution.

On March 2, 1965 at 6:20 p.m. the evening meal was ending at Bordeaux Jail. Rivard and a fellow prisoner, André Durocher, asked permission to get hoses from the furnace room to water the outdoor rink. This was not an unusual request and it did not occur to the officer who granted permission that the outdoor temperature was an exceptionally mild 4 degrees Celsius (11). Watering the rink was therefore not only useless but ridiculous. Nor did the officer bother to get authorization from his immediate superiors, knowing that Durocher had been watering the prison rink since the beginning of winter.

Accompanied by a guard, Rivard and Durocher went to the heating plant to get the hoses, where the door was opened by one of the men in charge. The guard went to the corner where the hoses were hung and turned on a light. Durocher climbed the steps and took down two hoses. Rivard took one and started towards the door. Durocher got down and 20 feet from the stairs pulled a pistol on the guard who, seeing the gun, made a move as though to attack.

"Don't be foolish," Durocher told him. "This is serious."

The guard raised his hands. The gangster also covered the young furnaceman with his gun. While he made the two men lie face down and tied their hands and feet with adhesive tape, Rivard went to get the other furnaceman and made him lie down beside the two others. When they were all bound, Rivard and Durocher forced them to hop into the room beside the shooting range. Rivard got some electrical wire and tied the three men to a bench. Then he put on the guard's hat. The two prisoners then broke down the door of

---

11. 40°F.

the shooting range. They were in the courtyard.

An armed guard was posted on the west wall of the prison. The footbridge on the small interior wall permitted him to see in all directions. About 7:15 p.m. he saw a guard coming in his direction... It was Rivard wearing the cap he had taken. Approaching the sentinel, Rivard pointed a revolver at him, a fake revolver carved from wood and blackened with shoe polish. At the same moment, Durocher came up from behind and attacked the sentinel. The two prisoners threw him down on the footbridge and tied him up with adhesive tape and electrical wire.

With a ladder from the heating plant they easily scaled from the small interior wall to the large exterior wall. They carried the guard's 12-gauge shotgun and the hoses with which they let themselves down from the big wall. Then they ran across the fields around the prison and a few minutes later arrived at Poincarré Street, where they abandoned the shotgun on the grounds of a private home. They walked to Edouard-Valois Street, where a car happened to be making a regulation traffic stop. Without hesitation the two escapees opened the car door and forced the driver, an

(Photo Allô Police)

Bordeaux Jail from which Lucien Rivard and André Durocher escaped.

accountant, to let them in. Rivard took the wheel and sped to Saint-Michel Boulevard a few miles away. There they let the hostage out and continued alone, but not before they had asked for his telephone number and given him $2 for a taxi. Half an hour later, with his usual suavity, Rivard phoned the accountant and told him where he could find his car.

Back at the prison, barely five minutes after the escape of the two prisoners, the guards managed to free themselves and sound the alarm. Less than half an hour later the most famous manhunt in the history of Canadian police began. The moment the escape was known, the RCMP, Quebec Provincial Police and Montreal Police mobilized all available men and organized a coordinated operation. Later that evening, three federal ministers held a press conference in Ottawa to announce that absolutely no effort would be spared to recapture Lucien Rivard, the main figure of the Dorion inquiry. Justice Minister Guy Favreau and his fellow ministers of Transport and Immigration announced that warnings of the escape had gone out to the United States, to rail and airline companies in Canada, to all police forces in the country, all immigration services and border posts. All Canadian airports were under surveillance and main highway routes in Quebec had been blocked. Special measures were being taken to locate Lawyer Pierre Lamontagne and ensure his protection.

In Quebec, Attorney General Claude Wagner, a newcomer to politics, ordered an immediate inquiry into the circumstances surrounding the escape. He assigned one of his assistants, Jacques Ducros, to interrogate all the prison guards in the presence of officers of the RCMP and the Provincial Police. The investigation continued all night. The following afternoon in the Quebec legislative assembly, Mr. Wagner recounted the smallest details of the escape, carrying realism to the point of exhibiting in the Chamber the wooden revolver covered with black polish. Assembly members, though shocked and astounded by Rivard's audacity, could not withhold laughter at some of the humorous aspects of the affair. They could not believe their ears. The Attorney General also announced at that time that the assistant-governor of the prison and six guards had been suspended for the duration of the investigation. But he blamed the escape primarily on over-crowded prison conditions. The whole affair was also being scrutinized in the House of Commons in Ottawa by federal Members of Parliament. The Opposition had succeeded in adjourning regular business for an emergency debate in which serious accusations, without much foundation, were aimed at the Justice minister who was already on the carpet with the Dorion inquiry.

The Rivard affair quickly took on large proportions right across Canada, but particularly in Quebec. On March 4 it over-flowed again when Attorney General Wagner revealed to the assembly that Rivard had written to Bordeaux Jail governor Albert Tanguay to apologize for the trouble he had caused him! Here is the text of the letter:

"Dear Sir,

Just a few words to tell you it is not true that André Durocher and I stole $25 from one of your guards. I have never taken a cent from anyone poorer than I am. I had saved $460 during my eight and a half months in detention and my friend Durocher had done the same. It would have been a pleasure for us to give them $25 because those poor devils are paid starvation wages. It's also false that we used violence on them, even lighting cigarettes for them before we left and checking to make sure their bonds were not too tight.

"You've always been good to everybody at Bordeaux. We bitterly regret all the trouble we're causing everybody. You certainly don't deserve it, but I could see no other solution. I see that I can't get justice here. I am innocent. I have never seen or known this famous Michel Caron, the prisoner in Texas. Mr. Tanguay, there were never any officers or guards who helped in any way in our escape. It's known that they spend their time selling themselves to each other for a better position or a better salary.

"To sum up, do not punish your men on our account. They were perhaps guilty of negligence, but certainly not of helping us to escape. The 12-gauge (gun), I hope they gave it back to you, as we left it on a lawn at Poincarré Street and Valois when we borrowed Mr. Bourgeois' car and we did not molest him either. If I'm lucky, I'll be far away when you receive this letter. The escape was decided on quite suddenly about 4 p.m. yesterday, March 2, with no assistance either from outside or inside. Hoping you believe me and that this letter will help you to clarify matters. Once again, excuse us.

Devotedly yours
A. Durocher, L. Rivard
Signed: Lucien Rivard."

The reading of this letter provoked great laughter in the House and in the country. Police authorities however, were not amused. Since the escape, hundreds of people had called police to report sightings of the escapees in every imaginable place. They had been seen on the Pacific coast, in Florida, in a Montreal hotel, a Trois-

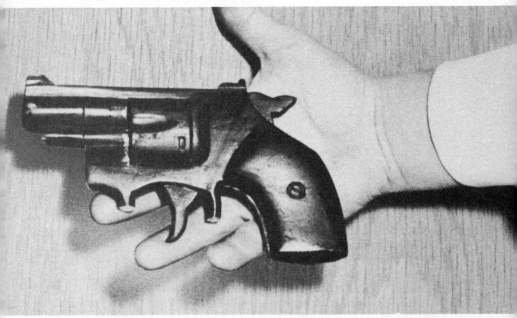

The wooden revolver covered with black polish used in the Rivard-Durocher escape.

Letter which Rivard forwarded to his wife via Spain. (Photos La Presse)

Rivières hotel, on an island in Rivière-des-Prairies, in the monastery at Saint-Benoît-du-Lac, on the islands of Saint-Pierre and Miquelon, in Mexico, Peru, Spain, New Brunswick... everywhere! Whenever the reports seemed plausible, they were checked. The F.B.I., the U.S. Bureau of Narcotics, U.S. Customs, Interpol, had been cooperating since the first hours of the escape. But the fugitives could not be found. The RCMP in Montreal had called at least 72 men off regular squad duty to look for Rivard. Eighteen of them were assigned to constant, uninterrupted surveillance of the comings and goings of Rivard's wife.

Members of the Narcotics Squad naturally played a key role in this gigantic manhunt. On March 5, for example, with representatives from the provincial and municipal police, they planned the 40 or so raids made the next morning on the homes of friends and acquaintances of the narcotics chieftain. A special force of 120 policemen paid visits to people like Vic Cotroni, his younger brother Frank, Emile Hogue, William Lamy, Blackie Bisson, Butch Munroe, Lou Grégoire, Gaston Clermont, Larry Buckszar, Gérard Turcot, Paul Delaney, Gaston Ethier, Gerry Turenne, Eddy Lechasseur and several others. Even the residence of the mayor of Auteuil, Adrien Dussault, a close friend of Rivard and of Gaston Clermont, was searched. So were the prison cells in Chomedey. The primary purpose of this operation was to create a climate of tension among Rivard's close associates, which might eventually encourage some of them to offer useful information.

As a result of the raids, six people were held for questioning, including Bill Lamy who was found in possession of false automobile registrations and of Canada savings bonds coupons of dubious origin. Lamy, wanted since mid-February in connection with a $340,000 cigarette robbery, had already admitted to the Dorion inquiry that he had supplied $17,000 towards the $60,000 fund collected the previous summer for Rivard's bail.

Over the next week, another score of raids were made and this time it was Eddy Lechasseur's turn to be taken to Provincial Police cells. Lechasseur, who had been seen several times with Mrs. Rivard, was charged with possession of an offensive weapon — in this case a blackjack found in a drawer in his apartment. It was a minor offense, but provided another opportunity to question one of Rivard's cronies. Rivard, in the meantime, was not letting himself be forgotten. On Thurday, March 12, the *Toronto Telegram* had exclusive publication of another letter from Rivard, this one addressed to his wife Marie and mailed from Vancouver. The letter contained little of interest to police, except for Rivard's stated intention to change his hiding-place and to write again in about two weeks. The Toronto newspaper paid Mrs. Rivard $3,000 for the letter. She had also announced that henceforth she would charge a fee for every interview she granted to journalists. On March 9, she had been paid $500 for a press conference at the *Queen Elizabeth Hotel.*

Two days before publication of this second letter, the federal government had put a price on Rivard's head. A reward of $15,000 was offered for information leading to the arrest of the famous fugitive. The Justice Minister explained that the government was posting this reward because it wished to honor the extradition commitment it had made to the United States. The day before, Judge Pierre Badeaux of Court of Appeal had rejected the second habeas corpus application in view of the non-appearance of Rivard. In the Quebec legislature, the debate went on for several days, mainly on a non-confidence motion by the Union Nationale opposition party which had earlier been refused an emergency debate. Gradually, however, calm was restored. Until mid-April there were no important developments in the police investigation. Information, anonymous or otherwise, continued to flow in, but none of it led anywhere.

On April 13, Marie Rivard made the news again when she declared she had received another letter from Lucien, this one from Barcelona, Spain. The RCMP verified the authenticity of the letter and noted that Rivard seemed well-informed on what was being written about him in Montreal. In his letter, he noted that he was being called "Petit Arsène," an expression which had been used by some French-language newspapers in Montreal. This led some to believe that Rivard might not be in Spain at all, but still in Quebec. This letter, as well as the one from Vancouver, could easily have been mailed by someone else in an attempt to throw police off the trail. But this third letter from Rivard was really the fourth. On March 30 he had sent a postcard to the prime minister of Canada, Lester B. Pearson:

Montreal, March 30, 1965

"Honorable Lester B. Pearson,
I leave Windsor tonight for Vancouver. I hope the road is clear for me now. I'm sorry I'm giving everybody so much trouble. But as you know, life is short. I have no intention of spending the rest of my life in prison. Please give my best wishes to my good friend, the MP Guy Rouleau.

Yours sincerely,
Lucien Rivard."

As the RCMP were examing Rivard's latest letters, U.S. Customs investigators were meeting Michel Caron. Caron supplied the names of several friends of Rivard and André Durocher with whom, as he had already admitted to Narcotics Squad agents, he had committed several robberies. He said that Rivard had confided to him once that he knew someone in the Marseilles region who helped underworld fugitives by hiding them in a castle. This information was communicated to the French central office for narcotics via Interpol. Later another rumor floating up from the underworld was also passed on to Interpol. This one recalled that Rivard had supposedly said at one time that if he ever had serious problems he would seek refuge on one of the islands off Portugal where his friend Batista, the ex-Cuban dictator, had settled.

Early in May, Georges Lemay, a one-time friend of Rivard, was arrested on a yacht at Fort Lauderdale in Florida. He had been wanted by police for several months for a $560,000 robbery at a Montreal branch of the Bank of Nova Scotia in 1961. Rumors spread after this arrest that Rivard was hiding out somewhere near Lemay's lair. Some people even reported to the F.B.I. that they had seen him in the vicinity with Durocher. But these reports were disproved a week or so later, when the Narcotics Squad learned that Emile Hogue had met Rivard somewhere in the Montreal area. This was a piece of hard information and the surveillance squads assigned to Rivard's friends were advised to increase their vigilance.

On May 28 one of Hogue's men was seen at Rivard's home. Accosted by police, he explained that Hogue had asked him to deliver a small heater to Mrs. Rivard. Seven days later the Montreal Police morality squad received a tip: André Durocher was living in Apartment 2, at 5855 Christophe-Colomb Street. The city police rushed to the address about 5:30 p.m., burst into the apartment and found Rivard's companion in escape. Durocher was with his wife and had two loaded revolvers on hand as well as three home-made bombs. But he had no time to use them. Taken to Montreal police headquarters, Durocher told detectives and two agents from the Narcotics Squad that he and Rivard had gone to Spain after their escape, then to Florida where they had hidden out not far from Georges Lemay's place....

After a few hours of interrogation however, Durocher changed his story and admitted he had been lying. He then said that Rivard was still in the Montreal region and had advised him, in case of arrest, to say that the two had separated two weeks earlier in Spain. Durocher stated that after the escape, which had been managed with the help of Eddy Lechasseur, he and Rivard had fled to western

Canada in a private plane. They had landed in Winnipeg and had driven from there to Vancouver by car, where Rivard had asked a friend to mail a letter. He had also asked another friend who was going to Spain to mail a letter to his wife from there. All this was intended to create confusion, said Durocher. Later the two had returned to Quebec to hide out in a Laurentian cottage at Lac L'Achigan. Rivard had left there about the end of May and had gone to another hideout, where he was still staying.

Durocher added that a man named Vincent Blais, alias Paul Leboeuf, helped Rivard in the Laurentians. Blais was responsible for the contacts with Mrs. Rivard. He also looked after supplies, along with another man named Fred Cadieux who was staying with Rivard. At the end of May, Cadieux had bought a Jeep station-wagon with $500 given to him by Rivard. Durocher also stated that every weekend when they were in the Laurentians, Rivard received a visit from Murielle Beauchamp, who was called Mimi, the secretary of one of Rivard's lawyers.

The police were puzzled. but they had no choice: all Durocher's statements would have to be checked. On the evening of June 2, a special squad of 80 RCMP and Provincial Police officers arrived at Lac L'Achigan to inspect the place described by the gangster. The cottage was occupied but not, unfortunately, by Rivard and his pals. Instead the police surprised a group of young people, freshly graduated from law school, enjoying their vacation in the cottage owned by the father of one of the graduates. Confused and angry at being so stupidly deceived, the officers confronted Durocher again. He stuck by his story. He would neither explain the apparent contradictions in it nor provide further details. In spite of this incident, other leads were checked. Vincent Blais had been located and was being kept under constant surveillance. But Mimi Beauchamp and Fred Cadieux could not be found. For the next month, nothing much could be added to the files except for a few interviews with underworld informers.

Early in July, Narcotics Squad agents decided to see Durocher again. They got in touch with their colleagues in the municipal bureau of criminal investigations who had Durocher in custody. The bureau replied, however, that for the time being they preferred to permit no further interviews with the prisoner. Curious, the federal agents delegated one of their men, Constable J.D. Farrell, to the Montreal Police. It was then learned that Durocher had revealed more of his secrets, particularly on the subject of a $1 million robbery of a Montreal postal truck on May 31, 1964. City detectives were hoping to obtain more details and for that reason did not wish to upset their man by subjecting him to other interrogations. Durocher had already told city police that he did not appreciate the way the federal agents had treated the information he had given them. Durocher explained that he had deliberately lied about the Lac L'Achigan cottage just to see how the agents would react. They had fallen into the trap and raided the place immediately. If Rivard had been captured, he would certainly have deduced that his fellow-escapee had turned him in.

Another factor induced prudence in the city police. A reliable informer had told them that Durocher had assassinated André Paquette, the gang leader in the postal truck robbery, and his girlfriend Alice Rioux. Durocher was said to have hidden the bodies of the victims in one of his Laurentian hideouts in the Saint-Sauveur – Morin Heights region. The prisoner was still unaware that police knew his crime. The detectives, before confronting him with what they knew, wanted to get as much information out of him as possible.

It was a delicate situation, but city police, nevertheless, were ready for close cooperation with the Narcotics Squad. On the afternoon of July 7 there was another meeting between the detectives and the two RCMP representatives, Constable Farrell and Corporal Gilles Poissant who had also learned from a confidential source the previous night of the murder of André Paquette. The second meeting established that on the whole Durocher had told the truth about his movements, and Rivard's, after the escape from Bordeaux Jail. He had clearly indicated to municipal police the location of three other summer cottages in the Piedmont region used by Rivard and André Paquette. One of these cottages had been rented by a man named Roland Phoenix, 40, the brother of Alice Rioux, and was to be used only in an emergency.

The investigation by city detectives had also identified Rivard's main contact in Montreal. It was Sébastien Boucher, 41, a good friend of Fred Cadieux. These two men were suspected of having staged the bold robbery of $164,000 in gold ingots near Kirkland Lake, Ontario on the preceding June 11. Information coming to the Narcotics Squad suggested that Rivard was no stranger to the organization of this robbery or to another which had reaped $125,000 worth of cigarettes.

Sébastien Boucher lived with his wife Jackie in Apartment 2 at 5210 Saint-Hubert Street in Montreal. Police had bugged his home soon after he had been located and in this way had confirmed that Cadieux was constantly in touch with Boucher and was visiting him twice a week. The police believed that Cadieux was the link with

Rivard and that Rivard had left the Laurentians after the murders of Paquette and his girlfriend. Another man, Richard Tinsley, known as Wire, was also in contact with Boucher. He was suspected of having replaced Vincent Blais after Blais realized he was being watched by the RCMP. The wiretap also revealed that Boucher had made the necessary bail arrangements for Eddy Lechasseur who had been in custody since mid-March. In a conversation with Jackie, Lechasseur had even asked for news of "the little baby," Rivard.

With this information in hand, federal and municipal police officers thought it advisable to consult with Provincial Police so that the task force which had been set up after the escape, and which had become more or less inactive, could resume its functions. Representatives of the three police forces met again on July 8. Provincial Police detectives revealed that they also were aware of the murder of the Paquette couple and that the motive, according to their information, was money — a hoard of $34,000. Durocher was believed to have had an accomplice, Conrad Brunelle, another thief who had been charged the previous year, with his wife, in the robbery of a Quebec City lingerie shop. Paquette had helped him to get bail, using Fred Cadieux as a go-between.

At the July 8 meeting, arrangements were made for pooling all information and planning investigations and surveillance of suspects, especially Boucher. The RCMP assigned its specially-created surveillance team for this purpose. The team members, the best in the business, were identified under the code name "Cannon." The next day they began their task of day-and-night surveillance of

(*Photo Allô Police*)

Sébastien Boucher at his court appearance following his arrest at the Woodlands cottage.

The woodlands chalet where Rivard had been hiding out.

Fred Cadieux, one of those arrested in the raid on the chalet.

Cadieux, Boucher and Mimi Beauchamp who in the meantime had been re-located.

Permanent observation points were set up around Boucher's home on Monday, July 12. The same day, the city police's wiretap revealed that Mimi Beauchamp did not know she was being followed and that she intended to take a day off during the week, probably Thursday. Fred Cadieux, who had not been heard from since the start of the operation, also telephoned Jackie Boucher. He told her his companion was fine and asked for news of Murielle. He added that he thought the young woman might be under police surveillance and said he would meet "Sébastien" in Montreal on Thursday.

Over the next two days, the Cannon team kept Boucher constantly in sight, despite his many movements around the city. They made special note of his meetings with the man named Richard Tinsley, with Bill Lamy and another individual who had just come back from Paris.

On Thursday about 9:50 a.m. Fred Cadieux arrived at Boucher's place. A half-hour later he left, driving a blue Jeep station-wagon. Seventeen detectives from the Cannon team took up discreet pursuit. Cadieux made their task easier by driving slowly and stopping on various errands. At 11:20 a.m. he stopped his vehicle at a liquor store on Earnscliffe Avenue at Queen Mary Road where he bought a case of liquor. Then Cadieux continued on his way, crossing the Mercier bridge and taking Highway 3 toward Chateauguay. He stopped at the Towers shopping centre in the small town and bought some groceries. The agents noticed he bought more than would be required for one person. At 12:30 p.m. Cadieux continued west on Highway 3. Half an hour later, reaching the town of Woodlands, he stopped on the grounds of an elegant summer cottage less than half a mile from the shores of Lake Saint-Louis. Because of the terrain, the Cannon team was unable to maintain direct watch on the premises. Instead it took measures to ensure that no one could leave without being seen.

With no further delay, the Narcotics Squad officers called in their provincial and municipal colleagues. They all gathered at 3 p.m. in the office of Superintendent J.-Raoul Carrières, in charge of RCMP criminal investigations in Quebec. Analysis of the situation led them to conclude that Rivard was probably in the Woodlands cottage, but that it would be better to wait for news from the Cannon team, rather than rush things too much. The federal agents however, despatched one of their pilots to make aerial photos of the area in anticipation of a police raid. The day of July 15 ended with no one leaving the cottage.

The next morning about 9 o'clock, Cadieux came out and got into his Jeep. He drove to Chateauguay, bought more groceries, and came back to the cottage about 10:30 a.m. At that hour, the three police forces were meeting again in Superintendent Carrières' office at RCMP headquarters in Montreal. The time had come to act, and the operation was assigned to Sergeant Sehl of the Narcotics Squad. The plan was to move a force in quickly and quietly to encircle the cottage and block access roads. Fifty-three men — 26 of them from the RCMP — were mobilized with all the necessary technical gear: tear gas, dogs, an airplane, three outboards. The operation was to begin at 4:55 p.m. and the cottage was to be entered and searched by 5:05 p.m.

At 3:20 p.m. while Sergeant Sehl was giving last-minute instructions to the raiding party at RCMP headquarters, the Cannon team saw Fred Cadieux leave the cottage again and drive toward Chateauguay. About 20 minutes later Cannon advised the radio operator that Cadieux was returning to Woodlands with Sébastien Boucher.

At 5 p.m., the 53 officers from the RCMP, Provincial Police and Montreal police were in position around the cottage. Their arrival and deployment had been carried out without a hitch. Three minutes later Sergeant Sehl gave the signal for the raid by charging into the cottage himself, his pistol in hand. The surprise was almost total! Cadieux and Boucher, in bathing suits, were sitting in the living room. Rivard was standing there, also in his bathing suit. The three men had been about to go for a swim and were not armed! By the time they realized what was happening, it was too late ... they were already in handcuffs! The vast manhunt had ended. Rivard had kept the country in suspense for 136 days.

The search of the cottage, which had been rented a few days earlier by Cadieux, turned up $16,515, which proved to be part of the loot from the famous postal truck robbery in May 1964.

The investigation showed that the day after their escape from Bordeaux Jail, Rivard and Durocher had joined Paquette in the cottage at Piedmont where they hid out. Paquette had arranged for one of his men, Vincent Blais, to escort the fugitives to the cottage. Rivard disguised himself as a woman on that occasion.

Paquette, Rivard and Durocher stayed together there for six weeks until Durocher took advantage of his companions' absence to rape his host's girlfriend, Alice Rioux. When Rivard learned of the incident, he sent Durocher away before Paquette's return. Durocher joined up with Conrad Brunelle and with a couple of other gangsters, they pulled a series of holdups around the province. They were the ones who held up another postal truck at Richmond on May 11. But that job only brought them $6,000.

As for Rivard, he had withdrawn to another Laurentian cottage at Saint-Hippolyte. On May 21, he threw a party at his cottage attended by Mimi Beauchamp, André Paquette and Alice Rioux, Sébastien Boucher and his wife Jackie, and Freddy Cadieux. That was the night Paquette and his girlfriend were murdered. Returning to their own cottage after Rivard's party, they surprised Durocher and Brunelle attempting to steal the rest of the loot from the postal truck robbery. Durocher shot the couple in cold blood and buried the bodies not far from the cottage. When Rivard learned of the murder, he decided to change his hiding-place. (12)

After the Woodlands cottage had been searched, Rivard and his pals were brought to Montreal. That night six U.S. Customs investigators arrived in the city. The next morning, to general surprise, Rivard was arraigned before Sessions Court Judge T.A. Fontaine. The attorney acting for the Quebec Justice department agreed to withdraw charges of escaping and armed robbery against Rivard so that the extradition order could be carried out as quickly as possible. (13) Free of all Canadian court proceedings, Rivard was given into the custody of the RCMP until the new federal Justice minister, Lucien Cardin, personally signed the extradition papers. Lawyer Pierre Lamontagne, still representing the U.S. government, attended the arraignment.

For five days Rivard was questioned at length by federal and provincial detectives but he refused to talk. On the evening of July 21 therefore, Justice minister Cardin signed the extradition order. About 2:30 p.m. on the sixth day, the Mister Big of Canadian drug trafficking was taken to Dorval airport, then in an RCMP Beechcraft plane to Plattsburg, in New York State where U.S. Customs agents took him into custody. He arrived in Houston at

---

12. For the next few months, Durocher toured the province denouncing his former accomplices. In March 1966 Conrad Brunelle committed suicide, leaving a note accusing Durocher and denying any participation in the Paquette-Rioux murders. Three months later Durocher also took his own life after indicating where the bodies had been buried.

13. Fred Cadieux and Sébastien Boucher were charged with being accessories after the fact. On March 11, 1966, Cadieux was sentenced to two years in prison to be served concurrently with a total of 10 years imposed in December 1965 for various charges of fraud. Boucher was sentenced to a month in prison and a fine of $1,000 on November 24, 1966.

The morning after his arrest, Lucien Rivard is taken to the Palace of Justice, Montreal.

(Photo Allô Police)

(Photo Allô Police)

noon the next day where his accomplices who had been extradited in May — Charles-Emile Groleau, Raymond Jones and Julien Gagnon — were already being held. That afternoon he appeared before federal Judge Ben C. Connally who fixed bail at $500,000 and set trial for September 13.

Two days before the trial began, Narcotics Squad agents in Montreal and Toronto arrested Bill Lamy and Dominique Baccari, known as Nick the Greek, along with about 30 pushers they had been supplying.

This round-up was the result of an arduous undercover operation launched at the beginning of the year by two young agents from the Toronto section of the Narcotics Squad. Over five months they had gathered enough evidence against 30 or so Toronto pushers and distributors of marijuana, hashish and heroin. At the end of May they came to Montreal where their Toronto contacts gave them easy entry to the world of drugs and addicts. A month

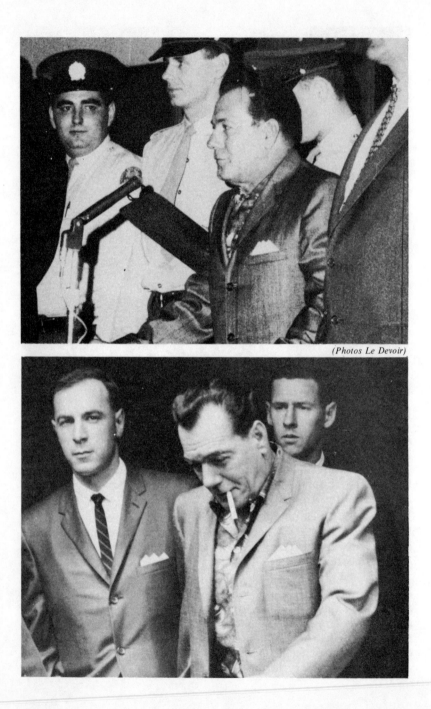

(Photos Le Devoir)

later, after a series of contacts with many pushers, most of them shoplifters or prostitutes, they made a connection with Dominique Baccari, a dealer who supplied Toronto and Vancouver as well as Montreal.

Because of their experience and the contacts they had made previously, the two undercover agents were able to adorn their propositions with realistic details and Baccari accepted them without question. They were soon able to engage in friendly debates with him over the state of the drug markets in Canada's big cities. When they first asked for heroin, Baccari said he would have to get it in New York, and on his return, he supplied them with 30 capsules. Two weeks later he showed them a secret compartment in his car, containing 350 capsules he was to deliver to Vancouver. He agreed to sell them 25 for $125.

The Baccari investigation completed, the undercover agents set out on the trail of Bill Lamy, one of Rivard's close associates. Thanks to an addict who was a mutual friend, one of the agents managed to meet Lamy but it took six weeks to get enough evidence for his arrest. Nearly every day Lamy would make an appointment with the agent and then cancel it. He would communicate only by telephone, using public booths so his address could not be traced. Lamy thought he was constantly being followed, which was not in fact true. Finally the police officer managed to visit Lamy in his apartment on August 24, where the trafficker complained about the sad state of the market:

"The European traffickers who usually supply us haven't budged since their last shipment was seized and Lucien was arrested. (14)

---

14. The seizure Bill Lamy referred to was probably that of the 28 kilos of pure heroin recovered at Montreal on March 24, 1965. On that occasion the Narcotics Squad assisted by the U.S. Bureau of Narcotics arrested five Frenchmen, four of whom were employed by Air France. In mid-January, the Bureau of Narcotics had notified the RCMP of the possibility that Roger Loiseleur, an Air France flight steward, might be involved in drug trafficking and with the New York Mafia. The U.S. agents knew that on August 3, 1964, he had delivered 17 kilos (37 pounds) to another Mafia courier. New information indicated that on March 23 another Russo agent was to take delivery of a new supply in Montreal. On March 22, the Narcotics Squad located the courier and established constant surveillance on his movements as well as those of Loiseleur. Loiseleur was arrested on the evening of March 24 as he was about to deliver four kilos to a room in the *Queen Elizabeth Hotel*. That morning he had already delivered six kilos to Russo's man but the federal agents took advantage of the courier's brief absence to seize the merchandise. The Bureau of Narcotics and the RCMP agreed not to arrest the courier, Carmine Paladino, in order to keep intact certain sources of information. He was kept under observation and was eventually arrested in

My man is in prison now and he's the only one who knows exactly where the drugs are stored. I tried to get a passport to go to France but they wouldn't give me one. I have contacts over there, but they won't come here because they think they're being watched all the time. There are even policemen dressed as longshoremen watching the docks."

If Lamy could not supply the undercover agent with heroin for the moment, he could supply codeine. He had part of the eight kilos (17 pounds) taken the previous winter at Dorval airport at the same time as gold ingots had been stolen. The codeine had been kept hidden for a long time so as not to attract any police attention, but now that the market was dry, the drug was being brought out for sale. Lamy asked for $5,000 a kilo (2.2 pounds) of codeine. He went to get it in a Cherrier Street building and turned it over to the agent in the lobby there. The Narcotics Squad decided that another transaction would be necessary to strengthen the evidence, which meant another two weeks of hide-and-seek between Lamy and the undercover agent. The deal was made on the evening of September 11 and immediately afterwards the arrests were made.

In Texas, the trial of Rivard and his three henchmen began as scheduled. It lasted seven days. On September 21, after three hours of deliberation on the testimony of Michel Caron and Roger Beauchemin, the 12 jury members from Laredo gave their verdict: guilty. Judge Connally pronounced the sentences on November 12. Lucien Rivard was sentenced to 20 years in penitentiary and fined $20,000; Julien Gagnon and Raymond Jones, his couriers, got 15 years and fines of $5,000; Charles-Emile Groleau, the intermediary, got 12 years and a fine of $5,000. In Montreal, three days earlier, Dominique Baccari had pleaded guilty and was sentenced to seven years in prison.

A year later, on September 15, 1966, Bill Lamy was given a three-year sentence and fined $5,000. Finally, in Hartford, Connecticut, the Milford hairdresser, Frank Coppola was sentenced to 12 years in prison on September 26, 1966. (15)

March 1966. The surveillance of Loiseleur had also resulted in the identification of four other accomplices. They were arrested the following day, March 25, 1965, after 18 kilos of heroin (39 pounds) had been found in their car. The investigation continued until the end of 1965, with further arrests in New York and Paris, including that of Henri La Porterie, the man in charge of the ring and a close associate of Paul Mondolini.

15. Coppola appealed his case however and after a number of other trials was finally acquitted.

The last act in the Rivard affair was played on Janauary 9, 1967 when Paris agents of the French central office for narcotics arrested Paul Mondolini, "the Mexican King of Narcotics." At the beginning of 1965, just before Rivard's escape, the U.S. Bureau of Narcotics arrested a Columbus, Georgia man who had received a refrigerator brought back from France with the household furnishings of a U.S. Army major. Nineteen pounds of heroin destined for the Miami Mafia were found in the refrigerator's double walls. The investigation led to the arrest of several Frenchmen, including the nephew of Marseilles' crime lord Joseph Orsini, one-time partner of Antoine d'Agostino. In exchange for reduced sentences, some of the accused exposed Paul Mondolini as one of the key leaders of the ring, along with two other Corsicans whose names had come up during the *Saint-Malo* investigation in 1955, Marcel Francisci and Achille Cecchini.

At the time of his arrest at Orly airport, Mondolini had just arrived from Marseilles. Police had been looking for him since the arrest of Michel Caron. He was charged with having brought into the United States, over the previous five years, ten tons of heroin with a street value of $9 billion.

Chapter 10

Before and After Expo 67

The arrest and sentencing of Lucien Rivard and several of his colleagues resulted in a marked slowdown of local gangsters' activities in heroin trafficking, both internationally and nationally. Fear of meeting the same fate no doubt induced many traffickers to be cautious about attempting to take over where Rivard and his gang had left off. But the main reason for the slowdown was the loss of the indispensable contacts with French suppliers. They were mistrustful men and few Montrealers could claim to have their confidence. Re-establishing the connection would almost certainly require the aid of Rivard himself or of Pep Cotroni. Only they could renew the links with the French underworld.

In September 1966 the RCMP Narcotics Squad was informed of resumed traffic in white heroin (French heroin) between Montreal and Toronto. With their numerous contacts in the underworld, the federal agents were able to identify the dealers within a few days. A Montrealer named Albert Teitlebaum, 38, was said to be delivering heroin capsules to several Toronto users. The information coming to police was that he worked for the well-known Peter (The Russian) Stepanoff who had been Pep Cotroni's chief lieutenant. Stepanoff, who had been sentenced to eight years in prison in 1960 for receiving stolen bonds, had been released on June 18, 1965, and little was known of his activities since then. He was believed to be associated in heroin trafficking now with Paul Duval, 51, long-time friend of Emile Hogue (Lépine) and former crony of Maurice Cloutier who had been shot down in October 1962. Cloutier, it will be recalled, was supplying certain Toronto wholesalers in 1961 and 1962 as well as distributing heroin in the Montreal market. He had been getting his supplies from Jean-Paul Tremblay, Roger Laviolette and some of Rivard's men.

On October 28, 1966, Teitlebaum arrived in Toronto to make

another heroin delivery. Detectives from the local section of the Narcotics Squad had been notified and were keeping an eye on him. The trafficker registered at a motel and then went into the city to meet a customer. While he was out federal agents discreetly searched his room and found 90 ready-for-sale heroin capsules in his baggage. They carefully took a few samples of the white powder and returned to their observation post. Teitlebaum returned to the motel a short time later and then left with the merchandise. Police had the proof that he was handling heroin but preferred to wait and observe additional deliveries to strengthen the case and to avoid tipping off Stepanoff and Duval to the police operation.

Teitlebaum made other deliveries to Toronto on November 4, 5 and 9. Each time, RCMP investigators managed to take samples without being noticed. On the last trip the agents, unable to maintain surveillance any longer, took 77 of the 84 capsules the trafficker had brought with him. When Teitlebaum discovered that his unsold heroin had disappeared, he rushed back to Montreal in confusion. Narcotics Squad agents expected that Stepanoff and Duval would suspect their courier of double-crossing them.

They were, therefore, not surprised to learn on November 21 that Stepanoff and Duval had just come to Toronto themselves. The two men spent the evening in the city without meeting anyone and about midnight went to check in at the *Holiday Inn* on Highway 27. The following afternoon an addict went to see Stepanoff and said he had a friend who was interested in buying substantial amounts of heroin. The addict did not know that his friend was really an undercover agent from the Narcotics Squad. Stepanoff agreed to the proposal and arrangements were made for a first meeting that night at the *Lord Simcoe Hotel.*

Thus, Corporal Jim Porter was introduced to Stepanoff about 10:30 p.m. After a short discussion, the trafficker said he was prepared to sell 100 capsules immediately at a price of $750. The undercover agent asked Stepanoff to come with him to his hotel, the *New Toronto* on Lakeshore Boulevard to get the money. Porter handed over the $750 there and the two men returned to the *Holiday Inn* where the agent was asked to wait in the bar.

Stepanoff then rejoined Duval who had never left the hotel room. A few minutes later federal agents who had been watching the room saw the two men emerge and, with the aid of a stool, retrieve a large white envelope from a trap in the corridor ceiling. Stepanoff then rejoined Corporal Porter and they returned to the *New Toronto Hotel* where the delivery of the drug was made in a washroom.

About 15 minutes later, towards midnight, Stepanoff returned alone to the *Holiday Inn.* As he entered the hotel, two police officers arrested him. A few seconds later Duval was also arrested. In his pants pocket police found the $750 in marked bills which Porter had given to Stepanoff. The trap in the corridor ceiling was searched. It yielded another 249 capsules of heroin. A large number of empty plastic capsules were found in Duval's car. Albert Teitlebaum was arrested in Montreal during the night and was brought to Toronto the next day to appear in criminal court with his two bosses. By the beginning of 1968, all three had been sentenced to terms of 5 to 7 years in prison.

This was not a large ring of traffickers, but it had been growing. In Stepanoff's Montreal apartment, a sheet of paper showed that he had serious plans to renew links with Pep Cotroni's former contacts: Jean-Baptiste Croce in France and Angelo Sonessa in New Jersey. At the time of the arrests, however, these new contacts had not yet been made. According to underworld information, the heroin which had been seized had been supplied by another of Rivard's friends who had recently received a concession for the business from Rivard.

In any case, the major questions remained to be answered: how, by whom and at what level was French heroin being brought to Montreal again? That was the new puzzle facing the Narcotics Squad.

Unfortunately for federal police authorities, it was not a time for solving puzzles but for providing security. The 1967 Universal Exposition in Montreal was starting and police staff had to be assigned in priority to the protection of the numerous foreign dignitaries attending. To meet these new requirements, the RCMP had to strip staff from its special services, including the Narcotics Squad. The squad was reduced from 30 men to eight men in one move. In the spring of 1967 experienced officers suddenly found themselves in scarlet RCMP tunics patrolling the site of Man and His World! For six months, the Narcotics Squad ceased functioning.

It was an unhoped-for opportunity for traffickers. How much advantage did they take of it? It's difficult to say. But judging by two seizures made just after Expo and further information obtained as late as 1971, Montreal during the months of festivities was a major, if not the major, port of entry for heroin on the continent.

On October 26, 1967, Michel Bernard and his wife Yvonne, owners of a bar on Voltaire Boulevard in Paris, arrived at Dorval airport on a visit to Montreal. Narcotics Squad agent Réginald

Pruneau and U.S. Customs agent Fred Cornetta who were at the airport checking international arrivals, noticed that the couple seemed extremely nervous. The woman kept making strange gestures at her husband. Intrigued by this behavior, the two agents asked Customs officers to make a careful examination of the Parisians' luggage. When this was done, each piece of luggage was soon seen to be equipped with a false bottom, solidly glued to the base and concealing 16 small plastic sacks each containing a pound of white power. In total, $8 million worth of pure heroin. (1)

On December 12, 1967, again on the advice of RCMP and U.S. Customs officers, Dorval officials intercepted an Italian-Argentinian, Vincenzo Caputo, who was on his way to New York from Paris. A false bottom in his suitcase concealed 6 kilos (14 pounds) of pure heroin.. The next day four other Italian-Argentinians, unaware of the arrest, presented themselves at Dorval Customs with identical suitcases. Like Caputo, they had come from Paris and were headed for New York. It didn't take officers long to find the 26 kilos of heroin they were carrying. A bit later an accomplice who had managed to get through Customs was arrested at the *Queen Elizabeth Hotel* in possession of four more kilos of heroin. (2) Within

---

1. Michel Bernard was making his second delivery of heroin. On July 30 of the same year, he came to Montreal with an old friend, Jacques Vermeulen, a well-known gangster from Lyon. After checking in at the *LaSalle Hotel* the two friends rented a car and left for New York to meet another French gangster, Jacques Baudin, better known as Pierre Andrieux. All three had suitcases loaded with heroin which had been supplied to them by two Corsican crime chiefs, Paul Pasqualini and François Marazzini, proprietors of the *Versailles* bar in Madrid. Baudin, the leader of the trio, then contacted a representative of the Corsicans, Claude-André Pastou, who was responsible for delivering the heroin to the New York buyer Peter Alicea. The ring started up by Pasqualini and Marazzini brought in several hundred kilos of heroin before it was broken at the end of 1971. In total, about 60 people and six different countries were involved in this conspiracy.

2. Carmine Russo was the one arrested at the *Queen Elizabeth Hotel.* The investigation revealed that his brother Michel, a crime chief in Buenos Aires, Argentina, had organized the movements of the couriers. Michel, of Neapolitan origin, was a partner of the big boss of the South American connection, Joseph-Auguste Ricord, a Corsican who dealt with Joseph Orsini of Marseilles. Michel Russo was arrested in Argentina in 1972 as a shipment of 100 kilos of heroin (220 pounds) was being prepared for the United States. The investigation also established that Vincent Caputo and his friends were associated with Ciro Casoria and Antonio Vista of Italy. These two in turn had close links with organized crime in New York through Giovanni Coppola, owner of the *Italseda Import-Export Corporation* on 14th Street. In 1968, Coppola was arrested in New York in possession of $50,000 in counterfeit U.S. currency. His name was then linked to that of a Neapolitan gang leader, Antonio Spavone, who managed a textile firm.

a week nine other persons were arrested in New York, Boston and at the U.S.–Canadian border. All had come from Europe via Montreal and brought a total of 40 kilos of heroin.

From the large amounts involved in these post-Expo seizures, The Narcotics Squad realized that international traffickers had been taking advantage of the situation and so had Montreal dealers who had started up new trafficking rings. The Squad urgently needed to get back to work and redouble efforts to catch up with the situation. It did so with more determination than ever, starting with the information that had been gathered by the few agents who had remained on duty with the Squad. Very soon, however, an incident shattered spirits and spread dismay in the ranks.

In February 1968, a 25-year-old policeman named Orest Kwasowsky who had been in the RCMP only five years appeared before the operations chief of the Squad and told how he and a colleague had succumbed to the temptation of collaborating with drug traffickers in New York.

The affair began on May 28, 1967, with the arrest of a Marseilles couple who arrived from Paris with six kilos of heroin hidden under bandages on their bodies. They were Marius Frontieri and Joséphine Koutouderas. The RCMP, which was supporting the U.S. Bureau of Narcotics in this operation, also arrested a New York club operator, Viviane Nagelberg, known as an important drug distributor. She had come to Dorval airport to take delivery of the heroin. (3)

Because there was insufficient evidence to lay charges against the New York woman and her companion, Lucky Esposito, two young Narcotics Squad investigators, Orest Kwasowsky and Roger Mourant, were assigned to escort them to the U.S. border. A specialist in seduction (she compromised about 40 federal and municipal police in New York) Viviane Nagelberg persuaded the two RCMP agents to give her a tour of Expo 67 before taking her to the border. The visit stretched into a long and hearty meal and resulted in the wily American woman inviting the two policeman to come and see her in New York. There, besides having a good time, they could discuss at their ease the advantages offered by the narcotics trade.

---

3. On June 18, 1967, one of the men in charge at the Marseilles end, Lucien Amabile, was arrested at Marignane airport in Marseilles as he was about to leave for Montreal with $11,000. Three of his accomplices, Dimitrio Porcino, Baptiste Pourcel and Joséphine Ballestra, managed to escape.

A few weeks later the two police officers went to New York. Kwasowsky had thought to bring with him a bit less than an ounce of heroin, the remains of a sample used for analysis. Viviane Nagelberg was pleased and gave them $500 for their initiative. Stimulated by their quick profit, the two young agents were easily persuaded that they could make a lot more money as participants in drug trafficking than they could by working to fight it! Back in Montreal, they kept their eyes open for a chance to make a profitable transaction. In December, following a large seizure at the airport, they conceived a plan to steal part of the confiscated drugs.

They finally undertook to carry out their plan on a February evening in 1968. The next day Mourant and another officer were to transport six kilos of heroin (14 pounds) to Ottawa to be destroyed. Mourant managed to get custody of the stock for a few hours to steal two and a half kilos (6 pounds) and replace them with flour. His accomplice decided he wanted no further part in the plan. Mourant carried on alone, later taking the heroin to New York where Viviane Nagelberg and her husband bought it for $27,000 cash.

At Ottawa, the 6 kilos would normally have been destroyed without delay, but Kwasowsky's confession intervened. Instead, a new analysis was made which showed that the drugs which had been 98 per cent pure when they were seized, now contained only 38 to 50 per cent heroin. When confronted with these facts, Mourant confessed and agreed to testify against the Nagelberg couple. In spite of this, the Court of Appeal, in June 1969, revised the two-year prison term imposed on Mourant by a lower court and sentenced him instead to ten years in penitentiary. The Court of Appeal also sentenced Kwasowsky to eight years instead of the three imposed by the lower court. In New York, the Nagelbergs were sentenced on June 18, 1970, to 15 years in prison and a $15,000 fine.

This whole affair, naturally, caused deep dismay among members of the RCMP whose reputation for integrity was a matter of great pride to them. Among Narcotics Squad members, it was anger mixed with shame. In the past few weeks agents had succeeded in infiltrating two important heroin trafficking gangs, one operating internationally, the other nationally. Interesting results were expected, but RCMP authorities decided to abandon the operations as a security measure for its undercover agents.

Any further investigation of promising leads would have to wait another few months.

Chapter 11

The Mafia Makes a Comeback

On the morning of August 27, 1968, as on most mornings, the Montreal liaison officer of the U.S. Bureau of Narcotics and Dangerous Drugs (BNDD) called the Narcotics Squad for assistance. (1) He wanted to verify certain information gathered by Brooklyn agents who for some months had been investigating two notorious criminals, Ronnie Carr and Joseph Bartelomio Dalli, suspected of heavy involvement in heroin traffic. Surveillance of their movements had shown them to be in regular contact with a prominent dealer, Carmen De Angelis, known for his relations with one of the most active drug traffickers in the New York region, Angelo Tuminaro, or Little Angie. (Tuminaro has been mentioned earlier in this book as the client of Pep Cotroni, of the Frenchman Jean Jehan and as the mysterious "Uncle Harry" of *The French Connection*.)

Seeking more information on the Dalli-Carr contacts, BNDD agents examined their telephone records. They discovered that Dalli frequently called a Montreal number, 672-7444. The RCMP Narcotics Squad in Montreal was asked to identify the person at that number, which it did without delay. Squad members knew their job was just beginning when they discovered the number belonged to an old acquaintance — Thomas Pythel, 44, former messenger for Pep Cotroni and Lucien Rivard. His file showed that he had already been in contact with Carmen De Angelis in February 1963.

---

1. On April 8, 1968, in order to reassure a public frightened by the increasing use of drugs of all kinds, the U.S. government broadened the jurisdiction of the Bureau of Narcotics to suppress traffic in amphetamines, cannabis derivatives, barbiturates, benzedrine and many other substances. The administration of the Bureau changed hands and was brought under the authority of the Justice department which had also taken over the Bureau for the Control of Drug Abuse from the department of Health, Education and Welfare.

Son of Ukrainian immigrants, Thomas Pythel had gradually climbed the rungs of the underworld ladder until he was finally associating with some of the biggest names in organized crime. Early in 1961 he had been sent to prison for possession of bonds stolen in the famous $3,750,000 robbery at the *Brockville Trust & Savings* company in May 1958. This robbery was the work of specialists in the Cotroni-Stepanoff organization. At the time, Pythel was a friend of René Robert, Pep Cotroni's jack-of-all-trades. In May 1966, Pythel was acquitted, after two trials, of another charge of receiving bonds stolen in an $80,000 robbery at a private home in a Montreal suburb in August 1964.

He had previously been arrested in Vancouver in July 1960 on a narcotics charge but was released for lack of evidence. On that occasion the RCMP arrested a local trafficker, Michael Fulton, who had possession of 23 ounces of heroin and 517 counterfeit $20 bills. Fulton had been seen with Pythel a few hours before his arrest and that had led to the arrest of Pythel. The investigation showed that Pythel made frequent trips to Vancouver where he met some of the top narcotics traffickers. In Montreal he was in constant contact with Lucien Rivard and many of his cronies, particularly Bill Lamy. Checks with airline companies also revealed that on June 23 and July 14, a few days before Fulton's arrest, Pythel had shipped two packages to Montreal, each weighing one pound. The packages, declared to contain printed material, were addressed to Pythel's associate Lawrence Zolton Buckszar, owner of two small printing shops, *Lomar Printing* and *Aldo's Printing*. Of Rumanian origin, Buckszar had been known to the RCMP and BNDD since 1958 when he was doing a lot of traveling with Lucien Rivard, especially to Cuba. In 1961 he was a director of *Certes Holding Ltd.* whose president was meat millionaire William Obront, since identified as the banker for the Cotroni organization.

After the arrest of Fulton, who had been working for the notorious trafficker Alexander-Robert MacDonald, Pythel began dealing with other Vancouver gangsters in the autumn of 1960, notably Gordon Kravenia and Stanley Lowe, considered the most active heroin distributors on the Canadian west coast. This association ended with Pythel's own conviction and sentencing early in 1961. In January 1963, less than a month after his release from Saint Vincent de Paul penitentiary, Pythel attempted to re-establish links with Kravenia. But Kravenia had also been arrested for possession of 156 heroin capsules and on March 29 was sentenced to five years in prison. Pythel then gave up his plans to operate in Vancouver.

At the time the BNDD had asked for help in tracing the Montreal telephone number, in August 1968, the RCMP suspected Pythel was implicated in the counterfeiting of Canadian Pacific travelers cheques, several specimens of which had shown up in New York. The federal agents speculated that the telephone calls between the Montrealer and De Angelis' partners might be connected to this racket. But the BNDD had become convinced that a narcotics transaction was imminent and that a meeting was to take place that same day between Pythel and his New York associates. Staff Sergeant Jacques Plante therefore, the new commander of the Narcotics Squad, immediately mobilized specialists from the surveillance section. Pythel and his closest henchmen were quickly located and kept in sight until the end of the afternoon, when the BNDD reported that a hitch of some kind would prevent the New York traffickers from getting to Montreal. The information was that the meeting had been put off for a few days.

On September 9, the BNDD advised the Narcotics Squad that Joe Dalli would be coming to Montreal the next day or within a few days to meet a certain Don. (2) The Montreal agents were certain that this would be Dominique Séville, 44, called The Lawyer, an active member of the local Mafia with close links to the powerful Luigi Greco. A specialist in stolen bonds, Don Séville was proprietor of a used-car business. During Expo he had been one of the managers of the *Béret Bleu* (formerly *Café Roméo*), one of the Cotroni clan's main night clubs run by Jimmy Soccio, Roméo Bucci and the bookie Moe Yacknin.

Knowing Séville's close relationship to Pythel, the RCMP surveillance team put a watch on his movements. The next morning about 10:30 it was learned that Dalli had left New York an hour earlier with an unknown man and was on his way towards the Canadian border. Federal agents immediately started out to find Pythel. They located him about 1:30 p.m. on the road to Plattsburg, New York. Arriving there, Pythel entered the *Howard Johnson*

---

2. Five days earlier, on September 4, Customs officers at Dorval airport, with the guidance of Narcotics Squad Sergeant Paul Sauvé, arrested a Marseilles baker, Paul Antonorsi, 29, who arrived from Amsterdam with six kilos of heroin (13 pounds) in two false-bottomed suitcases. The affair started in France where the BNDD had infiltrated an agent into a gang of Corsican traffickers. The undercover agent had convinced Antonorsi's boss that he had a cousin in Montreal who could sell to the Americans. An exchange of letters had even been arranged with the Narcotics Squad to convince the French dealer of the seriousness of the agent's offer. The affair resulted in the six kilo shipment and the arrest of Antonorsi.

Thomas Pythel

William Obront

Dominique (The Lawyer) Séville

Little Joe Horvath

restaurant where he stayed only a few minutes. Then, apparently satisfying himself that he wasn't being followed, he returned to Quebec. He went to *Le Bocage* motel on Taschereau Boulevard on the Montreal South Shore where he met an unknown person. Less than half an hour later he returned to Plattsburg, first to the *Howard Johnson* restaurant, then to the *Holiday Inn* where Dalli and his companion were installed. Shortly after, the RCMP agents and their colleagues from the BNDD, U.S. Customs and New York State Police noted the arrival of the stranger from *Le Bocage* motel.

The four-man meeting lasted about an hour. About 8:20 p.m. Pythel and the unknown from the motel left the *Holiday Inn* and drove towards Montreal, one behind the other, while RCMP agents followed both at a discreet distance. At the Champlain border post, police moved in. U.S. Customs officers there found $70,000 in Pythel's car and $3,630 in the unknown man's car. He was identified then as Claude Bourdeau, 31, a habitual criminal who had recently been released on parole.

The U.S. agents in the meantime had lost track of Dalli and his companion. They alerted the police Highway Patrol, however, and Dalli's Cadillac was intercepted near Schroon Lake, about 100 miles from Plattsburg. Five kilos of pure heroin (11 pounds) were found hidden in the spare tire in the trunk of the car. Dalli's companion was identified as Stanley Simmons, a friend of Ronnie Carr.

The four traffickers were taken to the Clinton County Jail, New York, and the next day appeared in court at Plattsburg where bail was set at $300,000 in total. The two Americans were able to obtain their release by posting bail of $50,000 each. But Pythel had to wait two weeks before his bail of $100,000 was reduced to $50,000. Bourdeau was freed a bit later on bail of $25,000 but as soon as he returned to Canada he was arrested and jailed again for breaking parole.

Pythel resumed his activities around the end of October. At the same time, the BNDD learned that the De Angelis—Dalli group was expecting another delivery of heroin from Montreal very soon. And this time it would be a 100-kilo cargo! On November 7 the Narcotics Squad was at Dorval airport when Joe Dalli arrived in Montreal. After a brief chat with Don Séville who had come to meet him, the New Yorker went to *Ruby Foo's* restaurant where he was seen with Pythel. He stayed in Montreal only a few hours, returning to New York the same afternoon. Over the next few months several other meetings took place between Dalli, Pythel and a Montreal truck driver who was Pythel's representative and had agreed to deliver the merchandise to New York. In mid-January and again in mid-February there were indications that a transaction was imminent. At Quebec City where Pythel had a good friend, everything was being done to find a European courier. But nothing came of all these efforts. The negotiations were never concluded and on June 13, 1969, Pythel and Dalli were both sentenced to 20 years in prison. (3)

By that time, nevertheless, the investigation by the RCMP and the BNDD had made considerable progress. During the autumn, it had been established that Pythel was again supplying the west coast through an old friend, Joseph (Little Joe) Horvath, 39. The RCMP Narcotics Squad had a file on Horvath who had been closely linked since the beginning of 1968 to an important gang of Vancouver traffickers led by Edward Ponak and including people like Eugene Sherban, Frank Ferron and Conrad William Gunn.

The youngest child of a family of Hungarian immigrants, Horvath grew up in an environment of prostitutes and gangsters in the red light district. From adolescence he kept company with the biggest names in the underworld such as the Cotroni brothers, Luigi Greco and others. His first major confrontation with the law came in 1949 following a robbery with violence. At that time he called himself Joe Valentine and earned some special attention by escaping just before his trial. When he was finally captured he was sent to prison for five years. A burglary specialist, he had been questioned in April 1967 about the famous Trans-Island Street tunnel affair for which the youngest Cotroni brother, Frank and several of his men were charged. (4) During Pep Cotroni's trial for receiving stolen bonds in 1960, Horvath's brother Alexander (the brothers claimed they worked together as bricklayers) testified for the defense but his version of events was not accepted.

As soon as Horvath's name was mentioned after Pythel's arrest, the Narcotics Squad checked his long distance phone calls and discovered he had made several calls to 266-9278 in Paris just a few

---

3. In Saint Vincent de Paul penitentiary, Claude Bourdeau still does not know whether or not he will some day be extradited to the United States for trial on heroin trafficking charges. Stanley Simmons, who skipped bail in May 1969, was not convicted and sentenced until 1972.

4. Frank Cotroni and his men were charged with conspiring over several months to dig a tunnel under Trans-Island Street, in northwestern Montreal, which was to emerge in the vaults of a branch of City and District Savings Bank of Montreal. City police discovered the plot before the tunnel could be finished. The estimated loot, if the plan had succeeded, would have been $5 million to $6 million. Cotroni was acquitted in August 1971, but several of his men were found guilty.

days before the Pythel-Dalli transaction. He had also phoned "Eugene," one of Edward Ponak's men in Vancouver. Later, at the end of November and in mid-December, he had called several places in New York and again to Vancouver, to Edward Ponak's brother. The dates of these calls and the numbers which had been given to long-distance operators were transmitted to the BNDD in the States and the central office for narcotics in France for further investigation.

While the phone number checks were being made, an important development occurred. On January 29, 1969 a former French docker was arrested at Dorval airport in possession of five kilos of heroin (11 pounds) in plastic bags hidden in two false-bottomed suitcases. Bumps in the lining of the suitcases had attracted the attention of Customs officers. Michel Papagallo, a port guard in Marseilles, had come from Paris claiming to be looking for work in the port of Quebec. It was pointed out to him that the port of Quebec was closed during the winter season and furthermore, that the port of Montreal was much bigger and more interesting. Papagallo gave a different story to RCMP investigators: his destination was actually Quebec City's airport where he was to deliver the suitcases to someone who was waiting there and with whom he would make contact by using a copy of the magazine *Paris-Match*. (5) He said the suitcases were supposed to contain French currency which a certain Jeannot, whom he had met at the Marseilles race track, wanted to get into Canada on the quiet. The Narcotics Squad then remembered that Thomas Pythel had spent two days in Quebec City under an assumed name just a few days before his arrest and the seizure of the first five kilos of heroin. The records of the *Congress Inn Hotel* showed that he made about 30 telephone calls but unfortunately it was impossible to find out to whom.

At the time they were advised of Papagallo's arrest, the French central office for narcotics and the BNDD were on the trail of a gang of traffickers which would lead to Pythel's partner, Joe Horvath. On June 27, 1968, one of Paul Mondolini's representatives, Jacques Bousquet, a wealthy Parisian contractor, had been arrested in

---

5. Papagallo agreed on the afternoon of his arrest to go to Quebec City with Narcotics Squad investigators and contact the man who was waiting for him. Unfortunately, a Customs officer anxious to announce the seizure, telephoned a radio station which quickly put the news on the air. The controlled-delivery project had to be abandoned.

France after shipping to New York a Citroen DS convertible containing 112 kilos of pure heroin (246 pounds). (6)

It had been noted then that the drug was contained in a new type of plastic bag in the form of a long tube. Research on the origin of these new packages led, in February 1969, to the *Electromagnétic* company in Pantin, France. Two men with criminal records, Roger Gabeloux and Dominique Giordano had just bought a machine for sealing the new type of plastic bags. Learning that the two gangsters intended to take the machine to Nice, the investigators notified the local police who intercepted the men's vehicle on February 20. The police searched the vehicle and checked the identities of its owner, after which the gangsters no doubt decided that they'd better get rid of the machine. Gabeloux, in fact, went back to Pantin on March 10 to buy another machine, 200 metres of polyethylene sacks and a vacuum machine. French investigators hiding near the *Electromagnétic* plant intended to follow Gabeloux to find out where and to whom he would deliver the equipment. The trail was lost however when the agents' vehicle had a collision with another car.

After losing Gabeloux, the investigators turned for help to the central files of the judiciary police. There they learned that several years earlier, Gabeloux had been mixed up in a counterfeiting affair with two other Parisian criminals, Alain Vavasseur and Lucien Tridard. According to the files, Tridard was still living in his apartment at 13 Roger-Salengo Street in the Paris suburb of Montmartre.

With no other clues available, the police followed up on the apartment lead, which was fortunate because there they picked up Gabeloux' trail again. About ten days later, on March 21, it was learned that Vavasseur was preparing a trip to Nice or Marseilles to collect a substantial stock of heroin. Tridard's apartment was then put under constant surveillance by the BNDD, the central office for

---

6. Bousquet admitted that the Citroen had made seven Atlantic crossings in three years and had transported 730 kilos of heroin (1,600 pounds), enough to supply the U.S. black market for four to six months! At the end of Chapter Nine, it may be recalled, there was reference to a seizure at Columbus. The three Frenchmen arrested in that affair, Jean Nebbia, Louis Douheret and Nonce Luccaroti, nephew of the famous Joseph Orsini, had made statements in exchange for reduced sentences. They named the following as responsible for the traffic: Jacques Bousquet, Achille Cecchini, Paul Mondolini, Marcel Francisci and Michel-Victor Mertz, a double agent for the French secret services. Mertz started in the narcotics traffic with his wife's stepfather, Charles Martel, an influential procurer in Marseilles and Paris and an associate of Paul Carbone and François Spirito, the first big chieftains of the narcotics trade whose exploits are described in an earlier chapter.

narcotics, French Customs and a special squad from the judiciary police in Paris.

The surveillance teams were reinforced on the morning of March 25. Vavasseur had returned and it had been learned that his three partners were about to leave. About 12:15 p.m. Gabeloux and Tridard were still in the apartment when a Peugeot 204 driven by Vavasseur turned into Salengo Street. As he neared Tridard's apartment, Vavasseur passed a surveillance car with three agents in it. He seemed curious about the occupants of the car, made as if to slow down, then drove away in a burst of speed. A few minutes later Gabeloux came out of the apartment and met Vavasseur in a tobacco shop nearby. After a short talk the two men came back to the apartment and it was then that police authorities decided to move in on them. The sudden arrival of a score of policemen provoked near-panic in the building. Gabeloux and Vavasseur tried to escape in the confusion but were quickly arrested. Tridard, still in pyjamas, tried to flush the drugs down the toilet and the bathtub, but only succeeded in blocking the plumbing and spilling heroin all over the place. Some of the drug had already been packed in the four Samsonite special suitcases found in the kitchen.

Gabeloux, Vavasseur, Tridard and a fourth Parisian, René Quintin de Kercadio (who was arrested a month later on the basis of incriminating notes found in the Salengo Street apartment) had been preparing a shipment of 25 kilos of pure heroin (55 pounds) to Joe Horvath in Montreal for March 27 and 28. Documents found on the traffickers, especially a half-portion of a Canadian banknote, their confessions, police verifications, records of telephone calls to Montreal and Europe, clearly established Horvath's responsibility as well as the impressive dimensions of the ring.

After their release from prison for their parts in the counterfeiting affair, Tridard, Gabeloux and Vavasseur had been hired by Dominique Giordano and two other Corsicans, Antoine Perfetti and Charles Nicolai, who had started a flourishing narcotics ring in collaboration with Joseph Boldrini in Marseilles, a former member of the Croce-Mondolini ring. (7) For several months, with de Kercadio, they had worked as go-betweens and couriers for the Corsicans. Then they had broken away and formed their own team, also supplied by Boldrini. Horvath, learning that they could supply

---

7. Joseph Boldrini was a co-conspirator in the case of the Lebanese Samil Khoury, in which Pep Cotroni was also charged in Paris in March 1957. (See Chapter Five).

the best stuff made in Marseilles, let himself be persuaded to do business with them. In that way he could count on regular and larger supplies.

Horvath's record of telephone calls showed that his calls to Paris on August 20 and 23, 1968 and on January 14 and February 26, 1969, had been made to the home of Charles Nicolai's girlfriend. (8) He had also called on January 10 and 14, on February 14 and 26 and on March 11 to a certain Mr. Dumont on Chaudrat Street in Paris. This man was later identified as a partner of Nicolai, Giordano and Perfetti. On March 4, finally, Horvath had called Montrouge, Tridard's home, where the 25-kilo seizure was later made.

The French traffickers had also telephoned Montreal a few times. On February 24 and March 2, Tridard had phoned the *Motel Diplomate;* on March 7 and 8, Gabeloux and de Kercadio had called the *Séville Hotel,* the *Motel Diplomate* and the *Hotel International;* finally, on March 17, de Kercadio had called three times from Brussels airport to the *Hotel International* at Dorval. All these calls preceded or followed trips to Montreal by Tridard and Gabeloux who had delivered to Horvath an undetermined amount of pure heroin between March 6 and 15.

After the arrest of Tridard and his gang, and the revelation of their links with Corsican traffickers in Marseilles and Paris, the central office for narcotics, the BNDD and the RCMP agreed not to undertake immediate, open investigations of Horvath's activities in Montreal or of Boldrini's in Marseilles. There was no point in scaring them out of the action and besides, the two men were already on the alert because of the arrests and seizures. The police objective was still to break the Nicolai ring as quickly as possible.

First results from this new phase of the investigation came on the following April 26. Close surveillance by agents of the central office for narcotics and the BNDD led to the interception at Orly airport of a messenger from the Corsican gang, Joseph-Antoine Ettori, who was about to board a plane for Montreal with five kilos of heroin (11 pounds) hidden in his false-bottomed Samsonite suitcase. Subsequent search of the trafficker's home produced another Samsonite suitcase with ten $100 Canadian bills hidden in it. This showed that Horvath's method was to send the Samsonite

8. The files of the French central office for narcotics linked Charles Nicolai to Marcel Francisci, a partner of Paul Mondolini, and to the brothers Dominique and Jean Venturi.

cases to France containing his down payment. His French suppliers loaded the suitcases with heroin and sent them back to him in Montreal where, finally, they were returned to Paris with the final payments for the last shipment and advance money for the next.

This new arrest encouraged police to take an interest in the apartment of the mysterious Mr. Dumont of Chaudrat Street who had received telephone calls from Horvath, including a recent one on May 1. As in the case of Tridard's apartment, surveillance of the Dumont premises showed that a new shipment of heroin was being prepared. The French central office finally raided the place on the late afternoon of May 13 and caught Nicolai and Perfetti in the act of hiding five kilos of pure heroin in the big suitcases. The traffickers had on hand all the necessary equipment for the delicate operation. A few minutes later, unaware of the arrest of his accomplices, Mr. Dumont himself walked into his apartment. His identity papers showed him to be in reality Joseph Sbragia, of Marseilles, brother of a close collaborator of old Joseph Orsini. It was later discovered that it was he who took delivery of the drugs from the couriers arriving in Montreal and then delivered it to Horvath's representatives. His last trip to Montreal was on March 18, a week after a telephone call from the Montrealer. (9)

In the weeks following the police successes in France, the RCMP and the BNDD obtained important new information on the composition and ramifications of Joe Horvath's ring in Canada and the U.S. In June, at the time Thomas Pythel was being tried, it was clearly established that Horvath had gone into association with the Cotroni clan through Nicola Di Iorio, Angelo Lanzo and Frank Dasti and with them, was dealing directly with influential members and associates of the powerful Gambino family in New York.

Nicola (Cola) Di Iorio, 47, was considered Vic Cotroni's most brilliant lieutenant. Born in Montreal, he did his basic training in

---

9. Dominique Giordano was not charged in this affair, but in August 1970 he was arrested for his part in another ring operating from Nice. Among those arrested with him were: Serge Constant, a young insurance agent who had delivered two shipments of drugs to the United States ; Jean and Dominique Audesio; Marcel Galvani, one of the chiefs of the Service d'Action Civique in Nice, a Gaullist organization which acted as a kind of special parallel police force in the fight against terrorism; Homère Filippi. All were implicated in the big network organized by the Corsican gangsters in Madrid, Paul Pasqualini and François Marazzani. Michel Bernard, arrested in Montreal in October 1967 also worked for this ring. A few weeks after the arrest of Bernard and his wife, Giordano came to Montreal with Claude-André Pastou, Jacques Baudin (Pierre Andrieux), Alexandre Pietrini and Joseph Cartier.

the service of Jimmy Soccio, Diodato Mastracchio and Giuseppe Cocolicchio before being brought under the direct authority of the godfather, on the same level as Luigi Greco. Endowed with superior intelligence and an innate sense of organization and public relations, he quickly became an indispensable counsellor to the senior Cotroni. Their intimates called them "The Egg" and "The Little Egg." Di Iorio, proprietor of the *Café Métropole* on St. Catherine Street West, supervised the interests of the family in night clubs, prostitution, gambling houses, bookmaking, loansharking and several other rackets. He had a wide range of friends and supporters in political and police circles. He was also on very good terms with Lucien Rivard's friends. In 1958 he was co-owner, with Blackie Bisson, of a blind pig on St. Lawrence Street. (10)

Di Iorio's own chief lieutenant for the past few years had been Angelo Lanzo, 41, a formidable strongman who had started as a club doorman for Jimmy Orlando and then became manager of gambling dens and debt-collector for Giuseppe Cocolicchio. He made the headlines in 1952 when he was sentenced to two months in prison for running, on Cocolicchio's behalf, the Cotroni organization's biggest gambling joint at the time, the *Ramsay Club* at 1410 de Bullion Street. Lanzo's importance in the underworld grew considerably when he was put in charge of the *Chez Paree* night club in 1966 and later of others such as the *Casa del Sol*, the *Little Club* and the *Café Métropole*. From that time he was seen more often in the entourage of Vincent Cotroni.

Frank Dasti, 55, was one of the most respected figures in the underworld and one of the oldest members of the Cotroni brothers' organization. He made his start with them, alongside men like Soccio, Mastracchio, Bizanti, Orlando. From 1951 to 1958, he was one of the shareholders in the *Béret Bleu (Café Roméo)* with Roméo Bucci, Peter Adamo and William Obront. In 1955, Dasti was on the books of the Narcotics Squad and the U.S. Bureau of Narcotics as a close collaborator of Pep Cotroni and Lucien Rivard. He was then considered to be one of the people in charge of local traffic. From the early 1960s, Lanzo was manager of the *Victoria Sporting Club,* the organization's biggest gambling house which employed, among

---

10. This establishment was closed that same year by Montreal police following a series of articles in *Le Devoir*. Narcotics Squad investigators had paid a visit to the newspaper's then director, Gérard Filion, to tell him of the total lack of cooperation they encountered from the Montreal police morality squad and the Quebec liquor police. Corruption in these forces was general at that time.

Nicola Di Iorio (top left) and his associates, Angelo Lanzo (top right) and Frank Dasti (bottom).

(Photos Michel Auger)

others, the Mastracchio brothers, Butch Munroe (an old pal of Lucien Rivard) and Joe Horvath.

Dasti was first linked to the new heroin ring when police were checking the identity of the person who had occupied a room in the *Americana Hotel* in New York on March 12 and 13 when Horvath had made phone calls to the room. Dasti and his wife had been in room 4821 while Horvath and his wife were in room 722. On May 9, the Narcotics Squad learned that Dasti was in New York again, this time at the *Park Sheraton Hotel*. The agents believed he was there to negotiate with buyers, as Horvath had been denied entry to the United States. They notified the BNDD which put Dasti under surveillance. That night he was observed as he met for an hour with a man named George Prince, later identified as Guido (The Bull) Penosi, a well-known trafficker from the Gambino organization. In 1964, the McClellan Senate committee on organized crime and illicit traffic in drugs had mentioned him as one of the associates of his brother-in-law Anthony Castaldi, an underworld leader from East Harlem in Manhattan and a collaborator of Big John Ormento, one of the Cotroni organization's old customers.

Dasti stayed in New York three more days, returning to Montreal May 12, the night before the arrests in Paris of Nicolai, Perfetti and Sbragia. This was his third trip to New York since the beginning of 1969. The second had been made between April 12 and 16, ten days before the arrest of Joseph-Antoine Ettori at Orly airport.

Records of Dasti's long-distance telephone calls also revealed that he was in regular touch with Penosi and two other New York mafiosi, Paul Oddo and Stephan Panepinto. BNDD files described Oddo as a henchman of Guido Penosi and a former courier for Robert Angelo Guiponne (also exposed by the McClellan Committee as a partner of Anthony Castaldi and others. (11)

As for Panepinto, alias Steve Murray, he was a 60-year-old gangster whose name had often come up in RCMP and Bureau of Narcotics investigations, notably in the case of Diodato Mastracchio and Pep Cotroni. An old crony of Carmine Locascio, one of the most important drug traffickers in the U.S., Panepinto had been sentenced to 15 years in prison in 1964. He was also an employee of *Jard Products Inc.* of New York, owned by Dominic Dioguardi, son of John (Johnny Dio) Dioguardi, an influential member of the

---

11. Such as Joseph Valachi and Rocco Sancinella, a former Pep Cotroni customer.

Paul Oddo   Guido Penosi

Lucchese-Tramunti family and a delegate to the Apalachin summit. (12)

Besides Dasti's numerous calls to Penosi, Oddo and Panepinto in February, March and April, there had also been a telephone conversation on January 14 between Horvath and another well-known mafioso in Miami, Salvatore Di Pietro, a member of the Genovese family and associate of Carlo Gambino's men. (13) On the same day he called Di Pietro, Horvath also telephoned twice to Paris to the homes of Charles Nicolai's girlfriend and Joseph Sbragia. Coincidence? Furthermore, on May 14, the day after the arrests of Nicolai, Perfetti and Sbragia, Horvath went to the *Café La Source,*

---

12. The 1965 seizure at Columbus, Georgia, of 90 kilos of heroin hidden in a refrigerator belonging to a major in the U.S. Army, had led to charges and the conviction of Frank Dioguardi, Johnny Dio's brother. Frank, who lived in Miami, and Anthony Sutera, met emissaries from Jacques Bousquet and Paul Mondolini at the *Americana Hotel* in Manhattan. Bureau of Narcotics agents installed in the next room recorded the meeting and a week later carried out the seizure at Columbus. Note that Johnny Dio was a major ally of the powerful labor leader James Hoffa who disappeared in late summer 1975.

13. Salvatore Di Pietro was on file as a partner of Ernesto Barese, a former messenger for Lucky Luciano doing business with the Toronto Mafia. He was also tied in with Alfred Guido and Joseph Tedeshe, important heroin distributors on the lower east side of New York and customers of Angelo (Little Angie) Tuminaro's gang.

on Guy Street in Montreal, for a business meeting. (14) There was no proof the meeting had been called to discuss the narcotics traffic, but such was the suspicion...

These were all valuable clues. For the RCMP Narcotics and Criminal Investigations squads, they were the barometer of the vitality of the Montreal underworld at the beginning of the 1970s and of its notable use of telephone communications. After exhaustive analysis, the federal police launched an impressive wiretapping and electronic eavesdropping operation in mid-June of 1969 in an attempt to gather all possible information on the drug trafficking activities of the Cotroni-Di Iorio organization. A recent experience, incidentally, had just proved the effectiveness of this kind of police operation.

At the end of April, city police detectives decided to tackle the Di Iorio gang which was controlling the night club business. Over the next month they raided some of the biggest downtown clubs such as *Pal's Café*, owned by the bookie Moe Yacknin; the *Béret Bleu*, belonging to Roméo Bucci and Jimmy Soccio; and *La Casa del Sol*, owned by Irving Goldstein and Angelo Lanzo. (15) Infractions of the law noted during the raids led the Montreal Police to install five wiretaps at the beginning of June on telephones in the *Café Métropole*, Di Iorio's headquarters. This brought quick results. In less than a week, information of exceptional importance had come into the possession of police.

Because of these convincing results, the RCMP undertook a vast project of special surveillance combining electronic eavesdropping at several strategic locations and the tailing and close observation of the movements of key people. Called *Operation Vegas*, the project

---

14. With Nicola Di Iorio, Angelo Lanzo, Michel Pozza (Luigi Greco's right-hand man), Sonny Applebaum and Thomas (The Moose) Solarik, a friend of Thomas Pythel.

15. Over the next three years, hundreds of raids were made on bars in Montreal and in the province. Thousands of violations were listed of federal and provincial tax laws, and of laws governing unemployment insurance, pensions, sales tax, amusement tax, public health and hygiene, safety in public places, sale of alcohol, the criminal code and municipal bylaws. More than 400 establishments were closed, of which 250 belonged directly or indirectly to underworld figures. Furthermore, accounting analysis of banking documents seized in the first raids led to a gigantic investigation of transfers of funds among members of the Montreal underworld. In two years transfers were discovered totalling more than $125 million of which more than $89 million appeared on the accounts of the meat magnate William Obront, leading many to identify him as the banker for the Cotroni organization.

The czar of the American Mafia, Don Carlo Gambino.

was set up with the special collaboration of the technical services of the Quebec Provincial Police which was administering a new police information bank, The Quebec Research Bureau on Organized Crime. (16)

The Narcotics Squad quickly put to use the new information being obtained which revealed more secrets of the Dasti-Horvath ring, despite the increased caution in the underworld as a result of recent arrests and seizures. In early summer of 1969 it was learned that the two traffickers were busy reorganizing supplies of heroin from Europe and distribution methods in New York and on the Canadian west coast. Because of the arrest of his suppliers in Paris, Horvath went to Europe on July 19 to meet various people in London, Barcelona, Rome and especially Munich. He returned to Montreal on August 5 and on August 14 met Vincent Cotroni himself. The meeting seemed important, for it took place in Cotroni's car. Police had already noted that the boss of the Montreal Mafia preferred this kind of meeting which made electronic eavesdropping difficult.

Dasti, in the meantime, had gone to New York on August 13 where that evening he met a man identified by BNDD agents as Paolo Gambino, the brother and one of the lieutenants of the czar of the American Mafia. One agent, posted near the two mafiosi in the lobby of the *Park Sheraton Hotel,* even managed to overhear scraps of conversation about the Thomas Pythel case and the costs involved in that affair. Leaving Gambino, Dasti handed him a large sum of money in U.S. currency.

The next day Dasti met his old friend Steve Panepinto first, and then Guido Penosi, again using the lobby of his hotel as a meeting place. He and Penosi discussed Pythel's situation and the financial consequences of the recent seizures for each gang. The matter of future transactions was also raised and Dasti told his companion that he could supply unlimited quantities of merchandise. He also talked about his "guy" who had gone to Germany and about the shipment which had not yet arrived — an apparent reference to Horvath's trip to Europe.

On August 15, Dasti met Panepinto again in the lobby of the *Park Sheraton.* Again, a BNDD agent managed to get close enough

---

16. Between 1973 and 1975 Quebec Provincial Police wiretaps for Operation Vegas provoked a series of public scandals involving corruption of politicians, policemen and civil servants, notably by the Nicola Di Iorio gang.

to hear: "I talked to the guy but since everything isn't settled yet, I didn't do anything."

Dasti returned to Montreal on August 17.

Throughout the autumn of 1969 nothing could be added to the dossier. There were no new developments until December 1. On the morning of that day the RCMP learned that one of Penosi's henchmen was on his way to Montreal to meet Dasti. About 11 a.m. a surveillance team of federal police followed Dasti to *La Parisienne Motel* on Taschereau Boulevard. On arrival, the agents spotted Horvath's car in the parking lot. Dasti stayed only five minutes and then went to the *Victoria Sporting Club* where a few minutes later he was joined by Horvath and the man identified as Paul Oddo, from the Bronx.

About 2 p.m. Horvath and Oddo returned to the motel. A half-hour later Horvath left again. A short time later Oddo and an unknown man also left and drove into downtown Montreal. The tailing team lost the New Yorkers until about 6 p.m. when they were seen again in the bar of *La Parisienne*. Dasti, in the meantime, had been seen with Nicola Di Iorio in the *Pierre* barber shop on St. Catherine Street East, a gathering place for the Cotroni clan. Finally, about 7 p.m., Oddo and his companion boarded an Air Canada flight for New York.

It was later learned that the discussions with Dasti, Horvath and Oddo had centred on the question of price. The Penosi group argued that they could buy heroin in New York for the same price as the Montrealers were asking and would not have to take the responsibility for transporting it from Montreal to the United States. After these discussions with Oddo, it was learned that Dasti and Horvath were in close communication with Frank Cotroni, one of the lieutenants of the oldest Cotroni brother Vic, and with Salvatore Di Pietro in Miami. Then in early January 1970 Di Iorio, Lanzo and Dasti made a trip to Miami where they had several meetings with Guido Penosi.

While these contacts with the American Mafia were being made, Horvath undertook a series of consultations with an old friend in Vancouver, Raymond Shephard, who had just been released from Wilkinson Road penitentiary and was on good terms with the Edward Ponak gang. Throughout the spring of 1970 Horvath increased his contacts with his Vancouver friends, but the RCMP was unable to obtain enough information to take action. That would have to wait . . .

Chapter 12

Lucien's Friends

The Narcotics Squad uncovered a new heroin ring at the beginning of 1969. At the time Thomas Pythel was negotiating new arrangements with Dalli, Joe Horvath and Frank Dasti were multiplying their contacts with associates in Paris, New York and Miami. On January 29, federal agents at Dorval airport awaited the arrival of William Faulder (Fats) Robertson, a Vancouver gang leader recently entered upon the narcotics scene. Short of stock after police seizure of his last shipment of heroin, he came to Montreal to meet new suppliers. He got off the plane and went directly to the home of Lucien Rivard's two old friends, Jean-Louis (Blackie) Bisson and Robert (Bob) Tremblay, in the Montreal suburb of Duvernay. Tremblay, who had been sentenced at Vancouver to 20 years in prison in the autumn of 1955 had just returned to Montreal after being freed on December 28. With his wife and daughter, he had moved in with his old friend.

Robertson stayed in Montreal for a week, constantly under police surveillance. Two days after his arrival he was joined by one of his Vancouver partners, Rolland Trudel. They spent most of their time with Tremblay and Bisson, either at their home or at the Ontario Street East restaurant called *Les Amusements Maisonneuve* which was Bisson's legitimate business front. Several times during his Montreal stay, Robertson met a man named Tony Lazarov at Bisson's home. Lazarov was an old friend of Thomas Pythel and Joe Horvath. His recent contacts with Dante Gabriel Gasbarrini and Johnny Papalia of Hamilton, two important figures in the Ontario Mafia, had sparked a great deal of interest in the RCMP and BNDD. Police officers remembered that in 1963 Papalia had been sentenced to ten years in prison in New York for his role in the international heroin ring he had set up with Alberto Agueci and Mafia leaders in Salemi, Sicily and in New York and Buffalo. Gasbarrini had been sent to prison for seven years in October 1949, at Vancouver, for distributing heroin for his father-in-law Antonio (Tony) Sylvestro and for Tony's brother Frank. At the time, Gasbarrini and Johnny Papalia had been Mafia leaders in Hamilton, with Johnny's father Anthony. (1)

On the evening of February 2, while Robertson was at the Bisson-Tremblay home with Trudel, the police surveillance team near the house noticed a suspicious-looking automobile. A check with the motor vehicle bureau showed it to be registered to Nicola Di Iorio who, as we have seen, had been associated with Bisson in a St. Lawrence Boulevard blind pig ten years earlier. In May, when the links between Di Iorio, Dasti and Horvath became evident, police wondered again why a car belonging to Vic Cotroni's right-hand man had been seen near Bisson's home on February 2.

Robertson returned to Vancouver on February 3. On January 20, nine days before he left for Montreal, he had been questioned about the murder the previous evening of one of his collaborators, Lucien Mayer. Mayer's body was found, with throat cut and head bashed in with an iron bar, a few hours after he had met Robertson and two other gang members, Bunta Singh and William Victor Hansen. Mayer had been arrested in June 1955 with Bob Tremblay when Tremblay was trying to take control of the Vancouver heroin market for Lucien Rivard. He had also been sentenced to 20 years in penitentiary. (2) The rumor in the underworld was that Mayer had become a police informer.

In the weeks following Robertson's return from Montreal, federal and municipal police in Vancouver noted a sharp increase in his gang's activities. Members met several times in various underworld hangouts. On March 5, Robertson flew to Montreal again where he was greeted at the airport by Bob Tremblay and driven directly to Bisson's home. The three men spent most of the next day together and another meeting took place between Bisson and Lazarov. On the afternoon of March 7, after leaving Bisson, Tremblay and Robertson slipped away to the *Café du Nord.* There they met another old friend of Rivard, Bill Lamy, who had been released from prison on October 2, 1968. Two other men who could not be identified were in on the discussion. When it ended, Tremblay and Robertson went to Tony Lazarov's place and all three moved on to the bar in the *Mount Royal Hotel* to continue the talk.

---

1. Gasbarrini was sentenced in 1949 with Carmen Chiovitti, John and Frank Smokler, Jake Golohar, Irving Hess, Mike Cushman, Benny Ugar, Nick Augustino and Steve Bohack.

2. See Chapter Four.

Blackie Bisson

Bob Tremblay

William Robertson

Rolland Trudel

Tony Lazarov

Conrad William Gunn

277

The surveillance operation ended the next afternoon when Tremblay took Robertson to the airport for his flight to Vancouver.

Back home, Robertson held talks with his partner Trudel and his other main satellites, Philip Michael Smith and Bernie Lewis. On the afternoon of March 14, the special surveillance team in Vancouver was able to inform the Narcotics Squad in Montreal that Robertson was at that moment on the telephone with Bob Tremblay and someone named Charlie. With the help of the number supplied by the west coast agents, the Montreal detectives quickly located Tremblay in the *Time Square* café on Bleury Street. When they arrived, Tremblay was still on the phone to Robertson. Bill Lamy and "Charlie," who would be identified later, were standing by. When the phone call ended, agents established close surveillance on Tremblay and Charlie until their departure for Vancouver a week later. But then things became complicated.

When Tremblay arrived at Vancouver airport on March 21, he was met by Robertson. The two went to the *Georgian Towers Hotel* where they joined Charlie who had returned with two grey Samsonite suitcases. A few minutes later, the three men left the hotel in a car driven by Robertson who easily lost the police tail. Police agents, unable to pick up the suspects' trail, decided to locate other gang members and follow their movements. The operation continued for two days and finally brought results: on March 25 an important local wholesaler, Nelson Burney Woods, was seen taking delivery of 60 capsules of heroin from a cache on East Third Avenue. This dealer was arrested later, at the end of the investigation. Tremblay and Charlie, meanwhile, returned to Montreal on March 23 and 25, respectively, and shortly afterwards Robertson and Trudel took a flight for Jamaica.

In April, the Vancouver police Narcotics Squad located more of the Robertson gang's heroin caches. These discoveries added to the evidence the RCMP was accumulating against the representatives, wholesalers and dealers of the gang. On May 2, Robertson returned to Canada and in Montreal had meetings with Tremblay, Bisson and Kenneth Moore who was a trafficker from Burlington, Ontario and well known in Toronto and Vancouver. The next day RCMP agents noted a long meeting between Tremblay and Moore at the *Seaway Hotel*. Charlie joined in the meeting towards the end. Then Tremblay and Moore met Blackie Bisson in the hotel parking lot.

No further information could be gathered at the time, but three days later, Vancouver police discovered the bullet-ridden body of Wallace Jack Tadich, a member of the Robertson gang, in a room at the *Rainbow Auto Court*. He had replaced Trudel a few weeks earlier and rumors were circulating about some kind of betrayal. The next day, searches carried out in city bars where Philip Michael Smith had been seen on the day of the murder, uncovered another cache containing 800 capsules of heroin. Robertson and Trudel dropped out of circulation after the murder of Tadich and the discovery of the heroin.

Their trail was picked up during the summer in Australia. By the time they returned to Vancouver at the end of the year, the RCMP had already completed part of its investigation. On January 2, 1970, Robertson and Trudel were arrested and charged with conspiracy in the trafficking of heroin, along with Philip Michael Smith, Bernie Lewis, Nelson Woods and Bob Tremblay. Tremblay was arrested in Montreal and brought to Vancouver to appear in criminal court. All the accused were granted bail. A few months later, because of certain legal technicalities, the proceedings against Tremblay, Robertson and Trudel were halted.

Tremblay and Bisson, according to the information being received by the RCMP, the BNDD and the French central office for narcotics, were not greatly affected by the Vancouver charges. In fact, they had already, at the beginning of September 1969, begun dealing with another west coast group led by the brothers Douglas and Donald Palmer and William Conrad Gunn, friends of Edward Ponak.

On September 16 and 17 the Narcotics Squad observed meetings in Montreal between Douglas Palmer and the Bisson-Tremblay duo. At the end of the winter of 1970, Robertson was reorganizing his operations with the help of another Vancouver trafficker, Jérôme Roman Trojan, and was again in contact with Tremblay and Bisson.

At the beginning of March, the French central office for narcotics advised the RCMP that Bill Lamy had been in Paris a few months earlier, from December 22 to 26. A routine investigation had revealed his presence at the *Hilton Hotel* but there was no information on whom he had met. The Narcotics Squad, suspecting that Lamy might have gone to Paris to establish contacts with French suppliers, put a close watch on this old friend of Lucien Rivard. It was a good move, because on the morning of March 11 federal agents observed Lamy's departure for the Bahamas. The BNDD was notified and managed to put a tail on Lamy. He was seen several times meeting a young man of about 30, apparently of Corsican origin. As soon as Lamy returned to Montreal information which might lead to the identification of the Corsican was transmitted to the French central office for narcotics.

After a long and laborious inquiry, the French authorities sent an interesting report to Montreal at the beginning of June. The person Lamy had met in the Bahamas in March (and perhaps in Paris in December) was Louis Litoro, (3) born in January 1941 in Sainte-Lucie de Tallano, Corsica. He was a nephew of the big chief of French gambling, Jean-Baptiste Andréani, and was on police files as a confidant of Paul Mondolini and Henri La Porterie, both known as former suppliers to Lucien Rivard. In January 1969 he had completed a five-year sentence for theft and since then, he and his brother Joseph had been moving in drug trafficking circles. Louis Litoro was also a friend of Roger Loiseleur, the Air France steward who had been arrested in Montreal in 1965 in connection with the seizure of 28 kilos of heroin (61 pounds). The subsequent investigation in France led to the arrest of La Porterie and his sentence of four years in prison for setting up the narcotics ring with Mondolini. It will be recalled that Lamy, while dealing with an RCMP undercover agent in August 1965, had remarked on the consequences of the arrests of Loiseleur and his accomplices in Montreal.

The information about Litoro inclined the Narcotics Squad toward the belief that Lucien Rivard might be involved in his friends' efforts to re-establish links with the French networks. But the immediate concern was to find out if Lamy's meetings had produced any results or were about to produce results. If so, substantial shipments of heroin could be expected over the next few months.

In Vancouver, meanwhile, things were not going well for Fats Robertson. On June 29, the RCMP arrested four of his men, including his new representatives Jérôme Roman Trojan and William Howard Wilson, and seized three kilos of pure heroin, two kilos of codeine and 10,000 gelatin capsules ready for use. On July 5, his new partner Keith Anderson, came to Montreal to meet Bob Tremblay and Blackie Bisson. Federal agents assumed that Anderson had come to discuss future supplies and the recent seizures in Vancouver. In Montreal he met a certain individual several times, but the federal agents were unable to identify this person or keep him under surveillance.

Two weeks later the French central office notified the RCMP that Louis Litoro would be coming to Montreal soon and that he had already spent several weeks in the city in the spring of that year. The Narcotics Squad immediately took up the chase. On August 22,

---

3. A pseudonym.

agents trailed Bisson and Tremblay to the *Alpine Inn* at Sainte-Marguerite in the Laurentians, where the two old friends of Rivard met a third man, identified from photos as Louis Litoro. There were two women with the group. They were identified as the girlfriends of Tremblay and the Corsican, Litoro. After this meeting, special surveillance squads were assigned to follow the suspects. A week later the same group met in a south shore restaurant. Federal agents, who had lost the Corsican's trail for several days, were also there. They were also watching the next day when Litoro paid a visit to Bill Lamy at his summer cottage at Lake Bellevue, Mont-Rolland and when Litoro and his girlfriend boarded a flight for Paris on August 31.

On September 6, Rolland Trudel was in Montreal to meet Bob Tremblay. The information from Vancouver was that Trudel had gone on his own again and was supplying traffickers on the U.S. west coast who were dealing with black wholesalers in Seattle and Los Angeles. Six days later, Robertson and Anderson also came to Montreal to meet Bisson. Because of their recent setbacks, no doubt, they were obviously cautious and mistrustful. The overworked RCMP surveillance teams were unable to witness anything very significant in their movements.

Until February 1971, the Narcotics Squad had to abandon its investigation of the Bisson-Tremblay-Lamy gang because of developments in the Dasti-Horvath case and the administrative upheaval provoked by the October Crisis. (4) Agents learned later that two seizures of pure heroin by Customs officers at Dorval airport, on November 29 and 30, had a considerable effect on Rivard's friends. The two couriers who were arrested, Joel Marcel Bédouin and Jacques Eisembarth, had come from Paris each carrying four kilos of heroin (8.8 pounds) hidden in false-bottomed suitcases. Later checks by the French central office for narcotics showed that Bisson had gone to Marseilles at the end of October and had stayed in France for about two weeks. He had met Litoro, as well as Bédouin who had already made two trips to Montreal.

At the end of January 1971, Vancouver informers told the RCMP of an abundance of heroin on the west coast and feverish

---

4. On October 5, 1970, James Cross, the British trade commissioner in Montreal, was kidnapped by a terrorist group of Le Front de Libération du Québec (FLQ). Five days later, on October 10, another FLQ cell kidnapped the Quebec Minister of Labor and Immigration, Pierre Laporte. Laporte was found dead on October 17, in the trunk of an automobile at Saint-Hubert airport on the south shore. James Cross' life was spared and he was freed on December 3 in exchange for safe conduct to Cuba for his kidnappers.

activity by the gangs involved in supply and distribution in the local market. On January 26, a Palmer brothers representative, Thomas Duncan, was arrested in Vancouver following seizure of three kilos of heroin (6.6 pounds) obtained in Montreal a few days earlier. The Narcotics Squad in Montreal set up special surveillance teams to try to find out what Bisson and his gang were doing. For two weeks the surveillance yielded nothing of particular interest, but on February 13, patience was rewarded: Bisson and his wife were followed to Dorval airport where they boarded a flight for New York.

In New York, the couple were given an appropriate welcome, without their knowledge, naturally. They were spotted and followed by BNDD agents who had been alerted by the RCMP in Montreal. Bisson was observed making several contacts with an important narcotics trafficker from the lower east side, Salvatore (Toto) Nuccio. Nuccio, with his five brothers and a score of notorious gangsters (most of them with files in the BNDD), was a member of the famous Mulberry Street gang, sometimes known as the Nuccio gang. He was on file as a close associate of Charles Tuzzolino, a former client of Little Angie's brother, Frank Tuminaro. Nuccio was also linked to the celebrated Di Palermo brothers, the oldest (Joseph) being another former client of Pep Cotroni who dealt with him through Carmine Galente. There was another interesting and perhaps more important detail: the oldest Nuccio brother, John, had spent a lot of time in Atlanta penitentiary with Lucien Rivard.

These discoveries encouraged the RCMP to take an even closer interest in Bisson and his gang. On March 21, Bisson and his wife took a flight to France. When they returned to Montreal nine days later, French police reported that Bisson had been in frequent contact with members of the La Porterie-Mondolini gang. Surveillance of Bisson and his men continued in Montreal. As a result, Bob Tremblay was seen meeting several times with members of the Palmer brothers gang and with another Montreal trafficker, Walter Guay, known to police as a friend of Lucien Rivard and his henchmen. Guay was known in the underworld as a fence for stolen jewelry, an independent man, well-educated and refined. In December 1960, he had been sentenced to four years in prison for heroin trafficking in Montreal.

In the early evening of April 6, a police tail was put on Walter Guay. At about 7 p.m. he left his Towers Street home and went to Bisson's restaurant where he met Tremblay. They talked for about 20 minutes then separated and went home. The next morning just before 11 o'clock, Guay left his house and went to the *Green Garden* restaurant on St. Catherine Street, one of the spots favored by

Edward Ponak

Salvatore Nuccio

Walter Guay

George William Turner

Peter Lahosky

Sally Ruggerio

Rivard's friends. Guay talked with various people there until mid-afternoon. Then he left the restaurant with an unknown man and placed a package in the trunk of his Cadillac. Guay bought some brown paper in a pastry shop, took his friend home to Saint-Denis Street, then returned to his own apartment where he stayed for the rest of the night. On April 8, Guay went down town again to meet another person and the two returned to Guay's apartment late in the afternoon.

On the 9th, police surveillance began about 7 a.m. At 9 a.m. Guay went to the *Green Garden* and then to a jewelry store nearby where he met an unidentified person. They talked for a few minutes and Guay returned to the *Green Garden* where he met two other men. A bit later, four more people, including a woman, joined him. He went to his apartment early in the afternoon to get a bag which he took to the CN station where he rented a locker. Then he had a drink in a Bavarian restaurant. About 2:40 p.m. he returned to the station, bought a ticket for Vancouver and checked his baggage. With plenty of time before departure, he left the station and while he was gone, federal agents searched his bag. They found two kilos of pure heroin in a small plastic bag wrapped in aluminum paper.

Samples were taken and arrangements made for agents to follow Guay to Vancouver on the same train. Everything went smoothly until April 11 when the agents realized that Guay was no longer on the train. His suitcase was still there, however, and the police officers continued the trip in order to keep this piece of evidence in sight.

In Vancouver, the bag was put in the unclaimed luggage room. As a precaution, the agents had taken the heroin and replaced it with lactose. Meanwhile, Guay had been located in Montreal and took a flight for Vancouver that same day. He was visibly nervous when he arrived on April 12, and finally returned to Montreal without making an attempt to recover his baggage. He came back to Vancouver two days later however, this time with a suitcase identical to the first one. The next morning, about 8 o'clock on April 15, he went to the station to claim his suitcase, showing the matching piece he had brought to prove it was his.

When he got the bag, the trafficker stored it in a station locker and left in a taxi. For about 20 minutes he had the driver take him around the city, without stopping, then back to the CN station. Apparently satisfied with his diversionary tactic, he reclaimed his suitcase from the locker and went by taxi to the Pacific bus terminal. There he put the bag in another locker, number 610, and returned to his hotel.

About 9:30 that night the surveillance team at the bus terminal saw an unknown man with long, blond hair pick up the suitcase. At about the same time, Walter Guay was spotted outside. The agents watching his hotel had not seen him leave. The young man with the suitcase joined Guay. Luck was with the two suspects again. Police lost the trail of their car in traffic.

The next day special surveillance was ordered on the homes and hangouts of members of the Palmer gang. On the night of April 17 or 18, detectives observed Edward Eugene Stenson and his wife filling gelatin capsules in their kitchen. The agents knew that Stenson had been in Montreal the day Guay took delivery of a suspicious-looking package at the *Green Garden* restaurant. They decided to raid the Stenson home and seize the merchandise. But a disappointment awaited them inside: there was only one of the five pounds of lactose the agents had substituted, and no trace of Guay's suitcase.

Eight days later another gang member, John Albert Smith, the man who had picked up Guay's suitcase at the Pacific terminal, was put under surveillance. Over the next two days he was seen with his brother Andrew, also a member of the gang; with Stenson, who had been freed on bail; with Thomas Duncan, who had previously been arrested on January 26 and with George William Turner, the Palmer brothers' new partner who had visited Montreal frequently since the beginning of the year, the last time with Stenson.

No further arrests or seizures resulted from Walter Guay's delivery, but agents were able to add evidence to the dossier they had been compiling since February 1969. A year later, in June 1972, these files would form the basis for charges of conspiring to traffic in heroin against Douglas and Donald Palmer, George William Turner, Edward Eugene Stenson, Thomas Duncan, John Albert Smith, Robert Allen Porter, Michael John Watson, Clifford Luthala and Walter Guay. (5)

---

5. Nearly four years passed before justice was done in this case. Various judicial difficulties delayed the trial until the beginning of 1976. In the meantime, Frederic Thomas Ford, one of the key witnesses for the prosecution, narrowly escaped an attempt on his life in January 1975, when he was seriously wounded by shots fired by unknown persons. He recovered and testified at the trial which ended on March 22, 1976 with verdicts of guilty against seven of the accused. On April 7, 1976 the brothers Donald and Douglas Palmer were sentenced to life imprisonment, while Walter Guay, Thomas Duncan, John Albert Smith and Robert Allen Porter were sentenced to 20 years each. Clifford Luthala got five years in prison. George William Turner skipped bail and was not available for trial.

In May 1971, after Guay's return to Montreal, agents watching the activities of Bisson and Tremblay noted another visit by Douglas Palmer. There was no doubt that he had come to complain about the lactose which had been delivered to him instead of heroin. At that time, too, another lead was becoming interesting. It was learned that Tremblay was in frequent contact with Joseph-Marcel Perron, a headwaiter in a hotel, who might be sent to France soon to pick up a cargo of heroin. On May 25, a special surveillance squad reported that Perron had cancelled the reservations he had made at the beginning of the month for the May 28 sailing of the *Empress of Canada* to Liverpool. He had made new reservations for June 16.

RCMP agents were convinced these reservations were related to heroin traffic and kept a close watch on the traveler. On the sailing day, strangely enough, Perron remained in Montreal. It was Blackie Bisson and his wife who left for Paris, and not by ship but by plane! The French central office for narcotics was alerted and was able to verify Bisson's new round of meetings with the La Porterie-Mondolini gang.

Back in Montreal the following week, Bisson and Tremblay had more meetings with Perron, who then made another reservation on the *Empress of Canada* for July 15.

This time Perron actually made the trip. So did Corporal Léonard Massé, a member of the Narcotics Squad assigned to follow him. On board, the agent noticed that Perron, the presumed courier, was accompanied by two other Montrealers. The passenger list identified them as Stanley Los, 30, a sporting goods merchant and Roger Martel, 36, a taxi driver. Like Perron, they each travelled with a suitcase and a trunk.

The *Empress of Canada* reached Liverpool on July 21. While Perron and his companions checked in at the *Adelphi Hotel,* Corporal Massé reported to his boss, Staff Sergeant Gilles Poissant who had been preparing for the arrival for two days with the help of colleagues from the narcotics section of Scotland Yard. The surveillance arrangements worked smoothly and the three Montrealers were followed to Paris on July 26. They left their trunks at the *Gare du Nord Hotel* but stayed at two other hotels, probably waiting for contacts to approach them. Two days later they picked up their trunks and transferred them to the Saint-Lazare station. On August 1, Perron hired a car and the next day, after storing the trunks in it, lent it for a few hours to a Frenchman who had met him at the *Celtic Hotel* where Perron was staying. When he got the car back, the trunks were gone. Unfortunately, police had also lost sight of them.

Between August 2 and 13, Perron, Los and Martel visited Belgium, Holland, Switzerland, Germany and Italy. Their return to Paris coincided with another visit to France by Blackie Bisson. On August 14, Perron met his French contact again and, as before, lent him his car. A few hours later the car and the three trunks were brought back to him. The next day Martel and Los went to the *Gare du Nord* to arrange shipment of the trunks to London. Customs officers, alerted by police, conducted a meticulous search and discovered false bottoms in the trunks concealing a total of 18 kilos of pure heroin (40 pounds) with a market value of about $20 million! The two Quebec travelers were arrested, along with Perron who was waiting for them in his hotel. Bisson, who had not been seen in their company, was able to leave freely two days later.

Under interrogation, Perron refused to identify the persons in charge of the transaction. But he admitted having made a previous trip to Paris at the end of December 1970 and being paid $5,000 for bringing back two suitcases containing several kilos of heroin.

Verification of records showed that he had left Montreal December 21 and returned January 9, via London and Halifax. Perron also admitted that he himself had recruited Los and Martel in Montreal for $5,000 each. On March 28, 1972, a Paris court sentenced him to 13 years in penitentiary to be followed by a five-year prohibition from visiting France. Los and Martel got ten years each and a similar prohibition.

The Bisson-Tremblay activities seemed to be slowed by this hard blow. Only a few communications with Joe Horvath attracted the attention of the Narcotics Squad. But in mid-September the BNDD warned of the presence in Canada of two traffickers who were wanted in the United States. One of them, John Machebroda, from Ontario, had been in Lewisburg prison with Lucien Rivard and might be trying to contact Rivard's friends in Montreal. (6) No trace of the two fugitives could be found, but on September 27, while routinely shadowing Bob Tremblay, federal agents spotted a New Yorker known to the BNDD, Salvatore (Sally) Ruggerio. Tremblay met him in a large, north-end shopping centre, just before the American went to Dorval airport to take a flight to New York. No more was heard from him in Montreal. For several months nothing significant was noted in the activities of Bisson, Tremblay and

---

6. John Machebroda, alias John Mansfield, was arrested August 24, 1970 at Alburg, Vermont, in an automobile with two Montreal holdup specialists, Ronald Bernard and William McAllister.

Lamy. On January 14, 1972 the Vancouver section of the Narcotics Squad advised Montreal agents that one of Rolland Trudel's men, George Charles Cresswell, was in Montreal to make a heroin purchase. Cresswell, registered at the *Dorval Hilton Hotel* under an assumed name, was located late that night on his way to the CN station with a package under his arm. He took a train to Toronto, then a flight to Vancouver where he was arrested in possession of one and a half kilos of heroin — enough to earn him a 20-year prison sentence.

On January 26, it was the turn of the Narcotics Squad's Winnipeg section to go into action. On the basis of confidential information, investigators in Manitoba followed Peter Lahosky, an old customer of the Rivard organization, to the Saint-Boniface station where he met Georgette Grenier, Emile Hogue's wife, who was bringing him a half-pound of heroin (250 grams). The delivery lady and the old chief were arrested together. Georgette was sentenced to 20 years in prison, while Lahosky was given life imprisonment. As for Hogue, who had been seen with Bisson and Tremblay several times since 1969, he faded out of the picture and no more was heard from him. (7)

Another seizure, also affecting Rivard's friends, was made in Vancouver on March 9, 1972, involving 14 kilos (30 pounds) of heroin. Eight days earlier, an emissary from Keith Anderson named Dale Clifford Larson had met Blackie Bisson at the *Diplomate Motel* in Montreal. Tremblay accompanied his partner, but waited outside in the car. Two days later, federal agents who had put a close watch on Larson, saw a stranger with a large suitcase arriving on foot at the motel about 10 p.m. Shortly afterwards, Larson came out with the same suitcase and went to the Voyageur terminal where he boarded a bus for Ottawa. Four Narcotics Squad agents made the trip with him, which took them first to Ottawa, then to Winnipeg, Calgary and Vancouver. The trafficker was arrested on the night of March 9 after he had delivered the merchandise to two other members of Anderson's gang. Anderson himself had a narrow escape, for he had lined up a meeting with his men for the next day. A few days later he was located in Montreal with Bisson.

In the month following this police action, little new information was obtained, though one piece of news was worth noting: the

---

7. Emile Hogue had already been given a scare by the 1969 arrests in British Columbia of Clovis Chapdelaine, former messenger for Jean-Paul Tremblay, and Marcel Servant, a Montreal wholesaler. Servant was known particularly to the RCMP as the main supplier of heroin to Montreal addicts in the mid-sixties. He was also known to have close links with Hogue.

Bisson-Tremblay association had broken up because of a quarrel of unknown origin. Narcotics Squad agents noted that the two men went their separate ways after the rupture. Bisson ceased practically all his associations with his former accomplices, while Tremblay continued to keep company with notorious traffickers like Walter Guay, some of Lucien Rivard's former cronies, and some new figures like Eddy Chiquette who was implicated in the importing of a ton of hashish in September 1973. Bill Lamy, who sometimes worked on his own, died in hospital on June 13, 1972 following an operation related to cirrhosis of the liver. He had been an alcoholic for a very long time.

Chapter 13

Listening in on
the Traffickers

For a long time the RCMP had suspected Frank Cotroni, the youngest of the four brothers, of active involvement in narcotics traffic. His name had often come up alongside that of his brother Giuseppe in investigations by the Narcotics Squad and U.S. services. In July 1955, it will be recalled, Paul Mondolini had taken refuge in Montreal and was first located by police as he and Frank Cotroni were on their way to Pep Cotroni's home. Frank was 25 at that time, totally devoted to Pep whom he served in many ways. He had often been seen with Lucien Rivard and other international traffickers associated with his brother. In December 1956, when Pep made his first trip to Paris, two advance reservations had been made, one of them for Frank. But at the last moment Frank's place had been taken by Lucien Ignaro, a Corsican from the Mondolini gang. After Pep's arrest in 1959, the Narcotics Squad was approached by one of Frank's representatives, offering to yield up the trafficker's cache of heroin in exchange for clemency in court. A package of heroin had even been placed under a balcony as proof that the offer was serious. In 1961 Frank's strong-arm crew tried to intimidate Lucien Rivard into putting his French contacts into service with the Mafia. For a while, armed guards had to patrol the approaches to Domaine Idéal to protect Rivard's property. After Rivard had been sentenced to prison, Frank's name came up several times in connection with international drug trafficking. At the beginning of 1968 he was linked to the drug racket again during an investigation of the presence, in Toronto, of a prominent Sicilian mafioso, Tomasso Buscetta, who was wanted in Italy for a double murder and in Colombia for trafficking involving 14 kilos (30 pounds) of heroin. (1)

---

1. In the sixties, Tomasso Buscetta had been one of the most efficient killers of La Barbera brothers gang in Palermo which controlled the narcotics and cigarette

It was learned then that since about 1966 Frank had been associated with a great friend of Buscetta, Giuseppe Catania, called Pino, another Sicilian who lived in Mexico and dealt in the drug traffic.

In December 1969 therefore, when Frank Dasti and Joe Horvath began keeping regular company with Frank Cotroni, federal agents assumed there was a connection with narcotics trafficking. The assumption became a certainty three months later, on March 25, 1970, when police listened in on a telephone conversation between Horvath and Dasti, who was vacationing in Miami. The call was made from the *Victoria Sporting Club* and the conversation went like this:

"What's going on?" asked Little Joe. "Are you having so much fun you're forgetting us. Didn't you get the message yesterday? I called you."

"Oh, that was you . . . why didn't you leave your name?" replied Dasti.

"You should have known it was me since it was a long distance call."

"How would I know it was you? Long distance, long distance, the other guy could have called me long distance."

"Anyway, I managed to get in touch with the Big Guy, you know. Like he says, the shares in New York, the unlisted shares, they're worth 11, you understand . . . I talked to him. I said 9 . . . Finally, it was certain. I was supposed to get an answer today. I did get one . . . But it's not sure the guy wants to sell, you understand. Now nothing's going to happen until next week. I'm telling you, I really fixed that asshole. I told him right in front of the other guy: 'You're a bullshitter, an asshole, you're a joker.' "

"Who are you talking about? The same dog as last time? I told you not to talk to that guy anymore."

"I know, apparently his guy is here. I told him . . . I'll buy at nine bucks a share. Christ, they're unlisted shares. Y'know, if I can make two bucks on the damned shares . . . He's going to give me an answer because it looks good. The way the Big Guy was talking."

"How come it takes him so long to call?"

---

traffic and shared control of rackets in the Sicilian capital with Salvatore Greco's gang. The murders he was involved in occurred during an armed confrontation between these two rival gangs. The relative peace established between the two clans was broken when Greco's men trespassed on La Barberas' narcotics territory.

"I don't know, the other guy didn't come back yet."

"Is he coming back?"

"I think so."

"Where are you? At the barbotte?"

"Of course! Where did you think I was . . ."

Obviously, the language was coded and full of double meanings. But after nearly a year of listening to that kind of talk through the electronic devices of Operation Vegas, investigators from the Narcotics Squad had learned to understand and interpret the language of the traffickers. Surveillance operations and other investigations over the months had validated their interpretations. This time the message was clear: Horvath was telling Dasti about the progress of talks with Frank Cotroni (the Big Guy) for the purchase of a stock of narcotics (unlisted shares). Little Joe was offering $9,000 a kilo and hoped to make a profit of $2,000 a kilo after the sale in New York.

Horvath and Dasti, left in short supply after the arrest of their suppliers in Paris in the spring of 1969, had approached Frank Cotroni who would be able to obtain certain quantities of drugs. The conversation indicated that Cotroni was acting through an intermediary. Horvath and Dasti mistrusted the go-between and apparently was recounting in the telephone call how he had tongue-lashed the man in Cotroni's presence as a "bullshitter," a liar and a guy who made promises but never produced. The agents knew the man in question was Guido Orsini, one of Cotroni's confidants, because a few minutes before Horvath called Miami, he had tried several times without success to call Orsini at the *Sorrento Bar,* one of the gang's hangouts.

Guido Orsini came to Canada in 1958 at the age of 24. He first attracted notice in 1964 in an affair of counterfeit Canadian money which implicated one of the best-known pizzeria owners in Montreal. Orsini's name also came up later during an investigation of a heroin ring operating between Montreal and Toronto. He was a protégé of Palmina Puliafito, Cotroni's sister, and in July 1966 he obtained incorporation papers for the *Café Rugantino* on Hutchison Street, which shortly changed its name to *Villa de Cesare.* (2) In

---

2. At the opening on October 24, 1966, a grand reception sponsored by the Cotronis brought together a panoply of public, judiciary and underworld personalities. The cloakroom, as in other cabarets owned by the Organization, was in charge of *Marilard Enterprises,* owned by Vic Cotroni's mistress, and the cash register at the bar was supervised by Michel Cotroni, the family's least-known member.

1969, becoming an impresario, Orsini opened the *Club Circolo (Italian Canadian Amusements Inc.)* at 6823 St. Lawrence Boulevard. Officially, this was the property of one of his best friends, Santo Mendolia, who also acted under the authority of Frank Cotroni.

The latest information about Orsini concerned his participation in an illegal entry ring for Italian immigrants organized by Frank Cotroni and Tomasso Buscetta. The racket was aimed at supplying new recruits to the New York Mafia which was suffering from the americanization of the sons of Little Italy. The children of immigrants, detached from ancestral values and direct knowledge of ghetto poverty, no longer had respect for the old chiefs or the ambition of their elders. The cohesion and vitality of Italian-American crime families had been seriously affected. In this operation, aimed at reinforcing traditional values, Cotroni clan members had responsibility for welcoming Sicilian immigrants, Calabrians and others, sent to Montreal and Toronto by Buscetta's friends, and then facilitating their passage to the United States by supplying false papers and necessary technical aid. According to official estimates, hundreds of immigrants have already passed into the United States through this operation.

On December 9, 1969, U.S. Customs officers at Champlain intercepted Tomasso Buscetta and two New York mafiosi, Giuseppe Tramontana of Brooklyn and Anthony Settimo of Queens. All three were traveling in a car belonging to Montrealer Matteo Scanzano, in which police found lottery tickets, pornographic films and a Playboy magazine bill in Frank Cotroni's name. During interrogation, Buscetta, who had four Canadian passports on him and was traveling under the name of Roberto Cavallaro, managed to escape and return to Canada. The investigation revealed that Tramontana, owner of *Tony's Pizzeria* in Hackettstown, New Jersey, a centre for the immigrant racket, had rented three rooms since November in a Montreal hotel where Frank Cotroni had a permanent suite. The day after the arrests at the border, Guido Orsini and a young gangster named Antonio Di Genova came to collect the baggage of Tramontana and his friends and pay the hotel bill. (3) On January

---

3. Antonio Di Genova was murdered in a bar in Montreal's Italian quarter on September 14, 1973. His death was linked to that of another young trafficker of Italian origin, Angelo Facchino, shot down in the street on September 2, 1973, by two Cotroni gang members, Gallo Moreno and Antonio Carmine Vanelli. Di Genova, a partner of Vanelli, was a victim of Facchino's friends. Facchino, in turn, was said to have been involved in the murder of two of Di Genova's friends, Mario Cambrone and Salvatore Sergi who were eliminated in July 1973.

14, New York police shadowing Tramontana intercepted one of Buscetta's sons, Antonio, and discovered that he lived with his mother and two sisters at the home of Rosario Gambino, a young cousin of the powerful boss of the American Mafia.

The Horvath-Dasti conversation of March 25, 1970 encouraged the Narcotics Squad to concentrate on establishing the kind of heroin sources available to Cotroni and Orsini. Agents worked from the theory that there must be a link between the immigrant racket and the narcotics racket and that Cotroni had probably taken advantage of his relations with Buscetta to launch large-scale drug operations.

The day after the Horvath-Dasti conversation, Champlain Customs officers noted the entry into the United States of Giuseppe Tramontana, who said he had been in Montreal. Horvath had probably been referring to Tramontana when he said on the phone — "apparently his guy (Guido's) is here." Since the beginning of March, the BNDD in New York had been investigating Carlo (The Baron) Zippo, a Neapolitan suspected of being the head of a new heroin ring. Buscetta had been carrying a paper bearing Zippo's name on it when he was arrested with Tramontana and Settimo at the Canadian-U.S. border in December.

In addition, there was the visit to Acapulco in late February and early March by Frank Cotroni, his oldest brother Vic, the organization's financial counselor Irving Ellis, the number two man and dauphin of the clan Paolo Violi, Jimmy Orlando and the lawyer

---

In August 1975, as he was questioned during a case he had brought against two Quebec Provincial Police officers, Vic Cotroni denied having told his right-hand man, Paolo Violi, that Cambrone and Sergi were aides to Di Genova. He also denied ever giving any order to seek out those responsible for the murders.

However, it has since become possible to get to the bottom of these incidents and clarify the role of the Montreal Mafia leaders, thanks to phone wiretaps by the Montreal Urban Community Police produced as evidence in November 1975 before the Quebec Commission of Inquiry into Organized Crime.

These murders followed a quarrel over narcotics transactions between the young "piciotti" of the Mafia — Di Genova and his friends — and a small gang of French-Canadian traffickers with whom Angelo Facchino was working. On July 13 and 31, 1973, Vic and Frank Cotroni, with Paolo Violi, discussed the assassination of their young protégés Cambrone and Sergi and what action might be taken to avenge them. Then followed the murder of Facchino and after that the riposte from the French-Canadians. After the death of Di Genova, the Cotroni brothers, Paolo Violi, Joe Di Maulo and some of their soldiers met in the *Windsor Hotel* to discuss their next move in the conflict. In spite of Violi's desire to massacre the French-Canadians, it was decided to end the war in order to avoid further bloody reprisals. As for the executioners Moreno and Vanelli, it was learned that Violi, with the complicity of a prison guard, had sent them a message advising them to admit their guilt. This they did.

Guido Orsini

Santo Mendolia

Giuseppe Tramontana

Tomasso Buscetta

Ilvero Aniello Santella

Giuseppe Indelicato

Raymond Daoust. (4) This visit was the occasion for a summit conference with Meyer Lansky on the subject of the possible legalization of gambling casinos in Quebec. The Narcotics Squad was particularly interested in the numerous meetings between Frank Cotroni and Buscetta's good friend, Pino Catania who had even made the rental arrangements for the villa in which Frank was staying. Catania had been closely and constantly associated for a long time with the main importer of heroin and cocaine in Mexico, Jorge Asaf y Bala. They had even been partners in a shirt-making company, *Le Duc Shirts,* in Mexico City. It may be recalled that in the early fifties Bala, known as the Mexican Al Capone, was one of the major figures in the Antoine d'Agostino gang. Catania also had close contacts with another influential Montrealer, Nicholas Rizzuto who, incidentally, had received several telephone calls from *Brasitalia Import-Export Company* on 46th Street in New York, a firm used by Carlo Zippo as a legal front.

On April 28, a second important conversation was held. Guido Penosi telephoned Dasti at the *Victoria Sporting Club.*

"Where are you?" asked Dasti.

"In town," replied the New Yorker.

"Will you be there long?"

"Yes."

"I'll be going there on the 11th."

On May 6, about 3 p.m., Dasti phoned home and said to his wife:

" ... The guys are in town. I think I can finish the deal today. It's not as much as I thought at first. They didn't have the exact money. They'll take what we have here. I think I'll make two (5) but

---

4. On March 5, 1970, journalist Michel Auger of *La Presse* exposed the summit meeting in Acapulco and the presence there of lawyer Raymond Daoust. Daoust confirmed his presence in Acapulco at that time but vigorously denied any participation in the meeting. He acknowledged however that he had met by chance, on beach or street, some of the people who had been identified by the police. Threatened with libel suits, *La Presse* chose to retract and apologize to the celebrated criminal lawyer on March 28, 1970. In November 1974, Morton Shulman of Toronto, a New Democratic Party member of the Ontario legislature, revived the affair. He declared in the legislature that lawyer Daoust had participated in the Acapulco meeting in his role as intermediary between crime chieftains and politicians likely to support the establishment of gambling casinos in Quebec.

5. $2,000.

I'd like to have made the whole lot. I would have made five if the other load had come but it won't be here till summer . . ."

As soon as it was recorded, this conversation was communicated to the Narcotics Squad which immediately organized a surveillance team to locate Dasti and follow him. It was no easy task. The trafficker was not spotted until about 8:30 p.m. as he was on his way home. The hope of observing an important meeting was slight, and it disappeared entirely the following morning when Dasti went to his bank and deposited a large sum of money. The deal had already been made and there was nothing more to do but wait for the next development.

It came rather quickly. That same day Frank Cotroni, Guido Orsini, Santo Mendolia and three other Montrealers went to Toronto. (6) Over the next three days they made contact with several Ontario mafiosi, including Nicolas D'Elia and Ilvero Aniello Santella, two notorious traffickers. Santella's file showed him to be in close association with another Ontario trafficker, Giuseppe Indelicato who had been deported to Canada from the U.S. in 1958 after serving a two-year term in New York for smuggling a kilo and a half of heroin. D'Elia was listed on police files as the right-hand man of Rocco Zito, a Toronto Mafia boss. (7) When the Montrealers returned home, Dasti left immediately for New York, where he met Penosi and his partners.

On May 22, during a telephone conversation, Dasti told Penosi that he'd be receiving "something interesting" very soon.

"This time they told me it was guaranteed," he said. "When? I don't know. In a couple of days, maybe next week . . . At the end of the week I'll give you a number where you can call me."

---

6. The other three Montrealers were identified by police as Giovanni Mollo, Giacomo Cirelli and Claude Dubois, who would make the headlines a few years later (see closing pages of this book).

7. Rocco Zito and Giuseppe Indelicato had close links with each other and both had important contacts with high-level figures in New York and Montreal. On May 4, 1970, at the *Holiday Inn* in Toronto, the two of them met Paolo Gambino, brother of the top man in the American Mafia, who had just been to Montreal. Several years earlier, on September 10, 1964, Frank Cotroni, with his older brother Vic and Paolo Violi, met an old Sicilain mafioso in Montreal by the name of Antonio Manno, brother-in-law of Nick Rizzuto. Agents shadowing the visitor noted that he was accompanied by a group of people who used a car registered in the name of Giuseppe Indelicato. The previous year, on August 25, 1963, Paolo Violi attended an important meeting in Hamilton with about 30 people including Rocco Zito and Nicolas D'Elia.

On May 31 Dasti told Penosi he had met "the guy" the night before and had been assured that "it" would be arriving within the week. On June 6 Dasti explained to his customer that "it hasn't arrived yet" but that "the guy will be arriving this week" and he'd have an answer on Saturday. A week later the Montrealer asked Penosi to call him back the next night at the agreed place. The Narcotics Squad knew the place was a hotel, but didn't know which one. The team assigned to shadow Dasti was not able to find the hotel in time for the call.

On June 25, a U.S. border patrol near Rouse's Point, N.Y., intercepted an old Chevrolet with Quebec licence plates. The driver, Nicola Maturo, 24, who had a criminal record, was arrested, questioned and held for deportation. In the car, registered in the name of Guido Orsini's brother-in-law Giovanni Di Blasio, police found some capsules of cocaine, a New York City traffic ticket issued to Matteo Scanzano, an immigration certificate in the name of Giuseppe Romano (Tramontana's partner in *Tony's Pizzeria* in Hackettstown) and a naturalization certificate in the name of Guido Orsini.

On July 7, just before noon, Frank Cotroni telephoned Dasti at the *Victoria Sporting Club.*

"Hello," said Dasti, "why didn't you leave at 11:15?"

"I couldn't. But don't worry. I'm going to sell the house. I'm supposed to see it before two o'clock."

"O.K., I'll call you back in five minutes."

Five minutes later:

"I just called the "notary" about the house," said Cotroni. "He's gone. We won't know until after four o'clock if it's going to be tomorrow or later."

"I've got to have an answer before I can make the arrangements."

"The notary is going to do his best to be there."

"We better see each other today."

"Well, good, come at six o'clock."

"O.K., anyway I'll make arrangements with him for eleven in the morning."

A little later, early in the afternoon, Guido Penosi called from New York to speak to Dasti at the *Victoria Sporting Club.*

"Anything new?" asked Penosi.

"Everything is being arranged tonight," replied Dasti. "Call me back tomorrow morning at 11 o'clock, at the number you know."

The next morning a surveillance team followed Dasti into the lobby of the *Bonaventure Hotel* where he received a call on one of the four phones there. Federal agents were not able to tape the conversation, but later in the day, one of the Operation Vegas listening devices picked up the essential parts of a conversation among Dasti, Angelo Lanzo and another influential member of the organization. It was learned that the three mafiosi were about to conclude a transaction for 12 kilos of heroin (26.5 pounds) which they estimated would bring them $144,000. Dasti himself was thinking of going to New York to supervise the deal and make sure no problems arose over payment. The delivery was to be made in three stages and after each one, Dasti and his cashier-bodyguard would deposit the money in the hotel safe.

On July 9 Dasti telephoned Santo Mendolia's *Circolo Club.* Orsini answered and told him there would be another delay:

"You'll have to wait till I call... I want to talk to you. There's nothing serious, just a few details, you understand? I'll explain it to you. When I explain, you'll see that these things can happen... It's not that I'm thinking of waiting a week or two, it would be just a day or two, you understand... Because they need me for a deal. Anyway, Frank, I have to see you to explain because somebody's arriving tonight."

The next day Penosi telephoned.

"I haven't been able to get the shit yet," explained Dasti, "but the lawyers are working on it."

"Dammit, I'm getting fed up with these delays! I've been waiting on you for a year and all you do is put me off."

"I know, but it's not my fault. I promised I'd arrange this for you. Call me back next Monday night (July 13) at seven at the same number."

Later in the day, Dasti met Orsini at the *Circolo Club,* and later still, Orsini met Frank Cotroni at the same place.

On the morning of July 13, Orsini left his home and drove toward the U.S. border with another member of the organization, Dominico Cordileone and another unidentified man. U.S. customs and immigration officials, notified by the RCMP, intercepted the trio shortly after they had crossed the border without inspection, using a secondary road. Considered undesirables, Orsini and Cordileone were jailed for illegal entry into the United States and were sentenced later in the week to three months in prison. They appealed the sentences, however, and were freed on bail of $1,500. The third man in the trio, Giuseppe Romano, Tramontana's partner,

Vic Cotroni (head of table) surrounded by friends André Lufty, Paolo Violo, his brother Frank and Claude Faber.

Frank Cotroni (left) and Carlo Arena.

was a U.S. citizen and was freed shortly after his arrest. While Orsini was being held, Cotroni telephoned Dasti to ask him if he knew what had happened to the guy who was supposed to go to see the "notary." Dasti said he knew and the two men arranged to meet.

The border incident created further delays in the planned heroin deal. No one wanted to take any risks. On his return to Montreal, Orsini had a meeting with an angry Dasti, who blamed him for all the trouble. Orsini defended himself, complaining that the business had cost him $9,000 in lawyers' fees and bail for himself and the two others. Dasti had to go to New York on July 22 to explain the new delay to Penosi. The BNDD noted that the meetings were tense and that Penosi was much annoyed at the way things had turned out. Penosi had recently been charged in Miami with income tax offenses. He had serious financial problems and no doubt hoped to solve them by the narcotics transaction.

Giuseppe Tramontana was in Montreal on August 10 for a meeting with Frank Cotroni. In late afternoon he and Guido Orsini boarded a flight for Rome. Italian police and the BNDD informed the RCMP that on their arrival they had checked into the *Claridge Hotel* and had been contacted shortly afterwards by three men, two of them Montrealers named Carlo Arena and Giacomo Ciccirello who were known to police as Frank Cotroni's henchmen. Orsini and Tramontana returned to America early in September, just as certain events were developing.

The BNDD had learned in mid-August that Guido Penosi and Paul Oddo had quarreled and broken up their partnership. This, however, was not believed to have affected their relationship with Dasti. In addition, on August 30, New York police and the FBI arrested Tomasso Buscetta and his son Benedetto, 22, as they were driving in their car after a meeting with the Neapolitan Carlo Zippo. Charged with illegal entry into the U.S., Tomasso was kept in cells waiting for the Italian government to follow up on its request for extradition. (8) Meanwhile, Zippo had dropped out of sight.

On October 5, an unknown man telephoned Dasti at the *Victoria Sporting Club* and advised him that he was not far away, at

---

8. U.S. Immigration hoped for quick deportation of Buscetta who had been sentenced in absentia in Palermo to a long term in prison. But the Italian government neglected to follow up its original request for extradition. After several months of preventive detention, Buscetta was freed on bail and deported to Mexico. From there he made his way to Sao Paulo, Brazil where he became owner of a taxi fleet and a restaurant chain, as well as a member of the gang of the Corsican Joseph-Auguste Ricord. In 1972, after a confession by the French

the *Oscar Motel* on Taschereau Boulevard. Dasti replied that he would go there right away. A few minutes later the man called back and asked Horvath to tell Dasti to call him again. While these calls were being made, the Narcotics Squad established surveillance at the *Oscar Motel*. This produced no results the first day, but the next morning about 9:30, agents saw Dasti entering the motel restaurant where he met Paul Oddo and an unidentified man.

Corporal Gary Lagimodière, of the RCMP criminal investigation bureau and Kevin Gallagher of the BNDD casually walked into the restaurant where they heard Dasti saying to the stranger:

"I've been in this business a long time. Let them do what they have to do and we'll do what we have to do."

The stranger's reply was inaudible but Dasti, shaking his fingers in front of him, spoke loudly:

"Five! I'm telling you five."

At that moment, Oddo leaned toward the Montrealer and said something in a low voice. Dasti moved closer to his companions and continued the discussion more discreetly. Meanwhile, outside, other members of the surveillance team spotted another stranger who seemed to be keeping a look-out around the motel.

The meeting lasted until 11:20 a.m. Dasti left by himself and the stranger from outside joined Oddo and his companion. Fifteen minutes later the three visitors took the highway to the U.S. At the border, Customs officers took the identification of the two unknown men. The first, the one Dasti had been talking to, was Anthony Vanacora. Born in 1923 and residing on 105th Street in New York, he was on file at the BNDD as a heroin trafficker, for which he had been sentenced to ten years in prison in 1954. He was known to be associated with Anthony Verrzino and Anthony Baratta (father and son) who had been sentenced to 15 years for drug trafficking. The second stranger was identified as Vincent James Altamura, 38, of Long Island, N.Y. His BNDD file showed charges for crimes of violence, as well as his close relations to a narcotics dealer named George Stewart and another trafficker named John Campopiano, alias Johnny Echoes.

---

trafficker Claude-André Pastou, Buscetta was finally arrested with his son Benedetto; two of his men, Guglielmo Casalini and Paolo Gigante, who were friends of Carlo Zippo; several Frenchmen, including Christian David, Ricord's right-hand man and a collaborator with the French secret services. Buscetta was deported to New York, from where he was extradited to Italy.

Oddo had evidently come to Montreal to introduce his new partners to Dasti. But Dasti still had the problem of finding the merchandise. Orsini's efforts still had not produced results and Dasti had to keep putting off the people like Horvath who kept harassing him for supplies. On November 3, Dasti went back to New York for three days where he met Steve Panepinto, William Castaldi (Antonio's son and Penosi's brother-in-law) and Penosi himself. The night before he returned to Montreal, Dasti telephoned Orsini at the *Circolo Club* to get a progress report:

"Is your guy ready?" asked Orsini.

"Sure, no problem," said Dasti.

"How many tomatoes does he want?"

"As many as you've got!"

"Even if it's 30?"

"Thirty, fifty."

"Perfect, perfect!"

"Look, I'm warning you, if you screw me again somebody's head is going to roll. Anyway, I'm going to see my guy again."

"Don't worry, Frank. It's so close it could even be tomorrow."

Back in Montreal, Dasti was in touch with Orsini several times. From these meetings the Narcotics Squad concluded that Orsini had not yet received his "tomatoes." Dasti became increasingly impatient. So did Horvath. For them, Frank Cotroni's right-hand man was no more than a swindler.

On November 10 there was a meeting of Frank Cotroni, Orsini and Horvath. Dasti could not be there, but afterwards Orsini called him and told him everything was going well and he must be patient. "Joe will explain everything to you," he said. Dasti then telephoned Frank Callachi — a partner of Penosi and the Castaldis — at Pelham Bay General Hospital in New York where he was undergoing treatment and asked him to tell the guys that another delay could be expected. The next day, the BNDD agent hospitalized in the same room as Callachi was able to report that Callachi had received a visit from William Castaldi. Three days later, Castaldi telephoned Dasti to get the latest news:

"Don't get mad," said Dasti, "we've got a little problem."

"Nobody's mad," replied Castaldi. "We're ready and we'll wait."

"So far everything's going well. There's just a little problem we're going to fix up soon."

In fact, Dasti no longer had much confidence in Orsini. On November 17 he burst into laughter when Orsini told him:

"It'll give you a heart attack when this thing gets going. I got to make my deals. You know, he calls me every night. And there's always little problems coming up. Now I'm starting another deal, you wouldn't believe where it comes from."

Unlike Dasti, the Narcotics Squad took Orsini's words seriously. On December 1 Orsini telephoned Christian Dewalden in Rome, owner of a cosmetics firm and the luxurious *Piper Club*. He advised Dewalden that he would arrive in Italy in two days and already had $1 million in reserve at a Milan branch of a Montreal bank. Earlier, on November 28, Santo Mendolia had called Switzerland to tell an important international trafficker, Salvatore Catalano, that his friend would meet him in Italy soon. Catalano, a Brooklyn resident, had been exposed in 1963 by Italian authorities as a dangerous member of the Mafia. He was on BNDD files as an associate of Tomasso Buscetta, Pino Catania, Anthony Settimo, Carlo Zippo, Giuseppe Tramontana and several other U.S. and Italian crime chiefs. He had been under police surveillance since his arrival in Europe.

Guido Orsini left Montreal with his wife on December 2. Officially, he was going to Italy to recruit performers for the New Year's show being organized by Palmina Puliafito, his fairy godmother in the Cotroni clan. In Rome he was met by the nightclub operator Dewalden and Franco Ferruzzi, one of Catalano's men. That same day Catalano was meeting an important delegation from the Italian Mafia. (9)

---

9.   The delegation included Gaetano Badalamenti, Alfredo Bono, Michel and Giusto Sciarabba, Angelo Consentino and Pietro Sorci. Two of these were of special importance — Badalamenti and Sorci. Sorci was on BNDD files as a partner of Cristoforo Rubino and the brothers Ugo and Salvatore Caneba, associates of Lucky Luciano as mentioned earlier in this book. He also had close links with Giovanni Maugeri, of Milan, a partner of the Corsicans Dominique Albertini and Antoine Galliano who had been involved in the Saint-Malo affair. On January 10, 1957, it will be recalled (see chapter Five), Maugeri was arrested in New York with Charles Campo. On June 4, 1958, an undercover operation led to the arrest for heroin trafficking of Vito Badalamenti and his cousin Caesar. Originally from Cinisi, Sicily, the Badalamentis were also known to police for their roles in cigarette smuggling and their strong presence in the fruit and vegetable markets in the regions of Palermo and Trapani. After his release from prison, Gaetano's cousin Caesar settled in Detroit where he became proprietor of a real estate agency, on good terms with Giuseppe Indelicato. According to RCMP files, in mid-June 1970, an influential Montreal mafioso, Nicholas Rizzuto, who had links with Pino Catania and Carlo Zippo, telephoned Caesar Badalamenti's home. In the Mafia, obviously, the lines of communication are complex, but they always interconnect.

The next day Catalano and Orsini, followed by Italian police and the BNDD, left Rome for Milan. For a few days they made the rounds of Milan automobile dealers, no doubt looking for vehicles to be used for the transport of heroin. On December 6 Catalano telephoned a Milanese friend, Nicola Greco, whose cousin Vincenzo lived in Montreal, was a friend of Orsini and the Cotronis, and worked at the *Dante Pizzeria* across from the *Circolo Club*. When Catalano called, a man named Frateluzza was at Nick Greco's place.

"Call Pino Catania in Mexico," Catalano told him. "Tell him to start a new company that needs sardines, tomatoes and dough (pasta). We'll send him 100 kilos of macaroni every month."

"Salvatore," said Frateluzza, "I don't understand what you're talking about."

"That doesn't matter. Just tell that to Pino. He'll understand."

The day after this conversation, the Italian police decided to make a move. Catalano had been suspected of involvement in a cigarette smuggling affair for some time. The police therefore put him under house arrest. This didn't seem to affect Orsini's operations. He continued his business with Ferruzzi's help. On December 18, Orsini called Santo Mendolia at the *Circolo Club* and said:

"I've been looking at cars and I think I'm going to buy a Ferrari ... If Eligio could come to Italy and bring back the car, that would be perfect. Try to talk him into it and tell him if he needs money, we can help. He's got to agree because the car is good. He did it before. It's not like he'd be doing it for the first time ... When we're finished with the car we can sell it ... Anyway, pal, don't worry, and tell the other pal that I've already got it. I bought all the neckties. I bought 30 of them. I hope you'll be happy. There's ten for you and ten for him and 10 for the other guys."

"Yes, Guido, but if the Ferrari guy, Eligio, if he doesn't want to go, how will the neckties get here?"

"Don't worry about nothing. If that happens we'll think about it then ... Anyway, if that happens it wouldn't be too good because I haven't got room to bring them with me on the plane."

"What are you going to do if you haven't got a car?"

"Don't worry."

The Narcotics Squad immediately notified Italian police and the BNDD of this conversation. Ferrari dealers were visited to find out who might be in the market for such a car. It was learned that a young woman had bought a Ferrari in Rome for delivery in Milan to a man named André Cuvillier. Cuvillier was a regular customer at Christian Dewalden's *Piper Club* and a crony of well-known French traffickers. (10) His Ferrari was tailed by police, without significant results, until its trail was lost in the Turin region. The RCMP meanwhile, had identified Eligio. He was Eligio Siconolfi, owner of a garage on St. Catherine Street West who was often seen with members of the Cotroni gang at the *Circolo Club*.

During this time, Orsini maintained contacts with his Montreal associates. On December 10 he telephoned Carlo Arena who had accompanied him on a previous trip to Italy with Tramontana. Orsini again mentioned his 30 neckties which he was about to send to Montreal and said that everything was going well. Two days later he called Mendolia again.

"I'm very happy with my trip," he said.

"Listen, Guido, I'm not too sure about Eligio."

"Oh, well, talk to Santo (11) about it and tell him to find someone else to come to Italy and bring back the Ferrari. Tell him to talk to Carlo."

In Montreal, Mendolia kept busy. On December 14 he telephoned Toronto, to Aniello Santella, and told him that Guido had given him a blank cheque to deal with certain matters. He added that Guido would be calling him on the telephone the next afternoon and that the other guy would be there too for the call. Orsini did call the next day, and after talking to Mendolia for a few minutes, he spoke next to Frank Cotroni who was also present.

"Everything's fine," said Guido. "I'm even going to be able to take a vacation. But don't worry, the deal will be made before that. I'll be able to come back with no problem."

"Have you finished everything?" asked Cotroni.

"I've done everything, I haven't forgotten anything. The only thing I've still got to do is to contact someone tomorrow to decide who's going to carry the things, since he's already got them here. To ship them I'm going to ask for help from someone at the Liquor Board. You know the guy from the other side, he's left all this entirely up to me. I'm responsible for everything now. Tomorrow

---

10. Such as: Ange Simonpieri, a top man in the Corsican underworld who was arrested the following autumn; Maurice Rosen and Jacques Baudin, alias Robert Andrieux, a henchman of Dominique Giordano who was a former supplier to Joe Horvath.

11. Frank Cotroni.

I'm getting in touch with a company in Milan and if they can help me it could leave during the week and everything would be perfect. I could be back home for Christmas. But if they can't help me, I'll have to arrange something myself and find somebody to bring back the car. You know, it's not just one or two bottles, it's 30."

"Yeah, anyway, I already saw the notary about the wine." (12)

"Don't worry, everything's going fine."

"Listen, I'm leaving for Mexico on Friday (13) and I think I'll be back about the 8th." (14)

"Me, I'll be back before then."

"Anyway, if you want to call me there, ask Santo (15), I'll leave him the telephone number."

"There's one thing, Frank. I'm going to need some money to buy the car and continue the trip. Even more if I have to look after shipping the car and finding someone. I just want to put a down payment on the car, the rest could be paid in 40 days. I know the guys in the garage, I think it can be done like that. You know, the cosmetics company knows the Ferrari well and maybe it will help me."

The day after this call from Orsini, Paul Oddo and Anthony Vanacora telephoned Dasti at the *Victoria Sporting Club*.

"How are things going?" asked Vanacora, after Oddo had talked with Dasti for a few minutes.

"Fine. I talked to him three days ago and he said everything was going fine."

"You know, the guys down there are getting impatient for news. Would you mind if I called you every two or three days to find out what's happening?"

"No, no, that would be fine."

On December 18 two other important conversations were taped by the Quebec Provincial Police Operation Vegas. In the first one, Mendolia and Arena telephoned Orsini.

"Hello, Guido," said Arena. "How's it going?"

"Fine, fine."

---

12. In this case, the notary referred to by Cotroni was Frank Dasti.

13. December 18.

14. January 8.

15. Mendolia.

"Catocchi will be leaving for Rome on the night of the 22nd. He's bringing you $700. Five hundred of it is Frank's."

"Good. But you know, over here, they (16) won't leave me alone for a minute."

"Yeah, did they ever see you with the other guy who'll be going over?"

"Never, never."

"Anyway, be careful. Here's Santo."

Mendolia brought Orsini up to date on certain financial problems, then told him of newspaper articles in recent days about the immigrant racket.

"In the Italian and American newspapers, they brought out articles about the immigrant operation. They know everything. They mention lots of names, Frank's, yours, and others too."

"Now I know why the police came to see me and kept me for an hour," said Orsini.

"You should come back as soon as possible before something happens to you."

"I've got too many neckties here. I've got to finish what I started first."

"Be careful."

The same day Horvath and Dasti discussed Orsini's trip.

"I don't trust him," said Dasti. "He's always promising, promising, but nothing ever gets done."

"I know. But I talked to him and he said this time it was going to work."

As a result of these conversations, additional important information came to the Narcotics Squad. A friend of Luigi Greco (17) told Matteo Scanzano that Orsini was under constant surveillance in Italy and so were the people he was seeing. The friend thought that if Orsini had an operation going and intended to bring something back, he'd better give up the idea. Scanzano contacted Carlo Arena and Santo Mendolia soon afterwards and gave them the message. The two men immediately cancelled the reservations they had made a few days earlier for their trip to Rome to meet Orsini. In Italy, the BNDD learned that Franco Ferruzzi,

---

16. A reference to police surveillance.

17. No relation to Nicola Greco and his cousin Vincenzo.

Catalano's partner, had also been warned that he was in danger in Rome.

On December 20, Mendolia telephoned Orsini again who was then at Porto Dascoli.

"Don't touch anything," he warned Orsini. "Be very careful. The police know everything. I told you, in the articles they talked about you and the others."

Matteo Scanzano, who was with Mendolia, also urged Orsini to be careful.

"Who told you that?" demanded Orsini.

"Greco did. He got it from the police."

Orsini asked his friends to try to find out more. If the police and journalists were aware. of the immigrant operation, that didn't necessarily mean that they knew of the real reasons for his trip to Italy. He attributed the attention he was getting from the Italian police to his contacts with Catalano who had been arrested at the beginning of the month.

On December 23, the Montreal impresario Tony Catocchi (pseudonym), a great friend of the Cotroni family, arrived in Rome and was met at the airport by Orsini. He brought the money Frank Cotroni and Mendolia had sent to Guido. There was no indication that he knew what the money was to be used for. The same day, two other Montrealers arrived in Rome: Staff Sergeant Gilles Poissant and Sergeant Paul Sauvé, of the Narcotics Squad had come to lend a hand to their colleagues in the Italian police and the BNDD.

On December 28, Orsini again telephoned Mendolia and Arena.

"When are you coming back?" Mendolia asked immediately.

"Come on, what are you most interested in — the food parcels or me?"

"The food parcels!"

The Good Lord gave them to me and I won't let them go. I won't leave here before they do."

Arena then informed Orsini that Frank Cotroni would be returning to Montreal earlier than expected to attend the funeral of one of his brothers-in-law. But he would be going back to Mexico right afterwards and would return to Montreal on the planned date.

Another trans-Atlantic conversation took place a few days later. Guido then explained to Mendolia that the delivery had been delayed and wouldn't be made until the end of January. He did not know whether the merchandise would be delivered directly to

Canada, via Halifax, or sent through another country such as Mexico. If it went through another country, the profits would be reduced because of the percentage payable to Pino Catania. Mendolia again recommended caution, adding that it was through "the cook," Vincenzo Greco, of the *Dante Pizzeria,* that they had learned that police were on to the affair. Vincenzo's cousin Nicola, in Italy, had told him he was under constant surveillance there.

Another conversation was intercepted on January 4. In brief, Mendolia informed Orsini that he had seen Cotroni who was happy but also advised caution. Guido said he had "done everything from A to Z" and had finished the deal. He still did not know when he would come back. The night before, Eligio Siconolfi had arrived in Rome with an assortment of Quebec licence plates. Agents immediately began shadowing him, and followed him to Milan the next day where he bought a Ferrari for $5,360 and drove it back to Rome. Police lost track of him on the highway however, and he was not relocated until January 11 at the *Reggina Carlton Hotel.*

Orsini and his wife returned to Montreal on January 19. On arrival, he went immediately to the *Dante Pizzeria* where he met Frank Cotroni and heard the latest developments. Cotroni told him he had met Catania during his trip to Mexico and had been offered a stock of cocaine. Pino had even come to Montreal to discuss the deal and Dasti was at that moment in New York to negotiate the sale to Oddo and Vanacora. The Narcotics Squad and the BNDD were aware of some of the details of this deal, again as a result of the Operation Vegas wiretaps. Since December 30 more than a dozen revealing conversations had been intercepted by Quebec Police technicians, implicating Frank Dasti, Frank Cotroni, Joe Horvath, Paul Oddo, Anthony Vanacora and Frank Callachi. The one on December 30 between Dasti and Oddo went like this:

"You know what I used to give you?" asked Dasti. "Could you use the other? Understand?"

"You mean the damaged goods?"

"No, no, no, the other."

"Oh! I know what you mean."

"It begins with C."

"Yeah, I know... We might arrange something. Do you know the prices? If you could give me an idea, I could ask around."

"Prices, prices, they're about the same."

"About the same? Yeah, well I don't think so. It's a lot lower here," (18) said Oddo.

"Anyway, we'll find out."

"O.K. . . . anything new on the other thing?"

" . . . I just blew another deal," said Dasti. (19)

"Ah, shit!"

"There's something that isn't working right . . . I don't know where . . . Anyway it'll be fixed up."

"O.K.," said Oddo, "I'll find out about that other deal there."

"Yes. They did me a favor. They put this one in my hands." (20)

"Ah! I know what you mean."

"Ah? You understand eh?"

"I'll do my best," said Oddo.

"Let me know because the guy's going to be there in New York in a couple of days. In five or six days."

The next day Oddo called to find out how many "suits" were available. "I could get a couple of dozen," Dasti told him. Callachi then called and Dasti asked him to call back Saturday, January 2. The night before that, Oddo indicated that he was ready to buy the lot, depending on the price, and Dasti had asked him to come to Montreal for discussions, adding that in the meantime he would try to arrange things with his guy. Cotroni had called Dasti afterwards and Dasti had told him that his "guy" was ready.

On January 2, Vanacora telephoned Dasti and asked him if he would be prepared to lower the price if someone bought the whole stock, instead of just five kilos. He explained that there was a ready supply of cocaine in New York at the time, and therefore the price should be lower. Dasti repeated that his friends had offered him this deal to help him catch up a bit and if he could complete it, he might then be able to follow up with the other projects that had been planned. He asked Vanacora to see what he could do and made arrangements to meet him in Montreal on the following Monday.

---

18. Like any good salesman, Oddo was seeking the best possible price. As a general rule, cocaine was more expensive and more difficult to obtain than heroin. In North America it is considered a de luxe drug.

19. Dasti was probably thinking of Orsini's trip to Italy, which produced no results.

20. Dasti meant that Cotroni had chosen him as intermediary, to make up for Orsini's abortive trip to Italy.

Paul Oddo   Anthony Vanacora

This meeting actually took place two days later than that, on Wednesday, January 6, at the *Osteria Del Panzoni,* a Metcalfe Street restaurant. It was observed by Narcotics Squad agents. Afterwards Dasti told his wife he would be going to New York soon to collect the second payment of $20,000, the first one of $10,000 having already been remitted to "the other guy."

The following day, Pino Catania arrived in Montreal and on the night of January 8 met Frank Cotroni and Dasti at the *Pescatore Restaurant* on Stanley Street. A special RCMP surveillance team had also been arranged for this meeting. On this occasion, as he had done during the meeting with the New Yorkers, Dasti telephoned his wife, this time to ask her to pack their bags for the trip to New York.

When Orsini met Cotroni at the *Dante Pizzeria,* Dasti was in New York ready to meet Oddo and Vanacora. The New York meeting took place in late afternoon in front of the *Drake Hotel.* BNDD agents who had been shadowing the Montrealer since his arrival saw Vanacora hand Dasti a small package which Dasti quickly placed inside his coat. It appeared to be a payment for the merchandise.

Dasti spent the entire afternoon of the next day, January 10, alone in the lobby of his hotel. Extremely nervous, he seemed to be waiting for someone. At 6:30 p.m., no one having contacted him, he went to dinner with his wife and an hour later left the hotel, alone, in a taxi. Traffic was heavy at that moment and the BNDD tailing squad lost him. The agents were furious with themselves, especially when Dasti called his wife shortly after 7:30 p.m. to tell her he had to meet some people and would be held up for a while. The police were certain that Dasti was delivering the drugs to his clients at that moment. Patrols were sent out to try to locate him, or Oddo or Vanacora, but without success. Dasti returned quietly to his hotel, alone, about 10 p.m. and went to bed.

The next morning about 10 o'clock Dasti went to the *Jerome Cafeteria* in the Bronx where he talked for an hour with Vanacora and his son Dominique. Then he returned to his hotel. For the rest of the day the BNDD noted nothing unusual. In his hotel room however, Dasti was trying to telephone Cotroni in Montreal. The RCMP was aware of these attempts through listening agents. When Dasti finally managed to reach Cotroni at home early the next morning, the conversation revealed that once again the traffickers had been successful. Dasti said in effect that the deal had been completed and that the guy (probably the courier) had left with part of the money. The final payment would apparently be brought to

Montreal by the New Yorkers during the week, Dasti not wanting to run the risk of carrying such a large sum of money himself. The conversation also confirmed Joe Horvath's interest in the deal. The night before, after meeting Cotroni, he had telephoned Dasti.

Dasti was back in Montreal by noon the following day. He met Cotroni first, then he went to the *Victoria Sporting Club* and telephoned his wife and Steve Panepinto. In this way the Narcotics Squad learned that Vanacora and Paul Oddo were expected in Montreal that evening and that Dasti intended to return to New York in a few days to discuss another deal with Panepinto. During the evening, an RCMP team spotted Frank Dasti and Frank Cotroni in the *Laurentien Hotel.* The two mafiosi seemed in bad humor. Cotroni made several telephone calls and berated the respondents in Italian. About 9 p.m. Dasti left and went to the airport where he waited in vain for the arrival of the New Yorkers.

Elsewhere on that day, January 13, there were interesting developments on Orsini's trip to Italy. He received a telephone call from Eligio Siconolfi who asked:

"What have you done to me? I was followed by five people who accused me of stealing 20 kilos from you."

"They must be cops."

He was right. BNDD agents in powerful American cars had followed Siconolfi's every move in Rome. Thinking his followers were Orsini's enemies, Siconolfi went to the police station to complain. The U.S. agents were "arrested," but so was Siconolfi and during his detention he was made to believe that Guido, Santo and Matteo were impatiently awaiting his return to Montreal.

Following the call from Siconolfi, Orsini telephoned Franco Ferruzzi in Italy and told him "the trip went well except for the fact that the police followed our friend." He added:

"Remember what I told you about the things I was supposed to send?"

"Yes," replied Ferruzzi.

"Well, everything's off. (21) Also, don't be surprised if you get a visit and are questioned about me."

"Don't worry, no problem."

Cotroni left for Mexico soon after Dasti had returned to Montreal. On January 15 Oddo telephoned to complain about the

---

21. Meaning that the operation in Italy was cancelled for good.

quality of the merchandise delivered to New York.

"You know what?" he said to Dasti. "It's badly spoiled... They'll have to throw some out. They're losing on each one..."

"Wait a minute!"

"I tell you they're in bad shape, Frank, I saw them..."

The next morning Oddo returned to the charge:

"... It's gummy. I don't know what the hell it is. It's like gum, sticky... I saw it with my own eyes. I know it's spoiled. They'll have to get rid of some of it, you know. They'll have to cut part of it."

"In that case, leave it alone, I'll arrange for someone to go and pick it up. I paid for that stuff. There's no problem. Give it back to me."

"That's not for me to decide," said Oddo. "But there's a loss. With the 'figure,' they said 18, it went up to 19, then up to 20. And that was final. They won't go no further. Now it's up to you to decide Frank, what you want to do... It's not for me to decide, Frank, you know what I mean."

"Anyway, you know what to do," said Dasti.

"What? Because I've got it well hidden. But the place is risky. The woman there bothers me. I've got to get it out of there, understand. Now it's up to you to decide what you're going to do. I don't know."

"Yeah, well, you understand, I can't make a decision just like that, so fast."

"I understand," said Oddo. "It's the same for me, I can't decide, you understand."

"My guy will be calling me today. I don't know what time."

"Good, well listen, tell him I saw to that myself."

"Can you wait till tomorrow?"

"I can leave it there till tomorrow."

After this call, Dasti telephoned Cotroni in Mexico to explain the situation.

"I've got to know what to do," said Dasti. "The guys are in a jam down there, and they don't want anything to do with it... Because what's happened is it takes two to make one... I've got to sign a contract for two years. That makes 14,000."

"It's 7,000 a year. So for two years that makes 14,000," repeated Cotroni. (22)

"That's it," continued Dasti. "That's what absolutely has to be done to arrange the business... Because it's gone bad, the guy can't do anything with it and besides, he doesn't want to waste time. You know how it is, they're nervous."

"Me, I don't know what to say to him," replied Cotroni. (23) "I don't care, it wouldn't bother me to give them that, but it's because after, maybe they wouldn't want to deal with us again..."

"... Well, listen, I can't take chances with these guys. I don't want to burn them. And they're in a jam. I can't hold them by the throat, eh? Listen, those guys aren't liars."

"What do you think then?"

"They're not liars, that's all I'm telling you. Anyway, I'll see about it, see what he can do. He's supposed to call me at 1:30. That's why I wanted an answer."

"O.K., do whatever you think," said Cotroni.

At 1:30 p.m., as planned, Oddo telephoned Dasti at the *Victoria Sporting Club.*

"Listen," Dasti said immediately, "you don't have to say anything. Everything you told me is O.K."

"Everything I said is O.K.?"

"Yeah, leave it like that for this time." (24)

"O.K., we'll come down tomorrow to bring it to you."

Oddo kept his word. The next afternoon he arrived in Montreal with Vanacora and Altamura. The Narcotics Squad knew they were in town but decided not to establish surveillance. If the traffickers found out they were being followed they might cancel or postpone their next transaction. It was a wise decision. On January 19, Oddo telephoned Dasti again to ask him if he had any news on "other deals." The Montrealer could not give him an immediate answer but promised to keep him advised of developments.

Shortly after this, Orsini got in touch with Dasti to tell him to call Cotroni in Mexico right away. Like a faithful soldier, Dasti

---

22. Cotroni understood that the price had been cut in half from the original agreement, to $7,000 a kilo instead of $14,000.

23. Cotroni is no doubt referring to Catania.

24. Dasti preferred to lose money rather than good customers.

obeyed instantly:

"I'm meeting the guy tomorrow, you know," Cotroni said. (25) "I just want to see him about the lease there."

"Yeah, well, the lease is ended."

"Did you get the thing?"

"Yes."

"Good, I'll call you back and tell you what to do. I'm going to see him tomorrow, I'll see what he wants. If he wants it, I'll call you and we'll send it for delivery," said Cotroni.

"Ask him what he wants to do about the other business there . . . Because they're waiting . . . You've got to sign a contract to pay only so much . . . He has to build, you know, then it costs him five, six, seven . . . It's got to be a contract like that or it's no good."

"Yeah, I understand. That's O.K."

"Me, I'll look after the rest."

"Right . . . Call back the guy, you know, the one who just called you there . . . Tell him, you know he's supposed to come and join me Friday . . . Ask him if he could come tomorrow instead . . . That would be better for me . . . Don't tell him anything besides that."

"O.K., goodbye."

Naturally, Dasti did as Cotroni asked and got in touch with Orsini. The next day Orsini telephoned Cotroni to tell him he would be there on the 22nd with the money the other would give him. On the 21st he called Dasti who arranged to meet him the next morning in Berke's pharmacy on St. Catherine Street West. There Dasti would give him $14,000 in small bills.

At 10 a.m. on January 22, Sergeant Paul Sauvé of the Narcotics Squad and special agent Kevin Gallagher of the BNDD and an RCMP surveillance team witnessed the meeting. Dasti arrived ten minutes before Orsini and another gang member, Pasquale Di Pilla, 34. (26) The trio chatted for a few minutes, then Dasti left alone and went to the bank branch beside the pharmacy. He returned ten minutes later with a small box in a paper bag which he gave to Orsini. At that moment the agent Gallagher casually entered the drug store carrying a brief case which concealed a precision camera. Working the shutter release in the handle of the case, he got a dozen

---

25. Cotroni is referring to Catania.

26. Di Pilla was arrested the following July in Toronto for possession of two kilos of heroin.

or so candid photos of Dasti handing over the parcel to Orsini. Five minutes later the gangsters left the place.

Orsini took a flight for Mexico that night and met Cotroni and Pino Catania at the *Presidente Hotel.* Three days later he was back in Montreal after a stopover at Toronto airport where he met Aniello Santella and one of his partners, Fortunato Bartuccio. Since December, Santella had been in constant touch, through Mendolia, with the Cotroni gang and Giuseppe Tramontana on the subject of the immigrant operation and the investment he had made in Orsini's trip to Italy. (27) Before Orsini departed for Mexico, he had talked on the telephone to Santella about a certain sum of money which was to be sent to Ferruzzi in Italy. On that occasion Santella had told Orsini of a new proposition by Tramontana, who had been engaged as representative for another group of U.S. traffickers. These dealers had about 40 pounds of heroin to distribute, but were demanding cash. Santella was in financial difficulties himself, but thought his friend in Montreal might help to make the deal. Orsini had then called Tramontana to tell him he would take all the "neckties" he had. Then he had put Mendolia in charge of the affair until his return to Montreal. Santo had been in touch with Santella to arrange the meeting at Toronto airport and had then gone to New York to meet Tramontana and his two new partners.

The day after his return to Montreal, Orsini multiplied his approaches to Tramontana, Santella and Dasti to try to organize a new transaction at the lowest possible price and if possible without putting up any money at all. He also asked Tramontana to lower his demands and agree to a transaction in two stages, to allow time to sell the first lot and raise the money necessary for the second. Santella was prepared to take five kilos immediately, at $13,000 each, which he counted on selling at $15,000, but Orsini was not willing to pay that much unless the merchandise was delivered directly to New York. Dasti was ready to approach his regular customers but doubted they would pay more than $10,500 a kilo. Tramontana added that his price would be lower in Montreal than in Toronto. But he said his friends had another customer in mind in Toronto and he couldn't guarantee that the other one would not get the contract, especially since his friends did not wish to sell for less

---

27. The same day Orsini returned to Montreal, Siconolfi's Ferrari arrived in New York where it was searched from top to bottom. Nothing was found because the traffickers had cancelled the transaction. The car was brought to Montreal via Detroit and was seized by the RCMP because it had not been declared.

Candid film showing the exchange of money between Frank Dasti and Guido Orsini in Berke's Pharmacy in Montreal.

than $12,000. The best he could do was wait a day so that Orsini could talk to his own friends.

This meeting took place on the morning of January 27 in the lobby of the *Laurentien Hotel.* For half an hour, closely observed by a Narcotics Squad surveillance team, Orsini, Mendolia and Dasti bitterly debated the offer that had been made. Orsini had previously met with Santella who had explained that the sellers in this affair were all originally from the same village in Italy and before helping anybody else, they would help each other, as was the custom among Italians. Orsini made no attempt to hide his anger at these Americans, promising that the next time his boss would see to it that they did business with him first. He swore that sooner or later he would find out the identity of the mysterious Toronto buyer. For the moment however, all he could do was hope that Tramontana would call him back, as agreed. He could then go to Toronto to meet his friends.

That afternoon, after the meeting in the *Laurentien Hotel,* Orsini telephoned Pino Catania in Mexico:

"You know your friend the doctor, across the water there, do you think he'll agree? . . . I've already written to him," said Orsini.

"Don't worry . . . I think it'll be all right."

"Anyway, the others there, the notary (28) and his friends, they didn't want to listen . . ."

"Yeah, but they didn't want to lose money."

"Yeah, I hope it goes better with the doctor."

"I think it will . . . Call me back next Wednesday. Maybe I'll have some good news," said Catania.

"O.K."

By that time Italian police had intercepted the letter Orsini had mailed on January 11 to Catania's friend. It read as follows:

" . . . Concerning the artists who were expected in Canada, I am the one who cancelled the arrangements. I thought it would be the best solution. Concerning the things we discussed together about Montesilvano, everything is going very well. The prospectus I saw and the information I received seemed very, very interesting. You will soon receive word on this matter. At the moment, a group of friends are in San Remo and as soon as possible they will get in touch with you or go to see you personally. On that matter, do not worry.

"This will become the basis for a close and active cooperation."

In the meantime, Orsini put all his hopes in Catania to the point of advising Dasti that he might be getting a bit of stuff, even though he had no real idea of how that could be arranged. Always anxious to impress, he declared that the merchandise would be less expensive than that of Tramontana and his friends who, incidentally, had made a deal with their client in Toronto. The local section of the Narcotics Squad had done a good job on that affair. Though it had been unable to prevent the transactions, it had succeeded in identifying Tramontana's partners, and possibly also

---

28. This refers to Tramontana.

the buyer.

The federal agents had noted the arrival in Toronto on January 26 of two New Yorkers, Pietro Misuraca, 44, and Anthony Castiglione, 30. Castiglione was particularly well-known to the BNDD because of his close relations with the two big names in Palermo — Pasquale Fretto and Giuseppe Gaglia, considered by Italian police to be important traffickers of drugs. In Toronto, (while Castiglione travelled back and forth between Toronto, Montreal and New York) Misuraca was seen frequently with Antonio Sciortino, 37, of Islington. Unknown to the Narcotics Squad until then, Sciortino's name, however, had been previously recorded because his car had been seen in suspect circles. (29)

For some time the RCMP had been receiving information indicating that Benedetto Zizzo had started a heroin ring between Italy and the U.S. Misuraca's association with Sciortino in Toronto added a clue to the files. A fresh investigation was therefore launched into the activities of this newcomer. Over the next few months it would bring to light important connections.

Meanwhile, on February 1, an unexpected incident shook the plans of the Montreal Mafia. Frank Cotroni was arrested and imprisoned by Mexican police, following a complaint by an Acapulco jeweler concerning jewelry worth $2,080 which had been purchased on a credit card, presumably stolen. This was, in fact, a mistake. The jewels had been bought by another Montrealer, a salesman of Larousse encyclopedias who had lent his convertible Cadillac to a friend. The friend had driven it to Mexico where he left it for an evening with his friend, Frank Cotroni. The jeweler's wife thought she recognized the jewel buyer when police located Cotroni with the Cadillac. Cotroni had to wait 12 days to get the misunderstanding cleared up, but then another complaint was lodged against him. The American Express company accused him of using stolen credit cards during his stay in Acapulco in the winter of 1970. This time the Mexican police decided to cut things short and on February 15 Cotroni was deported to Canada. Three days later, in a luxurious suite at the *Holiday Inn* in Montreal, Frank Cotroni called a press conference and explained his Mexican adventures to about a hundred reporters and photographers, under the floodlights of camera crews from four television stations.

---

29. People in these circles were closely linked to Benedetto Zizzo, former partner of the Agueci brothers who were arrested in 1961, and brother of the Mafia boss of Salemi, Sicily. See Note 2, page 156, Chapter Seven.

He came out of it with the honors of war, but that was not enough to reassure Pino Catania who had taken the first steps to obtain Cotroni's release in Mexico. Catania feared the incident had attracted too much police attention to him and his partner Asaf y Bala. On February 23, therefore, he announced to Orsini that all current projects were being postponed.

Over the next two months the activities of Montreal traffickers linked to the Cotroni clan were sharply reduced. They kept in touch with their clients and contacts, but nothing of much interest came to the ears of Narcotics Squad agents. The police were concentrating on the gambling joints and cabarets of the Nicola Di Iorio gang. In mid-March, as nightclub raids continued, Quebec Provincial Police succeeded in closing the Organization's two largest gambling clubs, Dasti's *Victoria Sporting Club* and Roméo Bucci's *Blue Stripe Mountain Riders.*

Not until May 6 did anything happen to rekindle the zeal of the RCMP investigators. But on that day a wiretap of a phone conversation revealed that Dasti had been in contact with Paul Oddo to ask him and "the other guy" to come for a meeting in Montreal. The New Yorker promised to come the next day and to bring with him a series of public pay phone numbers for a new communications code to thwart police curiosity.

A surveillance team was put on Dasti and another on the *Laurentien Hotel* where the meeting was to take place. But on the assigned day neither Oddo nor Vanacora showed his face in Montreal. The only interesting incident, in fact, was a brief Dasti-Horvath meeting in the parking lot of a west-end shopping centre. But the next day, May 8, the BNDD learned that Paul Oddo had left New York by plane. He arrived at Dorval airport where he was met by Dasti. The two pals chatted for an hour in the airport parking lot then drove downtown, where agents lost them in the traffic. Late in the afternoon the BNDD reported Oddo's return to New York and his meetings with Vanacora and other well-known traffickers.

The Narcotics Squad in Montreal, unaware of the content of these latest talks, decided to organize closer surveillance of Dasti's movements. As a result, Dasti was observed about 12:40 p.m. on May 20 in a public phone booth in the *Red Cap* tavern on St. Lawrence Boulevard. When he left the premises, Constable Réginald Beers noted the phone number — 279-0192. A check was then made to see if any long distance calls had been made from that number. A few minutes later police learned that only one long distance call had been made in the past hour from the 279 exchange. At 12:33 p.m., a call had been made from 279-0132, in Steve's restaurant on St. Catherine Street, to 364-2481 in New York. The BNDD went to work on that number and shortly learned that while the subscriber was not known to them, his address was the same as Paul Oddo's...

During the afternoon the Narcotics Squad was notified that Dasti was impatiently awaiting an important call from the U.S. Additional information that evening indicated that Horvath had called Dasti and that Dasti had given him a tongue-lashing because his telephone line was always busy. Horvath told him he was with "The Lawyer," Dominique Séville and that Séville would be waiting for news from him. The investigators recalled that at the beginning of the month Horvath and Séville had contacted Blackie Bisson to offer him about 30 pounds of heroin they had obtained in Toronto. Bisson, Lucien Rivard's old friend, refused the offer because of the bad quality of the merchandise.

A bit later that evening, Frank Cotroni telephoned Dasti and asked him if he had any news from his nephew on the estimate for his car. The ex-manager of the *Victoria Sporting Club* replied that he would have word about 9 or 9:30. Federal agents knew that Dasti's nephew, René Di Fruscia, owned a garage on St. Lawrence Boulevard, *Monte Carlo Auto Body,* and that Dasti was spending most of his time there since police had closed his gambling club. Their theory however was that Cotroni's call had been made in code and probably had to do with the activities of Horvath and Séville.

This theory was strengthened within the next hour, as Horvath and Cotroni phoned Dasti again to ask if he had any news. Dasti replied that he was still waiting.

Finally, in late evening, Dasti got a call from Anthony Vanacora:

"I scored," said the New Yorker. "I've got everything."

"Good, O.K., give it to him and let him leave."

"He'll be leaving in about an hour, but I'm losing 10,000. Some was missing from each one. I weighed them myself with the guys. Since he's O.K., I'm taking the loss, but you tell your guy it's stupid to try that."

"Yeah, are you sure?"

"Listen, in each one there was supposed to be 34, but there was only 32."

"I'm going to look after that, but let him go... Call me tomorrow morning... I want to go to bed, they've been bothering me here all day."

"I hope you can fix this up."

"Yeah, yeah, don't worry . . . goodbye."

By these words, the Narcotics Squad knew they had failed again. The traffickers had once again brought off a transaction. And they were proud of it. Shortly after Vanacora's call, Horvath telephoned for a third time and Dasti told him the outcome of the affair.

"Oh, Francesco!" exclaimed Little Joe. "I could kiss you."

But business is serious, and after asking Horvath to notify the others, Dasti blamed him for lying and exaggerating the weight of the merchandise. Vanacora said that each package which should have contained 34 ounces contained only 32, which meant an interesting side profit for Horvath. Dasti knew it and didn't like that kind of dealing, which blemished his good reputation.

"If a man weighs 150 pounds you shouldn't say he weighs 180 pounds," he said.

But since Dasti seemed content to bawl him out without demanding compensation, Horvath accepted the reproach and the two accomplices had a meeting the following day.

After each transaction, Dasti often went to New York to see his clients and to enjoy a good time with his wife, who was from the U.S. and liked going home. The RCMP was not surprised, therefore, to see him leave for New York with his wife on June 6. On his three-day stay, the BNDD observed his meetings in turn with Paul Oddo and Anthony Vanacora, Steve Panepinto, and William Castaldi, one of Guido Penosi's men. (30)

This visit to New York was followed a week and a half later by Paul Oddo's brief visit to Montreal during which Dasti introduced him to Frank Cotroni and Guido Orsini. This meeting was considered significant by the Narcotics Squad: it indicated perhaps a resumption of supplies through Cotroni and Orsini, who had not been very active since wintertime.

More confirmation of this theory came a bit later in the summer. On August 20 it was learned that Dasti and Santo Mendolia were taking steps to recuperate a refrigerated trunk belonging to a friend, Mauro Zanetti, which had been seized by a

---

30. At the time of this trip to New York, Guido Penosi was awaiting results of his appeal against his sentence of 45 months in prison pronounced in December 1971 for tax evasion. He finally lost the appeal and was imprisoned in 1972.

bailiff. According to police information, the truck was soon to be used to transport a shipment of drugs to New York. Federal agents knew already that Oddo had called Dasti several times since mid-July to remind him that his guys were waiting.

Hoping to learn more, Sergeant Sauvé and Constable Beers set up a watch around the service station where the truck was being kept. They waited all day of August 21 but the traffickers made no attempt to come to get the truck. The next morning they concluded they were wasting their time and that the traffickers had out-foxed them again. But Oddo telephoned Dasti to tell him his guy had arrived during the night and that the clients were checking the 32 one-pound packages one by one. The New Yorker said he hoped that this time the merchandise would conform to the agreement. He thought the courier could start back for Montreal before noon. Oddo assured the Montrealer that everything seemed to be in order even though the packaging had not been done in the proper way. Finally, he promised to come to Montreal that night or the next day.

With the help of other telephone conversations, intercepted both before and after this one, the RCMP established that the courier was Lucien (The Cat) Madère, a former employee at the *Victoria Sporting Club*. They also established that Mendolia had arranged his trip, and that the merchandise had been supplied to Dasti by Horvath and Séville.

Oddo arrived in Montreal on August 23 about 8 o'clock in the morning. He met briefly with Dasti, gave him a small package, and left again for New York. Dasti repaid the call with a visit to New York two days later and on September 9 the New Yorker came again to Montreal, apparently to discuss the tampering with the merchandise which had occurred again. On this subject, Dasti warned Horvath about Séville's procedures and Little Joe promised to look into it.

On September 19 Dasti went back to New York. The BNDD noted his presence, and Panepinto's, at the funeral of a high-ranking member of the New York Mafia, James Plumeri, alias Jimmy Doyle, a captain in the family of Carmine Tramunti (successor to Gaetano Lucchese). The chieftain had been murdered three days earlier over a conflict with Carlo Gambino about control of the garment industry. Panepinto's bosses, the Dioguardis, were nephews of the dead man.

On October 1, another telephone conversation between Oddo and Dasti was overheard:

Benedetto Zizzo

Antonio Sciortino

Vito Adamo

Baldassare Accardo

Salvatore Reggio

Antonio Aguano

"I'll have a new shipment of fruit for you very soon," said Dasti. "It won't be packaged like the last time. I promise you that... I spoke to my people and I can explain what happened the last time."

Nine days later Oddo telephoned to find out how things were going and Dasti replied:

"The deal looks good. I should have more news in a couple of days. I'll know then what's what, but everything is O.K."

But by October 15 Dasti's mood had changed:

"I'm waiting, waiting, and everything should be ready. I'm waiting for those assholes. They were supposed to bring the car and the assholes didn't show up. It's supposed to be three or four cars."

The supplies for this new deal were to come from Italy via Toronto through Cotroni, Orsini and Mendolia. In September these men had made contact with Vito Adamo, Salvatore Reggio and Baldassare Accardo, three henchmen of Benedetto Zizzo and Antonio Sciortino. They had made arrangements to buy part of a heroin shipment which the Torontonians had sent for. Antonio Aguano was supposed to bring back the merchandise. Strange as it may seem, he appeared to be the most influential member of the Toronto gang, at least according to information arising from the current police investigation there. During the summer, Zizzo and Reggio had many bitter discussions about the method to be used for importing the stuff. Finally the two mafiosi turned to Don Toto, that is, Aguano, for a final decision. Aguano decided to go to get the merchandise himself in a new Ford of that year. He intended to return on September 16 via Halifax with the merchandise concealed in a secret compartment built into his car's gas tank.

On October 17, two days after Dasti's latest talk with Oddo, Cotroni, Orsini and Mendolia met Vito Adamo and Salvatore Reggio in Montreal at the *Casa d'Italia* restaurant. Previous information gathered by the Toronto section of the Narcotics Squad indicated that the discussion centred on the delay in delivery of the merchandise and on the price demanded by the Torontonians, which was considered too high. In any case, the meeting quickly proved to be futile. Aguano returned at the beginning of November, empty-handed. In Italy an incident involving his car had unnerved him and later someone had warned him that his car would be searched and gone over with a fine-toothed comb. Not wishing to risk another seizure (the gang had already been hit by one in New York in August), he decided to cancel the operation.

But the absence of the heroin did not prevent the RCMP from taking action. On November 11, Aguano, Adamo, Accardo and

Reggio were arrested at a farm in a Toronto suburb and charged with conspiracy to traffic in heroin. Two were convicted and sentenced. Adamo, called the Philosopher, who had been released for lack of evidence, was assassinated in Naples on January 24, 1973, because he was suspected of being an informer for the RCMP. The investigation, begun when Anthony Castiglione and Pietro Misuraca arrived in Toronto at the beginning of 1971, led on January 27, 1973, to the arrest of Benedetto Zizzo, Antonio Sciortino, Antonio Codispoti, Vito and Francesco Cutrona, Nicola and Gaetano Asaro and Francesco Bellitti. (31)

The Cotroni gang members were greatly disappointed by the failure of the Toronto transaction. On November 17, 1971, Mendolia got in touch with Castiglione to find out how to contact "The Blond," Giuseppe Tramontana. Later he called Pietro Misuraca in Louisiana:

"I've got some work for the both of us," he said.

"Good. I've decided that my shares and yours will be ten each ... Remember, you're the one who started this ... The second time I was in Montreal I was willing to accept the $10,500. It wasn't right because I had promised people to sell the stuff and the price was to be $11,500 ... If I hadn't promised the stuff to others ..."

"If I could, I'd be glad to give you $14,000. Remember, Pietro, when you left Montreal, you told me to try to get $10,000 each."

"That's true, but things have changed."

Mendolia then asked Misuraca to give him an address so he could write to him. The next day Misuraca called back:

"There's nothing new, but it's possible I'll be there before the end of the year."

"We'll wait for you. Will you be ready?" asked Mendolia.

"Don't ask me when we'll be ready. The first chance we get, it'll be for you."

"I'll call you again tomorrow."

The next day Mendolia was unable to reach Misuraca. He tried again for several days without success. But finally, in mid-December, he contacted Tramontana and went to meet him in New York. His trip was preceded and followed by meetings with Dasti and Orsini. But these approaches led nowhere. Or if they did, the RCMP never heard about it. At the beginning of 1972, the Narcotics Squad

---

31. All received heavy sentences except for Sciortino, who was acquitted.

learned that Aniello Santella, who had been deported to Italy, was preparing to come to Montreal to arrange a new transaction with his friends there. In October, Orsini had travelled to Italy again and met Santella. On February 24, 1972, Santella arrived in New York but was not allowed to continue on to Montreal. U.S. Immigration officers took him into custody and released him only when he agreed to accept voluntary deportation to Italy.

At the time of these latest developments, several joint investigations by Canadian, U.S. and French police were being concluded. Some of them would have strong repercussions on the Cotroni clan.

Chapter 14

Artists on Stage

In early April of 1971, the RCMP Narcotics Squad, at the request of U.S. Customs investigators, began looking for a musician named Henri Tailler. This man was suspected of being involved in a heroin delivery when he came to Montreal in the winter of 1969 as part of the troupe of the French singer Johnny Halliday.

On April 22, 1969, Customs officers at Boston's Logan airport had by chance arrested a French immigrant who was carrying six kilos of pure heroin. Emile Alonzo, in exchange for the clemency of the courts, confessed his role in an important French narcotics ring. In September 1968 he had joined his half-brother Armando Gagliani in New York who had introduced him to two other Frenchmen, Jean-Claude Kella and Guido Rendel with whom he entered the heroin traffic. In mid-1969 Alonzo met another member of the gang, Laurent Fiocconi, known as Charlot, who had come from Europe to arrange a drug shipment from Montreal to New York. A hitch in plans had developed: the man named Tailler who had undertaken the task of picking up the merchandise in Montreal was unable to carry it out. Fiocconi then assigned the task to Rendel and asked Alonzo to go along with him. Alonzo went to Montreal. He did not see Tailler, as Rendel was responsible for making the contact. But once that was done, Alonzo went to the *LaSalle Hotel* to take delivery of two guitar amplifiers belonging to the Johnny Halliday troupe. Twenty-three kilos of pure heroin (50 pounds) had been concealed in the amplifiers. For the transport to New York, Rendel and Alonzo removed the merchandise from the sound equipment and hid it beneath the back seat of their car. The trip back was made without incident. Alonzo then went to Paris where Fiocconi and Rendel gave him the six kilos of heroin he was transporting when arrested.

Alonzo's confession was not made all at once. He began by identifying the main actors by pseudonym and he left out several interesting details, such as the identity of the man known as Henri Tailler and the fact that the drug had been concealed in amplifiers accompanying the Johnny Halliday group. It took U.S. Customs months to establish the real identity of the traffickers. The earliest information transmitted to the RCMP mentioned a certain "Taillefer" and other similar-sounding names.

On one detail however, Alonzo had quickly come clean — the origin of the heroin. He declared it had been supplied by a "chemist" well-known in the French underworld, Georges Albert Veran, who had been arrested a month before in Marseilles after discovery of an illegal laboratory and seizure of 135 kilos of morphine-base (290 pounds) and 20 kilos of pure heroin (44 pounds). Veran had previously been arrested in October 1964 in a laboratory for transforming morphine-base to heroin along with the overseer of the premises, Joseph Césari, half-brother of Dominique Albertini who was the underworld's first great "chemist." Césari made the best heroin on the market and supplied, among others, the Paul Mondolini ring. Veran was sentenced to only three years in prison on that occasion, but Césari was given seven years and a large fine.

According to Alonzo, Veran who was known in Marseilles as Le Vieux, was a good friend of his half-brother Gagliani and was supposed to have a very good contact in Canada. He had supplied several heroin shipments to America via Canada as well as the lot received by the musician Tailler. In July 1969 the RCMP searched unsuccessfully for evidence of a trip he was said to have made to Montreal.

Not until April of 1971 did Alonzo's full and detailed statements reach the Narcotics Squad. The investigation quickly centred on the Montreal promoters of Johnny Halliday's tour. No one knew any musician by the name of Tailler. There was, however, a Marseilles stage artist named Edmond Taillet who was a friend of one of the members of the Halliday troupe. This artist, furthermore, had provoked a small incident: his amplifiers had arrived with those of the Halliday group and had been sent in error to Sherbrooke which was the first stop of the Halliday tour. Taillet had moved heaven and earth in an attempt to get his amplifiers brought back to his hotel immediately. He had been to Montreal several times since 1969 but never given a show there. At the time of this incident, he had been in New York but went to Montreal on April 5 and left again the next day.

All these elements led federal agents to suspect that Edmond Taillet might be the wanted trafficker. Arrangements were therefore made to shadow him on his next visit to Montreal. On April 24 it was learned that he had made reservations for five days at the *LaSalle Hotel* and that he had received a telegram that month which read: "THE SQUIRREL IS WAITING FOR THE NUTS."

Taillet arrived at Dorval airport at 8:35 p.m., April 25, 1971. He passed the Customs examination, then went to his hotel where a young woman came to meet him. The next morning he telephoned Marseilles. Federal agents installed in the next room heard him ask someone named Etienne if a certain person had been sick and had vomited. He then said he was waiting to continue the voyage and asked if all was going well. Taillet next made a telephone call to Paris.

In late afternoon a man, perhaps a Parisian, came to his hotel room. Their conversation left no doubt about the nature of their activities. Taillet spoke of his next trip to New York and asked if the "girl" he was to meet on April 30 had arrived. They talked of a large sum of U.S. money which would be sent to Marseilles in suitcases and about methods of getting through French Customs without being searched. At one point there was discussion of the advantages in using an automobile for certain operations. While his visitor was still there, Taillet received a telephone call in which he said he would be happy to get in touch with "Michel" because he had a message for him from Marseilles. He told his caller that "Michel" was now living with the Montreal actress Danielle Ouimet. Taillet's visitor left early in the evening and the rest of the night was calm.

On April 27, Taillet went to the *Chez Clairette* restaurant owned by a friend from Marseilles, then returned to his hotel. He received a visit from an unidentified couple who left late in the afternoon in a luxurious Corvette convertible. A check of the licence plates showed the vehicle to be registered to Michel Mastantuano, 28, of 2055 Saint-Mathieu Street in Montreal. Agents followed the car to Habitat 67, the elegant apartment buildings put up during Expo 67. The apartment the couple entered had been rented in the name of Danielle Ouimet. The young woman's companion was evidently the Michel for whom Taillet had brought a message from Marseilles. Shortly after his arrival at Habitat 67, the driver of the Corvette made another quick return trip to the *LaSalle Hotel.*

Taillet left his hotel on April 28 carrying a briefcase, a travel bag and a liquor-bottle container. He went to Dorval airport and took a flight to New York. Notified by the RCMP, New York Customs investigators took him into custody on his arrival, charging him the next day with having delivered 23 kilos of heroin to Guido

Rendel and Emile Alonzo. At first Taillet refused to talk for fear of reprisals against his family but finally he, too, agreed to cooperate with investigators. His statements threw light on one of the largest and most complex heroin rings ever put into operation by French traffickers.

Edmond Taillet got his start in the drug trafficking world in September 1968 when an acquaintance he met several times in Marseilles cabarets suggested he could get rich quickly by delivering heroin to Montreal in his luggage or instruments. The acquaintance was a Corsican gangster named Joseph Marro whom Taillet had first met a few years earlier in *Le Versailles* cabaret. They had sat together at the table of the club's boss, Antoine Guérini, a godfather of the Corsican underworld. (1) Taillet, attracted by the prospect of easy money, accepted Marro's proposal.

Following instructions, he then bought an amplifier and a guitar and turned them over to Marro. A few days later he picked up the amplifier (now loaded with heroin) and a false-bottomed suitcase (also loaded with heroin). He made his first delivery in Montreal to a man he had already been introduced to in Marseilles. Taillet learned later that this was Edouard Rimbauld, a detective story novelist who wrote under the name of Louis Salinas. Taillet was paid $1,125 when he returned to France after his first job.

Towards February 1969, Marro asked him to think of some way of sending a shipment in musicians' gear. Taillet then suggested the idea of mixing two heroin-filled amplifiers in with the instruments of Johnny Halliday's orchestra. Marro liked the idea and the project took shape. Taillet recruited an old friend, Jacques Bec, a show producer who was in financial difficulties. Through him he arranged to have his instruments transported with those of the Halliday group. Edouard Rimbauld was to receive the merchandise in Montreal again, but at the last moment he was unable to make the trip. Guido Rendel, alias Ricard, was therefore given the assignment and in exchange for the 25 kilos, he remitted $138,000 to Taillet. The money was brought back to Marseilles and handed over to Marro and his two bosses, Joseph (Le Frisé) Mari and Jean-Baptiste (Bati) Croce, both long-time associates of Paul Mondolini, Ansan Bistoni and Pep Cotroni. Because he had declined to deliver the

---

1. See Note 14, page 49, Chapter Two. As the oldest and head of the family, Antoine Guérini was the leading figure in the Marseilles and Corsican underworld until his assassination on June 23, 1967. Just before his death, he was said to have had a serious dispute in a Paris gambling joint over a heroin deal.

merchandise directly to Boston himself, Taillet was paid only $8,000 instead of the $12,000 to which he would have been entitled.

At the end of April or the beginning of May 1969, Croce went to Paris and organized a new mission for Taillet. He was given the responsibility of going to New York to collect the payment from the U.S. buyer. Taillet did so and returned with $150,000 given to him by a Puerto-Rican named Antonio Flores. Marro and Croce then asked him to go to Montreal and make the acquaintance of an unmarried woman with a car. He would invite her (with her car) on a pleasure trip to France. While touring in the South of France, Taillet would arrange to put the car into Marro's hands for one night. Then the woman could take a ship for Montreal with her car on board.

Taillet went to Montreal in June 1969. At the *Chez Clairette* restaurant he came to know another Marseillais who was a waiter there, Michel Mastantuano. He also renewed acquaintances with a musician friend, Jean Cardon, an accordionist at *Chez Babette* restaurant. Cardon introduced him to girls and he set his designs on Noella, a barmaid in an Old Montreal club. He courted her as planned and she became his mistress. In less than a week the young divorcée, mother of two children, was ready to go to France. Her trip was quickly organized with Marro and Croce meeting the costs. In Paris, Jacques Bec again agreed to take part in the operation, and accompanied Taillet and Noella to Marseilles.

Edmond Taillet   *Jacques Bec*

When Marro and his men had done their work, the trio returned to Paris and arrangements were made to ship the car, and the 27 kilos of heroin concealed in it, back home. In Montreal at the beginning of July, Taillet and Bec got in touch with Mastantuano and Cardon to pick up the car at the docks. It was finally the accordionist Cardon who undertook to pick up the car and store it at his place until Taillet and Bec were ready to leave for New York. The delivery to the U.S. was made without problem. Taillet travelled to New York by plane, while Bec and Noella drove there in the car. The heroin was turned over to Antonio Flores and his brother Tony who made an initial payment of $200,000. Taillet returned to Montreal to pay Cardon and to arrange with Mastantuano to break things off with Noella. That was not too difficult: she had fallen into the trap set for her which was enough to justify her "dismissal." The young woman was crushed, but business is business. Taillet received $20,000 for his work, out of which he paid Bec and Cardon whom he had hired without the knowledge of Marro and Croce.

For Taillet's fourth mission, Marro asked him to return to Montreal to meet a Jean-Pierre Buffa who was awaiting orders before proceeding to New York. He agreed and worked with the courier on the delivery of a car to a certain Anthony Segura. During the operation, Buffa gave him to understand that about 30 kilos were involved and that Buffa had been recruited in Lyon by Ricard (Guido Rendel).

Back in Paris with the money, Taillet got Marro's agreement to another seduction operation. He had met another young woman in Montreal, Ginette. He proposed to buy her a car and to bring her to France for a repeat of the first scenario. Bec, already familiar with this script, was brought in again and in Montreal Ginette introduced him to Rose-Marie. The operation might, therefore, bring in twice as much. The two friends had no trouble buying the cars, but since Marro and Croce had not been warned of the change in plans, only one car was shipped abroad. In France everything went smoothly, except for an emergency which took Rose-Marie back to Montreal in the middle of the trip. The delivery to New York was made in mid-October. Ginette, who thought she was going to pick up a suitcase of money, drove the car, while Taillet and Bec travelled by plane. The 50 kilos were delivered to Segura by Taillet in exchange for two payments totalling about $270,000.

About ten days after Taillet had brought the money back to France, Marro and Croce told him they had certain friends who were looking for a buyer. They had agreed to send someone to New York to introduce these friends to Segura. A car and a courier were already in place for a transaction. Taillet went there and made the exchange with a representative of the buyer. At the beginning of January, he returned to New York to collect another payment from Segura. At that time the project involving the second automobile, Rose-Marie's, had been put on the shelf by Croce and his lieutenant. Taillet and Bec tried to revive the project at the end of January 1970 by bringing the girl and her car to France, but Marro declared it was too soon. Rose-Marie was sent home to Montreal and the operation had to wait. In March the Corsicans definitely cancelled the project. Taillet sold the car, which angered Bec who decided to break up with him and join another gang of traffickers.

Taillet himself became inactive after that, but resumed his activities in February 1971 when Marro got in touch with him again. At a meeting in Marseilles with Marro, Croce and Mari, Taillet was offered a very interesting trip on which he would not be required to transport any merchandise personally. He was to meet another Frenchman, Etienne Mosca, who would give him an envelope which he in turn would hand over to Segura. The envelope contained the ticket for the parking lot where a Citroen would be left, containing 93½ kilos of heroin (205 pounds) with a street market value of about $100 million. The New Yorker would then hand over another envelope containing the key to the car and the money, which Taillet would then give to Mosca. Taillet would be paid $8,000 on his return to Paris. He accepted the proposition and went to New York, via Montreal, on April 5. On his return to New York on the 25th he was to meet again with Segura who, by then, would have received the merchandise. During his stay in Montreal, Taillet met Michel Mastantuano who was aware of his activities and who confided that he himself had gone into the narcotics business. Taillet guessed that he had joined up with Jacques Bec. As for the Parisian who had come to see Taillet in his hotel room, that was the accordionist Jean Cardon.

Taillet's confession was far from complete on June 15, 1971, when the French central office for narcotics asked the RCMP to make a careful check on the automobile of a Parisian gangster which was en route to Montreal on the liner *Alexander Pushkin.* A routine check of passengers leaving Le Havre revealed that Edouard Batkoun, 40, of Paris, who described himself as a coffee importer, was traveling with his 72-year-old mother and had shipped his Fiat car with him. Of Algerian origin, Batkoun was known to judiciary police as a procurer. In 1965, he owned a Calais café which was a hang-out for gangsters and prostitutes. He had no known means of support other than pimping and gambling.

339

The *Alexander Pushkin* arrived at Montreal on June 21. As soon as it docked, Sergeant Paul Sauvé and Constable Réginald Beers, of the Narcotics Squad, boarded with a specially-trained dog and began an examination of the suspect Fiat. The animal seemed not to sense anything in particular, but one of the investigators lifted the back seat and noticed a badly-adjusted bolt under the left mudguard. The panel was removed, and the agents discovered plastic sacks containing the precious white powder. The right panel and the doors of the vehicle were then removed. A total of 25 sacks was discovered: 50 kilos or 110 pounds of heroin valued at more than $50 million. It was the second largest seizure of heroin ever made in Canada, the largest being the seizure of 62 kilos in the luggage of the diplomats Juan Aritzi and Salvador Pardo-Bolland in 1962.

Batkoun was arrested when he returned to get his car, after taking his mother to the home of her sister who lived in Montreal. Brought to criminal court, he swore he had no knowledge of the contents of his car.

He was acquitted in October when his defense raised a reasonable doubt about his guilt by arguing that he had not had control over his vehicle during the eight days of the ocean crossing. Anyone could have placed the heroin in his car without his knowledge. After the trial, he returned to France with his Fiat, unfortunately for him. Alerted by the RCMP, French Customs officers made a scrupulous search of his car and managed to scrape up a trace of heroin, less than one-hundredth of a gram. He was charged with exporting narcotics and the Paris tribunal concluded that he was aware of the cargo hidden in his car. The investigation carried out in Paris and Marseilles established that he was working for two Corsicans, Maurice Castellani and Albert Francesconi. (2)

Furthermore, two days after the seizure of the 50 kilos, the French Central office for narcotics advised the RCMP that another Corsican trafficker, Paul François Graziani, a friend of Francesconi, was in Montreal at the *Bonaventure Hotel* waiting to be contacted by a certain Janvier. The police made discreet inquiries and learned that Graziani had been at the *Bonaventure* since June 14. He had arrived in Montreal on the 12th and stayed two days at the *Laurentien Hotel.* He spent his days in his room or beside the pool and had advised hotel employees that he was waiting for a very important telephone call. Agents entered his hotel room while he

---

2. Francesconi was known as a partner of Louis Litoro and Henri La Porterie, suppliers to Blackie Bisson and Bob Tremblay.

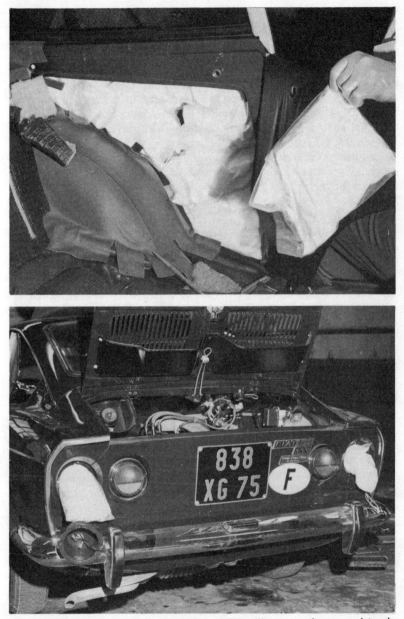

Sacks of heroin valued at more than $50 million are discovered in the panels and doors of Edouard Batkoun's Fiat.

was out to make a careful search of his baggage. They found nothing of particular interest, but Graziani returned to his room before they could leave. The agents tried to pass themselves off as hotel employees checking the air-conditioning, but the Frenchman's suspicions were aroused. On June 27 he left the *Bonaventure* to register at the *Berkeley Hotel* on Sherbrooke Street West. The next day agents followed him to a Metro station where he met an unknown person. His trail was lost in the Metro but he returned to his hotel a bit later with a bag of mechanical toys. On the morning of June 29, he met the same person on St. Catherine Street and in the afternoon he went to Dorval and took a flight to Paris. It was learned later that the unknown person he had met was André Arioli, manager of the *Chez Clairette* restaurant and accomplice of Michel Mastantuano.

The same day however, the French central office informed the Narcotics Squad that when Graziani returned to France he was warned that one of his associates, Félix Rosso, had been meticulously searched on his arrival three days earlier. Rosso was no doubt the Janvier that Graziani was to have contacted in Montreal. The RCMP could discover no trace of a visit to Montreal by Rosso. They remembered, however, that on the day Batkoun was arrested, U.S. Customs officers at Champlain had reported the entry into the U.S. of a Félix Rosso and a Robert Gauthier, of Montreal, in a 1970 Renault. The two men had a large sum of U.S. money on them and travelled to Plattsburg, then to New York. On June 17, the U.S. Customs office at Dorval airport had advised the BNDD that Rosso had left Montreal for New York and Miami.

On July 15, French police informed Staff Sergeant Gilles Poissant of the Narcotics Squad that Michel Mastantuano had been in Paris with Danielle Ouimet for at least five days, and that Graziani had called him at his hotel the night before. The conversation went like this:

"The people think it's a lot, too much for right away, understand?"

"Yes. What are they going to do now?"

"Don't worry. I talked to them and they're making arrangements to take everything."

"Splendid! What's going to happen after?"

"Don't worry. The final step will be taken soon. I'll talk to you again . . ."

The central office for narcotics also learned in its investigation that the Graziani-Rosso tandem was linked to the boss of *Le Consul* bar in Paris, Joseph (Jo le Boxeur) Signoli, a Marseillais and friend of old Joseph Orsini as well as a member of the previously-mentioned organization, le Service d'Action Civique (S.A.C.). This was a gaullist, extreme right-wing organization which recruited many of its shock troops in the underworld. Under Signoli's direction, Graziani and Rosso hoped to organize a shipment of 200 kilos of heroin (440 pounds) to the United States, using a private ship. About this time, the RCMP learned through gossip columns in Montreal's entertainment journals that Michel Mastantuano and Danielle Ouimet planned a sailing trip in the Caribbean at the end of the summer. For this purpose the actress's fiancé had undertaken construction of a 36-foot ship with his friend Robert Gauthier. Federal agents speculated that this would be the same Gauthier who had accompanied Rosso to New York. They recalled that Edmond Taillet, when questioned about the Mastantuano-Ouimet couple, had said the young Marseillais was acquainted with traffickers and was possibly involved in narcotics traffic himself.

In August, periodic checks on Gauthier's movements showed him to be spending a lot of time at his shipyard. Mastantuano and Danielle Ouimet returned to Montreal on the 10th. For closer surveillance of their actions, Corporal Ernest Bacqué of the Narcotics Squad made discreet approaches to rent an apartment at Habitat 67. The high rent, but especially the lack of vacancies, forced a delay in this project. On September 20, the BNDD alerted the RCMP to the arrival in Montreal of Richard Berdin, one of Joseph Signoli's men. In mid-summer, French investigators had learned that Berdin was to be one of the ring's representatives in New York. An informer told them early in September that he planned another trip to New York and that at least six cargos of heroin were ready for shipment.

Berdin arrived at Dorval at 6:35 p.m. from Brussels and took a taxi to the *Ritz-Carlton Hotel* where he registered under the name of Gilbert Kemmoun. He spent the evening and the night in his room under constant surveillance by three agents from the Narcotics Squad and the BNDD. At noon the next day he went to Dorval airport and took a flight to New York where he checked in to the *Abbey Victoria Hotel*. Customs investigators were aware that two French liners, the *France* and the *Raffaello*, were scheduled to arrive in New York on September 22. Two special investigating teams from U.S. Customs were assigned to a search of the two ships. While Berdin met an unidentified man in front of the Air France offices, the teams found 82 kilos of heroin (180 pounds) in a 1970 Ford Galaxie. The car belonged to a Sicilian from Queens, Giuseppe

Giacomazzo, who was returning with his lady friend from a tour of Italy which had taken him to Naples, Rome, Genoa and Turin. Caught red-handed, Giacomazzo agreed to cooperate and to proceed with the delivery of the merchandise as planned to Frank Rappa, co-owner of a small pizzeria in Hope Lawn, New Jersey and an associate of members of the Gambino family. On September 25 and 26, Customs investigators arrested Rappa, Berdin, and Lorenzo D'Aloisio, Giacomazzo's brother-in-law.

The BNDD and the French central office for narcotics were still far from satisfied. They would have preferred more patience on the part of the Customs investigators. It was not this delivery to Frank Rappa they had been waiting for, but seven others destined for a much more important buyer. (3) Nevertheless, they realized their hoped-for results over the next few months, thanks in part to Richard Berdin's prompt confession which filled in the gaps in the information already gathered about Mastantuano.

Berdin's adventures in the drug trade began in March 1970 when an underworld friend, Francis Scapula, offered the opportunity to join him in working for Joseph Signoli and his partner Alexandre Salles. Signoli and Salles had decided to join up with the well-seasoned gang of Laurent Fiocconi and Jean-Claude Kella. Berdin's task was to recruit casual travelers who would deliver heroin from France to the United States for $1,000 a kilo. He linked up with André Labay, an industrial adventurer, half-crook and half-secret agent who undertook to transport heroin to the United States in automobiles he would supply himself.

The first operation got underway about the end of April. Berdin got about 30 kilos from Scapula which he supplied to Labay, who then asked Berdin to go to the *Fontainebleau Hotel* in Miami. He would call Berdin there to tell him how the merchandise would be delivered. In Paris, before he left, Berdin met Scapula, Signoli and Salles who were accompanied by Fiocconi and Pierre (Gros Pierrot) Simeoni, a specialist in armed robbery and muscle jobs. He was introduced to the man he would deliver the merchandise to in New York. He was Jean (Petit Jeannot) Dumerain, a former prison mate. Everything went off as planned. When Dumerain got the 37 kilos of heroin (81 pounds) he passed them to Jean-Claude Kella, Fiocconi's partner who had the precious connection with the New York buyer and had lived in the U.S. for a year under an assumed name. Berdin

3. Over the years, a certain rivalry arose between the BNDD and the U.S. Customs service, to a point where suppression of the international drug traffic was often

received $37,000, of which $27,000 went to Labay. It had not been Labay who had taken the Bentley automobile to the U.S., but one of his friends, Raymond Moulin. A few years earlier, when Labay had been chief of the secret service for President Tschombe, of Congo-Kinshasa, Moulin had been his bodyguard.

After this delivery at the end of May, Berdin stayed in the U.S. for three months, as agreed beforehand, to take delivery of all the heroin shipped by Labay. The second load of 70 kilos (154 pounds) arrived around the end of June or the beginning of July 1970 in the same way as before, except that Berdin turned over the heroin to Signoli himself. With Signoli at the time was a man named Guy, identified later as Guido Rendel, alias Ricard, the replacement for Kella who had been arrested in Italy with Fiocconi. Signoli came back to New York about the beginning of August, with another Corsican, André Andréani, called le Grand Dédé who was to replace Rendel after the next shipment — a Mercedes stuffed with 72 kilos of heroin (158 pounds) which Labay and Moulin were sending in the care of a certain Jean-Claude Demeester. While his accomplices were receiving the stuff, Berdin went to Port Arthur, Texas, where a sailor was to deliver another 25 kilos to him. He didn't dare take personal possession of the drugs, as he had been searched by Customs officers on his descent from the plane. When the transaction was completed, he sent back to France part of the proceeds of the last sale, about $200,000.

A few days after his return to Paris, Berdin went to Marseilles with Scapula to meet Salles and a few others to settle a few disputes. Then he took a couple of weeks vacation during which he became involved in a serious auto accident which put him in hospital for a prolonged period of convalescence. He remained in constant touch with his friends however, and by the beginning of December he was back in the United States waiting to receive another shipment from Labay. This assignment had been given to him by Salles and Signoli and one of their henchmen, Francis (Le Belge) Vanverbergh who was representing the Fiocconi-Kella team. Berdin went to New York and met Salles and Signoli. Then with André Andréani and another

---

seriously compromised. Bureaucratic jealousies between the two organizations permitted several traffickers to slip out of the net, sometimes because of failure to share important information, sometimes because of hasty arrests by one organization which "burned" some current investigation by the other. Caught in between, foreign services, and particularly the RCMP Narcotics Squad had to perform feats of diplomacy so as not to offend the sensibilities of one or the other organization.

Corsican, Félix Rosso, he went to Fort Lauderdale, Florida, to take delivery of merchandise brought in by two sailors. Back in New York, the heroin was delivered to a buyer named Louis, identified by the BNDD as Louis Cirillo, who described himself as a baker from the Bronx but who had links with the big crime bosses Carlo Gambino and Thomas Eboli. While Salles, Signoli, Andréani and Rosso returned to France, Berdin went to Miami to pay $100,000 to the two sailors.

Shortly after his return to New York, Berdin met Andréani who had returned to prepare for the next shipment from Labay and Moulin. Berdin then learned that the operation was directed from Marseilles by old Joseph Orsini, who had taken steps to find them a buyer in the U.S. (4) The two Parisians had been interested in finding their own customer. They no longer wished to be dependent on clients of Fiocconi and Kella and resented the large share of profits claimed by these two men. The next shipment was also brought in by Jean-Claude Demeester: 102 kilos of heroin (224 pounds) concealed in an old 1949 Cadillac which came to the U.S. by way of Canada. The car had been thoroughly searched by the RCMP when it passed through Montreal but nothing had been found. (5) Nevertheless, Demeester had been panic-stricken by the search. He abandoned the car at Boston and returned to Paris. There he was ordered to return to Boston, pick up the car and deliver it to Berdin, Andréani and Moulin. When the heroin was unloaded, Andréani was surprised to find only 102 kilos instead of the expected 167. Berdin learned later that the missing 65 kilos were located by another member of the ring, Maurice Castellani, whose name had come up at the time Batkoun was arrested in Montreal. Andréani was assigned to deliver the heroin to the Mafia customers while Berdin remained alone in New York.

At the beginning of February, Signoli arrived in New York on a false passport and he and Berdin met Jacques Bec, impresario for the entertainers Les Charlots and former partner of Edmond Taillet in the Jean-Baptiste Croce ring. Bec told them of the expected arrival of a car he had sent to France with one of his friends, Michel Mastantuano. There had been some delay because the ship carrying

---

4. Orsini introduced Signoli to an individual who was to find him a U.S. buyer. This individual, though Orsini was unaware of it, was an undercover agent for the BNDD. The traffickers however, discovered the trap in time to avoid it.

5. The drugs were hidden in secret compartments, expertly welded into the vehicle's chassis. The car would almost have had to be taken apart to find them.

the automobile had been stuck in ice in the St. Lawrence River. This cargo finally reached New York in mid-February. With Bec, Berdin met Mastantuano near the *Holiday Inn* on 57th Street. Mastantuano entered the hotel and emerged a few minutes later with a man who left almost immediately. Berdin took the wheel of the car, a Ford parked in front of the hotel, and with Bec and Mastantuano went to meet Signoli who was waiting with Cirillo's representative near 50th Street. The group then travelled in procession to a small suburban villa where the exchange took place. That night or the following day, Signoli handed Berdin $100,000 which he, in turn, gave to Bec and Mastantuano. Berdin had only a brief glimpse of the young woman who took Bec's share back to France.

When Berdin himself returned to France, he met another underworld acquaintance, Dominique Mariani, a young procurer who was well aware of Berdin's activities and had even offered to provide couriers. In September or October of 1970 he had agreed to meet one of Mariani's couriers in a Champs Elysées restaurant, *Fouquet's,* owned by Marcel Francisci, a highly-ranked chieftain associated with Paul Mondolini and the Venturi brothers. Berdin went to the restaurant, spotted the courier in question, but since Mariani himself had not shown up, did not make himself known to the individual. When he saw Mariani again in the spring of 1971, Mariani told him the courier in question had just been arrested in the U.S. with a Volkswagen van containing about 40 kilos of heroin. (6)

Berdin remained inactive for a few months after his meeting with Mariani, until July 1971 when he went to Marseilles to collect the 15 kilos owed to him by the Salles-Signoli team for his work on previous shipments. He had split from the group after the last operation in New York and was associating with another Paris gang centred on the *Picpus* bar. The men who frequented this bar – Jean (Petit Jeannot) Dumerain, Pierre (Gros Pierrot) Simeoni, Antoine

---

6. This was Roger Delouette, ex-agent of the Service de documentation extérieure et de contre-espionnage (S.D.E.C.E.), the French CIA, who was arrested April 5, 1971, at Port Elizabeth, New Jersey, as he was about to pick up his van containing 44.5 kilos of pure heroin. After his arrest, Delouette accused his former boss in the secret service, Colonel Paul Fournier of organizing the drug shipment with Mariani. U.S. authorities' desire to extradite Colonel Fournier provoked a quarrel between Paris and Washington. In 1973 Claude Pastou, a member of the Joseph-Auguste Ricord gang in South America, declared that it was he who was to receive the drugs from Delouette and that Colonel Fournier had nothing to do with the affair, the supplier being the trafficker Jean-Baptiste de Bono.

Grisoni and André Lajoux — had decided to start their own network. (7) In Marseilles it had been Robert (Le Noir) Di Russo, one of Salles contacts, who had given Berdin the drugs owing to him. Back in Paris, Berdin had entrusted the supply to his new partner, Petit Jeannot. (8)

He himself undertook no new operations until September 18, when he went to Lyon with Grisoni and Lajoux. The trip was the result of discussions begun a few days earlier with a gang from Lyon which was proposing that the Picpus gang take charge of a loaded car already en route to the U.S. and sell the merchandise through its regular customers. This was the first shipment in a series of eight organized by Italian-Americans spending vacations in Italy or France. At Lyon, Berdin was introduced to the man who would hand over the car to him in New York. A rendezvous was arranged for September 22, in late afternoon, in front of the Air France offices in New York. Before leaving from Brussels, Berdin met, in Paris, the person to whom he would give the money belonging to the Lyon group. This was an airline pilot who made several trips a month to the U.S.

The sequel to this story, which took place in Montreal and New York, is known, except perhaps for the fact that the representative of the Lyon gang advised Berdin in New York that the operation could not go on. He had noticed police patrolling around the car brought in by the courier Giacomazzo. Berdin was arrested because unlike the Lyon representative, he did not abandon all immediately, but instead returned to his hotel to collect his things before leaving.

André Labay did not participate in the Lyon affair, but on September 19 on his return from Haiti, where he had strong support,

7. In July 1969, André Lajoux was involved in a shipment of heroin which came to the attention of the RCMP. A Parisian couple traveling on the liner *Cristoforo Colombo* were carrying a stock of heroin without their knowledge. During the crossing the man discovered the drug by chance in his luggage and raised an angry storm which obliged ship authorities to lock him up. The shipping company advised the BNDD of the incident and the ship which was scheduled to sail non-stop to New York put in at Halifax. There two members of the Narcotics Squad from Montreal boarded and persuaded the couple to cooperate by continuing to New York as though nothing had happened. The two Parisians stayed at the *Sheraton Hotel* and while they were absent from their room a man showed up to pick up their luggage. He was met there by two BNDD agents who tried to conceal their identity. The stranger excused himself, explaining that he had come to the wrong room. He was later identified as André Lajoux.

8. Robert Di Russo was assassinated along with two accomplices in Marseilles on

he told Berdin he had the chance to bring 100 to 400 kilos of heroin into the U.S. with the complicity of Customs officers at New York. After talking to Grisoni about this, Berdin organized a meeting with an old friend, Roger Preiss, known as Eric, who had introduced him to Francis Scapula in 1968. Preiss knew the New York buyer because he had already worked with Joe Signoli. Labay and Preiss agreed to remain in close contact and to study opportunities for future deliveries organized and financed by the Picpus gang. Berdin learned during his work in the ring that Edouard Batkoun's Fiat was being awaited in Montreal at that time by Antoine Grisoni, and in the United States by André Lajoux. (9)

By the end of September 1971, Berdin's confession was in the hands of the French central office for narcotics, which quickly organized surveillance on several traffickers he had named, particularly André Labay and Roger Preiss who were believed to be preparing early shipments. On October 6, Labay was shadowed in the Champs-Elysées area as he got into a rented Volkswagen parked near Montaigne Avenue. Three others were in the neighborhood to watch him leave: André Lajoux, Antoine Grisoni and Georges Burait. Labay drove towards the west autoroute and arrived at his home in the Grandes Terres residence at Marly-le-Roi. In the parking lot he was surrounded by a horde of policeman and arrested without resistance.

In the trunk of the small automobile police found five expensive suitcases which had been purchased a few hours earlier. They contained in total 106 kilos or 233 pounds of heroin. The next day Burait, Grisoni and Lajoux were arrested in Paris, while Preiss, who had given Labay the keys to the Volkswagen, was collared on his arrival in New York.

Preiss also talked willingly to police. On October 19, as his friend Berdin had done, he appeared before a grand jury for the southern district of New York and testified about his participation in the Signoli ring. He told how Signoli had taken him to Montreal at the beginning of August, on Berdin's recommendation, to handle the last phase of the heroin shipment. There he was introduced to a man he identified as Michel Mastantuano. On August 13 he left Montreal

---

September 5, 1972. He was believed to have double-crossed some underworld associates by delivering them a supply of sand instead of the morphine-base which had been contracted for.

9. At the end of 1974, Berdin published a detailed account of his misadventures in international trafficking: *Nom de code, Richard,* Paris, Gallimard, 1975.

for Miami where Signoli joined him. During the week he spent in Florida, the Corsican introduced him to his client, Louis Cirillo and Cirillo's assistant, John Anthony Astuto. He met them several times in Miami and in New York when he arrived with Signoli on August 21.

Two days later Preiss said he accompanied Signoli to a meeting with Astuto in front of their hotel and they went to a suburban villa. During the drive there he noticed they were being followed by a car driven by Mastantuano. On arrival at the villa, Mastantuano drove his car into the garage and for the next five hours they worked at unloading the 80 kilos of heroin which had been hidden in the car. Later that day, Cirillo came himself to give Signoli a suitcase containing $300,000. Back in France he met Berdin and was introduced to Labay with whom he organized the 106-kilo shipment supplied by the Picpus gang which was seized at Marly-le-Roi.

Following the grand jury testimony by Preiss and Berdin, the district attorney's office indicted Michel Mastantuano for bringing into the United States 100 kilos of heroin on February 17, 1971, and 80 kilos on August 23. The RCMP immediately put Mastantuano under watch. On October 26, the U.S. consul in Montreal, Leonard F. Willems, appeared before Judge Kenneth C. Mackay of Superior Court to file a written accusation against Mastantuano and request his extradition to the United States. A warrant for his arrest was issued and two days later Narcotics Squad officers burst into the apartment of Danielle Ouimet and arrested the young actress and her fiancé, Mastantuano.

After a long interrogation, the young woman was freed, while her fiancé was jailed. She went immediately to the *Bonaventure Hotel* to meet her lawyer, Raymond Daoust, who was accompanied by Frank Cotroni. The defense was quickly organized. At his appearance in court the following day, Mastantuano declared his innocence and his intention to fight to the limit against extradition. The legal proceedings lasted nine months. At first, the Marseillais received help from Frank Cotroni in exchange for his promise to make his contacts for heroin supplies in France available to the Cotroni organization. Nearly every time Mastantuano appeared in court, until March 1972, federal agents observed meetings between Cotroni or Horvath and Mastantuano's friend André Arioli who was himself implicated in the affair but still at liberty. At these meetings attempts were made to extract money from Mastantuano by holding out the possibility of an intervention by influential politicians. These approaches ceased when Cotroni and Horvath realized they were not going to get what they hoped for.

By May 1972 Mastantuano was defeated and financially ruined. He changed lawyers, engaging Nikita Tomesco, to whom he pledged his fiancée's Citroen DS 21, which had already been used to transport heroin. Earlier, one of his lawyers had tried to arrange the theft of the vehicle, but the plan failed when the thief could not get the machine started and was almost arrested by a police patrol. On June 9, Mastantuano finally abandoned the legal battle and accepted extradition. On August 17, 1972, he made a long statement to BNDD agent Anthony S. Pohl who was acting as special commissioner for the international rogatory commission set up at Paris in November 1971. In the presence of representatives of the French central office for narcotics, U.S. Customs and the BNDD, he exposed his accomplices and gave a detailed account of his own part in the gigantic international narcotics ring.

Mastantuano said he got into the heroin traffic in May 1970. Before that he had kept company with Edmond Taillet but had not taken any direct part in the operations. His début was made when Jacques Bec, who had broken with the Jean-Baptiste Croce gang and joined up with friends of Joseph Orsini, suggested he go to Paris to discuss important business. In France, Bec explained what he would be expected to do. He was to buy a Citroen DS 21, load it with heroin, ship it to Canada and then convey it to New York. The job would bring $1,000 a kilo and since there were about 40 kilos to deliver, there would be $40,000 to be shared equally between the two men. The risks, after all, seemed minimal, and Mastantuano accepted the offer and began work immediately.

He went to the Citroen firm and ordered a DS 21 which, for convenience sake, he put in the name of his new conquest, Danielle Ouimet, a young actress he had met at the *Chez Clairette* restaurant. She was with him in Europe at that time and was negotiating a film contract. He returned to Montreal to get the certified cheque required for payment of the automobile. As the 5,000 francs (about $1,200) given to him by Bec was not enough, he decided to ask for help from his friend André Arioli who worked with him at *Chez Clairette.* Attracted by the prospect of easy profits, Arioli willingly lent the necessary $3,000. The money was deposited in Miss Ouimet's bank account and the certified cheque was issued.

Back in Paris, Mastantuano and Bec worked out final details of the operation and waited for delivery of the Citroen, which came on June 30. Bec's bosses were not yet ready, so Mastantuano went to visit his fiancée in Brussels where she was filming *Le rouge aux lèvres.* Bec telephoned him two weeks later to say he was taking the car to Biarritz right away where the organization's mechanics would conceal the heroin in it. Mastantuano undertook to bring the car back to Paris and ship it to Montreal where it arrived at the beginning of September. At his request, Miss Ouimet agreed to pick up the car in port, which produced a bit of a scene. She noticed scratches on the body of the car and expressed her outrage in loud and clear terms. The car was stored in the garage of Mastantuano's building on Saint-Mathieu Street until September 27 when the young actress drove it to New York. Mastantuano and Bec took charge of it there with André (Le Grand Dédé) Andréani. The 40 kilos of heroin were to be delivered to the villa of an important Gambino family member, Anthony Stassi in New Jersey. (10) The drugs had been hidden in the chassis, under the floor and under the seats of the car.

Bec and Mastantuano shared the $40,000 handed over by Andréani and immediately began planning their next operation. This time Arioli was asked to buy a new car in Quebec and ship it to France, which he did, via Amsterdam. In Paris, Arioli received instructions to leave the car, a Ford Galaxie 500, in a certain parking lot and wait until he received word to pick it up at the Bayonne station. Confident that everything was going smoothly, Mastantuano, still accompanied by Danielle Ouimet (who, by the way, had agreed to bring Bec's money to France for him), returned to Montreal. About December 20, Bec telephoned from Paris. He was furious: the Ford loaded with heroin had been parked at the station for two days and Arioli could not be found. Mastantuano said he would look after it and three days later he returned to Paris with Arioli who had gone home to Montreal while waiting. The car was picked up and consigned to a shipping company. Mastantuano then returned to Montreal for Christmas. He went back to France with his fiancée a week later to spend New Year's with his parents in Marseilles. While he was there he had a visit from Arioli who announced that the car had broken down. Arrangements would have to be made to bring the shipper in to make the necessary repairs.

The group was back in Montreal by mid-January, awaiting the arrival of the Ford when another unexpected development occurred:

---

10. Anthony Stassi, 61 in 1970, was the younger brother of Joseph Stassi who was arrested following the seizure of 10 kilos of heroin at Houston, Texas on November 7, 1962. This seizure was mentioned in the chapter on the Rivard affair. The heroin had been supplied by Paul Mondolini and his partners who were then installed in Mexico. Joe Stassi was considered as important a figure as Salvatore Giglio in North American heroin trafficking. In April 1975, they were indicted for their activities in 1970. Also indicted were the Frenchmen Claude Otvos, a cellmate of Joe Stassi, and Jean (Uncle) Guidicilli.

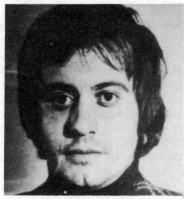

Alexandre Salles

Joseph Signoli

Michel Mastuantuano

André Arioli

Felix Rosso

André Lajoux

The Soviet freighter carrying the car was stuck in the ice in the St. Lawrence River. Bec had to go to New York to reassure his bosses and his clients. Finally, on February 10, Arioli got possession of the Ford and prepared to deliver it to New York where Mastantuano had arranged to meet him at the *Holiday Inn* on 57th Street. He made the trip on the 16th with a girlfriend, another Montreal actress who was probably unaware of the real reasons for the visit. At the scene, Mastantuano met Bec who introduced him for the first time to his boss, Joe Signoli, and another member of the ring, Richard Berdin. The four men took charge of the delivery of the 80 kilos to Anthony Astuto, Louis Cirillo's representative. Back in Montreal the $80,000 was split up: Bec took $52,000, the rest going to Mastantuano who gave $10,000 to Arioli and $1,000 to another friend, Robert Gauthier who had accompanied him to New York by car. Bec did not hesitate to call again on the good services of Danielle Ouimet to bring his loot back to France for him.

Pleased with the success and profitability of his new activities, Mastantuano decided to launch the next deal himself. Towards the end of April 1971, he went to Paris to explain his project to Bec. With the agreement concluded, he returned to Montreal to find a car and someone to ferry it. He approached the singer Daniel Guérard who, without asking too many questions, agreed to ship a car to France and bring it back later for $7,000 plus the cost of buying the car. Mastantuano had decided not to make the Montreal-Paris run himself, but he found himself obliged to go to France on an urgent request from Bec. Signoli needed him for a special mission. A Fiat 124 loaded with heroin was being held up in Montreal because its Italian driver could not get a visa to enter the United States. The driver had to be replaced with someone who could take the car to New York with the cooperation of two other gang members, Félix Rosso, who was already on the scene, and Paul Graziani who was about to join him. Mastantuano would get

---

11. "Mister Félix" was later identified as Louis Santoni, former Corsican policeman who had turned to drug trafficking. He was arrested following the seizure in Marseilles on February 20, 1972 of 423 kilos (930 pounds) of pure heroin hidden in a crab-fishing boat, *le Caprice des temps*. This was the largest seizure ever made anywhere in the world. It led to charges against the boat's captain, Marcel Boucan, Alexandie Orsatelli, an old Corsican gangster, his mistress Marcelle Agavanian, his bodyguard Toussaint Astolfi, Mathieu Péraldi (Santoni's man), and Laurent Fiocconi, associated with the Signoli gang. The name of the chemist Joe Césari, half-brother of Dominique Albertini, was mentioned as the possible manufacturer of the seized heroin. Sold in the streets of New York, the 930 pounds of heroin would have brought in a half billion dollars.

$40,000 for the job.

Following his instructions, he returned to Montreal and began looking for a Fiat identical to the one containing heroin so that licence plates could be switched. He soon realized it would be impossible to obtain such a car quickly enough. He then went to another friend, the accordionist Jean Cardon who had already worked with Taillet. For $6,000 Cardon agreed to lend his garage and his own car and even to drive it to New York. The drugs were then transferred from the Fiat to Cardon's station wagon, this operation being performed, naturally, with as much secrecy as possible. Meanwhile, Danielle Ouimet accepted another chore. This time she went to Miami for Félix Rosso and delivered a letter and a photo of an individual to a "Mister Félix." (11) She received $200 for making the trip.

On June 21, the day after she returned, the delivery of the 70 kilos of heroin was made. Cardon drove alone to New York, while Mastantuano travelled with the young actress. Rosso drove in a car with Robert Gauthier and their entry into the U.S. was noted by Customs officers at Champlain who, it will be recalled, notified the RCMP. Graziani elected to stay in Montreal, since one of his cousins had already been implicated in a narcotics affair in the States. (12) In New York, Mastantuano took over the delivery with Rosso and another Corsican, Jean (Uncle) Guidicilli, a replacement for Signoli who was under summons in Paris for possession of a false passport. The money, nearly $1 million in cash, was brought back to Montreal by Cardon, Rosso, Mastantuano and Miss Ouimet. The loot was split up but Graziani, who knew he was being watched by the RCMP, entrusted his $100,000 to Mastantuano and his fiancée until they arrived in France at the beginning of July.

In Paris, Mastantuano attended a stormy meeting with Graziani, Signoli and a man named Joe who seemed to be the boss. Joe and Signoli berated Graziani for leaving their money in Montreal. Signoli ended by telling him: "Be at headquarters, *Fouquet's,* at the usual time." This was the restaurant owned by Marcel Francisci. Mastantuano went to Marseilles after this incident where he met two of Graziani's partners who hung out at the bar *Les Catalans.* The next day Graziani came to join him and more meetings were held with Signoli and members of the gang.

---

12. This cousin would be Gabriel Graziani, one of Dominique Venturi's men who was with Antranik Paroutian, supplier to Pep Cotroni and Peter Stepanoff around 1958. See Chapter Five and end of Chapter Six.

Mastantuano spent the rest of July on vacation with his fiancée and her parents. Before leaving he told Daniel Guérard, who was still waiting in Paris, that he could pick up his Barracuda at Bayonne station and send it back to Montreal. Towards the end of the month he joined Bec in Marseilles. Their relationship had deteriorated and Bec, to prove his good faith and Signoli's reliability, arranged a meeting with an important figure in the Corsican Mafia, Marcel (le Politicien) Rossi. Rossi, a leader of the Service d'Action Civique in Marseilles, declared that he was associated with Marcel Francisci and Dominique Mariani, the friend of Roger Delouette, and that these people would be taking over control of heroin in France. During the conversation there was particular interest in the construction of the sailboat *Jisan* which Mastantuano had undertaken three months earlier with his friend Robert Gauthier. In the beginning, the project had been conceived for the production of a documentary television series, but the keel of the ship was also to be designed to conceal large quantities of heroin. Signoli had financed part of the construction costs.

Shortly after this meeting Mastantuano returned to Montreal where Signoli awaited him and introduced him to another man, Roger Preiss, using the pseudonym Patrick. The three men met a few times in Danielle Ouimet's apartment while waiting for the arrival of the Barracuda. This time there was no delay and the car arrived on the expected date, August 19. Two days later Daniel Guérard drove the car to New York where Mastantuano, again with his fiancée, took charge of it. The delivery was made in the manner already described by Preiss, in the presece of another Corsican, Marius Lastrayoli, known as le Petit, a friend of Signoli. It was Mastantuano's last operation before his arrest. He did meet Jacques Bec again in September but no concrete project was developed for the immediate future.

On September 8, 1972, following Mastantuano's confession, André Arioli was arrested in Montreal and a request for his extradition was made. Unlike Mastantuano, he did not contest it and was escorted to New York on October 23. He refused however, to cooperate with U.S. authorities. But that was of no great importance: sufficient evidence had already been made available in the statements by Emile Alonzo, Edmond Taillet, Richard Berdin, Roger Preiss, Michel Mastantuano and several others arrested in France and the United States. As a result, about 60 of the most active and important international traffickers were charged or exposed. The French connections which, as we have seen, were cross-linked at several levels, were the most affected. Between 1972 and 1975 most of the traffickers mentioned in this chapter were sentenced in France or the U.S. to terms ranging from five years in the case of Mastantuano to 25 years for Fiocconi and Kella. Top stars in the crime world like Jean-Baptiste Croce, Joe Signoli, Alexandre Salles, Félix Rosso, Paul Graziani, Antoine Grisoni, André Lajoux, Jean Guidicilli, Louis Cirillo, Anthony Astuto, Anthony Segura, Joe and Anthony Stassi and many others were among those convicted. Joseph Bernard (le Frisé) Mari, brought down by cancer on August 6, 1973, escaped conviction. So did Etienne Mosca who committed suicide on May 6, 1974. Albert Bistoni, Croce's old companion in arms, was shot down in a Marseilles bar on March 31, 1973, a few hours after the jailing of his partner. Joseph Orsini, the guiding light of one of the great rings, died a natural death in 1972.

Chapter 15

A Taste for Danger

On November 9, 1971, special agent Kevin Gallagher of the BNDD's liaison office in Montreal called on the Narcotics Squad for help in dealing with a double agent. This man spoke no English and was on a special mission in the city. Staff Sergeant Gilles Poissant, who was in charge of the Squad and was already familiar with some of the details of the affair, went with his U.S. colleague to see the agent. The man he met was an old acquaintance – Roger Gabeloux, one of Joe Horvath's former suppliers. He had been arrested in Paris in March 1969 as he was about to ship 25 kilos of pure heroin to Montreal. After serving a 30-month sentence he had been freed from Fresnes prison the preceding September 29.

Gabeloux, on his release, had offered his services to BNDD agents posted in Paris. Two main reasons motivated this decision which he explained later in a book: his own crisis of conscience over the ravages caused by heroin; and the prospect of living a new adventure which would permit him to satisfy his real passion, gambling. (1) His first approach was to one of his old accomplices, René Quintin de Kercadio, who was called Le Boiteux, or the Lame One. They were adventurers of the same stripe and together in prison had constructed many a project for the future. (2) They first

---

1. *Le Jockey,* by Philippe B., Paris, Editions Oliver Orban, 1974. This book is his account of his adventures in the service of the BNDD and the RCMP. Neither service would ever admit officially that Roger Gabeloux, alias Philippe B., was one of its double agents.

2. In his book, Gabeloux claims that his partner de Kercadio was also a double agent for the RCMP and the BNDD though he did not know that when they were associates. If events seem to confirm this, neither of the services, as in the case of Gabeloux, will do so: nor did de Kercadio himself ever make such a claim. His nickname—Le Boiteux (the Lame One) stems from a knee injury he received in an aircraft accident in Algeria.

decided to renew contacts with Joe Horvath and offer him a first shipment which they would finance with the support of a gang of procurers led by Daniel Marquet. For heroin supplies, they had the advantage of direct relations with two big Marseilles suppliers, Théodore Marininchi, a new acquaintance of Gabeloux, and Joseph Boldrini, their former supplier (who has been mentioned earlier in this book). (3)

That was the plan for the first project. But their possibilities were quickly expanded. Through their friends in the underworld, they had been in contact with a Greek, Jean Glaros, who for a month had been looking for ten kilos of heroin for Montreal buyers. At the end of the summer, Jean-Marc Guillet, a young Montrealer in his twenties, told them he knew people interested in finding a serious supplier who could provide them with regular shipments at $10,000 a kilo. While he was on vacation in Paris, Guillet introduced Glaros to an emissary from the Montrealers, Rolland Pannunzio, who had been assigned to conclude the necessary agreements. He had already obtained a three-kilo lot through a Parisian cabaret operator, Jos Biggi, but it was not enough and furthermore, was of bad quality. Anxious to give full satisfaction to his client who had promised him a return of $500 a kilo, Glaros was delighted to meet Gabeloux and de Kercadio and to introduce them to the Quebecer. The two pals agreed to set up a regular supply network on condition that they be allowed to meet the man in charge in Montreal. Pannunzio replied that if they could not meet the big boss himself, whom he identified by the initials L.G., he would put them in touch with the man responsible for heroin operations, Conrad Bouchard. The two Frenchmen agreed.

Pannunzio and Bouchard were on police files in Montreal as associates of the Cotroni clan. Their common protector was the powerful Luigi Greco, number two man of the local Mafia and former partner of Carmine Galente and Giuseppe Cotroni. From the evidence, he would be the L.G., the big boss who was financing the affair.

Of the two gangsters, Bouchard was certainly the better known. A formidable person, without respect for the laws of man or God, Bouchard was detested even by certain elements of the underworld. He owed much of his success to the close relations he had been able to establish with the high chiefs of the local Mafia. He first won their favor by singing Italian operatic arias in their nightclubs, and

---

3. See Chapters Five and Six.

then proved himself working alongside Peter Stepanoff and Pep Cotroni in robberies, receiving stolen bonds and narcotics traffic. In 1959 when Pep Cotroni was arrested, his name was frequently mentioned. He and Greco were named as co-conspirators in this affair by the New York grand jury. (4)

In 1966 Bouchard was implicated in two huge frauds, one of $110,000 at a Quebec City branch of the Provincial Bank in September 1963, the other of $269,000 at *Canadian Acceptance Corporation* in Montreal in the spring of 1965. At the same time, he was charged in a $723,000 holdup at a Laval branch of the Provincial Bank and for receiving part of the proceeds of another bank robbery. Strangely enough, for all these crimes, he was sentenced to only 30 months in penitentiary, which has always intrigued observers of the criminal justice scene. On his release from prison he was arrested again in June 1969 for conspiring to manufacture and distribute hundreds of thousands of false six-cent stamps. Out on bail, he was implicated again a year later in a million-dollar fraud involving a bank and two firms of stockbrokers. (5) Finally, on July 27, 1971, he was charged with using five false American Express cheques and a stolen credit card. His arrest (and that of two U.S. associates of the Mafia) prompted a police raid and search at the home of his neighbor, Luigi Greco.

Pannunzio, in contrast, was a handyman and docile follower who until January 1971 had been proprietor of a bar, the *Café Boul' Mich*, on Saint-Michel Boulevard in the north end of Montreal. The place was closed during the crack-down on nightclubs carried out by Montreal and Provincial Police. Bouchard had begun frequenting the bar on his release from prison in 1968 and had linked up with Pannunzio with whom he launched into various deals.

Gabeloux and de Kercadio, at their first meeting with Pannunzio, learned the operating procedures of the ring organized by Bouchard. The merchandise was simply shipped by parcel from Bourget airport. When the freight was unloaded at Dorval airport, all parcels remained on the freight dock for a while. At that moment

---

4. See Chapter Six, page 150.

5. Frank Cotroni played an important behind-the-scenes role in this affair by putting Theodore Aboud into Bouchard's clutches. Aboud was a small-time gangster in trouble with loan-sharkers. In April 1973, appearing before the Quebec Commission on Organized Crime, Aboud declared that Bouchard's lawyer, Raymond Daoust, had counselled him in 1970, suggesting names of foreign countries where he could take refuge after the fraud. The celebrated lawyer denied these declarations.

Roland Pannunzio

Conrad Bouchard

Louis Greco

Joseph Boldrini

Jean Glaros

Frank Cotroni (left), Conrad Bouchard (centre), and Raymond Daoust (right) during a night out in Mexico.

an airline employee who was in league with the gang was responsible for picking up the right parcel using the invoice number issued by the shipping company in France. This method pleased Joseph Boldrini, and when de Kercadio went to see him, he agreed to provide the first ten kilos at 13,000 francs a kilo (about $12,000 a pound). Boldrini also declared his willingness to supply an additional ten kilos on credit. Marininchi, for his part, said he would supply on credit a first stock of 30 to 50 kilos, when he was met separately for the Horvath operation.

Delighted with their progress in Marseilles, Gabeloux and de Kercadio had to face an unexpected development on their return to Paris. Glaros informed them that Pannunzio had lost, at the gambling table, all the money he had been given to buy the first ten kilos. The Greek had to get help from another friend to provide the means for Pannunzio to get back to Montreal. On the night of his departure, Glaros had talked on the telephone for the first time to Bouchard from a bar in the Paris suburb of Boulogne where he and Pannunzio usually met. This club, the *O-K-Bec,* frequented by Quebecers visiting Paris, was owned by Bouchard's friend, Roger Mollet, a former associate of Marius Martin and Jean Jehan in *La*

Cave restaurant in Montreal. (6) Bouchard told Glaros he was furious with Pannunzio and would reimburse his friend on the next mission. He was satisfied, despite everything, with the deal, and added that he was getting together more money and would send a new emissary soon. He said he would call back in a few days.

Gabeloux and de Kercadio took advantage of this incident to make their first contact with Bouchard, announcing their participation in the shipment of five additional kilos. When Bouchard called back to the *O-K-Bec,* de Kercadio was there to take the call. The deal was made: a second emissary, Jean-Marc Guillet, would be in Paris at the end of October with the necessary money and he was delighted at the participation of his new suppliers. There was another slight delay, but on November 7 Guillet arrived in Paris with money for ten kilos. As soon as he got the funds advanced by Daniel Marquet's gang of procurers, de Kercadio placed an order for 15 kilos with Boldrini and plans were made for Glaros and Jean-Marc to ship the parcel on November 10, the day after Gabeloux left for Montreal.

On November 9, in the BNDD offices in Montreal, the chief of the Narcotics Squad gave his go-ahead to a collaboration with Gabeloux. According to Gabeloux' testimony, the RCMP undertook to ensure his protection and facilitate his task, on condition that he report regularly on everything he did so as to make things easier for RCMP surveillance teams and permit strict control of the operation. In the matter of the 15 kilos, it had already been agreed that the five kilos financed by the double agent and his friends would be sold to Bouchard. They would not be included with the ten others, as the RCMP and the BNDD would try to keep track of them right to the end hoping to identify Bouchard's clients in the U.S. As for the parcel of ten kilos paid for by the Montrealers, the Narcotics Squad would prevent their pick-up at Dorval airport, but in a manner that would not raise suspicions, so as not to compromise the large shipment expected to follow.

While waiting for de Kercadio to arrive so they could contact Bouchard, Gabeloux was to renew acquaintances with Joe Horvath. On the morning of November 10, he went to Horvath's home in the northwest suburb of Pierrefonds. He had an excellent motive for the visit, as Little Joe still owed $8,000 on a transaction dating back to early 1969. The welcome was warm and the conversation turned quickly to the subject of mutual interest. Vain and self-satisfied,

---

6. See Chapter Seven, page 161.

Horvath explained that he had gone into a new kind of business — trafficking in hashish — which was almost as profitable as heroin when the dealer knew what he was doing. For months he had been importing hundreds of kilos using a system similar to Bouchard's. According to Horvath, his system was as safe as the one he had put into operation for heroin a few years earlier. At that time, he told Gabeloux, the Frenchman in charge would telephone and using an agreed code, give the name and the day of arrival of the courier with the heroin-stuffed Samsonite luggage. On landing at Dorval airport, the courier's instructions were to take a taxi to the *Motel Diplomate*, rent a room and wait patiently for developments. The courier was unaware that he was being watched, from the time he left the airport, by two of Horvath's men whose job it was to control the operation right to the final stage. Each man drove a car, one in front of the taxi leading the other way, the other behind it, making sure there was no police tail. If everything seemed normal, and only then, they telephoned the courier soon after his arrival at the hotel to get his room number. Half an hour later, without passing the reception desk, one of the supervisors would join the courier in his room. He would emerge soon afterwards carrying the two Samsonite cases emptied of their contents except for the two and a half to three kilos of heroin concealed in false sides and bottoms of each. With no further delay, Horvath's two representatives would get in their cars, and one protecting the other, would drive to a house in east end Montreal where Horvath awaited them. There, in a small basement garage, was a mini-laboratory concealed behind a sliding wall. After expert analysis confirmed the quality of the merchandise, Horvath handed the money, along with two new Samsonite cases, to one of his men to be taken back to the French courier. For Horvath, it was child's play. (7)

This description confirmed the suspicions of French and Montreal police during the 1969 investigation. It added some interesting details, however, which had not been known.

As for his hashish network, Horvath naturally believed it to be foolproof. It delighted him to think that police had been running in circles for a year, enraged by the smell of hashish in many Montreal bars and restaurants, but unable to break the system.

But as foxy and talented as Horvath was, the Narcotics Squad had nevertheless penetrated his secret five months earlier. Since then nearly a dozen investigators had been working all-out to collect the

---

7.   *Le Jockey,* o.c.

evidence to arrest him and his accomplices, several young hoodlums associated with the redoubtable motorcycle gang, Satan's Choice. The hashish was shipped from Afghanistan by a Montrealer who lived there and who communicated with Horvath and the others through ingeniously-coded telegrams.

Horvath had been without a heroin supplier for some time. He was therefore counting on Gabeloux to re-launch him in the market. Not particularly generous, his first offer was only $7,000 a kilo, but finally he agreed to pay $8,000 which was still much less than the price offered by Conrad Bouchard.

De Kercadio arrived in Montreal on November 13. As was only natural, Gabeloux was there to welcome his partner, while agents from the Narcotics Squad and the BNDD watched from the sidelines. De Kercadio was carrying a suitcase and a travel bag containing the first five kilos. The two men took a taxi to the *Chateau Champlain Hotel.* By then Jean Glaros had also arrived at Dorval airport and was met by Rolland Pannunzio who, like a good host, showed him a bit of the city and took him to his Gouin Boulevard home before accompanying the visitor to the *Holiday Inn.*

The surveillance teams picked up nothing special that night, but at 8 o'clock the next morning the three Parisians met at the *Laurentien Hotel.* An hour and a half later they met Jean-Marc Guillet at the corner of Dorchester and Peel Streets and all four went to a restaurant in the Italian quarter on Jean Talon Street. At

Louis Henri   *James Episcopia*

10:30 a.m., an unidentified man in a Renault picked them up there and drove them to another restaurant on Jean Talon. They spent an hour there and then took a taxi to Guillet's home. During the afternoon no one left the apartment except Guillet who came out three times to make telephone calls from nearby restaurants. Between the second and third call, about 3 p.m., a 1971 Chevelle automobile was seen moving in a suspicious manner around the building. The agents, assuming that the driver was checking to see if police were watching the area, thought it wise to pull back. When they moved in again a bit later, the Chevelle was parked nearby and the driver had disappeared. About 5:50 p.m., agents at the rear of Guillet's building saw Gabeloux, de Kercadio, Glaros and the Chevelle driver (whom they now identified as Conrad Bouchard), come out of the building, cross the backyard and climb over the fence surrounding the property. They were obviously trying to leave the place without being seen, but of course, they did not succeed. The two Frenchmen returned to their respective hotels while Bouchard was allowed to go his way without being followed.

Thanks to Gabeloux, the Narcotics Squad knew that the group's next meeting would be that night in the *Napoli* restaurant on Jean Talon. But before that, Bouchard was supposed to send someone to get the five kilos of heroin de Kercadio had left in a room at the *Laurentien Hotel*. Three investigators were assigned to keep a close watch on the room. At 7:30 p.m. an unknown man entered the room carrying a brown paper bag. A few moments later he came out with the same sack, no doubt having changed its contents. In any case, the agents in the lobby were alerted and given a brief description of the man. He was spotted as he got out of the elevator but quickly lost himself in the crowd. The agents were unable to recover his trail.

The loss was not as serious as the agents first thought. At the *Napoli,* during dinner, Bouchard announced that he would not pay for the five kilos until he had received the parcel. His New York client preferred to make only one trip. But if the ten kilos had not arrived within eight days he would pay for the first delivery so as not to upset Gabeloux' supplier who was offering credit for a large shipment to come. In either case, therefore, it would still be possible to identify the U.S. buyers eventually.

A few days passed. On November 19 the group met for dinner again, this time in the *Chateau Champlain,* and as usual when Bouchard was present, champagne flowed throughout the feast. The ten kilos had not yet arrived and some people were getting impatient. The next day, Saturday, both the RCMP and the traffickers learned that the parcel sent by Glaros and Guillet was being delayed by a work slowdown by Alitalia airline employees in Rome. Reassured, Bouchard then agreed to pay for the five kilos the following week. The delay gave Gabeloux time to introduce Horvath to de Kercadio at the downtown apartment de Kercadio had rented. The meeting took place without the knowledge of Bouchard who still bore a grudge against Little Joe for an old doublecross. On November 27 Bouchard met Gabeloux and de Kercadio and told them the five kilos had been delivered to the U.S. He arranged to meet them the following night at the Dorval *Hilton* to make the payment which would be brought by a messenger from New York.

The Narcotics Squad, naturally informed about this meeting, intended to be there too. The Squad had made good use of its time in the past three weeks. Through surveillance, it had succeeded in locating and identifying the man who had come to get the five kilos from the room at the *Laurentien Hotel.* He was Louis Henri, until then known mainly for his counterfeiting activities with Bouchard. He was said to be crafty, intelligent, and less impulsive than his boss. On November 22, five days before Bouchard announced that the heroin had been delivered to his clients, Henri had gone to New York where the BNDD observed him in the company of two notorious traffickers, Robert Perrette of the Natale Evola gang, and James (Jimmy Legs) Episcopia of the Joseph Colombo family. (8) In June 1956, Episcopia had been sentenced to three years in prison for drug trafficking, while Perrette was known to police as an associate of Benny Marchese of Connecticut who worked for Guido Penosi's brother-in-law, Anthony Castaldi. (9)

On the morning of the 28th, several hours before the meeting at the *Hilton,* RCMP agents watched airport arrivals and departures, hoping to spot anyone who would be bringing the money back from New York for Bouchard. About 1 p.m. they saw Louis Henri board a flight for New York. Forty-five minutes later he was met by Perrette and Episcopia and driven to a luxury apartment in Lower Manhattan. The three men stayed there about 20 minutes, then drove towards Brooklyn. In the region of King Highway and 12th Street, the BNDD agents abandoned their pursuit after noticing that

---

8. In the early sixties, Joseph Bonanno quarreled with Mafia chiefs and was ousted from his family. Other chiefs took over from him, including Natale Evola, a friend of Vito Genovese. Joseph Colombo replaced Joseph Profaci who died in 1962.

9. Benny Marchese was sentenced to seven years in prison in September 1958 for supplying heroin to his nephew Michel, in Los Angeles.

the three men seemed to have become suspicious about being followed. Henri returned to Montreal at the end of the afternoon without bringing anything back and immediately met with Bouchard.

At 4:40 p.m., Bouchard's wife, Lorraine Brunet, and a friend Richard Goulet, a garage owner who was also a friend of Frank Cotroni, took a flight to New York where they, too, met Episcopia and Perrette. They returned to Dorval shortly after 8 p.m. and joined Bouchard who was waiting with Gabeloux and de Kercadio in *La Crémerie* bar of the *Hilton*. Goulet handed Bouchard a leather purse remarking, according to Gabeloux, that it was all there. The money was then given to the two Frenchmen who split it between them in the men's room. Gabeloux then took his leave, went to the airport to board a flight for Paris via New York. The New York detour was necessary because the double agent had agreed with de Kercadio to send a telegram to Daniel Marquet pretending that the heroin had been seized and that they could not reimburse Marquet. Before he left, Gabeloux advised Staff Sergeant Poissant that he would be going to Marseilles to place an order with Théo Marininchi. As soon as the merchandise was ready, de Kercadio would join him with the $100,000 Bouchard and his friends had decided to invest in the operation. Another order would be placed with Joseph Boldrini, which would make a total cargo of about 60 kilos (132 pounds) with a street value of more than $60 million.

While Gabeloux put the plan into operation in France, as well as smooth-talking Marininchi into giving him 25 kilos on credit, de Kercadio and Bouchard went to Acapulco where they met the New Yorkers Perrette and Episcopia. Gabeloux found out from Glaros where his partner was and called him there, learning that Boldrini had already been contacted and was not averse to the idea of advancing credit. The two cronies agreed to meet in Paris around the middle of December after the 25 kilos from Marininchi had been delivered. In the meantime, there was only one dark cloud: the parcel of ten kilos had still not arrived. The two Parisians did not know, however, that the parcel addressed to "Marc Tillet, professeur," and containing, according to the declaration, books and personal effects, had been at Dorval since November 26 under constant watch by the Narcotics Squad.

De Kercadio and Bouchard returned to Montreal on December 4. The next morning they had a meeting which was also attended by Bouchard's wife, Guillet, and Henri. About 1 p.m. at the Air Canada depot at Dorval, Corporal Favreau (since promoted to inspector) noted the arrival of a taxi driver to pick up the suspect parcel. The driver presented a note signed by a certain "Professor Marc Tillet" and was given the package. He then went to the Customs office and filled out the usual documents. At that moment, at the *Skyline Hotel,* Sergeant Paul Sauvé and Corporal Réginald Beers rented room 905 and asked the reception clerk to do them a small favor: if a Frenchman with a limp came to rent a room, they wished him to be given one next to theirs. About 2:15 p.m. de Kercadio entered the hotel lobby and asked at the desk for a room. He was given number 903. Fifteen minutes later, the taxi driver who had picked up the parcel arrived at the hotel and met Le Boiteux (de Kercadio—the Lame One). The two men entered the elevator with the parcel and five minutes later the driver returned alone to the main floor, empty-handed. As soon as he left the hotel, the two federal agents went to the room they had rented. About 4 p.m., noting the departure of the Frenchman, Sergeant Sauvé obtained a key to the room and with Sergeant Léonard Massé entered it to make an inspection.

The room and the furniture were searched. A newspaper had been left on one of the tables and there was a brown suitcase in the wardrobe. The suitcase was placed on the bed and opened. It was divided into two compartments. One contained the wrapping paper from the parcel and 20 one-pound sacks of white powder; the other contained the remains of the cardboard box. Everything was carefully replaced in the suitcase and the suitcase was put back in the cupboard. The two agents then left the room taking care to lock the door. An hour later they returned and Sergeant Massé took some samples of the white powder. Mixed with the acid "Marquis," the powder turned purple. The test was conclusive: it was heroin. Back in their room the agents signaled with flashlights to their colleagues outside the hotel that their mission was accomplished.

About 6 p.m. one of the surveillance team agents observed de Kercadio's arrival in the hotel bar. The trafficker seemed nervous: he kept getting up, going to the window and separating the drapes to look outside. Bouchard showed up after about 15 minutes. He saw de Kercadio but before joining him he went outside to give a sign to Louis Henri who had arrived with him and was waiting in his Cadillac. Bouchard and de Kercadio talked for about 45 minutes. During the conversation, de Kercadio placed a key on the table. Bouchard picked it up and went out to give it to Louis Henri. He came back five minutes later and soon he and de Kercadio left. An agent seated nearby heard the Frenchman say to Bouchard: " . . . you'll call me then, as soon as you can."

In the lobby the two men separated and Bouchard left the hotel. At that moment, on the ninth floor, an agent observed Louis Henri leaving de Kercadio's room with the brown suitcase, and joined him in the elevator to go down to the lobby. There Henri asked the desk clerk to call a taxi and went outside to wait for it. Bouchard, who had parked his Cadillac in the lot in front of the hotel, got out of his car and walked towards the entrance. On his way in he winked at Henri, then joined de Kercadio in the bar where he talked for about five minutes before leaving again. In the meantime, Henri's taxi had come. Henri put the suitcase on the back seat of the taxi and got in front with the driver. The vehicle headed east on Cote-de-Liesse, then took Lajeunesse Boulevard to the *Maxime Motel* which was owned by Gerry Turenne, Lucien Rivard's former partner.

There Henri went inside for a few minutes, leaving the suitcase in the car. Then he returned to get the suitcase and went back into the motel. Ten minutes later, at 7:15 p.m., Bouchard also arrived with a girlfriend and his brother-in-law Claude Racicot. The three entered the motel bar. At 7:20 p.m. Bouchard came out and took a quick drive in his car on Lajeunesse Boulevard. Three minutes later he was back in the bar. At 7:50 p.m. Louis Henri came out of the bar and took a small blue suitcase from the trunk of Bouchard's Cadillac, then went back into the motel. A few minutes later a taxi arrived, Henri got in with the blue suitcase and the taxi drove north, followed immediately by Bouchard in his car. The taxi stopped at the corner of Papineau Avenue and Henri-Bourassa Boulevard. Henri got out with the blue suitcase and joined Bouchard in his car. The two men drove around the area for a while, until Henri got out at Lajeunesse and Crémazie Boulevards and took a taxi. Bouchard returned to the motel and a few minutes later Henri also arrived, without the blue suitcase. All these manoeuvres, no doubt, were attempts to find out if any federal agents were in the area and watching operations.

The taxi waited in front of the bar. Less than five minutes later Bouchard came out, got in his car, started the motor and waited. Ten minutes later Henri came towards the taxi from behind the building carrying, this time, the brown suitcase. He got in the taxi which headed north, followed by Bouchard. Because of the location of the motel, only one RCMP surveillance car was able to follow the two cars at first. The suspect cars turned west on Fleury, then south on Berri. At Sauriol Street, Bouchard turned east while the taxi continued on Berri. But by then other police vehicles had joined the pursuit and followed Henri's taxi, while the first police car followed Bouchard back to the motel, and then to his home.

At 8:30 p.m. the taxi stopped at the corner of Berri and Jarry Streets. Henri got out with the brown suitcase and walked towards the Metro station. Three agents quickly followed and got into the same train. At the next station, Jean Talon, Henri got out and took a bus. One of the agents took the same bus. Henri got off at Durocher and Jean Talon Streets and began walking. The agent did not dare follow him on foot for fear of being seen. But he did see the suspect get into another taxi. He quickly communicated his position using his radio-transmitter. His colleagues returned to their cars, converged on the area, but could not locate the taxi. The agents, annoyed with themselves, had no choice but to abandon the game for the time being...

Surveillance teams were in place in front of Bouchard's home very early the next morning, December 6. About 10 a.m., the trafficker left with his wife and went to a bank which he entered alone. In order to avoid attracting attention, at a time when proof of the transaction was already sufficient, the surveillance was temporarily withdrawn. It resumed three days later, on December 10, in time to witness the departure for Acapulco of Bouchard and de Kercadio with two young women. The BNDD surveillance later reported their meetings with Richard Goulet who was also in Acapulco. On the night of December 13-14 Gabeloux, who was waiting in Paris, received a call from Marininchi who told him the 25 kilos he had ordered would arrive soon. A few hours later he got a telephone call from de Kercadio. After a few comments about Bouchard's incredible ostentation, de Kercadio said he would be in Paris on the morning of the 16th with the $100,000 the U.S. buyers would be paying to the Montrealers.

Goulet left Mexico by plane for New York on the morning of the 15th. He arrived at Kennedy airport in mid-afternoon and met Episcopia and his 20-year-old son Joseph. At 5 p.m. the three took a flight to Acapulco and joined Bouchard. De Kercadio arrived on schedule in Paris the following day. He was met by Glaros and the two went to see Gabeloux who had received the 25 kilos from Marininchi's emissaries the night before. The next step was a brief visit of about twelve hours to Marseilles by de Kercadio, where he obtained Boldrini's agreement to supply 45 kilos, ten of them on credit. It was agreed that Gabeloux would pick up the merchandise in Marseilles on the 22nd, following a meeting at Orly airport with Boldrini's partner, Etienne Matteuci, who would collect the money. He and Glaros would then prepare the shipment of 60 of the 70 kilos. Ten kilos would be kept in reserve in case things went wrong, and could eventually be offered to Joe Horvath.

Everything went as planned. At that time, December 21, the pleasure-loving de Kercadio rushed back to Acapulco to rejoin Bouchard. Gabeloux, when he had possession of the merchandise, contacted the Paris office of the BNDD and arranged with U.S. agents for the surreptitious seizure of the 60 kilos. On the morning of the day before Christmas, he and Glaros went to the freight office at Bourget airport and deposited Bouchard's three big Samsonite suitcases at Iberia airlines transit sheds. The cases were addressed to: "M. Garcia Faustino Morales, International Airport Dorval, Montréal, P.Q., Bureau restant, Dorval airport." When the registration of the packages had been completed, the double agent and his companion left the airport and returned to Paris. On the way they stopped at a post office where Gabeloux telephoned de Kercadio in Acapulco to give him the number of the manifest bill which the airline employee accomplice would need in order to make the pick-up at Dorval. The two partners hoped to meet each other in Montreal at the end of the year.

In the meantime however, agents of the French central office and the BNDD carried out the process of seizing the 60 kilos of heroin at Bourget airport. The news was announced in *France-Soir* of December 26, and as agreed, the seizure was attributed to the flair of Customs officers whose curiosity had been aroused by the unusual use of Samsonite suitcases to transport old books. The discovery was publicly ascribed to pure chance, and the investigation continued.

For Gabeloux, the hardest part was to come. After notifying Glaros, he telephoned de Kercadio and Bouchard in Acapulco. Alarmed, they decided to join him in France. They said they would be there in two or three days and that they themselves would take on the task of announcing the bad news to Boldrini in Marseilles. In the meantime, Gabeloux was to report the fiasco to Marininchi who was unaware that his 25 kilos were part of the 60 kilos which had been seized. On December 28, Gabeloux arrived at Avignon station where Marininchi was waiting. Marininchi signaled him to follow and the two men got into a Citroen DS 22. A few minutes later a man of about 30 joined them. The Marseillais introduced him as Michel, one of his partners in the affair. In fact, the man was Paul Diaz, a gang leader with important interests in an illegal laboratory. (10)

---

10. In November 1973, Paul Diaz was arrested and charged in connection with the detection of an illegal heroin laboratory in the Marseilles region on March 29, 1972. The investigation led to the arrest of two Corsican traffickers, Christian

In his book, Gabeloux describes this meeting on a country roadside as delicate. The suppliers were displeased: the two Parisians had been dealing with another supplier without their knowledge, and furthermore, the shipment had not been carried out precisely according to the agreement. Samsonite suitcases had been used instead of wooden cases as agreed beforehand. The double agent explained that he had no choice: de Kercadio had promised his former supplier that he would make a deal with him, and the Montreal buyer preferred the suitcases in order to make things easier for the man who would recuperate the merchandise at Dorval. To prove his good faith, Gabeloux played his best card. He said he still had five kilos and would deliver them to Montreal himself. The entire proceeds of $50,000 would go to compensate Marininchi and his friend. The two men, aware of the risks of such an operation, were satisfied. They proved it by confiding to the double agent that they had agreed to act as intermediary for another Marseilles gang in the sale of a stock of 96 kilos of heroin already stored in Puerto Rico. The individual who was to introduce the U.S. buyer to their friends had been arrested on another matter and the liaison had been broken. If Gabeloux and his partner could arrange this sale through their contacts in Montreal, everything would be squared.

For the moment, the negative effects of the sale were therefore neutralized on the Marininchi side. But Boldrini still had to be faced. When de Kercadio and Bouchard arrived in France they met with Gabeloux and agreed to Marininchi's proposition. Then they, too, went to Marseilles on the night of December 29. Agents on duty for the French central office for narcotics and the BNDD noted their presence at Boldrini's home at the same time as Etienne Matteuci. They prolonged the stay for a few days before returning to Paris where they made frequent visits to Roger Mollet's bar, the *O-K-Bec*.

For the five-kilo transaction, Bouchard and de Kercadio went back to Montreal on January 13 and registered at the *Bonaventure Hotel*. The following day Gabeloux also arrived and checked into the *Chateau Champlain* in one of the two rooms reserved by the

---

Simonpieri and Joseph Fabiano. Fabiano was also implicated with Diaz and two other Marseillais in the murder of a gangster named Raymond Bortoli who was suspected of being behind a series of arrests made by the French central office for narcotics. Finally, three weeks after Diaz was charged, his wife, a lawyer and member of the Bar at Marseilles, was charged with possession of objects acquired through the proceeds of narcotics sales. Note that Christian Simonpieri was the nephew of Ange Simonpieri, one of the big bosses of the Corsican underworld who was mentioned in Chapter Thirteen in connection with Guido Orsini's trip to Italy in December 1970.

Narcotics Squad. This time the Squad expected to be able to intervene. Federal agents had learned that de Kercadio had said nothing to defend his partner during the meetings with Boldrini and were determined to prevent him from concluding this deal. They therefore asked Immigration officers to keep de Kercadio in their custody from the morning of January 14 on, under pretext of an identity check.

When Gabeloux arrived in the afternoon, he was told of these measures by the police officers and by Bouchard who called to ask how the trip had gone and if he had the merchandise with him. There was no problem about the heroin: he had the five kilos. He had even brought it in himself in his travel bag, which did not enthuse the federal agents who had not been told in advance how he intended to transport the drug. An alert Customs officer checking his bag could have created a very complicated situation. Bouchard and Gabeloux agreed to wait a while, to see what would happen to de Kercadio, before making the exchange. They did not have to wait long, for de Kercadio was released at 5 p.m., when Immigration offices closed for the day.

Soon after that, he called Gabeloux and asked him to come to meet Bouchard at the *Bonaventure.* The meeting dealt mainly with methods of making the exchange. Following instructions from the RCMP, Gabeloux insisted that the operation take place at the *Chateau Champlain,* but the Montrealer considered that much too dangerous. He wanted Gabeloux to take a taxi to a certain bar where the owner would give him a letter containing the final instructions. The double agent wanted no part of this method, despite the advice of his partner to do what Bouchard was suggesting. They all agreed to think about it some more and to meet again at midnight in *L'Escapade* restaurant in the *Chateau Champlain.* Gabeloux returned to his room and reported to the chief of the Narcotics Squad. That night he kept the appointment with Bouchard who was accompanied by Louis Henri and one of his U.S. buyers, James Episcopia. Episcopia and his partner Perrette had been staying at the *Queen Elizabeth Hotel* for the past two days under their own names. De Kercadio was not at this meeting. His detention by Immigration officers had made him nervous and he was leaving for Acapulco at 7 o'clock the next morning on grounds that his presence in Montreal could be dangerous for the group. The meeting at *L'Escapade* lasted late into the night. Federal agents noted that Henri got up a number of times to make calls from a public telephone. When the meeting ended, the participants had agreed to proceed with the transaction in the morning.

Shortly after 8 o'clock on the morning of Saturday, January 15, Bouchard telephoned Gabeloux to ask him to come to his room in the *Bonaventure* right away. When he arrived 20 minutes later, Louis Henri was there too. Henri left a few minutes later, however, when Bouchard began to explain how the transaction was to be made. Gabeloux was to go back to his room to get the stuff immediately and go to room 1128 at the nearby *Queen Elizabeth Hotel.* The New York mafiosi had a suite on the same floor of that hotel. Henri, after making sure he wasn't being followed, would bring the $50,000 to the room and the exchange would be made.

Gabeloux agreed and returned immediately to his room at the *Champlain* where he found the chief investigator for the Narcotics Squad and briefly explained the operation to him. Less than 20 minutes later, Gabeloux entered the lobby of the *Queen Elizabeth Hotel,* suitcase in hand, and went to the indicated room, using the key Bouchard had given him. About the same time, three federal agents arrived at the hotel and spotted Louis Henri, carrying nothing, just as he entered an elevator. At 9:40 a.m., Henri was back in the lobby and left the hotel. Five minutes later he returned and took the elevator to the 11th floor. A Narcotics Squad agent followed him, got off at the 11th floor and waited in the corridor. In the room, the sacks of heroin were being counted and the exchange was going ahead. It was after 10 a.m. when Henri emerged from the room with the large suitcase. The agent who was shadowing him took the same elevator but on the ground floor let him go his own way. As Henri hailed a taxi, Corporal Gilles Favreau and other RCMP members moved in and arrested him. In the suitcase they found the five kilos of heroin packed in ten plastic bags. In Henri's pocket they found the hotel bill for the room in which the exchange had just been made.

About 10:20 a.m., Sergeant Sauvé and two other Squad members posted at the *Bonaventure* went to Bouchard's room and arrested him. Police already had evidence against him gathered during the previous 10-kilo transaction. When they burst into the room, Bouchard tried to hide an address book in the waistband of his underwear, but it fell on the floor instead. He put his foot on the book, too late. It was confiscated by the officers.

At the time of his arrest, Henri was about to go to the Voyageur Bus Terminus to deposit the suitcase in a locker. He would then have brought the key to Bouchard who would have given it to one of the two U.S. buyers. The first time, on December 5, when he had lost his police trackers, Henri had delivered the suitcase of heroin himself to the two New Yorkers who were waiting for him at the

Pont-Viau Hotel. This time, following the arrests, the buyers quickly realized that something had gone wrong and without waiting for what was due to them, rushed home to New York. As for Gabeloux, he returned to his room with the money and that night took a plane for Paris.

On Monday morning, January 17, Bouchard and Henri appeared in Criminal Court accused of conspiring to import heroin and of possession and trafficking in narcotics. Bail was refused them. In Paris meanwhile, Gabeloux met Jean Glaros who had heard the news in a telephone call from de Kercadio in Acapulco the previous night. But the Greek was mainly interested in a new transaction he had already mentioned to Gabeloux after the 60-kilo seizure. His friend Jean-Marc Guillet had quarreled with Bouchard and separated from him. But he had found another connection in Montreal and was working for a group of Italians, who were also looking for a reliable and regular supply of heroin. They were prepared to pay $13,000 a kilo (more than $6,000 a pound). Preliminary contacts had already been made with Gabeloux, and Guillet's new friends were ready to buy his remaining five kilos and even pay for them in advance. The shipping method would follow the Bouchard formula except that the merchandise would be sent in a normal parcel using another company in Italy rather than in France. During the latest transaction in Montreal, Guillet had come to Paris and introduced Glaros to the Italian representative assigned to negotiate the deal.

Now all that remained was for Gabeloux to meet Guillet and the Italian. That noon he met Guillet with Glaros in a Greek restaurant and arranged to meet the Italian two days later in the *Marignan* restaurant on the Champs-Elysées. They met as planned, in the presence of Glaros and his friend Antoine Diamentides, an old tailor whose home was being used to store the five kilos and who had helped Pannunzio after his disasters at *L'Aviation* gambling club. (11) By the time lunch was over, the deal was made: Gabeloux and Glaros would bring the five kilos to Milan by car a few days later and turn them over to the Italian in exchange for $65,000 after the parcel had been shipped to Montreal.

This deal, however, went no further. Early on the evening of January 21, investigators from the French central office for narcotics

---

11. *Le Jockey*, pages 217 to 227. The Narcotics Squad was never informed by Gabeloux of his meeting in Paris with the Italian from Montreal. It was thought this person might be Guido Orsini. Subsequent events tend to confirm that, especially since the double agent identified the man in his book as "Guido."

arrested Glaros and Diamentides and seized Gabeloux' five kilos. This blow put at least a temporary end to the double agent's collaboration with police services. Gabeloux had also learned that de Kercadio had aroused suspicions about him among the Marseilles suppliers. He decided not to reimburse Marininchi with the $50,000, but to take a prolonged vacation instead.

In America, the RCMP and BNDD were concentrating on de Kercadio and Jean-Marc Guillet. In de Kercadio's case, he was suspected of attempting to negotiate on his own for the sale of the 96 kilos of heroin stored in Puerto Rico. Now that he had managed to discredit his partner with the Marseilles suppliers, he would no doubt be in a position to negotiate this deal. The police also knew that he was still in contact with Bouchard through his wife and one of his henchmen, Jean Duval, a good friend of Louis Henri. He met Duval twice in the first half of February in New York and at the second meeting the BNDD noted the presence of Perrette and Episcopia.

As for Guillet, it was particularly important to get positive identification of the Italian group in Montreal he was now working for. Since his approach to Gabeloux had failed and his friend Glaros had been arrested, he would possibly try to make an approach to de Kercadio. Careful surveillance of his movements showed him to be in close contact with Guido Orsini and Santo Mendolia. Guillet, engaged to an Italian girl from Montreal, spent many hours at Alfredo Gagliardi's travel agency which was also frequented by Frank Cotroni's men.

On February 20, the Narcotics Squad was advised of de Kercadio's presence in Montreal at the *Ritz Carlton Hotel.* A special surveillance was organized and the investigators were able to rent an adjoining room. On February 21, Guillet turned up at de Kercadio's room with Guido Orsini and Santo Mendolia. From what police could gather, it seemed to be a preliminary meeting for Guillet to introduce his new friends to de Kercadio. Certain deals were discussed, notably the possibility of sending an emissary to Marseilles to meet de Kercadio and provide him with the money necessary for negotiations with Boldrini and Marininchi. A stock of about ten kilos would then be shipped to Montreal by de Kercadio to be delivered to Orsini after he paid the difference on the sale price. Over the next four days, other meetings took place between de Kercadio and Frank Cotroni's men. On February 25, just before the French trafficker took a flight to Acapulco, a Narcotics Squad team observed a last meeting with Orsini, Mendolia and Guillet.

In Mexico, the BNDD noticed nothing significant in de Kercadio's activities. The day after his arrival he married a young Mexican girl of 18 and spent all his time with her. It was a short honeymoon however. On February 29 he took a flight to Paris via New York. On arrival in France he was shadowed by detectives from the French central office for narcotics with the aid of BNDD representatives and an RCMP officer. He stayed in Paris only two days before going to Marseilles to meet Joseph Boldrini. On March 4, the police noticed with interest the arrival of Théo Marininchi and Paul Diaz. Their presence at Boldrini's home at the same time as de Kercadio disproved Gabeloux' reports which had Boldrini and Marininchi as competitors rather than partners.

About 7 p.m. on March 5, de Kercadio left Boldrini's home and went to the *Hotel de Noailles,* where he met an Italian later identified as Alfredo Del Zoppo, an emissary of the mafioso Albert Pantani of Merceville, New Jersey. According to RCMP and BNDD reports, Pantani had come to Montreal on February 26 and had met Guido Orsini and Santo Mendolia at the *Motel Diplomate.* Del Zoppo was probably the courier assigned to bring de Kercadio the down payment for the new supply of heroin. This theory was strengthened when de Kercadio returned immediately to Boldrini's home after a brief meeting with the Italian.

The next day, about 1 p.m., Paul Diaz arrived at Boldrini's. Half an hour later he left with de Kercadio. They drove around Marseilles for a while until Diaz stopped his car at Place de la Rotonde and let de Kercadio out. Diaz drove away but about five minutes later, came back to get de Kercadio and drove him to the Saint-Charles station. When he boarded the train for Paris, de Kercadio was carrying a travel bag which he did not have when he left Boldrini's home. Police were sure the bag contained heroin, but preferred not to intervene until other members of the ring had been identified. Unfortunately, coordination problems between surveillance teams permitted de Kercadio to lose his police shadows shortly after his return to Paris. They tried to retrace him without success. They even established special surveillance at Orly and Bourget airports and at other European airports frequently used by international traffickers.

The Narcotics Squad in Montreal, which had delegated one of its men to France, was advised of the latest developments. Early in the evening of March 7, a call from the French central office suggested that de Kercadio might already be in Montreal. Investigators immediately made the rounds of hotels looking for any sign of the Frenchman. Surveillance teams were also assigned to follow Guido Orsini and Santo Mendolia. The federal agents had been working on the search for an hour when a desk clerk at the *Ritz Carlton* informed them that a Frenchman with a limp had arrived with two suitcases late in the afternoon and had asked for the keys to two rooms reserved in the names of "Claude Rouchaud, 157, avenue de Neuilly, Paris, France," and "Pierre Roy, 270, Boulevard Aristide-Briand, Paris." The employee did not know if the individual had remained in the hotel, but he had not seen him come out.

This information was immediately passed on to those in charge of the operation, who had also just learned from other investigators that Orsini and Mendolia, along with Jean-Marc Guillet, had arrived at the *Berkeley Hotel* a few minutes earlier and had gone to a room occupied by a "C. Roy, of Trois-Rivières." At the *Ritz Carlton,* investigators got instructions to see if de Kercadio was in either of the two rooms, and if not, to search them discreetly. They telephoned the rooms and when no one answered proceeded with the search. In room 716, in the name of Claude Rouchaud, they quickly discovered, in a bureau drawer, a brown briefcase containing about ten sacks of white powder each weighing about a pound. In room 918, rented to Pierre Roy, a black case rested on the wardrobe shelf: it also contained about ten sacks of white powder of the same weight. The agents took a few samples of the powder, submitted them to the "Marquis" test, and confirmed the analysis: all in all, about 20 pounds of heroin. A special surveillance operation was quickly organized at the *Ritz Carlton.*

Meanwhile, at the *Berkeley Hotel,* Orsini, Mendolia and Guillet were still in the room rented in the name of Claude Roy. They finally left in mid-evening and only then, when the occupant of the room went to the hotel bar, was he identified, as expected, as de Kercadio. About midnight he went back to his room and was still there at noon the next day when Orsini and Mendolia came to join him. The meeting lasted for about an hour, until Orsini and Mendolia left together and went to the *Monte Carlo Auto Body* on Saint-Laurent Boulevard, the new headquarters of Frank Dasti.

About 4 o'clock that afternoon, a stranger entered room 716 at the *Ritz Carlton.* A few minutes later he emerged with the brown briefcase and hurried to the hotel parking garage where he took the wheel of a 1967 Buick with Quebec licence plates. A tailing operation was rapidly organized, but the stranger was crafty and obviously suspicious. Furthermore, he was being protected by a 1969 Pontiac which had followed him from the start; police recognized the occupants of this car as Guido Orsini and Santo Mendolia. The

Frank Dasti (above), Santo Mendolia (bottom left) and Guido Orsini in front of Dante Pizzeria.

(Photos Michel Auger)

two vehicles headed north on Park Avenue. At Saint-Viateur an evasive action confused the police pursuit and the Buick was lost. All surveillance teams were alerted and a description of the suspect and his car was broadcast over police radios. At 4:40 p.m., agents concealed near *Monte Carlo Auto Body* saw the suspect Buick and its driver emerge from Dasti's hang-out. The charge was resumed in haste but the quarry was again lost in the dense, rush-hour traffic. For most of the night, agents patrolled the city trying to locate the Buick, but without success. The car and its driver could not be found.

The next morning, March 9, Orsini and Mendolia returned to the *Berkeley Hotel* and met de Kercadio again in his room. The meeting was shorter than that of the previous day and afterwards, the two mafiosi went to the *Sonesta Hotel.* While Orsini waited in the car, Mendolia went to meet a man recognized as Antonio Merola of Toronto, a former messenger for Aniello Santella. Mendolia left and the Torontonian drove away from the *Sonesta* in his own car, a black, 1968 Buick parked nearby. He arrived at the *Ritz Carlton,* parked in front of the hotel and went up to room 918. A few minutes later he emerged with the black case which he placed beside him in his car. Then he drove north, in a manner designed to shake any pursuers, finally arriving at the *Bélanger Hairdressing Salon,* which he entered with the valise. This establishment belonged to Palmina Puliafito, one of Cotroni's two sisters, and was managed by Guido Orsini's wife.

At 1 p.m., an hour and a half after Merola's arrival, police watching the area noted a stranger coming out of the building with a briefcase and getting into a 1972 Buick. He drove west on Bélanger Street and lost his police pursuers when he took Cote-des-Neiges Road. Twelve minutes later Merola also came out of the *Salon Bélanger,* went to his car and displaced the back seat. Then he went back into the salon. At 2:05 p.m. another man came out. He was identified as Fortunato Bartuccio, one of Aniello Santella's partners whom Orsini had previously met in January 1971. He carried a large black plastic bag which he placed under the back seat of Merola's car. He then replaced the seat and drove north to Metropolitan Boulevard, heading in the direction of Toronto. The pursuit was withdrawn when he left the island of Montreal and the Ontario section of the Narcotics Squad was alerted.

Hardly ten minutes after his departure, Frank Dasti arrived at the *Salon Bélanger* and stayed there until 4 p.m. While he was there, several members of the Cotroni organization made brief visits. The same thing had happened the night before at *Monte Carlo Auto Body.*

Antonio Merola left the Salon early in the evening and took a flight from Dorval airport to Toronto. By the time he arrived, agents had been posted around Bartuccio's home. They saw Bartuccio drive up, remove the black plastic bag he had taken from *Salon Bélanger*, store it in his garage and drive away. When he left, the agents entered the garage and found in the bag two small paper sacks each containing a pound of heroin. Everything was put back in place and the surveillance continued. At 11 p.m. Bartuccio returned home with Merola and went to the garage to get one of the paper sacks. The two men drove off again, but did not get far. They saw they were being followed and in an attempt to escape, drove impetuously into a dead-end street. With nowhere to go and nothing else to do, they tried to save themselves by throwing the bag of heroin into the street. But it was no use. They were caught. A few months later Merola was sentenced to ten years in penitentiary while Bartuccio, after making a confession and denouncing his accomplice, took advantage of his release on bail to flee to Italy.

Of the ten kilos supplied by Boldrini and his partners, only one had been seized. René Quintin de Kercadio returned to France immediately, and the French central office for narcotics took up the chase.

Two weeks later, on March 25, the Quebec Provincial Police learned from one of its Operation Vegas wiretaps that Paul Oddo would be coming to Montreal the next day to meet Frank Dasti and Guido Orsini. The exchange of conversation indicated that another transaction was imminent. Two days earlier, on the night of March 23-24, U.S. Customs officers at Champlain had intercepted Mauro Zanetti, a friend of Dasti and Orsini. (12) The search of Zanetti's truck had produced nothing but Dasti and Oddo seemed to be upset by it. This incident, apparently, would be on the agenda for the talks in Montreal. Meanwhile, in France, the French central office noted that de Kercadio had gone to see Joseph Boldrini in Marseilles again and that he was spending a lot of time in Paris with Roger Mollet.

From the morning of March 26, while agents watched Dorval airport for arrivals from New York and Europe, Montreal hotels were being checked for evidence of the presence of foreign traffickers. At the *Hotel Martinique*, it was learned that a Roger Mollet had made a reservation on March 20 for a "Claude Frontin,

---

12. Zanetti owned a small fruit and vegetable store. He was the owner of the famous refrigerated truck which was kept under surveillance in August 1971 during a previous transaction with Oddo and Anthony Vanacora.

Paris, France," leaving an address and phone number: "4202 Kindersley Avenue, 459-4499." On March 22, someone had come to occupy room 303 and the bill had been paid the next day. At *La Salle Hotel* a Parisian named Roger Mollet had occupied room 544 since March 21; and at the *Seaway Hotel,* room 422 had been occupied since March 22 by a "C. Roy, Williams Street, Trois-Rivières." This room had been reserved on March 20 by a stranger who had left, for reference, the phone number 459-4499.

The connection between these various scraps of information was not lost on Narcotics Squad investigators, who recalled that the name "C. Roy, of Trois-Rivières" had been used at the *Berkeley Hotel* at the beginning of the month by de Kercadio.

The suspicions raised by these "coincidences" caused police to search the two rooms which were still being occupied. In the first one, nothing significant was found, but in the second, agents found a small suitcase containing about ten sacks of white powder, about five kilos of heroin in all. The agents then speculated about what they might have found in the room at the *Martinique* if they had been able to visit it four days earlier. Still, they were reasonably satisfied with progress so far, and proceeded with surveillance of the *Seaway Hotel* and especially of room 422.

At 5:55 p.m. on the same day, an unknown person of about 30 entered that room. Less than two minutes later he emerged carrying nothing. On the ground floor, agents saw him enter the bar to talk for a few minutes with a young man who seemed to be of Italian origin, and then leave the hotel. The young Italian then took the elevator and entered room 422, using the key which had been given to him by the other man in the bar. He came out a few minutes later carrying the suitcase containing the heroin and got in the elevator. Agents on the ground floor were preparing to react when they suddenly noticed Guido Orsini and Santo Mendolia in the lobby. Trying not to be seen, the agents backed off a bit, still doing their best to keep an eye on things. About 15 minutes passed and the young Italian had not yet come down to the lobby. The two mafiosi then left. The agents regrouped and realized that the young messenger had slipped through their fingers, probably by getting out of the elevator on the mezzanine and leaving the hotel by some other route. Patrols were organized but none of the suspects could be traced.

At 8:25 p.m. Paul Oddo arrived at Dorval on an Eastern Airlines flight. He went directly to the *Chateau Champlain* where he had stayed on his last trip March 10. At about the same time Mauro Zanetti left Montreal again in his refrigerated truck headed for New

York. He was not stopped at the border, and in New York, he went directly to the Hunt's Point market. BNDD surveillance observed no suspicious meetings. In Montreal, Oddo did not meet Frank Dasti until the morning of the following day. The meeting began in the lobby of the hotel and continued in the New Yorker's room where Orsini and Mendolia joined them. The latter two did not stay long. At 12:15 p.m. they left with Dasti. As they left, Corporal Claude Savoie, who was in the adjoining room with colleagues Ernest Bacqué and Réginald Beers of the Narcotics Squad and Kevin Gallagher of the BNDD, heard Oddo say: " . . . Park Sheraton. O.K., I'll be seeing you."

In mid-afternoon Dasti returned to the *Chateau Champlain* to see Oddo in his room. Shortly afterwards the two mafiosi came down to the bar where they were joined by Orsini. They talked for about half an hour, until it was time for Oddo to go to Dorval to catch his flight to New York. He went directly home on arrival, without meeting any of his regular friends.

The reference to the *Park Sheraton* was surely significant for the investigators. It probably meant a meeting there and perhaps even the exchange of the five lost kilos would take place at the *Sheraton Hotel* on 56th Street. From 9 a.m. on March 28, therefore, a BNDD surveillance team was posted there. A check of the hotel register showed that an old employee of Frank Dasti, Lucien (The Cat) Madère had checked in that morning at 7:25. At 9:10 a.m. Oddo showed up in the lobby and then left alone a few minutes later. An agent went up to the 25th floor where Madère's room was located and about 9:45 a.m., saw Madère coming out of the service elevator. A hotel employee advised him to use the elevator reserved for guests and Madère did so, going down to the lobby for a few minutes before returning to his room.

At the time of these events, Sergeant Paul Sauvé of the Narcotics Squad was communicating important information to the BNDD. Quebec Provincial Police technicians had just listened in on a dozen or so conversations recorded the previous evening, overnight and that morning on Operation Vegas instruments. These showed that Madère was definitely on a heroin delivery mission in New York. He himself had hidden the merchandise in the spare tire of his car, following Dasti's suggestion, and the transaction was to be completed that morning. During the night, Orsini and Mendolia in turn had communicated with Dasti to check on how things were going. Once given assurance that all was well, they discussed the trip Mendolia was to make to New York in the morning and his scheduled meeting with Madère to receive a "message" for Dasti.

The last conversations had been recorded between 9 and 9:45 a.m. from the wiretap at *Monte Carlo Auto Body*.

Shortly after 9 a.m., Oddo called Dasti to tell him that he had arrived at the hotel but did not see Madère. The Montrealer assured him Madère was there and gave him his room number as well as a brief description. Oddo ended the conversation by remarking that he thought he had spotted police agents and that there was a lot of "heat." Orsini then called Dasti who told him not to worry, his guy had already checked in. Finally, Dasti telephoned Madère's wife who said that Lucien had called her at 9:30 a.m. to say he was up and was waiting "for him to come."

Oddo returned to the *Sheraton* in New York at 10 a.m. He went first to the restaurant where he made a phone call and then took the elevator. One surveillance team waited in the lobby while another kept watch in the garage near the Montrealer's car. Twenty minutes later Oddo and Madère came out of the elevator together. At the desk Madère asked for his car to be brought and he and Oddo went outside to wait. Five minutes later an employee brought the car around. Madère tipped him and got in the car while Oddo took the wheel. Before the car could move off, a score of BNDD agents erupted from their hiding places and arrested both men. The trunk of the car was immediately opened and the spare wheel taken out. The heroin was inside it: ten kilos or 22 pounds of the white powder contained in 20 small plastic sacks. On the street, it would add up to $10 million worth of destructive drug addiction.

Later that day another check of the register at the *Sheraton Hotel* showed Santo Mendolia listed as a guest. But since he had not been seen with the two others, he was not arrested. There was another interesting discovery: the car Oddo had driven to the *Sheraton* belonged to the wife of Nicholas Pisanella, an important New York trafficker known as a retainer for William Castaldi and Frank Stassi. Stassi, like his brothers Joseph and Anthony, was an associate of the famous Louis Cirillo, the buyer for Michel Mastantuano and his gang.

In the hours following the arrests, several other revealing telephone conversations were intercepted, four of which were calls from Dasti and Orsini to Madère's room. The bosses were worried and wanted to know what had happened to their courier. A BNDD agent who spoke French took charge of answering the phone. It was a burlesque situation. The mafiosi, trying to find out what was going on, could not understand why a stranger kept answering the telephone. They tried to pass themselves off as a friend asking where Lucien was, as a son, and even as a "Mountie," but each time the

Frank Dasti (left) with Nick Visceglia.

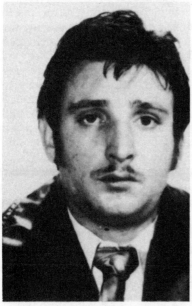

Antonio Merola   *Lucien (The Cat) Madère*

agent gave the same reply: "Lucien has gone out. He'll be back soon." Dasti and Orsini finally understood what had happened. From then on their only worry was: will Lucien talk?

But he did not talk. On May 18, 1972, The Cat was found guilty, along with Oddo, by a federal court in New York. They were sentenced respectively to six and ten years in penitentiary.

These arrests were a serious worry to Frank Cotroni and his men, but did not slow down their activities. At the end of April, one of Oddo's trusted aides, Nick (Nick The Noose) Visceglia, came to Montreal twice to meet Frank Dasti. Nothing resulted from these meetings, but the RCMP knew that Guido Orsini, who was in daily contact with Dasti, was increasing his approaches to a friend in Toronto, Vito (The Philosopher) Adamo to negotiate the sale of 13 kilos of heroin obtained from a French supplier. The Narcotics Squad suspected René Quintin de Kercadio of being involved in this affair because the BNDD, alerted by the French central office, had spotted him shortly before in New York. Unfortunately the shadowing operation did not succeed and he was lost from sight after two days. At the time of the talks with Visceglia and Adamo, it was not known if he was still in the U.S. or had returned to France.

At the beginning of May, RCMP detectives in Toronto learned that Adamo was in New York with a man from Detroit. According to the information available, the trip was intended to negotiate the purchase of 13 kilos which Orsini's supplier had already delivered there. The BNDD was informed and attempted to locate the suspects. In Montreal at this time, the Narcotics Squad was receiving additional information. According to this, Dasti had tried in vain to negotiate a sale to Oddo's friends, but the thing had fallen through because of unacceptable demands by the New Yorkers. They had asked that Dasti's courier be held as hostage until the transaction was concluded and the merchandise stored in a safe place. Orsini, meanwhile, was said to be in contact now with Anthony Castiglione of New York, who was also a friend of Vito Adamo and, as we have seen, a partner of Pietro Misuraca and Giuseppe Tramontana.

This information was also transmitted to the BNDD. Special surveillance operations were established by U.S. detectives and results were quickly produced. On May 9, Castiglione and one of his partners, Camillio Rizzuto, were arrested as they came out of the *Sheraton Motor Inn* with 13 kilos of heroin.

Two days later, on May 11, the RCMP exposed Joe Horvath's hashish ring. the chief himself and five young people in their twenties — Neil Faierman, Peter Gold, Harvey McLintock, Linda Kosow and Abdul Wahid — were arrested and charged with conspiring to import hashish. A seventh person, Bob Roy from Kaboul in Afghanistan, but originally from Montreal, was cited in the charges. Begun in June 1971, the investigation by federal detectives led at the end of January 1972 to the discreet seizure at Dorval airport of two stocks of hashish of 106 and 109 kilos, valued at more than $2 million. The seizures were backed up on February 19 by raids on the homes of several gang members, including Joe Horvath's. This permitted the completion of the documentary evidence which had been accumulated by police over an eight-month period. Arraigned in Criminal Court on the same day of their arrests, Horvath and his accomplices were immediately freed on bail of $5,000 each. This had the main effect of allowing Little Joe to resume his heroin activities immediately with his friends in the Cotroni clan and with the Palmer brothers gang in Vancouver.

Five days after Joe Horvath was charged, Guido Orsini went to Toronto with three other members of the organization: Antonio Di Genova and Dominico Cordileone (names already familiar) and Elpido Voverio, a young recruit. (13) They registered on the late afternoon of May 17 at the *Sutton Place Hotel.* Towards midnight, Antonio Merola, who was free on bail at the time, came to get them and take them to the *Beverley Hills Hotel* where Vito Adamo was waiting. He, in turn, took them to the *Sam Marco* brasserie on St. Clair Avenue. There a three-way conversation involved Orsini, Merola and Adamo, while the others seated nearby kept a respectful silence as befits ordinary soldiers. Information obtained by the Toronto section of the Narcotics Squad indicated that the main subject of conversation was the arrests of Castiglione, Merola and their partners and the subsequent effects on heroin supplies. Orsini believed that even if his French supplier might be somewhat indisposed by the latest developments, he would continue to deal with him. He hoped to be able to prove that very soon.

---

13. See Chapter Twelve.

Chapter 16

A Quebec Film: Produced by the RCMP

Jean-Pierre Buffa, a 27-year-old Frenchman from Lyon, landed at Dorval airport at 12:55 p.m. on Wednesday, June 28, 1972. Three years earlier, at about the same time of year, he had arrived in Montreal with an automobile containing 60 pounds of heroin which he later delivered to New York on the instructions of the Marseilles entertainer, Edmond Taillet. Buffa, a good friend of Paul Diaz (partner of Théodore Marininchi and René Quintin de Kercadio) was coming to Montreal this time to conclude a deal for about ten kilos.

Staff Sergeant Gilles Poissant, in charge of the Narcotics Squad, had been awaiting his arrival for some days. When Buffa presented himself to Immigration and Customs officers at the airport, a surveillance team already had him under observation. He answered the usual questions with assurance and stated that he intended to visit Montreal and Quebec City before taking a vacation in the Caribbean. Since the beige suitcase he carried contained nothing incriminating, he was wished a cordial welcome. Buffa went to the Royal Bank branch at the airport. Then he bought a popular gossip newspaper and went to make a call from a public phone booth. He bent down to pick something up from the floor of the booth, came out, entered another booth, came out again and walked towards the metal lockers. He opened locker 605, without inserting any money beforehand, and placed his beige suitcase inside. Two federal agents standing nearby noted that the locker already contained a black briefcase. That did not seem to surprise Buffa, who locked the door and then made a casual tour of airport shops.

Notified of his intention to go to Quebec City, Sergeant Léonard Massé checked with Air Canada and Québecair. He learned that Buffa had a reservation on Air Canada flight 520 leaving Montreal at 5 p.m. and scheduled to arrive at Ancienne Lorette airport 40 minutes later. A special RCMP team was immediately sent to

Quebec City to await the traveler and follow him. Meanwhile, the local detachment of the Squad checked hotels and motels and within an hour learned that Buffa had reserved a room at the *Motel L'Habitation* on Laurier Boulevard. Police immediately reserved the adjacent room.

Just before 4 p.m. Buffa returned to locker 605, removed his beige suitcase and the briefcase. He checked the suitcase at the baggage counter, bought his ticket and waited for his flight, keeping the briefcase with him. A Narcotics Squad agent boarded the plane with him and kept him in sight during the flight. In Quebec City, Buffa took a taxi to *L'Habitation,* entering room 28 at 6:25 p.m., still carrying the briefcase. An hour and a half later he left the motel in a taxi, empty-handed, and went to the *Clarendon Hotel,* where he used the telephone at the reception desk. An agent got close enough to hear him say: "You're on the fifth floor, are you . . . Good, I'll come up." He got in the elevator. No one followed him, but all the exits were watched.

Sergeant Massé, who had come from Montreal to supervise the operation, took advantage of Buffa's absence from his room to pay it a short visit with three other agents. They had no trouble finding the briefcase. It was lying on the bed. It contained 17 plastic sacks of heroin powder, about eight and a half kilos or 19 pounds. Samples were taken for chemical analysis and everything was put back in place as before.

Buffa left the *Clarendon* at 8:55 p.m. and went to a bar nearby. An hour later he returned to his motel. Technical devices installed by federal agents permitted them to listen in on everything that was said in the next room. The trafficker made several telephone calls before going to bed, none of them very important. There was a question about his beige suitcase, which he had been unable to locate when he landed at Ancienne Lorette. It was brought to the motel and he picked it up at the reception desk before he turned in. The first interesting calls took place just before seven o'clock the next morning. The first was from an unknown person who woke him up and reminded him what he had to do immediately afterwards. The police equipment received only sounds made in Buffa's room, so the agents had to reconstitute conversations based only on what Buffa himself was saying. The second call was made by Buffa to Montreal to tell a certain "Santo" where he was staying. This person made note of the room number and announced the time of his arrival. Using the number obtained through the long distance operator, agents identified the man as Santo Mendolia.

After these two calls, Buffa left the motel in a taxi and got out in front of the *Chateau Frontenac Hotel* where he telephoned again from a public booth. He returned immediately to his motel and made arrangements to rent a car. About 9:30 a.m. he went to the airport by taxi to pick up the rented car, and was back in his room at 11 a.m. Ten minutes later he loaded his beige suitcase and the heroin-filled briefcase into the trunk of the car. At 11:45 a.m. a taxi driver brought him a package and a letter. At 1:45 p.m. Guido Orsini and Santo Mendolia entered room 28.

The room had been well bugged, and agents heard everything:

"Bonjour! How's it going?" said Buffa.

"Fine," answered Orsini.

"Good. What time is it now? At least two o'clock?"

"It's a quarter to two."

"A quarter to," put in Mendolia, in one of his rare interventions.

"We were held up because there was a lot of traffic."

"Well, good, let's get to the point. It's about the bottles. (1) You know about it?" asked Buffa.

"Yes, yes."

"Good, I'll tell you briefly what's happening. I had Claude on the phone, Claude or Richard, whatever you like. (2) So, then I give you this and you, well, you've got them, haven't you?"

"What?" asked Orsini.

"The two colts." (3)

"Ah, we're supposed to give them to you?"

"Well, if you haven't got them, it doesn't matter."

"Then . . ."

"In any case, he'll be there," said Buffa. "Apparently there was a little difficulty there, there are problems in France . . . We had a lot of trouble getting the business . . . We had some small problems, problems of production . . . transport. He had to go to Switzerland. Well, anyway, it's not serious, it's not your problem, it's his problem.

---

1. Drugs.

2. This was René Quintin de Kercadio. In his book, *Le Jockey,* Roger Gabeloux called his former partner Richard. In Montreal, during the Bouchard deal, de Kercadio lived at the *Richelieu Towers* under the name of Claude Hernandez.

3. The money.

He tries to arrange things as best he can and he does pretty well ...
Good, so, we had to do this for you in two stages, that is, we had to
bring part of it up here and maybe Pierre will bring another part
here. I don't think you're here to buy a kilo or two, so, anyway, he
probably didn't tell you but he has to sell to you at $9,000."

"Yes, he told me," said Orsini.

"He told you. He told you about everything. Good, well listen,
send me a guy in half an hour with the capital. I'll give it to him."

"Oh là là, oh là là!" replied Orsini. "I come from Montreal,
Jean-Pierre. I don't come from Quebec City."

"I'm really pressed for time. I called you the day before
yesterday. You were advised yesterday."

"Yes, yes, perfect, that's what I did. But don't forget that he,
before, he telephoned me last week and he told me—Tuesday, I
arrive, with nothing. Saturday or Sunday, Jean-Pierre will arrive
with the necessary. Me, I told him, what's going on, that's three
times I've had the person come here. You understand. So I told him,
I'll wait till he comes and then I'll make the arrangements. When
you called yesterday to say you had arrived, well I started right
away to get things going. My friend and I, in Montreal, he tried to
contact the person. Well, he has to come from outside, he's not from
Montreal. Then the time it takes to get down here, for him to do
what he has to do ... You'll have to forget it for tonight, Jean-
Pierre ... I'd like to do it right now if I could, but while I'm here
talking to you, the other person is trying to reach my guy. I had him
come down three times because Claude or Richard, as you wish, had
given me an appointment."

"Well then, listen," said Buffa, "what we need first, it's for you
to give me the exact details. You tell me what time, what day, if it's
after Sunday or before Sunday."

"I'd like it to be tomorrow. So you should tell me where I can
reach you tonight or tomorrow to tell you exactly what time the
person will be coming, understand? He knocks at the door, the same
thing that was done the other day. He comes in, he gives you the
money. As for you, you won't be here with the 'body' and me I
won't be here either. You count your money and when it's counted
you take the keys and say, Here you are friends, go and get it."

"Yes, yes, agreed, agreed!"

"But I want you to be relaxed. Two big guys, understand. While
one goes to get the things, the other stays here for two minutes, five
minutes ... What I want is that you don't have the bottles with you.

The bottles, they stay in the back. That's for your protection and ours."

"Good! So you'll telephone me?"

"I'll call for you."

"Have you got a telephone number to give us?" asked Mendolia. "Richard's number, have you got it?"

"Oh, I haven't got it yet," replied Buffa. "He's supposed to call me today because he's moving around a lot."

"Anyway, you tell him that I really need his telephone number," said Orsini. "You tell him that I've got a real good market, besides the one I'm interested in here... I have a really good friend in Mexico. I talked to him. He's a friend. You can trust him just as though he were me. If you've got a way into Mexico to sell bottles, it would be a pleasure for me to help out my friend."

"Good, we'll see about that with Richard, eh!"

"For our deal, I want you to understand. I'm trying to do it as soon as possible. If there's a delay, it's because I had the person come three times to the *Hotel des Gouverneurs*. I don't want to look like a clown again. He comes from New York, this guy."

"... But I'll be getting into trouble too. The thing is, we've got to do it as quickly as possible."

"Jean-Pierre, it doesn't depend on me, it depends on the guy who has to come from New York. If I can get in touch with him, he might decide to leave right away. That would mean that the young guy could be here tomorrow morning."

"Well, if it doesn't take long, that'll be good. You call me back here..."

"... Jean-Pierre, could I ask you something a bit touchy? If you want to answer, you can, if you don't, you don't have to. This is between friends."

"Yeah, go ahead."

"Here in Montreal, are you legit, are you legally here or...?"

"There's no problem," replied Buffa.

"Well, you know, I don't see why we come to Quebec City instead of Montreal. For Richard, I understand, I told him so myself—don't touch Montreal any more, because he's hot. But for you, it's not the same."

"This is what he prefers for now."

"Anyway, do as you wish. But if you decide, I could suggest some places . . ."

"Good, well, that's it, then," interrupted Buffa. "You call me at 10 o'clock. If I go to Montreal I'll call you, but it's not sure, it's not at all sure, it will depend on my business in Quebec. But if I go to Montreal I'll call you before 10 o'clock .. Anyway, you try to fix things for tomorrow morning "

"Yes, yes."

"O.K., perfect, Bonjour!"

Orsini and Mendolia left the *Motel L'Habitation* at 2:10 p.m. Mendolia took with him the package the taxi driver had delivered earlier. They returned to Montreal that afternoon and went directly to the *Dante Pizzeria*. Buffa, when his visitors had left, went to get the suitcase and briefcase and brought them back to his room. He received a telephone call, possibly from his partner Claude, for he summarized the discussion he'd just had with the Montrealers. Buffa's remarks indicated that his partner was displeased with the delay and that there would be no question of going to Montreal to conclude the deal. He apparently advised Buffa to demand a straight yes or no answer from Orsini when he called.

In effect, that's what Buffa did that night when he received a call from Montreal. He told the caller that he had to leave for France soon and was unable to wait because he needed the money from this transaction to conclude another one. He said that if Orsini could not arrange the deal within two days the whole thing would be put off until July 12. Furthermore there was no question this time of doing the deal in Montreal. The caller promised the insistent Frenchman that he would call back the next morning.

The day of June 29 ended with more calls to Buffa from his partner and from a friend in Montreal, Jean Duval (the former associate of Louis Henri and one of Conrad Bouchard's men). Duval was known to be in close contact with de Kercadio following the arrest of his boss and probably met Buffa through him.

At 6:30 a.m. on Friday, June 30, a telephone call woke Buffa. The caller informed him that he had agreed with the Montrealers to wait till the end of the afternoon to give them the chance to find the necessary money. They mustn't appear to be too hard! After breakfast, Buffa telephoned Air France and Air Canada and reserved a seat on a flight to Guadeloupe on Sunday, July 2. At 11:10 a.m. he received the anxiously-awaited call from Montreal. His replies indicated to listening agents that Orsini and Mendolia had not yet solved their problems. They could only buy four kilos and asked that the transaction be made in two stages so they could buy the whole lot reasonably quickly. Buffa was receptive, but made it clear that everything must be concluded by the following morning and that the first payment must be made right away, before the end of the afternoon. In any case, he could not make the decision by himself. He would have to talk to his partner and would call them back with the answer at noon.

The partner called immediately afterwards. Buffa described the earlier conversation and left the decision up to him. The partner preferred to make the transaction in one stage only. In spite of that, when someone (Orsini or Mendolia) called Buffa at noon, the trafficker tried to give him a chance: he would be meeting someone at about 4 p.m. to hand over the merchandise, unless in the meantime a messenger from Montreal arrived, in which case something could be arranged. Buffa said he would then explain to his partner that he had to do it that way because their guy was already en route when they called. The proposition seemed to satisfy the Montreal caller, especially since Buffa assured him that if it did not work this time, there was still the possibility of a complete transaction on July 12 and 13. They agreed to talk again at 2 p.m.

The more telephone calls that were made, the more apparent it became to investigators that each party in the deal was trying his best to stack the cards in his own favor. Just after his last conversation with the Montrealers, for example, Buffa got another call from his partner and told him he had rejected Orsini's and Mendolia's proposition. It was not easy for the agents to reconstruct conversations of which they heard only one side, but they managed to follow the progress of the negotiations.

At 12:40 p.m., the trafficker left his room carrying the beige suitcase and the briefcase. He put them in the trunk of his rented car and returned to the motel for lunch. Then he carried the cases back into his room. He next reserved a room at the *Motel Universel* for July 12 and 13. Just before 2 p.m. he received another call in which he announced that he would be in Montreal that night and would telephone Santo to tell him where they could meet. Then he made arrangements with his partner to store the heroin in a safe place until his return. During the afternoon he made several trips back and forth between his motel and various potential storage places for the heroin-filled briefcase. He came back to the motel three times and went twice to a *Laurier Place* restaurant, before deciding at about 5 p.m. to deposit the briefcase in locker number 577 at the Palais station. He then returned by taxi to the *Bambou* restaurant at *Laurier Place,* staying there only a few minutes. He continued in the same taxi to his motel and then left for Montreal at the wheel of his rented car, constantly followed, of course, by several police surveillance cars.

He arrived in Montreal about 8 p.m., parked his car on Saint-Marc Street near St. Catherine, and entered the *Alpenhaus* restaurant. An hour later he left alone and disappeared in the night-time traffic. The agents let him go, knowing that he did not have the heroin with him. It was preferable, anyway, not to risk being seen, which might cause Buffa to change his plans. That was why he had not been followed in the *Hotel Clarendon* and the *Laurier Place* restaurant in Quebec City. Two days later, as planned, Buffa left Montreal for the West Indies.

In Quebec, as soon as Buffa had left the Palais station, a Narcotics Squad agent with the cooperation of employees there, removed the briefcase from the locker and put it in a secure place. It remained in the possession of the RCMP until the morning of July 12 when it was taken back to the station and left in the baggage room where Buffa would expect to be picking it up. Buffa came in at about 1:45 p.m. that same day. It was a federal agent disguised as a baggage room worker who handed him the briefcase and asked him if it belonged to him. His affirmative reply was carefully noted.

At the *Motel Universel* on Sainte-Foy Boulevard, where Buffa went immediately afterwards, the Narcotics Squad was already well installed. The agents had taken two rooms, one adjacent to the trafficker's and the other directly across the hall, so that all activities could be more easily observed. The shadowing team was dispersed in the area, ready for any eventuality. The electronic listening devices were in place, and immediately proved useful. As soon as he arrived in his room, Buffa began making long distance calls to Montreal to Orsini and Mendolia. Both were out but the message was left and finally at 3:16 p.m. one of the Montrealers called back. A meeting was arranged for that evening.

Again, Orsini and Mendolia arrived from Montreal by car. It was 6:40 p.m. when they entered Buffa's room, number 239. The greetings were brief and Buffa quickly got down to business with Orsini:

"So are you ready?" asked the Frenchman. "There's no problem I hope. Because that would really mess me up, you know."

"No, no, there's no problem any more. The buyer is already here. You've just got to give us a little time... The guy has already left New York. When he gets to Montreal, he'll take his car and drive here. I get the money and bring it to you, and you tell me where the thing is. After that the two cars go to get it. That's all there is to it."

"Good. Work it out the way you want, it'll have to be finished by tomorrow night because tomorrow I've got to go back to Paris. I've got appointments there. I've got a meeting with Claude, I absolutely have to see him. Me, I don't want to wait around here a week, eh!"

"Oh no, oh no."

"There's no question of that! Tonight I have to go to Montreal, but I have to be back here tomorrow."

"What time do you want us to call you tomorrow, and where?" asked Orsini. "Here or in Montreal?"

"Well, call me here at 10 a.m."

At that moment the telephone rang. It was Christian, another of Buffa's friends. Apparently he wanted to know if the agreed plan was still valid, because Buffa asked him to wait a minute as he asked Orsini:

"Whatever happens, tomorrow it will be finished?"

"Yes, yes, it'll be done tomorrow. I just needed the day," replied Orsini.

"When will you know exactly what time you'll be arriving?"

"Tomorrow morning at 10 o'clock or maybe even tonight. You're going to Montreal tonight, I'll call you tonight."

"Good, perfect."

Buffa returned to the telephone and said:

"Hello, good, so there's no problem. I think there's no problem for tomorrow. I don't know exactly when. I'll know tonight or tomorrow morning. Anyway, it will be all done tomorrow, I don't know the exact time."

Buffa hung up and continued the discussion with Orsini:

"Good," said Buffa, "I warned you he would call. He went to Switzerland and saw Claude and told him nothing had been done."

"There's something that bothers me, Jean-Pierre, just one thing," said Orsini. "It's this business of going fast, fast, fast. It's the only thing that bothers me. For the rest, there's no problem."

"No, no, wait a minute Guido, be reasonable! I left, I told you I'd be back on the 12th. You had eight days..."

"That's perfect, I told you that when he arrived, the person would be ready... As for me, the only thing I can promise is my word of honor that tomorrow it will be done. That's all. It's tomorrow. Give me the chance for the guy to get here with the damned money."

"What I'm asking for is an exact time. If you don't give me an exact time I'll have to be locked up here all day and that screws me up."

"You won't have to lock yourself up here, no."

"And furthermore, I want to know for sure that there's no problem. I've got to know that it's working, oiled, greased and running smoothly, understand?"

"For tomorrow, the guy will be here. He's leaving Montreal to come here. As for me, I've got to come from Montreal. He's got to come here and I've got to come here before him. I have to give you the money first, don't I? That's how it's done. There's no other way. I'll borrow the money from the others and I'll come here and give it to you. When I've given you the money, you tell me where the thing is. I'll tell my guy, he'll be there. The guy takes the merchandise, and he goes. And I go too. That's all, Jean-Pierre. The only thing is, I need until tomorrow. I'm not asking for a century. So don't worry about me. I'll be ready tomorrow."

"Good, O.K., you've got all day tomorrow. But don't give me any story tomorrow night about saying you're going to have to wait another day."

"Don't worry."

"Good then, agreed. Now about the five others. You have five to pick up, do you want to pick them up in three or four days?"

"Yes, and then?"

"They're here too, eh!" said Buffa.

"In Quebec?"

"Yes, yes. But you can't get them right away because I have to go through an intermediary."

"I understand your point of view," said Orsini. "It's a good thing you told me, so tomorrow I can start collecting my money."

"In three or four days, it'll be here. I have to go back to France first. I've got to bring back the capital. I've got a lot of deals ... I've got to go back, but I'll return here for you. Anyway, from now on you'll only have to deal with one person. It will be me, practically every time."

"From today on."

"From today on, it will be me nearly every time. As for Claude, you won't likely see him again, or very seldom."

"Say hello to him for me," put in Orsini.

"He's got a problem with his leg. It seems they operated on it and all that. (4) For the time being, I think he won't be showing up over here."

"I don't blame him. He's wise."

"As for me," explained Buffa, "I've always got him behind me. It's not me who makes the decisions, they're always his deals. You're his clients. Me, I just helped him out to sell off some of his merchandise. You understand. On the other hand, as far as Italy is concerned . . . "

"Yes, yes, Italy. You know, the same person who's coming here to take eight or ten, he's got a brother in Italy who's interested in this. And apart from him, I have another guy in mind who called me, I called him and he's ready right away. Now if the others ask for a date, we're always ready. Is there a date that you prefer?"

"Ah, no, I couldn't give them a date right now. I haven't been in France. I don't know at all how my affairs are there. With what's happened, I don't know how things have gone."

"Listen, Jean-Pierre, it's because the first time, I want to be there, understand. Because I know both parties, understand what I mean."

"They can work with big quantities?"

"Sure, always," said the Montrealer. "And on the Mexico thing, is that agreed?"

"No, it's not possible. We can't."

"Ah, that's too bad!"

"Unless it goes by the islands."

"For me that's impossible. To get into New York, there's always checking. For the dates, when will you be ready? We've got to arrange that because if the merchandise from Claude comes here and I'm in Italy with you, nothing can be done here."

"Well, there, you've got five or six kilos. I'm supposed to pick those ones up, it's true. But I won't pick them up for the moment. I can't go and get them. As soon as these ones are gone I'm going

---

4.   This detail about Claude's or Richard's leg is a good indication that the man in question was René Quintin de Kercadio.

back to France. The others, they're here I admit that. As I told you, I've got to do my work, then I'll come back and give you the five and after that, I'll go back to France again. But that changes nothing with your five. It should only take a couple of days."

"No, but Claude, isn't he going to be sending more merchandise?"

"Ah, as for that, I don't know," replied Buffa. "Did he tell you he'd be sending some? Now if you want some I can make you a present. But if you want to take 10 or 15 kilos, that's nothing. We couldn't get you more than that."

"Ten to 15, I'm ready to take that out every two weeks. Every 15 days."

"Ah, let's say at the end of the month. Could you do it for the end of the month?" asked Buffa.

"That's a good idea. For the end of the month, you bring in ten to 15. When we've handled that, we can leave right away for Italy."

"There'll be no problem on my side, when we're there, if the guy doesn't have any problem. You know, I've got certain obligations to him."

"I'm glad to do it that way. Everybody will be happy."

"O.K., then, for tomorrow, I don't know. Your American, did you advise him? You told him didn't you, for God's sake?"

"Yes, yes, don't worry."

"You know me, I like to have lots of advance notice. My schedule is worked out a week in advance at the minimum. That way you always have a week available. The only thing I want is not to stay here for days and days. You're notified in advance. You know it, it arrives, you pay me, it's simple. Good. Claude there, he'd call you and say 'I'm here', but I don't work like that. I warn you in advance and say in so many days, I'll be there."

"That's perfect, Jean-Pierre. And when you tell me, 'I've arrived', then I call New York. He comes and everybody keeps faith. Like now, I hope to be ready tomorrow at two o'clock, or three or four, but I want the whole day in case he calls and says he'll be there at five o'clock ... All I want every time is two days after you arrive, that's all. Because the only trouble I have with those guys is that I never know if it will take them a day, a day and a half, or half a day. I never know with them. And I can't blame them. Don't forget we're in America, Jean-Pierre. I need a day or two, but never more than two days."

"But no matter what," said Buffa, "there's one thing sure, if ever anything happens, a problem or whatever, don't come and tell me any stories. Tell it to me straight. Like tomorrow, if there's something, tell me."

"For tomorrow, no problem!"

"Good, so you'll call me then?"

"When we get to Montreal."

"Agreed! That's fine, keep well. Au revoir," said Buffa.

Orsini and Mendolia left the *Motel Universel* at 7:25 p.m. and drove back to Montreal. Forty-five minutes later Buffa came out and got in his rented car, heading, as he had promised, to Montreal. He was followed as far as Exit 161 of the Trans-Canada Highway when the federal agents were ordered to abandon the pursuit. At the motel, Corporal Ernest Bacqué had just located the briefcase and the heroin hidden under the stove. There was therefore no point in following the trafficker and risking his discovery of the surveillance.

Buffa came back to the *Motel Universel* the following morning. At 9:40 a.m. he was in his room. Until late afternnon his only activities were a few telephone calls which indicated the matter was in progress. At 6:10 p.m. he went out to place the briefcase in the trunk of his car. In doing so he opened the case and agents watching through binoculars thought they saw that it was empty. He returned to his room after moving his car.

Thirty-five minutes later Orsini and Mendolia arrived in a Buick. At the same time a Fiat with Ontario licence plates carrying two strangers was observed in the parking lot. The two men got out of the car and waited while the Montrealers went to Buffa's room. Soon Mendolia came out and took a black briefcase, smaller than Buffa's, from the trunk of the Buick. He went back inside with it. A few seconds later Orsini came out and took Buffa's briefcase back into the room. The younger stranger from the Fiat then went to Buffa's room and came out a minute later with the smaller briefcase which he put in the trunk of his car. These two men then drove away. As they reached Sainte-Foy Boulevard, Orsini and Mendolia joined them in their car. The two cars drove one behind the other to the *Hotel des Gouverneurs.*

About 7:30 p.m. Orsini returned to the *Motel Universel.* All his movements and those of the others had been closely watched since the beginning of the operation. As he neared Buffa's room, agents saw a third stranger emerge from the room with the large briefcase and get into a Rambler. Orsini left the grounds first, followed by the stranger who stopped before long at a garage to get gas. Three minutes later Orsini separated from the Rambler and went to rejoin Mendolia and the two men from the Fiat at the *Hotel des Gouverneurs.*

Five minutes later the four traffickers were on the road to Montreal. The weather was bad. It was pouring rain but the Buick and the Fiat stayed close to each other at high speed, not even separating during the worst of the storm. In a way, that made it easier for pursuing agents to keep them in sight. The Rambler was also being followed. For much of the trip, an airplane participated in the surveillance. The Buick was still preceding the Fiat on arrival at Montreal. After passing through the Lafontaine tunnel they took different routes to arrive at the corner of Repentigny and Chauvin Streets. There the two cars stopped and Mendolia got out to let another passenger out, a sixth person unidentified for the moment who had never been seen until then. This stop, it was noted, was made near the residence of Orsini's and Mendolia's boss, Frank Cotroni. Later, the mystery passenger was identified as Carlo Arena, a young recruit to the gang. The procession moved off again and took the Metropolitan Boulevard. At the Saint-Michel exit, the two cars left the elevated highway and drove on to 11th Avenue. The Fiat stopped at the Esso garage at the corner of Crémazie Boulevard and the Buick continued to Jarry Street where it stopped. It was about 10:10 p.m. and Staff Sergeant Poissant judged that it was time to intervene. This was also the view of the commander of the Narcotics Squad, Inspector Roger Perrier who would not normally participate directly in an operation, but wanted to be in on this one. The order was given. Federal agents quickly surrounded the traffickers and arrested them. In the Fiat they found the small briefcase which contained seven of the 17 sacks of heroin sold by Buffa. The two occupants were identified: the younger was Vincenzo Balsamo, from Windsor, Ontario; the other, his boss, was John Fecarotta, of Detroit.

At 10:30 p.m. the Rambler was just entering the Lafontaine tunnel. Narcotics Squad agents waited for it at the other end. It was intercepted with no trouble and the five kilos of heroin it was carrying were seized. The man in the car was identified as Tibor Korponay, 33, whose official employment was as a handyman at *Au Vieux-Montréal* restaurant, property of Thomas (The Moose) Solarick, a friend of Horvath and Thomas Pythel.

In Quebec City, Jean-Pierre Buffa had already been arrested. When Orsini and Korponay left, he too had come out of the motel with a package in his hands. He was followed by Sergeant Massé who had instructions to see if Buffa met anyone, and if so, to arrest him and his accomplice. Buffa drove into the centre of town. Lost in the traffic, he was spotted and arrested a bit later as he emerged alone, almost running, from the *Chateau Frontenac Hotel*. His rented car was located soon after in a nearby street. The front door on the passenger side had not been locked and the lock of the open glove compartment was on the floor. There was no trace of the package he had been carrying. It was learned later that it contained the payment for the heroin, $76,000.

In Criminal Court five days later Judge Guy Guérin refused bail to all the accused except Fecarotta who was ordered nervertheless to remain in Quebec. The judge's decision was made after he had viewed the film taken at the *Motel Universel* on the late afternoon of that July 13. All the comings and goings of the traffickers at the *Motel L'Habitation* and the *Motel Universel* had been videotaped from the beginning by the Narcotics Squad, which had spared no effort to get the evidence, at last, on Orsini and Mendolia. The police also hoped to be able to charge Frank Dasti, for they had learned that it was to him Orsini was referring on June 28 when he told Buffa that "my friend in Montreal" was trying to contact the New York buyer. But events worked again in Dasti's favor when police decided there was insufficient evidence against him. But the RCMP hoped it would be just a case of postponed action, for they had learned the identity of the New York buyer and knew that Dasti was still in contact with him. (5)

The former proprietor of the *Victoria Sporting Club* had moved since the arrest of his messenger Lucien Madère and his client Paul Oddo. Dasti had set up housekeeping in a west-end restaurant, the *Pizzeria Tower* on Décarie Boulevard. The new manager of this place was a friend of the gang, Vincenzo Greco, a former cook at the *Dante Pizzeria*. He was associated with Michel Cotroni, the least-known of the brothers, who was manager of the *Décarie Pub* located above the pizzeria. On July 12, when Buffa was trying to reach Orsini and Mendolia, he had telephoned several places, but especially to the *Pizzeria Tower*. After the arrests, a search of Mendolia's home turned up some interesting documents, including a note bearing the name of the *Motel L'Habitation,*

---

5. During Buffa's stay in Guadeloupe, Dasti and Orsini contacted several people to offer the 8½ kilos. The Narcotics Squad noted with interest the meeting at the *Hotel April* on Sherbrooke Street East between Dasti and Roger (Le Français) Denizet. Denizet's name had come up often since 1948, notably as an accomplice of Antoine d'Agostino, Jean-Claude Laprès, Marius Martin, Jean Jehan, Roger Laviolette, Anatole Ethier and Lucien Rivard. It will be recalled that he was arrested in Vancouver in 1948 in possession of one kilo of pure heroin.

Buffa's room number, and the name and telephone number of the *Pizzeria Tower.*

Dasti's new headquarters, a centre of interest for police services concerned with Mafia activities in Montreal, had also become the object of special surveillance, both physical and technical. In this way the Narcotics Squad in June was able to identify a new face in the trafficker's entourage: Joseph Santini, a visitor from the U.S. permanently installed in a suite at the *Décarie Plaza Hotel* right beside the *Pizzeria Tower.* (6) Between June 4 and July 11 this man had often made use of the public telephone in the *Pizzeria* to make long distance calls to three different places in Fort Lee, New Jersey and to New York to a certain "Patsy." Checks by the BNDD revealed that Patsy was really Pasquale Falcone, a mafioso with the Gerardo Catena—Thomas Eboli organization, successors to Vito Genovese.

Patsy Falcone owned the *Aquarius* bar on Hammersly Avenue in the Bronx. He was also impresario for several well-known *Columbia Records* artists, and was known to be on friendly terms with notorious racketeers from East Harlem, the Bronx, New Jersey and Pennsylvania. (7) Falcone had regular contacts with an important gang of heroin traffickers led by Louis Boyce and his brother-in-law Gaetano Licata. In 1970 Patsy was in financial difficulties and one of his employees at the *Aquarius* bar, Anna Licata-Boyce, introduced him to her husband, Louis Boyce. Boyce, a big narcotics dealer and owner of two construction firms in Mount Ephram and Lawnside, New Jersey, helped Falcone get on his feet again through the sale of three kilos of cocaine. In December 1971 Customs investigators arrested Boyce for conspiring to traffic in narcotics. Immediately after that his wife's brother, Gaetano Licata, a hardened mafioso, took the succession. Installed at the *J.C. Bar* in Philadelphia, a gangsters hangout, Licata began by dismissing his

---

6. It was later learned that Joseph Santini was none other than the well-known American mafioso Joseph Averso, who was particularly active in heroin-importation from Latin America. Originally from Cliffside, New Jersey, Averso had been wanted by police since July 1971 following the arrest of the son of the Panamanian ambassador to Taiwan.

7. In February 1973, Falcone's relations with the artistic director and vice-president of *Columbia Records,* David Wynsaw, caused the Federal Strike Force against Organized Crime, in Newark, to begin an investigation of the possible infiltration of the record industry by the Mafia. The investigation led to the dismissals of Wynsaw and *Columbia Records* president Clive Davis by the directors of the *Columbia Broadcasting System (CBS),* which created a national scandal on corruption and deception in the lucrative recording industry of the U.S.

brother-in-law's partner, Guy Diviaio, and reorganizing the supply system for Boyce's clients. According to the BNDD, Licata was capable of distributing about 40 kilos of heroin a month. In May and June 1972, he had received at least a dozen long distance calls from Falcone's home in Fort Lee, New Jersey. Several of these calls were made just before and just after other calls to Falcone from Joseph Santini in Montreal.

In connection with the Santini calls, the Narcotics Squad had communicated the following information to the BNDD: on June 4 Santini called Falcone to talk about the trip he was to make to Canada to pick up the "package." On June 13, Santini called Falcone to talk about a trip he was to make to Canada to take delivery of "the pillow case." Santini added that he would see no one unless "they" had the money and were ready to close the deal. On June 15 Santini spoke to Patsy to find out when "the guy down south" would get out of prison. In his opinion the guy should not be trusted because he found it strange that he had been sentenced to only six months in prison. They should be careful before they brought him back to Canada. On July 10 Santini called the *3rd Rail Pub* and asked Mario there if Patsy was still around and if he had given him the money. When he got the answer Santini told Mario to give the money to Patsy. On July 11, the day before Buffa returned to Quebec, Santini spoke to Falcone to find out when he would be coming to Canada. He told him he wanted to see him that night or the next day at the latest. He advised him to go to see "the guy" and ask for the money and to bring it with him. He told Patsy to tell "the other guy" that they had something for him. On this subject, Santini ended by telling Patsy: "I can't talk to you about that on the phone. I'll tell you about it when I see you."

But Falcone arrived too late and the merchandise was sold to others, with the consequences already described.

On July 28, special agent Michael James Campbell of the Newark BNDD presented an official request to Chief Judge James A. Coolahan of the New Jersey judicial district for authorization to install a listening device on the telephone at the residence of Pasquale Falcone in Fort Lee. Thanks to information provided by the RCMP the request was immediately granted. Within a week the relations of the *3rd Rail Pub* with Gaetano Licata, Joseph Santini and Mario had been considerably clarified. In addition, it was learned that Falcone was in regular contact with another gang of drug traffickers, the Salerno brothers in East Harlem. Of the five Salerno brothers, three were before the courts for trafficking in heroin and cocaine.

At the end of August, while the BNDD's wiretap was still functioning, the Narcotics Squad in Montreal learned that Frank Dasti had made contact with the French trafficker René Quintin de Kercadio through Jean-Marc Guillet. At that moment in fact, Guillet was in Tunis meeting with de Kercadio. (8) On August 30, Sergeant Paul Sauvé of the RCMP and special agent Kevin Gallagher of the BNDD's Montreal office, were at Dorval airport to await Guillet's arrival. He was not on the plane, but another interesting party was: Claude Dewachter, a member of Daniel Marquet's gang of procurers which, it will be recalled, financed de Kercadio and Roger Gabeloux when they got out of prison in the autumn of 1971. The Canadian and U.S. investigators recognized Dewachter and knew that he had linked up with de Kercadio. The double agent Gabeloux had returned to Paris in June and met his former partner. He learned then that de Kercadio had finally reimbursed Marquet and his associates and was again their partner in heroin traffic. Another important point: while de Kercadio was staying at the *Berkeley Hotel* in Montreal at the beginning of March, Dewachter was returning to France after a stay in Quebec. In mid-May after the arrests of the New Yorkers Castiglione and Rizzuto, Dewachter and Marquet accompanied de Kercadio to Montreal.

This time Dewachter came to Montreal alone. He passed through the Customs inspection without incident and took a taxi to the *Bonaventure Hotel* where he registered in his real name. Sergeant Sauvé and agent Gallagher did not let him out of their sight. Shortly after taking his room, he left the hotel and went to the *Pizzeria Tower.* The agents noted he had not changed his clothing except for one additional detail: he now wore a bright red tie. Perhaps that was to be a sign of recognition. At 7 p.m., 15 minutes after his arrival at the *Pizzeria,* Frank Dasti approached him and a lively discussion began. For about ten minutes the two agents observed as much as they could. But it would have been difficult to continue the surveillance without being noticed, so they withdrew. The next morning they learned that Dewachter had checked out of the hotel without even using his room and had gone back to Paris.

---

8. The RCMP and other Montreal police services noted in the spring and summer of 1972 that Jean-Marc Guillet regularly frequented a real estate investment firm called *Les Immeubles Tempo Ltée,* which was really the legal cover for the new activities of Jimmy Soccio and Giuseppe (Pep) Cotroni, freed from prison in April 1971. Two of the many projects undertaken by the *Tempo* firm were the construction of a housing complex and establishment of a gambling casino in Tunis.

Jean-Pierre Buffa

John Fecarotta

Tibor Korponay

Daniel Marquet

Claude Dewachter

Sebato Falgiano

Two days later, early on the morning of September 2, Frank Dasti telephoned Falcone's home. He wasn't there, but the phone was answered by a young friend, Anthony Del Vecchio. A heroin user, Del Vecchio had been an informer for the BNDD since July. He advised the Montrealer to call back a little later, about 9 a.m., and then made several calls trying to reach his boss. At 8:50 a.m. Patsy called him and told him to ask Dasti to give a telephone number where he could be reached at 10 a.m. This was done and Dasti gave the young man the number of the telephone in the lobby of the *Décarie Plaza Hotel* where he was at that moment (under observation by two officers of the RCMP and the BNDD). Dasti ended the call by saying: "O.K., but tell Patsy to call, it's important."

On September 6, Gaetano Licata called Falcone and they discussed the imprisonment of Louis Boyce. During the conversation Patsy indicated he was expecting a call "from the other side" on Friday the 8th. He got the call on the night of the 7th. Again, Falcone was out and Del Vecchio took the message from Dasti, who was waiting impatiently for Patsy's call because he had people with him who were waiting for answers. At 8:30 p.m., after two fruitless attempts to reach Patsy, Del Vecchio called Dasti back to ask him to be patient. Dasti repeated that he wanted Patsy to call as soon as possible. Shortly afterwards, Falcone called home and Del Vecchio gave him the message. He replied that he would call from his home in the Bronx.

Falcone got in touch with Dasti at the *Pizzeria Tower* on Saturday, September 9, asking him for a delay in the deal in progress because he could not get funds immediately. Dasti reluctantly agreed and said he would call back the next day. Then Patsy telephoned Francine Berger, who, along with her sister Wally, was an accomplice of Patsy, according to Del Vecchio. In mid-July, Falcone and Wally Berger had come to Montreal to meet Dasti. Del Vecchio had come with them and there had been discussion of heroin transports to be made in the future by the Berger sisters. Dasti's method was as follows: Falcone and one of the girls would drive to Montreal while Del Vecchio would come by plane. Once the heroin had been purchased, Del Vecchio and the girl would take it back to New York in the car while Patsy returned by plane. In his call to Francine, Patsy declared that "the person over there wants to do the affair all at one time." The young woman replied that she could not do it like that. In her view, someone should go to get part of it, and the next day someone else would go to get the rest. Falcone said it could not be done that way because "the guys want someone to wait there with them until the thing arrives and then turn over the money."

On September 10, Dasti called Falcone who told him he had met the people the night before and that they could not bring the money. Dasti suggested he try to reach "the guy" who might be able to do something. But Patsy said he had tried and the guy could not be found. At the end Dasti said he would call back the next morning. When he did, Falcone said that he had reached "the guy" who was supposed to call him back. Dasti asked him to let him know what happened one way or the other. Shortly afterwards, Licata telephoned Patsy and asked what was new. Falcone replied that the guy from "the other side" had called and had "five things" at a price of $75,000. Licata replied that he had the man and the bread and all he needed was the word. The things were there, said Falcone, it was just a matter of going to get them. Licata said that was fine with him. The conversation ended with Patsy's assurances that the arrangements had been made by Joe (Santini), who was in Europe at that moment to attend his mother's funeral. (9) Licata did not know the people in Canada but Falcone said he would make all the arrangements. The two men agreed to talk again the next day.

On Tuesday, September 12, at 9 a.m., Patsy advised Dasti that he had nothing from the guy and was going to have to "let this one go." Dasti was floored: he had made all the arrangements with Joe and now he was not there. In any case, he expected to be receiving something else in about two weeks and advised Falcone to start getting his money together right away.

The five-kilo transaction therefore did not take place. According to Del Vecchio, Falcone had made diligent efforts to find funds for the operation, even contacting several racketeers in the New York area. Telephone conversations with Dasti resumed on September 25. Before that, Licata and Santini (who was still in Italy) had been in contact with Falcone to find out how things were going and to indicate they were impatient for results. Licata in particular pressed Patsy to act quickly and to get him something, no matter what. Santini asked him if he was still in contact with Dasti, to which Patsy replied that he was.

On September 22, early in the morning, Falcone telephoned the *Pizzeria Tower* but Dasti was not there, so he left a message. Three days later, on Monday the 25th, Dasti returned the call:

---

9. Joseph Averso, alias Santini, was able to visit Italy on a false passport obtained in Montreal through the good services of Frank Dasti.

"You called me?" he asked.

"Yes," replied Patsy, "I wanted to know if the orchestra is still in town."

"The what?"

"The orchestra. I wanted to know if you still had them there."

"No, we got what we wanted. I can't talk to you like this."

"I had some news from our friend. (10) He's going to call me back this week. I think he'll be back soon."

"Where is he?"

"Somewhere in Italy, I don't know exactly where. He'll be coming to my place next week ... I wanted to talk to you anyway. I wanted to know if you could arrange to get the whole group together."

"Yes, yes," replied Dasti, who understood he was being asked if he was ready for another transaction.

"We'll have to make the arrangements."

"Somebody has got to come down there and talk to you. There's no use talking on the phone like this."

"Let's start making arrangements right now, maybe I could come to see you. Anyway, I'll call you back before Thursday."

Patsy received a call the next day, September 26, from an unidentified man who asked him "what's going on?". He replied he thought he could arrange the thing for the following Friday and in any case would be able to give an answer on Thursday. "I talked to him yesterday," said Falcone, "and I'll know definitely on Thursday. I'll call you at home if it's for Friday." On the subject of another affair in progress between them, Falcone said "everything's fine on the western front." On the 27th, Licata called Falcone and asked if he had heard anything from the guys. Patsy replied that "everything is fine" and that they could still get five things.

Falcone called Dasti at the *Pizzeria Tower* at 5:30 p.m. on Thursday the 28th:

"Is everything O.K." he asked.

"If it's O.K. for you it's O.K. for me," replied the Montrealer, who said he would call back the next morning when he had all the details for the trip to Montreal.

---

10. Santini.

"It's the whole group, eh, a five-piece group?"

"Yes, Yes."

Falcone next received a call from Spiro Venduras, a trafficker from Los Angeles, California. He told him he had just received a call from his guy who was to call back the next day. He would know then where things were. Venduras asked him if he had news of Santini and Patsy said he expected a call from him soon. In the meantime he would be sending him a little "bread."

At 9:40 a.m. on September 30, Dasti telephoned Falcone and talked to Del Vecchio. The young man said his boss was busy and would be back the next day. Dasti insisted that he call back if possible that afternoon. About 1 p.m. Falcone called home and Del Vecchio told him that Dasti and Venduras had called. He asked Patsy if he would be leaving or making arrangements soon because he had a reception to go to that night. The mafioso told him:

"Oh, don't worry about what's going to happen there, we probably won't be going until next week ... Even if it happens this week, we can't bring it back right away, it would have to be left there for a while ... You can't bring it back just like that, you know ... You have to leave it there for a while and bring it back a little at a time to different places, understand ... "

Dasti got in touch with Falcone on October 7 and announced that he had "ten girls" available. Patsy expressed great interest but finally he could not go to Montreal. According to Del Vecchio, Falcone was unable at the time to get financial backing from outside and his own funds were tied up elsewhere. He thought a transaction could take place as soon as Patsy's problems were settled. In the meantime, the Montrealer was looking elsewhere. Dasti contacted his old friend Steve Panepinto. In a telephone call early in October, Panepinto told Dasti his friend would call soon. "So much the better," said Dasti, "I've got something very good for him."

On October 10, in the morning, Dasti told his wife on the phone that his "guy" was arriving from Europe that afternoon. A Narcotics Squad surveillance team was hastily despatched to Dorval airport. About 4 p.m. Claude Dewachter arrived on a flight from Frankfurt, Germany. He immediately hailed a taxi and went directly to the *Pizzeria Tower* where Dasti awaited him. From their observation posts, agents noticed that Dasti kept checking to see if he was being watched. They suspended the surveillance in order to avoid being seen themselves.

The next night, after midnight, an unknown person called Dasti and asked how to get to the *Pizzeria Tower*. This man, apparently from the States, said he had arrived and had checked into a South Shore motel. Dasti gave him directions and the stranger said he would be there in about two hours. Sergeant Sauvé and Corporal Claude Savoie hastened to the vicinity of the pizzeria. They suspected something was going to happen because Dasti was up late, contrary to his habits, and had not yet gone home. A black Cadillac with New York licence plates pulled up and parked in the cross street beside the restaurant. A stranger got out and entered the pizzeria where Dasti was waiting. While the two men talked, the RCMP contacted the BNDD's liaison officer in Montreal, Jack McCarthy, to check on the ownership of the Cadillac. The information was quickly supplied: the de luxe vehicle belonged to Sebato Falgiano, alias Sammy Feet, 59, a mafioso from Queens, New York. (11) Discreet patrols ascertained that the Cadillac had been moved onto the parking lot of the *Décarie Plaza Hotel,* beside the pizzeria and stayed there during the night.

About 11:30 a.m. on October 12, after several unsuccessful attempts which seemed to irritate him, Dasti managed to reach young Carlo Arena on the phone. He told him his guy had come during the night and wanted to conclude the transaction. Arena promised to do his best. Dasti next called Frank Cotroni to advise him of events. He took the occasion to complain that he had been unable to reach Arena all night and that this had made the client very nervous. At 1:30 p.m. Dasti called room 1004 in the *Décarie Plaza Hotel* and a feminine voice told him: "Sammy has gone downstairs for a few minutes." During the afternoon Arena called Dasti several times and promised that "the contracts" would be delivered to the hotel for 4 p.m. Federal agents kept close watch on the black Cadillac.

Dasti and Falgiano were observed about 6 p.m. in conversation on the sidewalk in front of the pizzeria. At that moment a woman got into the Cadillac and drove to the front of the restaurant to pick up the two mafiosi. The Cadillac headed towards the South Shore. Agents lost the car in traffic momentarily but found it again on Champlain bridge. There seemed to be only one person in it then.

11. A member of the old Genovese family, Falgiano was co-owner of the *Savoie* restaurant in New York. His police files indicated association with the brothers Anthony and Joseph Russo, two well-known traffickers. It will be remembered that in March 1965, Air France employees who had been supplying Joseph Russo, alias Joe Fats, were arrested in Montreal (See note page 245). In 1955, with Settimo Accardo, alias Sam Accardi, and Frank Digregerio, Joseph Russo was arrested following a BNDD undercover operation. The three cronies were each sentenced to four years in prison.

Frank Dasti (right) with Steve Panepinto in New York.

The vehicle turned on to Highway 15 in the direction of Plattsburg, N.Y. About 20 miles from Montreal the Cadillac left the autoroute and turned left towards the small village of Saint-Philippe. There the Cadillac made a U-turn and returned to Highway 15 and headed back to Montreal. Near Laprairie the car turned on to Marie-Victorin Boulevard and made an extensive tour before coming back to Highway 15. A traffic signal at the approach to the autoroute permitted agents to note that the woman was still driving the car and that Falgiano was in the back seat seemingly busy with something. Back on Highway 15 Falgiano and his companion once more headed for Plattsburg, and again made the detour to Saint-Philippe and back before leaving definitely this time for the U.S.

The car arrived at the border at 8:05 p.m. and crossed without incident. Soon afterwards it stopped at a garage where Falgiano made a phone call. The BNDD had now taken up the pursuit and followed the Cadillac to Tarreytown, about a dozen miles from New York, before making the interception and arrests. In the armrests of the back seat, the agents found ten kilos of heroin.

415

Falgiano was sentenced to ten years in penitentiary and three years of special probation on January 19, 1973.

For two months after this police action things were quiet. Dasti in particular seemed nervous and suspicious, as he sensed the vise slowly tightening around him. On December 13 the BNDD notified the Narcotics Squad that Pasquale Falcone seemed ready to resume talks with Dasti and had arranged to go to Montreal the next day with Gaetano Licata. The night before, Daniel Marquet had arrived in Montreal with, presumably, a stock of heroin and was staying at the *Mount-Royal Hotel.* The French central office for narcotics, whose investigation was making rapid progress, had informed the RCMP of Marquet's trip, while also requesting that he not be arrested in Montreal if that could be avoided. Such an arrest might compromise the chances, considered to be excellent, of breaking the entire ring of procurers in France. Montreal investigators agreed, for they suspected, with the BNDD, a possible Canada-U.S. conspiracy which would implicate Dasti. For that, they would have to permit the heroin to be delivered.

An RCMP surveillance team was at Dorval airport at 6 p.m. on December 14 when Falcone and Licata arrived together. One of them carried a briefcase. They took a taxi to the *Dupont and Smith* restaurant in front of the *Mount-Royal Hotel.* Dasti was waiting for them in the bar. The three men talked until 8:45 p.m. and then left in Dasti's car. The Montrealer drove his clients to the airport and went home when they left for New York.

A few hours before this meeting an incident had almost spoiled everything. During the afternoon Montreal Urban Community Police intercepted a telephone call by Frank Dasti from an Ontario Street tavern. The mafioso asked an unidentified person to go to a Frenchman's room in the *Mount-Royal Hotel* and pick up a package for him. The city police, having recognized Dasti's voice, rushed to the hotel intending to search the room and, if possible, seize the mysterious package. Fortunately a Narcotics Squad contact was on the scene and knew of the federal investigators' interest in Daniel Marquet. Sergeant Paul Sauvé arrived in time to persuade his city colleagues not to proceed with their project. The surveillance operation was then able to continue with success.

At noon on December 16, the BNDD advised the Narcotics Squad that Gaetano Licata was on his way to Montreal in a Thunderbird with a woman and a child. RCMP agents picked up his trail on the outskirts of the city about 4 p.m. but the task of following him was difficult. It had been snowing steadily since morning and visibility was almost zero. Near the *Bonaventure Hotel* agents lost sight of the trafficker and were unable to relocate him. All the parking lots in the area were checked without success. Finally the agents began checking hotels by telephone. After four or five calls it was learned that a certain L. Fresca, from the U.S., had rented room 4090 in the *Sheraton Mount-Royal Hotel.* That would be Licata; two days earlier he had used the same name when he came with Falcone to meet Dasti.

That evening Sergeant Sauvé managed to rent the adjacent room. He waited all night for Licata to show up, but in vain. He learned only later that the mafioso had rented another room in the name of his female companion who was not known to police. The next morning surveillance teams set a close watch on Dasti, which took them to the lobby of the *Sheraton Mount-Royal* and then to one of its bars where Licata was finally re-discovered. This was the first of several meetings that day, all of them in the hotel. Federal agents, who had still not found Licata's Thunderbird, concentrated on the hotel and on Dasti's movements.

On Monday morning, December 18, the first task for the surveillance teams was to check the places frequented by Dasti. At noon, his car was seen at the corner of St. Catherine and Saint-Dominique Streets. At 2:05 p.m. the Thunderbird was seen at the west entrance to the *Mount-Royal Hotel.* Licata was there with the woman and the child, a little girl of 5. He helped the porter put the two suitcases in the trunk of the car. The threesome then left, driving north to the elevated highway, then east to autoroute 40 heading towards Trois-Rivières. The agents were beginning to wonder where they were going. But at the second tollgate, as they saw Licata studying a road map, they understood that he had taken the wrong road. He asked for directions, then went into the autoroute police station. Finally, he turned back in the direction from which he had come, made the South Shore and took the Eastern Townships autoroute towards Sherbrooke. At 5 p.m. he drove off the autoroute and went to Granby. There he stopped at a garage to ask for directions and then went to eat with the woman and child in a Main Street pizzeria. During the meal he seemed not to notice the presence of police officers who had followed him from Montreal.

After supper the couple and the little girl drove off again, stopping a few minutes later at the *Motel Kiko Bar.* Licata removed the suitcases from the car and they went into the motel. It was 6:42 p.m. At 8:50 p.m. the trio left the motel with the suitcases and continued on the highway towards Sherbrooke. Twenty minutes later, at a tollbooth, Licata asked for directions to Vermont. He was told to leave the autoroute at Eastman and take Highway 39, which he did. At 11:30 p.m., after another half-hour restaurant stop, the Thunderbird and the surveillance vehicles arrived at the border gate at Highwater. At that point Licata and his companion were arrested. In one of the suitcases police found the ten kilos of pure heroin they were looking for. Brought back to Montreal, the two adults were interrogated. That quickly led to freedom for the young woman, who was totally unaware of Licata's activities. Licata was charged in Criminal Court, pleaded guilty in May 1973 and was sentenced to 25 years in penitentiary.

Meanwhile, on December 19, just a few hours after Licata had made his first appearance in Montreal court, Frank Dasti and his wife were on the road to New York. Dasti was not enthusiastic about the trip, but he had no choice. His wife insisted on spending Christmas with her parents and of the two, she always had the last word.

The BNDD, pressed to act by the RCMP which thought the time had come, showed up at the *Park Lane Hotel* the following morning and spotted Dasti in the lobby about 11 o'clock. After making a phone call, Dasti went back to his room, coming down 20 minutes later with his wife. He hailed a taxi. He and his wife got in the cab which was driven by special agent Michael Pavlick of the BNDD. A few minutes later Mrs. Dasti left her husband while she went off to do some shopping. Dasti then immediately told the driver he knew he was one of the hotel's special guards. The policeman did not deny it and began chatting with his passenger. The two men spent all afternoon together talking about Dasti's activities and relationships, while Dasti passed himself off as a professional gambler and bookie.

About 5 p.m. Pavlick took the trafficker back to the hotel and they agreed to meet later. And they did that rather soon. Less than an hour later the police agent telephoned Dasti — who suspected nothing — and asked him to meet in the lobby, pretending to have an interesting proposition for him. Dasti arrived and Pavlick, with other federal agents, arrested him on a warrant which had just been issued at Newark, New Jersey. It was a temporary indictment prepared solely to justify the detention of Dasti until the grand jury hearings. He was accused of having used, between January 1 and December 20, 1972, all the communications facilities between States, including telephone and mails, to promote the commission of an illegal act, that is, traffic in narcotics. Dasti was baffled . . . His bail was set at $250,000.

He was still in prison on February 6, 1973, when the grand jury at Newark ordered his indictment, and those of Pasquale Falcone, Joseph Averso, alias Santini, Anthony Del Vecchio, Francine and Wally Berger, Spiro Venduras and Fort Lee gangster Mattew Terrigno, on 26 separate counts.

In France, it was the turn of the central office for narcotics to strike a blow. On December 30, 1972, following a surveillance operation in cooperation with the BNDD which had led as far as Marseilles, Daniel Marquet, Claude Dewachter, Roger (Le Kik) Alboreo and Pierre Tomassi were all arrested as they prepared another shipment of 15 kilos of heroin to Montreal.

Chapter 17

Big Peroff

On January 22, 1973, Staff Sergeant Guy Houde, formerly with the RCMP Narcotics Squad but then commander of the Counterfeit Squad, got a request from the U.S. Secret Service for information on a Montreal gangster known as The Moose. The night before, an informer named Frank Peroff had been in touch with Frank Leyva, in charge of the Secret Service's liaison office in Paris. Peroff claimed to have $500,000 in false U.S. banknotes and said he could get $2 million more. The source of the fake money was said to be The Moose.

Peroff had been in Rome for the past six months on a double agent operation among international forgers. On a January day in 1973, as he strolled near the Excelsior Hotel, he happened to meet Louis Coté, an acquaintance from Montreal and a partner of his old friend Conrad Bouchard. (1) Peroff had met Bouchard in the Bahamas in 1970. They became friends as well as partners in various undertakings involving counterfeit money, receipt of stolen bonds and fraud. Bouchard's sudden arrest in January 1972 had put an end to their cooperation.

---

1. Louis Coté was one of Conrad Bouchard's most faithful sidekicks. He joined him in a series of crimes in the early sixties, notably two huge frauds of $110,000 and $269,000 and a $723,000 bank robbery. In November 1962, Coté was freed for lack of evidence in connection with the murder of the drug dealer Maurice Cloutier. In June 1972 the Quebec Liquor Control Board closed the *Café Jean-Lou* on Saint-Laurent Boulevard because Coté had taken over there. A year earlier the owner and the organist had been beaten up for refusing to pay protection to a gang of extortionists. Gerry Turenne, Lucien Rivard's former partner, later took control of the café and "suggested" to the proprietor's widow that Louis Coté should be hired as manager. It may be recalled that Turenne's *Motel Maxime* was once used by Bouchard and Louis Henri to harbor a stock of heroin.

During the chance meeting in front of the Excelsior Hotel, Coté told Peroff that Bouchard had been free on bail since the beginning of June and was anxious to link up with him again. (2) Coté took Peroff to a telephone booth and they called Bouchard, who was delighted to hear from his former colleague in the Bahamas. The two men telephoned each other several times over the next few days. During these calls Bouchard had mentioned his friend, The Moose, who was then in Amsterdam and later went to Rome with a man named Mike where they met Peroff.

The Moose and Mike told Peroff they had a stock of half a million dollars in false $100 and $50 bills and were counting on him to convert it into real money. The two gangsters added that they were not acting for Bouchard, even though they had worked for him in the past. During a recent narcotics operation, Bouchard had made an error which cost them the pretty sum of $40,000. He was trying to repair this blunder by putting them in touch with Peroff. He had given them the counterfeit money at a good price, knowing that his friend Peroff could get rid of it for them. As proof, The Moose and Mike showed Peroff $28,000 in false banknotes. Peroff accepted the deal and at a later meeting, the two cronies turned over to him the rest of the stock: $408,750.

Normally, Peroff would have had no scruples about doing this favor for Bouchard's friends, but at that time he had a problem because of his suspicious activities in Rome. He thought he was being followed and watched. Peroff feared he would be arrested while in possession of the counterfeit money, so thought it wiser to contact agent Frank Leyva whom he had worked with in the spring of 1972. He told him his story, and in exchange for a good cover, offered to cooperate with the Secret Service again. The agent agreed and put him in touch with agent Mario Cozzi in the Customs liaison office of the U.S. Embassy in Rome. Peroff was to give the fake banknotes to Cozzi.

Staff Sergeant Houde and his men in Montreal were well versed in Conrad Bouchard's counterfeiting activities. Bouchard, since his release on bail, was suspected of having chosen counterfeiting as a way of getting himself on his feet again. (3) The false $100 and $50

---

2. Bouchard's release on bail pending his heroin-trafficking trial was his fourth such release since 1969. Granted by magistrates, without taking public interest into consideration, these releases were almost authorizations to continue profiting from the rackets. In addition to bail, Bouchard managed about 50 trial postponements over the years, probably a record in Canadian judicial annals. This situation was vigorously denounced in several newspapers at the end of 1973.

bills had appeared in Montreal at the end of October and the beginning of November 1972. The arrest of two passers and the seizure of $400,000 in false $50 U.S. bills on January 3, 1973, confirmed RCMP suspicions that Bouchard was the guiding spirit behind the operation. (4)

As for his friends, The Moose and Mike, police had no doubt they were Thomas Solarick and Nicolas Silverman (Mike), two Rumanians well-placed in the Montreal underworld. Solarick was a hard nut, known as swindler, receiver, smuggler and enterprising trafficker. An old friend of Thomas Pythel and Joe Horvath, he was also on good terms with the bosses of the Cotroni clan. Silverman, for his part, was known for keeping company with Horvath's entourage. He owned some businesses, including the *Fisher Art Gallery* in Greenfield Park on the South Shore. As mentioned earlier, Solarick was owner of the restaurant *Au Vieux Montréal* where he employed Tibor Korponay, one of the accused in the Orsini affair.

This information was of the greatest interest to the U.S. Secret Service, just as the information from Peroff was of great interest to the RCMP, and particularly to the Narcotics Squad. The narcotics transaction mentioned by the informer was already known to the Montreal agents: the losses suffered by The Moose in that affair had been the work of the double agent Roger Gabeloux.

In mid-September 1972 Gabeloux had renewed contacts with the traffickers' milieu and linked up with a Corsican leader in Paris, Joe Biggi. Though he was aware of the rumors circulating about Gabeloux' double role, Biggi agreed to help him finance the purchase of ten kilos of heroin.

Three weeks later, Gabeloux showed up at the *O-K-Bec* bar and sought out the boss, Roger Mollet, who to his great surprise welcomed him with open arms. Given Mollet's receptive attitude, Gabeloux pressed his luck and asked him to call Montreal and tell

---

3. In the counterfeit racket with the right contacts, a small fortune can be amassed quickly with less risk than in drug trafficking. Putting in circulation $500,000 in false $100 or $50 bills would bring the operator profits of about $20,000. The amount of money would be manufactured in three days at a cost of $5,000 and the operator would sell the lot for five per cent of its face value. Some distributors resell the bills for 15 per cent of value, others for 30 per cent. Some sell them in financial markets at full value, realizing enormous profits.

4. One of the arrested passers was Antonio Zuccaro, 25, of the U.S. He had made the false $100 bills with funds advanced by Bouchard. On February 16, 1973, Secret Service agents exposed the clandestine printing shop at Passaic, New Jersey.

Bouchard he (Gabeloux) wished to speak to him. The contact was made and on October 20 Gabeloux went to Montreal to meet Bouchard. He explained that he had a new drug deal going and wanted to see if Joe Horvath was interested. Bouchard, who considered Little Joe a personal enemy because of an old dispute, advised Gabeloux to drop him and deal instead with his successor. This guy, said Bouchard, had been on the circuit for ten years and was just getting back into business after an interruption of four years. He paid top price of $12,000 a kilo (more than $5,400 a pound).

This friend was Solarick. He agreed to work with Gabeloux but did not want to see him in Montreal. He would meet him in Paris, for he had already arranged a trip to France to buy five kilos at Marseilles prices which he intended to ship to Quebec himself via Belgium. On the morning of November 13 Solarick was in Amsterdam and telephoned Gabeloux to arrange a meeting the following day at Lille. The two men met, along with Tony, a friend of the Montrealer, and worked out the details of their first deal. The transaction would take place in Marseilles and Solarick and his friend, if they wished, could attend at a distance. The price for the five kilos paid in advance, according to the advantageous prices quoted at Marseilles, was $22,000, that is $4,400 a kilo or $2,200 a pound. The ten other kilos, half of which were being financed by Joe Biggi, would be bought at the same price at Marseilles but were to be delivered to Montreal by Gabeloux and sold there for $12,000 a kilo. Solarick would give his share of the money to Gabeloux in Marseilles, just before the transaction.

At that time, the RCMP and the BNDD had not yet been informed of the deal. In this matter Gabeloux was not acting as a double agent. No one knew it yet, but he had decided to make some quick money by double crossing everybody. He did not intend to let the police in on anything unless he actually succeeded in obtaining the merchandise, which he strongly doubted would happen.

On his return to Paris after meeting Bouchard, Gabeloux got in touch with an old Parisian trafficker, nicknamed Pépère, who had the necessary contacts in Marseilles and agreed to provide the desired 15 kilos. (5) But this old crook had linked up with Biggi in order to cheat him. Gabeloux knew this and was preparing to cheat them first.

---

5. Pépère's real identity was never made known to the RCMP but many thought him to be Roger Coudert, the old trafficker who had often made the headlines and whose name has frequently been mentioned in this book.

On November 14, after the agreement at Lille, Gabeloux returned to Paris with Solarick and Tony, whom he introduced that night to Joe Biggi at the *Café de la Paix*. The gangsters got along well and nothing remained in the way of the transaction. The next afternoon, after a final meeting, Solarick and Tony took the road for Marseilles. The next night Gabeloux, with Biggi's $22,000, boarded the train with Pépère and two other gangsters who would act as intermediaries. About noon on November 16, Pépère went to a hotel near the Saint-Charles station to await the call from Gabeloux advising when his Montreal client would arrive with the money. The exchange was then supposed to take place in a bar. Gabeloux, however, had different plans.

One of his friends, a stranger to drug trafficking, was already waiting at the station for him with a suitcase containing 15 kilos of talcum powder. This was the junk that would be handed over to Solarick in exchange for his $22,000!

At 12:30 p.m. Gabeloux met Solarick and Tony as agreed in the lunchroom of the Saint-Charles station. The buyers were nervous and impatient. They felt uncomfortable in Marseilles. They looked as though they would really prefer to rush back to Lille immediately without even waiting for the merchandise. But since they had no intention of cancelling the transaction, they proposed instead that Gabeloux bring the stuff back by train himself, which would be safer than by car. The adventurer hastily agreed. This was beyond his wildest hopes. Before they left, the two gangsters gave him the money. The caper had succeeded. With $44,000 in his pocket, Gabeloux bowed to his luck and dropped out of circulation. (6).

On January 25, 1973, three days after the Secret Service had asked the RCMP for information about The Moose, Frank Peroff turned over $436,750 in false currency to the U.S. Customs agent in Rome, Mario Cozzi. Solarick and Silverman, who were still in

---

6. Four days after Solarick's mishap, Bouchard was arrested in Montreal, along with several other prominent underworld figures such as Jimmy Soccio, John Lia (a former manager at Frank Dasti's *Victoria Sporting Club*), and Sébastien Boucher (one of the accomplices in Lucien Rivard's escape). The arrests were made in a raid on *Les Immeubles Tempo Ltée* by the morality squad of the city police and the Commission of Inquiry into Organized Crime. This firm, as mentioned, had been the "cover" for Giuseppe (Pep) Cotroni since his release from prison in 1971. He himself had been on the premises until just a few minutes before the raid. The arrival of police interrupted a crooked card game in which the gangsters were attempting to pluck two carefree businessmen who had just made an interesting financial score. Bouchard and the other vultures had decided to take it away from them.

Rome, soon returned to Paris and then to Montreal, while keeping in touch with the double agent Peroff. As for Peroff, he was in Paris on February 2 meeting with other representatives of U.S. Customs and the BNDD. He let them know that Solarick and Silverman had come to Europe not only on a counterfeit money operation, but also on a heroin-trafficking deal. The fake money was to be used to pay the French suppliers. On January 27, before they left, they had told him that their heroin transaction was going well and that they were going back to Montreal to get the necessary money.

In view of this new information, the BNDD and U.S. Customs persuaded Peroff to work with them. That same day, from an office in the U.S. Embassy in Paris, Peroff telephoned Solarick in Montreal. Solarick advised him to stay put, because he would be going to France the next day. In Montreal the RCMP was tailing Bouchard and observed his brief meeting with Solarick. On February 3, Peroff contacted Solarick at the modest *Hotel de Rome* on Constantinople Street in Paris, near the Saint-Lazare station and met him later in a Chinese restaurant. Two other Montrealers were present: Julia Kovacz Szige, a Hungarian singer who was Silverman's girlfriend, and Kalev Amon, a Turkish immigrant. Silverman was expected soon. Amon was known to the Narcotics Squad as a henchman of the Jewish hashish trafficker, Isaac Eskanasi. (7)

On February 4, Solarick confided to Peroff that another of his partners, The Kraut, would be coming from Montreal with the rest of the money for the heroin purchase. Two days later, Solarick confirmed that the heroin would be shipped to Montreal with oil paintings purchased in Paris. The Kraut, meanwhile, had arrived: he was Werner Patek, a retainer of Joe Horvath and his friend Raymond Shephard. Solarick, Silverman and Patek were placed under surveillance on Wednesday, February 7 by agents of the French central office, the BNDD and U.S. Customs. The traffickers were travelling in a Peugeot 204 rented a week earlier by Kalev Amon. All day long, the Montrealers toured the art galleries of Paris.

---

7. Isaac Eskanasi, whose real name was Itshak Eliyahu Ashkenazi, had been interrogated by the RCMP in connection with several shipments of hashish and cocaine brought to Montreal for him by women, including the former lady ambassador from Panama. Her son, without her knowledge, was helping the trafficker by transporting drugs in his mother's diplomatic bags. After his interrogation by the RCMP, Eskanasi thought it wise to leave Canada and return to Israel.

The next morning Solarick and Silverman bought about 30 paintings of no great value in an art gallery near the *Hotel de Rome,* and brought them back to their room. Half an hour later Patek arrived on foot at the parking lot nearby where the Peugeot was parked. He took a brown leather suitcase from the trunk and went directly to Solarick's room. Silverman was already there. That was the moment the French central office agents chose to act. A score of policemen burst into the room and arrested the three traffickers who were busily removing the 20 half-kilo sacks of heroin from the suitcase. Later, Silverman's girlfriend was also arrested.

The Narcotics Squad in Montreal, informed of the coup by French police, made a raid on Kalev Amon's home. Small traces of heroin were discovered there, enough to bring charges against the trafficker. But a little later, in view of the insignificant amount of heroin found, the charges were withdrawn. In France, however, Amon was charged on the same counts as the others and on October 25, 1974, he was sentenced in absentia to the same term as Solarick, Patek and Silverman, ten years in penitentiary. (8)

After the arrests, Peroff returned to Rome where his wife and five children were living. But scarcely a week later he left on another mission, at the urgent request of BNDD and U.S. Customs agents. He arrived in Montreal on February 15 with the task of finding out from Conrad Bouchard if the 10 kilos seized at the time of Solarick's arrest constituted the whole or only a part of the heroin bought in France by the Montrealers. During his 12 days in Montreal, the double agent got no precise answer to this question, but Bouchard was seriously considering sending him to Marseilles to take delivery of an important stock of heroin directly from an illegal laboratory. The trafficker came up with this idea when Peroff led him to believe he had a pilot's licence and owned a private aircraft. (9)

Back in Rome on February 27 Peroff reported to the representatives of the BNDD and U.S. Customs and persuaded them

8. Amon went back to Europe and was arrested in Spain. As this book was being written, he was to be extradited to France.

9. Frank Peroff was seen by U.S. and Canadian police officers as a con man, a peerless bluffer, and a highly-accomplished liar. Bouchard was cut from the same cloth. This created many problems for investigators who could never be sure how much truth there was in Peroff's reports. Agents, for example, doubted the truth of the story about a large stock of heroin to be bought directly from an illegal laboratory. Whether this was Bouchard's brainchild or Peroff's made little difference, because police knew that in Marseilles at that time there was a severe drug shortage and even French traffickers were having difficulty getting supplies.

to arrange his next trip to Montreal in a private jet, which would surely impress Bouchard and his friends and convince them of the possibilities of transporting large quantities of heroin. On March 16 the double agent and his family returned to New York at the expense of the U.S. agencies, leaving behind $10,000 in unpaid bills. Peroff's extravagant life style became a bit of a problem for the police in the weeks to come. In the next three days Peroff had several telephone conversations with Bouchard and on March 20 he arrived at Dorval airport on a Lear jet piloted by two agents of U.S. Customs. The Narcotics Squad had reserved rooms at the *Martinique* and that night Bouchard and one of his partners, Claude Lemoyne, owner of *Longue Pointe Auto Body,* a small garage on Hochelaga Street, came to see the double agent in his room. After an hour or two of talk, Peroff took them to the airport and gave them a guided tour of the jet, inside and out. Bouchard was very impressed, especially when the double agent pointed out the numerous nooks and crannies in which heroin could be hidden. At the end of the evening, Bouchard arranged to meet Peroff for lunch the next day at *Moishe's Steak House* on St. Lawrence Street. This place, belonging to a former associate of Carmine Galente and of Luigi Greco at the *Bonfire* restaurant, was much-favoured by the leaders of the Montreal underworld.

On March 21, Peroff met Bouchard and Lemoyne at the restaurant and was introduced to an important person, Giuseppe (Pep) Cotroni. Cotroni was accompanied by his chauffeur and all-purpose man, Dominic Torrente. After the introductions, the discussion proceeded in Italian between Cotroni and Peroff. Peroff was subjected to close interrogation on his contacts in the international underworld and was asked about the possibilities of the Lear jet, his methods of smuggling and his plans for bringing the heroin into America. Following his instructions, Peroff stressed the point that he intended to transport the merchandise directly into the United States. Cotroni, for his part, thought about two weeks would be necessary to amass enough heroin to make the trip profitable. In the meantime he had a deal going with some Americans and he asked Peroff to stand by for a trip to Windsor. The double agent agreed, not knowing what else to do. After lunch, just before Pep left, he took the double agent aside and told him he liked him. Peroff's smooth talk had paid off.

Later that afternoon Bouchard had a talk with a Quebec City restaurant owner, which ended on a bitter note. He decided he had to go to Quebec and asked Peroff to take him there by plane. Not wanting to displease Bouchard, the double agent agreed. Late that

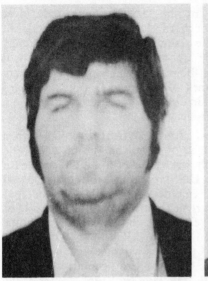

Claude Lemoyne

Louis Côté

Pep Cotroni and his trusted aide Jimmy Soccio.

429

afternoon the Lear jet, piloted by the U.S. Customs undercover agents, left Dorval carrying Bouchard, Lemoyne and Peroff. At Quebec City the meeting with the restaurant owner, Roger Dulude, lasted only an hour and the group returned to Montreal about 10 p.m. Before leaving the airport Bouchard telephoned Pep Cotroni who ordered him to deliver a stock of heroin to Detroit. Bouchard was hardly enthusiastic, but couldn't get out of it. The double agent agreed to take him there in the plane.

The next afternoon Bouchard arrived at Dorval airport with a brown leather suitcase, accompanied by Lemoyne and his old friend Louis Coté. Once in the aircraft, he asked Peroff to set the course for Windsor instead of Detroit. The Lear landed at Windsor airport at 4:35 p.m. The pilot and copilot remained on board while the four passengers were driven to the *Pizzeria Colosseo* on Ottawa street. At 5 p.m. Bouchard, alone, left the restaurant and walked to the home of a young Italian woman on nearby Gladstone Street. The surveillance team already knew that this young woman was the cousin of John Fecarotta from the U.S. who had been arrested in the Orsini affair and was out on bail. On January 17 in Montreal, the city police had stopped her for an identity check when she was with old Jimmy Soccio, Pep Cotroni's trusted aide. Feracotta's Oldsmobile was parked in front of the Gladstone Street house.

The Montrealer remained in the house for a little more than an hour and a half. About 6:55 p.m. he left, still carrying the suitcase, and joined Peroff and his accomplices in the pizzeria. They left immediately for the airport, and by 7:30 p.m. the Lear jet was en route to Montreal. At the same time, the police who had remained on surveillance at the Gladstone Street house saw Fecarotta emerge, get into his Oldsmobile and drive to a furniture store. When he left there late in the evening he was stopped by a patrol car of the city police, asked for his identification, and given a ticket for speeding. By then the double agent and his companions had already landed in Montreal. Bouchard, very nervous, drove around the city for two hours before going home, hoping to shake any police trackers. Peroff thought Bouchard had sold five kilos to Fecarotta for $30,000. The police thought the transaction had not yet taken place and that the operation had only been a preliminary meeting.

The next day the double agent returned to New York. Before leaving he reported that Bouchard was expecting a visit soon from a Frenchman to arrange final details of a shipment of 100 kilos of heroin (220 pounds). The merchandise would be destined for Fecarotta who would have $200,000 at his disposal. The heroin would then be sold to various clients in Detroit, Chicago and New

York. Once the arrangements were made, the plan called for the double agent to go to France in "his jet," with Coté and Lemoyne, to receive the merchandise and bring it to America. The method and detail of the return transport had been left to Peroff.

In the succeeding weeks Peroff called Bouchard often to keep in contact. Reports from the double agent indicated that Bouchard mainly discussed his trial, which was still being delayed, future transactions of heroin, and the means of acquiring the funds necessary to finance a big affair of 100 kilos. One of the means considered was a deal in stolen bonds. Bouchard suggested that Peroff negotiate the sale and distribution of a stock of Simpson-Sears "debentures." On police advice, Peroff declined to get involved in the stolen securities racket.

While these telephone conversations were going on, relations between Peroff and the U.S. agencies continued to deteriorate. The double agent became more and more demanding and his family's expensive tastes were aggravating police officers, who began to doubt the success of the project. For them, Peroff was just a big spoiled kid with nothing on his mind but high living.

In spite of these problems, Peroff came back to Montreal on April 25. He stayed only three days, during which he met Bouchard and his friends and telephoned Raymond Shephard, a partner of Horvath and a friend of Solarick and the two others who had been arrested with him in Paris. These arrests, in fact, were the subject of the telephone conversation, as Shephard raised the question about the possibility of Peroff being an informer. Shephard, whom Peroff knew by the nickname of "John the Doctor," said he had purchased the French police files on the Solarick case. He claimed he had seen Peroff's name, address and telephone number in the files, and wondered why Peroff had never been arrested or interrogated. But Bouchard had confidence in Peroff and finally, Shephard too was satisfied with the explanations. He even asked if it would be possible to use the Lear jet to bring back from France 40 kilos of heroin from the original stock bought by Solarick. In later meetings with Peroff between April 25 and 28, Claude Lemoyne asked him to try to find a "chemist" who could operate an illegal lab in Quebec for transforming morphine-base. In that way the Montreal traffickers need no longer be at the mercy of the Marseillais and the Corsicans.

Many an American trafficker dreamed of the day when he would no longer be dependent on supplies from overseas. But the Narcotics Squad doubted that this was the real intention of Bouchard and his gang. Agents were beginning to think that the flashy display of all these beautiful projects was only intended to maintain liaison with Peroff until he could be used in the best way at the best time. His possibilities for aerial transport were a major asset and Bouchard had already let it be known that he might want to flee the country in the plane if he lost his court battle. (10) The Lear jet was a trump card for the traffickers. Federal agents, U.S. and Canadian, were also skeptical of the talks with Bouchard about a big hashish importation.

These talks had begun at the end of April, during a meeting between Bouchard and Peroff, and were continued more seriously about the middle of May. Bouchard had proposed that Peroff go to Morocco in his plane to pick up a ton and a half of hashish and bring it back to Florida. U.S. narcotics agents hastily discouraged this project because they could not operate in Morocco. Peroff then asked Bouchard to suggest another plan and the Montrealer, who claimed to have several underworld backers for the deal, proposed Pakistan. This too was unacceptable. Pakistan was at war and neither Canadian nor U.S. agents believed government authorities there would be able to cooperate in a controlled operation. The RCMP began thinking about ending the double agent's activities and sending him back to the U.S.

Peroff came back to Montreal however, and at a meeting at Bouchard's home on May 16 he made it clear that he intended to drop the hashish project. He was Jewish and had no taste for a trip to a Moslem country. Furthermore, he would need an advance of $30,000 to fit out his plane before he could undertake any drug-transporting flight. Bouchard took the news badly. He was particularly indignant about the demand for money (which was really a police demand) and warned Peroff that the Italians would not let him get out of the deal like that. Then he relaxed a bit, not wanting to burn his bridges, and remarked that an advance of

---

10. At this time Bouchard, never much bothered by scruples, was hoping to free himself from the charges by trying to implicate federal agents in heroin trafficking, with the complicity of certain journalists. His targets were the chief investigator for the Narcotics Squad, Gilles Poissant, his colleague Staff Sergeant Paul Sauvé and the prosecutor in the case, Réjean Paul. Bouchard was convinced de Kercadio was a double agent and tried to show that the Narcotics Squad used him to set a trap and build a false case against Bouchard himself. With the help of so-called private investigators, who were no more than professional criminals and friends of the Milieu, Bouchard accused the RCMP of using public funds to buy and import narcotics. He also implied that Gilles Poissant had benefited personally from the sale of narcotics. Bouchard and his friends managed to bring this matter to the stage of preliminary hearing in criminal court, where it ended with the rejection of the false charges against the Narcotics Squad.

$10,000 might be possible. Bouchard said it might also be possible to consider a trip to Israel instead of to Pakistan, suggesting that the hashish project was only a test. The real objective was the importation of morphine-base, a project he claimed to have been working on for months.

Two days later Bouchard, Lemoyne and Coté came to get Peroff in his room at the *Seaway Hotel* and took him to a tavern for a confrontation with Thomas Solarick's nephew. The nephew accused Peroff of being responsible for his uncle's arrest. Once again the double agent had to do some fast talking, but he managed to convince his accusers that he was no informer. Police agents were alarmed by this incident. To avoid needless risk, they ordered Peroff to return to New York on the pretext that urgent repairs had to be made to his aircraft. As soon as he got back to New York, Peroff telephoned Bouchard in order to reassure him and keep the contact open. The Montrealer was in good humor. He indicated that the hashish project had been dropped, but that he and his friends were thinking of reviving the heroin operation. He said the merchandise would be picked up at a place already familiar to Peroff. That probably meant Rome. The double agent had further telephone conversations with Bouchard on May 22 and 23. By then Bouchard was talking about a shipment of 200 kilos of heroin (440 pounds) in an operation that could take place in about two weeks. The Montrealer suggested that Peroff get in touch with one of his clients in New York, James (Jimmy Legs) Episcopia, to explore possibilities of financing at that end. Episcopia was also involved in the stolen or counterfeit bond racket which Bouchard thought might be useful in obtaining funds for the heroin purchase.

Peroff joined his wife and children at the end of May in Puerto Rico, where they had been installed at the expense of U.S. Customs. Throughout June he kept in regular contact with Bouchard, without slackening his free-spending ways. On June 24 Bouchard had succeeded in getting another three-month adjournment of his trial on heroin-trafficking charges. He intended to use the time to make a financial killing with 150 kilos of heroin brought in from Rome.

The United States government made major administrative changes in its anti-narcotics forces on July 1 which, incidentally, had a considerable effect on Peroff's undercover operation with the Bouchard gang in Montreal. The U.S. created a single federal agency, the Drug Enforcement Administration (DEA) by combining the two long-time bitter rivals—the drug investigation section of the Customs Service in the Treasury Department and the Bureau of Narcotics and Dangerous Drugs (BNDD) of the Justice Department.

The new Drug Enforcement Administration, which also absorbed the former offices of Drug Abuse Law Enforcement and National Narcotics Intelligence, came under the authority of the Justice Department.

The immediate consequence of the fusion for Peroff was the change in authority over the Bouchard operation. Peroff's supervisor, agent Richard Dos Santos of U.S. Customs, got a new boss. This was John J. O'Neil, a former officer of the BNDD, who soon intervened in the double agent's action.

On July 6 Peroff telephoned Bouchard from the home of a neighbor, the DEA having temporarily suspended his own telephone service. The agent took the precaution of recording the conversation. Bouchard's words were explosive; he stated that the financier Robert Vesco would advance funds to finance the huge heroin operation he and his friends were planning. Bouchard explained that Vesco's right-hand man, the Montreal businessman Norman LeBlanc who had already been implicated in a gigantic $110 million fraud, was on close terms with one of Bouchard's partners. This partner was "like a father to LeBlanc." Bouchard added that there would be an important meeting the next day, after which Peroff's services would probably be required to pick up Vesco's money in Costa Rica.

The double agent could hardly believe his ears. He, like everybody else, knew that Vesco had been indicted in May by a federal grand jury in New York for complicity with the former Attorney General of the United States, John Mitchell, and the former Secretary of Commerce, Maurice Stans, in an attempt to influence the Securities and Exchange Commission following a $250,000 contribution to President Richard Nixon's re-election campaign. In 1972 the Securities and Exchange Commission had accused Vesco and LeBlanc of a $224 million swindle involving mutual funds of *Investors Overseas Service* (IOS). These two men together controlled a great number of firms in several Caribbean countries, including the powerful *Bahamas Commonwealth Bank* in Nassau. Peroff had previously given his opinion of Vesco to agents of U.S. Customs and the Detroit Organized Crime Strike Force. Answering questions about criminal activities in the Bahamas, Peroff described Vesco as influential and powerful, with connections in organized crime.

Bouchard's latest statements about Vesco's involvement stimulated the double agent's interest and he kept in telephone contact with the Montrealer. In these conversations Bouchard confirmed the project and asked Peroff to stand by with his plane for an early flight to Costa Rica where Norman LeBlanc was to provide a sum of $300,000. As for the Montreal gangster who was like a father to LeBlanc, Bouchard identified him as Pep Cotroni. Peroff recorded a conversation in which Bouchard said he would probably have to go to Europe himself and was trying to obtain a false passport.

DEA agents hardly knew what to think of Peroff's reports on what Bouchard was saying. The Narcotics Squad in Montreal, brought in on the affair, thought there was no truth in Bouchard's story. The agents considered it a bluff to retain Peroff's interest and to keep him available, and available particularly perhaps, in case Bouchard had to make a hasty departure from the country. (11) The U.S. agents shared this opinion, by and large, but were not quite sure what to do. It was a delicate question, with broad political implications. No one wished to become involved in the Watergate affair, or to leave himself open to possible charges of holding up a criminal investigation. Nor did anyone wish to invest time and money in a far-fetched cause.

Peroff though, was convinced or pretended to be convinced that Bouchard was telling the truth. He demanded a private plane for his use and upward revision in his remuneration. He did not want the Bahamian government to be informed of his mission because he was sure Vesco would learn about it and that would endanger him and his family. Even though DEA agents were not strong believers in Bouchard's truthfulness, the delicate nature of the investigation gave Peroff the opportunity to negotiate the same financial deal with the new agency that he had enjoyed with Customs. John O'Neil, in charge of his file, agreed to let Peroff go to Costa Rica on a commercial flight. But there would be no question of using a costly private Lear jet. The Narcotics Squad, in the meantime, let it be known they had no wish to see Peroff in Montreal just then.

On July 17 Peroff left San Juan with his family for New York. At the airport the two agents who met him reproached him for transporting his family at the expense of the service without getting prior permission. There was an argument, and finally the agents walked away leaving Peroff to fend for himself. Insulted, he went immediately to a phone booth and called the office of the special Watergate prosecutor, Archibald Cox, who was not there at the time.

---

11. On June 4, 1974, Bouchard admitted to Staff Sergeant Sauvé and Corporal Savoie of the RCMP that the whole Vesco affair was no more than a strategy to keep Peroff interested. The night the double agent called, Bouchard had just read a newspaper article on the financial manipulations of Vesco and LeBlanc. He used the information to impress Peroff and get him to play along.

The double agent settled his family into the Hilton Hotel at John F. Kennedy airport and tried again to reach Cox. He also telephoned, without success, to the offices of the commissioner and assistant commissioner of Customs Services, intending to complain about the attitude of DEA agents in the Bouchard affair. The next day, after several more attempts, he finally spoke to John R. Wing, one of the prosecutors in the Mitchell-Stans case. He described his role of double agent in detail, stressing an apparent loss of interest by DEA agents since Bouchard had mentioned Robert Vesco's name. Next Peroff called the White House to speak to J. Fred Buzhardt, President Nixon's special counsel in the Watergate affair. He was referred to Peter Grant, a Secret Service agent assigned to the protection of the president and White House officials. Peroff told his story again. Finally, on July 20, he got in touch with the Narcotics Squad in Montreal and declared that the transaction was imminent. He even claimed to have spoken to the person who would hand him the money in Costa Rica and insisted that all the arrangements had been made for the meeting.

These calls revived a few memories. They reminded some people that Peroff had been wanted in Florida since April 7, 1972, for cashing two cheques without sufficient funds. (12) New York police therefore arrested the impetuous double agent in his *Hilton Hotel* room on July 22 and took him to the Queens County house of detention. He was freed on bail three days later, thanks to the intervention of the DEA. The day after that, the new agency recognized him officially for the first time: his new code name was SC1-3-0419. On July 27 Peroff was sent to Montreal again to meet Bouchard. His instructions were precise: he must demand a $30,000 advance, claiming it was needed for repairs to his aircraft; he must establish, once and for all, the truth or falsity of Bouchard's statements and the seriousness of his intentions. Agents also wanted to find out if Bouchard was planning to leave Canada and what his immediate plans were. At the request of the Narcotics Squad, the DEA supplied Peroff with a description of a Lear jet available at Atlanta, in order to make it easier to learn about Bouchard's future projects.

About 10:30 a.m. on July 28, Bouchard and Louis Coté went to the double agent's room in the *Hotel Martinique*. The meeting lasted five hours. Bouchard was not happy about the presence of his "friend" in Montreal, and feared that would compromise the whole

---

12. The arrest warrants were later shown to be invalid, as they were related to a civil litigation, not a criminal offense.

affair. Peroff insisted that without financial help he would be unable to go to Costa Rica by plane. The machine needed repairs and there could be no flight until they were made. Bouchard said he might be able to provide $10,000. He claimed to have discovered a contact who would buy seven kilos of heroin at $10,000 each. If he could make the purchase that weekend, and sell the merchandise, he would have the money needed to repair the jet. (13) Bouchard explained that he could not ask Cotroni for the money because that might upset the negotiation with Vesco and LeBlanc. But to prove his good faith, he made several calls to various possible financiers. None of them wished to advance the money. Only one solution remained: a loan shark. Bouchard promised to get busy on that immediately. Soon after he left, in fact, Peroff got a telephone call from a man asking for the description of his aircraft.

Peroff telephoned Bouchard the next day, Sunday, and was told there were problems in raising the $10,000. But Bouchard said that by Monday noon he should be able to bring Peroff $5,000 or at the very least, $3,000. The two men arranged another meeting, but it never took place. The Narcotics Squad decided the comedy had gone on long enough and it was time to end a useless and costly exercise.

The federal agents had already warned the double agent they would not let him stretch out his stay in Montreal merely to benefit from fat fees for as long as possible. On July 30, at 10 a.m., following another fruitless call to Bouchard, Peroff was invited to pack his bags and leave Montreal immediately. Peroff called Bouchard from New York the next day, in the presence of a DEA agent. He apologized for his sudden departure which he explained by claiming that the aviation company had repossessed his Lear jet because of his financial difficulties. Bouchard was furious. He told Peroff that if he were in Montreal he'd have him taken care of. This conversation put a final end to the Bouchard narcotics investigation.

Peroff, however, kept busy in August. He took on an undercover assignment for the district attorney's office in Queens County, New York, something he had promised to do in exchange for his quick liberation the month before. Exploiting the situation, as usual, Peroff volunteered to share with judicial authorities his alleged knowledge of the sabotage of the Bouchard investigation. He made his case so

---

13. The RCMP thought this statement by Bouchard might be a trap to find out if Peroff was an informer. If Customs and police controls were tightened at the airport on the weekend, on information about the imminent arrival of a courier, that would indicate Peroff's real identity.

well that at the end of September the district attorney for the southern district of New York, Paul J. Curran, ordered an inquiry. The inquiry was to determine if the Bouchard-Vesco dossier could be re-examined and if charges of a deliberate cover-up by federal agents were well-founded. Curran's assistant, Arthur Viviani, was put in charge of the inquiry, which lasted until November 13. It did not move quickly enough for Peroff: on October 4, irked by what he considered to be undue delay, he contacted the permanent sub-committee on investigations of the Senate government operations committee. The committee, under the chairmanship of Senator Henry M. Jackson, took an immediate interest in the affair.

Peroff contacted the RCMP again at the end of October to report that Bouchard had spoken to him recently of prospects for a fake-money deal. The Counterfeit Squad, in fact, had noted a new series of counterfeit bills coming into circulation in Montreal and Bouchard was the prime suspect. Two Narcotics Squad agents used to dealing with Peroff visited him in New York and asked him to renew contacts with Bouchard. Peroff, harboring no grudges, willingly headed for Montreal.

On November 2 he met two U.S. Secret Service agents. His task would be to introduce one of them to Bouchard and the agent would do the rest. The meeting took place the next day. Bouchard and agent Dominic Germano, who was passing as a loan agent for Chase Manhattan Bank, got along well. Bouchard said he had $500,000 in counterfeit money to dispose of. He was in serious financial trouble and his legal costs were running high.

Agreement was reached at a second meeting on November 4. That evening a taxi driver was to deliver 820 counterfeit Canadian $100 bills in exchange for $2,500 in authentic money. At 7 p.m., as agreed, the messenger with the merchandise showed up at Germano's room at the *Vermont Hotel,* and was arrested by an officer from the RCMP Counterfeit Squad. Federal agents then arrested Bouchard at his home. (14)

The bail hearing a few days later after Peroff had returned to the U.S., led to the divulging of Peroff's real identity by the Secret Service agent Germano. A photo taken at Windsor airport during the visit to John Fecarotta was introduced as evidence that Bouchard had violated the terms of his previous bail. The activities

---

14. In mid-July 1975 Rolland Pannunzio was charged by the RCMP counterfeit squad with possession of instruments for the manufacture of false banknotes. His fingerprints were found on plates used to make false Canadian $100 and $50 bills.

Noise can harm
health—Page B-2

The Montreal Star

TOMORROW'S FORECAST: Cloudy, showers (Page A-4)   72 PAGES   TUESDAY, NOVEMBER 27, 1973   105th yea

We can prove it, says policeman

Cotroni 'Montreal's godfather'

By PAUL DUBOIS

Vincent Cotroni was described today as the "godfather" of the Montreal underworld.

"He is the 'Godfather' and this is not a figment of our imagination — this is fact and we can prove it," QPP Cpl. Bernard Couture told the Quebec inquiry into organized crime this morning.

Cpl. Couture, a surprise witness when the inquiry resumed today fol-

lowing a series of postponements, has been head of a special squad assigned to follow suspected underworld figures and wiretap their conversations.

"Wiretaps have permitted us to realize that Vincent Cotroni — beyond the shadow of a doubt — is the head of the local underworld," he said under questioning from special prosecutor Guy Dupre.

Cpl. Couture said that he, along

with other members of his squad, had kept close tabs on underworld suspects in the past six years. He added he was now in a position to prove that the Montreal underworld is divided into four separate organizations.

"And the heads of those organizations — the four lieutenants — report directly to Vincent Cotroni," he testified.

He said three of these groups are

headed by Paolo Violi, Nicolas (Cola) Di Iorio and Frank Cotroni. The fourth had been headed by the late Louis Greco, he added, but did not say who had taken over since Greco's death.

"From 1971 to 1972, Vincent Cotroni has met with Di Iorio and the other three lieutenants about 210 times that we knew of.

See COTRONI, Page A-2

Heroin plot alleged

Montreal men, Vesco linked

By MORTON MINTZ
© The Washington Post

WASHINGTON — An undercover narcotics worker says he was forced into hiding to protect his life after telling the White House of a scheme for smuggling 100 kilograms of heroin with the alleged financial backing of financier Robert Vesco.

The undercover man, Frank Peroff, has told his story to investigators for the Senate permanent investigations subcommittee and to a federal grand jury in New York City, informed sources said.

...learned that Peroff backed ...eedings of

C
an
wi
Ca

OTTAWA
night appealed
that mandatory
January.

He also told t
had approved a f
a gallon increas
heating oil and g
the Ottawa Valley
1

As he appeared
turn down thermos
Christmas lights, a
Mr. Macdonald w s
first phase of the g
gram to meet the e
winter.

Mr. Macdonald s
still some uncertai
to the extent of sh
ada will suffer.

But, he stated, th
...ed "that the fe

Inside
Tod

METRIC
public
Page /
SGWU
is am
EDITO
tack
GREE
agai
PERU
in
A-1
MIL
2u
SPN
Fi
M

Drug prober doubts Vesco involvement

By SUSANNA McBEE
© The Washington Post

WASHINGTON — A top government drug investigator said yesterday he has no evidence indicating that financier Robert L. Vesco planned to back a $300,000 scheme to smuggle 100 kilograms of heroin into the United States.

George Brosan, acting chief inspector of the U.S. Drug Enforcement Administration (DEA), said in an interview that he is convinced by his talks with agents working on the case that Vesco had nothing to do with such a scheme.

While Brosan said he wants to see

written reports on the investigation, he stressed: "I can't find anything indicating this guy is involved in junk."

The charge, which Vesco has called "a foul and sneaking lie," was made last summer by an informant named Frank Peroff to customs bureau agents and later to DEA agents in New York. (As of July 1, the 500-member narcotics unit of customs was merged into the newly formed DEA.)

Because the charge was not pursued, the Senate permanent subcommittee on investigations has sought to

See PROBER, Page A-2

not
n lob
oll,
b
pro
would
r
or
he k
in th
oil supp
r 125,00
e's ultim
end on
East p
could be
e over t

f the Arab
l producti
rels," Mr.
government
tion warren
ancing."
Macdonald sa
oil to Mont
t make up pa
long as the r

additional 50,
an be piped to
ent via the Po
real, and the g
sed quantities t
t markets.
Despite these arra

See WINTER, 1

Late
markets

'not easy'

The slide was halted this after...

guerr...
eration Organization.
They met in the great hall in m...

ever w

110,00

of the double agent, in fact, were getting a good deal of attention in a number of places. On November 25, the Vesco affair broke into the open and *The New York Times* revealed the nature of the inquiry conducted by the Senate permanent sub-committee on investigations. Twelve days later Viviani, heading the inquiry by the district attorney's office, concluded that the investigation into the heroin operation could not be re-opened to try to determine Vesco's possible involvement. The cover-up charges against the DEA agents were also judged to be unfounded. On December 13 a special joint committee of U.S. Customs and the DEA reached the same conclusions following an internal investigation. This committee even blamed Peroff's personal extravagances for the abandonment of the Bouchard investigation.

The Senate sub-committee produced its report in March 1975, after public hearings in the spring of 1974. The charges of a government cover-up were dismissed and the report stated there was no evidence to indicate that Vesco and LeBlanc had tried to finance a heroin transaction. The report concluded however, that Peroff was justified in saying that the conduct of U.S. federal anti-narcotic agents had been one of the main reasons for the failure of the Bouchard investigation. The sub-committee also concluded that Peroff was right in claiming that the U.S. agents had not explored the Vesco-LeBlanc lode as thoroughly as they should have.

Senator Jackson and his colleagues naturally did not extend their inquiry into the conduct of the Royal Canadian Mounted Police, and no member of the Narcotics Squad was invited to appear before the sub-committee. The report however, did raise questions about the consequences of identifying Frank Peroff in the Montreal court as a double agent and informer. However justifiable this decision was in the eyes of the Canadian authorities, said the report, to identify Peroff as an informer put his life and the lives of his family in danger. The report also reproached the administrator of the DEA, John R. Bartels Jr. for his unreserved acceptance of statements made by Bouchard during an interview with Narcotics Squad agents on June 4, 1974. The sub-committee did not declare that these statements were false, only that the DEA authorities had accepted them too readily as true.

On April 16, 1975, Narcotics Squad investigators sent a report to RCMP authorities explaining the circumstances which led to the unmasking of Peroff in the courtroom. Peroff had already agreed to testify against Bouchard if that became necessary. Réjean Paul, the prosecutor for the federal Justice department at the bail hearing, believed that Peroff had agreed to having his role divulged. He had therefore questioned the U.S. Secret Service agent on Peroff's real identity in an attempt to convince the court of the dangers of granting any further bail to Conrad Bouchard. (15) In that respect, the attempt was wholly successful.

---

15. In early 1975, Réjean Paul became chief prosecutor for the Quebec Commission of Inquiry into Organized Crime, headed by Judge Jean-L. Dutil.

Chapter 18

The Sicilian Sings

Frank Dasti finally got out of prison on bail on June 1, 1973. On that day Judge James A. Coolahan, of the federal court in Newark, New Jersey, agreed to reduction of bail from $250,000 to $100,000, and Dasti's wife and his nephew René Di Fruscia put up the required sum. Since his arrest on December 20, 1972, they had worked without cease with Joe Horvath to raise the money and to convince Dasti's friends and associates in the underworld to help him. It was no easy task because Dasti's bosses were not pleased with him. Vincent Cotroni had many meetings on this matter with his closest aides, his brother Frank, Nicola Di Iorio and Angelo Lanzo. They were not quite sure what attitude to take, according to information filtering in to the RCMP and the Quebec and Montreal police forces. Frank Cotroni was more anguished than the others: he had plunged deeply into the drug traffic with Dasti. He knew he would be cooked if Dasti talked. But Dasti was an old and ever-faithful member of the Organization. He would be much less dangerous at liberty than in a cell at the federal detention centre in New York.

On June 17, Dasti's trial, with those of his co-accused, Pasquale Falcone and the others, was put off to the autumn assizes. This was Judge Coolahan's decision, in light of the huge amount of publicity surrounding the *Columbia Records* scandal and the difficulty in finding a judge available to hear the case. Frank Dasti took advantage of the delay to return to Montreal. He had only one thing in mind: to do everything possible to avoid being returned to the United States. He was even prepared to appear before the Quebec Commission on Organized Crime (CECO) and to do whatever was necessary to earn a sentence for contempt of court.

His best hopes lay with his political connections. Dasti was a seasoned election worker, like most underworld leaders. He approached two figures in the government party — Jean-Jacques

Côté, a tavern owner and political organizer, and René Gagnon, executive assistant to the Quebec minister of immigration. His relations with these men went back to the autumn of 1969 when they were running Pierre Laporte's campaign for the leadership of the Quebec Liberal Party. The campaign was in serious financial difficulties at that time, and the organizers had called on the help of Frank Dasti and his boss, Nicola Di Iorio.

During the general election in Quebec in April 1970, Côté and Gagnon (who was an official Liberal candidate) again came to Dasti and Di Iorio for help. A meeting even took place between the mafiosi and Pierre Laporte who, though defeated for the leadership, remained a party stalwart. It was said later that Laporte did not know that the crime chiefs would be at the meeting and furthermore, that the meeting was brief. (1) Members of the Cotroni gang thought the politicians owed them something and they weren't shy about asking for payment. Their first demand was for the appointment of a man favorable to them as head of the Quebec Provincial Police morality squad. Di Iorio was being hampered by a small and diligent group of city and provincial police. He wanted an end to police raids on night clubs and gambling houses belonging to the Organization. In 1971, when his *Victoria Sporting Club* was closed, Dasti demanded quick and energetic action to quash the legal procedures taken by provincial investigators against him and his managers.

Each time, René Gagnon and Jean-Jacques Côté took steps to help their "benefactors." Political organizers, members of the legislature, judges and policemen were approached, but the hoped-for results were not attained. The main reason for failure, though the gangsters and their friends still did not know it in June 1973, was the famous Operation Vegas of the RCMP Narcotics Squad and the Quebec Provincial Police. The wiretaps, installed at first to collect information on drug trafficking and illicit gambling, also sparked police interest in people like Jean-Jacques Côté and René Gagnon as early as the fall of 1969. In May 1970, the new leaders of Quebec,

---

1. Pierre Laporte was killed in October 1970, a week after he was kidnapped by a terrorist group of the Front de Libération du Québec (FLQ). A few hours before his body was discovered, his friends René Gagnon and Jean-Jacques Coté met Frank Dasti who offered Mafia assistance to find the hostage. The Cotroni clan felt itself to be a particular target of the FLQ whose manifesto, broadcast on Radio-Canada, spoke of "the election riggers, Simard and Cotroni." René Gagnon said later than Nicola Di Iorio had told him he had been personally threatened by the FLQ. The FLQ, like many other people, knew of the help the Liberals got from Di Iorio's men in the April 1970 elections and would not forgive them for it.

Premier Robert Bourassa and his Justice Minister Jérôme Choquette, were briefed on the information so far obtained. Not wishing to provoke scandal or to tarnish the party's image of respectability, they decided not to get rid of their embarrassing colleagues, but to permit the Provincial Police to continue the investigation. (2) The Justice Minister in particular gave strong support to the police action and took steps to see that the corridor games played by Côté and Gagnon were "delicately" nullified.

On July 5, 1973, a Provincial Police surveillance team observed a meeting of Dasti, Gagnon and Côté at Côté's tavern on Côte-des-Neiges Road. The meeting ended just before noon: the mafioso and the executive assistant left the premises separately. Later testimony given at CECO hearings by two of the participants indicated that the meeting was held to discuss ways of preventing Dasti's return to the United States.

Dasti, in fact, had asked Gagnon as soon as he returned to Montreal if some means could be found through Gagnon to prevent his court appearance in the U.S. The tavern owner made some inquiries of his friend in the cabinet office and was told that nothing could be done, only the federal immigration department could intervene. The anxious Dasti wanted to speak personally to Gagnon and the tavern meeting was arranged for that purpose. Gagnon again told him plainly that he'd better get a lawyer, but also promised, so as not to upset Dasti too much, that he'd see what he could do.

But events gave Gagnon no time to do anything, and wiped out Dasti's hopes. Even as these men met in the tavern, a political bomb was exploding in the national assembly at Quebec City. Robert Burns, parliamentary leader of the Parti Québécois, revealed the ties between the Mafia and the Liberal Party and spoke of the famous meeting of April 16, 1970 attended by Pierre Laporte, the late minister of labour and immigration. These revelations followed articles in the daily newspaper Le Devoir about the existence of Operation Vegas and about the evidence it had turned up, in April and May 1971, of collusion between Cotroni clan members and the

---

2. Bourassa and Choquette said later that the decision not to remove Coté and Gagnon was taken on the recommendation of the Quebec Provincial Police special intelligence chief, Hervé Patenaude, who later became assistant director of the force. Patenaude was said to have believed that any action against the two Liberal organizers would have endangered Operation Vegas and the investigations by the Narcotics Squad. Many others believed, however, that it would have been possible, if desired, to put Jean-Jacques Coté and René Gagnon on the sidelines with no effect on police projects.

Nicola Di Iorio (left) and Vincent Cotroni (right).

Frank Dasti   *Jorge Asaf y Bala*

new Montreal police chief, Jean-Jacques Saulnier, Mayor Jean Drapeau's favorite. The Quebec Police Commission had launched an inquiry into the conduct of Chief Saulnier in the winter of 1972 following an earlier series of articles in *Le Devoir,* but the Operation Vegas tapes had not been admitted as evidence. The government was now being asked for explanations.

For the rest of the summer, attention was concentrated on the sequels to the Laporte and Saulnier affairs and on other revelations of internal problems in the police force and in the Commission of Inquiry into Organized Crime. The political climate was supercharged, and friends of the Mafia didn't dare make a move. Jean-Jacques Côté did tell Dasti on August 8 that he had met Gagnon and that "things were settling down on the U.S. affair," but this was only a bluff. The Liberal organizer was merely trying to stall Dasti's threat to tell everything he knew about political corruption if he did not get the help he was seeking. It was a desperate situation for Dasti. Even though, like most crime leaders, he shunned the limelight, he did take to granting interviews to journalists and justifying himself in public.

A last attempt was made on August 28. Harassed by Dasti, Jean-Jacques Côté agreed to arrange another meeting with René Gagnon. That night at Côté's home, the immigration minister's executive assistant met for the last time with Dasti and his boss, Di Iorio. Provincial Police detectives attached to CECO were on hand to film the meeting discreetly, part of which took place outside Côté's home. Four months later Côté testified at CECO hearings that he wanted Dasti to realize once and for all that he and Gagnon could do nothing to help him. "I wanted to end the bluff," he said. During the meeting, Dasti explained his case in detail and displayed a firm conviction that Gagnon could help him. But Gagnon told him clearly that he could do nothing, after explaining the differences between the provincial and federal immigration services. At that point Di Iorio said to Dasti: "I've been telling you for a long time that nothing can be done and that you should get a lawyer." (3) Dasti was greatly discouraged. At 58, he did not want to go to prison, perhaps never again to see his wife, who was ill. He repeated that he would make all kinds of statements against the Liberal Party if he were forced to go back to the United States.

But events continued to work against him. On September 15 *Le Devoir* revealed the details of the August 28 meeting and made

---

3. Testimony by Jean-Jacques Coté before CECO, December 19, 1973.

public for the first time Dasti's efforts to prevent his return to the U.S. for trial. The news upset the Bourassa government and the minister of immigration, Jean Bienvenue, felt obliged to suspend his executive assistant. Until then, the only step the government had taken was to ask CECO to give priority to the Laporte affair. Dasti, finding himself again in the public spotlight, panicked. He had only two weeks left before his trial. In desperation, he called the Parti Québécois member of the legislature, Robert Burns, parliamentary leader of the separatist party. Promising "hot" information on the Liberals, he asked Burns to demand his immediate appearance before CECO. He proposed to meet him the next morning. Sensing danger, Burns consulted with his friends and finally declined the offer.

Dasti had lost. On Monday, October 1, he was in Newark for his trial with Pasquale Falcone, Spiro Venduras and the sisters Francine and Wally Berger. Young Anthony Del Vecchio was the main witness for the prosecution. His testimony confirmed the numerous telephone conversations legally recorded by the BNDD (now called the DEA). The trial ended on October 11 and the jury declared all the accused guilty except for Francine Berger, who was acquitted. On October 31, Judge Frederick Lacey, who had described the accused as the garbage of the world, sentenced Dasti on three counts totalling 20 years in penitentiary. He was also fined $20,000 and subjected to special regulations in case of parole after serving 12 years. Falcone was sentenced to 10 years in prison and a fine of $10,000. The others benefited from the clemency of the court: Spiro Venduras was given two years in prison; Wally Berger got five years and Anthony Del Vecchio received a five-year suspended sentence.

Dasti's conviction created consternation among his friends and accomplices in Montreal. They wondered if the old trafficker, who felt he had been abandoned by them, would betray them. Vic and Frank Cotroni, Nicola Di Iorio and Angelo Lanzo (4) met at *Moishe's Steak House* on the evening of November 8. Dasti's Montreal lawyer, Léo-René Maranda was there too. As they were

4.   A coronary thrombosis struck Angelo Lanzo on May 19, 1974 in an apartment where he had hidden out to avoid an order to testify at CECO. Nicola Di Iorio also tried to get out of CECO's reach but was arrested in New Brunswick and later sentenced to a year in prison for refusing to testify. Vic Cotroni was given the same sentence in June 1974. Both were freed on bail while awaiting results of their challenge to the constitutionality of CECO in the Supreme Court of Canada. The Supreme Court upheld the constitutionality of the Quebec inquiry in March, 1976, which meant that the men would have to complete their sentences for contempt.

(Photo La Presse)

Frank Cotroni (shunning photographers) at the time of his arrest.

about to leave after eating, nearly a dozen Narcotics Squad agents burst into the restaurant and arrested Frank Cotroni. At the same time another team of federal investigators arrived at Guido Orsini's home and arrested him. He had been free on bail for the past year. A few hours earlier Judge James K. Hugessen of Superior Court had authorized the arrest of the two leaders on the strength of an official request from the U.S. government for their extradition in connection with a cocaine deal in December 1970 and January 1971. A federal grand jury in New York had just indicted Cotroni and Orsini, along with Dasti, Paul Oddo, Jorge Asaf y Bala, and Claudio Martinez, the courier, on the testimony of a key figure in the whole affair, the Sicilian Giuseppe (Pino) Catania. (5)

Catania had been arrested on August 20, 1973 at Houston, Texas, after he was expelled from Mexico for fraudulently disposing of his wife's jewelry. The trafficker had been en route to Italy, his country of origin, on an Air France plane, but DEA agents and Mexican police had arranged for an unscheduled stop on U.S. territory. When the plane landed, Catania was taken off and arrested. In exchange for clemency, he made a complete confession, recounting in detail his participation in six international narcotics transactions involving 330 kilos of pure heroin (726 pounds) and nine kilos of cocaine, for a total value of half a billion dollars. In the affair involving the Cotroni group, Catania supplied evidence that police had been unable to obtain mainly because of the previously-mentioned failure of the surveillance on Dasti on January 10, 1971. (6)

Here is a reconstruction of the statement Catania made to special agent Ronald E. Provencher of the DEA in Brooklyn:

> My name is Giuseppe Catania. I was born in Palermo on December 12, 1933. In 1950 I left Italy as a stowaway on a ship bound for Argentina. I worked in a garage and then in a plastics company in Buenos Aires. In 1953 I met two Neapolitans, Carlo Zippo and Michel Russo (7). In 1959 I left Buenos Aires and went to live in Santiago, Chile, for a few months and then I settled in Mexico where I worked as a salesman of clothing material. Between October 1964 and March 1966 I lived in Toronto where I also worked selling clothing and clothing material. I went back to Italy, via

---

5. A seventh man was indicted in this affair, Anthony Vanacora to whom Paul Oddo had sold cocaine.

6. See Chapter Thirteen.

7. Michel Russo's name has been mentioned several times in this book. An associate of members of Joseph Auguste Ricord's Corsican gang, he was the brother of Carmine Russo, one of the six Italian-Argentinians arrested in Montreal in December 1967.

Montreal, on March 7, 1966 and returned to Canada four months later, via New York. In November 1966 I returned to Mexico.

In Mexico in 1963 or 1964 a countryman had introduced me to Tomasso Buscetta, who was also in the clothing business. When I went to Canada, Buscetta brought me to Montreal and introduced me to Frank Cotroni, Frank Dasti and Guido Orsini. We met at the *Casanova* restaurant (8). On a visit to New York in 1966 I introduced Buscetta to Carlo Zippo. When I returned to Mexico at the end of 1966 I met Jorge Asaf y Bala and his brother Alfredo, through a Mexican industrialist in textiles. Asaf loaned me $1,600 for my business and through my association with him I learned later that he was involved in the narcotics traffic, especially with a man named Jorge Moreno Chauvet. (9)

On March 18, 1967, I went to meet Buscetta in Laredo, Texas. He had contacted me beforehand and wanted me to help him to get into Mexico City to have some plastic surgery done. I brought him to Mexico City with me and he had two operations, one on March 23 and the other in June. Then he returned to the United States. In January 1968 Asaf and I became partners in a custom shirt shop called *Camiseria Le Duc,* on Hamburgo Street in Mexico City. About a year later, around the beginning of March 1969, Asaf asked me to help him with some financial problems by contacting Buscetta to see if he would buy 25 kilos of heroin. I went to New York and made the arrangements with Tomasso who was then in the pizza business. When I got back to Mexico around the middle of March I told Asaf that Buscetta would be sending somebody down to make the final arrangements and meet the Mexican driver who would be delivering the heroin.

A few days later Buscetta telephoned me to say that Giuseppe Tramontana would be coming to meet me soon. I told Asaf and then he introduced me to Felipe Deguer who was of Arabian origin like himself. Tramontana arrived on March 21 and I introduced him to Deguer in a small restaurant near my place of business. He only stayed one day. He arranged for Deguer to deliver the merchandise to an address in Pennsylvania and then he went back to the States the next day. On March 25 Tomasso called me on the phone to say it was all over and everything had gone well. I went back to New York a month later to get the payment, but Buscetta wouldn't pay because he said the merchandise was no good and could not be sold. I met him again in June and he told me the same thing so then I went to Montreal and met Guido Orsini. He asked me if I knew anyone who could supply cocaine or heroin and I told him about my problems with Buscetta. Orsini said he would try to find a buyer for the 25 kilos. I went back to New York and told Buscetta about this possibility, but a few days later Orsini called and said he hadn't been able to find a buyer. So I went back to Mexico City.

In July Asaf introduced me to a Cuban, Alcibiades Garcia Vasquez who was willing to sell merchandise for him in New York. I met Buscetta and we

---

8. Later known as the *Villa Di Cesare.*

9. Jorge Moreno Chauvet, it may be recalled, was an associate of Paul Mondolini in Mexico in 1964 and a supplier to Lucien Rivard. He was among the co-conspirators in the Rivard affair. Asaf y Bala had been a partner of Mondolini's former boss, Antoine d'Agostino.

arranged a meeting with Tramontana in San Antonio, Texas. Finally Vasquez went to New York and at the end of the month I went back to San Antonio to get a payment of $14,000 from Buscetta's son, Antonio. I was in contact with Tomasso all summer, trying to get paid for the 25 kilos. At the end of August he told me he had sold half a kilo to Orsini and that Orsini had $4,000 for me. I went to Montreal in September and Orsini gave me the money. Before going back to Mexico in October I made a trip to Europe, first to Italy and then to Germany where I met Buscetta. When I gave the $4,000 to Asaf I told him the merchandise was bad quality and the guys were not able to sell it.

Buscetta came to see me in Mexico in February 1970. He'd just come from Spain and he told me he had obtained some heroin in Europe which should soon be arriving in Mexico. He asked me to see if Asaf could sell it for him. I talked to Asaf and he agreed. The merchandise arrived about two weeks later and I took delivery of it with Buscetta, Asaf and his brother Alfredo. There were 89 kilos. I know it was a Frenchman who sold the stuff to Tomasso because I heard him talking French several times. I even saw the guy once. A month later, when Asaf had still not found a buyer, part of the 89 kilos were delivered to New York for Buscetta by Felipe Deguer.

Tomasso went back to New York at the end of March and a few days later Carlo Zippo came to see me in Mexico City. He wanted to meet the courier who would be delivering the merchandise to him. Asaf and I introduced him to Alphonso Saucedo. The delivery was made on April 8. A couple of weeks later Asaf told me that Claudio Martinez, who already knew Buscetta and Zippo, would be leaving to deliver the remainder of the 89 kilos. Claudio left a few days later, but he had car trouble and I had to go to New York to help him. The merchandise was finally delivered and Buscetta gave me $7,000 which I gave to Asaf. Tomasso also let Asaf have nine kilos as compensation for the 25 kilos which had not been paid for. Asaf gave me a 1961 Mercedes which I sold for a profit. This was my first payment since Asaf's loss on the 25-kilo deal.

In December 1970 Asaf asked me if I could find a customer for a little cocaine he had for sale. His price was $11,000 a kilo. I knew Frank Cotroni was staying at the *Presidente Hotel* and I told Asaf I'd talk to him. I met with Cotroni and spoke to him about buying nine kilos of cocaine. He was interested but said he would have to talk to some of his friends before giving an answer. I met him again two or three days later and he said he and his friends would be interested provided the price was right and the stuff was delivered to New York. I gave him the price and said we'd deliver the merchandise. He said he would let me know soon, and at the beginning of January when we met in Mexico City again, he accepted the deal. We agreed that I would contact him in Montreal when I was ready to deliver the cocaine to New York. I told Asaf about the agreement and he said Martinez would deliver the stuff by car to New York. I made arrangements with Martinez to meet at the *Ramada Hotel* in Dallas on January 9.

I went to Montreal on about January 7 and checked in at the *Holiday Inn* on Sherbrooke Street. The next night I met Cotroni and Frank Dasti at the *Pescatore Restaurant.* Cotroni told me I was to meet his friend in New York and deliver the merchandise to him. I arranged to meet Dasti in front of the *Buitoni Restaurant* on Broadway on January 10. I went back to my hotel after this meeting and the next day I took a flight to Dallas. There were travel delays and I didn't get there till the next morning. I went to the

Ramada Hotel right away and Martinez was waiting for me with the nine kilos of cocaine he had brought in his car. We took a flight together to New York and checked into the *Taft Hotel*.

Martinez and I met Dasti at the agreed place early that evening. It was cold and we went to talk in one of the restaurants in the *Taft*. I told Dasti we were ready but he said the merchandise was to be delivered to somebody else. He got up and made a phone call and when he came back he said he would show me the guy who was to receive the cocaine in a few minutes. About half an hour later we left the restaurant and went to the hotel lobby. There Dasti pointed out the man. I know now that it was Paul Oddo. Dasti went to talk to him. Then he came back and told me to deliver the stuff to him in one hour at the *Riverside Plaza Hotel*. Dasti gave me the address before he left. I went up to our room with Martinez to get the travel bag containing the drugs. Then I took a taxi alone to the *Riverside Plaza*. Dasti was waiting for me at the entrance and gave me the room number, 718. I went up. Oddo opened the door and I quickly gave him the bag. I came back down right away and joined Dasti in the lobby. He told me he would contact me tomorrow.

Early the next morning Dasti telephoned me to ask me to meet him in the lobby. When we met he told me to go to the same place as last night to get the payment. Before I left I told Dasti that Martinez and I were leaving the *Taft* and that he could contact us later at the *Waldorf-Astoria*. Martinez and I both went to the *Riverside Plaza*. I went up alone to room 718 and Oddo gave me a shoe box containing $43,000. Later in the afternoon Dasti called me to tell me that if I wanted the rest of the money I'd have to stay in New York for a few days. I knew that Cotroni would be coming to Mexico City soon so I told Dasti to have him bring the rest of the money with him. He agreed and I took a flight back to Mexico City the next day and handed over the money to Asaf. Martinez flew back to Dallas to pick up his car.

Three days later, on January 15, Cotroni arrived and came to see me at my office. He gave me $7,000 and said the New Yorkers had complained about the quality of the stuff. He said he'd do his best to get the rest of the money for me as soon as possible. Then he left for Acapulco. I gave the $7,000 to Asaf y Bala. About a week later Orsini arrived in Mexico City and Cotroni came to meet him there. I met them in a room at the *Presidente Hotel*. Cotroni gave me another $14,000 and we talked about possible heroin deals. I told them they'd have to pay the $35,000 they still owed on the cocaine before we could talk about any more deals. I said I needed it to buy heroin in Europe. They agreed then, but they never did pay me, even though I made repeated demands for months. All I ever got was $500 from Orsini when I made a trip to Montreal in May 1972.

In July 1971 Carlo Zippo and Tomasso Buscetta stopped off to see me in Mexico. They were on their way to Rio de Janeiro from New York. Buscetta gave me $10,000 as a bond of friendship and told me they could send merchandise if we could find buyers in Mexico City. I spoke to Asaf and he said he had a good client who could take any amount of heroin. I gave Buscetta and Zippo our agreement and told them I had a good contact at the airport to smuggle the stuff in. We agreed he would call me when everything was ready. In the middle of August, they asked me to come and meet them in Rio, which I did. Tomasso had his son Benedetto with him. They asked me to go to Naples via Rome to meet a Corsican named Michel Nicoli. (10) I arrived in Naples on August 21 and early that evening, about 7:30, met Nicoli in the lobby of the *Orient Hotel.* We talked and then he introduced me to a Frenchman who later helped me prepare the shipment of 50 kilos of heroin hidden in two trunks of textile I had purchased for my business. The merchandise was addressed to Alphonso Saucedo and was to be picked up by my contact at the airport at the beginning of September. I returned to Mexico via London and Montreal. But on September 8 Zippo, who was in Mexico City too, told me there were some shipping problems in Italy. I had to go back to Naples to fix things up with Nicoli and the Frenchman and I returned to Mexico about September 30. The merchandise arrived about a week later and Saucedo picked it up. Then Zippo and I met Asaf and he gave us $450,000. Part of the money was given to Nicoli who came to Mexico a few days later, and Zippo was to send Buscetta his share through a bank transfer.

Zippo then began organizing another delivery. Around November 1971 a certain Felice Bonetti, one of Buscetta's men in South America, came to Mexico City to meet Zippo and arrange for a shipment of 120 kilos. Lucien Sarti, a Corsican, arrived a few days later to make the deal. I met him at his hotel, the *Maria Isabel,* with Zippo and Nicoli, then I went to see Asaf to find out how he wanted the delivery to be made. On the morning of November 30, as planned, Asaf's brother Alfredo parked a Ford Falcon on Hamburgo Street near Lancaster, then brought me the keys. Shortly afterwards Renzo Rogaï, one of Sarti's men, came to meet me in my office. Carlo Zippo was with me. The three of us went to Hamburgo Street and I gave the car keys to Rogaï. He drove away in the car.

Late that afternoon, as agreed, Rogaï joined Zippo and me in a snack bar. We saw Sarti and another guy, Jean-Paul Angeletti, arrive in the Ford, park it and walk away, leaving the keys on the dashboard. (11) Rogaï left us then and not long after, Alfredo came to get the car. Zippo and I went to meet Sarti at his hotel and after that I went alone to see Asaf who told me the merchandise was on its way to its destination. About a week later, Asaf began making the payments. There were about four or five of them. In all, Nicoli, Zippo and I gave Sarti $800,000. The last payment of $40,000 was given to Rogaï after Sarti had gone.

In December, Sarti telephoned me and Zippo from Rio. He was ready to send two packages by air. I gave him Saucedo's name, and contacted my friend, Antonio Hernandez of *Trans Cargo International,* so he'd be ready to receive the merchandise. The stuff arrived at the beginning of January and Saucedo went to pick it up. The two packages were taken to Alfredo's home and I went there with Zippo to check the merchandise. There were 46 kilos. Asaf payed us $332,000 and we gave $275,000 to Rogaï, according to the agreement with Sarti. On this deal and the 120-kilo deal Buscetta, Zippo,

---

10. Nicoli, one of Joseph Auguste Ricord's key men, had been wanted in the U.S. since 1968, when he skipped bail of $50,000 to avoid trial on narcotics trafficking charges. Following Ricord's imprisonment in March 1971, Nicoli reorganized the South American network with Buscetta and other members of Ricord's gang.

11. Jean-Paul Angeletti was one of Joseph Auguste Ricord's two chief lieutenants. The other was François Chiappe, called François les Grosses Lèvres (Big Lips), a good friend of Antoine Guérini of Marseilles.

Asaf y Bala and I split $500,000 equally. That was the last deal I was involved in. Sarti and Angeletti had problems with the Brazilian and Bolivian police and came to take refuge in Mexico City. Sarti proposed another 300-kilo deal but the delivery was never made. (12) In July 1972 another trafficker, Julio Juventino Lujan, offered to sell me 50 kilos of cocaine a month.

Asaf was ready to buy the stuff, but didn't want to advance the money. The transaction never took place. (13)

In Montreal Frank Cotroni and Guido Orsini appeared before Judge Ruston B. Lamb of Superior Court the day after their arrest. Sitting as extradition commissioner the judge declared that in this matter the burden of proof was reversed and that the accused must prove to the satisfaction of the court that their release on bail would be justified. The lawyers for the two men differed with this decision and applied for a writ of habeas corpus. But on November 21 Judge James Hugessen rejected their demand. In the meantime Judge Lamb accepted under reserve the affidavit signed by Catania and heard arguments from prosecution and defense. He announced his decision on December 11, 1973, ordering the extradition of Cotroni and Orsini, on grounds that the attorneys representing the U.S. authorities had established a prima facie case against the accused.

Cotroni's lawyers appealed the decision within the two-week period allowed by the law. The appeal division of Federal Court began its hearing on December 17. Orsini did not appeal the Lamb decision since his trial in Montreal had priority and if found guilty, which seemed almost certain, he would be serving his sentence in Canada. The three judges of the Federal Court confirmed the validity of Cotroni's extradition order on January 25, 1974. The only remaining hope was an appeal to the Supreme Court of Canada, for which permission had to be sought.

---

12. In Bolivia and Brazil, U.S. agents just missed Angeletti and Sarti. But through confidential information they learned of the presence of the two Corsicans in Mexico in April 1972. On the evening of April 27, Mexican police agents surrounded Sarti's refuge in a residential section of Mexico City. When the trafficker emerged from the house, police challenged him, but he refused to surrender. The Corsican was killed in the subsequent shootout. Angeletti was arrested that same night. Shortly afterwards, Sarti's girlfriend Helena Ferreira, who was being held in Brazil, confessed and provided important details leading to the arrest in October 1972 in Brazil of Michel Nicoli and two other members of his gang, François Antoine Canazzi and Christian David. David was a gangster from Bordeaux and a former collaborator of the French secret services. He was suspected of taking part in the assassination of the Moroccan leader Ben Barka, in November 1965. He was also behind the Delouette affair in the spring of 1971.

13. Most of the traffickers exposed by Giuseppe Catania were charged in various countries, but primarily in the U.S. where a federal grand jury in Brooklyn handed down two series of indictments involving a total of 25 persons.

While these steps were being taken, Cotroni polished his image. Certain obliging journalists wrote about his generosity towards the poor and towards his cellmates at Christmas and New Year's!

"It may be remembered," wrote one of them, "that Cotroni was in the habit of providing Christmas food baskets to poor families. Despite his imprisonment at 1701 Parthenais Street since November 8, he still contributed to the food baskets this year. Furthermore, Cotroni wanted his cellmates to benefit from his generosity too. He bought 50 pairs of slippers for them, a dozen transistor radios, and many Christmas stockings containing various articles for prisoners, articles aimed at brightening their Christmas celebrations. This was not the first time Cotroni has been generous to his companions in misfortune. A few years ago, when he was arrested in Acapulco, Mexico for possession of false credit cards and jailed for about two weeks, we noted that he paid for the operation on a prisoner who had been injured by a policeman and whose leg was threatened with gangrene. Cotroni also made prison life more agreeable for his cellmates by getting changes in food and entertainment. Three other Montrealers who were in the Acapulco prison at that time, and who were unknown to Cotroni until then, also enjoyed his good deeds."

Cotroni's friends and associates came readily to his aid in his fight against extradition. In bars and restaurants frequented by gangsters special collections were solicited from those who wished to give moral and financial support to their good friend Frank. Some who were not enthusiastic about donating allowed themselves to be persuaded by friendly warnings from the collectors. Several benefit dinners were also held in city bars. A $100 a plate banquet was held on April 3 at *Casa Renaldo* on Hutchison Street, one of Frank Cotroni's hang-outs. This was attended by more than 100 persons whose names were in the files of the Quebec Research Bureau on organized crime. Unfortunately for them, the police were aware of the banquet. About 10:30 p.m. fifty or so city police led by Morality Squad detectives burst into the restaurant and arrested most of the diners. Among those who spent the rest of the night in jail were: Nicodemo Cotroni, Frank's oldest son; Michel Cotroni, his brother; Paul Emile and Pierre Désormiers, his brothers-in-law; Jean Di Iorio, Nicola's son; Carlo Arena; Claude Faber; Richard Goulet; Willy Johnston; Eugène Lefort; Jean-Claude Lelièvre; André Lufty; Julio Ciamarro; Richard De Massino; Irving Goldstein; Joe Toddaro; Salvatore and Nicodemo Macei; Georges Cherry; Réal Morency; Philippe Pandolfi, and many others. Most were freed after questioning.

Rumors had been circulating for the past two weeks about an open contract said to have been issued for the assassination of Pino Catania. As a result, DEA agents and U.S. federal marshals had set up exceptionally strong surveillance and protection.

On April 11 Judge James Hugessen in Montreal rejected a second application for habeas corpus by Cotroni's lawyers. On April 29 in Ottawa, the Supreme Court granted permission to appeal the extradition order but only on one of the two counts, the charge of conspiracy. Judges sitting as extradition commissioners had often held that conspiracy was an extraditable offense within the terms of the U.S.-Canadian treaty on extradition. But no appeal court in Canada had ever been called upon to confirm or set aside those decisions. The highest court in the land therefore decided to take this opportunity of examining the question in more depth, since it also concerned the cases of several other Canadian traffickers wanted in the United States. But the Supreme Court refused Cotroni permission to appeal on the cocaine trafficking charge. No matter how the Court ruled on the conspiracy question therefore, Cotroni was going to be extradited to the U.S. to stand trial. His half-victory was merely a stay of the U.S. proceedings, though a prolonged one, for the Supreme Court began its hearings on the matter only in the autumn and its decision was not expected until early in 1975.

When the decision did come, the Montreal underworld was in mourning. Little Joe Horvath had died of throat cancer in Saint-Luc Hospital the night before. He was 45. There was a kind of irony in the fact that all of Horvath's narcotics enterprises had just been exposed and dismantled by the RCMP and the DEA. He had been arrested by the RCMP Narcotics Squad for the second time on March 1 for extradition to the U.S. on charges of trafficking in heroin and cocaine. A federal grand jury in Milwaukee, Wisconsin had indicted him on February 26, 1974 for conspiracy to traffic in narcotics with his Montreal partner Raymond Shephard, his Vancouver friends George William Turner and the brothers Douglas and Donald Palmer and some of their men, and the two U.S. buyers, Albert and Gudrum Herrman. The offenses were said to have been committed by Horvath and Shephard between October 10, 1972 and February 1, 1973, at Milwaukee and Montreal. (14) Hospitalized after his arrest, Horvath could not meet the requirements for bail.

---

14. On May 31, 1974, Judge James Hugessen rejected an extradition request for the habitual criminal Raymond Shephard, stating that the evidence to be presented against him would be insufficient to warrant a guilty verdict by a jury in Canada.

To add to Horvath's worries, Sessions Court in Montreal had rejected, a week before this arrest, his motion for a withdrawal of the charges of international trafficking in hashish laid against him in May 1972 by the Narcotics Squad. Three of his accomplices in the hashish affair had already been sentenced to prison and his trial was to start on April 10. It was postponed however, because of his illness. Federal agents, meanwhile, had just received information that Horvath had revived his hashish trafficking ring. Since the beginning of November 1973 he had brought 11 shipments into Montreal totalling 850 kilos or 1,870 pounds.

During a routine check at Dorval airport on February 22, 1974, the hashish section of the Narcotics Squad, under Sergeant John Leduc, discovered four cartons in the warehouse of an import-export firm called *Emery Air Freight*. The boxes contained 148 kilos (325 pounds) of cannabis derivative. They had arrived from Amsterdam two days earlier, supposedly containing textiles for a company called *Wilkinson Agency* on Bleury Street. A quick police check showed that this company did not exist. The agents waited for two weeks for someone to claim the merchandise and then contacted Dutch police for a check on the sender listed on the shipping documents, a certain M.S. Felman, of 20 Bloemgracht Street in Amsterdam. This turned out to be a fictitious address, but it was learned that Felman had already shipped ten similar cargos since November 1973 to various Montreal firms. The RCMP investigation showed that none of these companies existed. Furthermore, neither Felman nor any of the receiving companies was listed in the central files of the Customs service. This led to the suspicion that an employee of *Emery Air Freight* was in league with the traffickers. Informers advised the Narcotics Squad that Horvath was the organizer of these shipments. A detail from Horvath's May 1972 trial was then recalled, when it was proved that the hashish involved at that time had also been brought to Montreal through *Emery Air Freight*.

The evidence was based largely on the statement by a U.S. trafficker Albert Herrman who was cooperating with the DEA in exchange for favorable treatment. In the U.S. such promises of clemency were frequent and accepted by the courts. Judge Hugessen ruled that such practices should not be tolerated in Canada. This book demonstrates however, that the practice is one of the most effective weapons against international traffickers. It brought about the arrest in Milwaukee of George William Turner, who was found guilty by a jury. (He managed to flee the U.S. however.) In Vancouver, to avoid problems with extradition, the RCMP brought new charges against the Palmer brothers and their henchmen, then called in the DEA's cooperating witness to testify in Canada. This tactic led to the conviction of Palmer and his accomplices in April 1976.

Lucien Rivard is greeted by journalists at Dorval airport upon his release from prison, January 17, 1975.

Edwin Pearson   *Raymond Sheppard*

Horvath played his role right to the end. He called Narcotics Squad investigators to his hospital bed and told them he was ready to make a full confession. In fact, he was hoping to take upon himself all the blame for the Milwaukee charges in order to clear his accomplices. But he died without managing to do that.

A week after Horvath's death, another unexpected event surprised the Montreal drug-trafficking world. Guido Orsini made an about-face before Judge Yves Mayrand and pleaded guilty to the charges of trafficking in heroin laid against him in July 1972. The French trafficker Jean-Pierre Buffa had been the first to confess in November 1972 and had been sentenced to 20 years in prison. He tried later to re-open his case, claiming that he had not acted as a drug trafficker but as an auxiliary to an RCMP double agent. It didn't work. The Appeal Court was not taken in by Buffa's claims. Orsini tried a similar ploy in asking for the clemency of the court. According to his lawyer, Orsini was merely the helpless victim of two double agents — Buffa and de Kercadio — who had incited him and seduced him into crime. Besides, Orsini was said to be suffering from an incurable illness, a cancer of the bladder for which he had been under treatment since 1970.

The judge handed down Orsini's sentence on July 3, 1974: 22 years in prison. "It is evident that a police informer had succeeded beforehand in infiltrating this organization," said the judge. "But whether or not there was a double agent in no way diminishes the responsibility of the accused and his consent to continuing and concluding the transaction. In this type of case, the police must frequently resort to the use of double agents..." Four months earlier, Conrad Bouchard who had also been caught in the net of a double agent, had been sentenced to life imprisonment. (15)

The other suspects in the Orsini affair were dealt with later. Frank Cotroni's case came before the Supreme Court of Canada on October 7, 1974 and on the 23rd the decision was handed down. The nine judges of the highest court ruled unanimously that conspiracy is

---

15. In France, six weeks after Bouchard's conviction, the central office for narcotics and the DEA struck a hard blow by arresting the Marseillais Joseph Boldrini, 63, and Etienne Matteuci, 53, following seizure of 20 kilos of heroin in a baggage locker at the Gare de l'Est in Paris. These two Corsicans were known to be heroin suppliers to The Lame One, (René Quintin de Kercadio) and to the double agent Roger Gabeloux. A third trafficker, Jacques Lacoste, 50, of Paris, was also arrested in this roundup. Two others, Jérôme Leca, Boldrini's old henchman, and Roger Gosselin, managed to escape. The first three were sentenced on June 18, 1975 to terms of 12 to 17 years in prison while the two others, still on the loose, were sentenced in absentia to 15 years each.

an extraditable offense under the U.S.-Canada treaty and therefore the appellant's claim was rejected. Immediately following the decision, Staff Sergeant Paul Sauvé and Corporal Claude Savoie of the Narcotics Squad and two agents from the DEA collected Cotroni from the Parthenais Street detention centre and escorted him quietly to Dorval airport. In New York, Cotroni appeared before chief judge Jacob Mishler of the federal court for the district of Brooklyn who fixed a trial date in mid-November. Bail was set at $1,500,000. Cotroni pleaded not guilty. Unable to post the bail money, he was taken to cells.

Judge Mishler began preliminary proceedings on November 16, which centred mainly on the admissibility of 17 telephone conversations recorded by Quebec Provincial Police technicians during Operation Vegas. Cotroni's lawyers, who included the celebrated Moses Polakoff, formerly Lucky Luciano's lawyer, strenuously objected to the introduction of the tapes. The defense lawyers were even preparing to have criminal charges brought against the Provincial Police in Montreal in an attempt to have the wiretap records first introduced as evidence in Canada. That would delay the start of the New York trial which had been set for January 6. The tactic would also bring Cotroni temporary freedom as a result of the reduction in bail which would be required by U.S. law. The law in general prevents the continued detention of a suspect if court proceedings have not begun within two months. This defense strategy did not succeed. The Montreal judge dealing with the matter rejected the complaint signed by the wife of Frank Dasti who was one of the men charged with Cotroni. Judge Mishler accepted the legality of the Operation Vegas recordings and the New York trial began on the scheduled date with Pino Catania's shattering testimony. (16)

---

16. Another trafficker who had become an informer for the DEA, George Stewart, also testified at Cotroni's trial. He had been arrested for narcotics trafficking in 1970 and in January 1971 was working as a double agent among wholesalers and distributors of cocaine and heroin in New York. He had then been in on a cocaine transaction between James Altamura, Joseph Cordovano and Alvin Lee Bynum, a big wholesaler. After Frank Cotroni's extradition in November 1974 a DEA agent who had worked with Stewart studied the wiretaps from Operation Vegas. He discovered, noting the conversations about the bad quality of a cocaine shipment, that the merchandise sold by Cordovano and Bynum was in fact the same merchandise previously sold by Cotroni and Dasti to the Oddo-Vanacora team. These last two had passed the drug on to their friend Altamura, who in turn had passed it to Cordovano. It was Altamura in fact, who came to Montreal on January 14, 1971 to hand over the first $7,000 which Cotroni gave to Pino Catania in Mexico. Thanks to Stewart and Catania, the agents were able to arrest traffickers at every link in the smuggling chain, from the Mexican supplier Jorge Asaf y Bala to the New York wholesaler, Alvin Lee Bynum.

The defense tried everything to discredit and intimidate the witness, but without success. Through the work of Edwin Pearson, a Montreal private investigator who had already been mixed up in Conrad Bouchard's efforts to discredit the chief investigator for the Narcotics Squad, certain photographs and two letters were introduced in court by the defense. Catania had sent these recently to his wife and daughter in Mexico but they had never reached them. Since these documents appeared to have been stolen from the postal services, Judge Mishler raised questions in open court about Edwin Pearson's role. He even considered summoning Pearson immediately before a grand jury to get to the bottom of the matter. The incident ended there, however, for the Montrealer had made a hasty departure from the Brooklyn court house. The trial lasted nine days and on the evening of January 21, the 12 jurors pronounced verdicts of guilty against Cotroni and Dasti.

The two men were sentenced on March 24. Frank Cotroni, 44, was sentenced to 15 years in prison and a fine of $20,000. Dasti was also given a 15-year sentence, which did not affect his situation as he was already serving a 20-year sentence for trafficking in heroin. Judge Mishler, in pronouncing sentence, noted that he had not taken into account a pre-sentence report describing Frank Cotroni as one of the most important Mafia figures in Canada. He had similarly set aside about 40 letters from Quebec businessmen, religious organizations and a journalist describing the donations made by Cotroni to various works of charity. (17) The judge declared that he had been guided simply by the evidence presented to the court, which demonstrated that Cotroni was the leader of this drug-trafficking network. He had also given no weight to a letter sent by a juror six weeks after the trial. This juror, a woman, affirmed that after long reflection she no longer believed the accused were guilty.

Before sentence was pronounced, Cotroni himself addressed the judge:

"I'm no saint, but I swear to you that I'm no bum either. I never took part in drug trafficking. I'm a good father of a family and if I'm sent to prison my home could break up. I've been married for 22 years and I'm a good father of a family. I have six children, three of them still very young. The older ones, two boys and a girl, had to

---

17. In the hours preceding the sentencing, several devout members of Montreal's Italian colony gathered together to implore divine intervention on behalf of the youngest Cotroni boy.

quit school because of all the bad publicity about me. My oldest boy is getting married soon and I'd like to be there to stand up with him as his father. (18) I've been kept in prison now for 17 months already and in my case that's as hard as five or six years in prison. If you decide to put me in jail, I wish you would order that they put me in a prison near the Canadian border so I can be closer to my family. In closing, if I didn't testify at my trial, it was because I wanted to avoid problems with the income tax guys ..."

In U.S. law, prisoners become eligible for parole after serving one-third of their sentence. But in practice most of those convicted of offenses related to organized crime are not granted parole before serving two-thirds of their sentence. That meant that Frank Cotroni would be in jail for five to ten years and would not return to Quebec before 1980, perhaps not before 1985, unless, of course, the Court of Appeal, where Cotroni's lawyers continued his legal battle, altered the Mishler judgment.

On March 16 Anthony Vanacora was sentenced to four years in prison on each of two counts of purchasing cocaine from Paul Oddo and tax evasion. Oddo, who like Dasti had already been convicted, was unable to stand trial because he was suffering from cancer. Jorge Asaf y Bala was still waiting in a Mexican prison for his extradition to the U.S. As for Giuseppe (Pino) Catania, who was liable for a 20-year term in prison, he received a five-year suspended sentence at the hands of Judge Mishler.

---

18. Frank's oldest son, Nicodemo Cotroni, married Bob Tremblay's daughter in the summer of 1975. Tremblay was chief lieutenant to Lucien Rivard who was released from prison on January 17, 1975. Rivard returned to Montreal and immediately re-established links with his old friends, and particularly with Tremblay.

Chapter 19

A Rather Violent Business

The smashing of the Frank Cotroni ring, not surprisingly, was only a step in the long march against international drug traffickers. For the Narcotics Squad it meant no more than a brief pause; its members knew that broken rings always re-formed and re-connected.

On October 1, 1973, a month before Frank Cotroni was indicted, an undercover operation among Montreal heroin and cocaine pushers led to the arrest of 20 people, most of them black. Among them were several well-known procurers like Charlie Chase, a former Canadian boxing champion, George Desmond, Gordon Griffith and Howard Jones.

On January 12, 1974, a Puerto Rican gang leader from New York named Ramon Ramirez, alias Ramon Ortiz, was arrested near the Blackpool border post as he returned to the U.S. with four kilos of heroin in the spare tire of his elegant Jaguar. Ramirez had entered Canada that morning and had been shadowed by an RCMP team led by Sergeant Léonard Massé, on a tip from the DEA. He first went to a South Shore motel and the apparently met his Monteal supplier. The supplier was not arrested because the surveillance team did not observe the actual transaction. The federal agents kept watch on the motel, thinking their man was still inside. They realized their error several hours later when Ramirez returned to the hotel by taxi, carrying a package. His later arrest and the seizure of the heroin was followed by an investigation on his application for bail, which revealed Ramirez to be a good friend of Walter Guay, who was linked to Bob Tremblay, who in turn was closely linked to Lucien Rivard. The New Yorker, in fact, had been known to the RCMP since June 1972.

Three and a half months later, on April 22, 1974, two young Montrealers named Michel Angell and Jean-Claude Renaud were

465

arrested after receiving two pounds of heroin sent from Thailand in two pairs of skis. The Narcotics Squad knew that the drugs had been destined for two leaders of the Satan's Choice motorcycle gang (1) and for a member of the Cotroni organization who was arrested a few months later when a hashish-trafficking ring was broken up.

Imports of French heroin into Canada had greatly diminished since the arrests of the big men in Montreal. Indispensable contacts with the French underworld had been cut off and in addition, the European networks were facing serious problems themselves. A series of arrests had hampered the activities of the French rings and there was also a severe shortage of primary material. The Turkish government had restricted production of the opium poppy after repeated pressures from U.S. authorities who estimated that 80 per cent of the 10 to 13 tons of heroin consumed annually in the United States was manufactured in Marseilles from opium poppies grown in Turkish fields. (2) Lately, large quantities of heroin from south-east Asia had been appearing on the market in Europe, Montreal and elsewhere in America, originating primarily in the famous golden triangle, the border regions of Burma, Laos and Thailand.

The seizure of the kilo of heroin in the skis led to a combined operation by the RCMP and the anti-drug section of the Thailand police. On June 21, 1974 three persons were arrested in Bangkok: Jonal Ricky Nicols, a Montreal addict turned pusher and then international trafficker; his girlfriend Holly Linn Hislot; and a Thai gangster named Sam Viriyanet. Six ounces of number 4 white heroin were seized at the same time. (3) Nicols, linked up with young recruits to the Cotroni organization, was on his fifth heroin-buying

---

1. Satan's Choice was a gang of tough bikers solidly entrenched in narcotics traffic of all kinds, and in league with Joe Horvath.

2. On June 29, 1971, when the Turkish government published its annual list of provinces authorized to plant the opium poppy, it came as a surprise to the peasant growers. The government authorized plantings in only four provinces, instead of seven as in the previous year. And it also decreed that the 1972 harvest would be the last in Turkey. From the autumn of 1972 it would be forbidden to cultivate the opium poppy or produce opium.

3. In south-east Asia, clandestine laboratories produced two kinds of heroin: the white, number 4, has at least 90 per cent purity; the purple or brownish, number 3 (rock heroin or brown sugar), is much less pure. This distinction only exists in south-east Asia, as European illegal labs produce only white heroin. Mexico, however, also produced brown heroin with a degree of purity, at the source, of only 60 to 70 per cent.

Gordon Griffith

Howard Jones

Charlie Chase

Richard Nicols

Wayne Martin

Ernesto Nitolo

trip to Thailand. Like many others, he had been tempted by the incredibly low prices in the producing countries. (4)

These arrests gave rise to other developments. On January 30, 1975, four young Italian-Quebecers were arrested, including the apparent leader, Ernesto Nitolo. An RCMP undercover agent passing as a Toronto trafficker had succeeded in purchasing four lots of Thailand heroin number 4 valued at about half a million dollars.

At the end of April 1975, after Nicols had been sentenced to ten years in prison in Bangkok, four of his accomplices were arrested in Montreal for helping him sell heroin and cocaine to another RCMP undercover agent in January 1974: Janet Murray, a girlfriend of Nicols; Kenny Terreskowiz, a friend of the brothers Wayne and Ronald Turner who were arrested with the gang of black procurers in October 1973; Michael O'Connor; and Steve Roseberg who, unwittingly, had introduced the police agent to the others after meeting him in Toronto. Roseberg's friend, Hamid Reza Manousheri, was arrested on March 29, 1974 in possession of a pound of heroin imported from Iran a couple of weeks earlier.

Another Montreal addict, Wayne Martin, went to Bangkok on June 4, 1975. Over the previous two years he had made nearly a dozen similar trips. Like Nicols, he was associated with the Satan's Choice leaders and with a Halifax gang. On this trip he bought four ounces of white heroin on his arrival and mailed it immediately to Quebec. Anti-narcotics agents of the Bangkok police and two RCMP detectives had Martin under surveillance. He was arrested on June 18 after buying another three ounces of heroin from two Chinese women who had brought the merchandise from the Chonburi region (favored by Thai traffickers because of the presence of "rich" Americans). In Montreal, police seized two more ounces sent by mail, to go with the three ounces confiscated at Dorval airport on May 19 from a young Halifax woman who Martin had recruited as a courier in Amsterdam. In February 1976 Martin was sentenced to four years in prison in Thailand. A month later in Montreal his wife, a heroin addict like him, was sentenced to ten years in prison for conspiracy in his importing ring.

---

4. In Thailand an ounce of number 4 heroin sells for $100. The Montreal trafficker mixes one ounce of heroin with lactose to get five ounces which he sells for about $2,400 each, for a gross profit of about $10,000. Intermediaries cut the heroin again, tripling its volume and producing 224 grams at $120 each or 896 "spoons" at $45 each. The ounce of heroin bought for $100 in Bangkok therefore has a street value in Montreal of more than $40,000.

In Europe the Dutch capital had replaced Marseilles as the hub of the international traffic in heroin, and holding the upper hand were the leaders in the Chinese quarter of Amsterdam, along with the great chieftains of the Hong Kong crime world. (5) Most of the important Chinese traffickers were members of the Tch'ao-Tcheou sect, a community in south-east China on the border of Canton and Foukien provinces. Their organization resembled those of the Mafia families and the Corsican gangs: they exerted comparable political and economic influence, were united by cultural ties and dialect, and remained in contact with each other despite their dispersion in the Chinatowns of big cities all over the world. With other Chinese organizations, the Tch'ao-Tcheou dominated the networks for collection, manufacture and distribution of opiates through south-east Asia. Before the Second World War a good part of the North American traffic in opium and its derivatives was in the hands of Chinese leaders on the Pacific Coast who were supplied by Chinese sailors working on merchant ships. After the war south-east Asia became a negligible source of supply for two main reasons: the competition from European heroin and the difficulty of coordinating Chinese suppliers and white distributors. In recent years the crackdown on European suppliers and the shortage of low-cost opiates from the Middle East had removed the first obstacle to Asian sources, while the U.S. presence in south-east Asia removed the second.

On July 3, 1975, a 26-year-old Dutchman named Eric Jan Doorn was arrested at Dorval airport when Narcotics Squad agents opened some of his cigarette packages and found two and a half ounces of number 3 brown heroin and an ounce of number 4 heroin. Doorn had actually arrived from Amsterdam two days earlier and had been detained by Immigration officers who judged that the $90 he had was insufficient for the stay he intended to make in Quebec. It was while he was being held for deportation that RCMP investigators were called in.

---

5. In recent years, Hong Kong traffickers have linked up with countrymen in Vancouver to establish an important heroin network. On March 28, 1975 the Vancouver section of the Narcotics Squad arrested two men, one of them a 42-year-old Chinese named Fook Hing Clifford Jung, in connection with a heroin seizure of 8½ pounds. The drug had been concealed in 36 batteries shipped from Hong Kong. On September 21, 1975 King Sing Tai, 21, of Hong Kong, was arrested in Vancouver carrying four pounds of number 3 heroin. The RCMP and Vancouver police also arrested six other people, including a woman, over the next few days. All were charged with conspiracy to import heroin. The Hong Kong–Vancouver heroin connection, according to Narcotics Squad specialists, was the most active in Canada as this book was being published.

The latest significant intervention by the Narcotics Squad in Montreal, on the international trafficking level, came on February 26, 1976. On that day two foreign travelers, Joseph Muraro, 27, an Australian, and Neils Christian Severin, 27, a Dane, were arrested as police seized a pound and half of pure Thai heroin. The merchandise had a street value of $15 million, because of the current shortage, which made it the most important seizure by Montreal federal agents since the arrest of the Puerto Rican Ramon Ramirez on January 14, 1974. The two suspects had only recently arrived in Canada, but had been quickly spotted through the RCMP's contacts among traffickers and heroin users. Close police surveillance led to raids on a safety deposit box at the *Toronto-Dominion Bank* at University and de Maisonneuve Streets and on the Peel Street apartments of the Dane and the Australian.

Despite this seizure, heroin was still available on the Montreal market and the Asiatic network continued to feed the 700 to 1,000 local heroin addicts, and the other 15,000 scattered across Canada, especially in Vancouver and Toronto. Other small-time Montreal traffickers were still going overseas − directly to Bangkok or Amsterdam − to buy small amounts of Thai heroin.

Furthermore, (and this was of great interest to the Narcotics Squad, the DEA and the French central office for narcotics,) many big-time Montreal traffickers had recently re-established their links with French and Italian colleagues. The Turkish government, angered by U.S. policy in the Cypriot crisis of 1974, had again authorized the cultivation of opium poppies. Much of the first new harvest in the summer of 1975 had certainly gone to illegal laboratories in the south of France, despite government controls on the crop. The Franco-Quebecois connections could soon be expected to resume their activities. There were reasons to believe, however, that from then on these networks would be better organized and more difficult to expose.

In the meantime, traffic in other drugs was in high gear. Hashish, for example, was always in demand. Its popularity had been increasing steadily for the past ten years and many a crime chief had followed Joe Horvath's example by investing a lot of money and energy in the business. The number two man in the local Mafia, Luigi Greco, lost $200,000 in March 1972 when British Customs officers seized 3,395 pounds of hashish in the port of Manchester. (6) This seizure was followed by a Narcotics Squad

6. Luigi Greco was accidentally killed a few months later, on December 7, 1972, as he and some workers were replacing the floor of his pizzeria. The funeral, as tradition prescribed, was the occasion for an impressive gathering of the cream of

operation in Montreal and Lebanon which led to the arrest of 12 persons, including some well-known in the Frank Cotroni entourage, such as Albert Numi, alias Albert Di Carlo, and his brother-in-law Frank Zaurini. (7)

This affair began on March 6, 1972, with a telephone call from British Customs officer Sam Charles, who had found the 3,395 pounds of hashish three days earlier while inspecting a container. The drug, with a street value of more than $15 million, was contained in 260 cases of tinned fruit on the freighter *SS Manchester Crusader* which had left Beirut on January 25. The cargo was destined for a Montreal firm, *Oriental Food Importing* on Montcalm Street and came from a Lebanese shipping firm, *Beirut Trading Agency and Commission.* The *Oriental Food Importing* company was a fiction, as was soon discovered by Sergeant Gilles Favreau and his men in the hashish section of the Narcotics Squad. It was decided to permit the normal delivery of the cargo to Montreal, after most of the hashish hidden in the cases had been removed. Only 35 pounds of the drug was left intact, and the freighter resumed its journey on the night of March 7-8.

As the ship steamed towards Montreal, federal agents visited the customs broker engaged for clearing the cargo through customs and learned that the duty had been paid 16 days earlier by a certain Harry. The person had left a telephone number, 728-0582, where he could be reached when the merchandise arrived. This was the number of an infamous discotheque, *The Flip Bar,* on Papineau Avenue, owned buy Luigi Greco's nephew, Tony Carbone. (8) The agents were told that the merchandise, after clearing customs, was to be delivered to the *Alberjac Company,* whose Masson Street address

---

the underworld. Greco's protégé, Conrad Bouchard paid his last respects in a noteworthy way by singing Schubert's moving "Ave Maria" at the religious ceremony.

7. Frank Zaurini had been acquitted of grievous assault in January 1955 and convicted of keeping a gambling house in February 1964. But he attracted more attention over incidents involving Frank Cotroni and his henchmen. In November 1967, a hotel porter was murdered and two of Cotroni's men, Jacques Pacetti and Claude Faber, were called to testify at the coroner's inquest. The two men, through their lawyers, presented the alibi that at the time of the murder they had been attending a celebration for one of their friends. Zaurini and Albert Numi had also attended the reception. In June 1970, another party gathering of Frank Cotroni's friends was interrupted by police, and Zaurini was among the guests. Both these festive occasions were held at the *Renaldo* restaurant on Saint-Hubert Street, owned by a friend of the Cotronis, Philippe Pandolfi.

8. Tony Carbone was known to police as one of Paolo Violi's men. Violi in turn was Vic Cotroni's chief lieutenant and considered the dauphin of the organization.

corresponded with the rear entrance of another firm, *Vincent Packing Inc.* Frank Zaurini, it was learned later, was an invisible partner in *Vincent Packing.*

The *Manchester Crusader* anchored in the Port of Montreal on March 18, 1972, and the RCMP immediately established a special surveillance. Two days later, a police officer pretending to be a transport company representative, called *The Flip Bar* and asked to speak to Harry. At that moment a secretary from the Narcotics Squad office who had agreed to play the role of secret agent was sitting in the bar not far from the telephone. She was to observe the man who answered the telephone, Tony Carbone. Carbone told the caller that Harry was not there, and then took the message: the cases of tinned goods would be delivered that afternoon.

The truck driver transporting the cargo was accompanied by a federal agent, while other agents took up positions to observe the delivery at the rear of *Vincent Packing.* It was then that Zaurini and Numi were spotted for the first time. Numi, with two of the owners and two helpers, unloaded the cases, while Zaurini patrolled the area obviously watching for signs of police surveillance. When the delivery truck left, some of the cases were loaded on to a small truck belonging to one of Numi's helpers and taken to the home of his brother-in-law, Primo Salcito. (9)

Shortly after midnight, while several of the suspects were celebrating in a restaurant, the RCMP moved in. The remaining 35 pounds of hashish were seized in the cases stored at Salcito's place, and all the suspected accomplices were arrested, except for Carbone and Greco.

They were all released on bail over the next few weeks, but the investigation continued in an attempt to identify and charge the

---

The *Flip Bar,* known as a hang-out for drug traffickers and an important distribution centre, was closed a few months later by the Quebec Liquor Control Board after a public inquiry on this affair. On November 20, 1975, Carbone was publicly questioned on his relations with Violi when he appeared before the Quebec Commission on Organized Crime.

9. Don Salcito, Primo's brother, was the Montreal leader of the Hotel and Restaurant Employees and Bartenders International Union (AFL-CIO/CLC), Local 120. Tony Carbone, in his testimony before the Quebec Commission on Organized Crime, admitted that he and Paolo Violi had helped this union to organize workers in several establishments in Saint-Léonard, one of the fiefs of the Montreal Mafia. Primo Salcito himself had been seen several times with Paolo Violi. At the beginning of 1976, following numerous complaints of improper activities, the Quebec Federation of Labor vainly attempted to conduct an internal inquiry into the affairs of this union.

Frank Zaurini

Albert Numi

Hassib Mefrige

Tony Carbone

Donald Côté

Robert de Courcy

gang's Lebanese suppliers. Two Narcotics Squad agents went to Beirut in October, 1972. They provided local police with enough information to arrest four well-known traffickers: Amine Halim Chaoubah, Gaby Suidan, Antoine Abon Zeid and Charalambos Roussakis.

The details of the conspiracy could now be reconstructed. In mid-november 1971 Zaurini went to Lebanon with a friend from the Cotroni gang, Irving Goldstein, and another friend of Lebanese origin, Hassib Mefrige, known as Hapse. (10) Mefrige had been expelled from Blue Bonnets race track in May 1971 and was known to the RCMP for his links with another Lebanese, Saghie Fouad, the brother of a trafficker who had been arrested twice in Halifax and a partner of Gaby Suidan's brother. Fouad had the assignment of delivering $60,000 to Amine Halim Chaoubah for the purchase of the hashish and for his participation in the operation. Chaoubah took the money to the Baalbek valley, celebrated throughout the world for its cannabis plantations, and negotiated a deal with an important local chief, Antoine Abon Zeid. Chaoubah looked after the shipment from Beirut, with Gaby Suidan who added to it his personal shipment of 125 pounds of hashish for his own profit. Suidan's merchandise arrived in Montreal, without the knowledge of police, at the same time as Zaurini's. Chaoubah and Fouad had both been in Montreal when the RCMP arrested the Zaurini gang. They quickly left the country.

While the Montreal investigators were in Lebanon, they discovered that two earlier shipments had already been delivered to the fictitious company, *Oriental Food Importing*. Forty-eight cases of jellied fruit had been delivered on June 21, 1971. Another 126 cases sent by the same gang followed on September 16 of that year.

But the Zaurini affair is celebrated in police annals for another reason, namely the man's escapades while out on bail before his trial. City and Provincial Police surprised Zaurini in the company of Frank Cotroni when they raided the *Speakeasy Disco* at the *La Salle Hotel* on October 17, 1972. Also present were several of Cotroni's men, including Hassib Mefrige and Gallo Moreno, who would later be charged with the murder of a minor drug dealer, Angelo

---

10. Goldstein, a former employee of Solomon (Solly Silver) Schnapps, had been a nightclub manager for Nicola Di Iorio and Angelo Lanzo for many years and an organizer of chartered gambling junkets for Frank Cotroni. On May 29, 1972, Quebec Provincial Police detectives observed an important meeting in the *Sirloin Barn* restaurant, near *Blue Bonnets* race track, attended by Vincent Cotroni, Paolo Violi, Nicola Di Iorio, Angelo Lanzo, William Obront and Irving Goldstein.

Facchino. Zaurini was arrested and accused of violating his bail conditions, which prohibited association with known criminals. He was also accused of going to a summer cottage beyond the geographic limits set in the conditions of bail. At this cottage police had seen a car belonging to Dominique Ricci, Tony Carbone's right-hand man. Despite the infractions, Zaurini's bail was continued. His first trial ended in a hung jury on March 14. (11)

Still on bail awaiting his second trial, Zaurini was arrested a third time on May 18, 1973, at the *Speakeasy Disco* again, this time in the company of Frank Cotroni's old friend, Joe Di Maulo. (12) Freed again, he was arrested again on August 16 when he was found in the company of a couple of gangsters. The court decided four times was enough, and ordered Zaurini to stay in prison. At his trial on September 14 he pleaded guilty and was sentenced to seven years in prison. Three of the other suspects in the affair were acquitted, and charges against two others were withdrawn.

Three days before Zaurini was sent to prison, the RCMP had exposed another important deal in the international traffic in hashish. For close observers of the scene, this new case emphatically confirmed that the so-called "soft drug" market had been invaded by the big-time mob leaders.

Narcotics Squad agents had seized 1,705 pounds of hashish on September 11, 1973, and arrested three well-known underworld gangsters. They were Edouard (Eddy) Chiquette, already sentenced to a total of 23 years in prison to be served concurrently or consecutively, who was known to police for his close relations with Bob Tremblay; Jacques Picard, a high-spirited young repeater; and

---

11. During the first trial, the chief Crown prosecutor, Louis-Philippe Landry, called a surprise witness, the president of *Vincent Packing*. This was Jacques Cloutier, who testified that Zaurini had asked to borrow his warehouse for a few hours for a big celebration of the baptism of a friend's son. Zaurini, godfather of the child, had then given Cloutier an envelope containing $5,000, telling him: "See all these people? They're your friends. But if you do anything sneaky, they'll be your enemies."

12. Joe Di Maulo and Frank Cotroni had been mixed up together in several previous incidents. In September 1960 they and two others, including Michel (The Penguin) Di Paolo, had been arrested for possession of dangerous weapons. Di Maulo had been questioned by the coroner when Claude Faber and Jacques Pacetti were arrested in 1967. In 1970 he was arrested again with Zaurini at the *Renaldo Restaurant*. But Di Maulo had never been implicated in any narcotics affair. His brother Jimmy however, who was doing a life term for murder, had been involved in the heroin traffic. Théodore Aboud, a reformed criminal, testified at the CECO hearings that Jimmy Di Maulo had asked him some years earlier to help market two kilos of heroin he had in his possession.

Robert de Courcy, who was once a foreman in the Port of Montreal. At the time of their arrests, the three men had just stored a large supply of hash in a rented garage on Lepailleur Street, in east-end Montreal. Police had tailed them from Dorval airport where they had collected 12 wooden cases from the Air France warehouse. The cases were supposed to contain kitchen utensils.

But the actual contents had been discovered three days earlier, almost by accident. Sergeant John Leduc, who had recently become head of the international hashish section of the Narcotics Squad, noticed a familiar name on the shipping documents for the cases which had come to Montreal from Beirut via Orly Airport in Paris. The name was "S. Daou," a Lebanese who had transported two lots of hashish to Beirut airport in the spring of 1971 which were later stolen from Dorval airport.

An Air France representative at Dorval had asked the RCMP in mid-May 1971 to investigate the disappearance of two suitcases weighing 58 and 97 kilos which had arrived on April 18 and May 15 respectively. According to the shipping documents, both cases had been sent by the same person, Jalal Abdo, of Beirut. The man who brought the cases to Beirut airport gave his name as S. Daou. The cases were addressed to two different places in Montreal, both of which turned out to be fictitious. The Narcotics Squad transmitted its information to Lebanese police, and continued its investigation of the theft. A cleaning company employee told the police that he had seen a man in uniform, on two occasions, taking a suitcase from the Air France warehouse after regular working hours. The man was identified as a supervisor for *General Aviation Service,* which handles baggage at Dorval.

The agents began shadowing the suspect, which led to his arrest on July 13, 1971, as he attempted to clear through Customs another shipment of 210 pounds of hashish from Beirut. A few days earlier Joe Horvath had been overheard in a conversation which indicated that this shipment was for him. By the time of Denis Coghlan's arrest, the Lebanese police had also made some progress. Jalal Abdo, the sender of the first two lots, was arrested on June 22, 1971 as he prepared to ship 440 pounds of hashish to Montreal. He was a former Syrian policeman who had fallen in with a gang led by a man named Georges Zattar.

All these details came to Sergeant Leduc's mind when he noticed the name S. Daou on the shipping documents more than two years later. The cases related to the documents were checked and the huge shipment of hashish was found. Police agents disguised as airport employees waited for someone to claim the cases. In the meantime, Lieutenant Richard Séguin, of the Montreal Urban Community Police drugs section, advised his RCMP colleague on September 11 that his men were following Eddy Chiquette and his friends. There were indications that the Chiquette gang was expecting a big shipment of drugs. When the city police were given details of the RCMP operation already in progress, they withdrew the surveillance to avoid any risk to the operation's success.

A little later that same night, a man employed by a firm of customs brokers showed up at the airport and completed the documents necessary for clearing the cargo. He then gave the documents to another man whom he later claimed he did not know. Less than an hour later Jacques Picard arrived at the Air France warehouse in a truck and drove off with the 12 wooden cases. Eddy Chiquette watched from his car, then followed Picard's truck to the Lepailleur Street garage, where Robert de Courcy was waiting.

After the arrests and seizure, the RCMP learned that Chiquette and his two accomplices were only the sub-contractors for getting the merchandise out of Dorval. The 12 cases of "kitchen utensils," according to seized documents, were consigned to *Happy Life Distributors,* a firm belonging to another well-known person, Bella Klein, who had been close to the late Luigi Greco. Klein had recently visited the Middle East with Donald Côté, another friend of Greco and the Cotronis who had also been seen at different times with Chiquette and his gang. (13)

On November 11, 1973, at about 2:30 a.m., four men broke into Côté's summer home at Sainte-Anne-des-Plaines and shot to death his wife, his five-year-old son, and an employee who was sleeping on the sofa in the living room. Côté, the killers' target, escaped death by diving quickly under the bed. Three days later, a few hours before the funeral of the Côté mother and child, Montreal police

---

13. Donald Côté began making headlines in Montreal in the early sixties when he and others were charged with the murder of Rocky Pearson, a South Shore gang leader. He was freed for lack of evidence, and on July 12, 1963 was himself the target of an attempted murder in front of the Maisonneuve Hospital. His name cropped up again in 1968 in connection with influence-peddling in the granting of a liquor licence to a well-known Laurentian ski resort. In May 1969 his alleged participation in an extortion matter was mentioned during public hearings by the Quebec Municipal Commission investigating the affairs of the Montreal suburb of Anjou. A witness testified that he had been forced to sell his taxi company to the Anjou police chief who was in league with the Mafia, and that Donald Côté had been present at the time. Pep Cotroni's daughter was said to have worked in the jewelry shop managed by Côté when her father was in prison. According to police files, Côté had close links with Paolo Violi. Côté and two friends were charged on October 22, 1973, with receiving $1 million worth of stolen bonds.

found the charred and mutilated bodies of Eddy Chiquette and Robert de Courcy in the trunk of a burning car. Warrants for their arrest had been issued earlier that day by the Provincial Police in connection with the massacre at Sainte-Anne-des-Plaines. Investigators believed the Sainte-Anne murders to be a reprisal for the refusal of those who had financed the 1,705 pounds of hashish to help Chiquette and his friends defray legal costs for their defense. (14) A warrant had also been issued for Jacques Picard, also suspected of taking part in the triple murder, but the 25-year-old bandit had managed to escape his pursuers for the moment. He was arrested in June 1974 in New York State following a series of armed robberies and was sentenced to ten years in prison in April 1975.

The assassinations of Chiquette and de Courcy led, ironically, to two more substantial drug seizures. On the death of the two men, federal and city agents proceeded with the seizure of a 750-pound shipment of hashish at the Port of Montreal. For two weeks they had been watching and waiting for Chiquette and his friend to come to claim the merchandise, which had also been sent from the Middle East.

Then on the evening of February 27, 1974, city police confiscated 1,000 pounds of phenobarbital, an extremely dangerous tranquilizer. (15) The drugs, originally destined for a pharmaceutical firm, were part of a stock of 2,090 pounds stolen during a strike at the Port of Montreal in June 1972. This robbery had been organized by de Courcy, who was a foreman-checker in the port at that time. Part of the loot had been put into circulation on the black market, and part had been recovered by police. What remained had been stored by de Courcy in a rented shed. He sent the monthly rental payments to the owner by taxi, and when he was killed, the

---

14. On November 17, 1975, Donald Côté and his accomplice Henri Aubry were arrested for the murders of Eddy Chiquette and Robert de Courcy, after an arduous investigation by Montreal Urban Community detectives. Four days earlier a New Jersey mobster named Joseph Rodriguez had testified that he and two Newark mafiosi, Ray Rieno and his son Ray Jr. had executed the two Montrealers. The order for the executions, according to the testimony, had been placed by Donald Côté, who had the assistance of his friend Henri Aubry and Louis Greco, son of the late Luigi. Côté was sent directly to trial on a preferred indictment, but was granted bail in the meantime when a judge decided that his freedom would not be a danger to the public. In the U.S. the Rienos also had to face trial for the murder of a 69-year-old mafioso, Emmanuel Cammarata, in Miami on September 2, 1972.

15. Phenobarbital is highly poisonous in its pure state. Two adolescents who had ingested some had to be hospitalized with severe brain damage.

The Montreal Star *reports the murders of Chiquette and de Courcy.*

Police examine the 1,000 pounds of phenobarbital recovered from a robbery organized by de Courcy.

payments naturally stopped. The owner then notified police who entered the shed and found the stocks of stolen phenobarbital.

A few days earlier the Lebanese police informed the RCMP of the arrest of Jamil Nahra, of Beirut, who had shipped the 1,705 pounds of hashish. The man had operated with the complicity of four Lebanese Customs officers and a notorious trafficker, Fouad Abi Zeid, who had died two months before the arrests. He was believed to be related to the Zeid who had been mixed up in the Zaurini affair.

In mid-August, another large seizure directly involved the Canada-Lebanon connection. On August 8, acting on a tip, the RCMP intercepted a West German, Rudolph Becker, when he arrived at Dorval airport with a false Australian diplomatic passport and two suitcases containing 74 pounds of liquid hashish. (16) Becker had come from Damas, Syria, with stopovers at Amsterdam and New York. He knew he was now in deep trouble, and agreed to cooperate with the Narcotics Squad. He first exposed the intermediary in the deal, Hamin Habdul Hamid, a Palestinian who claimed to be a member of the Palestine Liberation Organization (PLO) and had travelled on the same plane as Becker with a false diplomatic passport from Yemen.

Hamid's trail was picked up when he contacted the German Becker, now a double agent, and police kept him under constant surveillance. Fares Bassile, a Lebanese from Ottawa, got in touch with Hamid on August 10 and took him to the federal capital for meetings with the presumed buyer, Mike Saikelys, a businessman from the Lebanese colony in Ottawa. The next day Hamid and Bassile returned to Montreal and met Becker at the *Holiday Inn*. They were arrested there, as they handed Becker $10,000. In Ottawa, Saikelys was also arrested.

Immediately after this operation, the Narcotics Squad struck a death blow at another international hashish trafficking ring, using a wiretapping warrant for the first time (a new federal law had just legalized wiretaps authorized by court warrants). Agents arrested the apparent leader of this ring, Valentino Morielli, and four other suspects, Thomas Martel, Giachino Delladonne, Pietro Raschella and Eugène Saint-Jacques, following seizure of 100 pounds of hash at Dorval airport. Raschella and Saint-Jacques were baggage

---

16. Liquid hashish is ten times as toxic as solid hashish and, naturally, more expensive. Its price was $25 a gram on the Quebec black market compared to $10 for solid hashish. The 74 pounds of liquid hash in Becker's suitcases therefore had a street value of about $828,650.

handlers for *General Aviation Service.* For months federal agents had suspected them of being in league with international traffickers.

The investigation, begun in May 1973 on information from the U.S. BNDD, ended on September 3, 1974 with the arrest of Eugène Saint-Jacques. He was caught in possession of two suitcases sent from Karachi, Pakistan, after having switched their shipping tickets from international to domestic to avoid Customs inspection.

This hashish ring had been affected directly or indirectly since April 1973 by nearly a dozen police actions in Montreal, Paris, Frankfurt, London and Karachi. A total of 20,958 pounds of hashish had been seized and several suspects had been arrested, including Joseph Martellino, another Cotroni clan henchman. Martellino had been exposed by the work of the Quebec Provincial Police and morality squad officers in Montreal, and had been sentenced to seven years in penitentiary.

Other operations in 1975 confirmed the importance of the international traffic in hashish through Montreal. Five Montreal area residents were arrested by the RCMP on February 13 as they transferred 1,100 pounds of hashish from a DC-7 to three high-priced cars at Dorval airport. The suspects were John James Graham, presumed to be the leader, James Filler, Moishe Shulman, David Greenberg, and Christopher Neil Richardson, from Britain. The aircraft had been chartered for the occasion and had brought the merchandise from Beirut, where the hash had cost $15,000. The market value of the lot in Montreal was between $750,000 and $900,000, or $1,500 to $1,800 a pound. The street value was about $2,240,000, or $280 an ounce.

Sergeant Leduc's men intervened again on March 10, seizing three cardboard boxes containing 165 pounds of hashish. The key figure in the Dorval airport ring, Ronald Fewtrell, was arrested along with three accomplices, his nephew Pierre Temar, his partner and fund-raiser Jerry Rovam, and a customs broker company employee named Philippe Aubert. (17) In January, federal agents learned that about ten shipments of portable calculators had been sent from Amsterdam to a Montreal company, *J. Bourbonnais et Fils,* in care of the brokers *David Kirsh Ltd.* addressed to two

---

17. The names of Fewtrell's accomplices have been changed because their judicial procedures had not yet reached the stage of preliminary hearing and because their identification in a detailed account might interfere with a fair and impartial trial.

different and fictitious places. (18) Dutch police, who had been asked to cooperate in the investigation, advised the RCMP on March 6 that three cartons supposedly containing calculators had just been shipped to *J. Bourbonnais et Fils* in Montreal, through *David Kirsh Ltd.* The boxes arrived that same day and were transferred from the KLM warehouse to the *Kirsh Ltd.* depot, under the constant watch of Narcotics Squad agents.

Four days later Philippe Aubert, who was in charge of the depot where the boxes were being kept, had a meeting with Fewtrell, who, incidentally, was a former municipal policeman. Shortly afterwards, Pierre Temar arrived in a rented car to collect the merchandise. He then drove the car to the parking lot of the *Bonaventure Arena* across from the *Skyline Hotel* and took a taxi to meet Fewtrell at his headquarters in the *Satellite Restaurant.* It was here that airport employees wanting to make a little extra on the side met Fewtrell to propose their deals.

While Temar was still with his uncle, Jerry Rovam, a contractor from the South Shore, arrived at the arena parking lot. He scanned the whole area for a long time, before taking the risk of opening the rented car and removing the three boxes. He was arrested on the spot. The three others were also immediately arrested. Searches at the homes of Fewtrell and Temar turned up several portable calculators identical to those which had been shipped to the importer, *J. Bourbonnais et Fils.* The calculators had no doubt been placed in the hashish boxes so that they could eventually be returned to the *David Kirsh Ltd.* warehouse, cleared through Customs, and finally delivered to *Bourbonnais et Fils* or, in other words, to Fewtrell. A telephone number found on Fewtrell when he was arrested was the same number used by the brokers to inform *Bourbonnais et Fils* that the merchandise had arrived. It was actually a telephone answering service, which sent its bills to the home of Fewtrell's girlfriend in Lachine.

The shipper of the hashish was arrested shortly afterwards in Amsterdam. He was a 25-year-old Montrealer named Andrew McCowan, who worked for Fewtrell.

This affair produced rather spectacular repercussions a few months later, in the early summer of 1975. The Toronto daily, *The Globe and Mail,* quoted a secret RCMP report to the effect that about 60 Dorval airport employees (Customs officers, brokers,

---

18. It should be emphasized here that the *Kirsh Ltd.* firm and its directors had nothing to do with the traffic in drugs.

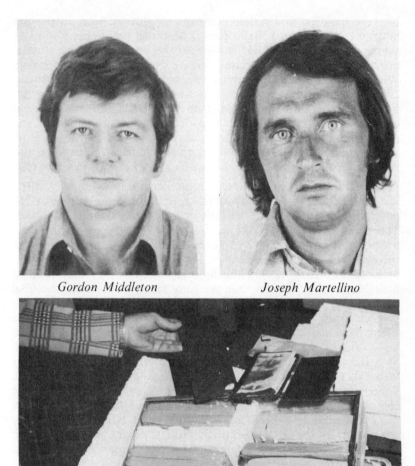

Gordon Middleton   *Joseph Martellino*

(Photo Le Devoir)

Suitcase containing hashish led to the arrest of Joseph Martellino.

483

baggage handlers and airline company employees) were in the pay of drug traffickers, and that a former Montreal policeman was at the centre of the ring. The newspaper reported that the former policeman had been associated with a Narcotics Squad informer, William Brown, who had been assassinated in Montreal on August 29, 1974, on his return from a trip to Morocco and Spain. On this trip he was said to have tried to negotiate purchase of large quantities of hashish. He had been accompanied by Fewtrell and another Canadian, Allan B., 25, who was arrested in Montreal on July 9, 1975 when 340 grams of marijuana were seized at his home. A few hours before his death, Brown had met Fewtrell in a bar. (19)

Federal agents arrested another six persons on March 21, 1975, in Montreal and in the Ottawa-Hull region, following seizure of 250 pounds of liquid and solid hashish with a retail value of $1,400,000. The Ottawa-Hull section of the Narcotics Squad had been on the trail of this gang for several years. Agents had learned the week before that a new shipment of drugs had arrived from Lebanon or Syria on February 12. On the morning of March 21 they notified their Montreal colleagues that the gang members were in Montreal to pick up the merchandise. Montreal agents first spotted the suspects near *Blue Bonnets* race track and followed them to the *Claire Terminal* customs clearing station on Pullman Street. There they watched the loading of cases on to a truck presumably rented by a Lebanese from Ottawa, Souhil Baroud. The merchandise was then taken to the home of a Montrealer, on Papineau Avenue. Police surprised him there as he and a 23-year-old accomplice were concealing the drugs in a briefcase. During the transit to his home, the Montrealer had been followed by Souhil Baroud, his brother Zaki, and Gérard E. Despard, of Hull. Despard was arrested in Montreal with the two Papineau Avenue suspects. The Baroud brothers were arrested in Ottawa.

Two other Montrealers, Roger Dutrisac, 46, and his brother Marcel, 37, were arrested on May 13 on a farm near the Ontario border. At that moment they were removing 415 pounds of hashish hidden in 315 wooden tables shipped to Montreal from New Delhi, India. Two suspected accomplices, Cyrille Morgan, 49, and Nicole Lagacé, 27, were also arrested for looking after some of the shipping procedures. A week later Nadie Meland and Kevin Murphy were arrested by the Narcotics Squad in Montreal for importing from the

---

19. When a Narcotics Squad agent revealed this meeting, Fewtrell told the court he could not be under suspicion for Brown's murder because Brown had been one of his best friends . . .

same Indian shipper 50 wooden tables each containing one pound of hashish.

Harry Louis Yacknin, brother of bookie Moe Yacknin (one of Bella Klein's associates), had 300 pounds of hashish in his Cadillac when he was arrested on May 16 at a South Shore motel. Federal detectives were tipped off by a maid who happened to see the merchandise. Police were unable to locate a young man believed to be involved in this affair. The suspicions of another room maid in another motel in September 1974 had already enabled the drugs section of Montreal Urban Community Police to confiscate nine bundles containing 400 pounds of marijuana.

On July 9, 1975, another large cargo, 320 pounds of hashish worth about $1,440,000 on the black market, was seized at Dorval airport by Customs officers and the Narcotics Squad. This came about through the regular search of parcels arriving from countries recognized as large drug producers. In this case the merchandise had been shipped from Nepal via Paris to a fictitious address in Montreal. Before making the seizure, the federal agents waited in vain for four days for someone to claim the four wooden cases falsely described as containing books and handicrafts. A month later another seizure was made in roughly the same manner. In the latter case the wooden boxes had been shipped from Karachi, Pakistan, via Paris, and contained 220 pounds of hashish.

At the end of August, police of Copenhagen, Denmark, broke up a ring of traffickers who had been sending 440 pounds of Pakistani hashish to Canada every month. Couriers for the ring were recruited in European discos and the gang leaders paid the return air fare to Pakistan plus about $5,000 on delivery of the merchandise to Copenhagen.

The Narcotics Squad crowned an arduous, 16-month investigation on the evening of September 16, 1975, by seizing 1,400 pounds of hashish and arresting 18 persons, including several young businessmen with no criminal records and a Quebec Provincial Police detective. (20) The drug, which came from Morocco by ship

20. The accused were: Michel Lachapelle, 28, former fireman and later owner of a garage, *Milac Auto*, on Gouin Boulevard West; his wife, Monique, 27; his brother Luc, 25; Paul Bergon, 28, president of *Mirabel Alarm*, who was one of the suspects found in the warehouse; his brother Claude Bergon, 32, director of the exclusive Sainte-Rita private school, who was also in the warehouse; Jean-Marie Caron, 30, a Quebec Provincial Police officer; his brother Bernard Caron, 31; Pierre-Paul Gauthier, 42, co-owner of a service station and driver of the motorized trailer; José Dias, 28, driver of the all-purpose van; Carol Ménard, co-

via Le Havre, France, had been ingeniously hidden in compartments built into the gas tanks of a motorized house trailer and a cross-country vehicle. Federal agents had been preparing for a long time, and when the merchandise arrived at the Port of Montreal, they launched a gigantic operation called "Zapata." About 130 police officers were involved in constant surveillance of the suspects, who were taking exceptional precautions themselves. When police closed in at the end, three of the suspects were happily removing bars of hashish from the gas tank of one of the vehicles in an isolated suburban warehouse. The all-purpose vehicle had been left at the docks to be picked up later, while a third machine, another trailer, was in Europe on its way to Morocco. (21)

Less than 24 hours after this spectacular police round-up, one of the largest ever made in Canada, the Narcotics Squad arrested Ronald Fewtrell for the second time since the beginning of 1975. This time the key man in the shady deals at Dorval airport was charged with conspiracy in the importation of 90 pounds of hashish seized in Montreal on August 24. A BOAC freight supervisor named Robert McLone was charged with him. Two suspected accomplices, Anthony Guiol, 28, and Gordon Thomas Albert, 35, had been arrested earlier. Their appearance in Criminal Court had produced evidence of an interesting link with the suspected leader of another gang of international traffickers, George Gordon Middleton, who had been arrested at Dorval on February 13. Middleton, in fact, had put up part of their bail, which earned him another charge for having declared in court that no charges were pending against him. Fewtrell decided to cut matters short and pleaded guilty on October 6. Two days later he was sentenced to ten years in prison.

Drug traffickers always think they can do better than others, but the ones who never get caught are rare. The desire for gain is so strong however, that even those who have been publicly exposed, often return to the action.

---

owner of a chic clothing boutique and Dias' boss; Léo Aubut, 50, owner of the *Carnival M.F.G. Company* of Sainte-Thérèse; Slobodan Gravilovick, 30, a welder and the third person arrested in the warehouse; Charles Giroux, 28, Quebec civil servant; Jean Brais, 28; Gérald Bond, mechanic; Jacques Beaudin, 36; Sheila Cross, Claude Bergon's girlfriend; Gaétane Villeneuve, 22, Bernard Caron's girlfriend. Three days after the arrests, all were released on bail totalling half a million dollars. None of the suspects contested the high bail suggested by the prosecution, which strengthened the impression that the ring was well-organized and had abundant resources. Michel Lachapelle alone, the suspected leader, had to put up bail of almost $150,000.

486

On February 25, 1976, James Filler and David Greenberg, two of George Gordon Middleton's companions, were surprised again by Narcotics Squad agents who arrested them in possession of a ton of high-quality Moroccan hashish. Four others were arrested with them, including Lawrence Schlear and Larry M. Morrisson, two armed robbers out on parole. Schlear, who on the surface had become an honest garage operator, organized the hashish importation in much the same manner as that of the previous year. A twin-motored aircraft of the Lodestar type had been chartered to facilitate and accelerate transportation of the merchandise. The federal police moved in soon after the plane had been unloaded.

Between January 1, 1973 and August 1, 1975, 5,674 pounds of hashish and 4,736 pounds of marijuana were seized in Quebec by the RCMP, yet the traffic continued with increasing vigor. Other drugs were also widely available and were rapidly expanding in use. Cocaine, for example, had revived in popularity in recent years, to the point where a special section of the Narcotics Squad was created to combat the increasing cocaine traffic. Two experienced officers, Sergeant Gilbert Bishop and Corporal Raymond Boisvert were put in charge, and several important interventions and arrests have since been made.

A New Yorker of South-American origin, Gilberto Morales, was arrested in Toronto on August 10, 1973 with 27½ pounds of cocaine. Montreal detectives had been following him for some days, since they had seen him receiving the merchandise in Montreal. The drug had been brought to Montreal by two Chileans working for an influential gang of Santiago traffickers led by Carlos Baeza. Baeza and several Chilean and U.S. accomplices had been indicted in New York in 1974 in connection with a huge international conspiracy.

Three Bolivians, one of them carrying a diplomatic passport,

---

21. Four days after the Montreal arrests Spanish police, on information from the RCMP, caught up with the third vehicle and its two occupants. The police found $34,000 hidden in the special compartment in the gas tank. The money was for purchase of another cargo of hashish in Morocco which would have been shipped to Montreal in the same manner as those which had been seized by the Narcotics Squad. Federal agents estimated the travelers had enough money to buy 600 pounds of hashish which would have had a street value in Montreal of $2,700,000. Before this third vehicle had left Montreal for overseas, two agents had a chance to dismantle the gas tank and note the presence of the money and of nearly a dozen sand bags each weighing about 40 pounds. The sand was to be switched for hashish on the return trip, so the total weight of the vehicle would remain about the same going and coming.

were arrested in Montreal on August 5, 1974. (22) This came about after an undercover operation by two agents from the RCMP and the U.S. Drug Enforcement administration (DEA), and the prior arrest in Toronto of the Montreal buyer, a black named Jade Beasley. The Bolivians had been carrying four kilos of cocaine (8.8 pounds) with a black market value of about $6 million. (23)

Three more kilos were seized later in Toronto in connection with this affair. These were sold to RCMP undercover agents by Beasley's wife, who had been arrested with her husband but released on parole to look after their children. Apparently the merchandise had been intended in the first place for wholesalers in Seattle and Hawaii.

On August 11 and 12, 1974, DEA agents in San Juan, Puerto Rico arrested three young Montrealers who had just taken delivery of about ten pounds of pure cocaine. All 25 years of age, they were Johann Meyer, John Skelcher and David Murray. The arrests followed a tip from the RCMP which had been on the track of the three men since the beginning of June 1973. Police investigation had indicated that the trio directed an international cocaine network with connections in South America, the Caribbean, the United States and Canada. The RCMP's undercover operation ended with the arrest of 20 people, and led to charges against several of Meyer's associates who had been dealing with black procurers involved in the network. A month later the Narcotics Squad arrested a couple from Bogota, Colombia and seized their six false-bottomed suitcases which each contained a kilo of "coke." The couple had arrived five days before their arrest, and had met one of Meyer's partners, as well as Herman Cortes, who represented the Colombian supplier and was to supervise this deal and another for which he and two accomplices were later arrested in Vancouver. (24)

22. Alberto Sanchez Bello, 32, had just become private secretary to a close aide of the Bolivian chief of state, Hugo Banzer. Bello's arrest and trial in Montreal created a political scandal in La Paz which resulted in his boss's dismissal.

23. In June, 1975, a Montreal trafficker could buy a kilo of pure cocaine for $8,000 in Bogota, Colombia, and resell it in Montreal for $35,000 to $40,000. Mixed with two kilos of dextrose or lidococaine, the kilo would become six and a half pounds of product 36-40 per cent pure, which could be sold for $17,000 to $20,000 a pound. The wholesaler buying a pound would cut it once or once and a half and sell it for $1,700 an ounce, $100 a gram or $50 a "spoon" (quarter-gram). A kilo of pure cocaine could produce 29,568 spoons after being cut several times, which adds up to a street value of $1,478,000 a kilo.

24. On November 6, 1973, Herman Cortes was arrested at Vancouver airport with his Venezuelan courier, Fernando Garcia Hernandez and the U.S. buyer, John Vincent Liberto. A kilo of cocaine was found in Hernandez' belt.

The investigation by the RCMP and the DEA continued after Meyer's arrest in Puerto Rico, and led to charges being laid against 15 important traffickers in Detroit on April 27, 1975. The leader of the Detroit gang, Robert Charles Wind, was one of the major clients of the young Montreal leader, Johann Meyer.

The cocaine traffic provoked another sweeping police action at the beginning of 1976. On February 19 and 20 a year-long undercover operation by the RCMP ended in the arrest of about 50 people, including Paolo Cotroni, Frank's 20-year-old son. The carefully-planned raids struck a hard blow at the cocaine, cannabis and LSD distribution rings in the Laurentians, north of Montreal.

The investigation had been launched in March 1975 when a Montreal member of the Narcotics Squad had begun hanging out in the nightclubs of the Laurentian resort area. The agent gradually introduced himself into drug-user circles and one day managed to make direct contact with the young Cotroni, who lived in Sainte-Adèle and was already greatly respected in certain company. Cocaine transactions were quickly concluded and this led the young Cotroni to introduce the undercover agent to several of his friends, including Eric Knitel, 30, said to be his partner, Wayne Bourassa, Serge Limoges, Douglas McLeod, Réal Garneau, Gilles Venditolli and others. The work of the undercover agent and of the colleague who joined him during the investigation established the links between many of the arrested suspects and the top levels of the Montreal underworld.

Traffic of amphetamines (speed), LSD, and other synthetic drugs was also flourishing in Quebec, with spectacular repercussions in 1974 and 1975. On the afternoon of April 28, 1974, Sergeants Gérard Gravel and Renaud Lacroix of the Narcotics Squad crowned a five-month long investigation by exposing a speed manufacturing laboratory in the Joliette region directed by leading members of the Satan's Choice motorcycle gang from Montreal. (25) Five members of the gang were charged: Joseph (Sonny) Lacombe, the suspected leader, his brother Philippe, Michael Rowan, Kevin O'Brien and Kim Clow. When police raided the abandoned and isolated house

---

25. A month before, the Toronto section of the Narcotics Squad had dismantled a first illegal speed lab at St. Catharines, Ontario, operated by a Satan's Choice gang. Nine people were arrested, including two Quebecers. Another speed lab was broken up in Ontario on September 21, 1975. This lab, on an abandoned farm at Barry's Bay, could produce large quantities of methamphetamines. The raid by the RCMP, Ontario Provincial Police and Metro Toronto Police turned up an arsenal of weapons, a radio set for receiving police calls, and a radar system to warn of the approach of "unauthorized" vehicles.

used as the laboratory, two of the suspects were busily producing 200 pounds of speed with a street value of $1,200,000. (26) The investigation showed that half the product was destined for the U.S. market, the remainder for the Montreal and Quebec markets.

Another illegal speed lab was dismantled by the RCMP and MUC police at the beginning of 1975. Five hundred pounds of methamphetamines were seized at a farm at Saint-Alexis-des-Monts after a two-month investigation by city police, and three people were arrested: Guy Corriveau, Douglas Malony and Paul Granito. This group however, had nothing to do with the activities of the Satan's Choice gang who were associated instead with another formidable gang of bikers, The Devil's Disciples. In recent years the Disciples had taken control of distribution of drugs in many key parts of Montreal. But at the beginning of 1975, the gang was torn by internal dissension.

Police date the beginning of this war, directly related to the drug traffic, from January 19, 1975, when the bullet-ridden body of 19-year-old Philippe Beereens was found in his suburban Montreal apartment. The victim was a partisan of Gilles Forget, 28, one of the two leaders of the rival gangs and the main supplier of ingredients for the illegal speed labs. A few days before his death, Beereens had been followed by federal agents as he delivered ingredients from Forget to a new laboratory. Forget had first been arrested by the RCMP in September 1973 following a seizure of speed. Charged with conspiracy in the trafficking of drugs Forget, like many others, took advantage of his release on bail to intensify his activities. Beereens' murder, according to information gathered by police, followed the threats of death he had made in the *Brasserie Iberville* against Claude Ellefsen, known as Johnny Halliday (27), the 28-year-old former leader of the Devil's Disciples and Forget's rival. In the underworld, Halliday was known as the strong man of Saint-Louis Square, a favoured hang-out for Montreal's francophone drug-users. (28) Halliday had close links with some of the Satan's Choice leaders and was also close to some of Lucien Rivard's former

---

26. In Canada, speed retails at $2,500 to $3,500 a pound, while in the U.S. traffickers pay up to $5,000 a pound. Sold at $10 a "spoon" (about three-quarters of a gram) a pound of speed ultimately realizes $90,000.

27. No relation to the French singer, except that Claude Ellefsen was a devoted fan of the performer.

28. On February 24 and 25, 1975, federal agents made a thorough sweep of Saint-Louis Square (near the centre of Montreal), arresting more than a dozen young drug pushers linked to the Devil's Disciples. The round-up resulted from a year-long undercover operation by three agents of the Narcotics Squad.

Exterior and interior of house in which the Satan's Choice gang produced speed.

allies in Laval. When police broke up the speed laboratory at Joliette, Halliday and two friends were believed to have linked up with Forget to start a new laboratory. Each side was to invest $22,000 in the enterprise but Halliday had apparently not paid his share. War broke out because of that.

As might be expected, Forget retaliated for Beereens' murder. On the evening of March 30, a bomb exploded in the Piedmont Cottage shared by Halliday, his bodyguard Pierre McDuff, 32, and a young woman. The three occupants suffered only slight injuries. The nitroglycerine charge used by the bombers had been placed near the door, inside the garage which was beneath the cottage. The attempt would probably have had murderous results if anyone had attempted to use Halliday's car, parked nearby. The would-be killers had done a professional job, linking the car's starter to another nitro bomb hidden under the hood.

This failed attempt was followed by a similar attack on April 23 against Gilles Auger, 27, a former Devil's Disciple in Forget's entourage and a drug pusher for Forget. The bomb placed under the hood demolished his fancy Cadillac parked on Boyce Street in the east end. Auger also escaped death, but he lost an eye. Three days later the bullet-ridden body of Claude Brabant, 38, was found beside a country road. He had been a drug dealer with Halliday's gang who had joined up with Forget after a dispute with the boss. He had been the Devil's Disciples speed salesman to U.S. customers, particularly in Boston. Brabant had been arrested on February 8 at his cottage at Saint-Calixte, after an undercover operation by the RCMP and the DEA. Eleven pounds of speed had been seized, and soon after, police became aware of his rupture with Halliday. After Brabant's assassination, it was the turn of José Martindale, 33, former president of the Devil's Disciples who was in close partnership with Halliday. Forget's minions had seen Martindale with one of Halliday's bodyguards, Jean-Pierre Aspirot. Forget decided to attack Martindale, but the first target was Aspirot, who was shot at in a shopping centre parking lot. Martindale was on his guard from then on. Children playing near his home on April 29 discovered a home-made bomb in the culvert at the entrance to his yard. The bomb was dismantled safely.

A few days later, on May 9, the decomposing corpse of another Devil's Disciple, Réal Girard, was pulled from the St. Lawrence River. This murder, however, was not linked to the current war. Then on the evening of May 28 two killers waited at the country home of Guy Filion, 25, one of Halliday's partners. His girlfriend Ginette Pelletier entered the house first and was killed in a hail of bullets. But Filion, who was following, escaped without harm by running and hiding in a ditch in front of the house. The story in the underworld was that this attack was not related to the Halliday-Forget war. It concerned instead a quarrel Filion was having with a gang of cocaine pushers operating from a Lajeunesse Street bar in the north end of the city.

Two hired killers renowned in the underworld cornered Gilles Forget and his chief lieutenant Pierre (Nap) Saint-Jean, 29, in the *Brasserie Iberville* on the night of June 11-12. Forget and Saint-Jean were cold-bloodedly murdered. The night before, the two victims had taken part in the kidnapping and murder of five young people allied with the Halliday gang. The five had been at the *Brasserie Iberville* when they were forced to leave and get into a Cadillac. They have not been seen since. It is said their bodies were buried in such a way that they would never be found.

Less than 24 hours after the murder of Forget and Saint-Jean, city detectives arrested five well-known individuals: Jean-Paul Mathurin, a young gangster and waiter at the Brasserie; Gilles Lavigne, the manager of the establishment; Michel (Mike) Blass and Armand (Ti-Man) Auger, two notorious criminals; and Ronald Proulx, a friend of the gang. All were sent to trial on preferred indictments authorized by the Quebec attorney-general. The most famous of the gang was Michel Blass. On the previous January 24, his younger brother Richard had been shot down by police, three days after 13 people had been murdered in a bar called *Le Gargantua*. The victims had been locked up in a storage cupboard and the club had then been set on fire. The news of the massacre went around the world and horrified the public. Mike himself had been held by police for several days in connection with the affair.

The quick intervention by city police in the Forget-Saint-Jean murder investigation can be explained by the presence of wiretaps which had been installed for some time at certain places of interest, including the *Brasserie Iberville*. Given the nature of some of the conversation overheard on the evening of June 11, a surveillance team of city police took up positions around the Brasserie. The four policemen had tailed Blass, Mathurin and Auger when they left the place after the fusillade of bullets and drove off at top speed.

On July 22, Judge Charles Phelan of Superior Court freed two of the accused on bail, Mathurin and Lavigne, who were both employed at the *Brasserie Iberville*. According to the judge, they could not be considered a danger to society. Three days later, at 8:25 a.m., 15 minutes after the north-end Brasserie had opened, three armed men burst in and locked the 11 occupants — including the

The body of Gilles Forget being taken from the Brasserie D'Iberville *where he was murdered by two hired assassins.*

manager and three other employees — in the toilets. Then they blew the place up with dynamite. But before the explosion, the hostages managed to break down the doors and escape what would have been a terrible carnage. Police investigators considered the attack to be the reaction of Forget's friends to the release on bail of his suspected murderers who were employed at the Brasserie. Judge Phelan dealt with Michel Blass' application for bail that same day, and proved more severe. The judge denied bail to Blass after a police officer gave an account of the latest attack. But officially the judge based his decision on the fact that Blass was already on bail awaiting trial for a jewel robbery when he was arrested for the double murder. (29)

A few days before the Brasserie employees, Mathurin and Lavigne, were released on bail, two drug pushers linked to Forget's gang were assassinated. Joseph Minotti and Yvon Saint-Pierre, both 20, were killed about a week apart, on July 9 and 17. Almost immediately city detectives issued warrants for the arrest of two Devil's Disciples, in particular Pierre Paré, 27. On February 6, 1975, Paré had been stopped by federal agents when he was with Gilles Forget. The two bikers, suspected of delivering an order of speed, had to be released because the drug was found in a garbage can and not on their persons. One of the theories about the murders of Minotti and Saint-Pierre (who shared an apartment with a third man) was that they had shown they could not be trusted in transactions with Forget's friends. It was even said that Saint-Pierre had informed on some traffickers in order to take over their deals when they were arrested.

A more likely explanation has been established: Saint-Pierre wanted to contact the police to give information about the disappearance of Johnny Halliday's five young friends and the place where the bodies had been hidden.

---

29. After deliberating for 18 hours, a jury of eight men and four women pronounced its verdict on February 13, 1976: Jean-Paul Mathurin was declared guilty of the two murders in the *Brasserie Iberville.* Michel Blass, 31, acquitted of the murder of Pierre Saint-Jean, was found guilty of manslaughter in the death of Gilles Forget. Ti-Man Auger, 43, was found guilty on two manslaughter charges, while Ronald Proulx, 34, was acquitted of all charges. Gilles Lavigne, suspected of conspiracy in organizing the reprisals, was to stand trial later. The *Brasserie Iberville* trial almost provoked another murder. Marcel Godon, a friend of Jean-Guy Giguère who had helped organize the June 12 slaughter, testified for the prosecution against Michel Blass. On December 30, 1975, before the trial began, an attempt was made on his life, but the bullet wound in his stomach was not fatal.

Jean-Guy Giguère (top), one of Halliday's best friends, was fatally shot.

The Brasserie D'Iberville after the bombing on July 25, 1975.

(Photos Allô Police)

496

The same day Saint-Pierre was murdered, another person linked to the Devil's Disciples disappeared from circulation. Renée Larose, 16, Pierre Saint-Jean's girlfriend, was at her sister's home on the afternoon of July 17 when a young man telephoned. The young girl, apparently frightened, then told her sister she was going out to meet the caller. She left in hurry, not even stopping to put on shoes, and has not been seen since . . .

The destruction of the *Brasserie Iberville* came eight days after her disappearance, but even that did not slake the thirst for vengeance of the friends of Gilles Forget and Pierre Saint-Jean. On the morning of July 31, Halliday's bodyguard Pierre McDuff, who has survived the bomb attack in the Piedmont cottage, was shot in the face and killed. He had just driven his Corvette out of his garage on Chapleau Street in the east end when two men blocked his way with their car. One of them got out to perform the execution.

A similar scene was enacted on the morning of August 27. Jean-Guy Giguère, 34, a partner of Ti-Man Auger and one of Halliday's best friends, was shot and killed by a high-powered bullet as he got into his car parked near his home. Giguère had narrowly escaped in a bomb attack on April 1, 1975, carried out for Le Petit Ritz, a tough gang of east-end professional thieves he had once been associated with. Following this failed attempt, according to underworld rumors, Giguère and Ti-Man were given $25,000 by Halliday to get rid of Gilles Forget and his friends. In exchange, the former leader of the Devil's Disciples undertook to help Giguère in his war with the Petit Ritz gang. Strangely enough, however, some people thought that Giguère's murder was the work of Halliday. One of Giguère's relatives received an anonymous telephone call and thought he recognized the voice that said: "We got the dog Jean-Guy and you're going to taste it next." But Giguère was liked and respected by many. Someone close to him told a journalist on the day after his death: "I swore on Jean-Guy's tomb that those who killed him will die in their turn."

Another skirmish in the war that was tearing apart the Devil's Disciples occurred in mid-afternoon on Sunday, August 24. Jean-Pierre Aspirot, 22, who had already survived an attempt on his life, was at the *Astro Bar-salon* in the north end with two of his men. For some unknown reason, the bikers had it in for the manager of the place. There was a scuffle, the manager opened fire on his assailants and killed Aspirot. The *Astro Bar-salon* was known to police as a notorious hang-out for drug pushers.

Two days later, suspicious residents called police about a van parked in front of the funeral parlor where Aspirot's body was resting. Two young men were standing beside it and seemed to be waiting for something or someone. City police arrived and questioned them. One was Daniel Lafortune, 21, the apartment-mate of Joseph Minotti and Yvon Saint-Pierre. He had been wounded himself in the gunfire that had killed Minotti. In the van police found a fully-loaded hunting rifle. Some believed that Aspirot's friends had prepared themselves to fight off another murderous raid. Others thought that Aspirot's enemies were preparing to attack his brother, Jean-Claude. Whatever the case, the two young men denied that the van was theirs. They explained that they were merely waiting for the funeral parlor to open so they could pay their last respects to their friend Aspirot . . .

Finally, on Sunday, September 29, a tenant reported to police that he had just heard shots in his apartment building on 26th Avenue in the Rosemount district. City police entered one of the apartments and found the body of Pierre Barrette, 24, said by some to have recently become Claude Ellefsen's (Johnny Halliday) new bodyguard. The young man had been killed by shotgun blasts in the head and chest while his hands were tied behind his back.

Aside from these "incidents," several other murders had been directly related to the Devil's Disciples drug-trafficking operations.

The charred bodies of Claude Chamberland, 39, and his 22-year-old girlfriend were found on May 20, 1974 in a burned trailer home in Laval. Both had been shot with a pistol before the fire. Chamberland, a swindler and bookie, had been close to Halliday who had a trailer home not far from his. The trailer Chamberland had been occupying belonged to Gilles Brochu, one of Lucien Rivard's former comrades. According to police investigators, Chamberland had been involved in a narcotics affair with the Devil's Disciples and had been executed by Pierre McDuff, Halliday's chief lieutenant. One of his close friends had been murdered a month earlier at Stoke, in the Eastern Townships.

On the night of July 21, 1974, two killers walked into *La Fontaine de Johannie* restaurant on Saint-Denis Street near Saint-Louis Square and shot down Jean-Claude Arbour and Jacques Morin, both 26. This was apparently their punishment for having trespassed on Devil's Disciples drug territory. Both men were known to the Narcotics Squad as drug pushers. Undercover agents had even succeeded in buying hashish, cocaine and heroin from Arbour. The double murder had a tragic consequence: in a rage at the murder of his brother, Jean-Paul Morin showed up at the wrong house that night and mistakenly killed the young civil servant who answered the door.

Next came the discovery of the remains of 20-year-old Ginette Caron in a country field on October 10. The young girl had been killed by a .38 calibre bullet in the head. As a drug-user who hung around Saint-Louis Square with Devil's Disciples gang members, she was apparently assassinated because she knew too much about the drug pushers.

On November 28, 1974, a Laval resident and owner of a small trailer home business disappeared. Jean Viau, 49, has not been seen since. Police inquiries indicated his disappearance may have had something to do with certain shady deals he was believed to be involved in with Johnny Halliday. Viau, who also kept company with some of Lucien Rivard's former cronies, was suspected of being implicated in the financing of at least six illegal labs for speed and LSD in Montreal, Toronto and Hull. Federal agents were particularly interested in his relations with certain chemical products firms.

Pierre Barrette's murder in September 1975 initiated a truce in the Devil's Disciples war. Traffic in speed, which had diminished considerably during the hostilities, quickly revived and the name of Claude Ellefsen, alias Johnny Halliday, was soon coming up in police investigations. Narcotics Squad agents believed the former leader of the Devil's Disciples had set up an illegal laboratory in the Montreal region and was planning another one in Quebec City.

Familiar with Halliday's habits, the agents assigned teams to close surveillance and soon identified some new suspects in his entourage. But they were not able to find the clandestine laboratory. That was the problem. For more than four months the Narcotics Squad were stymied in their efforts to unmask the illegal makers of methamphetamines. While shadowing Halliday and his partner José Martindale early in 1976, the agents came to the conclusion that the lab must be in the area of Pointe Calumet, about 30 miles from Montreal. But the suspects were always wary, and it was difficult to follow them to a final destination.

Patience was rewarded on Saturday, February 14, 1976, when agents followed Martindale to a house occupied by a young couple. The police were convinced they had found the illegal lab, and set up round-the-clock surveillance of the area, covering all access roads. The next evening, Martindale and Halliday were seen entering the suspect house.

It takes 18 hours to produce a batch of speed. When Martindale and Halliday did not emerge again until Monday night, February 16, 24 hours after they had gone into the house, police were sure that a batch of drugs had just been completed and was about to be distributed. The two former bikers were therefore arrested on the spot. Halliday was carrying a revolver, but offered no resistance. He was also carrying one of the 22 pounds of speed which had just been manufactured. These arrests were quickly followed by a series of police raids in the area, and in Quebec City where preparations were being made for a second laboratory. Five other persons were arrested, among them Jacques (Coco) Sénécal, 27, a Devil's Disciples member suspected of being the gang's distributor, and Gilles Boucher, 27, suspected of handling the supplies. In all, 2,200 pounds of chemical products were confiscated at Pointe-Calumet and Quebec City, enough to make $16 million worth of speed.

At Martindale's home, besides 15 cases of drug-manufacturing equipment, police found an electronic gadget capable of remote detonation of a bomb from as far away as one mile. Martindale, taken to RCMP headquarters, told agents that the war between members and ex-members of the Devil's Disciples would only end with the extermination of one camp or the other. Claude Ellefsen explained why he was carrying the revolver: "Some people are going to get blown up. The dynamite is no problem and I'm ready and able to kill to defend myself ..."

At the preliminary hearing of the two men, Judge Rhéal Brunet, former head of the Quebec Commission on Organized Crime, denied bail on grounds of public safety. The courtroom was closed to the general public for these proceedings, and armed agents guarded the doors.

The war of the Devil's Disciples, added to the Chiquette Affair massacre and the murder of the informer William Brown, dramatically demonstrated the violence surrounding the traffic in drugs, especially at the level of distribution and sale to users. In recent years in Quebec dozens of pushers and small-time traffickers have been murdered or brutally assaulted in constant, covetous disputes over control of key distribution centres.

Two motorcycle gangs in Sherbrooke, for example, Les Atomes and Les Gitans, fought each other openly in the streets of the city with knives, revolvers and baseball bats during the winter of 1974. Two young people were killed in this conflict which apparently broke out when one gang trespassed on the other's territory. Previously, the gangs had divided the city into two parts, each controlling drug distribution in its own district.

In Quebec City, the Pacific Rebels motorcycle gang had been at war since the beginning of 1974 with a local underworld gang involved in drug trafficking. Since then guns and bombs have killed a dozen persons. Four of the victims had nothing to do with drug trafficking: they were murdered by mistake.

In the Hull-Ottawa region a big gang of narcotics traffickers led by a former Montrealer, Jean-Claude Lesage, would tolerate no competition. In Hull on September 21, 1973, a drug dealer who had just got out of jail a week earlier was seriously injured when a bomb exploded in his car. A passenger was also slightly injured. A few days later, on October 4, another car was blown up at Vanier, near Ottawa. The three young people in the vehicle escaped unharmed. On November 13 the body of a young pusher, Conrad Carré, 24, was found in a wooded section of Touraine, a small town near Hull. A few days later, Quebec Provincial Police investigating the death arrested Jean-Claude Lesage and some of his henchmen, including Paul (Butch) Boucher, president of the Gatineau section of the Popeyes motorcycle club.

For lack of evidence, Lesage was released after the coroner's inquest, but in the meantime the RCMP and local police forces began a broad investigation of his activities and those of other traffickers in the district. The investigation, involving the work of three RCMP undercover agents, led to the arrest on February 21, 1974 of 37 dealers, pushers and distributors of heroin, cocaine, opium, speed, LSD, hashish and phencyclidine (PCP). (30) Further investigation followed this round-up and in mid-September 1974 another 28 persons were arrested, including Jean-Claude Lesage. Again, a dangerous undercover operation made the sweep possible.

The Lesage gang's drug supplies came almost exclusively from the powerful Dubois brothers clan in Montreal, according to evidence presented at public hearings of the Quebec Commission on Organized Crime in December 1975. The nine Dubois brothers, ranging in age from 28 to 45, had been famous or infamous in the Montreal underworld for several years. Through terrorist methods and family cohesion they had built a powerful criminal organization which today rivals that of the local Mafia. It was the recent decline in Mafia strength in fact, which enabled the Dubois gang to move beyond their local fiefdom in the south-west sector of Montreal and implant themselves in force downtown and in Old Montreal. Like other gangs in the Montreal underworld, they had previously worked for leaders of the Cotroni family.

---

30. Phencyclidine is an extremely dangerous tranquilizer for horses sold by drug traffickers as a substitute for mescaline which is almost non-existent on the Quebec black market. To camouflage the fraud, traffickers mix the phencyclidine with LSD and scorched flour.

The Organized Crime Commission heard public testimony from several witnesses on the Dubois family activities. From the evidence it appeared that trafficking in drugs, and particularly the control of distribution and sales, was one of their major enterprises. The Dubois brothers developed such power in this area, that at the time of writing they were believed to be in control of most of the key drug distribution points in the south-west and the city centre. With few exceptions, only dealers authorized by them may work in these districts, all must pay fees to those who grant the sales concessions, besides being required to buy their supplies from their wholesalers.

One of the main links in the Dubois organization chain, until the end of 1975, was the *Paul Calcé Agency*, Quebec's largest recruiting firm for gogo dancers and strippers. At the time of CECO's public hearings, this firm controlled 95 per cent of the market in Montreal and tolerated little competition. Witnesses testified that agency managers recruited many teen-age girls under 18, some of them became drug pushers for the Dubois gang.

In December 1973 and January 1974, the drugs section of the MUC Police seized nearly two million tenuate pills, a medicine used to reduce the appetite but which traffickers had been selling as an alternative to speed. The dealers could not be charged, since these pills were not on the list of controlled drugs of the Canadian Food and Drugs administration. But the men involved were publicly identified as Dubois gang associates through Montreal police wiretaps which were introduced as evidence at the Quebec Organized Crime Commission hearings.

The rise of the Dubois clan, naturally, was not exactly smooth and trouble-free. Many who resisted had to be brought to their knees with blows or threats, and some of them courageously testified at the Crime Commission. Former employees of the *Iroquois Hotel* in Old Montreal, among others, told how the Dubois had gradually taken over the place, first by slipping in a few of their own men as employees, and then by physically expelling all other staff members who did not cooperate with them. One ex-employee testified that gang members had lured him into a room and then deliberately gouged out one of his eyes. Once the Dubois gang had cleared out the "undesirables" and had the hotel under control, they invited in their drug pushers, in this case members of the motorcycle gang Les Mercenaires from the south-west sector of the city. In the summer and autumn of 1975 RCMP undercover agents managed to infiltrate the drug-dealing network at the *Iroquois Hotel*. The agents succeeded in making a number of important purchases, but the undercover operation had to be abandoned. Police had learned

aymond Dubois

Jean-Guy Dubois

Normand Dubois

laude Dubois

René Dubois

Roland Dubois

an-Paul Dubois

Adrien Dubois

Maurice Dubois

(Photos La Press.

reliably that two members of the Dubois gang had been assigned to assassinate the two police officers who were suspected of being informers.

Back in 1972-73, the Devil's Disciples motorcycle gang had carved out its own lucrative little kingdom in mid-town Saint-Louis Square. Outraged by this intrusion, the Dubois clan sent in a delegation of killers and strongmen to oust the bikers. The Disciples were not schoolboys however, and welcomed the messengers with baseball bats. But in spite of the resistance, the Dubois gang later established itself on the territory in force, mainly by interfering in the internal dispute which had divided the Devil's Disciples.

It would take too long to describe every violent event in the career of the Dubois brothers. It is enough to note, in closing, that from August 1974 until the beginning of 1976, their gangland operations were marked by a series of killings as savage and bloody as those of the Devil's Disciples. A dozen gangsters were eliminated in the conflict and several others narrowly escaped death. One of the major belligerents in this gang war was Pierre McSween, who later was a surprise witness at the Quebec Commission on Organized Crime. Largely through his detailed testimony, the Commission inquiry demonstrated that the Dubois brothers were not only the central figures in this gangland war, but also its main beneficiaries. As a result of these bloody conflicts, the Dubois brothers increased their prestige and renown in the underworld, where their tight grip remains clear and present despite the Commission's explosive revelations. To date, not one of the Dubois brothers has been charged with trafficking in drugs. It remains to be seen how long that will be so . . .

As this book was going to press, in fact, the Narcotics Squad in Montreal struck a hard, spectacular blow at one of the groups in the Dubois entourage. The Pommerleau brothers — Claude, Paul and Norman — and a Moroccan named Abdellatif Aziz, were arrested on April 25 and 26, 1976 after a long and arduous undercover operation by a young RCMP agent. (31) These men had also been wanted by

---

31. In December 1975 Claude Pommerleau, 29, was freed "with regret" by coroner Maurice Laniel, following an inquest into the murder of a Montreal drug pusher, 28-year-old Daniel Lapointe. Lapointe had been well known for his association with the Dubois brothers gang, as were Pommerleau and Yves Audette, 28, who was also freed after the inquest. Audette had previously been arrested on April 18, 1975 for possession of burglars' tools. Three other men were arrested with him, including the famous Georges Lemay, an old friend of Lucien Rivard and Claude Ménard.

The Montreal Star

FINAL

star action

PAGE A-4

TOMORROW'S FORECAST: Snow, rain (Page A-2) 68 PAGES

TUESDAY, DECEMBER 9, 1975

107th year, No. 256 PRICE FIFTEEN CENTS

PICTURE INTRODUCED: Photo submitted by newspaper publisher Jean-Jacques Mercier at today's crime inquiry shows (circled from left): Normand

Newsman testifies at probe

Dubois 'terrors of St. Henri'

By NORMAN PROVENCHER

Quebecers must 'cut out electric frills'

Weekend SPORTS
Section C

Bar owner defied protection racket in Dubois territory

By NORMAN PROVENCHER

Baby dies in London quest for hospital

LONDON (AP) —

The Montreal Star

FINAL

TOMORROW'S FORECAST: Cool (Page A-2) 52 PAGES

MONDAY, DECEMBER 8, 1975

107th year, No. 255 PRICE FIFTEEN CENTS

Probe focuses on Dubois clan

Murdered McSweens were gang 'dummies'

By NORMAN PROVENCHER

See DUBOIS, Page A-5

Pierre McSween ponders a question during today's session of crime inquiry.

Mayor still not ready

other police forces in connection with several large robberies and kidnappings of bank managers.

Back in May, 1974, the Narcotics Squad agent had taken a job in the air freight services of Air Canada, first at Montreal International Airport at Dorval, then at the newly-opened Mirabel Airport. For two years he cut himself off completely from his police colleagues, as he gradually penetrated the closed circle of about 15 Air Canada employees suspected of crooked operations during the past several years. Some of these employees were in positions of importance. At the same time they had close links with a well-known underworld figure, Claude Ménard, a former buddy of the late, notorious Richard Blass and a friend of the Johann Meyer who was arrested on a cocaine charge in Puerto Rico in August 1974.

In September 1975, one of Ménard's henchmen, in a panic after botching an assignment in South America, tried to kill him. But Ménard survived, and he and a friend, along with the Pommerleau gang, were charged with importing narcotics into Canada with the complicity of several Air Canada employees who also face charges. The shipments involved were for the most part hashish from Morocco, which had become the main Mediterranean port for international traffic in cannabis since the outbreak of the civil war in Lebanon.

The undercover agent succeeded in nullifying several drug operations by tipping off his colleagues in the Narcotics Squad. Just a few days before the investigation ended, for example, police were able to seize 100 pounds of hashish in Jamaica, and another 300 pounds had been seized at Mirabel Airport on February 7, 1976. Shortly before that, three Quebecers had been arrested in New York as they tested the delivery system from Toronto, using a sample of 20 pounds of hashish.

The criminal charges laid by the RCMP after the investigation relate specifically to trafficking in 450 pounds of hashish with a market value of nearly $1 million. Additional charges involve theft of merchandise valued at more than $2 million.

Some of the suspects in this case are believed to have been operating rackets for at least ten years, under cover of their employment with Air Canada. It was a ring in the service of several underworld gangs. The smashing of the ring, therefore, on the eve of the Olympic Games in Montreal, must be considered a police achievement of high importance.

Conclusion

One must keep company with the men of the Narcotics Squad for months to begin to understand the scope and meaning of the work they have done, and are continuing to do each day. The general public, who pay for police services, are largely unaware of what these officers spent in patience, devotion, determination and sacrifice to break up the narcotics combines which this book has attempted to describe. The policeman is often the target of prejudiced spirits, seen in caricature as a savage brute, without much intelligence, more likely to resort to force than to seek to understand. Such mercenary primates may still exist among policemen. But the peace officers who work behind the scenes, devoting a large part of their lives to the pursuit of the chieftains of the drug trade, are not in that category. It takes intelligence, finesse and wiliness to penetrate the secrets of the great narcotics networks. In that respect, the agents of the Royal Canadian Mounted Police, particularly those in Montreal, have acquired a professionalism over the years which today, it must be said, makes them the envy of more celebrated police forces around the world.

Of all those in Canada who are concerned with the underworld of crime, the investigators of the Narcotics Squad are certainly among the best-informed and the most-aware of the problems it creates. Their hundreds of infiltration missions into the underworld, their astonishing network of informers and double agents who cooperate with them, have given them an exceptional knowledge of the criminal world, its organization, hierarchy and, especially, its evolution. It comes as no surprise then, that on the whole the hardest blows against underworld leaders have been struck by the Narcotics Squad, whether at Vancouver, Toronto or Montreal.

If one makes a detailed analysis of the situation of the international narcotics traffic in Canada, the United States, or

507

France, it becomes evident that most of those who dabbled in this rather specialized trade were sooner or later unmasked and sent to prison. In some cases it took years of patient work, but so what! Few criminal activities entail such a high probability of failure. In spite of police efforts and successes, however, the traffic continues and drugs flow to the consumer market more abundantly than ever. Today, and for the past few years, professional gangsters no longer have the stage to themselves. Thousands of weekend or part-time traffickers — tourists, students, hippies, addicts — have invaded the market. Their presence complicates the situation and assures thousands of their friends and acquaintances of a constant supply of hashish, cocaine, speed, heroin. Many of these amateurs have never given a thought to the baneful consequences of their little combines. But just as the more powerful dealers, they contribute to the exploitation of man, and their motives are hardly more praiseworthy.

As we have seen, the profits made by those who traffic in drugs are astronomical and fortunes are quickly made. It's easy to understand why, despite the risks presented by the relentless work of police, there always have been and always will be professionals and amateurs willing to assume the role of suppliers to the millions of drug users. History shows that each time ringleaders were arrested and imprisoned, their henchmen, friends and partners soon took over their operations. One is almost tempted to say that the repression of narcotics traffic is useless and that it would be better to surrender to the inevitable.

If that solution might seem acceptable in respect to some of the so-called "light" drugs, it remains unthinkable when one considers the tragic effects of thousands of users of heroin, morphine, cocaine, amphetamines and so on. Can anyone seriously suggest that unscrupulous traffickers, concerned only with financial profit, be given a free hand to enslave the young and not-so-young who naively believe that happiness is found in drugs? The brutal rules of this "business" require not only that the demand be satisfied, but also that it be provoked, sustained and stimulated. One can easily imagine the heights drug usage might have reached had it not been for the battle waged to this day against traffickers of all description!

The drug problem, certainly, is far from being only a police problem, and must be approached in a manner that is not repressive. The psychological, sociological and cultural conditions which lead millions of people into the use of drugs, will not be changed by the work of anti-narcotic squads. There is dust, and there are the causes of the dust. We will not change our society significantly in a few days, unfortunately, and until efforts to attack the roots of the evil begin to bear fruit, we must continue to sweep up the dust. If we don't, the dirt will soon fill our entire house and make it impossible to live in.

Like most human activities, the battle against drug trafficking is a perpetual recommencement. Those who wage it know that. They wish, however — and they are right to do so — that the public would understand them a little better and support them a little more. Their use of informers, spies, promises of immunity, electronic eavesdropping and other police methods, do not meet with general favor. And yet, as this book showed, without those methods it would be impossible to carry out an effective battle against those exploiters of human misery, those underwriters of slow suicide, the traffickers in drugs, particularly heroin. Only those who know the daily anguish and drama lived by heroin addicts and users of other dangerous drugs can understand how important it is to give police officers the means to counteract the ever more subtle operations of the traffickers in narcotics.

Bibliography

Bandits à Marseille, Eugène Saccomano, Paris, Éditions Julliard, 1968.

Code Name Richard, Richard Berdin, New York, E. P. Dutton & Co. Inc., 1974.

The Corsican Contract, Evert Clark and Nicholas Horrock, New York, Bantam Books, 1974.

The Deadly Silence, Renée Buse, New York, Doubleday & Company Inc., 1965.

Don Carlo: Boss of Bosses, Paul Meskil, Toronto, Popular Library Edition, 1973.

Dossier D ... comme drogue, Alain Jaubert, Paris, Éditions Moreau, 1973.

Final Report of the Commission of Inquiry into the Non-medical Use of Drugs, The Ledain Commission Report, Ottawa, Information Canada, 1973.

French Connection: The world's most crucial narcotics investigation, Robin Moore, Boston, Little, Brown & Co., 1969.

The Heroin Trail, The Ugly Odyssey from Blossom to Bloodstream, New York, The staff and editors of Newsday, 1974.

The International Connection: Opium from Growers to Pushers, Catherine Lamour and Michel R. Lamberti, New York, Pantheon Books, Div. of Random House, Inc., 1974.

La Lutte internationale contre le trafic des stupéfiants, Problèmes politiques et sociaux, Paris, La Documentation française, nos. 222-223, April 12-19, 1974.

La Mafia, Martin W. Duyzings, Paris, Petite Bibliothèque Payot, 1966.

La Mafia: les vrais parrains, en collaboration, Revue Historia, Hors Série no. 28, Paris, Librairie Jules Tallandier, 1972.

Lansky, Hank Messik, New York, G.P. Putnam's Sons, 1971.

La Rage des goof-balls, Alain Stanké and Marie-José Beaudoin, Montréal, Éditions de l'Homme, 1962.

The Last Testament of Lucky Luciano, Martin A. Gosch and Richard Hammer, Boston, Little, Brown & Co., 1975.

Le Jockey, Philippe B., Paris, Éditions Olivier Orban, 1974.

L'Intouchable, Evert Clark and Nicholas Horrock, Paris, Collection Super Noire, Gallimard, 1975.

The Mafia is not an Equal Opportunity Employer, Nicholas Gage, New York, Dell Publishing Co. Inc., 1972.

Merchant of Heroin, Alvin Moscow, New York, The Dial Press Inc., 1968.

The Murderers : The Story of Narcotic Gangs, Harry J. Anslinger and W. Oursler, New York, Farrar, Straus & Cudahy, 1961.

Organized Crime and Illicit Traffic in Narcotics, Hearings before the Permanent Subcommittee on Investigations of the Committee on Government Operations, United States Senate; Eighty-Eight Congress; Part 1 to 5 and Index to Hearings; Washington, U.S. Government Printing Office, 1963, 1964 and 1965.

Peroff: The Man who knew too much, Frank Peroff and L. H. Whittemore, New York, William Morrow Inc., 1975.

The Politics of Heroin in Southeast Asia, Alfred W. McCoy, New York, Harper Colophon Books, 1973.

The Protectors, Harry J. Anslinger, New York, Farrar, Straus & Cudahy, 1962.

Rapport d'enquête sur la police de Montréal, Juge F. Caron, Montréal, Cour supérieure, Jugement no 3000, 1954.

Report of the Commissioner the Honourable Frederic Dorion, Chief Justice of the Superior Court for the Province of Quebec, Special Public Inquiry 1964, June 1965.

The Secret Lives of America's Most Successful Undercover Agent, Sal Vizzini and Oscar Fraley, New York, Arbor House Publishing Co., 1972.

Smugglers, Timothy Green, New York, Walker & Co., 1969.

Staff Study of the Frank Peroff Case, Permanent Subcommittee on Investigations of the Committee on Government Operations, United States Senate, Ninety-Fourth Congress, Washington, U.S. Government Printing Office, March 1975.

The Trail of the Poppy: behind the Mask of the Mafia, C. Siragusa, New Jersey, Prentice Hall, Englewood Cliffs, 1966.

Un Prêtre et son péché, Alain Stanké, Montréal, Édition de l'Homme, 1961.

Valachi Papers, Peter Maas, New York, G.P. Putnam's Sons, 1968.

World Drug Traffic and its Impact on U.S. Security, Hearings before the Subcommittee to investigate the Administration of the Internal Security Act and Other Internal Security Laws on the Committee on the Judiciary, United States Senate; Ninety-Second Congress; Part 1 to Part 7, Washington, U.S. Government Printing Office, 1972-1973.

Note: Non-exhaustive bibliography. To the preceding works must be added the hundreds of newspaper and magazine articles from Quebec, Canada, the United States and France.

Charts and Maps

FIGURE B.1

CONVERSION OF OPIUM INTO HEROIN

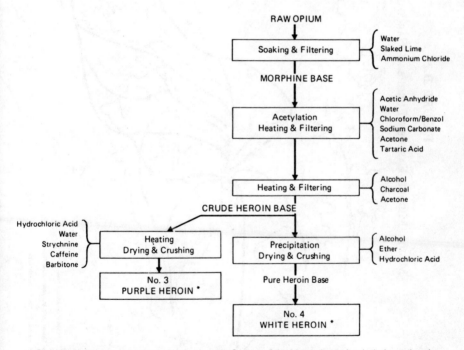

* European laboratories produce only white heroin, while Southeast Asian laboratories produce both the purple and white varieties. Usage of the terms 'No. 3' and 'No. 4' are, consequently, restricted to Southeast Asia.

Source: United States, Cabinet Committee on International Narcotics Control. *World Opium Survey 1972*. Washington, D.C.: July, 1972.

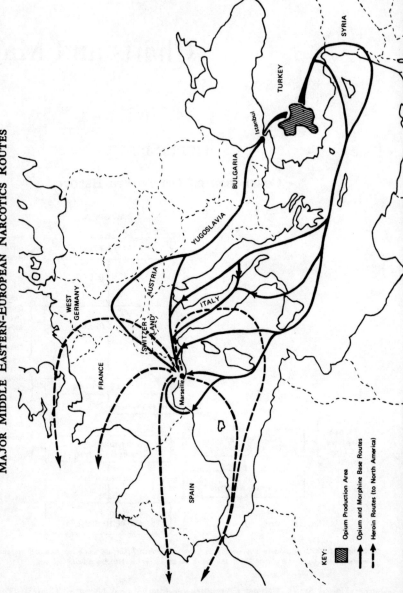

FIGURE B.2

MAJOR MIDDLE EASTERN-EUROPEAN NARCOTICS ROUTES

KEY:

 Opium Production Area

Opium and Morphine Base Routes

Heroin Routes (to North America)

MAJOR SOUTHEAST ASIAN NARCOTICS ROUTES

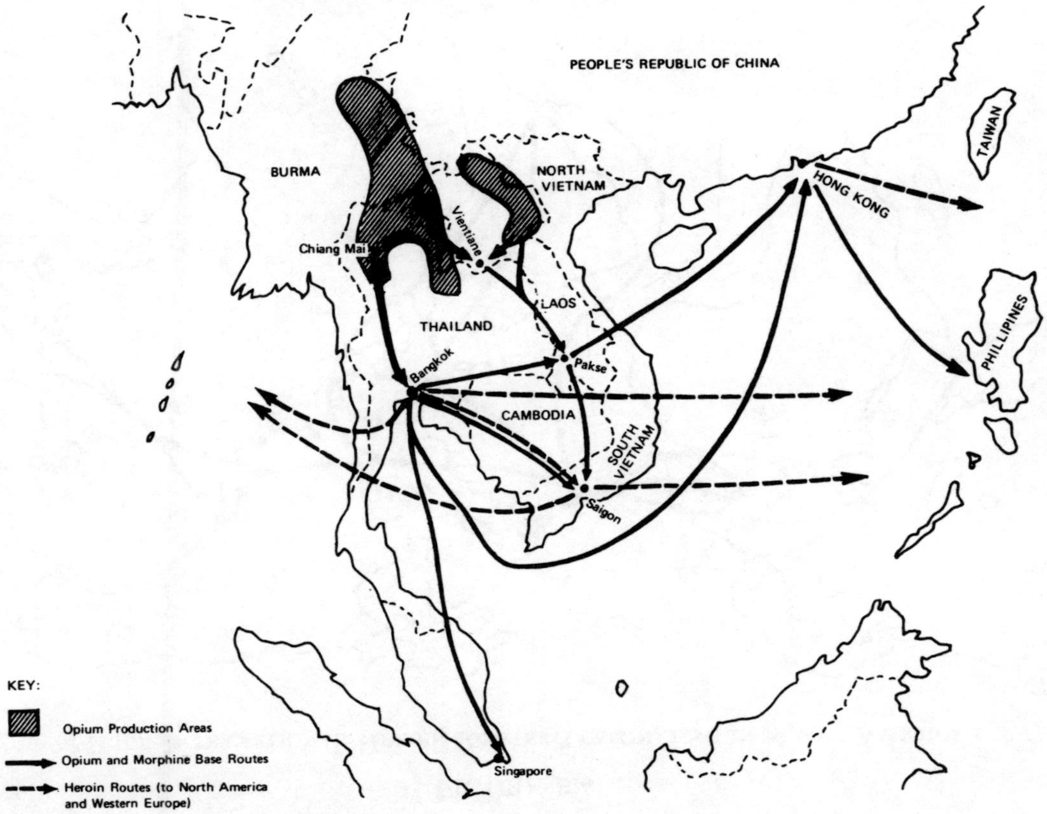

TAIWAN

PHILLIPINES

HONG KONG

PEOPLE'S REPUBLIC OF CHINA

NORTH VIETNAM

LAOS

SOUTH VIETNAM

Pakse

Saigon

CAMBODIA

THAILAND

Vientiane

Bangkok

BURMA

Chiang Mai

Singapore

KEY:

Opium Production Areas

Opium and Morphine Base Routes

Heroin Routes (to North America and Western Europe)

518

FIGURE B.4

MAJOR INTERNATIONAL HEROIN ROUTES TERMINATING IN NORTH AMERICA

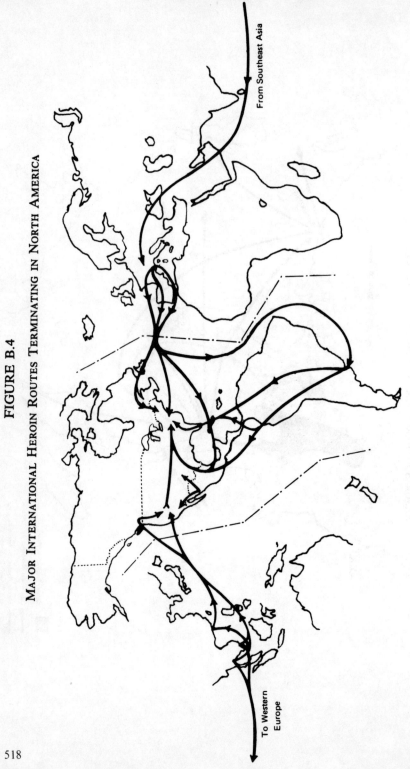

FIGURE B.5

TRADITIONAL PATTERN OF HEROIN DISTRIBUTION IN CANADA*
(1971–1972)

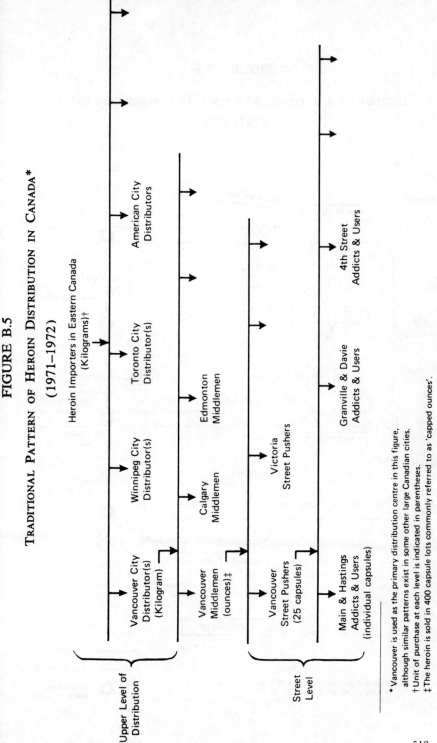

* Vancouver is used as the primary distribution centre in this figure, although similar patterns exist in some other large Canadian cities.
† Unit of purchase at each level is indicated in parentheses.
‡ The heroin is sold in 400 capsule lots commonly referred to as 'capped ounces'.

FIGURE B.6

STRUCTURE OF A TYPICAL CANADIAN CITY DISTRIBUTION SYSTEM
(1971–72)

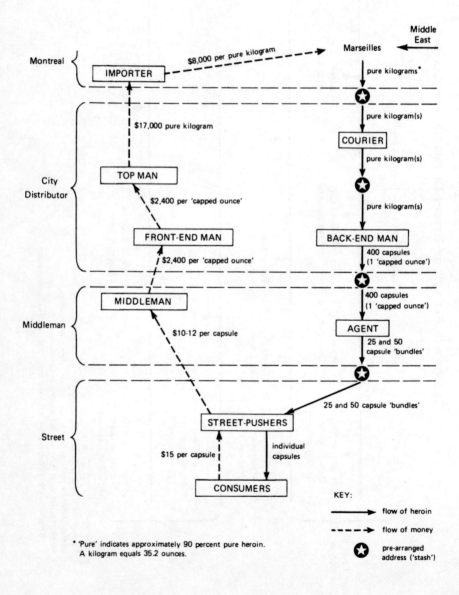

* 'Pure' indicates approximately 90 percent pure heroin.
A kilogram equals 35.2 ounces.

FIGURE B.7

MAJOR CANADIAN HEROIN ROUTES

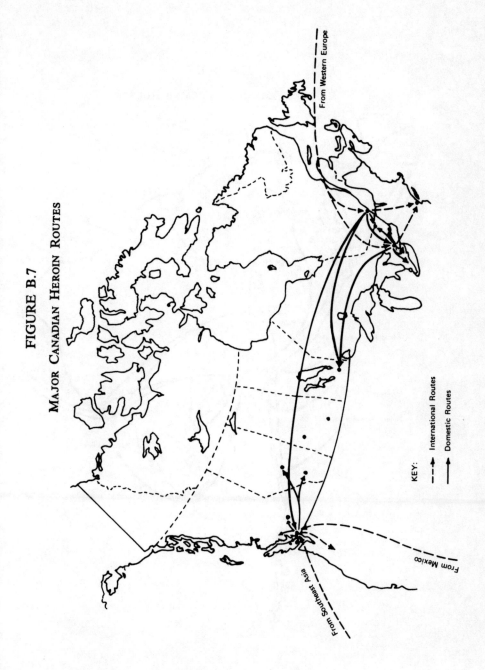

KEY:

- - - ▶ International Routes

——▶ Domestic Routes

From Western Europe

From Mexico

From Southeast Asia

FIGURE B.8

SOUTH AMERICAN COCAINE ROUTES

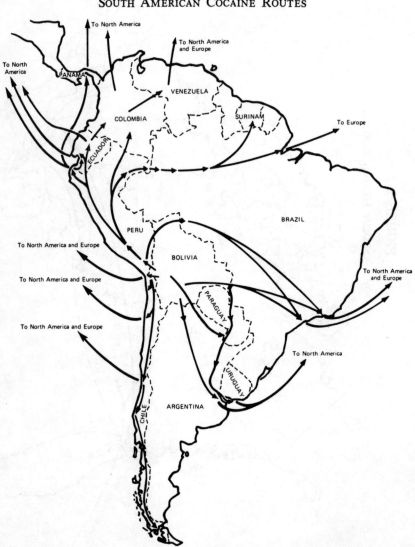

Index

Bender, Tony. See Strollo, Anthony
Benny the Sicilian. See Bellanca, Sebastiano
Bentvena, William 129, 150
Bercovitch, Léo 85
Berdin, Richard, alias Gilbert Kemmoun 343-350, 354, 356
Berger, Francine 410, 419, 448
Berger, Wally 410, 419, 448
Bergeron, Gérard 216, 217
Bergeron, Jean-Paul 211
Bergeron, Jeannette 216-218
Bergon, Claude 485, 486
Bergon, Paul 485
Bernard, Michel 251, 252, 265
Bernard, Ronald 287
Bernard, Yvonne 251, 265
Bernardini, Vincent 62
Bernstein, Joseph (Jos) 20, 22, 23
Bernstein, Sam 20
Bianca, Tony (pseudonym) 141
Bianchi-Maliverno, Robert-Thomas. See Maliverno, Robert-Thomas Bianchi
Bianco, Tony 79, 80
Biase, Patrick, alias Dave Costa, alias Jack Farraco 126-146, 148, 181-192, 194-196
Bienvenue, Jean 448
Biff, See Rinucci, Michel
Big John. See Ormento, John
Big Pep. See Cocolicchio, Giuseppe
Big Red. See Chesson, Cecil
Biggi, Jos 360, 423-425
Biondo, Joseph 48, 197
Bishop, Gilbert 487
Bisson, Jean-Louis, known as Blackie 67, 68, 86, 101, 104, 111, 155, 171, 232, 266, 275-282, 286-289, 325, 340
Bisson, Mrs. 282, 286
Bistoni, Ansan-Albert, known as Mister Albert 76, 95, 101, 103, 104, 106, 107, 112, 197, 336, 357
Bizanti, Angelo 50, 51, 55, 67, 266
Black, Archie 40
Blackie. See Bisson, Jean-Louis
Blain, Albert. See D'Agostino, Antoine
Blain, Madeleine. See Filleau, Suzanne

Blain, Marc-André (Judge) 146
Blais, Vincent, alias Paul Lebœuf 235, 237, 240
Blanka Benny. See Bellanca, Sebastiano
Blaschevitsch, Herbert, alias Herbert Suares 112
Blass, Michel (Mike) 493, 495
Blass, Richard 493, 506
Blond (The). See Tramontana, Giuseppe
Bloom, John 23
Bohack, Steve 276
Boisvert, Raymond 487
Boiteux (Le). See De Kercadio, René-Quintin
Boldrini, Joseph 107, 263, 264, 360, 362-364, 369, 372-375, 378, 379, 383, 460
Bolland, Salvador Pardo 193, 197, 340
Bolland, Salvador Pardo, Mrs. 197
Bonanno, Joseph, known as Joe Bananas 81, 82, 109, 117, 122, 128, 368
Bond, Gérard 486
Bonet, Fulgencio Cruz, known as Pancho 210
Bonetti, Felice 454
Bonilla, Alfonso 215, 221
Bono, Alfredo 305
Bootsie. See Di Pasqua, Anthony
Bortoli, Raymond 374
Boucan, Marcel 354
Bouchard, Conrad 139, 146, 150, 151, 183, 360-377, 393, 396, 421-428, 430-438, 440, 441, 460, 462, 471
Boucher, Gilles 500
Boucher, Jackie 236, 237, 239, 241
Boucher, Paul (Butch) 501
Boucher, Sébastien 236, 237, 239-241, 425
Bourassa, Robert 445, 448
Bourassa, Wayne 489
Bourbonnais, Charles 197
Bourdeau, Claude 259, 260
Bourgeois, Mr. 230
Bourget, Gerry 204
Bourvil 39

Palmer, Donald *279, 282, 285, 389, 457, 458*
Palmer, Douglas *279, 282, 285, 286, 389, 457, 458*
Palmeri, Giuseppe *156*
Pancho. See Bonet, Fulgencio Cruz
Pandolfi, Philippe *456, 471*
Panepinto, Stephan (Steve), alias Steve Murray *268, 269, 272, 304, 315, 326, 327, 413, 415*
Panico, Carmine *129, 150*
Panico, Salvatore *128, 129, 150*
Pannunzio, Rolland *360-363, 366, 377, 438*
Pantani, Albert *379*
Paoleschi, François *62*
Paoloni, Antonio, known as Planche *97, 98*
Papagallo, Michel *261*
Papalia, Anthony *276*
Papalia, Johhny *156, 157, 275, 276*
Papillon, Henri-Paul *31-34, 36, 42*
Paquette, André *236, 237, 240, 241*
Paquin, Nelson *52*
Parcouet, Georgette *94*
Pardo-Bolland, Salvador. See Bolland, Salvador Pardo
Paré, Pierre *495*
Paroutian, Antranik *113-118, 151, 156, 355*
Pasquale, Don. See Ania, Pasquale
Pasqualini, Paul *252, 265*
Pastou, Claude-André *252, 265, 303, 347*
Patek, Werner, known as The Kraut *426, 427*
Patenaude, Hervé *445*
Patrizzi, Joseph *76*
Paul, Réjean *432, 441*
Pavlick, Michael *418*
Pearson, Edwin *459, 462*
Pearson, Lester B. *225, 227, 233*
Pearson, Rocky *477*
Pellerin, Gilles *39*
Pelletier, Ginette *492*
Penguin (The). See Di Paolo, Michel
Penosi, Guido, known as The Bull, alias George Prince *268, 269, 272,*

273, 297-300, 302, 304, 326, 368
Peppe, The brothers. See Cotroni
Péraldi, Mathieu *354*
Perfetti, Antoine *263-265, 268, 269*
Peroff, Frank *421-423, 425-428, 430-438, 440, 441*
Perreault, Donald *52*
Perreault, Douglas *52*
Perreault, Frank *52, 53*
Perreault, Joseph-Raymond *155*
Perrette, Robert *368, 369, 375, 378*
Perrier, Roger *404*
Perron, Joseph-Marcel *286, 287*
Petillo, David *150*
Petit (Le). See Lastrayoli, Marius
Petit Jeannot. See Dumerain, Jean
Petrov, Larry *29, 115*
Petrula, Frank *60, 61, 81-83, 85, 88, 119*
Petrula, Mrs. Frank *83*
Phaneuf, Alain *189, 192, 193, 195, 196*
Phelan, Charles (Judge) *493, 495*
Philibert, Mister. See Venturi, Jean
Philosophe (le). See Adamo, Vito
Phoenix, Roland *236*
Picard, Jacques *475, 477, 478*
Pici, Joe *78*
Picpus (gang) *348-350*
Pietrini, Alexandre *265*
Pio. See Andréani, Jean-Joseph
Pirico, Francesco *76, 101*
Pisanella, Nicholas *386*
Planche. See Paoloni, Antonio
Plante, Jacques *257*
Plante, Pacifique, (Pax) *62, 81, 83, 85, 88, 89*
Ploune (La). See Turcot, Gérard
Plumeri, James. alias Jimmy Doyle *327*
Pohl, Anthony S. *351*
Poirier, Maurice *226*
Poissant, Gilles *200, 201, 216, 236, 286, 310, 342, 359, 369, 391, 404, 432*
Poitras, Maurice *188*
Polakoff, Moses *461*
Politicien (Le). See Rossi, Marcel
Polizzano, Carmine *128, 150*
Pollakowitz, Jack *20-23, 25, 26, 47*